1985

THE ENGLISH POETS
GENERAL EDITOR: CHRISTOPHER RICKS

Also available in this series

Robert Browning: The Poems, volume one
Robert Browning: The Poems, volume two
Robert Browning: The Ring and the Book
Edmund Spenser: The Faerie Queene
Henry Vaughan: The Complete Poems
William Wordsworth: The Poems, volume two
William Wordsworth: The Prelude
Sir Thomas Wyatt: The Complete Poems

William Wordsworth:
The Poems

VOLUME ONE

EDITED BY JOHN O. HAYDEN

NEW HAVEN AND LONDON
YALE UNIVERSITY PRESS

First published in 1977 in the United Kingdom in a paperback
edition by Penguin Books Limited in the series Penguin
English Poets. First published 1981 in the United States of
America by Yale University Press.

Printed in the United States of America.

Library of Congress Cataloging in Publication Data

Wordsworth, William, 1770–1850.
  The poems.

  (The English poets ; 7–8)
  Includes bibliographies and indexes.
  I. Hayden, John O. II. Title. III. Series:
English poets ; 7–8.
PR5850.F81   821'.7   81–2994
ISBN 0–300–02751–6 (v. 1)   AACR2
ISBN 0–300–02752–4 (v. 2)
ISBN 0–300–02754–0 (pbk. : v. 1)
ISBN 0–300–02755–9 (pbk. : v. 2)

10 9 8 7 6 5 4 3 2 1

Contents

8 2 1.71
W 9 2 5 p h
/

Table of Dates   *19*
Introduction   *23*
Further Reading   *31*

[An asterisk preceding a title indicates either questionable
or partial authorship. Brackets around a title signify the
unauthorized status of the title.]

Lines Written as a School Exercise at Hawkshead   *37*
Anacreon   *40*
The Dog – An Idyllium   *41*
[Septimius and Acme]   *42*
Translation of a Celebrated Greek Song   *43*
To Melpomene   *44*
The Death of a Starling   *44*
[Lesbia]   *45*
Beauty and Moonlight   *46*
Sonnet on Seeing Miss Helen Maria Williams Weep   *47*
Sonnet Written by Mr — Immediately after the Death
of his Wife   *47*
[A Ballad]   *48*
The Vale of Esthwaite   *50*
Extract from the Conclusion of a Poem   *66*
'What is it that tells my soul the Sun is setting'   *67*
On the Death of an Unfortunate Lady   *67*
A Winter's Evening   *68*

114, 633

Dirge Sung by a Minstrel *68*

[Fragments on a Heroic Theme] *70*

[Fragment of an Intended Poem on Milton] *72*

[Orpheus and Eurydice] *72*

[In Part from Moschus's Lament for Bion] *74*

[The Horse] *75*

Ode to Apollo *76*

An Evening Walk *77*

Written in Very Early Youth *88*

'When slow from pensive twilight's latest gleams' *88*

[Sonnet ('If grief dismiss me not')] *89*

Lines Written While Sailing in a Boat at Evening *89*

Remembrance of Collins *90*

Septimi Gades *91*

Descriptive Sketches [1850] *94*

'Sweet was the walk along the narrow lane' *114*

The Birth of Love *114*

[At the Isle of Wight] *116*

'In vain did Time and Nature toil to throw' *116*

'The western clouds a deepening gloom display' *117*

Guilt and Sorrow *118*

Inscription for a Seat by the Pathway Side *141*

[Translation of Horace's *Ode* III, xiii] *141*

[Imitation of Juvenal – Satire VIII] *142*

'The hour-bell sounds, and I must go' *147*

'The road extended o'er a heath' *147*

'No spade for leagues had won a rood of earth' *149*

The Convict *152*

[Fragment of a 'Gothic' Tale] *153*

Address to the Ocean *160*

Argument for Suicide *161*

The Borderers *163*

Animal Tranquillity and Decay *242*

[Fragment: 'Yet once again'] *242*

[Fragment: The Baker's Cart] *242*

Inscription for a Seat by a Roadside *243*

The Three Graves. Parts I* and II *245*

*Address to Silence *252*

Lines Left upon a Seat in a Yew-tree *254*

Incipient Madness *256*

The Farmer of Tilsbury Vale *257*

The Reverie of Poor Susan *260*

A Character *261*

A Night-Piece *262*

The Old Cumberland Beggar *262*

[Fragments from the Alfoxden Note-Book (i)] *268*

To My Sister *269*

Goody Blake and Harry Gill *271*

The Complaint of a Forsaken Indian Woman *275*

Her Eyes Are Wild *277*

The Idiot Boy *281*

The Last of the Flock *295*

We Are Seven *298*

Simon Lee *300*

'A whirl-blast from behind the hill' *303*

The Thorn *304*

[Fragments from the Alfoxden Note-Book (ii)] *311*

Lines Written in Early Spring *312*

Anecdote for Fathers *313*

Peter Bell *315*

Andrew Jones *351*

'I love upon a stormy night' *352*

'Away, away, it is the air' *354*

[Fragments from the Alfoxden Note-Book (iii)] *355*

Expostulation and Reply   355
The Tables Turned   356
Lines Composed a Few Miles above Tintern Abbey   357
There Was a Boy   362
*Alcaeus to Sappho   363
'A slumber did my spirit seal'   364
Influence of Natural Objects   364
'She dwelt among the untrodden ways'   366
'Strange fits of passion have I known'   366 ·
Nutting   367
The Danish Boy   369
Ruth   371
To a Sexton   379
Matthew   380
The Two April Mornings   381
The Fountain   383
'Could I the priest's consent have gained'   385
Elegy Written in the Same Place   387
Address to the Scholars of the Village School   389
Lucy Gray   392
Written in Germany   394
A Poet's Epitaph   395
Ellen Irwin   397
[Fragment: 'For let the impediment be what it may']   399
[Fragment: Redundance]   400
'Three years she grew in sun and shower'   400
The Brothers   402
To M. H.   414
Hart-Leap Well   415
*The Voice from the Side of Etna [The Mad Monk]   421

'There is an Eminence, – of these our hills' *422*
'It was an April morning: fresh and clear' *423*
Written with a Pencil upon a Stone *424*
The Idle Shepherd-Boys *425*
The Two Thieves *428*
'A narrow girdle of rough stones and crags' *430*
On Seeing Some Tourists *432*
Written with a Slate Pencil upon a Stone, the
Largest of a Heap *433*
The Oak and the Broom *434*
The Waterfall and the Eglantine *437*
Song for the Wandering Jew *439*
''Tis said, that some have died for love' *440*
For the Spot Where the Hermitage Stood *442*
The Seven Sisters *443*
To Joanna *445*
'When, to the attractions of the busy world' *448*
The Childless Father *451*
The Pet-Lamb *452*
Rural Architecture *454*
Michael *455*
[Fragments from the 'Christabel' Note-book] *468*
[Fragment: A Somersetshire Tragedy] *471*
[Fragment: 'Witness thou'] *471*
[Fragment from Dove Cottage Manuscript 44 (i)] *472*
Motto Intended for Poems on the Naming of
Places *472*
The Affliction of Margaret — *472*
The Forsaken *475*
The Orchard Pathway *475*
'I travelled among unknown men' *476*
Repentance *476*

The Manciple's Tale [– A Modernization] 478
The Prioress' Tale [– A Modernization] 485
The Cuckoo and the Nightingale [– A Modernization] 494
Troilus and Cresida [– A Modernization] 505
*Written in a Grotto 510
To a Young Lady 511
Louisa 511
The Sailor's Mother 512
Alice Fell 514
Beggars 516
To a Butterfly ('Stay near me') 517
The Emigrant Mother 518
To the Cuckoo ('O blithe New-comer!') 521
'My heart leaps up when I behold' 522
To H. C., Six Years Old 522
Ode: Intimations of Immortality 523*
The Sparrow's Nest 529
To a Sky-Lark ('Up with me!') 530
'Among all lovely things' [The Glow-Worm] 531
Written in March 532
The Green Linnet 533
To the Daisy ('In youth') 534
To the Daisy ('Bright Flower!') 537
To the Same Flower [The Daisy] ('With little') 537
The Redbreast Chasing the Butterfly 539
To a Butterfly ('I've watched you now') 540
[Fragments from Dove Cottage Manuscript 44 (ii)] 541
The Tinker 542
Foresight 543
To the Small Celandine ('Pansies, lilies') 544

*The Barberry-Tree *546*

To the Same Flower [The Small Celandine]
('Pleasures newly found') *549*

Resolution and Independence *551*

Travelling *556*

Stanzas Written in My Pocket-Copy *556*

1801 ('I grieved for Buonaparté') *558*

'Methought I saw the footsteps of a throne' *559*

'Great men have been among us; hands that
penned' *559*

'England! the time is come when thou shouldst
wean' *560*

'It is not to be thought of that the Flood' *560*

'There is a bondage worse, far worse, to bear' *561*

'When I have borne in memory what has tamed' *561*

To Sleep ('O gentle Sleep!') *562*

To Sleep ('A flock of sheep') *562*

To Sleep ('Fond words') *563*

'"Beloved Vale!" I said, "When I shall con"' *563*

'Brook! whose society the Poet seeks' *564*

'What if our numbers barely could defy' *564*

'There is a little unpretending Rill' *565*

'I find it written of SIMONIDES' *565*

'How sweet it is, when mother Fancy rocks' *566*

Personal Talk *566*

'Pelion and Ossa flourish side by side' *568*

'The world is too much with us; late and soon' *568*

To the Memory of Raisley Calvert *569*

'Where lies the Land to which yon Ship must go?' *569*

"With how sad steps, O Moon, thou climb'st the
sky" *570*

'With Ships the sea was sprinkled far and nigh' *570*

'It is no Spirit who from heaven hath flown' *571*

On the Extinction of the Venetian Republic *571*
A Farewell *572*
'The sun has long been set' *574*
Composed upon Westminster Bridge *574*
Composed near Calais *575*
Calais, August, 1802 *575*
Composed by the Sea-Side *576*
'It is a beauteous evening, calm and free' *576*
To Toussaint L'Ouverture *577*
Calais, August 15, 1802 *577*
September 1, 1802 *578*
Composed in the Valley near Dover *578*
September, 1802. Near Dover *579*
London, 1802 *579*
Written in London, September, 1802 *580*
Composed after a Journey across the Hambleton
Hills *580*
'Those words were uttered as in pensive mood' *581*
[Translation of Ariosto] *581*
Sonnet Translated from the Italian of Milton *584*
*Cantata, from Metastasio *584*
[Translations from Metastasio] *585*
'Nuns fret not at their convent's narrow room' *586*
[Translation of the Sestet of a Sonnet by Tasso] *587*
At the Grave of Burns *587*
Thoughts Suggested the Day Following *590*
Address to Kilchurn Castle *592*
Sonnet Composed at — Castle *593*
'Fly, some kind Harbinger, to Grasmere-dale!' *594*
To the Men of Kent. October, 1803 *594*
Anticipation. October, 1803 *595*
Sonnet, in the Pass of Killicranky *595*

Lines on the Expected Invasion 1803   596
October, 1803 ('One might')   596
October, 1803 ('These times')   597
October, 1803 ('When, looking')   597
To a Highland Girl   598
Yarrow Unvisited   600
At Applethwaite, near Keswick   602
'She was a Phantom of delight'   603
The Small Celandine   604
[Fragment: 'Along the mazes of this song I go']   605
Ode to Duty   605
The Matron of Jedborough and Her Husband   607
The Blind Highland Boy   610
Admonition   618
'Who fancied what a pretty sight'   618
'I wandered lonely as a cloud'   619
Address to My Infant Daughter, Dora   620
Yew-Trees   622
Vaudracour and Julia   623
[Fragment: 'There was a spot']   632
The Kitten and Falling Leaves   632
French Revolution   636
[Inscription for the Moss-Hut at Dove Cottage]   637
The Simplon Pass   637
The King of Sweden   638
Glen-Almain; Or, The Narrow Glen   638
Elegiac Stanzas Suggested by a Picture of Peele
Castle   639
'Distressful gift! this Book receives'   642
To the Daisy ('Sweet Flower!')   643
Stepping Westward   645
Elegiac Verses in Memory of My Brother   646

Fidelity *649*

Incident Characteristic of a Favourite Dog *651*

Tribute to the Memory of the Same Dog *652*

From the Italian of Michelangelo ('Yes! hope may') *653*

Rob Roy's Grave *653*

To the Sons of Burns *657*

The Solitary Reaper *659*

From the Italian of Michelangelo. To the Supreme
Being *660*

From the Italian of Michelangelo ('No mortal
object') *661*

*From the Italian of Michelangelo ('Well-nigh') *661*

From the Italian of Michelangelo ('Rid of a
vexing') *662*

Character of the Happy Warrior *662*

*The Cottager to Her Infant *664*

[Translations from Michelangelo. A Fragment] *665*

Michelangelo in Reply to the Passage upon His
Statue *666*

[Translation: 'Come, gentle Sleep'] *667*

The Waggoner *667*

Power of Music *691*

Stray Pleasures *693*

Star-Gazers *694*

'Yes, it was the mountain Echo' *696*

The Recluse. Home at Grasmere *697*

Water Fowl *717*

To the Evening Star over Grasmere Water *718*

To the Spade of a Friend *719*

[Fragment: 'The rains at length have ceased'] *720*

Lines, Composed at Grasmere *720*

The Horn of Egremont Castle *721*

Thought of a Briton on the Subjugation of
Switzerland   *725*
November, 1806   *725*
Song at the Feast of Brougham Castle   *726*
'Though narrow be that old Man's cares, and
near'   *731*
A Complaint   *731*
Song for the Spinning Wheel   *732*
'Through Cumbrian wilds, in many a mountain
cove'   *733*
A Prophecy   *733*
'O Nightingale! thou surely art'   *734*
To Lady Beaumont   *734*
Gypsies   *735*
To Thomas Clarkson   *736*
To the Poet, John Dyer   *736*
'Grief, thou hast lost an ever ready friend'   *737*
'Mark the concentred hazels that enclose'   *737*
'The Shepherd, looking eastward, softly said'   *738*
'Weak is the will of Man, his judgement blind'   *738*
Composed by the Side of Grasmere Lake   *739*
The Force of Prayer   *739*
The White Doe of Rylstone   *741*
Sonnet on Milton   *797*
[St Paul's]   *798*
The Tuft of Primroses   *799*
To the Clouds   *815*
Elegiac Stanzas Composed in the Churchyard of
Grasmere   *817*
[Pelayo]   *819*
Composed While the Author Was Engaged in Writing
a Tract   *821*
Composed at the Same Time   *821*

1810 ('Ah! where is Palafox?') *822*

'Hail, Zaragoza! If with unwet eye' *822*

'Is there a power that can sustain and cheer' *823*

'Avaunt all specious pliancy of mind' *823*

The French and the Spanish Guerillas *824*

'Say, what is Honour? – 'Tis the finest sense' *824*

'Call not the royal Swede unfortunate' *825*

'Look now on that Adventurer who hath paid' *825*

'Brave Schill! by death delivered, take thy flight' *826*

'Alas! what boots the long laborious quest' *826*

'And is it among rude untutored Dales' *827*

Feelings of the Tyrolese *827*

'O'er the wide earth, on mountain and on plain' *828*

*[Passage from John Wilson's *The Angler's Tent*] *828*

'Advance – come forth from thy Tyrolean ground' *828*

Hofer *829*

On the Final Submission of the Tyrolese *829*

Epitaph (from Chiabrera): 'Not without heavy grief' *830*

Epitaph (from Chiabrera): 'Destined to war' *831*

Epitaph (from Chiabrera): 'Pause, courteous Spirit!' *831*

Epitaph (from Chiabrera): 'There never breathed' *832*

Epitaph (from Chiabrera): 'O Thou who movest' *833*

Epitaph (from Chiabrera): 'Perhaps some needful service' *833*

[Epitaph on Tasso (Translated from Chiabrera)] *834*

Epitaph (from Chiabrera): 'Weep not' *834*

Epitaph (from Chiarera): 'True is it' *835*

Epitaph (from Chiabrera): 'O flower' *835*

[Epitaph (from Chiabrera): 'O Lelius'] *836*

'The martial courage of a day is vain' *836*

Indignation of a High-Minded Spaniard *837*

'In due observance of an ancient rite' *837*

Feelings of a Noble Biscayan *838*

The Oak of Guernica *838*

1810 ('O'erweening Statesmen') *839*

On a Celebrated Event in Ancient History *840*

Upon the Same Event *840*

Upon the Sight of a Beautiful Picture *841*

Epistle to Sir George Howland Beaumont *841*

Departure from the Vale of Grasmere *849*

View from the Top of Black Comb *850*

Written with a Slate Pencil on a Stone, on the Side of
the Mountain *851*

Inscription in the Grounds of Coleorton *852*

Written at the Request of Sir George Beaumont *853*

Inscription in a Garden of the Same *853*

For a Seat in the Groves of Coleorton *854*

1811 ('Here pause') *854*

1811 ('The power of Armies') *855*

Spanish Guerillas *855*

'The fairest, brightest, hues of ether fade' *856*

'Even as a dragon's eye that feels the stress' *856*

'Hail, Twilight, sovereign of one peaceful hour!' *857*

Composed on the Eve of the Marriage of a Friend *857*

Epitaph *858*

Characteristics of a Child Three Years Old *858*

[Fragment from Dove Cottage Manuscript 69] *859*

'Come ye that are disturbed, this steady voice' *859*

Maternal Grief *860*

November, 1813 *862*

'If thou indeed derive thy light from Heaven' *863*

'Surprised by joy – impatient as the Wind' *863*

APPENDICES
A: *Preface to* Lyrical Ballads, 1802   *867*
B: *Descriptive Sketches* 1793   *897*

Notes   *921*
Index of Titles   *1047*
Index of First Lines   *1057*

Table of Dates

1770   *7 April*   Born at Cockermouth, Cumberland to John Wordsworth, a Lawyer.

1771   Dorothy Wordsworth, his only sister, born (three brothers: Richard b. 1768, John b. 1772, Christopher b. 1774).

1776–7 Attends nursery school in Penrith, along with Mary Hutchinson, his future wife.

1778   *c. 8 March*   Ann Wordsworth, his mother, dies.

1779   Enters Hawkshead School.

1783   *30 December*   His father dies.

1785   Earliest extant verse written (aetat. 15).

1787   Attends St John's College, Cambridge.

1789   Spends long vacation with his sister and Mary Hutchinson.

1790   Spends long vacation on a walking tour of France and Switzerland with Robert Jones, a college friend.

1791   *21 January*   Receives B.A. degree.
        26 November   Leaves for stay in France.

1792   Meets Michel Beaupuy and has an affair with Annette Vallon.
        December   Returns to London.
        15 December   A daughter, Anne-Caroline, by Annette Vallon, born at Orleans.

1793   *29 January*   *An Evening Walk* and *Descriptive Sketches* published.
        August–September   Walking tour over Salisbury Plain to Bristol, and thence through part of Wales.

1795 *January* His friend Raisley Calvert dies, leaving Wordsworth a legacy.

August Meets Samuel Taylor Coleridge.

September Settles with Dorothy at Racedown, Dorset.

1797 *July* Moves to Alfoxden, Somerset, to be near Coleridge at Nether Stowey.

1798 *10 July* Visits Tintern Abbey.

September *Lyrical Ballads* published (4 poems by Coleridge included).

16 September Embarks for Germany with Coleridge and Dorothy.

1799 *May* Returns to England (Sockburn-on-Tees).

20 December Settles with Dorothy at Dove Cottage at Town-End, Grasmere.

1800 *January–September* John Wordsworth visits.

1801 *January* *Lyrical Ballads*, second edition (dated 1800), published in two volumes with the famous Preface.

1802 *Lyrical Ballads*, third edition, published with extended Preface and Appendix.

August Visits Annette Vallon and Caroline at Calais.

4 October Marries Mary Hutchinson.

1803 *18 June* A son, John, born (other children: Dora b. 1804, Thomas b. 1806, Catharine b. 1808, William b. 1810).

August–September Tours Scotland with Coleridge and Dorothy.

1804 Coleridge sails for Malta.

1805 *6 February* John Wordsworth drowns.

May *The Prelude* finished.

Lyrical Ballads, fourth edition, published.

1806 *August* Coleridge returns from Malta.

November Wordsworths move to Coleorton.

1807 *May* *Poems in Two Volumes* published.

July   Wordsworths return to Dove Cottage.

1808   *May*   Wordsworths move to Allan Bank, Grasmere.

1809   *May*   *The Convention of Cintra* tract published.

1810   *22 February*   *Essay on Epitaphs* published in *The Friend.*

October   Estrangement from Coleridge.

1811   *May*   Wordsworths move to the Rectory, Grasmere.

1812   *May*   Reconciliation with Coleridge.

Catharine and Thomas Wordsworth die.

1813   *March*   Appointed Distributor of Stamps for Westmoreland.

May   Wordsworths move to Rydal Mount, between Grasmere and Ambleside.

1814   Tours Scotland with his wife and Sara Hutchinson during the summer.

August   *The Excursion* published.

1815   *March*   *Poems* (first collected edition; in two volumes) published.

May   *The White Doe of Rylstone* published.

1816   *May*   *A Letter to a Friend of Burns* and *Thanksgiving Ode* published.

1817   *December*   Meets John Keats in London.

1818   *Two Addresses to the Freeholders of Westmoreland* published.

1819   *April*   *Peter Bell* published.

May   *The Waggoner* published.

1820   *May*   *The River Duddon* published.

July   *The Miscellaneous Poems of William Wordsworth* (4 volumes) published.

May–December   Tours Continent with his wife and Dorothy.

1822   *March*   *Ecclesiastical Sonnets* and *Memorials of a Tour on the Continent, 1820* published.

November   *A Description of the Scenery of the Lakes* published.

1827   *February*   Sir George Beaumont, patron, dies.

May Third collected edition of the *Poems* (5 volumes) published.

1831 *September–October* Tours Scotland with his daughter and nephew, Charles; visits Sir Walter Scott.

1832 Fourth collected edition of the *Poems* (4 volumes) published.

1834 *25 July* Coleridge dies.

1835 *January* *Yarrow Revisited and Other Poems* published.
Mental breakdown of Dorothy Wordsworth.

1836–7 Fifth collected edition of the *Poems* (in stereotype; 6 volumes) published.

1837 *March–August* Tours France and Italy with Henry Crabb Robinson.

1838 *June* One-volume edition of *The Sonnets* published.
21 July Receives D.C.L. from the University of Durham.

1839 *12 June* Receives D.C.L. from Oxford University.

1842 *April* Poems, *Chiefly of Early and Late Years* (with *The Borderers* and *Guilt and Sorrow*) published [volume VII of collected *Poems*].
July Resigns Distributorship of Stamps and receives pension.

1843 *April* Succeeds Southey as Poet Laureate.
Dictates notes on his poems to Isabella Fenwick.

1845 *November* Sixth collected edition of the *Poems* (1 volume) published.

1847 *9 July* His daughter Dora dies.

1849–50 Seventh collected edition of the *Poems* (6 volumes) published – the last edited by Wordsworth himself.

1850 *23 April* William Wordsworth dies.
July *The Prelude* published.

1855 *January* Dorothy Wordsworth dies.

1859 *January* Mary Wordsworth dies.

Introduction

William Wordsworth has in many respects been fortunate in his editors. William Knight, Edward Dowden, Nowell C. Smith, and Ernest de Selincourt have assiduously uncovered and pieced together poems from manuscripts, have chased down allusions, quotations, and variants; and they have been assisted in a good part of this work by the myriad of minor editors of selected editions. Any editor of Wordsworth's poetry begins his task with a large debt to the past. Yet there is a good deal of work still to be done, even in a modest collected edition such as the present one.

The production of a clear and accurate text is the major consideration; for the standard text edited by Ernest de Selincourt in five volumes contains a number of errors. The substantive errors, such things as incorrect wording and collocation, number over eighty; and the accidental, such as unnecessary or mistaken changes in punctuation, paragraphing, and capitalization, occur on almost every page.

With these problems in mind I have returned to Wordsworth's own last edition of 1849–50, complying with his own words (in a letter to Alexander Dyce, 30 April 1830): 'You know what importance I attach to following strictly the last Copy of the text of an Author.' Of those poems not included in his last edition, I have given the latest version printed elsewhere during his lifetime where such exists; and where the poem is extant only in manuscript I have given the latest manuscript version. By a quirk of fate, a few poems first printed after Wordsworth's death now are available only in that printed form, which I have followed. A handful of manuscript poems (*The Three Graves*, (Part I), '*There was a spot*', *Inscription for the Moss-Hut*, *The Cottager to Her Infant*, *In the First Page of an Album*, *The Lady Whom You*

Here Behold, Written in Mrs Field's Album, Upon the Sight of the Portrait of a Female Friend, and '*Prithee, Gentle Lady*') I have not been able to examine in manuscript, and for these have had to rely solely on later editions.

Once the text was determined, it was edited in a number of ways. The spelling has been modernized where it was merely archaic without a purpose. Hyphenated words, like *to-morrow,* and combinations of words, like *any one,* have been joined as one word, although an exception was made for *for ever,* which is often so spelled in Britain today. Where the sound of the word hasn't changed, obsolete spellings, such as *shew* (show) and *quire* (choir), have been modernized, but where the sound has changed as in *sate* (sat), I have left the spelling as I found it.

The capitalization has also been respected, because Wordsworth apparently used capitals as a form of emphasis. The major exception is the consistent capitalization of pronouns referring to God, which in the original texts are capitalized only occasionally.

At the Dove Cottage Library there is a legend still told of a professor who had written a chapter on Wordsworth's punctuation and had come to check the original texts as an afterthought. The chapter had to be dropped (or the title changed to 'De Selincourt's Punctuation'), for Wordsworth's punctuation was fairly thoroughly modernized by his last editor.

Wordsworth has been said to overpunctuate, yet de Selincourt *adds* as much as he takes away. It might be better to say that Wordsworth's punctuation is merely different from modern accepted practice; sometimes, for example, he apparently uses commas for a pause. I have been chary of meddling with Wordsworth's rhythms and have left most of his punctuation intact. Only where a reader today might become confused have I made changes: where a comma occurs between the subject and its adjacent verb or where one has been omitted between several items in a series.

Unless bracketed, the titles of the poems are those given them by Wordsworth in the last edition or in manuscript. I have changed the titles de Selincourt gave to other poems only when he overlooked a title provided by Wordsworth. The remaining titles originating with de Selincourt I have, however, placed in brackets to indicate their unauthorized status.

When poems have been printed from manuscript I have used brackets to show the state of the text. Where the brackets are empty a word or words were simply left blank by Wordsworth. A question-mark in brackets indicates that a word or words were written but are illegible. A word in brackets followed by a question mark signifies illegibility and conjecture; with the question mark preceding, a bracketed word represents a blank in the manuscript and a conjecture. Bracketed letters also represent blanks and conjecture.

Rather than exclude or place poems of questionable authorship in a special section, I have included them in the text with the other poems. An asterisk preceding a title in the table of contents and in the text indicates either questionable or partial authorship. The reader should consult the notes for further information.

The arrangement of the poems undoubtedly represents my most important editorial decision. Even though William Knight, the most authoritative editor before de Selincourt, arranged his edition in chronological order of composition, such order is still considered by some to be untraditional, if not positively fraudulent because counter to the poet's own wishes.

The main contender is of course Wordsworth's own system of categories, which he used in all the collected editions during his lifetime. Supporters of his system, however, have always been few; Wordsworth himself was perhaps its only enthusiast. Even Ernest de Selincourt has admitted that the system 'will not stand logical examination', with Wordsworth shifting poems from one category to another in the various editions. De Selincourt nevertheless chose the system because of its 'supreme value': namely that it was Wordsworth's. Yet Wordsworth could be a great poet without being a great editor.

Some of the objections previously raised against the order of composition no longer hold. Problems of dating, for example, have largely yielded to the efforts of modern scholars, especially Mark Reed.

And the new dates to some extent eliminate another objection:

that the main reason for Wordsworth's categories in the first place has been ignored – 'that one poem should shade off happily into another' (letter to Henry Crabb Robinson, 6 April 1826). For, as James Scoggins has pointed out in his study of the two most important of Wordsworth's categories, the arrangement of 'Poems of Fancy' and 'Poems of Imagination' very nearly follow the order of composition (*Imagination and Fancy* [1966], p. 74). In any event, Wordsworth's argument based on the supposed offensiveness of abrupt transitions from one kind of poem to another rests on the premise that such transitions *should* offend the reader, not that they in fact *do* so. I doubt very much if most readers read through a volume from cover to cover, or even from the beginning of one section to the end.

The most forceful objection to order by composition is that datings, no matter how accurate, mislead. In the case of longer poems written over a period of years no real problem occurs, since only *The Excursion* is involved to any extent and consequently is easy enough to remember. Like Knight, I have placed the poem at the beginning of 1814, when it was completed. As for short poems in a series, I have left intact seven series that were written and published as a series. Of the poems in each series, most were written during a short period; and the few other poems, I believe, present no difficulty.

But even with Wordsworth's short poems there is a serious problem, inasmuch as he revised many of his poems, some of them extensively. If the poems are studied for evidence of the evolution of his poetic style, the reader should consult de Selincourt's edition for variants before drawing too specific conclusions. The problems of ordering poems whose composition dates are very tentative or span a number of years should bring the reader who is seriously interested in Wordsworth's stylistic development to the head-notes of the poems to determine how definite the order of the poems involved is.

Moreover, even with a poet who revised less than Wordsworth and the dating of whose poems is more certain than his, the study of poetic evolution would pose very complex problems and would require extreme caution. Still, it is a mistake to consider stylistic development as the only thing that can be

examined from an arrangement by composition. Study of Words-
worth's developing interests in themes and forms, to the extent
that they can be seen as separate from style, is another advantage
of this arrangement.

Order of composition is in fact the standard method of
ordering the works of most poets. Wordsworth himself consid-
ered it the proper method 'in the case of juvenile poems or those
of advanced age' (letter to Henry Crabb Robinson, 27 April
1826). And chronology of composition is the method followed
in selected editions and in anthologies, surely the most common
forms in which Wordsworth's poems are read today.

By placing poems by date of composition, moreover, one of
the disadvantages of Wordsworth's system is circumvented,
namely the formation of the large clump of the poems that were
not in the 1849–50 edition. They form a separate 'category'
in de Selincourt's edition, a group of poems that have no literary
reason whatsoever for combination.

Chronology of composition, therefore, seems to me the most
reasonable of the methods for ordering Wordsworth's poems.
Even in the absence of the above arguments, it would have won,
I believe, by default: there is no other method that is as good.
Information concerning Wordsworth's categories are, however,
available in the head-notes to the poems.

The dates of composition of the poems written before 1815
are taken, often word for word, from Mark Reed's two studies
of Wordsworth's chronology, although I have sometimes
supplemented his lists with more specific terminal dates.
After 1815 the dates of composition are derived from my own
research.

The order of the poems in this edition, however, differs at
times from Reed's lists. Although I do follow Reed's codes and
their descending order of likelihood (probably, perhaps, pos-
sibly), unlike him I have usually given the probable dates
precedence in the placement of the poems and have given
priority to the composition of the bulk of a poem over the writing
of a few lines. Within a particular year, moreover, the poems
are given in the following order of dates of composition: 1) the
exact date, 2) the month, 3) the season, 4) whether early or late

within the year. Within a series of years, the poems are given by the earliest date of a substantial part of composition. For example, the dates of the poems of the year 1800 might read: 2 January 1800, 15 January 1800, January 1800, between January and April 1800, February 1800, early 1800, July 1800, summer 1800, 7 October 1800, probably 1800, possibly 1800, 1800–1801, probably 1800–1801. At times the ordering of the poems is thus only suggestive of the actual, unknown dates of composition.

Having ignored Wordsworth's wishes about the arrangement of the poems, I have been allowed by the format of this series of editions at least to follow his injunction that 'the poems should be left to speak for themselves' (letter to E. Moxon, 5 November 1845), with the notes placed at the end of the volumes. The scholarly sources for the information in the notes are usually not given unless the material is from an unfamiliar source (that is, not from a previous collected edition) or is merely speculative. Covering the same ground examined by so many editors does not allow for much that is original; consequently I take credit for little of the information in the notes beyond making numerous citations more definite.

Perhaps my principal contribution to Wordsworthian annotation is the limitation of the notes as strictly as possible to those that illuminate the text. The notes dictated by Wordsworth to Isabella Fenwick in 1843 have been especially trimmed to what is pertinent to the poems, either to their composition or to their meaning and form. The same is true of Wordsworth's own footnotes, except that I have been a bit more liberal in applying my rule. At the time of publication Wordsworth in these notes apparently thought he was aiding the reader in some way; the Fenwick notes, on the other hand, were originally intended only to satisfy the interests of Wordsworth's family and friends.

It is the nature of many of the annotations of Wordsworth's poems to point up the autobiographical nature of his poetry; this is especially true of the Fenwick notes. Such information, I believe, is useful in understanding the poems; but caution should be exerted not to treat the poems as if they are mere anecdotes from the life of the poet.

If a poem was printed in any collected edition before Wordsworth's death in 1850, the category to which he assigned it is given in the head-note to that poem at the rear of the volume. The first category date given is also the date of the first collected edition in which the poem appeared; if none is given and the date of first publication precedes 1850, the poem was not collected by Wordsworth. The poems first published in the *Lyrical Ballads* of 1798 and 1800 are cited as such in the head-notes, but often they were revised, and so care should be taken against reading them as if in their original forms. *The Prelude* has not been included in this edition, because it has already been published in an edition of its own by Penguin in 1971.

Few variants are given in the notes. Only those revisions of special interest are either noticed or quoted.

The Barberry-Tree is published with the consent of the Librarian on behalf of the Governing Body of Christ Church, Oxford; *Fragments on a Heroic Theme*, originally included in *The Early Wordsworthian Milieu*, ed. Z. S. Fink (1958) is published by permission of Oxford University Press: and *More may not be by Human Art Exprest* is reprinted from *Wordsworth's Pocket Notebook*, edited with commentary by George Harris Healey, copyright 1942, by Cornell University Press and used by permission of Cornell University Press.

I should like to acknowledge the generosity of the Dove Cottage Trustees in allowing me to publish new material from manuscripts under their care. Other libraries to which I am obliged for making available manuscripts in their possession are the British Museum; the Queen's Library, Windsor; Christ Church Library, Oxford; the Fitzwilliam Museum, Cambridge; the Pierpont Morgan Library, New York; the Huntington Library; and the Cornell University Library. The staffs of all these libraries were most helpful and generous with their time, as were also the staff of the Reading Room of the British Museum and the Interlibrary Loan Department of the Library of the University of California, Davis.

Perhaps my largest debt, in view of the immense work involved in producing an edition of this size, is to the typists who were so careful and concerned for the accuracy of text and notes.

Elaine Bukhari was responsible for the text, Betty Kimura for the notes. Several work-study assistants also helped with this edition at various stages; I should like to thank them all for their diligent services. My work at the Dove Cottage Library was more productive than otherwise might have been the case because of the generous advice of two scholars present at the time, Paul Betz and Beth Darlington. Robert Kirkpatrick of the University of North Carolina gave me help on one poem, and my old friend, George Dekker, of Stanford University, read the introduction and offered advice on the edition as a whole. I should also like to thank my wife, who helped with the examination of manuscript material and put up with many inconveniences during the production of this edition.

These volumes are dedicated to Donald Davie.

Further Reading

[For further reading concerning *The Prelude* specifically, see J. C. Maxwell's edition of *The Prelude* in this series.]

EDITIONS

[For editions published during Wordsworth's lifetime, see the Table of Dates.]

The Poetical Works of William Wordsworth, 6 volumes, 1857 [the first edition to contain the Fenwick Notes].

Matthew Arnold, ed., *Poems of Wordsworth*, 1879 [a selected edition with the well-known introduction].

William Knight, ed., *The Poetical Works of William Wordsworth*, 11 volumes (the last three volumes contain the *Life*), 1882–9 [superseded by the 1896 edition].

Edward Dowden, ed., *The Poetical Works of William Wordsworth*, 7 volumes, 1892–3 [The Aldine Edition].

Thomas Hutchinson, ed., *The Poetical Works of William Wordsworth*, 5 volumes, 1895 [basis of the Oxford Standard Authors edition].

William Knight, ed., *The Poetical Works of William Wordsworth*, 8 volumes, 1896.

A. J. George, ed., *The Complete Poetical Works of Wordsworth*, Houghton Mifflin Co., Boston and New York, 1904 [Cambridge Edition].

Nowell C. Smith, ed., *The Poems of William Wordsworth*, 3 volumes, Methuen, 1908.

Ernest de Selincourt and Helen Darbishire, eds., *The Poetical Works of William Wordsworth*, 5 volumes,

Clarendon Press, 1940–49 [revised ed., volumes I–III, 1952–4; the standard edition].

Philip Wayne, ed., *Wordsworth's Poems*, 3 volumes, 1955 [Everyman edition].

W. J. B. Owen and J. W. Smyser, eds., *The Prose Works of William Wordsworth*, 3 volumes, Clarendon Press, 1974.

BIBLIOGRAPHIES AND REFERENCE WORKS

Bernbaum, Ernest, James V. Logan, and Ford T. Swetnam, Jr., 'Wordsworth', in *The English Romantic Poets: A Review of Research and Criticism*, 3rd Rev. ed., ed. Frank Jordan, New York, 1972.

Cooper, Lane, *A Concordance to the Poems of Wordsworth*, 1911.

Hayden, John O., *The Romantic Reviewers 1802–24*, Routledge & Kegan Paul, 1969 [chapter 3].

Healey, G. H., ed., *The Cornell Wordsworth Collection: A Catalogue*, Cornell University Press, 1957.

Henley, E. F. and D. H. Stam, eds., *Wordsworthian Criticism, 1945–1964; An Annotated Bibliography*, New York Public Library, 1965.

Logan, J. F., *Wordsworthian Criticism: A Guide and Bibliography*, Ohio State University Press, 1961.

Peacock, M. L., Jr., ed., *The Critical Opinions of William Wordsworth*, Johns Hopkins Press, 1950.

Reed, Mark, *Wordsworth: The Chronology of the Early Years 1770–1799*, Harvard University Press, 1967.

—, *Wordsworth: The Chronology of the Middle Years 1800–1815*, Harvard University Press, 1975.

Smith, Elsie, ed., *An Estimate of William Wordsworth by His Contemporaries 1793–1822*, Blackwell, 1932.

Stam, David H., *Wordsworthian Criticism, 1964–1973; an Annotated Bibliography*, New York Public Library, 1974

Woodring, Carl, *Politics in English Romantic Poetry*, Harvard University Press, 1970 [chapter 4].

BIOGRAPHIES, LETTERS, AND JOURNALS

Broughton, L. N., ed., *Some Letters of the Wordsworth Family*, Cornell University Press, 1942.

—, ed., *Wordsworth and Reed: The Poet's Correspondence with His American Editor: 1836–1850*, Cornell University Press, 1933.

Burton, Mary E., ed., *The Letters of Mary Wordsworth*, Clarendon Press, 1958.

Coburn, Kathleen, ed., *The Letters of Sara Hutchinson*, Routledge & Kegan Paul, 1954.

De Selincourt, Ernest, ed., *Journals of Dorothy Wordsworth*, 2 volumes, New York, Macmillan, 1941.

—, ed., *The Letters of William and Dorothy Wordsworth: The Later Years*, 3 volumes, Clarendon Press, 1939.

Harper, G. M., *William Wordsworth: His Life, Works, and Influence*, 3rd ed., Scribners, 1929.

Margoliouth, H. M., *Wordsworth and Coleridge, 1795–1834*, Oxford University Press, 1953.

Moorman, Mary, ed., *Journals of Dorothy Wordsworth*, Oxford University Press, 1971 [The Alfoxden and Grasmere Journals].

—, ed., *The Letters of William and Dorothy Wordsworth*, arranged and edited by E. de Selincourt, 2nd ed., revised, Volume II. *The Middle Years, Part 1, 1806–1811*, Oxford University Press, 1969.

Moorman, Mary, and Alan G. Hill, eds., *Ibid.*, Volume III. *The Middle Years, Part 2, 1812–1820*, Oxford University Press, 1970.

Moorman, Mary, *William Wordsworth, A Biography: The Early Years, 1770–1803*, Clarendon Press, 1957.

—, *William Wordsworth, A Biography: The Later Years, 1803–1850*, Clarendon Press, 1965.

Morley, Edith J., ed., *Henry Crabb Robinson on Books and Their Writers*, 3 volumes, Longmans, Green, 1938.

Shaver, Chester L., ed., *The Letters of William and Dorothy*

Wordsworth, arranged and edited by E. de Selincourt, 2nd ed., revised, Volume I. *The Early Years, 1787–1805*, Oxford University Press, 1967.

Thompson, T. W., *Wordsworth's Hawkshead*, ed. Robert Woof, Oxford University Press, 1970.

Wordsworth, Christopher, *Memoirs of William Wordsworth, Poet-Laureate, D.C.L.*, 2 volumes, 1851.

SELECTED CRITICISM

Bateson, F. W., *Wordsworth: A Re-interpretation*, Longmans, Green, 1954.

Batho, Edith C., *The Later Wordsworth*, N. Y., Russell & Russell, 1963 [1933].

Beatty, Arthur, *William Wordsworth: His Doctrine and Art in Their Historical Relations*, 3rd ed., University of Wisconsin Press, 1960.

Bloom, Harold, *The Visionary Company: A Reading of English Romantic Literature*, 2nd ed., Cornell University Press, 1971 [Chapter 2].

Clarke, C. C., *Romantic Paradox: An Essay on the Poetry of Wordsworth*, Routledge & Kegan Paul, 1962.

Coleridge, Samuel Taylor, *Biographia Literaria*, ed. J. Shawcross, 2 volumes, Clarendon Press, 1907 [Chapters 4, 14, 17–20, 22].

Danby, J. F., *The Simple Wordsworth: Studies in the Poems 1797–1807*, Routledge & Kegan Paul, 1960.

Davie, Donald, *Selected Poems of William Wordsworth*, Hutchinson, 1962 [Introduction].

Davis, Jack, ed., *William Wordsworth*, Boston, Heath, 1963 [Collection of essays by various hands].

De Selincourt, Ernest, *Dorothy Wordsworth: A Biography*, Clarendon Press, 1933.

Dunklin, G. T., ed., *Wordsworth: Centenary Studies Presented at Cornell and Princeton Universities*, Princeton University Press, 1951 [Collection of essays by various hands].

Durrant, Geoffrey, *Wordsworth and the Great System: A Study of Wordsworth's Poetic Universe*, Cambridge University Press, 1970.

Ferry, David, *The Limits of Mortality: An Essay on Wordsworth's Major Poems*, Wesleyan University Press, 1959.

Garlitz, Barbara, 'The Baby's Debut: The Contemporary Reaction to Wordsworth's Poetry of Childhood', *Boston University Studies in English*, IV (1960), pp. 85–94.

Grob, Alan, *The Philosophic Mind: A Study of Wordsworth's Poetry and Thought 1797–1805*, Ohio State University Press, 1973.

Hartman, Geoffrey H., *Wordsworth's Poetry, 1787–1814*, Yale University Press, 1965.

Heffernan, James A. W., *Wordsworth's Theory of Poetry: The Transforming Imagination*, Cornell University Press, 1969.

Jones, John, *The Egotistical Sublime: A History of Wordsworth's Imagination*, Chatto & Windus, 1954.

Leavis, F. R., *Revaluation: Tradition and Development in English Poetry*, Chatto & Windus, 1936 [Chapter 5].

Marsh, Florence, *Wordsworth's Imagery: A Study in Poetic Vision*, Yale University Press, 1952.

Mayo, Robert, 'The Contemporaneity of the Lyrical Ballads', *Publications of the Modern Language Association*, LXIX (1954), pp. 486–522.

McMaster, Graham, ed., *William Wordsworth: Penguin Critical Anthology*, Penguin Books, 1972.

Miles, Josephine, *Wordsworth and the Vocabulary of Emotion*, University of California Press, 1942.

Owen, W. J. B., *Wordsworth as Critic*, University of Toronto Press, 1969.

Parrish, Stephen Maxfield, *The Art of the Lyrical Ballads*, Harvard University Press, 1973.

Perkins, David, *Wordsworth and the Poetry of Sincerity*, Harvard University Press, 1964.

Piper, H. W., *The Active Universe: Pantheism and the*

Concept of Imagination in the English Romantic Poets,
Athlone Press, 1962.

Rader, Melvin, *Wordsworth: A Philosophical Approach,*
Clarendon Press, 1967.

Read, Herbert, *Wordsworth,* Jonathan Cape, 1930.

Scoggins, James, *Imagination and Fancy: Complementary
Modes in the Poetry of Wordsworth,* University of Nebraska
Press, 1967.

Sheats, Paul D., *The Making of Wordsworth's Poetry
1785–98,* Harvard University Press, 1973.

Smith, James, 'Wordsworth: A Preliminary Survey',
Scrutiny, VII (1938).

Sperry, W. L., *Wordsworth's Anti-Climax,* Harvard University
Press, 1935.

Stallknecht, N. P., *Strange Seas of Thought: Studies in
William Wordsworth's Philosophy of Man and Nature,* 2nd ed.,
Indiana University Press, 1958.

Thomson, A. W., ed., *Wordsworth's Mind and Art,* Oliver
& Boyd, 1969 [Collection of essays by various hands].

Thorpe, C. D., 'The Imagination: Coleridge vs. Wordsworth',
Philological Quarterly, XVIII (1939), pp. 1–18.

Trilling, Lionel, 'The Immortality Ode', in *The Liberal
Imagination,* Secker & Warburg, 1951.

Willey, Basil, *The Eighteenth Century Background: Studies on
the Idea of Nature in the Thought of the Period,* Chatto &
Windus, 1941 [Chapter 12].

Woodring, Carl, *Wordsworth,* Boston, Houghton Mifflin
& Co. 1965.

Wordsworth, Jonathan, *The Music of Humanity: A Critical
Study of Wordsworth's 'Ruined Cottage',* Nelson, 1969.

—, ed., *Bicentenary Wordsworth Studies in Memory of John
Alban Finch,* Cornell University Press, 1970 [Collection of
essays by various hands].

Lines Written as a School Exercise at Hawkshead, Anno Aetatis 14

'And has the Sun his flaming chariot driven
Two hundred times around the ring of heaven,
Since Science first, with all her sacred train,
Beneath yon roof began her heavenly reign?
While thus I mused, methought, before mine eyes,
The Power of Education seemed to rise;
Not she whose rigid precepts trained the boy
Dead to the sense of every finer joy;
Nor that vile wretch who bade the tender age
10   Spurn Reason's law and humour Passion's rage;
But she who trains the generous British youth
In the bright paths of fair majestic Truth:
Emerging slow from Academus' grove
In heavenly majesty she seemed to move.
Stern was her forehead, but a smile serene
"Softened the terrors of her awful mien."
Close at her side were all the powers, designed
To curb, exalt, reform the tender mind:
With panting breast, now pale as winter snows,
20   Now flushed as Hebe, Emulation rose;
Shame followed after with reverted eye,
And hue far deeper than the Tyrian dye;
Last Industry appeared with steady pace,
A smile sat beaming on her pensive face.
I gazed upon the visionary train,
Threw back my eyes, returned, and gazed again.
When lo! the heavenly goddess thus began,
Through all my frame the pleasing accents ran.

' "When Superstition left the golden light
30   And fled indignant to the shades of night;
When pure Religion reared the peaceful breast
And lulled the warring passions into rest,

Drove far away the savage thoughts that roll
In the dark mansions of the bigot's soul,
Enlivening Hope displayed her cheerful ray,
And beamed on Britain's sons a brighter day;
So when on Ocean's face the storm subsides,
Hushed are the winds and silent are the tides;
The God of day, in all the pomp of light,
40   Moves through the vault of heaven, and dissipates the
         night;
Wide o'er the main a trembling lustre plays,
The glittering waves reflect the dazzling blaze;
Science with joy saw Superstition fly
Before the lustre of Religion's eye;
With rapture she beheld Britannia smile,
Clapped her strong wings, and sought the cheerful isle.
The shades of night no more the soul involve,
She sheds her beam, and, lo! the shades dissolve;
No jarring monks, to gloomy cell confined,
50   With mazy rules perplex the weary mind;
No shadowy forms entice the soul aside,
Secure she walks, Philosophy her guide.
Britain, who long her warriors had adored,
And deemed all merit centred in the sword;
Britain, who thought to stain the field was fame,
Now honoured Edward's less than Bacon's name.
Her sons no more in listed field advance
To ride the ring, or toss the beamy lance;
No longer steel their indurated hearts
60   To the mild influence of the finer arts;
Quick to the secret grotto they retire
To court majestic truth, or wake the golden lyre;
By generous Emulation taught to rise,
The seats of learning brave the distant skies.
Then noble Sandys, inspired with great design,
Reared Hawkshead's happy roof, and called it mine;
There have I loved to show the tender age
The golden precepts of the classic page;
To lead the mind to those Elysian plains

70   Where, throned in gold, immortal Science reigns;
     Fair to the view is sacred Truth displayed,
     In all the majesty of light arrayed,
     To teach, on rapid wings, the curious soul
     To roam from heaven to heaven, from pole to pole,
     From thence to search the mystic cause of things,
     And follow Nature to her secret springs;
     Nor less to guide the fluctuating youth
     Firm in the sacred paths of moral truth,
     To regulate the mind's disordered frame,
80   And quench the passions kindling into flame;
     The glimmering fires of Virtue to enlarge,
     And purge from Vice's dross my tender charge.
     Oft have I said, the paths of Fame pursue,
     And all that Virtue dictates, dare to do;
     Go to the world, peruse the book of man,
     And learn from thence thy own defects to scan;
     Severely honest, break no plighted trust,
     But coldly rest not here – be more than just;
     Join to the rigour of the sires of Rome
90   The gentler manners of the private dome;
     When Virtue weeps in agony of woe,
     Teach from the heart the tender tear to flow;
     If Pleasure's soothing song thy soul entice,
     Or all the gaudy pomp of splendid Vice,
     Arise superior to the Siren's power,
     The wretch, the short-lived vision of an hour;
     Soon fades her cheek, her blushing beauties fly,
     As fades the chequered bow that paints the sky.
     ' "So shall thy sire, whilst hope his breast inspires,
100 And wakes anew life's glimmering trembling fires,
     Hear Britain's sons rehearse thy praise with joy,
     Look up to heaven, and bless his darling boy.
     If e'er these precepts quelled the passions' strife,
     If e'er they smoothed the rugged walks of life,
     If e'er they pointed forth the blissful way
     That guides the spirit to eternal day,
     Do thou, if gratitude inspire thy breast,

Spurn the soft fetters of lethargic rest.
Awake, awake! and snatch the slumbering lyre,
110 Let this bright morn and Sandys the song inspire."
    'I looked Obedience: the celestial Fair
    Smiled like the morn, then vanished into air.'

Anacreon

Αγε, ζωγραφων αριστε

(*Imitated*)

Reynolds, come, thy pencil prove,
Reynolds, come and paint my love,
Shadowed here her picture see
Shadowed by the muse and me.
The muse who knows 'twere rash to dare
From life to paint a form so fair,
For sure so many charms combine
Half Apelles' fate were thine.
    Waving in the wanton air
10 Black and shining paint her hair;
Could with Life the canvas bloom
Thou mightst bid it breathe perfume.
Let her forehead smooth and clear
Through her shading locks appear,
As at eve the shepherd sees
The silver crescent through the trees;
Nicely bend the living line
Black and delicately fine,
As you paint her sable brows
20 Arched like two etherial bows.
    Gentle as a vernal sky
Soft and sleepy paint her eye
Trembling as the lunar beam
Sweetly silvering o'er the stream.
Now her lovely cheek adorn
With the blushes of the morn.
Give her lip the rose's hue

Moistened with the morning dew,
Paint it breathing love and joy,
30   Breathing bliss that ne'er can cloy.
        Let thy softest pencil throw
O'er her neck a tint of snow,
There let all the Loves repair,
Let all the Graces flutter there.
Loosely chaste o'er all below
Let the snowy mantle flow,
As silvered by the morning beam
The white mist curls on Grasmere's stream,
Which, like a veil of flowing light,
40   Hides half the landskip from the sight.
Here I see the wandering rill,
The white flocks sleeping on the hill,
While Fancy paints, beneath the veil,
The pathway winding through the dale,
The cot, the seat of Peace and Love,
Peeping through the tufted grove.
        Reynolds, Heaven directs the line,
Heaven inspires the fair design;
All but Life thy pencil gives,
50   Gods! she comes, the picture lives.

The Dog – An Idyllium

Quicquid est hominum venustiorum Lugete. –
Fies nobilium tu quoque. –

Where were ye, nymphs, when the remorseless deep
Closed o'er your little favourite's hapless head?
For neither did ye mark with solemn dream
In Derwent's rocky woods the white Moon's beam
Pace like a Druid o'er the haunted steep;
Nor in Winander's stream.
Then did ye swim with sportive smile
From fairy-templed isle to isle,
Which hear her far-off ditty sweet

10 Yet feel not even the milkmaid's feet.
    What tho' he still was by my side
    When, lurking near, I there have seen
    Your faces white, your tresses green,
    Like water lilies floating on the tide?
    He saw not, barked not, he was still
    As the soft moonbeam sleeping on the hill,
    Or when ah! cruel maids, ye stretched him stiff and chill.

    .   .   .   .   .

    If, while I gazed to Nature blind,
    In the calm Ocean of my mind
20 Some new-created image rose
    In full-grown beauty at its birth
    Lovely as Venus from the sea,
    Then, while my glad hand sprung to thee,
    We were the happiest pair on earth.

[*Septimius and Acme*]

(Catullus, XLV)

Septimius thus his [   ] love addressed,
His darling Acme in his arms sustained,
'My Acme, may I perish if my breast
Burns not for thee with love to madness strained,
And more – if I am not prepared to give
To thee such earnest love unchanged by time
As any human heart can feel and live,
Then may I roam through Lybia's burning clime
And meet alone the ravenous lion's roar.'
10 He spoke and at the word the God of love,
    The God of love, as from the right before,
    Sneezed from the left, and did the vow approve.
    But Acme, lightly turning back her head,
    Kissed with that rosy mouth the inebriate eyes
    Of the sweet youth, and kissed again and said:
    'My life, and what far more than life I prize,

So may we to the end of time obey
Love our sole master, as my bosom owns
A flame that with far more resistless sway
20   Thrills through the very marrow of my bones.'
She spoke and Love, as from the right before,
Sneezed from the left hand and the vow approved.
Needing no other omen to implore,
With mutual soul they love and are beloved;
His Acme only does Septimius prize
All Syria and all Britain's wealth above;
And Acme for Septimius only sighs,
And finds in him alone her sole delight and love.
Whoe'er a more auspicious passion saw,
30   Or any mortals under happier law?

Translation of a Celebrated Greek Song

– And I will bear my vengeful blade
With the myrtle boughs arrayed,
As Harmodius before,
As Aristogiton bore,
When the tyrant's breast they gored
With the myrtle-branded sword,
Gave to Triumph Freedom's cause,
Gave to Athens equal laws.
Where, unnumbered with the dead,
10   Dear Harmodius, art thou fled?
Athens says 'tis thine to rest
In the islands of the blest,
Where Achilles swift of feet
And the brave Tydides meet.
I will bear my vengeful blade
With the myrtle boughs arrayed,
As Harmodius before,
As Aristogiton bore,
Towering mid the festal train
20   O'er the man Hipparchus slain,

Tyrant of his brother men;
Let thy name, Harmodius dear,
Live through heaven's eternal year;
Long as heaven and earth survive
Dear Aristogiton, live;
With the myrtle-branded sword
Ye the tyrant's bosom gored,
Gave to triumph Freedom's cause,
Gave to Athens equal laws.

To Melpomene

[A FRAGMENT]

Come then in robe of darkest blue
And face of pale and sickly hue –
Who *Moon-like* guid'st the liquid swell
Of sounds that float upon the shell
At whose soft touch whate'er is mute
Talks with a voice like Pity's Lute
– Like what the Sailor's Widow hears
At Night dull-tingling in her ears
While touchèd by the *moon-raised* Surge
10 The wild rocks round her sing a wondrous Dirge,
That floats around thy poet's shell of bluest night
Which liquid words tender light
[   ] have a sound themselves and give a sound
              cetera desunt

The Death of a Starling – Catullus

(*Sunt lacrimae rerum – Lugete,* [*o*] *Veneres Cupidinesque*)

Pity mourns in plaintive tone
The lovely Starling dead and gone.
Weep, ye Loves, and Venus, weep
The lovely Starling fallen asleep.
Venus see with tearful eyes,

In her lap the starling lies,
While the Loves all in a ring
Softly stroke the stiffened wing.

.   .   .   .   .

Yet art thou happier far than she
10   Who felt a mother's love for thee.
For while her days are days of weeping,
Thou, in peace, in silence sleeping
In some still world, unknown, remote
The mighty Parent's care hast found,
Without whose tender guardian thought
No Sparrow falleth to the ground.

[*Lesbia*]

(Catullus, v)

My Lesbia let us love and live,
And to the winds my Lesbia give
Each cold restraint, each boding fear
Of Age and all her saws severe.
Yon sun now posting to the main
Will set – but 'tis to rise again;
But we, when once our [   ] light
Is set, must sleep in endless night.
Then come, with whom alone I live,
10   A thousand kisses take or give,
Another thousand – to the store
Add hundreds – then a thousand more,
And when they to a million mount
Let Confusion take the account,
That you, the number never knowing,
May continue still bestowing,
That I for joys may never pine
That never can again be mine.

Beauty and Moonlight

AN ODE

Fragment

High o'er the silver rocks I roved
To wander from the form I loved,
In hopes fond Fancy would be kind
And steal my Mary from my mind;
'Twas Twilight and the lunar beam
Sailed slowly o'er Winander's stream.
As down its sides the water strayed
Bright on a rock the moonbeam played.
It shone half-sheltered from the view
10 By pendent boughs of tressy yew,
True, true to love but false to rest,
So fancy whispered to my breast;
So shines her forehead smooth and fair
Gleaming through her sable hair.
    I turned to Heaven, but viewed on high
The languid lustre of her eye,
The moon's mild radiant edge I saw
Peeping a black-arched cloud below,
Nor yet its faint and paly beam
20 Could tinge its skirt with yellow gleam.
    I saw the white waves o'er and o'er
Break against a curvèd shore,
Now disappearing from the sight
Now twinkling regular and white;
Her mouth, her smiling mouth can show
As white and regular a row.
    Haste – haste, some god indulgent prove
And bear me, bear me to my Love.
Then might – for yet the sultry hour
30 Glows from the Sun's oppressive power,
Then might her bosom soft and white
Heave upon my swimming sight,

As these two Swans together ride
Upon the gently swelling tide.
Haste, haste, some god indulgent prove,
And bear me, bear me to my Love.

Sonnet on Seeing Miss Helen Maria Williams Weep at a Tale of Distress

She wept. – Life's purple tide began to flow
In languid streams through every thrilling vein;
Dim were my swimming eyes – my pulse beat slow,
And my full heart was swelled to dear delicious pain.
Life left my loaded heart, and closing eye;
A sigh recalled the wanderer to my breast;
Dear was the pause of life, and dear the sigh
That called the wanderer home, and home to rest.
That tear proclaims – in thee each virtue dwells,
10 And bright will shine in misery's midnight hour;
As the soft star of dewy evening tells
What radiant fires were drowned by day's malignant
    power,
That only wait the darkness of the night
To cheer the wandering wretch with hospitable light.

Sonnet Written by Mr — Immediately after the Death of his Wife

The Sun is dead – ye heard the curfew toll,
Come, Nature, let us mourn our kindred doom;
My Sun like thine is dead – and o'er my Soul
Despair's dark midnight spreads her raven gloom,
Yes, she is gone – he called her to illume
The realms where Heaven's immortal rivers roll
Who bids thy Sun, O Nature, shed the bloom
Of light and life upon a happier pole.
Yet soon thy Sun shall wake his sister light

And lo the shades of Darkness roll away;
She too shall soon from her [   ] height
Pour o'er my breast Religion's moonlight ray,
To cheer me through my long and lonely night
Till Heaven's bright Morn lead on the eternal day.

[*A Ballad*]

'And will you leave me thus alone
And dare you break your vow?
Be sure her Ghost will haunt thy bed
When Mary shall lie low.'

So spoke in tears – but all in vain
The fairest maid of Esthwaite's vale,
To love's soft glance his eye was shut
His ear to Pity's tale.

And oft at Eve he sought the bridge
10   That near her window lay;
There gayly laughed with other maids
Or sung the hour away.

She saw – and wept – her father frowned,
Her heart began to break;
And oft the live-long day she sat
And word would never speak.

Oft has she seen sweet Esthwaite's lake
Reflect the morning sheen;
When lo! the sullen clouds arise
20   And dim the smiling scene.

Reflected once in Mary's face
The village saw a mind more fair;
Now every charm was all o'erhung
By woe and black despair.

And oft she roamed at dark midnight
Among the silent graves;
Or sat on steep Winander's rock
To hear the weltering waves.

Her father saw and he grew kind,
30 And soon Religion shed
Hope's cheering ray to light her to
Her dark, her wormy bed.

For now her hour of Death was nigh,
And oft her waft was seen
With wan light standing at a door,
Or shooting o'er the green.

She saw – she cried – ''tis all in vain
For broken is my heart,
And well I know my hour is nigh,
40 I know that we must part.

Heaven told me once – but I was blind –
My head would soon lie low;
A Rose within our Garden blew
Amid December's snow.

That Rose my William saw – and plucked,
He plucked and gave it me;
Heaven warned me then – ah blind was I –
That he my death would be.

And soon these eyes shall cease to weep
50 And cease to sob my breath;
Feel – what can warm this clay-cold hand?'
– Her hand was cold as Death.

To warm her hand a glove they brought,
    The glove her William gave;
She saw, she wept, and sighed the sigh
    That sent her to her grave.

Her knell was rung – the Virgins came
    And kissed her in her shroud;
The children touched – 'twas all they durst
60   They touched and wept aloud.

The next day to the grave they went,
    All flocked around her bier;
Nor hand without a flower was there
    Nor eye without a tear.

The Vale of Esthwaite

[?] avaunt! with tenfold pleasure
I [?] the landskip's various treasure.
Lark, O Lark, thy Song awake
Suspended o'er the glassy lake
And see the mist, as warms the day,
From the green vale steals away;
And ah! yon lingering fleecy streak,
As breaks the rainbow, soon shall break;
Now like a [   ] silver zone
10 On the lake's lovely bosom thrown
Yet round the mountain tops it sails
Slow born[e] upon the dewy gales.
And on yon summit brown an[d] bare,
That seems an island in the air,
The shepherd's restless dog I mark,
Who, bounding round with frequent bark,
Now leaps around the uncovered plain,
Now dives into the mist again;
And while the guiding sound he hears
20 The [   ] shepherd lad appears
Who knows his transport while he sees
His cottage smoking from the trees,
[?] [knows?] the shepherd boy
And clasps his clinging dog for joy.

At noon I hied to gloomy glades,
Religious woods and midnight shades,
Where brooding Superstition frowned
A cold and awful horror round,
While with black arm and bending head
30   She wove a stole of sable thread.
And hark! the ringing harp I hear
And lo! her druid sons appear.
Why roll on me your glaring eyes?
Why fix on me for sacrifice?
      But he, the stream's loud genius, seen
      The black arched boughs and rocks between
      That brood o'er one eternal night,
      Shoots from the cliff in robe of white.
      So oft in castle moated round
40   In black damp dungeon underground,
      Strange forms are seen that, white and tall,
      Stand straight against the coal-black wall.
         Then musing onward would I stray
         Till every rude sound died away
         And naught was heard but at my feet
         The faint rill tinkling softly sweet.
      [   ] Gothic mansion stood
      In the black centre of a wood,
      [   ] ever of his rusted door
50   [   ] shield from death the wandering poor.

And oft as ceased the owl his song
That screamed the roofless walls among,
Spirits yelling from their pains
And lashes loud and clanking chains
Were heard by minstrel led astray
Cold wandering through the swampy way,
Who as he flies the mingled moan
Deep sighs his harp with hollow groan.
He starts the dismal sound to hear,
60   Nor dares revert his eyes for fear:
Again his harp with grating thrill

Shrieks at his shoulder sharp and shrill;
Aghast he views, with eyes of fire,
A grisly Phantom smite the wire.
Then fancy, like the lightning gleam,
Shot from wondrous dream to dream;
Till roused, perhaps the flickering dove
Broke from the rustling boughs above,
Or straggled sheep with white fleece seen
70   Between the Boughs of sombrous green,
Starting wildly from its sleep,
Shook the pebble from the steep
That gingling downward shrill and slow
[   ] in the Rill below. –

Lone wandering oft by Esthwaite's s[tream]
My soul has felt the mystic drea[m],
When Twilight, wrapped in dusky s[hroud],
Slow journeyed from her cave of cloud;
Where, as she sleeps the livelong day
80   And dreams of Philomela's lay,
Her Elfins round her feebly sing,
Or fan her face with silken wing.
Hark, o'er the hills with dewy feet
She comes, and warbles softly sweet,
With voice which was ordained to cheer
In Eden our first father's ear,
When first he saw day's regent drop
Behind the western mountain top;
And sure it soothed his anxious pain,
90   Sweet as the soft low-warbled strain
Of angels hovering round the bed
Where the dying rest their head,
That they may tempt without a fear
The night of Death so dark and drear.
While in the west the robe of day
Fades, slowly fades, from gold to grey,
The oak its boughs and foliage twines
Marked to the view in stronger lines,

Appears with foliage marked to view,
100 In lines of stronger, browner hue,
While every darkening leaf between,
The sky distinct and clear is seen.
But now a thicker blacker veil
Is thrown o'er all the wavering dale
[   ] assume
[   ] against the gloom
[   ] head seems to rear
[   ] the steeple near
[   ] woods and hills with hamlets graced
110 [   ] flat, and seem a level waste.
[   ] last of all the leafy train
[The?] black fir mingles with the plain.
While hills o'er hills in gradual pride
That swelled along the upland's side
From the blunt baffled Vision pass
And melt into one gloomy mass.
And on its bosom all around
No softly sunken vale is found,
Save those seen faintly [?that] combine
120 To form the Horizon's broken line.
      Now holy Melancholy throws
      Soft o'er the soul a still repose,
      Save where we start as from a sleep
      Recoiling from a gloom too deep.
Now too, while o'er the heart we feel
A tender twilight softly steal,
Sweet Pity gives her forms arrayed
In tenderer tints and softer shade;
The heart, when passed the Vision by,
130 Dissolves, nor knows for whom [n]or why.
If winds faint rippling paint it white
The long lake lengthening stretches on the night,
While many a dark [and?] sleeping bay
Blends with the shore and steals away,
With dew-drop eye and languid cheek
Pale as the dying western streak.

[*10 pages (about 500 to 550 lines) were removed from the notebook (D.C. MS. 3) at this point.*]

What though my griefs must never flow
For scenes of visionary woe,
I trust the Bard can never part
140 With Pity, Autumn of the heart!
She comes and o'er the soul we feel
Soft tender tints of Sorrow steal;
Each flaunting thought of glowing dye,
The offspring of a brighter sky
That late in Summer colours dressed
The laughing landscape of the breast,
Is dead, or tinged with darkened shades
In sickly sorrow droops and fades.
But, Charity, thy treasures show
150 A warmer tint and riper glow,
And richly teem with smiling store
For the long Winter of the poor.

How sweet at Eve's still hour the song
Of streams, the hills and vales among.
Wide as the Schoolboy's step the rill
Drops from the near rock tinkling shrill;
The Brook, scarce worth a bridge of stone,
Soothes the lulled ear with softer moan.
A deep majestic murmur shows
160 Where the slow solemn River flows;
The torrent like the raving shore
Swells the full choir['s] sullen roar.

.   .   .   .   .

Hoarse sound the swoln and angry floods
And high amid the rocky [woods?]
Moans the wet wind — my listening ear
The wild lone wailings seems to hear –
Of one who crazed with care and pain
Hung to her straw and clanking chain.

.   .   .   .   .

Yon hamlet far across the vale
170 Is decked in lustre soft and pale;
Hope, like this moon, emerging fair
On the dark night of sad despair
Till higher mounted cannot cheer
The sable mountains frowning near
Yet does she still all fondly play
On scenes remote with smiling ray.
'Tis thus the dawning queen of Night
While ineffectual is her light
To gild the mountains near arrayed
180 In gloomy blank impervious shade
Bounds o'er the gloom . . .

   .   .   .   .

How sweet in life's tear-glistering morn
'While fancy's rays the hills adorn,'
To rove as through an Eden vale
The sad maze of some tender tale,
Pluck the wild flowers and fondly place
The treasure in the bosom's face.
Yet ah! full oft the enchanting while
We crow'd the heart with pile on pile.
190 [   ] rising high
Well from the heart, they droop, and all is dry.

   .   .   .   .   .

To mark the white smoke rising slow
From the wood-built pile below,
Hang like a Spirit on its way,
Hang lingering round with fond delay
Round the dear Spot where late it fell,
And it had loved so long and well.
Methinks my rising soul would smile
With joy, to linger here awhile.

   .   .   .   .   .

200 The ploughboy by his gingling wain
Whistles along the ringing lane

And, as he strikes with sportive lash
The leaves of thick o'erhanging ash
Wavering they fall; while at the sound
The blinking bats flit round and round.

.   .   .   .   .

   The moaning owl shall soon
Sob long and tremulous to the moon
Who soon the dark grey cloud shall fold
In robes of azure white and gold
210 And to the sky a blue restore
Deeper than in the day it wore.

[*D.C. MS. 3 continues here.*]

But Lo the night while from [   ]
The [   ] owl screams her song
And mark the [pain?] of fear
Waves her black banner to the r[ear]
[   ] I the while
Looked through the tall and sable isle
Of firs that to a mansion led
With many a turret on its head;
220 And while the wild wind raved aloud,
And each his grim black forehead bowed,
And flung his mighty arms around
That clanged and met with crashing sound,
They seemed unto my fear-struck mind
Gigantic Moors in battle joined;
While each with hollow-threatening tone
Claimed the hoar castle as his own.
I started – and with wild affright
Turned on the pale-faced child of Night,
230 That wandering through the pathless skies
Shot by fits before my eyes.
Now hollow sounding all around I hear
Deep murmurings creep upon my ear;
No more the wild shrieks of the storm
Drive to its cell the startling worm.

Alone, the Spirit of the surge
Sings from the rocks the tempest's dirge,
While now and then the Fisher's skiff
Clanks its small chain against the cliff.
240 Green isles, steep woods, emerge to view
And white rocks shagged with sable yew
The solemn mists, dark brown or pale,
March slow and solemn down the vale;
The moon with sick and watery face
Wades through the skies with heavy pace.
　　Now did I love the dismal gloom
Of haunted Castle's panelled room
Listening the wild wind's wailing song
Whistling the rattling doors among;
250 When as I heard a rustling sound
My haggard eyes would turn around,
Which strait a female form surveyed
Tall, and in silken vest arrayed.
Her face of wan and ashy hue
And in one hand a taper blue;
Fixed at the door she seemed to stand
And beckoning slowly waved her hand.
I rose, above my head a bell
The mansion shook with solemn knell.
260 Through aisles that shuddered as we passed
By doors [?] flapping [　?　] the blast
And green damp windings dark and steep,
She brought me to a dungeon deep,
Then stopped, and thrice her head she shook,
More pale and ghastly seemed her look.
[　　　　　　　　　] showed
An iron coffer marked with blood.
The taper turned from blue to red
Flashed out – and with a shriek she fled.
270 With arms in horror spread around
I moved – a form unseen I found
Twist round my hand an icy chain
And drag me to the spot again.

But these were poor and puny joys
Fond sickly Fancy's idle toys.
I loved to haunt the giddy steep
That hung loose trembling o'er the deep,
While ghosts of Murderers mounted fast
And grimly glared upon the blast.
280 While the dark whirlwind robed, unseen,
With black arm reared the clouds between;
In anger Heaven's terrific Sire
Prophetic struck the mighty Lyre
Of Nature; with Hell-rouzing sound
Now shrieked the quivering strings around;
At each drear pause a hollow breath
Was heard – that sung of pain and Death,
While, her dark cheek all ghastly bright,
Like a chained Madman laughed the Night.
290 Again! the deep tones strike mine ear,
My soul will melt away with fear,
Or swelled to madness bid me leap
Down, headlong down, the hideous steep.
    Yet Ah! that soul was never blind
To pleasures of a softer kind.
    [   ]
    [   ]
Her tints so shadowy soft and pale
O'er lovely Grasmere's heavenly vale
300 While muttering low the wayward song
I sat the wild field-flowers among;
Through what sweet scenes did fancy rove
While thus her fairy dreams she wove.
Compared with fancy what is truth?
And Reason, what art thou to Youth?
Soft sleeps the breeze upon the deep
Sweet flowers, while all in peace you [sleep?]
[?] of the tempest which may blow
Tomorrow, and may lay you low.

.   .   .   .   .

310 While lighted by the star of eve
No more a curtain shall they form
Giving its shelter from the storm,
The moon retired, air blackened round,
And loud the tempest lashed the ground;
I tried the wide vault dark and blind
While Terror lashed me on behind,
While yelling loud the torrents white
Shot through the gloom upon my sight.
So in his hall in times of yore
320 Alone a Baron, wandering o'er
At midnight hour with melting gaze
The holy forms of other days,
Has marked slow creeping round the wall
A gloom as black as funeral pall,
And a tall Ghost of ashy hue
On every canvas met his view.
     The Demons of the storm in crowds
Glared through the partings of the clouds
While Satan, calling those around,
330 He trod the hills with thundering sound.
Pale, faint and dismal was the trace
Of human feature on his face.

    .   .   .   .   .

On tiptoe, as I leaned, aghast
Listening the hollow-howling blast
I started back – when at my hand
A tall thin Spectre seemed to stand.
Like two wan withered leaves his eyes,
His bones looked sable through his skin
As the pale moonbeam wan and thin
340 Which through a chink of rock we view
On a lone sable blasted eugh.
And on one bended arm he bore
What seemed the poet's harp of yore;
One hand he waved – and would have spoke,
But from his trembling shadow broke

Faint murmuring – sad and hollow moans
As if the wind sighed through his bones.
He waved again, we entered slow
A passage narrow, damp and low,
350 I heard the mountain heave a sigh
Nodding its rocky helm on high,
And on we journeyed man[y] a mile
While all was black as night the while,
Save his tall form before my sight
Seen by the wan, pale, dismal ligh[t]
Around his bones so [   ] shed
Like a white shroud that wraps [?the dead].
Now as we wandered through the gloom
In black Helvellyn's inmost womb
360 The Spectre made a solemn stand,
Slow round my head thrice waved his [?hand],
And [?   ] mine ear then swept his [?lyre]
That shrieked terrific shrill and [?dire]
Shuddered the fiend, the vault among
Echoed the loud and dismal song.
'Twas [done?]. The scene of woe was o'er;
My breaking soul could bear no more.
[?   ] when with a thunderous sound
That shook the groaning mountain round
370 A massy door wide open flew
[   ]
That [?][   ] my grisly guide
Each night my troubled spirit ride
[   ] unveil
To mortal ears the horrid tale
'Twere vain [   ]
Start from my body mad with fear
I saw the ghosts and heard the yell
Of every Briton [   ] who fell
380 When Edmund deaf to horror's cries
Trod out the cruel Brother's eyes
With [   ] heel and savage scowl,
While terror shapeless rides my soul,

[   ] together are we hurled
Far, far amid the shadowy world.
And since that hour, the world unknown,
The world of shades is all my own.

.   .   .   .   .

I saw
A dark and dreary vale below,
390   And through it a river [?strong]
In sleepy horror heaved along,
And many a high rock black and steep
Hung brooding on the darksome deep,
And on each sable rock was seen
A Form of wild terrific mien.
Ha! that is hell-born Murder nigh
With haggard, half-reverted eye,
And now aghast he seems to stare
On some strange Vision in the air,
400   And Suicide with savage glance
Started from his brooding trance,
Then sunk again, anon he eyed
With sullen smiles the torpid tide;
And moody Madness aye was there
With wide-rent robe and shaggy hair.
That streamed all wildly round his f[ace]

.   .   .   .   .

Peace to that noisy brawling din
That jars upon the dirge within,
Dear stream, forgive thy friend, for he
410   Before was never harsh to thee.
But ah! fond prattler, ah! the strain
No more, as wont, can sooth[e] my pain;
Cease, cease, or rouse that sullen roar
As, when a wintry storm is o'er,
Thy rock-fraught heavy heaving flood
Sounds dear, and creeps along the freezing blood.
'Tis dear – and still with merry song

Dashed from the rough rocks lively leaps along.
At sleepy noon what idler now
420   Shall pore upon the willow bough?
Upon thy bosom pleasure dancing,
Still retreating or advancing,
Still art thou dear, fond prattler, run,
And glitter in tomorrow's sun.

[*4 pages (about 200 to 225 lines) were removed from the
notebook (D.C. MS. 3) at this point.*]

No spot but claims the tender tear
By joy or grief to memory dear.
One Evening when the wintry blast
Through the sharp Hawthorn whistling passed
And the poor flocks, all pinched with cold
430   Sad-drooping sought the mountain fold
Long, long, upon yon naked rock
Alone, I bore the bitter shock;
Long, long, my swimming eyes did roam
For little Horse to bear me home,
To bear me – what avails my tear?
To sorrow o'er a Father's bier.
Flow on, in vain thou hast not flowed,
But eased me of a heavy load;
For much it gives my heart relief
440   To pay the mighty debt of grief,
With sighs repeated o'er and o'er,
I mourn because I mourned no more.
For ah! the storm was soon at rest,
Soon broke [   ] upon my breast
Nor did my little heart foresee
She lost a home in losing thee.
Nor did it know of thee bereft
That little more than Heaven was left.
   Thanks to the voice in whisper sweet
450   That says we soon again shall meet;
For oft when fades the leaden day
To joy-consuming pain a prey,

Or from afar the midnight bell
Flings on mine ear its solemn knell,
A still Voice whispers to my breast
I soon shall be with them that rest.
   Then may some kind and pious friend
Assiduous o'er my body bend,
Once might I see him turn aside
460 The kind unwilling tear to hide,
And may – for while the tempests blow,
And cold we tread this vale of woe,
So dearly shall man buy a shed
To hide but for an hour his head.
Nor is one wandering wish to roam
Fondly to his long, long home.
Ah! may my weary body sleep
In peace beneath a green grass heap,
In Churchyard, such at death of day
470 As heard the pensive sighs of Gray;
And if the Children loitering round
Should e'er disturb the holy ground,
Come, [oh?] come with pensive pace
The violated sod replace,
And, what would even in death be dear,
Ah! pour upon the spot a tear.
   Friend of my soul! for whom I feel
What words can never half reveal,
Thou too when musing by the side
480 Of thy Winander's darling tide,
While Hermit Eve in funeral stole
With holy thoughts inspires the soul,
Thou too shalt turn thine eager eyes
To where the Vale of Esthwaite lies
(That vale where first my eyes surveyed
Fair Friendship in thy form arrayed)
And ah! fond wish, methinks I see
One tender thought shall steal to me.
   But cease my soul, ah! cease to pry
490 Through Time's dark veil with curious eye,

That power who gave and only knows
The hour when these sad orbs shall close
May hold before me Nature's page
Till dim seen by the eyes of age;
Then basking in the noontide blaze
Here might I fix my feeble gaze
As on a Book, companion dear
Of childhood's ever merry year,
Retrace each scene with fond delight
500 While memory aids the orbs of sight.
 Perhaps my pains might be beguiled
By some fond vacant gazing child;
He the long wondrous tale would hear
With simple unfastidious ear
For while I wandered round the vale
From every rock would 'hang a tale,'
While he with questions dear and dear
Called tale from tale and tear from tear.
 Yet if Heaven bear me far away
510 To close the evening of my day,
If no vast blank impervious cloud
The powers of thought in darkness shroud,
Sick, trembling at the world unknown
And doubting what to call her own,
Even while my body pants for breath
And shrinks at the dart of Death,
My soul shall cast the wistful view
The longing look alone on you.
As Phoebus, when he sinks to rest
520 Far on the mountains in the west,
While all the vale is dark between
Ungilded by his golden sheen,
A lingering lustre softly throws
On the dear hills where first he rose.
[ ] For I must never share
A tender parent's guardian care;
Sure, from the world's unkind alarm,
Returning to a mother's arm;

Mist-eyed awhile upraise the head
530 Else sinking to Death's joyless bed,
And when by pain, by Death, depressed
Ah! sure it gentler sinks to rest.
As when a Ball, his darling toy,
Tossed upward by some watchful boy
Meets in its quick declining course
The well-known hand that gave it force,
Springs up again with feeble bound
Then softer falls upon the ground.
Sister, for whom I feel a love
540 What warms a Brother far above,
On you, as sad she marks the scene,
Why does my heart so fondly lean?
Why but because in you is given
All, all, my soul would wish from Heaven?
Why but because I fondly view
All, all that Heaven has claimed, in you?

What from the social chain can tear
This bosom linked for ever there,
Which feels, whene'er the hand of pain
550 Touches this heaven connected chain,
Feels quick as thought the electric thrill
Feels it ah me – and shudders still?
While bounteous Heaven shall Fleming leave
Of Friendship what can me bereave?
Till then shall live the holy flame,
Friendship and Fleming are the same.

[*4 pages (about 200 to 225 lines) were removed from the notebook (D.C. MS. 3) at this point.*]

Adieu, ye forms of Fear that float
Wild on the shipwreck of the thought,
While fancy in a Demon's form
560 Rides through the clouds and swells the storm,
To thee, sweet Melancholy, blind,
The moonlight of the Poet's mind,

Blind to the thousand worlds that lie
In the small orb of [   ] eye.

While Fancy loves apart to dwell,
Scarce through the wicker of her cell
Dares shoot one timorous winking eye
To cheer me drooping on my way;
And that full soon must I resign
570 To delve in Mammon's joyless mine.

Your hollow echoes only moan
To toil's loud din or Sorrow's groan.

What though your dreary gloom absorb
[   ] of the rolling orb
The muses gave when first they placed
Their pencil in the hand of taste?
[?] on the mental tablet throws
Each Beauty Art and Nature knows
In tints whose strength though time efface
580 He blends them into softer grace.

Extract from the Conclusion of a Poem,
Composed in Anticipation of Leaving School

Dear native regions, I foretell,
From what I feel at this farewell,
That, whereso'er my steps may tend,
And whensoe'er my course shall end,
If in that hour a single tie
Survive of local sympathy,
My soul will cast the backward view,
The longing look alone on you.

Thus, while the Sun sinks down to rest
10 Far in the regions of the west,
Though to the vale no parting beam

Be given, not one memorial gleam,
A lingering light he fondly throws
On the dear hills where first he rose.

'What is it that tells my soul the Sun is setting'

What is it that tells my soul the Sun is setting?
For not a straggling ray tell[s] her he is in the
Eas[t] or west[;] 'tis the brown mist which
descends slowly into the valley to [shed?] [?]
that burden of [ghosts?]. See where a
son of other worlds is sailing [s]lowly on the
lake – no! 'tis the taper that twinkling in the
cottage casts a long wan shadow over the [lake?].
Lo[ud] howls the village Dog. Spirit of these
10   Mountains [I see thee?] throned on Helvellyn, but
[thy?] feet and head are wrapped in mist.
Spirit of these mountains if thou can[st?]
bid the mist break from thy forehead, and nod
me thrice farewell. farewell[,] farewell. –
[For?] no more shall the ghosts leaning from
The [?   ] from the [howling of the wind?]
listen while thou instructed me in [thy?] law
of [Nature?]. Bid the mist break from thy brow,
an[d] thrice nod me a Farewell.

On the Death of an Unfortunate Lady

[A FRAGMENT]

Ah! have you seen a bird of sweetest tone
Freed by some infant from its prison gloom?
Quick to the treacherous [glass?] the [mourner?] flies –
Go make its little grave – it falls – it dies
And see him plant it round with flowers, and pour
An infant's [angel?] tear, an infant's sighs,
But ah! poor maid no penitential shower

Yet o'er thy grave shall bend the pensive flower
And Pity long shall weep at [Eve's?] funereal hour.

A Winter's Evening –

FRAGMENT OF AN ODE TO WINTER

– But hark! the Curfew tolls! and lo! the night
Mounts the black Coursers of the stormy North
    Now down the pathway brown
    I bend my pensive steps
       cetera desunt

Dirge Sung by a Minstrel

List! the bell-Sprite stuns my ears
Slowly calling for a maid;
List! each worm with trembling hears
And stops for joy his dreadful trade.
For nine times the death-bell's Sprite
Sullen for the Virgin cried
And they say at dead of night
Before its time the taper died.
    Mie love is dedde
10   Gone to her deathbedde,
    Al under the wyllowe tree.
When friends around her death-bed hung
To feed life's ebbing flood awhile,
The fell disease had chained her tongue
Yet still she gave – she gave – a smile.

So have we marked yon lake at Eve
When aye of Love we took our fill
With smiles the smallest rill receive
Though mute – it smiled – it dimpled still.
20   But now she is dead
    And laid in her grave,
    For ever to remain.

Low-mouldering does that eyebrow lie
Which I, lovelorn, must view no more,
Thrown o'er her soft dissolving eye
Thrown like a bridge all ivied o'er.
The Loves and Pleasures thence shall lean
No more like boys in smiling row,
To watch the God who bathed half-seen
30 In the blue crystal flood below.

Sweet when the red rose blossoms wild
Where hedge-rows bathed with may-morn dew
And flocks which never mark defiled
At rest within are sweet to view.

Her lips with sweeter fragrance glowed
And lovelier tenants did enclose
And from them sweeter music flowed
Than may-morn hedgerow ever knows.

Death like a Rock his shade has cast
40 Black o'er the chill vale of my days;
I view his lowering form aghast
Still as I tread through shadowy maze.

Maids yet unborn in secret there
Of Death forewarned shall pour the tear;
And children ere they lisp a prayer
Shall learn thy deathbed to revere.

And should some boy wild in the race
On thy green grave unweeting start,
Strange fear shall fly across his face
50 And home he goes with haunted heart.

And if a scattered flower be there,
Oft as they gather round thy sods
That flower the wandering group shall spare
And think it is a flower of God's.

*[Fragments: Drafts, Mostly or All for a
Poem on a Heroic Theme]*

His armour glittered in the [   ]
but fear sat on his forehead, as when
the sun shoots his beams upon
the side of Skiddaw or Helvellyn
but mists sette upon his head

.   .   .   .   .

His crest nodded dreadful on
his head like an oak
shook by the wind upon
the top of Teneriff –
10 As when the moon as she
raises her orb above the Horizon
rests upon the Branches of some
tall Oak, which grows upon
the summit of the Horizon

.   .   .   .   .

Mighty was the warr[ior?],
dreadful was his countenance,
yet it was tempered with the
placid serenity of deliberate
courage, as when a sunbeam
20 gilds the top a rugged rock –
or when the sun skirts with gold
the top of some dark cloud –
They gaze upon each other
like two rocks which rise
from the sea in dreadful majesty
they stand unmoved while the
[waves?] dash at their feet, and
the Storm howls round their
heads. —

30   Stood like a tower which at
dusky Evening the shepherd
views enlarged and magnified
by the darkness. —

.   .   .   .   .

His consort is sad, the smile of
Joy forsakes her face, as when
the black shade of the earth interposes
betwixt the sun and Moon –

.   .   .   .   .

Before Winter is expired
He loved the fair Elfrida, but
40   her Sire denied the completion
of their happiness, as, when
The Spring reclines upon the
lap of the Youthful Year, the
hoary Winter rears his icy arm
and dashes her from his embrace.
Soft South wind, warm rain. Evening.
Sun breaks out. Verdure. Birds. All human
Nature rejoices.
Spring. While oft the west
50   wind roars & brings hail
and blackens all the vale
while short gleams of sunshine
burst forth & serve to divide
the showers. Ev'n then 'tis
sweet when perhaps at Eve the
storm has ceased, the wind
yet blowing amid the trees
And the sun shining while
the clouds scowl down the sky
60   to meditate. . . .
Turrita nubes, shaped like towers.

[*Fragment of an Intended Poem on Milton,
Written in the Copy of* Paradise Lost
which Belonged to Wordsworth at Cambridge]

On Religion's holy hill
He built an altar, and the fire from heaven
Came down upon it. Round the growing flames
That filled the sense with fragrance gently rose
Soft sounds and [   ] and all the while were heard
Airs of high melody from solemn harp
And Voice of Angel in accordance sweet.
Anon the trump of God, with dreadful blast
Rocked all the mountain; on their flashing clouds
10 The silent cherubs trembled; undismayed
Stood the blind prophet and
                    cetera desunt

[*Orpheus and Eurydice*]

(Translated from Virgil's *Georgics*)

He wandering far along the lonely main
Soothed with the hollow shell his sickly pain;
Thee, thee, dear wife, he sung forlorn,
From morn to eve, and thee from eve to morn.

He pierced the grove where brooding darkness flings
A cold black horror from his [   ] wings,
To where Hell's King in griesly state appears
And round him hearts unmoved by human tears;
On as he passed and struck the plaintive shell
10 Ambrosial music filled the ear of hell.
    [   ] from the lowest bound
Of Erebus the shadows flocked around,
As birds unnumbered seek their leafy bower,
Driven by the twilight dark, or morning shower,

Boys, men, and matrons old, the tender maid,
And mighty heroes' more majestic shade.

.   .   .   .   .

Felt his dear wife the sweet approach of light
Following behind – ah why did Fate impose
This cruel mandate, source of all his woes?
20   When [   ] a sudden madness stole
His swimming senses from the lover's soul.
The deed might not in vain for pardon sue
If Hell the sweets of gentle pardon knew.
He paused, and treading on the edge of day
Mindless, his parting soul dissolved away,
He turned and gazed. [
                    ] and thrice a dismal shriek
From Hell's still waters thrice was heard to break.

.   .   .   .   .

Then she – 'what God our Ruin hath decreed,
30   And why, my Orpheus, why this desperate deed?
Once more I hear a dreadful voice, it cries
Come come away [   ]
Farewell my life, farewell my soul's delight,
A death-like darkness tears me from thy sight
But ah, my Orpheus, ah, no longer mine;
Thy fond Eurydice, no longer thine,
[Still?] through the gloomy door with eager pain
Stretches her powerless arm to thee in vain.'
What prayers or songs of weeping can now move
40   The cruel fates to grant again [his?] love?
Even now cold shivering in the boat she stood,
That slowly struggled through the torpid flood.
For seven long moons, by Strymon's desert side,
He wept unceasing to the hollow tide;
While overhead, as still he wept and sung,
Aerial rocks in shaggy prospect hung.
Meek grew the tigers when in caverns hoar
He sung his tale of sorrow o'er and o'er;

The solemn forest at the magic song
50 Had ears to joy – and slowly moved along.

So darkling in the poplar's shady gloom
Mourns the lorn nightingale her hapless doom;
Mourns with low sighs and sadly pleasing tongue,
Torn callow from their nest, her darling young;
All night she weeps, slow-pouring from her throat
Renewed at every fall the plaintive note,
Moans round the cheerless nest with pious love;
The solemn warblings sadden all the grove.
No maid the mourner's widowed bosom moves
60 He sickened at the thought of other loves;
Hopeless and sad, with never ceasing moan,
He trod the snowy Tanais all alone.
He loved through cold Rhipaean snows to roam,
Cold fields of ice and snow his only home;
[Reft?] of his dear lost partner did he plain
Given to his arms from Death, but given in vain;
For which sad dearer office coldly spurned
The fell Ciconian Matrons inly burned
[   ] to Bacchus, as they paid
70 Nocturnal orgies in the midnight shade;
Him, mourning still, the savage maenads found
And strewed his mangled limbs the plain around;
His head was from its neck of marble torn
And down the Oeagrian Hebrus slowly borne.
Then too upon the voice and faltering tongue
Eurydice in dying accents hung;
Ah! poor Eurydice, it feebly cried;
Eurydice, the moaning banks replied.

[*In Part from Moschus's Lament for Bion*]

Ah me! the lowliest children of the spring,
Violets and meekest snowdrops, when they lie
Nipped in the faded garden, soon again

Put forth fresh leaves and breathe another year,
But we, the great, the mighty and the wise,
Soon as we perish, in the hollow earth
Unwakeable, unheard of, undisturbed,
Slumber, a dull interminable sleep.
Never to come again the time of song
10 Nor [store?] of purple light, of scent and [   ].
Man's sweet and pleasant time, his morn of life,
Flies first, and come diseases on and age;
Widowed of Joy and Labor, till at length
Beat by the inclement storm of cruel Death
He finds a fearful refuge, none knows where.

At the sweet hour of prime the [   ] lark
Springs up, awaked by joy, and o'er the head
Of the tired labourer, like a mountain stream,
Sings discontinuous all day long, and joy
20 Drops down with him at Evening to his nest.
Labour and grief and Solitude and fear ...
                cetera desunt

[*The Horse*]

The foal of generous breed along the plains
Walks stately, balanced on his easy joints,
Round are his hips, his belly short, his neck
Lofty, and sharp his head with muscles swoln;
His breast exults luxuriant, all on fire,
No idle sound appals him of the herd,
First he devours the road, the stranger bridge
Attempts, and throws himself upon the threatening
        flood;
He hears the din of distant arms, his feet
10 Chafe, shudder his erected ears, his limbs
Tremble; beneath his nostrils clouds of fire
Forced down, collected, roll in wreaths, his mane
Redundant on his ample shoulder tossed

Floats to the right; strained like a bow, his [spine?]
Doubles, and unbroken, springing back, he scorns
The Earth; resounds the hoof of solid horn.
Such Cyllarus, who first received the rein
From Amyclaean Pollux, such, renowned
In Grecian song, the brother steeds of Mars;
20 Such great Achilles' car, so Saturn's self,
Fleet as his wife's approach, a horse's mane
Gave to the winds, and flying, with neighings shrill
Filled all the shaggy round of Pelion high.

Ode to Apollo

As the fresh wine the poet pours,
What asks he, Phoebus, what implores?
Not rich Sardinia with her seas of corn,
Nor herds in grateful prospect laid
In hot Calabria's chestnut shade,
Nor gold nor ivory from the realms of morn,
Nor fields where, kissed by Liris' tide
As still his evening waters glide,
Drops in the quiet stream the crumbling mold;
10 Let those who for the blessing pine
Prune with Calenian hook the vine
And the rich merchant drain from cups of gold
Wines from Assyrian produce given
Each year the darling care of Heaven
[Thrice?] from the Atlantic safe restored,
But me, a poet, olives feed,
And the light mallows of the mead
And simple endive crowns my frugal board.
Give me, Latona's honied boy,
20 My little blessings to enjoy,
Unbroken of frame, and oh! with mind entire,
Nor old to totter in a race
Of Shame, forgot by every grace,
Deserted by the Lyre.

An Evening Walk Addressed to a Young Lady

General Sketch of the Lakes – Author's regret of his Youth
which was passed amongst them – Short description of Noon –
Cascade – Noon-tide Retreat – Precipice and sloping Lights –
Face of Nature as the Sun declines – Mountain-farm, and the
Cock – Slate-quarry – Sunset – Superstition of the Country
connected with that moment – Swans – Female Beggar –
Twilight-sounds – Western Lights – Spirits – Night – Moon-
light – Hope – Night-sounds – Conclusion.

Far from my dearest Friend, 'tis mine to rove
Through bare grey dell, high wood, and pastoral cove;
Where Derwent rests, and listens to the roar
That stuns the tremulous cliffs of high Lodore;
Where peace to Grasmere's lonely island leads,
To willowy hedge-rows, and to emerald meads;
Leads to her bridge, rude church, and cottaged grounds,
Her rocky sheepwalks, and her woodland bounds;
Where, undisturbed by winds, Winander sleeps
10 'Mid clustering isles, and holly-sprinkled steeps;
Where twilight glens endear my Esthwaite's shore,
And memory of departed pleasures, more.

Fair scenes, erewhile, I taught, a happy child,
The echoes of your rocks my carols wild:
The spirit sought not then, in cherished sadness,
A cloudy substitute for failing gladness.
In youth's keen eye the livelong day was bright,
The sun at morning, and the stars at night,
Alike, when first the bittern's hollow bill
20 Was heard, or woodcocks roamed the moonlight hill.

In thoughtless gaiety I coursed the plain,
And hope itself was all I knew of pain;
For then the inexperienced heart would beat
At times, while young Content forsook her seat,
And wild Impatience, pointing upward, showed,

Through passes yet unreached, a brighter road.
Alas! the idle tale of man is found
Depicted in the dial's moral round;
Hope with reflection blends her social rays
30 To gild the total tablet of his days;
Yet still, the sport of some malignant power,
He knows but from its shade the present hour.

But why, ungrateful, dwell on idle pain?
To show what pleasures yet to me remain,
Say, will my Friend, with unreluctant ear,
The history of a poet's evening hear?

When, in the south, the wan noon, brooding still,
Breathed a pale steam around the glaring hill,
And shades of deep-embattled clouds were seen,
40 Spotting the northern cliffs with lights between;
When crowding cattle, checked by rails that make
A fence far stretched into the shallow lake,
Lashed the cool water with their restless tails,
Or from high points of rock looked out for fanning
     gales;
When school-boys stretched their length upon the green;
And round the broad-spread oak, a glimmering scene,
In the rough fern-clad park, the herded deer
Shook the still-twinkling tail and glancing ear;
When horses in the sunburnt intake stood,
50 And vainly eyed below the tempting flood,
Or tracked the passenger, in mute distress,
With forward neck the closing gate to press –
Then, while I wandered where the huddling rill
Brightens with water-breaks the hollow ghyll
As by enchantment, an obscure retreat
Opened at once, and stayed my devious feet.
While thick above the rill the branches close,
In rocky basin its wild waves repose,
Inverted shrubs, and moss of gloomy green,
60 Cling from the rocks, with pale wood-weeds between;

And its own twilight softens the whole scene,
Save where aloft the subtle sunbeams shine
On withered briars that o'er the crags recline;
Save where, with sparkling foam, a small cascade
Illumines, from within, the leafy shade;
Beyond, along the vista of the brook,
Where antique roots its bustling course o'erlook,
The eye reposes on a secret bridge,
Half grey, half shagged with ivy to its ridge;
70 There, bending o'er the stream, the listless swain
Lingers behind his disappearing wain.
– Did Sabine grace adorn my living line,
Blandusia's praise, wild stream, should yield to thine!
Never shall ruthless minister of death
'Mid thy soft glooms the glittering steel unsheath;
No goblets shall, for thee, be crowned with flowers,
No kid with piteous outcry thrill thy bowers;
The mystic shapes that by thy margin rove
A more benignant sacrifice approve –
80 A mind that, in a calm angelic mood
Of happy wisdom, meditating good,
Beholds, of all from her high powers required,
Much done, and much designed, and more desired, –
Harmonious thoughts, a soul by truth refined,
Entire affection for all human kind.

Dear Brook, farewell! Tomorrow's noon again
Shall hide me, wooing long thy wildwood strain;
But now the sun has gained his western road,
And eve's mild hour invites my steps abroad.
90 While, near the midway cliff, the silvered kite
In many a whistling circle wheels her flight;
Slant watery lights, from parting clouds, apace
Travel along the precipice's base;
Cheering its naked waste of scattered stone,
By lichens grey, and scanty moss, o'er-grown;
Where scarce the foxglove peeps, or thistle's beard;
And restless stone-chat, all day long, is heard.

How pleasant, as the sun declines, to view
The spacious landscape change in form and hue!
100 Here, vanish, as in mist, before a flood
Of bright obscurity, hill, lawn, and wood;
There, objects, by the searching beams betrayed,
Come forth, and here retire in purple shade;
Even the white stems of birch, the cottage white,
Soften their glare before the mellow light;
The skiffs, at anchor where with umbrage wide
Yon chestnuts half the latticed boat-house hide,
Shed from their sides, that face the sun's slant beam,
Strong flakes of radiance on the tremulous stream:
110 Raised by yon travelling flock, a dusty cloud
Mounts from the road, and spreads its moving shroud;
The shepherd, all involved in wreaths of fire,
Now shows a shadowy speck, and now is lost entire.

Into a gradual calm the breezes sink,
A blue rim borders all the lake's still brink;
There doth the twinkling aspen's foliage sleep,
And insects clothe, like dust, the glassy deep:
And now, on every side, the surface breaks
Into blue spots, and slowly lengthening streaks;
120 Here, plots of sparkling water tremble bright
With thousand thousand twinkling points of light;
There, waves that, hardly weltering, die away,
Tip their smooth ridges with a softer ray;
And now the whole wide lake in deep repose
Is hushed, and like a burnished mirror glows,
Save where, along the shady western marge,
Coasts, with industrious oar, the charcoal barge.

Their panniered train a group of potters goad,
Winding from side to side up the steep road;
130 The peasant, from yon cliff of fearful edge
Shot, down the headlong path darts with his sledge;
Bright beams the lonely mountain-horse illume
Feeding 'mid purple heath, 'green rings', and broom;

While the sharp slope the slackened team confounds,
Downward the ponderous timber-wain resounds;
In foamy breaks the rill, with merry song,
Dashed o'er the rough rock, lightly leaps along;
From lonesome chapel at the mountain's feet
Three humble bells their rustic chime repeat;
140   Sounds from the water-side the hammered boat;
And *blasted* quarry thunders, heard remote!

Even here, amid the sweep of endless woods,
Blue pomp of lakes, high cliffs and falling floods,
Not undelightful are the simplest charms,
Found by the grassy door of mountain-farms.

Sweetly ferocious, round his native walks,
Pride of his sister-wives, the monarch stalks;
Spur-clad his nervous feet, and firm his tread;
A crest of purple tops the warrior's head.
150   Bright sparks his black and rolling eye-ball hurls
Afar, his tail he closes and unfurls;
On tiptoe reared, he strains his clarion throat,
Threatened by faintly-answering farms remote:
Again with his shrill voice the mountain rings,
While, flapped with conscious pride, resound his wings!

Where, mixed with graceful birch, the sombrous pine
And yew-tree o'er the silver rocks recline,
I love to mark the quarry's moving trains,
Dwarf panniered steeds, and men, and numerous wains:
160   How busy all the enormous hive within,
While Echo dallies with its various din!
Some (hear you not their chisels' clinking sound?)
Toil, small as pygmies in the gulf profound;
Some, dim between the lofty cliffs descried,
O'erwalk the slender plank from side to side;
These, by the pale-blue rocks that ceaseless ring,
In airy baskets hanging, work and sing.

Just where a cloud above the mountain rears
An edge all flame, the broadening sun appears;
170 A long blue bar its aegis orb divides,
And breaks the spreading of its golden tides;
And now that orb has touched the purple steep,
Whose softened image penetrates the deep.
'Cross the calm lake's blue shades the cliffs aspire,
With towers and woods, a 'prospect all on fire;'
While coves and secret hollows, through a ray
Of fainter gold, a purple gleam betray.
Each slip of lawn the broken rocks between
Shines in the light with more than earthly green:
180 Deep yellow beams the scattered stems illume,
Far in the level forest's central gloom:
Waving his hat, the shepherd, from the vale,
Directs his winding dog the cliffs to scale, –
The dog, loud barking, 'mid the glittering rocks,
Hunts, where his master points, the intercepted flocks.
Where oaks o'erhang the road the radiance shoots
On tawny earth, wild weeds, and twisted roots;
The druid-stones a brightened ring unfold;
And all the babbling brooks are liquid gold;
190 Sunk to a curve, the day-star lessens still,
Gives one bright glance, and drops behind the hill.

In these secluded vales, if village fame,
Confirmed by hoary hairs, belief may claim;
When up the hills, as now, retired the light,
Strange apparitions mocked the shepherd's sight.

The form appears of one that spurs his steed
Midway along the hill with desperate speed;
Unhurt pursues his lengthened flight, while all
Attend, at every stretch, his headlong fall.
200 Anon, appears a brave, a gorgeous show
Of horsemen-shadows moving to and fro;
At intervals imperial banners stream,
And now the van reflects the solar beam;

The rear through iron brown betrays a sullen gleam.
While silent stands the admiring crowd below,
Silent the visionary warriors go,
Winding in ordered pomp their upward way
Till the last banner of their long array
Has disappeared, and every trace is fled
210 Of splendour – save the beacon's spiry head
Tipt with eve's latest gleam of burning red.

     Now, while the solemn evening shadows sail,
On slowly-waving pinions, down the vale;
And, fronting the bright west, yon oak entwines
Its darkening boughs and leaves, in stronger lines;
'Tis pleasant near the tranquil lake to stray
Where, winding on along some secret bay,
The swan uplifts his chest, and backward flings
His neck, a varying arch, between his towering wings:
220 The eye that marks the gliding creature sees
How graceful, pride can be, and how majestic, ease.
While tender cares and mild domestic loves
With furtive watch pursue her as she moves,
The female with a meeker charm succeeds,
And her brown little-ones around her leads,
Nibbling the water lilies as they pass,
Or playing wanton with the floating grass.
She, in a mother's care, her beauty's pride
Forgetting, calls the wearied to her side;
230 Alternately they mount her back, and rest
Close by her mantling wings' embraces prest.

     Long may they float upon this flood serene;
Theirs be these holms untrodden, still, and green,
Where leafy shades fence off the blustering gale,
And breathes in peace the lily of the vale!
Yon isle, which feels not even the milk-maid's feet,
Yet hears her song, 'by distance made more sweet,'
Yon isle conceals their home, their hut-like bower;
Green water-rushes overspread the floor;

240 Long grass and willows form the woven wall,
   And swings above the roof the poplar tall.
   Thence issuing often with unwieldy stalk,
   They crush with broad black feet their flowery walk;
   Or, from the neighbouring water, hear at morn
   The hound, the horse's tread, and mellow horn;
   Involve their serpent-necks in changeful rings,
   Rolled wantonly between their slippery wings,
   Or, starting up with noise and rude delight,
   Force half upon the wave their cumbrous flight.

250 Fair Swan! by all a mother's joys caressed,
   Haply some wretch has eyed, and called thee blessed;
   When with her infants, from some shady seat
   By the lake's edge, she rose – to face the noontide heat;
   Or taught their limbs along the dusty road
   A few short steps to totter with their load.

   I see her now, denied to lay her head,
   On cold blue nights, in hut or straw-built shed,
   Turn to a silent smile their sleepy cry,
   By pointing to the gliding moon on high.
260 – When low-hung clouds each star of summer hide,
   And fireless are the valleys far and wide,
   Where the brook brawls along the public road
   Dark with bat-haunted ashes stretching broad,
   Oft has she taught them on her lap to lay
   The shining glow-worm; or, in heedless play,
   Toss it from hand to hand, disquieted;
   While others, not unseen, are free to shed
   Green unmolested light upon their mossy bed.

   Oh! when the sleety showers her path assail,
270 And like a torrent roars the headstrong gale;
   No more her breath can thaw their fingers cold,
   Their frozen arms her neck no more can fold;
   Weak roof a cowering form two babes to shield,
   And faint the fire a dying heart can yield!

Press the sad kiss, fond mother! vainly fears
Thy flooded cheek to wet them with its tears;
No tears can chill them, and no bosom warms,
Thy breast their death-bed, coffined in thine arms!

    Sweet are the sounds that mingle from afar,
280 Heard by calm lakes, as peeps the folding star,
Where the duck dabbles 'mid the rustling sedge,
And feeding pike starts from the water's edge,
Or the swan stirs the reeds, his neck and bill
Wetting, that drip upon the water still;
And heron, as resounds the trodden shore,
Shoots upward, darting his long neck before.

    Now, with religious awe, the farewell light
Blends with the solemn colouring of night;
'Mid groves of clouds that crest the mountain's brow,
290 And round the west's proud lodge their shadows throw,
Like Una shining on her gloomy way,
The half-seen form of Twilight roams astray;
Shedding, through paly loop-holes mild and small,
Gleams that upon the lake's still bosom fall;
Soft o'er the surface creep those lustres pale
Tracking the motions of the fitful gale.
With restless interchange at once the bright
Wins on the shade, the shade upon the light.
No favoured eye was e'er allowed to gaze
300 On lovelier spectacle in faery days;
When gentle Spirits urged a sportive chase,
Brushing with lucid wands the water's face;
While music, stealing round the glimmering deeps,
Charmed the tall circle of the enchanted steeps.
– The lights are vanished from the watery plains:
No wreck of all the pageantry remains.
Unheeded night has overcome the vales:
On the dark earth the wearied vision fails;
The latest lingerer of the forest train,
310 The lone black fir, forsakes the faded plain;

Last evening sight, the cottage smoke, no more,
Lost in the thickened darkness, glimmers hoar;
And, towering from the sullen dark-brown mere,
Like a black wall, the mountain-steeps appear.
– Now o'er the soothed accordant heart we feel
A sympathetic twilight slowly steal,
And ever, as we fondly muse, we find
The soft gloom deepening on the tranquil mind.
Stay! pensive, sadly-pleasing visions, stay!
320 Ah no! as fades the vale, they fade away:
Yet still the tender, vacant gloom remains;
Still the cold cheek its shuddering tear retains.

The bird, who ceased, with fading light, to thread
Silent the hedge or steamy rivulet's bed,
From his grey re-appearing tower shall soon
Salute with gladsome note the rising moon,
While with a hoary light she frosts the ground,
And pours a deeper blue to Aether's bound;
Pleased, as she moves, her pomp of clouds to fold
330 In robes of azure, fleecy-white, and gold.

Above yon eastern hill, where darkness broods
O'er all its vanished dells, and lawns, and woods;
Where but a mass of shade the sight can trace,
Even now she shows, half-veiled, her lovely face:
Across the gloomy valley flings her light,
Far to the western slopes with hamlets white;
And gives, where woods the chequered upland strew,
To the green corn of summer, autumn's hue.

Thus Hope, first pouring from her blessed horn
340 Her dawn, far lovelier than the moon's own morn,
Till higher mounted, strives in vain to cheer
The weary hills, impervious, blackening near;
Yet does she still, undaunted, throw the while
On darling spots remote her tempting smile.

Even now she decks for me a distant scene,
(For dark and broad the gulf of time between)
Gilding that cottage with her fondest ray,
(Sole bourn, sole wish, sole object of my way;
How fair its lawns and sheltering woods appear!
350 How sweet its streamlet murmurs in mine ear!)
Where we, my Friend, to happy days shall rise,
Till our small share of hardly-paining sighs
(For sighs will ever trouble human breath)
Creep hushed into the tranquil breast of death.

But now the clear bright Moon her zenith gains,
And, rimy without speck, extend the plains:
The deepest cleft the mountain's front displays
Scarce hides a shadow from her searching rays;
From the dark-blue faint silvery threads divide
360 The hills, while gleams below the azure tide;
Time softly treads; throughout the landscape breathes
A peace enlivened, not disturbed, by wreaths
Of charcoal-smoke, that, o'er the fallen wood,
Steal down the hill, and spread along the flood.

The song of mountain-streams, unheard by day,
Now hardly heard, beguiles my homeward way.
Air listens, like the sleeping water, still,
To catch the spiritual music of the hill,
Broke only by the slow clock tolling deep,
370 Or shout that wakes the ferry-man from sleep,
The echoed hoof nearing the distant shore,
The boat's first motion – made with dashing oar;
Sound of closed gate, across the water borne,
Hurrying the timid hare through rustling corn;
The sportive outcry of the mocking owl;
And at long intervals the mill-dog's howl;
The distant forge's swinging thump profound;
Or yell, in the deep woods, of lonely hound.

Written in Very Early Youth

Calm is all nature as a resting wheel.
The kine are couched upon the dewy grass;
The horse alone, seen dimly as I pass,
Is cropping audibly his later meal:
Dark is the ground; a slumber seems to steal
O'er vale, and mountain, and the starless sky.
Now, in this blank of things, a harmony,
Home-felt, and home-created, comes to heal
That grief for which the senses still supply
10 Fresh food; for only then, when memory
Is hushed, am I at rest. My Friends! restrain
Those busy cares that would allay my pain;
Oh! leave me to myself, nor let me feel
The officious touch that makes me droop again.

'When slow from pensive twilight's latest gleams'

When slow from pensive twilight's latest gleams
'O'er the dark mountain top descends the ray'
That stains with crimson tinge the water grey
And still, I listen while the dells and streams
And vanished woods a lulling murmur make;
As Vesper first begins to twinkle bright
And on the dark hillside the cottage light,
With long reflexion streams across the lake.
The lonely grey-duck darkling on his way
10 Quacks clamorous; deep the measured strokes rebound
Of unseen oar parting with hollow sound
While the slow curfew shuts the eye of day
Soothed by the stilly scene with many a sigh,
Heaves the full heart nor knows for whom, or why.

[*Sonnet*]

(a Translation)

If grief dismiss me not to them that rest
Till the grey morn of age those starry fires
Unwatched extinguish, till the young desires
Forget those vermeil lips, that rising breast,
That cheek, those auburn locks which now exceed
The breathing woodbine's hues, till Time efface
With hand remorseless every angel grace
That bad[e] concealment on my spirit feed;
Haply my bolder tongue may then reveal
10 The prison annals of a life of tears;
And if the chill time on the softer joys
Smile not, a broken heart perchance may feel
Sad solace from the unforbidden sighs
Heaved for the fruitless lapse of vernal years.

Lines Written While Sailing in a Boat at Evening

How richly glows the water's breast
Before us, tinged with evening hues,
While, facing thus the crimson west,
The boat her silent course pursues!
And see how dark the backward stream!
A little moment past so smiling!
And still, perhaps, with faithless gleam,
Some other loiterers beguiling.

Such views the youthful Bard allure;
10 But, heedless of the following gloom,
He deems their colours shall endure
Till peace go with him to the tomb.
– And let him nurse his fond deceit,

And what if he must die in sorrow!
Who would not cherish dreams so sweet,
Though grief and pain may come tomorrow?

Remembrance of Collins Composed upon the Thames near Richmond

Glide gently, thus for ever glide,
O Thames! that other bards may see
As lovely visions by thy side
As now, fair river! come to me.
O glide, fair stream! for ever so,
Thy quiet soul on all bestowing,
Till all our minds for ever flow
As thy deep waters now are flowing.

Vain thought! – Yet be as now thou art,
10 That in thy waters may be seen
The image of a poet's heart,
How bright, how solemn, how serene!
Such as did once the Poet bless,
Who murmuring here a later ditty,
Could find no refuge from distress
But in the milder grief of pity.

Now let us, as we float along,
For *him* suspend the dashing oar;
And pray that never child of song
20 May know that Poet's sorrows more.
How calm! how still! the only sound,
The dripping of the oar suspended!
– The evening darkness gathers round
By virtue's holiest Powers attended.

Septimi Gades

1
Oh thou, whose fixed bewildered eye
In strange and dreary vacancy
Of tenderness severe,
With fear unnamed my bosom chilled
While thus thy farewell accents thrilled,
Or seemed to thrill mine ear;

2
Think not from me, my friend, to roam,
Thy arms shall be my only home
My only bed thy breast;
10 No separate path our lives shall know,
But where thou goest I will go,
And there my bones shall rest.

3
Oh! might we seek that humble shed
Which sheltered once my pilgrim head,
Where down the mountains thrown
A streamlet seeks, through forest glooms,
Through viny glades and orchard blooms,
Below, the solemn Rhone.

4
But if the wayward fates deny
20 Those purple slopes, that azure sky,
My willing voice shall hail
The lone grey cots and pastoral steeps
That shine inverted in the deeps
Of Grasmere's quiet vale.

5
To him who faint and heartless stands
On pale Arabia's thirsty sands,

How fair that fountain seems
Where last beneath the palmy shade
In bowers of rose and jasmine laid,
30 He quaffed the living streams.

6

As fair in Memory's eye appear,
Sweet scene of peace, thy waters clear
Thy turf and folding groves –
On gales perfumed by every flower
Of mountain-top or mead or bower
Thy honey people roves.

7
What finny myriads twinkle bright
Along thy streams – how pure and white
The flocks thy shepherds fold;
40 What brimming pails thy milkmaids bear!
– Nor wants the jolly Autumn there
His crown of waving gold.

8

Yes, Nature on those vivid meads,
Those [   ] slopes and mountain-heads,
Has showered her various wealth;
There Temperance and Truth abide
And Toil with Leisure at his side,
And Cheerfulness and Health.

9
No spot does parting Phoebus greet
50 With farewell smile more fond and sweet
Than those sequestered hills;
While as composing shades invest
With purple gloom the water's breast
The grove its music stills.

10

When shouts and sheepfold bells and sound
Of flocks and herds and streams rebound
Along the ringing dale,
How beauteous, round that gleaming tide,
The silvery morning vapours glide
60   And half the landscape veil.

11

Methinks that morning scene displays
A lovely emblem of our days,
Unobvious and serene;
So shall our still lives, half betrayed,
Show charms more touching from their shade,
Though veiled, yet not unseen.

12

Yes, Mary, to some lowly door
In that delicious spot obscure
Our happy feet shall tend;
70   And there for many a golden year
Fair Hope shall steal thy voice to cheer
Thy poet and thy friend.

13

Though loudly roar the wintry flood
And Tempest shake the midnight wood
And rock our little nest
Love with his tenderest kiss shall dry
Thy human tear and still the sigh
That heaves thy gentle breast.

Descriptive Sketches Taken During a
Pedestrian Tour Among the Alps [*1850*]

To the Rev. Robert Jones, Fellow of St John's College, Cambridge.

DEAR SIR,

However desirous I might have been of giving you proofs of the high place you hold in my esteem, I should have been cautious of wounding your delicacy by thus publicly addressing you, had not the circumstance of our having been companions among the Alps, seemed to give this dedication a propriety sufficient to do away any scruples which your modesty might otherwise have suggested.

In inscribing this little work to you, I consult my heart. You know well how great is the difference between two companions lolling in a post-chaise, and two travellers plodding slowly along the road, side by side, each with his little knapsack of necessaries upon his shoulders. How much more of heart between the two latter!

I am happy in being conscious that I shall have one reader who will approach the conclusion of these few pages with regret. You they must certainly interest, in reminding you of moments to which you can hardly look back without a pleasure not the less dear from a shade of melancholy. You will meet with few images without recollecting the spot where we observed them together; consequently, whatever is feeble in my design, or spiritless in my colouring, will be amply supplied by your own memory.

With still greater propriety I might have inscribed to you a description of some of the features of your native mountains, through which we have wandered together, in the same manner, with so much pleasure. But the sea-sunsets, which give such splendour to the vale of Clwyd, Snowdon, the chair of Idris, the quiet village of Beth-gelert, Menai and her Druids, the Alpine steeps of the Conway, and the still more interesting windings of the wizard stream of the Dee, remain yet untouched. Apprehensive that my pencil may never be exercised on these subjects, I cannot let slip this opportunity of thus publicly assuring you with how much affection and esteem, I am, dear Sir, Your most obedient very humble servant,

London, 1793. W. WORDSWORTH.

Happiness (if she had been to be found on earth) among the charms of Nature – Pleasures of the pedestrian Traveller – Author crosses France to the Alps – Present state of the Grande Chartreuse – Lake of Como – Time, Sunset – Same Scene, Twilight – Same Scene, Morning; its voluptuous Character; Old man and forest-cottage music – River Tusa – Via Mala and Grison Gypsy – Sckellenenthal – Lake of Uri – Stormy Sunset – Chapel of William Tell – Force of local emotion – Chamois chaser – View of the higher Alps – Manner of life of a Swiss mountaineer, interspersed with views of the higher Alps – Golden age of the Alps – Life and views continued – Ranz des Vaches, famous Swiss Air – Abbey of Einsiedlen and its pilgrims – Valley of Chamouny – Mont Blanc – Slavery of Savoy – Influence of liberty on cottage-happiness – France – Wish for the Extirpation of slavery – Conclusion.

Were there, below, a spot of holy ground
Where from distress a refuge might be found,
And solitude prepare the soul for heaven;
Sure, nature's God that spot to man had given
Where falls the purple morning far and wide
In flakes of light upon the mountain-side;
Where with loud voice the power of water shakes
The leafy wood, or sleeps in quiet lakes.

Yet not unrecompensed the man shall roam,
10 Who at the call of summer quits his home,
And plods through some wide realm o'er vale and height,
Though seeking only holiday delight;
At least, not owning to himself an aim
To which the sage would give a prouder name.

No gains too cheaply earned his fancy cloy,
Though every passing zephyr whispers joy;
Brisk toil, alternating with ready ease,
Feeds the clear current of his sympathies.
For him sod-seats the cottage-door adorn;
20 And peeps the far-off spire, his evening bourn!
Dear is the forest frowning o'er his head,
And dear the velvet green-sward to his tread:
Moves there a cloud o'er mid-day's flaming eye?
Upward he looks – 'and calls it luxury:'
Kind Nature's charities his steps attend;
In every babbling brook he finds a friend;
While chastening thoughts of sweetest use, bestowed
By wisdom, moralise his pensive road.
Host of his welcome inn, the noon-tide bower,
30 To his spare meal he calls the passing poor;
He views the sun uplift his golden fire,
Or sink, with heart alive like Memnon's lyre;
Blesses the moon that comes with kindly ray,
To light him shaken by his rugged way.
Back from his sight no bashful children steal;
He sits a brother at the cottage-meal;
His humble looks no shy restraint impart;
Around him plays at will the virgin heart.
While unsuspended wheels the village dance,
40 The maidens eye him with enquiring glance,
Much wondering by what fit of crazing care,
Or desperate love, bewildered, he came there.

A hope, that prudence could not then approve,
That clung to Nature with a truant's love,
O'er Gallia's wastes of corn my footsteps led;
Her files of road-elms, high above my head
In long-drawn vista, rustling in the breeze;
Or where her pathways straggle as they please
By lonely farms and secret villages.
50 But lo! the Alps, ascending white in air,
Toy with the sun and glitter from afar.

And now, emerging from the forest's gloom,
I greet thee, Chartreuse, while I mourn thy doom.
Whither is fled that Power whose frown severe
Awed sober Reason till she crouched in fear?
That Silence, once in deathlike fetters bound,
Chains that were loosened only by the sound
Of holy rites chanted in measured round?
— The voice of blasphemy the fane alarms,
60   The cloister startles at the gleam of arms.
The thundering tube the aged angler hears,
Bent o'er the groaning flood that sweeps away his tears.
Cloud-piercing pine-trees nod their troubled heads,
Spires, rocks, and lawns a browner night o'erspreads;
Strong terror checks the female peasant's sighs,
And start the astonished shades at female eyes.
From Bruno's forest screams the affrighted jay,
And slow the insulted eagle wheels away.
A viewless flight of laughing Demons mock
70   The Cross, by angels planted on the aërial rock.
The 'parting Genius' sighs with hollow breath
Along the mystic streams of Life and Death.
Swelling the outcry dull, that long resounds
Portentous through her old woods' trackless bounds,
Vallombre, 'mid her falling fanes, deplores,
For ever broke, the sabbath of her bowers.

More pleased, my foot the hidden margin roves
Of Como, bosomed deep in chestnut groves.
No meadows thrown between, the giddy steeps
80   Tower, bare or sylvan, from the narrow deeps.
— To towns, whose shades of no rude noise complain,
From ringing team apart and grating wain —
To flat-roofed towns, that touch the water's bound,
Or lurk in woody sunless glens profound,
Or, from the bending rocks, obtrusive cling,
And o'er the whitened wave their shadows fling —
The pathway leads, as round the steeps it twines;
And Silence loves its purple roof of vines.

The loitering traveller hence, at evening, sees
90 From rock-hewn steps the sail between the trees;
Or marks, 'mid opening cliffs, fair dark-eyed maids
Tend the small harvest of their garden glades;
Or stops the solemn mountain-shades to view
Stretch o'er the pictured mirror broad and blue,
And track the yellow lights from steep to steep,
As up the opposing hills they slowly creep.
Aloft, here, half a village shines, arrayed
In golden light; half hides itself in shade:
While, from amid the darkened roofs, the spire,
100 Restlessly flashing, seems to mount like fire:
There, all unshaded, blazing forests throw
Rich golden verdure on the lake below.
Slow glides the sail along the illumined shore,
And steals into the shade the lazy oar;
Soft bosoms breathe around contagious sighs,
And amorous music on the water dies.

    How blest, delicious scene! the eye that greets
Thy open beauties, or thy lone retreats;
Beholds the unwearied sweep of wood that scales
110 Thy cliffs; the endless waters of thy vales;
Thy lowly cots that sprinkle all the shore,
Each with its household boat beside the door;
Thy torrents shooting from the clear-blue sky;
Thy towns, that cleave, like swallows' nests, on high;
That glimmer hoar in eve's last light, descried
Dim from the twilight water's shaggy side,
Whence lutes and voices down the enchanted woods
Steal, and compose the oar-forgotten floods;
– Thy lake, that, streaked or dappled, blue or grey,
120 'Mid smoking woods gleams hid from morning's ray
Slow-travelling down the western hills, to enfold
Its green-tinged margin in a blaze of gold;
Thy glittering steeples, whence the matin bell
Calls forth the woodman from his desert cell,
And quickens the blithe sound of oars that pass

Along the steaming lake, to early mass.
But now farewell to each and all – adieu
To every charm, and last and chief to you,
Ye lovely maidens that in noontide shade
130 Rest near your little plots of wheaten glade;
To all that binds the soul in powerless trance,
Lip-dewing song, and ringlet-tossing dance;
Where sparkling eyes and breaking smiles illume
The sylvan cabin's lute-enlivened gloom.
– Alas! the very murmur of the streams
Breathes o'er the failing soul voluptuous dreams,
While Slavery, forcing the sunk mind to dwell
On joys that might disgrace the captive's cell,
Her shameless timbrel shakes on Como's marge,
140 And lures from bay to bay the vocal barge.

Yet are thy softer arts with power indued
To soothe and cheer the poor man's solitude.
By silent cottage-doors, the peasant's home
Left vacant for the day, I loved to roam.
But once I pierced the mazes of a wood
In which a cabin undeserted stood;
There an old man an olden measure scanned
On a rude viol touched with withered hand.
As lambs or fawns in April clustering lie
150 Under a hoary oak's thin canopy,
Stretched at his feet, with stedfast upward eye,
His children's children listened to the sound;
– A Hermit with his family around!

But let us hence; for fair Locarno smiles
Embowered in walnut slopes and citron isles:
Or seek at eve the banks of Tusa's stream,
Where, 'mid dim towers and woods, her waters gleam.
From the bright wave, in solemn gloom, retire
The dull-red steeps, and, darkening still, aspire
160 To where afar rich orange lustres glow
Round undistinguished clouds, and rocks, and snow:

Or, led where Via Mala's chasms confine
The indignant waters of the infant Rhine,
Hang o'er the abyss, whose else impervious gloom
His burning eyes with fearful light illume.

　　The mind condemned, without reprieve, to go
O'er life's long deserts with its charge of woe,
With sad congratulation joins the train
Where beasts and men together o'er the plain
170　Move on – a mighty caravan of pain:
Hope, strength, and courage, social suffering brings,
Freshening the wilderness with shades and springs.
– There be whose lot far otherwise is cast:
Sole human tenant of the piny waste,
By choice or doom a gypsy wanders here,
A nursling babe her only comforter;
Lo, where she sits beneath yon shaggy rock,
A cowering shape half hid in curling smoke!

　　When lightning among clouds and mountain-snows
180　Predominates, and darkness comes and goes,
And the fierce torrent, at the flashes broad
Starts, like a horse, beside the glaring road –
She seeks a covert from the battering shower
In the roofed bridge; the bridge, in that dread hour,
Itself all trembling at the torrent's power.

　　Nor is she more at ease on some *still* night,
When not a star supplies the comfort of its light;
Only the waning moon hangs dull and red
Above a melancholy mountain's head,
190　Then sets. In total gloom the Vagrant sighs,
Stoops her sick head, and shuts her weary eyes;
Or on her fingers counts the distant clock,
Or, to the drowsy crow of midnight cock,
Listens, or quakes while from the forest's gulf
Howls near and nearer yet the famished wolf.

From the green vale of Urseren smooth and wide
Descend we now, the maddened Reuss our guide;
By rocks that, shutting out the blessed day,
Cling tremblingly to rocks as loose as they;
200 By cells upon whose image, while he prays,
The kneeling peasant scarcely dares to gaze;
By many a votive death-cross planted near,
And watered duly with the pious tear,
That faded silent from the upward eye
Unmoved with each rude form of peril nigh;
Fixed on the anchor left by Him who saves
Alike in whelming snows, and roaring waves.

But soon a peopled region on the sight
Opens – a little world of calm delight;
210 Where mists, suspended on the expiring gale,
Spread rooflike o'er the deep secluded vale,
And beams of evening slipping in between,
Gently illuminate a sober scene: –
Here, on the brown wood-cottages they sleep,
There, over rock or sloping pasture creep.
On as we journey, in clear view displayed,
The still vale lengthens underneath its shade
Of low-hung vapour: on the freshened mead
The green light sparkles; – the dim bowers recede.
220 While pastoral pipes and streams the landscape lull,
And bells of passing mules that tinkle dull,
In solemn shapes before the admiring eye
Dilated hang the misty pines on high,
Huge convent domes with pinnacles and towers,
And antique castles seen through gleamy showers.

From such romantic dreams, my soul, awake!
To sterner pleasure, where, by Uri's lake
In Nature's pristine majesty outspread,
Winds neither road nor path for foot to tread:
230 The rocks rise naked as a wall, or stretch,
Far o'er the water, hung with groves of beech;

Aërial pines from loftier steeps ascend,
Nor stop but where creation seems to end.
Yet here and there, if 'mid the savage scene
Appears a scanty plot of smiling green,
Up from the lake a zigzag path will creep
To reach a small wood-hut hung boldly on the steep.
– Before those thresholds (never can they know
The face of traveller passing to and fro,)
240 No peasant leans upon his pole, to tell
For whom at morning tolled the funeral bell;
Their watch-dog ne'er his angry bark forgoes,
Touched by the beggar's moan of human woes;
The shady porch ne'er offered a cool seat
To pilgrims overcome by summer's heat.
Yet thither the world's business finds its way
At times, and tales unsought beguile the day,
And *there* are those fond thoughts which Solitude,
However stern, is powerless to exclude.
250 There doth the maiden watch her lover's sail
Approaching, and upbraid the tardy gale;
At midnight listens till his parting oar,
And its last echo, can be heard no more.

    And what if ospreys, cormorants, herons cry,
Amid tempestuous vapours driving by,
Or hovering over wastes too bleak to rear
That common growth of earth, the foodful ear;
Where the green apple shrivels on the spray,
And pines the unripened pear in summer's kindliest
        ray;
260 Contentment shares the desolate domain
With Independence, child of high Disdain.
Exulting 'mid the winter of the skies,
Shy as the jealous chamois, Freedom flies,
And grasps by fits her sword, and often eyes;
And sometimes, as from rock to rock she bounds,
The Patriot nymph starts at imagined sounds,
And, wildly pausing, oft she hangs aghast,

Whether some old Swiss air hath checked her haste,
Or thrill of Spartan fife is caught between the blast.

270   Swoln with incessant rains from hour to hour,
All day the floods a deepening murmur pour:
The sky is veiled, and every cheerful sight:
Dark is the region as with coming night;
But what a sudden burst of overpowering light!
Triumphant on the bosom of the storm,
Glances the wheeling eagle's glorious form!
Eastward, in long perspective glittering, shine
The wood-crowned cliffs that o'er the lake recline;
Those lofty cliffs a hundred streams unfold,
280   At once to pillars turned that flame with gold:
Behind his sail the peasant shrinks, to shun
The *west*, that burns like one dilated sun,
A crucible of mighty compass, felt
By mountains, glowing till they seem to melt.

But, lo! the boatman, overawed, before
The pictured fane of Tell suspends his oar;
Confused the Marathonian tale appears,
While his eyes sparkle with heroic tears.
And who, that walks where men of ancient days
290   Have wrought with godlike arm the deeds of praise,
Feels not the spirit of the place control,
Or rouse and agitate his labouring soul?
Say, who, by thinking on Canadian hills,
Or wild Aosta lulled by Alpine rills,
On Zutphen's plain, or on that highland dell,
Through which rough Garry cleaves his way, can tell
What high resolves exalt the tenderest thought
Of him whom passion rivets to the spot,
Where breathed the gale that caught Wolfe's happiest
     sigh,
300   And the last sunbeam fell on Bayard's eye;
Where bleeding Sidney from the cup retired,
And glad Dundee in 'faint huzzas' expired?

But now with other mind I stand alone
Upon the summit of this naked cone,
And watch the fearless chamois-hunter chase
His prey, through tracts abrupt of desolate space,
Through vacant worlds where Nature never gave
A brook to murmur or a bough to wave,
Which unsubstantial Phantoms sacred keep;
310 Through worlds where Life, and Voice, and Motion
        sleep;
Where silent Hours their death-like sway extend,
Save when the avalanche breaks loose, to rend
Its way with uproar, till the ruin, drowned
In some dense wood or gulf of snow profound,
Mocks the dull ear of Time with deaf abortive sound.
– 'Tis his, while wandering on from height to height,
To see a planet's pomp and steady light
In the least star of scarce-appearing night;
While the pale moon moves near him, on the bound
320 Of ether, shining with diminished round,
And far and wide the icy summits blaze,
Rejoicing in the glory of her rays:
To him the day-star glitters small and bright,
Shorn of its beams, insufferably white,
And he can look beyond the sun, and view
Those fast-receding depths of sable blue
Flying till vision can no more pursue!
– At once bewildering mists around him close,
And cold and hunger are his least of woes;
330 The Demon of the snow, with angry roar
Descending, shuts for aye his prison door.
Soon with despair's whole weight his spirits sink;
Bread has he none, the snow must be his drink;
And, ere his eyes can close upon the day,
The eagle of the Alps o'ershades her prey.

Now couch thyself where, heard with fear afar,
Thunders through echoing pines the headlong Aar;
Or rather stay to taste the mild delights

Of pensive Underwalden's pastoral heights.
340 – Is there who 'mid these awful wilds has seen
The native Genii walk the mountain green?
Or heard, while other worlds their charms reveal,
Soft music o'er the aërial summit steal?
While o'er the desert, answering every close,
Rich steam of sweetest perfume comes and goes.
– And sure there is a secret Power that reigns
Here, where no trace of man the spot profanes,
Naught but the *chalets*, flat and bare, on high
Suspended 'mid the quiet of the sky;
350 Or distant herds that pasturing upward creep,
And, not untended, climb the dangerous steep.
How still! no irreligious sound or sight
Rouses the soul from her severe delight.
An idle voice the sabbath region fills
Of Deep that calls to Deep across the hills,
And with that voice accords the soothing sound
Of drowsy bells, for ever tinkling round;
Faint wail of eagle melting into blue
Beneath the cliffs, and pine-wood's steady *sugh*;
360 The solitary heifer's deepened low;
Or rumbling, heard remote, of falling snow.
All motions, sounds, and voices, far and nigh,
Blend in a music of tranquillity;
Save when, a stranger seen below, the boy
Shouts from the echoing hills with savage joy.

When, from the sunny breast of open seas,
And bays with myrtle fringed, the southern breeze
Comes on to gladden April with the sight
Of green isles widening on each snow-clad height;
370 When shouts and lowing herds the valley fill,
And louder torrents stun the noon-tide hill,
The pastoral Swiss begin the cliffs to scale,
Leaving to silence the deserted vale;
And like the Patriarchs in their simple age
Move, as the verdure leads, from stage to stage;

High and more high in summer's heat they go,
And hear the rattling thunder far below;
Or steal beneath the mountains, half-deterred,
Where huge rocks tremble to the bellowing herd.

380   One I behold who, 'cross the foaming flood,
Leaps with a bound of graceful hardihood;
Another high on that green ledge; – he gained
The tempting spot with every sinew strained;
And downward thence a knot of grass he throws,
Food for his beasts in time of winter snows.
– Far different life from what Tradition hoar
Transmits of happier lot in times of yore!
Then Summer lingered long; and honey flowed
From out the rocks, the wild bees' safe abode:
390   Continual waters welling cheered the waste,
And plants were wholesome, now of deadly taste:
Nor Winter yet his frozen stores had piled,
Usurping where the fairest herbage smiled:
Nor Hunger driven the herds from pastures bare,
To climb the treacherous cliffs for scanty fare.
Then the milk-thistle flourished through the land,
And forced the full-swoln udder to demand,
Thrice every day, the pail and welcome hand.
Thus does the father to his children tell
400   Of banished bliss, by fancy loved too well.
Alas! that human guilt provoked the rod
Of angry Nature to avenge her God.
Still, Nature, ever just, to him imparts
Joys only given to uncorrupted hearts.

    'Tis morn: with gold the verdant mountain glows;
More high, the snowy peaks with hues of rose.
Far-stretched beneath the many-tinted hills,
A mighty waste of mist the valley fills,
A solemn sea! whose billows wide around
410   Stand motionless, to awful silence bound:
Pines, on the coast, through mist their tops uprear,

That like to leaning masts of stranded ships appear.
A single chasm, a gulf of gloomy blue,
Gapes in the centre of the sea – and, through
That dark mysterious gulf ascending, sound
Innumerable streams with roar profound.
Mount through the nearer vapours notes of birds,
And merry flageolet; the low of herds,
The bark of dogs, the heifer's tinkling bell,
420 Talk, laughter, and perchance a church-tower knell:
Think not, the peasant from aloft has gazed
And heard with heart unmoved, with soul unraised:
Nor is his spirit less enrapt, nor less
Alive to independent happiness,
Then, when he lies, out-stretched, at even-tide
Upon the fragrant mountain's purple side;
For as the pleasures of his simple day
Beyond his native valley seldom stray,
Naught round its darling precincts can he find
430 But brings some past enjoyment to his mind;
While Hope, reclining upon Pleasure's urn,
Binds her wild wreaths, and whispers his return.

Once, Man entirely free, alone and wild,
Was blest as free – for he was Nature's child.
He, all superior but his God disdained,
Walked none restraining, and by none restrained:
Confessed no law but what his reason taught,
Did all he wished, and wished but what he ought.
As man in his primeval dower arrayed
440 The image of his glorious Sire displayed,
Even so, by faithful Nature guarded, here
The traces of primeval Man appear;
The simple dignity no forms debase;
The eye sublime, and surly lion-grace:
The slave of none, of beasts alone the lord,
His book he prizes, nor neglects his sword;
– Well taught by that to feel his rights, prepared
With this 'the blessings he enjoys to guard.'

And, as his native hills encircle ground
450 For many a marvellous victory renowned,
The work of Freedom daring to oppose,
With few in arms, innumerable foes,
When to those famous fields his steps are led,
An unknown power connects him with the dead:
For images of other worlds are there;
Awful the light, and holy is the air.
Fitfully, and in flashes, through his soul,
Like sun-lit tempests, troubled transports roll;
His bosom heaves, his Spirit towers amain,
460 Beyond the senses and their little reign.

And oft, when that dread vision hath past by,
He holds with God himself communion high,
There where the peal of swelling torrents fills
The sky-roofed temple of the eternal hills;
Or, when upon the mountain's silent brow
Reclined, he sees, above him and below,
Bright stars of ice and azure fields of snow;
While needle peaks of granite shooting bare
Tremble in ever-varying tints of air.
470 And when a gathering weight of shadows brown
Falls on the valleys as the sun goes down;
And Pikes, of darkness named and fear and storms,
Uplift in quiet their illumined forms,
In sea-like reach of prospect round him spread,
Tinged like an angel's smile all rosy red –
Awe in his breast with holiest love unites,
And the near heavens impart their own delights.

When downward to his winter hut he goes,
Dear and more dear the lessening circle grows;
480 That hut which on the hills so oft employs
His thoughts, the central point of all his joys.
And as a swallow, at the hour of rest,
Peeps often ere she darts into her nest,
So to the homestead, where the grandsire tends

A little prattling child, he oft descends,
To glance a look upon the well-matched pair;
Till storm and driving ice blockade him there.
There, safely guarded by the woods behind,
He hears the chiding of the baffled wind,
490 Hears Winter calling all his terrors round,
And, blest within himself, he shrinks not from the sound.

Through Nature's vale his homely pleasures glide,
Unstained by envy, discontent, and pride;
The bound of all his vanity, to deck,
With one bright bell, a favourite heifer's neck;
Well pleased upon some simple annual feast,
Remembered half the year and hoped the rest,
If dairy-produce, from his inner hoard,
Of thrice ten summers dignify the board.
500 – Alas! in every clime a flying ray
Is all we have to cheer our wintry way;
And here the unwilling mind may more than trace
The general sorrows of the human race:
The churlish gales of penury, that blow
Cold as the north-wind o'er a waste of snow,
To them the gentle groups of bliss deny
That on the noon-day bank of leisure lie.
Yet more; – compelled by Powers which only deign
That *solitary* man disturb their reign,
510 Powers that support an unremitting strife
With all the tender charities of life,
Full oft the father, when his sons have grown
To manhood, seems their title to disown;
And from his nest amid the storms of heaven
Drives, eagle-like, those sons as he was driven;
With stern composure watches to the plain –
And never, eagle-like, beholds again!

When long familiar joys are all resigned,
Why does their sad remembrance haunt the mind?
520 Lo! where through flat Batavia's willowy groves,

Or by the lazy Seine, the exile roves;
O'er the curled waters Alpine measures swell,
And search the affections to their inmost cell;
Sweet poison spreads along the listener's veins,
Turning past pleasures into mortal pains;
Poison, which not a frame of steel can brave,
Bows his young head with sorrow to the grave.

Gay lark of hope, thy silent song resume!
Ye flattering eastern lights, once more the hills illume!
530   Fresh gales and dews of life's delicious morn,
And thou, lost fragrance of the heart, return!
Alas! the little joy to man allowed
Fades like the lustre of an evening cloud;
Or like the beauty in a flower installed,
Whose season was, and cannot be recalled.
Yet, when opprest by sickness, grief, or care,
And taught that pain is pleasure's natural heir,
We still confide in more than we can know;
Death would be else the favourite friend of woe.

540   'Mid savage rocks, and seas of snow that shine,
Between interminable tracts of pine,
Within a temple stands an awful shrine,
By an uncertain light revealed, that falls
On the mute Image and the troubled walls.
Oh! give not me that eye of hard disdain
That views, undimmed, Ensiedlen's wretched fane.
While ghastly faces through the gloom appear,
Abortive joy, and hope that works in fear;
While prayer contends with silenced agony,
550   Surely in other thoughts contempt may die.
If the sad grave of human ignorance bear
One flower of hope – oh, pass and leave it there!

The tall sun, pausing on an Alpine spire,
Flings o'er the wilderness a stream of fire:
Now meet we other pilgrims ere the day

Close on the remnant of their weary way;
While they are drawing toward the sacred floor
Where, so they fondly think, the worm shall gnaw no
    more.
How gaily murmur and how sweetly taste
560 The fountains reared for them amid the waste!
Their thirst they slake: – they wash their toil-worn feet,
And some with tears of joy each other greet.
Yes, I must see you when ye first behold
Those holy turrets tipped with evening gold,
In that glad moment will for you a sigh
Be heaved, of charitable sympathy;
In that glad moment when your hands are prest
In mute devotion on the thankful breast!

Last, let us turn to Chamouny that shields
570 With rocks and gloomy woods her fertile fields:
Five streams of ice amid her cots descend,
And with wild flowers and blooming orchards blend; –
A scene more fair than what the Grecian feigns
Of purple lights and ever-vernal plains;
Here all the seasons revel hand in hand:
'Mid lawns and shades by breezy rivulets fanned,
They sport beneath that mountain's matchless height
That holds no commerce with the summer night.
From age to age, throughout his lonely bounds
580 The crash of ruin fitfully resounds;
Appalling havoc! but serene his brow,
Where daylight lingers on perpetual snow;
Glitter the stars above, and all is black below.

What marvel then if many a Wanderer sigh,
While roars the sullen Arve in anger by,
That not for thy reward, unrivalled Vale!
Waves the ripe harvest in the autumnal gale;
That thou, the slave of slaves, art doomed to pine
And droop, while no Italian arts are thine,
590 To soothe or cheer, to soften or refine.

Hail Freedom! whether it was mine to stray,
With shrill winds whistling round my lonely way,
On the bleak sides of Cumbria's heath-clad moors,
Or where dank sea-weed lashes Scotland's shores;
To scent the sweets of Piedmont's breathing rose,
And orange gale that o'er Lugano blows;
Still have I found, where Tyranny prevails,
That virtue languishes and pleasure fails,
While the remotest hamlets blessings share
600 In thy loved presence known, and only there;
Heart-blessings – outward treasures too which the eye
Of the sun peeping through the clouds can spy,
And every passing breeze will testify.
There, to the porch, belike with jasmine bound
Or woodbine wreaths, a smoother path is wound;
The housewife there a brighter garden sees,
Where hum on busier wing her happy bees;
On infant cheeks there fresher roses blow;
And grey-haired men look up with livelier brow, –
610 To greet the traveller needing food and rest;
Housed for the night, or but a half-hour's guest.

And oh, fair France! though now the traveller sees
Thy three-striped banner fluctuate on the breeze;
Though martial songs have banished songs of love,
And nightingales desert the village grove,
Scared by the fife and rumbling drum's alarms,
And the short thunder, and the flash of arms;
That cease not till night falls, when far and nigh,
Sole sound, the Sourd prolongs his mournful cry!
620 – Yet, hast thou found that Freedom spreads her power
Beyond the cottage-hearth, the cottage-door:
All nature smiles, and owns beneath her eyes
Her fields peculiar, and peculiar skies.
Yes, as I roamed where Loiret's waters glide
Through rustling aspens heard from side to side,
When from October clouds a milder light
Fell where the blue flood rippled into white;

Methought from every cot the watchful bird
Crowed with ear-piercing power till then unheard;
630 Each clacking mill, that broke the murmuring streams,
Rocked the charmed thought in more delightful dreams;
Chasing those pleasant dreams, the falling leaf
Awoke a fainter sense of moral grief;
The measured echo of the distant flail
Wound in more welcome cadence down the vale;
With more majestic course the water rolled,
And ripening foliage shone with richer gold.
– But foes are gathering – Liberty must raise
Red on the hills her beacon's far-seen blaze;
640 Must bid the tocsin ring from tower to tower! –
Nearer and nearer comes the trying hour!
Rejoice, brave Land, though pride's perverted ire
Rouse hell's own aid, and wrap thy fields in fire:
Lo, from the flames a great and glorious birth;
As if a new-made heaven were hailing a new earth!
– All cannot be: the promise is too fair
For creatures doomed to breathe terrestrial air:
Yet not for this will sober reason frown
Upon that promise, nor the hope disown;
650 She knows that only from high aims ensue
Rich guerdons, and to them alone are due.

Great God! by whom the strifes of men are weighed
In an impartial balance, give thine aid
To the just cause; and, oh! do thou preside
Over the mighty stream now spreading wide:
So shall its waters, from the heavens supplied
In copious showers, from earth by wholesome springs,
Brood o'er the long-parched lands with Nile-like wings!
And grant that every sceptred child of clay
660 Who cries presumptuous, 'Here the flood shall stay,'
May in its progress see thy guiding hand,
And cease the acknowledged purpose to withstand;
Or, swept in anger from the insulted shore,
Sink with his servile bands, to rise no more!

Tonight, my Friend, within this humble cot
Be scorn and fear and hope alike forgot
In timely sleep; and when, at break of day,
On the tall peaks the glistening sunbeams play,
With a light heart our course we may renew,
670 The first whose footsteps print the mountain dew.

'Sweet was the walk along the narrow lane'

Sweet was the walk along the narrow lane
At noon, the bank an[d] Hedge-rows all the way
Shagged with wild pale green Tufts of fragrant Hay,
Caught by the Hawthorns from the loaded wain,
Which Age with many a slow stoop strove to gain;
And Childhood, seeming still most busy, took
His little Rake; with cunning side-long look,
Sauntering to pluck the strawberries wild, unseen.
Now too on melancholy's idle dreams
10 Musing, the lone spot with my Soul agrees,
Quiet and dark; for [through?] the thick wove Trees
Scarce peeps the curious Star till solemn gleams
The clouded Moon, and calls me forth to stray
Through tall, green, silent woods and Ruins grey.

The Birth of Love

When LOVE was born of heavenly line,
    What dire intrigues disturbed *Cythera's* joy!
Till VENUS cried, 'A mother's heart is mine;
    None but myself shall nurse my boy.'
But, infant as he was, the child
    In that divine embrace enchanted lay;
And, by the beauty of the vase beguiled,
    Forgot the beverage – and pined away.

'And must my offspring languish in my sight?'
10   (Alive to all a mother's pain,
The Queen of Beauty thus her court addressed)
  'No: Let the most discreet of all my train
Receive him to her breast:
  Think all, he is the God of young delight.'

Then TENDERNESS, with CANDOUR joined,
  And GAIETY the charming office sought;
Nor even DELICACY stayed behind:
  But none of those fair Graces brought
Wherewith to nurse the child – and still he pined.
20   Some fond hearts to COMPLIANCE seemed inclined;
  But she had surely spoiled the boy:
    And sad experience forbade a thought
On the wild Goddess of VOLUPTUOUS JOY.

Long undecided lay the important choice,
Till of the beauteous court, at length, a voice
Pronounced the name of HOPE: – The conscious child
Stretched forth his little arms, and smiled.
'Tis said ENJOYMENT (who averred
  The charge belonged to her alone)
30   Jealous that HOPE had been preferred,
  Laid snares to make the babe her own.

Of INNOCENCE the garb she took,
The blushing mien, and downcast look;
  And came her services to proffer:
And HOPE (what has not HOPE believed!)
By that seducing air deceived,
  Accepted of the offer.

It happened that, to sleep inclined,
  Deluded HOPE for one short hour
40   To that false INNOCENCE'S power
Her little charge consigned.

The Goddess then her lap with sweetmeats filled;
  And gave, in handfuls gave, the treacherous store:
A wild delirium first the infant thrilled;
  But soon upon her breast he sunk – to wake no more.

[*At the Isle of Wight. 1793*]

How sweet the walk along the woody steep
When all the summer seas are charmed to sleep;
While on the distant sands the tide retires
Its last faint murmur on the ear expires;
The setting sun [   ] his growing round
On the low promontory – purple bound
For many a league a line of gold extends,
Now lessened half his glancing disc de[scends]
The watry sands athwart the [?   ]
10 Flush [   ] sudden [?] not [   ]
While anchored vessels scattered fa[r] [   ]
Darken with shadowy hulks [   ]
O'er earth o'er air and oce[an] [   ]
Tranquillity extends her [   ]
But hark from yon proud fleet in peal profound
Thunders the sunset cannon; at the sound
The star of life appears to set in blood,
And ocean shudders in offended mood,
Deepening with moral gloom his angry flood.

'*In vain did Time and Nature toil to throw*'

In vain did Time and Nature toil to throw
Wild weeds and dust upon these crumbled towers;
Again they rear the feudal head that lowers
Stern on the wretched huts that crouch below.

'*The western clouds a deepening gloom display*'

The western clouds a deepening gloom display
Where light obscurely sleeps in purple streaks,
And see the slowly sinking orb of day
Dilating through the Darkness dimly breaks:
So traveller full before this central bridge
Whose lofty arch o'erlooks the winding dale
Yon towers with [chasing?] walls and broken ridge
More solemn gleam through Nature's [   ] veil:
So through the dim eclipse of antique days
10 Each moral image to that pile assigned
But half distinguished from [?   ] [cottage?]
More awful features to the darkened mind.
What though yon [trees?] perchance their voice have lent
To fill the shriek that pierced the murderer's ear
Or deeper groans by captive anguish sent
Till Nature stilled the cry that none could hear.
'Tis past and in this wreck of barbarous pride
Now mortal weakness only views the tomb
[?   ] though savage still to man allied
20 And o'er their terror breathes a softening gloom.
Now while the branches that depending flow
The weather [stains?] which streak the mouldering stone,
Draw from the streams [accordant?] [?   ] below
New tints of tender sadness not their own.
Yet while with lapse still as the moonlight beam
Below the [?   ] [at times?] the midnight hours
Should silence listening to this [?   ] stream
[Start?] at the [music?] of their [streaming?] flowers.
When [fragrant?] [?   ] [glistening?] [?   ]
30 With heedless music and unaltered smile
[?   ] fond regret the ravage shall excite
In musing sage or thought [?   ] toil.

Guilt and Sorrow;
or Incidents upon Salisbury Plain

ADVERTISEMENT, PREFIXED TO
THE FIRST EDITION OF THIS POEM, PUBLISHED
IN 1842.

Not less than one-third of the following poem, though it has from time to time been altered in the expression, was published so far back as the year 1798, under the title of 'The Female Vagrant.' The extract is of such length that an apology seems to be required for reprinting it here: but it was necessary to restore it to its original position, or the rest would have been unintelligible. The whole was written before the close of the year 1794, and I will detail, rather as matter of literary biography than for any other reason, the circumstances under which it was produced.

During the latter part of the summer of 1793, having passed a month in the Isle of Wight, in view of the fleet which was then preparing for sea off Portsmouth at the commencement of the war, I left the place with melancholy forebodings. The American war was still fresh in memory. The struggle which was beginning, and which many thought would be brought to a speedy close by the irresistible arms of Great Britain being added to those of the allies, I was assured in my own mind would be of long continuance, and productive of distress and misery beyond all possible calculation. This conviction was pressed upon me by having been a witness, during a long residence in revolutionary France, of the spirit which prevailed in that country. After leaving the Isle of Wight, I spent two days in wandering on foot over Salisbury Plain, which, though cultivation was then widely spread through parts of it, had upon the whole a still more impressive appearance than it now retains.

The monuments and traces of antiquity, scattered in abundance over that region, led me unavoidably to com-

pare what we know or guess of those remote times with
certain aspects of modern society, and with calamities,
principally those consequent upon war, to which, more
than other classes of men, the poor are subject. In those
reflections, joined with particular facts that had come to my
knowledge, the following stanzas originated.

In conclusion, to obviate some distraction in the minds
of those who are well acquainted with Salisbury Plain, it
may be proper to say that, of the features described as
belonging to it, one or two are taken from other desolate
parts of England.

I

A Traveller on the skirt of Sarum's Plain
Pursued his vagrant way, with feet half bare;
Stooping his gait, but not as if to gain
Help from the staff he bore; for mien and air
Were hardy, though his cheek seemed worn with care
Both of the time to come, and time long fled:
Down fell in straggling locks his thin grey hair;
A coat he wore of military red
But faded, and stuck o'er with many a patch and shred.

II

10 While thus he journeyed, step by step led on,
He saw and passed a stately inn, full sure
That welcome in such house for him was none.
No board inscribed the needy to allure
Hung there, no bush proclaimed to old and poor
And desolate, 'Here you will find a friend!'
The pendent grapes glittered above the door; –
On he must pace, perchance 'till night descend,
Where'er the dreary roads their bare white lines extend.

III

The gathering clouds grew red with stormy fire,
20 In streaks diverging wide and mounting high;
That inn he long had passed; the distant spire,

Which oft as he looked back had fixed his eye,
Was lost, though still he looked, in the blank sky.
Perplexed and comfortless he gazed around,
And scarce could any trace of man descry,
Save cornfields stretched and stretching without bound;
But where the sower dwelt was nowhere to be found.

IV

No tree was there, no meadow's pleasant green,
No brook to wet his lip or soothe his ear;
30 Long files of corn-stacks here and there were seen,
But not one dwelling-place his heart to cheer.
Some labourer, thought he, may perchance be near;
And so he sent a feeble shout – in vain;
No voice made answer, he could only hear
Winds rustling over plots of unripe grain,
Or whistling through thin grass along the unfurrowed
        plain.

V

Long had he fancied each successive slope
Concealed some cottage, whither he might turn
And rest; but now along heaven's darkening cope
40 The crows rushed by in eddies, homeward borne.
Thus warned he sought some shepherd's spreading
        thorn
Or hovel from the storm to shield his head,
But sought in vain; for now, all wild, forlorn,
And vacant, a huge waste around him spread;
The wet cold ground, he feared, must be his only bed.

VI

And be it so – for to the chill night shower
And the sharp wind his head he oft hath bared;
A Sailor he, who many a wretched hour
Hath told; for, landing after labour hard,
50 Full long endured in hope of just reward,

He to an armèd fleet was forced away
By seamen, who perhaps themselves had shared
Like fate; was hurried off, a helpless prey,
'Gainst all that in *his* heart, or theirs perhaps, said nay.

VII

For years the work of carnage did not cease,
And death's dire aspect daily he surveyed,
Death's minister; then came his glad release,
And hope returned, and pleasure fondly made
Her dwelling in his dreams. By Fancy's aid
60 The happy husband flies, his arms to throw
Round his wife's neck; the prize of victory laid
In her full lap, he sees such sweet tears flow
As if thenceforth nor pain nor trouble she could know.

VIII

Vain hope! for fraud took all that he had earned.
The lion roars and gluts his tawny brood
Even in the desert's heart; but he, returned,
Bears not to those he loves their needful food.
His home approaching, but in such a mood
That from his sight his children might have run,
70 He met a traveller, robbed him, shed his blood;
And when the miserable work was done
He fled, a vagrant since, the murderer's fate to shun.

IX

From that day forth no place to him could be
So lonely, but that thence might come a pang
Brought from without to inward misery.
Now, as he plodded on, with sullen clang
A sound of chains along the desert rang;
He looked, and saw upon a gibbet high
A human body that in irons swang,
80 Uplifted by the tempest whirling by;
And, hovering, round it often did a raven fly.

X

It was a spectacle which none might view,
In spot so savage, but with shuddering pain;
Nor only did for him at once renew
All he had feared from man, but roused a train
Of the mind's phantoms, horrible as vain.
The stones, as if to cover him from day,
Rolled at his back along the living plain;
He fell, and without sense or motion lay;
90 But, when the trance was gone, feebly pursued his way.

XI

As one whose brain habitual frensy fires
Owes to the fit in which his soul hath tossed
Profounder quiet, when the fit retires,
Even so the dire phantasma which had crossed
His sense, in sudden vacancy quite lost,
Left his mind still as a deep evening stream.
Nor, if accosted now, in thought engrossed,
Moody, or inly troubled, would he seem
To traveller who might talk of any casual theme.

XII

100 Hurtle the clouds in deeper darkness piled,
Gone is the raven timely rest to seek;
He seemed the only creature in the wild
On whom the elements their rage might wreak;
Save that the bustard, of those regions bleak
Shy tenant, seeing by the uncertain light
A man there wandering, gave a mournful shriek,
And half upon the ground, with strange affright,
Forced hard against the wind a thick unwieldy flight.

XIII

All, all was cheerless to the horizon's bound;
110 The weary eye – which, wheresoe'er it strays,
Marks nothing but the red sun's setting round,
Or on the earth strange lines, in former days

Left by gigantic arms – at length surveys
What seems an antique castle spreading wide;
Hoary and naked are its walls, and raise
Their brow sublime: in shelter there to bide
He turned, while rain poured down smoking on every
 side.

XIV

Pile of Stone-henge! so proud to hint yet keep
Thy secrets, thou that lov'st to stand and hear
120 The Plain resounding to the whirlwind's sweep,
Inmate of lonesome Nature's endless year;
Even if thou saw'st the giant wicker rear
For sacrifice its throngs of living men,
Before thy face did ever wretch appear,
Who in his heart had groaned with deadlier pain
Than he who, tempest-driven, thy shelter now would
 gain.

XV

Within that fabric of mysterious form,
Winds met in conflict, each by turns supreme;
And, from the perilous ground dislodged, through storm
130 And rain he wildered on, no moon to stream
From gulf of parting clouds one friendly beam,
Nor any friendly sound his footsteps led;
Once did the lightning's faint disastrous gleam
Disclose a naked guide-post's double head,
Sight which, though lost at once, a gleam of pleasure
 shed.

XVI

No swinging sign-board creaked from cottage elm
To stay his steps with faintness overcome;
'Twas dark and void as ocean's watery realm
Roaring with storms beneath night's starless gloom;
140 No gypsy cowered o'er fire of furze or broom;
No labourer watched his red kiln glaring bright,

Nor taper glimmered dim from sick man's room;
Along the waste no line of mournful light
From lamp of lonely toll-gate streamed athwart the
      night.

XVII

At length, though hid in clouds, the moon arose;
The downs were visible – and now revealed
A structure stands, which two bare slopes enclose.
It was a spot, where, ancient vows fulfilled,
Kind pious hands did to the Virgin build
150 A lonely Spital, the belated swain
From the night terrors of that waste to shield:
But there no human being could remain,
And now the walls are named the 'Dead House' of the
      plain.

XVIII

Though he had little cause to love the abode
Of man, or covet sight of mortal face,
Yet when faint beams of light that ruin showed,
How glad he was at length to find some trace
Of human shelter in that dreary place.
Till to his flock the early shepherd goes,
160 Here shall much-needed sleep his frame embrace.
In a dry nook where fern the floor bestrows
He lays his stiffened limbs, – his eyes begin to close;

XIX

When hearing a deep sigh, that seemed to come
From one who mourned in sleep, he raised his head,
And saw a woman in the naked room
Outstretched, and turning on a restless bed:
The moon a wan dead light around her shed.
He waked her – spake in tone that would not fail,
He hoped, to calm her mind; but ill he sped,
170 For of that ruin she had heard a tale
Which now with freezing thoughts did all her powers
      assail;

XX

Had heard of one who, forced from storms to shroud,
Felt the loose walls of this decayed Retreat
Rock to incessant neighings shrill and loud,
While his horse pawed the floor with furious heat;
Till on a stone, that sparkled to his feet,
Struck, and still struck again, the troubled horse:
The man half raised the stone with pain and sweat,
Half raised, for well his arm might lose its force
180 Disclosing the grim head of a late murdered corse.

XXI

Such tale of this lone mansion she had learned,
And, when that shape, with eyes in sleep half drowned,
By the moon's sullen lamp she first discerned,
Cold stony horror all her senses bound.
Her he addressed in words of cheering sound;
Recovering heart, like answer did she make;
And well it was that of the corse there found
In converse that ensued she nothing spake;
She knew not what dire pangs in him such tale could
   wake.

XXII

190 But soon his voice and words of kind intent
Banished that dismal thought; and now the wind
In fainter howlings told its *rage* was spent:
Meanwhile discourse ensued of various kind,
Which by degrees a confidence of mind
And mutual interest failed not to create.
And, to a natural sympathy resigned,
In that forsaken building where they sate
The Woman thus retraced her own untoward fate.

XXIII

'By Derwent's side my father dwelt – a man
200 Of virtuous life, by pious parents bred;
And I believe that, soon as I began

To lisp, he made me kneel beside my bed,
And in his hearing there my prayers I said:
And afterwards, by my good father taught,
I read, and loved the books in which I read;
For books in every neighbouring house I sought,
And nothing to my mind a sweeter pleasure brought.

XXIV

'A little croft we owned – a plot of corn,
A garden stored with peas, and mint, and thyme,
210 And flowers for posies, oft on Sunday morn
Plucked while the church bells rang their earliest chime.
Can I forget our freaks at shearing time!
My hen's rich nest through long grass scarce espied;
The cowslip-gathering in June's dewy prime;
The swans that with white chests upreared in pride
Rushing and racing came to meet me at the waterside!

XXV

'The staff I well remember which upbore
The bending body of my active sire;
His seat beneath the honied sycamore
220 Where the bees hummed, and chair by winter fire;
When market-morning came, the neat attire
With which, though bent on haste, myself I decked;
Our watchful house-dog, that would tease and tire
The stranger till its barking-fit I checked;
The red-breast, known for years, which at my casement
    pecked.

XXVI

'The suns of twenty summers danced along, –
Too little marked how fast they rolled away:
But, through severe mischance and cruel wrong,
My father's substance fell into decay:
230 We toiled and struggled, hoping for a day
When Fortune might put on a kinder look;

But vain were wishes, efforts vain as they;
He from his old hereditary nook
Must part; the summons came; – our final leave we took.

XXVII

'It was indeed a miserable hour
When, from the last hill-top, my sire surveyed,
Peering above the trees, the steeple tower
That on his marriage day sweet music made!
Till then, he hoped his bones might there be laid
240 Close by my mother in their native bowers:
Bidding me trust in God, he stood and prayed; –
I could not pray: – through tears that fell in showers
Glimmered our dear-loved home, alas! no longer ours!

XXVIII

'There was a Youth whom I had loved so long,
That when I loved him not I cannot say:
'Mid the green mountains many a thoughtless song
We two had sung, like gladsome birds in May;
When we began to tire of childish play,
We seemed still more and more to prize each other;
250 We talked of marriage and our marriage day;
And I in truth did love him like a brother,
For never could I hope to meet with such another.

XXIX

'Two years were passed since to a distant town
He had repaired to ply a gainful trade:
What tears of bitter grief, till then unknown!
What tender vows our last sad kiss delayed!
To him we turned: – we had no other aid:
Like one revived, upon his neck I wept;
And her whom he had loved in joy, he said,
260 He well could love in grief; his faith he kept;
And in a quiet home once more my father slept.

XXX

'We lived in peace and comfort; and were blest
With daily bread, by constant toil supplied.·
Three lovely babes had lain upon my breast;
And often, viewing their sweet smiles, I sighed,
And knew not why. My happy father died,
When threatened war reduced the children's meal:
Thrice happy! that for him the grave could hide
The empty loom, cold hearth, and silent wheel,
270 And tears that flowed for ills which patience might not
   heal.

XXXI

''Twas a hard change; and evil time was come;
We had no hope, and no relief could gain:
But soon, with proud parade, the noisy drum
Beat round to clear the streets of want and pain.
My husband's arms now only served to strain
Me and his children hungering in his view;
In such dismay my prayers and tears were vain:
To join those miserable men he flew,
And now to the sea-coast, with numbers more, we drew.

XXXII

280 'There were we long neglected, and we bore
Much sorrow ere the fleet its anchor weighed;
Green fields before us, and our native shore,
We breathed a pestilential air, that made
Ravage for which no knell was heard. We prayed
For our departure; wished and wished – nor knew,
'Mid that long sickness and those hopes delayed,
That happier days we never more must view.
The parting signal streamed – at last the land withdrew.

XXXIII

'But the calm summer season now was past.
290 On as we drove, the equinoctial deep
Ran mountains high before the howling blast,

And many perished in the whirlwind's sweep.
We gazed with terror on their gloomy sleep,
Untaught that soon such anguish must ensue,
Our hopes such harvest of affliction reap,
That we the mercy of the waves should rue:
We reached the western world, a poor devoted crew.

XXXIV

'The pains and plagues that on our heads came down,
Disease and famine, agony and fear,
300 In wood or wilderness, in camp or town,
It would unman the firmest heart to hear.
All perished – all in one remorseless year,
Husband and children! one by one, by sword
And ravenous plague, all perished: every tear
Dried up, despairing, desolate, on board
A British ship I waked, as from a trance restored.'

XXXV

Here paused she, of all present thought forlorn,
Nor voice, nor sound, that moment's pain expressed,
Yet Nature, with excess of grief o'erborne,
310 From her full eyes their watery load released.
He too was mute: and, ere her weeping ceased,
He rose, and to the ruin's portal went,
And saw the dawn opening the silvery east
With rays of promise, north and southward sent;
And soon with crimson fire kindled the firmament.

XXXVI

'O come,' he cried, 'come, after weary night
Of such rough storm, this happy change to view.'
So forth she came, and eastward looked; the sight
Over her brow like dawn of gladness threw;
320 Upon her cheek, to which its youthful hue
Seemed to return, dried the last lingering tear,
And from her grateful heart a fresh one drew:

The whilst her comrade to her pensive cheer
Tempered fit words of hope; and the lark warbled near.

XXXVII

They looked and saw a lengthening road, and wain
That rang down a bare slope not far remote:
The barrows glistered bright with drops of rain,
Whistled the waggoner with merry note,
The cock far off sounded his clarion throat;
330 But town, or farm, or hamlet, none they viewed,
Only were told there stood a lonely cot
A long mile thence. While thither they pursued
Their way, the Woman thus her mournful tale renewed.

XXXVIII

'Peaceful as this immeasurable plain
Is now, by beams of dawning light imprest,
In the calm sunshine slept the glittering main;
The very ocean hath its hour of rest.
I too forgot the heavings of my breast.
How quiet 'round me ship and ocean were!
340 As quiet all within me. I was blest,
And looked, and fed upon the silent air
Until it seemed to bring a joy to my despair.

XXXIX

'Ah! how unlike those late terrific sleeps,
And groans that rage of racking famine spoke;
The unburied dead that lay in festering heaps,
The breathing pestilence that rose like smoke,
The shriek that from the distant battle broke,
The mine's dire earthquake, and the pallid host
Driven by the bomb's incessant thunderstroke
350 To loathsome vaults, where heart-sick anguish tossed,
Hope died, and fear itself in agony was lost!

XL

'Some mighty gulf of separation passed,
I seemed transported to another world;

A thought resigned with pain, when from the mast
The impatient mariner the sail unfurled,
And, whistling, called the wind that hardly curled
The silent sea. From the sweet thoughts of home
And from all hope I was for ever hurled.
For me – farthest from earthly port to roam
360 Was best, could I but shun the spot where man might
    come.

XLI

'And oft I thought (my fancy was so strong)
That I, at last, a resting-place had found;
"Here will I dwell," said I, "my whole life long,
Roaming the illimitable waters round;
Here will I live, of all but heaven disowned,
And end my days upon the peaceful flood." –
To break my dream the vessel reached its bound;
And homeless near a thousand homes I stood,
And near a thousand tables pined and wanted food.

XLII

370 'No help I sought; in sorrow turned adrift,
Was hopeless, as if cast on some bare rock;
Nor morsel to my mouth that day did lift,
Nor raised my hand at any door to knock.
I lay where, with his drowsy mates, the cock
From the cross-timber of an outhouse hung:
Dismally tolled, that night, the city clock!
At morn my sick heart hunger scarcely stung,
Nor to the beggar's language could I fit my tongue.

XLIII

'So passed a second day; and, when the third
380 Was come, I tried in vain the crowd's resort.
– In deep despair, by frightful wishes stirred,
Near the sea-side I reached a ruined fort;
There, pains which nature could no more support,
With blindness linked, did on my vitals fall;

And, after many interruptions short
Of hideous sense, I sank, nor step could crawl:
Unsought for was the help that did my life recall.

XLIV

'Borne to a hospital, I lay with brain
Drowsy and weak, and shattered memory;
390 I heard my neighbours in their beds complain
Of many things which never troubled me –
Of feet still bustling round with busy glee,
Of looks where common kindness had no part,
Of service done with cold formality,
Fretting the fever round the languid heart,
And groans which, as they said, might make a dead man
    start.

XLV

'These things just served to stir the slumbering sense,
Nor pain nor pity in my bosom raised.
With strength did memory return; and, thence
400 Dismissed, again on open day I gazed,
At houses, men, and common light, amazed.
The lanes I sought, and, as the sun retired,
Came where beneath the trees a faggot blazed;
The travellers saw me weep, my fate inquired,
And gave me food – and rest, more welcome, more
    desired.

XLVI

'Rough potters seemed they, trading soberly
With panniered asses driven from door to door;
But life of happier sort set forth to me,
And other joys my fancy to allure –
410 The bag-pipe dinning on the midnight moor
In barn uplighted; and companions boon,
Well met from far with revelry secure
Among the forest glades, while jocund June
Rolled fast along the sky his warm and genial moon.

XLVII

'But ill they suited me – those journeys dark
O'er moor and mountain, midnight theft to hatch!
To charm the surly house-dog's faithful bark,
Or hang on tip-toe at the lifted latch.
The gloomy lantern, and the dim blue match,
420 The black disguise, the warning whistle shrill,
And ear still busy on its nightly watch,
Were not for me, brought up in nothing ill:
Besides, on griefs so fresh my thoughts were brooding
    still.

XLVIII

'What could I do, unaided and unblest?
My father! gone was every friend of thine:
And kindred of dead husband are at best
Small help; and, after marriage such as mine,
With little kindness would to me incline.
Nor was I then for toil or service fit;
430 My deep-drawn sighs no effort could confine;
In open air forgetful would I sit
Whole hours, with idle arms in moping sorrow knit.

XLIX

'The roads I paced, I loitered through the fields;
Contentedly, yet sometimes self-accused,
Trusted my life to what chance bounty yields,
Now coldly given, now utterly refused.
The ground I for my bed have often used:
But what afflicts my peace with keenest ruth,
Is that I have my inner self abused,
440 Forgone the home delight of constant truth,
And clear and open soul, so prized in fearless youth.

L

'Through tears the rising sun I oft have viewed,
Through tears have seen him towards that world descend
Where my poor heart lost all its fortitude:

Three years a wanderer now my course I bend –
Oh! tell me whither – for no earthly friend
Have I.' – She ceased, and weeping turned away;
As if because her tale was at an end,
She wept; because she had no more to say
450 Of that perpetual weight which on her spirit lay.

LI

True sympathy the Sailor's looks expressed,
His looks – for pondering he was mute the while.
Of social Order's care for wretchedness,
Of Time's sure help to calm and reconcile,
Joy's second spring and Hope's long-treasured smile,
'Twas not for *him* to speak – a man so tried.
Yet, to relieve her heart, in friendly style
Proverbial words of comfort he applied,
And not in vain, while they went pacing side by side.

LII

460 Ere long, from heaps of turf, before their sight,
Together smoking in the sun's slant beam,
Rise various wreaths that into one unite
Which high and higher mounts with silver gleam:
Fair spectacle, – but instantly a scream
Thence bursting shrill did all remark prevent;
They paused, and heard a hoarser voice blaspheme,
And female cries. Their course they thither bent,
And met a man who foamed with anger vehement.

LIII

A woman stood with quivering lips and pale,
470 And, pointing to a little child that lay
Stretched on the ground, began a piteous tale;
How in a simple freak of thoughtless play
He had provoked his father, who straightway,
As if each blow were deadlier than the last,
Struck the poor innocent. Pallid with dismay

The Soldier's Widow heard and stood aghast;
And stern looks on the man her grey-haired Comrade
    cast.

LIV

His voice with indignation rising high
Such further deed in manhood's name forbade;
480 The peasant, wild in passion, made reply
With bitter insult and revilings sad;
Asked him in scorn what business there he had;
What kind of plunder he was hunting now;
The gallows would one day of him be glad; –
Though inward anguish damped the Sailor's brow,
Yet calm he seemed as thoughts so poignant would
    allow.

LV

Softly he stroked the child, who lay outstretched
With face to earth; and, as the boy turned round
His battered head, a groan the Sailor fetched
490 As if he saw – there and upon that ground –
Strange repetition of the deadly wound
He had himself inflicted. Through his brain
At once the griding iron passage found;
Deluge of tender thoughts then rushed amain,
Nor could his sunken eyes the starting tear restrain.

LVI

Within himself he said – What hearts have we!
The blessing this a father gives his child!
Yet happy thou, poor boy! compared with me,
Suffering not doing ill – fate far more mild.
500 The stranger's looks and tears of wrath beguiled
The father, and relenting thoughts awoke;
He kissed his son – so all was reconciled.
Then, with a voice which inward trouble broke
Ere to his lips it came, the Sailor them bespoke.

LVII

'Bad is the world, and hard is the world's law
Even for the man who wears the warmest fleece;
Much need have ye that time more closely draw
The bond of nature, all unkindness cease,
And that among so few there still be peace:
510 Else can ye hope but with such numerous foes
Your pains shall ever with your years increase?' –
While from his heart the appropriate lesson flows,
A correspondent calm stole gently o'er his woes.

LVIII

Forthwith the pair passed on; and down they look
Into a narrow valley's pleasant scene
Where wreaths of vapour tracked a winding brook,
That babbled on through groves and meadows green;
A low-roofed house peeped out the trees between;
The dripping groves resound with cheerful lays,
520 And melancholy lowings intervene
Of scattered herds, that in the meadow graze,
Some amid lingering shade, some touched by the sun's
     rays.

LIX

They saw and heard, and, winding with the road
Down a thick wood, they dropt into the vale;
Comfort by prouder mansions unbestowed
Their wearied frames, she hoped, would soon regale.
Erelong they reached that cottage in the dale:
It was a rustic inn; – the board was spread,
The milk-maid followed with her brimming pail,
530 And lustily the master carved the bread,
Kindly the housewife pressed, and they in comfort fed.

LX

Their breakfast done, the pair, though loth, must part;
Wanderers whose course no longer now agrees.
She rose and bade farewell! and, while her heart

Struggled with tears nor could its sorrow ease,
She left him there; for, clustering round his knees,
With his oak-staff the cottage children played;
And soon she reached a spot o'erhung with trees
And banks of ragged earth; beneath the shade
540 Across the pebbly road a little runnel strayed.

LXI

A cart and horse beside the rivulet stood;
Chequering the canvas roof the sunbeams shone.
She saw the carman bend to scoop the flood
As the wain fronted her, – wherein lay one,
A pale-faced Woman, in disease far gone.
The carman wet her lips as well behoved;
Bed under her lean body there was none,
Though even to die near one she most had loved
She could not of herself those wasted limbs have moved.

LXII

550 The Soldier's Widow learned with honest pain
And homefelt force of sympathy sincere,
Why thus that worn-out wretch must there sustain
The jolting road and morning air severe.
The wain pursued its way; and following near
In pure compassion she her steps retraced
Far as the cottage. 'A sad sight is here,'
She cried aloud; and forth ran out in haste
The friends whom she had left but a few minutes past.

LXIII

While to the door with eager speed they ran,
560 From her bare straw the Woman half upraised
Her bony visage – gaunt and deadly wan;
No pity asking, on the group she gazed
With a dim eye, distracted and amazed;
Then sank upon her straw with feeble moan.
Fervently cried the housewife – 'God be praised,
I have a house that I can call my own;
Nor shall she perish there, untended and alone!'

LXIV

So in they bear her to the chimney seat,
And busily, though yet with fear, untie
570 Her garments, and, to warm her icy feet
And chafe her temples, careful hands apply.
Nature reviving, with a deep-drawn sigh
She strove, and not in vain, her head to rear;
Then said – 'I thank you all; if I must die,
The God in heaven my prayers for you will hear;
Till now I did not think my end had been so near.

LXV

'Barred every comfort labour could procure,
Suffering what no endurance could assuage,
I was compelled to seek my father's door,
580 Though loth to be a burden on his age.
But sickness stopped me in an early stage
Of my sad journey; and within the wain
They placed me – there to end life's pilgrimage,
Unless beneath your roof I may remain:
For I shall never see my father's door again.

LXVI

'My life, Heaven knows, hath long been burdensome;
But, if I have not meekly suffered, meek
May my end be! Soon will this voice be dumb:
Should child of mine e'er wander hither, speak
590 Of me, say that the worm is on my cheek. –
Torn from our hut, that stood beside the sea
Near Portland lighthouse in a lonesome creek,
My husband served in sad captivity
On shipboard, bound till peace or death should set him
    free.

LXVII

'A sailor's wife I knew a widow's cares,
Yet two sweet little ones partook my bed;
Hope cheered my dreams, and to my daily prayers

Our heavenly Father granted each day's bread;
Till one was found by stroke of violence dead,
600 Whose body near our cottage chanced to lie;
A dire suspicion drove us from our shed;
In vain to find a friendly face we try,
Nor could we live together those poor boys and I;

LXVIII

'For evil tongues made oath how on that day
My husband lurked about the neighbourhood;
Now he had fled, and whither none could say,
And *he* had done the deed in the dark wood –
Near his own home! – but he was mild and good;
Never on earth was gentler creature seen;
610 He'd not have robbed the raven of its food.
My husband's loving kindness stood between
Me and all worldly harms and wrongs however keen.'

LXIX

Alas! the thing she told with labouring breath
The Sailor knew too well. That wickedness
His hand had wrought; and when, in the hour of death,
He saw his Wife's lips move his name to bless
With her last words, unable to suppress
His anguish, with his heart he ceased to strive;
And, weeping loud in this extreme distress,
620 He cried – 'Do pity me! That thou shouldst live
I neither ask nor wish – forgive me, but forgive!'

LXX

To tell the change that Voice within her wrought
Nature by sign or sound made no essay;
A sudden joy surprised expiring thought,
And every mortal pang dissolved away.
Borne gently to a bed, in death she lay;
Yet still, while over her the husband bent,
A look was in her face which seemed to say,
'Be blest: by sight of thee from heaven was sent
630 Peace to my parting soul, the fulness of content.'

LXXI

She slept in peace, – his pulses throbbed and stopped,
Breathless he gazed upon her face, – then took
Her hand in his, and raised it, but both dropped,
When on his own he cast a rueful look.
His ears were never silent; sleep forsook
His burning eyelids stretched and stiff as lead;
All night from time to time under him shook
The floor as he lay shuddering on his bed;
And oft he groaned aloud, 'O God, that I were dead!'

LXXII

640   The Soldier's Widow lingered in the cot;
And, when he rose, he thanked her pious care
Through which his Wife, to that kind shelter brought,
Died in his arms; and with those thanks a prayer
He breathed for her, and for that merciful pair.
The corse interred, not one hour he remained
Beneath their roof, but to the open air
A burden, now with fortitude sustained,
He bore within a breast where dreadful quiet reigned.

LXXIII

Confirmed of purpose, fearlessly prepared
650   For act and suffering, to the city straight
He journeyed, and forthwith his crime declared:
'And from your doom,' he added, 'now I wait,
Nor let it linger long, the murderer's fate.'
Not ineffectual was that piteous claim:
'O welcome sentence which will end though late,'
He said, 'the pangs that to my conscience came
Out of that deed. My trust, Saviour! is in thy name!'

LXXIV

His fate was pitied. Him in iron case
(Reader, forgive the intolerable thought)
660   They hung not: – no one on *his* form or face
Could gaze, as on a show by idlers sought;

No kindred sufferer, to his death-place brought
By lawless curiosity or chance,
When into storm the evening sky is wrought,
Upon his swinging corse an eye can glance,
And drop, as he once dropped, in miserable trance.

Inscription for a Seat by the Pathway Side Ascending to Windy Brow

Ye, who with buoyant spirits blessed
And rich in vigour want not rest,
Look on this slighted seat – repose
From thoughtless joy and sigh for those
Who, bowed with age or sickness, greet
With thankfulness this timely seat;
And well admonished ponder here
On the last resting place so near
To you. Though Time his prey yet spares,
10 Your fervid blood shall be as theirs;
Your motion light, your spirits high,
Shall turn to feeble, cold, and dry.
Then go with watchful care, sustain
The languid steps of age and pain;
The thorny bed of sickness smooth;
So shall ye give new joys to youth,
And for your future selves prepare,
Through every change of years and care,
That rest which Virtue still must know,
20 And only Virtue can bestow.

[Translation of Horace's Ode III, xiii]

Bandusian Spring than glass more brightly clear,
Worthy of flowers and dulcet wine,
Tomorrow shall a kid be thine
Whose brow, where the first budding horns appear,

Battles and love portends – portends in vain,
For he shall pour his crimson blood
To stain, bright Spring, thy gelid flood,
Nor e'er shall seek the wanton herd again.
Thee Sirius smites not from his raging star;
10   Thy tempting gloom a cool repose
To many a vagrant herd bestows,
And to faint oxen, weary of the share,
Thou, too, 'mid famous fountains shalt display
Thy glory, while I sing the oak
That hangs above the hollow rock,
Whence thy loquacious waters leap away.

[*Imitation of Juvenal – Satire VIII*]

Ye kings, in wisdom, sense and power, supreme,
These freaks are worse than any sick man's dream.
To hated worth no Tyrant ere designed
Malice so subtle, vengeance so refined.
Even he who yoked the living to the dead,
Rivalled by you, hides the diminished head.
Never did Rome herself so set at naught
All plain blunt sense, all subtlety of thought.
Heavens! who sees majesty in George's face?
10   Or looks at Norfolk and can dream of grace?
What has this blessed earth to do with shame?
If Excellence was ever Eden's name?
Must honour still to Lonsdale's tail be bound?
Then execration is an empty sound.
Is Common-sense asleep? has she no wand
From this curst Pharaoh-plague to rid the land?
Then to our bishops *reverent* let us fall,
Worship Mayors, Tipstaffs, Aldermen and all.
Let Ignorance o'er the monster swarms preside
20   Till Egypt see her ancient fame outvied.
The thundering Thurlow, Apis! shall rejoice
In rites once offered to thy bellowing voice.

Insatiate Charlotte's tears and Charlotte's smile
Shall ape the scaly regent of the Nile.
Bishops, of milder Spaniel breed, shall boast
The reverence by the fierce Anubis lost.
And 'tis their due: – devotion has been paid
These seven long years to Grenville's onion head.

.   .   .   .   .

But whence this gall, this lengthened face of woe?
30 We were no saints at twenty, – be it so;
Yet happy they who in life's later scene
Need only blush for what they once have been,
Who pushed by thoughtless youth to deeds of shame
'Mid such bad daring sought a coward's name.
I grant that not in parents' hearts alone
A stripling's years may for his faults atone,
So would I plead for York – but long disgrace
And Moore and Partridge stare me in the face.
Alas! 'twas other cause than lack of years
40 That moistened Dunkirk's sands with blood and tears,
Else had Morality beheld her line
With Guards and Uhlans run along the Rhine,
Religion hailed her creeds by war restored,
And Truth had blest the logic of his sword.

Were such your servant Percy! (be it tried
Between ourselves! the noble laid aside)
Now would you be content with bare release
From such a desperate breaker of the peace?
Y[our] friend the country Justice scarce would fail
50 [To gi]ve a hint of whips and the cart's tail,
Or should you even stop short of Woolwich docks
Would less suffice than Bridewell and the stocks?

But ye who make our manners, laws, and sense,
Self-judged can with such discipline dispense,
And at your will what in a groom were base
Shall stick new splendour on his gartered grace.

The theme is fruitful nor can sorrow find
Shame of such dye but worse remains behind.
My Lord can muster (all but honour spent)
60 From his wife's Faro-bank a decent rent;
The glittering rabble, housed to cheat and swear,
Swindle and rob – is no informer there.
Or is the painted staff's avenging host
By sixpenny sedition-shops engrossed,
Or rather skulking for the common weal
Round fire-side treason parties en famille?
How throngs the crowd to yon theatric school
To see an English lord enact a fool.
What wonder? – on my soul 'twould split a tub
70 To view the arch grimace of Marquis Scrub;
Nor safe the petticoats of dames that hear
The box resound on Viscount Buffo's ear.
But here's a thought which well our mirth may cross
That Smithfield should sustain so vast a loss,
That spite of the defrauded Kitchen's prayers
Scrub lives a genuine Marquess above stairs,
And they who feed with this Patrician wit
Mirth that to aching ribs will not submit
Good honest souls! – if right my judgement lies
80 Though very happy are not very wise
Unless resolved in mercy to the law
Their legislative license to withdraw
And on a frugal plan without more words
[   ]
But whence yon swarm that loads the westren bridge,
Crams through the arch, and bellys o'er the ridge?
– His Grace's watermen in open race
Are called to try their prowess with his Grace.
Could aught but Envy now his pride rebuke?
90 – The cry is six to one upon the Duke.
St Stephen's distanced, onward see him strive
Slap-dash, tail foremost, as his arms shall drive.
With shouts the *assembled* people rend the skies.
– His Grace and his protection win the prize.

– Now Norfolk set thy heralds to their tools,
Marshal forth-with a pair of oars in gules.
– Though yet the star *some hearts* at court may charm
The nobler badge shall glitter on *his arm.*
   Enough – on these inferiour things:
100 A single word on Kings and Sons of Kings.
– Were Kings a free born work – a people's choice,
Would More or Henry boast the general voice?
What fool, besotted as we are by names,
Could pause between a Raleigh and a James?
How did Buchanan waste the Sage's lore!
– Not virtuous Seneca on Nero more.
A leprous stain! ere half his thread was spun
Ripe for the block that might have spared his son,
For never did the uxorious martyr seek
110 Food for sick passion in a minion's cheek.
To patient senates quibble by the hour
And prove with endless puns a monarch's power,
Or whet his kingly faculties to chase
Legions of devils through a key-hole's space.
– What arts had better claim with wrath to warm
A Pym's brave heart, or stir a Ham[p]den's arm?
But why for scoundrels rake a distant age
Or spend upon the dead the muse's rage?
The nation's hope shall show the present time
120 As rich in folly as the past in crime.
Do arts like these a royal mind evince!
Are these the studies that beseem a prince?
Wedged in with blacklegs at a boxer's show
To shout with transport o'er a knock-down blow,
'Mid knots of grooms the council of his state
To scheme and counter-scheme for purse and plate.
Thy ancient honours when shalt thou resume?
Oh shame! is this thy service boastful plume?
Go, modern Prince, at Henry's tomb proclaim
130 Thy rival triumphs – thy Newmarket fame.
There hang thy trophies – bid the jockey's vest,
The whip, the cap, and spurs, thy praise attest;

And let that heir of Glory's endless day
Edward, the flower of chivalry, survey
(Fit token of thy reverence and love)
The boxer's armour, the dishonoured *Glove*.

.　　.　　.　　.　　.

When Calais heard (while Famine and Disease
To stern Plantagenet resigned her keys)
That victims yet were wanting to assuage
140　A baffled conqueror's deeply searching rage,
Six which themselves must single from a train
All brothers, long endeared by kindred pain,
Who then through rows of weeping comrades went
And self-devoted sought the monarch's tent,
Six simple burghers – to the rope that tied
Your vassal necks how poor the garter's pride!
Plebeian hands the [　　] mace have wrenched
From sovereigns deep in pedigree intrenched.
Let grandeur tell thee whither now is flown
150　The brightest jewel of a George's throne.
Blush Pride to see a farmer's wife produce
The first of genuine kings, a king for use;

_____

Let Bourbon spawn her scoundrels, be my joy
The embryo Franklin in the printer's boy.

.　　.　　.　　.　　.

But grant
The bastard gave some favourite stocks of peers
Patents of Manhood for eight hundred years.
Eight hundred years uncalled to other tasks
Butlers have simply broached their Lordships' casks,
160　My Lady ne'er approached a thing so coarse
As Tom – but when he helped her to her horse –
A Norman Robber then, &c. &c.

.　　.　　.　　.　　.

Erroneously we measure life by breath;
They do not truly live who merit death.

Though Riot for their daily feast unite
Thy turtles [Wilston?] and thy Venison, Wright,
For them though all the portals open stand
Of Health's own temple at her Graham's command
And the great high-priest baffling Death and Sin
170 T' earth each immortal idiot to the chin,
Ask of these wretched beings worse than dead
If on the couch celestial gold can shed
The coarser blessings of a Peasant's bed.

'The hour-bell sounds, and I must go'

The hour-bell sounds, and I must go:
    Death waits! – again I hear him calling.
No cowardly desires have I,
    Nor will I shun his face appalling.
I die in faith and honours rich,
    But, ah! I leave behind my treasure
In widowhood and lonely pain –
    To live were surely then a pleasure!

My lifeless eyes upon thy face
10   Shall never open more tomorrow –
Tomorrow shall thy beauteous eyes
    Be closed to love, and drowned in sorrow.
Tomorrow Death shall freeze this hand,
    And on thy breast, my wedded treasure!
I never, never more shall live –
    Alas! I quit a life of pleasure!

'The road extended o'er a heath'

The road extended o'er a heath
Weary and bleak: no cottager had there
Won from the waste a rood of ground, no hearth
Of Traveller's half-way house with its turf smoke

Scented the air through which the plover wings
His solitary flight. The sun was sunk,
And, fresh-indented, the white road proclaimed
The self-provided waggoner gone by.
Me from the public way the common hope
10 Of shorter path seduced, and led me on
Where smooth-green sheep-tracks thridded the sharp
    furze
And kept the choice suspended, having chosen.
The time exacted haste and steps secure
From such perplexity, so to regain
The road now more than a long mile remote,
My course I slanted, when at once winds rose
And from the rainy east a bellying cloud
Met the first star and hurried on the night.
Now fast against my cheek and whistling ears
20 My loose wet hair and tattered bonnet flapped
With thought-perplexing noise, that seemed to make
The universal darkness that ensued
More dark and desolate. Though I had seen
Worse storm, no stranger to such nights as these,
Yet had I fears from which a life like mine
Might long have rested, and remember well
That as I floundered on, disheartened sore
With the rough element and pelting shower,
I saw safe-sheltered by the viewless furze
30 The tiny glow-worm, lowliest child of earth,
From his green lodge with undiminished light
Shine through the rain, and, strange comparison
Of Envy linked with pity, touched my heart,
And such reproach of heavenly ordonnance
As shall not need forgiveness. . . .
. . . The cotters' ponies pastured near
Mute as the ground, nor other living thing
Appeared through all the waste; only the geese
Were heard to send from far a dreary cry.

'*No spade for leagues had won a rood of earth*'

No spade for leagues had won a rood of earth
From that bleak common, of all covert bare;
From travellers' half-way house no genial hearth
Scented with its turf smoke the desart air,
Through which the plover wings his lonely course,
Nor aught that might detain the sight was there,
Only a blossomed slope of dazzling gorse
Gave back the deep light of the setting sun;
All else was dreary dark – sad course her feet must run.

10 Oft did her eye retrace the backward road
Some coal-team or night-going wain to spy;
The road's white surface, fresh indented, showed
The self-provided waggoner gone by;
She turned aside for nearer path and strayed
Onward, where numerous sheep-tracks green and dry
Thrid the sharp furze and after choice is made
Keep choice suspended – so, again she sought
With slanted course the road, a long mile now remote.

Her heart recovered but the time allowed
20 No further stay and, less, her late affright,
And from the rainy east a bellying cloud
Met the first star and hurried on the night;
The shower o'erblown she urged her lonely way,
The desart opening in the moon's pale light,
And marked at last a taper's twinkling ray
Then little hoped for; from the minster tower
The distant clock tolled out the morning's second hour.

It was a lofty bell that to the ear
Gave large command, and now from wicker hole
30 Of hut beneath, that taper twinkled clear,
And thence a sound of singing upward stole
So plaintive-sad, the cadence might agree

With one who sang from very grief of soul;
More likely at such hour the lullaby
Of some poor mother o'er a sleepless child;
The house was soon attained – it was a dwelling wild.

Gently she knocked and prayed they would not blame
A Traveller weary-worn and needing rest;
Strait to the door a ragged woman came
40 Who, with arms linked and huddling elbows pressed
By either hand, a tattered jacket drew
With modest care across her hollow breast,
That showed a skin of sickly yellow hue,
'With travel spent', she cried, 'you needs must be
If from the heath arrived; come in and rest with me.

How could I fear that I, whose winter nights
Won many a merry festival from sleep,
Should pine, in youth outliving youth's delights,
Here in the eye of hunger doomed to weep?
50 Here of my better days no trace is seen;
Yet in my breast the shadow still I keep
Of Happiness gone by, with years between;
And but that Nature feels these corporal aches
My life might seem a dream – the thing a vision makes.'

So, praying her to come more near, she threw
A knot of heath upon the embers cold,
Which with her breath [   ] anon she blew,
And talked between of that unfriendly wold.
Then from a mat of straw a boy she raised
60 Who seemed, though weak in growth, three winters old,
And with a fruitless look of fondness gazed
On his pale face and held him at her breast;
If nourishment thence drawn might lead at length to
    rest.

The stranger, whom such sight not failed to touch,
Tenderly said, 'In truth you are to blame

For you are feeble and 'twill waste you much;
That office asks indeed a stronger frame.'
At this meek proof of sympathy so given
Into the mother's eye a big tear came.
70 'To wean the boy', she said, 'I long have striven
But we are poor, and when no bread is nigh
It is a piteous thing to hear an infant's cry.'

At once a thousand dreams through memory rushed,
And from the heart its present sorrow chased,
While down her cheek, by feverish watching flushed,
The o'erflow of inmost weakness trickled fast,
– Her cheek, the beauty of whose doubtful hues
Showed like a rose, its time of blowing past,
Wet with the morning's ineffectual dews.
80 Then, while the stranger warmed her torpid feet,
So willing seemed her ear, she gan her tale repeat.

'A little farm, my husband's own demesne,
Beheld the promise of my bridal day,
And when the dancing eddy of the brain
Was past, through many months that rolled away
Their calmer progress, sober reason blest
Each hope that youth can feed or years betray.
Our farm was sheltered like a little nest,
No greener fields than ours could eye survey,
90 Pleasant the fields without, and all within as gay.

From homely labour and appearance plain
Round the light heart such steady pleasure shone,
Thankful I lived nor tongue pronounced me vain.
I bore my fortunes meekly and was one
Whom softened envy might have learned to bless,
Nor needed that these joys should all be flown
To teach my heart the claims of wretchedness
But [   ]
Nor may it well be said by one so fallen as I.
                    [*cetera desunt*]

The Convict

The glory of evening was spread thròugh the west;
  – On the slope of a mountain I stood,
While the joy that precedes the calm season of rest
  Rang loud through the meadow and wood.

'And must we then part from a dwelling so fair?'
  In the pain of my spirit I said,
And with a deep sadness I turned, to repair
  To the cell where the convict is laid.

The thick-ribbèd walls that o'ershadow the gate
10   Resound; and the dungeons unfold:
I pause; and at length, through the glimmering grate
  That outcast of pity behold.

His black matted head on his shoulder is bent,
  And deep is the sigh of his breath,
And with stedfast dejection his eyes are intent
  On the fetters that link him to death.

'Tis sorrow enough on that visage to gaze,
  That body dismissed from his care;
Yet my fancy has pierced to his heart, and pourtrays
20   More terrible images there.

His bones are consumed, and his life-blood is dried,
  With wishes the past to undo;
And his crime, through the pains that o'erwhelm him, descried,
  Still blackens and grows on his view.

When from the dark synod, or blood-reeking field,
  To his chamber the monarch is led,
All soothers of sense their soft virtue shall yield,
  And quietness pillow his head.

But if grief, self-consumed, in oblivion would doze,
30   And conscience her tortures appease,
'Mid tumult and uproar this man must repose;
   In the comfortless vault of disease.

When his fetters at night have so pressed on his limbs,
   That the weight can no longer be borne,
If, while a half-slumber his memory bedims,
   The wretch on his pallet should turn,

While the jail-mastiff howls at the dull clanking chain,
   From the roots of his hair there shall start
A thousand sharp punctures of cold-sweating pain,
40   And terror shall leap at his heart.

But now he half-raises his deep-sunken eye,
   And the motion unsettles a tear;
The silence of sorrow it seems to supply,
   And asks of me why I am here.

'Poor victim! no idle intruder has stood
   With o'erweening complacence our state to compare,
But one, whose first wish is the wish to be good,
   Is come as a brother thy sorrows to share.

'At thy name though compassion her nature resign,
50   Though in virtue's proud mouth thy report be a stain,
My care, if the arm of the mighty were mine,
   Would plant thee where yet thou mightst blossom
     again.'

[Fragment of a 'Gothic' Tale]

.   .   .   .   .

Along a precipice they wound their way,
And as the path conducted they must go
Where a loose plank across a torrent lay

Whose waves sent deafness from the chasm below;
His hand on the other's shoulder close applied
O'er the rude bridge the blind man tottered slow;
That passage thus accomplished, soon they gained
The platform of the cliff, for little space remained.

So pressing on to reach that ancient pile,
10 Forsaken now and subject to the sky,
Along the sable avenue they toil,
The wind still eddying round them fierce and high;
When, all unlooked for in that lonely place,
With furious steed a horseman galloped by
Come from the quarter which [   ]
    [   ]
    [   ]

And looking round [   ] cliff he view[ed]
(The moon forth-darting then the darkness broke)
20 A castle hang, on either side a wood
Waved in the roaring wind's tempestuous shock;
It seemed, thus perched, a dim-discovered form!
Like some grim eagle on a native rock
Clapping its wings and wailing to the storm.
Forthwith our travellers to that Castle high
Reared their laborious steps, no better mansion nigh.

Advancing on he saw a sullen light
Red as a star, but star it could not be;
Its station scarcely seemed to reach the height
30 Of oak full-grown or any forest tree;
The bright moon severed the black clouds in twain,
And gave him on the gateway's side to see
A man who stepped along, a tower to gain;
Where but the keystone seemed to link the arch
Else broken, on he crept, a high and perilous march.

When he had reached a tower on the other side
He turned and cast a short survey around,
And as he turned the youth a cutlass spied

As if to staunch the blood of recent wound;
40 The blind [man?] now impatiently inquired
If better covert might not there be found;
So leading him along, the youth retired
Behind a wall with trees secure and dark,
And stood of that strange sight the sequel there to mark.

By entrance through a broken window made
He saw that daring traveller disappear,
Nor single word of this discovery said
To his forlorn dependant standing near;
A full half hour the youth prolonged his watch,
50 But whether work it were whose after-fear
Must sleep upon the proof of sure dispatch,
Or that the lantern gave him to explore
Some other passage out, that man appeared no more.

'Troth', cried the boy, 'well need some favourite girl
Were looked for, this attendance to requite;
Poor service 'tis while winds around us whirl
Thus scantly roofed to weather out the night;
My legs with standing ache to the very bone
And many hours must pass ere morning light.
60 Be cheerful, comrade, think thou'rt not alone;
'Tis time to search, if here we must sojourn,
Some more commodious spot where we may sleep till
    morn.'

So saying, by the hand he led his charge
Through the dark passage of the ponderous keep,
That opened to a court of circuit large
Whose walls had scattered many a stony heap;
The unimaginable touch of time
Or shouldering rend had split with ruin deep
Those towers that stately stood, as in their prime,
70 Though shattered stood of undiminished height,
And plumed their heads with trees that shook before the
    night.

Beyond a spacious gap, in distance seen,
A second court its battlements upreared,
And 'cross this ample area's midway green
The youth with his attendant thither steered;
The chasm scarce passed, he cast his eyes around

[*four lines missing*]

''Tis not for me this business to gainsay',
Thus inly to himself the stripling spoke,
'To some close covert hence we must away,
80   For work is here which none may overlook.'
So towards the shadow of the eastern wall
His backward course incontinent he took;
When all at once, as at a demon's call,
The pile was troubled by a deeper blast
And with impervious clouds the moon was overcast.

Nor stayed the tempest here; the thunder stroke
Burst on the mountains with hell-rousing force,
And as the sulphurous bolt of terror broke
The blind man shuddered to life's inmost source;
90   For through the darkness of his brain the flash
With sudden apparition [?] the course.
Again the fleecy clouds together clash,
Revealing to the guide a short descent
That promised safe retreat, and thither down they went.

It was a spot where once a depth of stairs
Led to a dungeon far from any sound;
A den where feudal Lords of ancient years
The vassals of their will in durance bound;
And underneath a corner tower, appeared
[*one line missing*]
100   Amid the wreck that strewed the encumbered ground,
Two armed men, who 'cross the stones conveyed
A burden of such weight as asked their mutual aid.

[*four lines missing*]

But now filled up with earth, with grass o'ergrown,
Smooth was the passage to the vault profound.
'What change!' exclaimed the blind man guided down,
'How warm, how still! here, comrade, will we stay,
No better can betide till Morning bring the day.

    Methinks I could almost be happy now
To find us safe and warmly lodged at last,
110 And yet my soul within, I know not how,
Is sad to think upon the perils past.
Tonight and many other nights and days
I owe thee much, and wish thee better placed.
Good youth, my debt thy earning ill repays,
For twice this very evening, but for thee,
There had not been a hair betwixt my death and me.

    On the loose plank which spanned that roaring flood
How had we fared alone, my dog and I
Or 'mid the darkness of the deafening wood
120 When at full speed the horseman galloped by.
In truth from thee it comes that now I live;
My recompense should with thy service vie;
But little recompense have I to give,
Yet something have I stored to meet the hour
When crippling Age shall bring the wanderer to his
    door.

    Broken I am in health, and child have none,
And couldst thou be content our lot to share
Ere to the grave my wife and I be gone,
That store for thee might grow with thrifty care;
130 But on a stranded vessel thou wilt seem
To waste thy pains forlorn of inward cheer;
So oft I fancy, and myself I deem
A Burden to the earth whereon I tread
A poor and useless man and better with the dead.'

His hopes the youth to fatal dreams had lent
And from that hour had laboured with the curse
Of evil thoughts, nor had the least event
Not owned a meaning monstrous and perverse;
And now these latter words were words of blood·
140 And all the man had said but served to nurse
Purpose most foul with most unnatural food;
Each kindred object which, that night, had braced
His fluctuating mind, he busily retraced.

Up as they climbed, the precipice's ridge
Lessons of death at every step had given;
And at the crossing of the pendent bridge
With impulse horrible his heart had striven:
And now with black regret he cursed agen
The fragment which the winds had idly riven;
150 But chief that place and those mysterious men
Here seen, did for his bloody purpose plead,
Of every human fear disburdening the deed.

At length confirmed and to the work addressed
The youth broke silence; but the summons found
No answer; for betaken to his rest
The blind man sleeping lay upon the ground.
So nearer to his bed the stripling drew,
When in that ample dungeon's farthest bound
Dim sparks revealed a hand of fleshy hue,
160 And such the import which that phantom bore
That had it long endured his heart had beat no more.

But that grim shape, as if it ne'er had been,
Soon vanished [   ] and anon
In place of those dull sparks a light was seen
That from the cavern's depth came gliding on;
And now the legs as of a human frame
Appeared; and with that light which dimly shone
Forthwith a gloomy figure nearer came,

And, stopping short, replaced a kerchief bound
170 About his arm, that bled as from a recent wound.

Glad respite did that black Appearance give
When every inward vessel gan dispart
With ghostly terrors never sent to live
Amid the weakness of a mortal heart;
The pendent cutlass and the belt, descried
By what faint glare the lantern could impart,
Marked out the shape which he before had spied.
His work arranged, the man at distance short
Passed through the dark recess and sought the upper
    court.

180 And gone, he left the stripling light of soul,
Nor doubting but the hand that vault had shown
Was earthly, 'mid lamp-smothering vapours foul
So fashioned to his eye by sparkles thrown
On the thick air, from fire-detaining wood
Or flint whose sound the wind had made its own.

[*three lines missing*]

His ear, though often troubled, only felt
The low vault to the moaning gust reply;
His sight, though inly busy, only dealt
With darkness or the shapes of Phantasy;
190 At length he rose, by irksome thought impelled,
And looking up, in restless walk, on high
Above the dungeon's roof a star beheld
Whose sparkling lustre, through the crevice shed,
Sent to his fluttering heart a momentary dread.

At length, the open area to explore,
For in that vault no second foot appeared,
Up to the dungeon's mouth his course he bore.
The winds were passed away, the sky was cleared,
Nor did the court or silent walls present

200 Object or shape whose motion might be feared;
Only the crimson moon, her lustre spent,
With orb half-visible was seen to sink,
Leading the storm's remains along the horizon's brink.

So back he slunk and to the corner came
Where lay his friend devoted to the grave;
But as he gan to lift his murderous aim
A rumbling noise along the hollow cave
Was heard remote, succeeded by a sound
Of uncouth horror, to which echo gave
210 Such rending peal as made the vault rebound;
Nor whelming crash it seemed, or shriek or groan,
But painful outcry strange, to living ear unknown.

'Whence comes that uproar?' starting from his sleep
The sailor cried, nor could the other make
Reply, o'ercome with shock of horror deep;
And, when returning thought began to wake,
In bare remembrance of that sound there dwelt
Such power as made his joints with terror quake;
And all which he, that night, had seen or felt
220 Showed like the shapes delusion loves to deem
Sights that obey the dead or phantoms of a dream.
                    [*cetera desunt*]

Address to the Ocean

'How long will ye round me be roaring',
    Once terrible waves of the sea?
While I at my door sit deploring
    The treasure ye ravished from me.
When shipwreck the white surf is strewing,
    This spray-beaten thatch will ye spare?
Come – let me exult in the ruin
    Your smiles are put on to prepare.

Oh! thus that your voice had still thundered!
10   Your arms for destruction been spread!
My Charles and I ne'er had been sundered;
    But now had I pillowed his head.

The love which the waves must dissever,
    The hope which the winds might deceive,
Why these, my sole stay, could I ever
    Permit him this bosom to leave?

Oh! where are thy beauties, my lover?
    And where is thy dark flowing hair?
Oh God! that this storm would uncover
20   Thy body that once was so fair!
Through regions of darkness appalling
    It sunk as the hurricane whirled;
By monsters beset in its falling,
    The brood of the bottomless world.

Then ocean! thou canst not uncover
    The body that once was so fair;
And lost are thy beauties, my lover!
    And gone is thy dark-flowing hair!
Ye waters! I hear in your roaring
30   A voice from your deepest abode;
New victims in anger imploring –
    My hope be the mercy of God.

Argument for Suicide

Send this man to the mine, this to the battle,
Famish an aged beggar at your gates,
And let him die by inches – but for worlds
Lift not your hand against him – Live, live on,
As if this earth owned neither steel nor arsenic,
A rope, a river, or a standing pool.
Live, if you dread the pains of hell, or think

Your corpse would quarrel with a stake – alas
Has misery then no friend? – if you would die
10 By license, call the dropsy and the stone
And let them end you – strange it is;
And most fantastic are the magic circles
Drawn round the thing called life – till we have learned
To prize it less, we ne'er shall learn to prize
The things worth living for. –

The Borderers. A Tragedy

Dramatis Personae

MARMADUKE ⎫
OSWALD ⎪
WALLACE ⎬ Of the Band of Borderers.
LACY ⎪
LENNOX ⎭
HERBERT
WILFRED, Servant to MARMADUKE
Host
Forester
ELDRED, a Peasant
Peasant, Pilgrims, &c.
IDONEA
Female Beggar
ELEANOR, Wife to ELDRED

SCENE: Borders of England and Scotland
Time: The Reign of Henry III.

Readers already acquainted with my Poems will recognize, in the following composition, some eight or ten lines, which I have not scrupled to retain in the places where they originally stood. It is proper however to add that they would not have been used elsewhere, if I had foreseen the time when I might be induced to publish this Tragedy.

February 28, 1842.

ACT I

SCENE, *road in a Wood.*

WALLACE *and* LACY

LACY. The Troop will be impatient; let us hie
  Back to our post, and strip the Scottish Foray
  Of their rich Spoil, ere they recross the Border.
  – Pity that our young Chief will have no part
  In this good service.
WAL.   Rather let us grieve
  That, in the undertaking which has caused
  His absence, he hath sought, whate'er his aim,
  Companionship with One of crooked ways,
  From whose perverted soul can come no good
10 To our confiding, open-hearted, Leader.
LACY. True; and, remembering how the Band have
       proved
  That Oswald finds small favour in our sight,
  Well may we wonder he has gained such power
  Over our much-loved Captain.
WAL.   I have heard
  Of some dark deed to which in early life
  His passion drove him – then a Voyager
  Upon the midland Sea. You knew his bearing
  In Palestine?
LACY.   Where he despised alike
  Mohammedan and Christian. But enough;
20 Let us begone – the Band may else be foiled.   [*Exeunt*]

    [*Enter* MARMADUKE *and* WILFRED]

WIL. Be cautious, my dear Master!
MAR.   I perceive
  That fear is like a cloak which old men huddle
  About their love, as if to keep it warm.
WIL. Nay, but I grieve that we should part. This
       Stranger,
  For such he is –

MAR.   Your busy fancies, Wilfred,
  Might tempt me to a smile; but what of him?
WIL. You know that you have saved his life.
MAR.   I know it.
WIL. And that he hates you! – Pardon me, perhaps
  That word was hasty.
MAR.   Fy! no more of it.
30 WIL. Dear Master! gratitude's a heavy burden
  To a proud Soul. – Nobody loves this Oswald –
  Yourself, you do not love him.
MAR.   I do more,
  I honour him. Strong feelings to his heart
  Are natural; and from no one can be learnt
  More of man's thoughts and ways than his experience
  Has given him power to teach: and then for courage
  And enterprise – what perils hath he shunned?
  What obstacles hath he failed to overcome?
  Answer these questions, from our common knowledge,
  And be at rest.
WIL.   Oh, Sir!
40 MAR.   Peace, my good Wilfred;
  Repair to Liddesdale, and tell the Band
  I shall be with them in two days, at farthest.
WIL. May He whose eye is over all protect you!   [*Exit*]

    [*Enter* OSWALD (*a bunch of plants in his hand*)]

OSW. This wood is rich in plants and curious simples.
MAR. [*looking at them*] The wild rose, and the poppy,
    and the nightshade:
  Which is your favourite, Oswald?
OSW.   That which, while it is
  Strong to destroy, is also strong to heal –
                        [*Looking forward*]
  Not yet in sight! – We'll saunter here awhile;
  They cannot mount the hill, by us unseen.
MAR. [*a letter in his hand*] It is no common thing when
50   one like you
  Performs these delicate services, and therefore

    I feel myself much bounden to you, Oswald;
    'Tis a strange letter this! – You saw her write it?
OSW. And saw the tears with which she blotted it.
MAR. And nothing less would satisfy him?
OSW.   No less;
    For that another in his Child's affection
    Should hold a place, as if 'twere robbery,
    He seemed to quarrel with the very thought.
    Besides, I know not what strange prejudice
60   Is rooted in his mind; this Band of ours,
    Which you've collected for the noblest ends,
    Along the confines of the Esk and Tweed
    To guard the Innocent – he calls us 'Outlaws';
    And, for yourself, in plain terms he asserts
    This garb was taken up that indolence
    Might want no cover, and rapacity
    Be better fed.
MAR.   Ne'er may I own the heart
    That cannot feel for one, helpless as he is.
OSW. Thou know'st me for a Man not easily moved,
70   Yet was I grievously provoked to think
    Of what I witnessed.
MAR.   This day will suffice
    To end her wrongs.
OSW.   But if the blind Man's tale
    Should *yet* be true?
MAR.   Would it were possible!
    Did not the Soldier tell thee that himself,
    And others who survived the wreck, beheld
    The Baron Herbert perish in the waves
    Upon the coast of Cyprus?
OSW.   Yes, even so,
    And I had heard the like before: in sooth
    The tale of this his quondam Barony
80   Is cunningly devised; and, on the back
    Of his forlorn appearance, could not fail
    To make the proud and vain his tributaries,
    And stir the pulse of lazy charity.

The seignories of Herbert are in Devon;
We, neighbours of the Esk and Tweed: 'tis much
The Arch-impostor —

MAR.   Treat him gently, Oswald;
Though I have never seen his face, methinks,
There cannot come a day when I shall cease
To love him. I remember, when a Boy
90   Of scarcely seven years' growth, beneath the Elm
That casts its shade over our village school,
'Twas my delight to sit and hear Idonea
Repeat her Father's terrible adventures,
Till all the band of playmates wept together;
And that was the beginning of my love.
And, through all converse of our later years,
An image of this old Man still was present,
When I had been most happy. Pardon me
If this be idly spoken.

OSW.   See, they come,
Two Travellers!
100   MAR. [*points*] The woman is Idonea.
OSW. And leading Herbert.
MAR.   We must let them pass –
This thicket will conceal us.   [*They step aside*]

        [*Enter* IDONEA, *leading* HERBERT *blind*]

IDON. Dear Father, you sigh deeply; ever since
We left the willow shade by the brookside,
Your natural breathing has been troubled.
   HER.   Nay,
You are too fearful; yet must I confess,
Our march of yesterday had better suited
A firmer step than mine.
   IDON.   That dismal Moor –
In spite of all the larks that cheered our path,
110   I never can forgive it: but how steadily
You paced along, when the bewildering moonlight
Mocked me with many a strange fantastic shape! –
I thought the Convent never would appear;

It seemed to move away from us: and yet,
That you are thus the fault is mine; for the air
Was soft and warm, no dew lay on the grass,
And midway on the waste ere night had fallen
I spied a Covert walled and roofed with sods –
A miniature; belike some Shepherd-boy,

120 Who might have found a nothing-doing hour
Heavier than work, raised it: within that hut
We might have made a kindly bed of heath,
And thankfully there rested side by side
Wrapped in our cloaks, and, with recruited strength,
Have hailed the morning sun. But cheerily, Father, –
That staff of yours, I could almost have heart
To fling't away from you: you make no use
Of me, or of my strength; – come, let me feel
That you do press upon me. There – indeed

130 You are quite exhausted. Let us rest awhile
On this green bank.   *[He sits down]*

HER. *[after some time]* Idonea, you are silent,
And I divine the cause.

IDON.   Do not reproach me:
I pondered patiently your wish and will
When I gave way to your request; and now,
When I behold the ruins of that face,
Those eyeballs dark – dark beyond hope of light,
And think that they were blasted for my sake,
The name of Marmaduke is blown away:
Father, I would not change that sacred feeling
For all this world can give.

140 HER.   Nay, be composed:
Few minutes gone a faintness overspread
My frame, and I bethought me of two things
I ne'er had heart to separate – my grave,
And thee, my Child!

IDON.   Believe me, honoured Sire!
'Tis weariness that breeds these gloomy fancies,
And you mistake the cause: you hear the woods
Resound with music, could you see the sun,

And look upon the pleasant face of Nature –
HER. I comprehend thee – I should be as cheerful
150   As if we two were twins; two songsters bred
In the same nest, my spring-time one with thine.
My fancies, fancies if they be, are such
As come, dear Child! from a far deeper source
Than bodily weariness. While here we sit
I feel my strength returning. – The bequest
Of thy kind Patroness, which to receive
We have thus far adventured, will suffice
To save thee from the extreme of penury;
But when thy Father must lie down and die,
How wilt thou stand alone?
160   IDON.   Is he not strong?
Is he not valiant?
HER.   Am I then so soon
Forgotten? have my warnings passed so quickly
Out of thy mind? My dear, my only, Child;
Thou wouldst be leaning on a broken reed –
This Marmaduke —
IDON.   O could you hear his voice:
Alas! you do not know him. He is one
(I wot not what ill tongue has wronged him with you)
All gentleness and love. His face bespeaks
A deep and simple meekness: and that Soul,
170   Which with the motion of a virtuous act
Flashes a look of terror upon guilt,
Is, after conflict, quiet as the ocean,
By a miraculous finger, stilled at once.
HER. Unhappy Woman!
IDON.   Nay, it was my duty
Thus much to speak; but think not I forget –
Dear Father! how *could* I forget and live? –
You and the story of that doleful night
When, Antioch blazing to her topmost towers,
You rushed into the murderous flames, returned
180   Blind as the grave, but, as you oft have told me,
Clasping your infant Daughter to your heart.

HER. Thy Mother too! – scarce had I gained the door,
    I caught her voice; she threw herself upon me,
    I felt thy infant brother in her arms;
    She saw my blasted face – a tide of soldiers
    That instant rushed between us, and I heard
    Her last death-shriek, distinct among a thousand.
IDON. Nay, Father, stop not; let me hear it all.
HER. Dear Daughter! precious relic of that time –
190   For my old age, it doth remain with thee
    To make it what thou wilt. Thou has been told,
    That when, on our return from Palestine,
    I found how my domains had been usurped,
    I took thee in my arms, and we began
    Our wanderings together. Providence
    At length conducted us to Rossland, – there,
    Our melancholy story moved a Stranger
    To take thee to her home – and for myself,
    Soon after, the good Abbot of St Cuthbert's
200   Supplied my helplessness with food and raiment,
    And, as thou know'st, gave me that humble Cot
    Where now we dwell. – For many years I bore
    Thy absence, till old age and fresh infirmities
    Exacted thy return, and our reunion.
    I did not think that, during that long absence,
    My Child, forgetful of the name of Herbert,
    Had given her love to a wild Freebooter,
    Who here, upon the borders of the Tweed,
    Doth prey alike on two distracted Countries,
    Traitor to both.
210 IDON.   Oh, could you hear his voice!
    I will not call on Heaven to vouch for me,
    But let this kiss speak what is in my heart.

    [*Enter a* PEASANT]

PEA. Good morrow, Strangers! If you want a Guide,
    Let me have leave to serve you!
IDON.   My Companion
    Hath need of rest; the sight of Hut or Hostel

Would be most welcome.

PEA.   Yon white hawthorn gained,
You will look down into a dell, and there
Will see an ash from which a sign-board hangs;
The house is hidden by the shade. Old Man,
220   You seem worn out with travel – shall I support you?

HER. I thank you; but, a resting-place so near,
'Twere wrong to trouble you.

PEA.   God speed you both.

[*Exit* PEASANT]

HER. Idonea, we must part. Be not alarmed –
'Tis but for a few days – a thought has struck me.

IDON. That I should leave you at this house, and thence
Proceed alone. It shall be so; for strength
Would fail you ere our journey's end be reached.

[*Exit* HERBERT *supported by* IDONEA]

[*Re-enter* MARMADUKE *and* OSWALD]

MAR. This instant will we stop him –

OSW.   Be not hasty,
For sometimes, in despite of my conviction,
230   He tempted me to think the Story true;
'Tis plain he loves the Maid, and what he said
That savoured of aversion to thy name
Appeared the genuine colour of his soul –
Anxiety lest mischief should befall her
After his death.

MAR.   I have been much deceived.

OSW. But sure he loves the Maiden, and never love
Could find delight to nurse itself so strangely,
Thus to torment her with *inventions*! – death –
There must be truth in this.

MAR.   Truth in his story!
240   He must have felt it then, known what it was,
And in such wise to rack her gentle heart
Had been a tenfold cruelty.

OSW.   Strange pleasures

Do we poor mortals cater for ourselves!
To see him thus provoke her tenderness
With tales of weakness and infirmity!
I'd wager on his life for twenty years.

MAR. We will not waste an hour in such a cause.

OSW. Why, this is noble! shake her off at once.

MAR. Her virtues are his instruments. – A Man

250   Who has so practised on the world's cold sense,
May well deceive his Child – what! leave her thus,
A prey to a deceiver? – no – no – no –
'Tis but a word and then –

OSW.   Something is here
More than we see, or whence this strong aversion?
Marmaduke! I suspect unworthy tales
Have reached his ear – you have had enemies.

MAR. Enemies! – of his own coinage.

OSW.   That may be,
But wherefore slight protection such as you
Have power to yield? perhaps he looks elsewhere. –
I am perplexed.

260 MAR.   What hast thou heard or seen?

OSW. No – no – the thing stands clear of mystery;
(As you have said) he coins himself the slander
With which he taints her ear; – for a plain reason;
He dreads the presence of a virtuous man
Like you; he knows your eye would search his heart,
Your justice stamp upon his evil deeds
The punishment they merit. All is plain:
It cannot be –

MAR.   What cannot be?

OSW.   Yet that a Father
Should in his love admit no rivalship,

270   And torture thus the heart of his own Child –

MAR. Nay, you abuse my friendship!

OSW.   Heaven forbid! –
There was a circumstance, trifling indeed –
It struck me at the time – yet I believe
I never should have thought of it again

But for the scene which we by chance have witnessed.
MAR. What is your meaning?
OSW.   Two days gone I saw,
   Though at a distance and he was disguised,
   Hovering round Herbert's door, a man whose figure
   Resembled much that cold voluptuary,
280   The villain, Clifford. He hates you, and he knows
   Where he can stab you deepest.
MAR.   Clifford never
   Would stoop to skulk about a Cottage door –
   It could not be.
OSW.   And yet I now remember
   That, when your praise was warm upon my tongue,
   And the blind Man was told how you had rescued
   A maiden from the ruffian violence
   Of this same Clifford, he became impatient
   And would not hear me.
MAR.   No – it cannot be –
   I dare not trust myself with such a thought –
290   Yet whence this strange aversion? You are a man
   Not used to rash conjectures –
OSW.   If you deem it
   A thing worth further notice, we must act
   With caution, sift the matter artfully.
                  [*Exeunt* MARMADUKE *and* OSWALD]

SCENE, *the door of the Hostel.*

HERBERT, IDONEA, *and* HOST.

HER. [*seated*] As I am dear to you, remember, Child!
   This last request.
IDON.   You know me, Sire; farewell!
HER. And are you going then? Come, come, Idonea,
   We must not part, – I have measured many a league
   When these old limbs had need of rest, – and now
   I will not play the sluggard.
IDON.   Nay, sit down.
                        [*Turning to* HOST]
300   Good Host, such tendance as you would expect

From your own Children, if yourself were sick,
Let this old Man find at your hands; poor Leader,
                                    [*Looking at the dog*]
We soon shall meet again. If thou neglect
This charge of thine, then ill befall thee! – Look,
The little fool is loth to stay behind.
Sir Host! by all the love you bear to courtesy,
Take care of him, and feed the truant well.

HOST. Fear not, I will obey you; – but One so young,
And One so fair, it goes against my heart

310   That you should travel unattended, Lady! –
I have a palfrey and a groom: the lad
Shall squire you, (would it not be better, Sir?)
And for less fee than I would let him run
For any lady I have seen this twelve-month.

IDON. You know, Sir, I have been too long your guard
Not to have learnt to laugh at little fears.
Why, if a wolf should leap from out a thicket,
A look of mine would send him scouring back,
Unless I differ from the thing I am

320   When you are by my side.

HER.   Idonea, wolves
Are not the enemies that move my fears.

IDON. No more, I pray, of this. Three days at farthest
Will bring me back – protect him, Saints – farewell!
                                    [*Exit* IDONEA]

HOST. 'Tis never drought with us – St Cuthbert and his
    Pilgrims,
Thanks to them, are to us a stream of comfort:
Pity the Maiden did not wait a while;
She could not, Sir, have failed of company.

HER. Now she is gone, I fain would call her back.

HOST. [*calling*] Holla!

HER. No, no, the business must be done. –
What means this riotous noise?

330   HOST.   The villagers
Are flocking in – a wedding festival –
That's all – God save you, Sir.

[*Enter* OSWALD]

OSW.   Ha! as I live,
The Baron Herbert.
HOST.   Mercy, the Baron Herbert!
OSW. So far into your journey! on my life,
You are a lusty Traveller. But how fare you?
HER. Well as the wreck I am permits. And you, Sir?
OSW. I do not see Idonea.
HER.   Dutiful Girl,
She is gone before, to spare my weariness.
But what has brought you hither?
OSW.   A slight affair,
That will be soon dispatched.
340 HER.   Did Marmaduke
Receive that letter?
OSW.   Be at peace. – The tie
Is broken, you will hear no more of *him*.
HER. This is true comfort, thanks a thousand times! –
That noise! – would I had gone with her as far
As the Lord Clifford's Castle: I have heard
That, in his milder moods, he has expressed
Compassion for me. His influence is great
With Henry, our good King; – the Baron might
Have heard my suit, and urged my plea at Court.
350 No matter – he's a dangerous Man. – That noise! –
'Tis too disorderly for sleep or rest.
Idonea would have fears for me, – the Convent
Will give me quiet lodging. You have a boy, good
    Host,
And he must lead me back.
OSW.   You are most lucky;
I have been waiting in the wood hard by
For a companion – here he comes; our journey

[*Enter* MARMADUKE]

Lies on your way; accept us as your Guides.
HER. Alas! I creep so slowly.

OSW.   Never fear;
   We'll not complain of that.
   HER.   My limbs are stiff
360   And need repose. Could you but wait an hour?
   OSW. Most willingly! – Come, let me lead you in,
      And, while you take your rest, think not of us;
      We'll stroll into the wood; lean on my arm.
         [*Conducts* HERBERT *into the house. Exit* MARMADUKE]

      [*Enter* VILLAGERS]

   OSW. [*to himself coming out of the Hostel*] I have
      prepared a most apt Instrument –
      The Vagrant must, no doubt, be loitering somewhere
      About this ground; she hath a tongue well skilled,
      By mingling natural matter of her own
      With all the daring fictions I have taught her,
      To win belief, such as my plot requires.
                                    [*Exit* OSWALD]

      [*Enter more* VILLAGERS, *a* MUSICIAN *among them*]

370 HOST [*to them*]. Into the court, my Friend, and perch
      yourself
      Aloft upon the elm-tree. Pretty Maids,
      Garlands and flowers, and cakes and merry thoughts,
      Are here, to send the sun into the west
      More speedily than you belike would wish.

   SCENE *changes to the Wood adjoining the Hostel* –

      MARMADUKE *and* OSWALD *entering.*

   MAR. I would fain hope that we deceive ourselves:
      When first I saw him sitting there, alone,
      It struck upon my heart I know not how.
   OSW. Today will clear up all. – You marked a Cottage,
      That ragged Dwelling, close beneath a rock
380   By the brook-side: it is the abode of One,
      A Maiden innocent till ensnared by Clifford,
      Who soon grew weary of her; but, alas!
      What she had seen and suffered turned her brain.

Cast off by her Betrayer, she dwells alone,
Nor moves her hands to any needful work:
She eats her food which every day the peasants
Bring to her hut; and so the Wretch has lived
Ten years; and no one ever heard her voice;
But every night at the first stroke of twelve
390   She quits her house, and, in the neighbouring
        Churchyard
Upon the self-same spot, in rain or storm,
She paces out the hour 'twixt twelve and one –
She paces round and round an Infant's grave,
And in the Churchyard sod her feet have worn
A hollow ring; they say it is knee-deep –
Ah! what is here?

                    [*A female* BEGGAR *rises up, rubbing her
                    eyes as if in sleep – a Child in her arms*]
BEG.   Oh! Gentlemen, I thank you;
I've had the saddest dream that ever troubled
The heart of living creature. – My poor Babe
Was crying, as I thought, crying for bread
400   When I had none to give him; whereupon,
I put a slip of foxglove in his hand,
Which pleased him so, that he was hushed at once:
When, into one of those same spotted bells
A bee came darting, which the Child with joy
Imprisoned there, and held it to his ear,
And suddenly grew black, as he would die.
MAR. We have no time for this, my babbling Gossip;
Here's what will comfort you.   [*Gives her money*]
BEG.   The Saints reward you
For this good deed! – Well, Sirs, this passed away;
410   And afterwards I fancied, a strange dog,
Trotting alone along the beaten road,
Came to my child as by my side he slept,
And, fondling, licked his face, then on a sudden
Snapped fierce to make a morsel of his head:
But here he is, [*Kissing the Child*] it must have been
    a dream.

OSW. When next inclined to sleep, take my advice
    And put your head, good Woman, under cover.
BEG. Oh, Sir, you would not talk thus, if you knew
    What life is this of ours, how sleep will master
420   The weary-worn. – You gentlefolk have got
    Warm chambers to your wish. I'd rather be
    A stone than what I am. – But two nights gone,
    The darkness overtook me – wind and rain
    Beat hard upon my head – and yet I saw
    A glow-worm, through the covert of the furze,
    Shine calmly as if nothing ailed the sky:
    At which I half accused the God in Heaven. –
    You must forgive me.
OSW.   Ay, and if you think
    The Fairies are to blame, and you should chide
430   Your favourite saint – no matter – this good day
    Has made amends.
BEG.   Thanks to you both; but, Oh Sir!
    How would you like to travel on whole hours
    As I have done, my eyes upon the ground,
    Expecting still, I knew not how, to find
    A piece of money glittering through the dust?
MAR. This woman is a prater. Pray, good Lady!
    Do you tell fortunes?
BEG.   Oh Sir, you are like the rest.
    This Little-one – it cuts me to the heart –
    Well! they might turn a beggar from their doors,
440   But there are Mothers who can see the Babe
    Here at my breast, and ask me where I bought it:
    This they can do, and look upon my face –
    But you, Sir, should be kinder.
MAR.   Come hither, Fathers,
    And learn what nature is from this poor Wretch!
BEG. Ay, Sir, there's nobody that feels for us.
    Why now – but yesterday I overtook
    A blind old Greybeard and accosted him,
    I' the name of all the Saints, and by the Mass
    He should have used me better! – Charity!

450   If you can melt a rock, he is your man;
        But I'll be even with him – here again
        Have I been waiting for him.
    OSW.   Well, but softly,
        Who is it that hath wronged you?
    BEG.   Mark you me;
        I'll point him out; – a Maiden is his guide,
        Lovely as Spring's first rose; a little dog,
        Tied by a woollen cord, moves on before
        With look as sad as he were dumb; the cur,
        I owe him no ill will, but in good sooth
        He does his Master credit.
    MAR.   As I live,
        'Tis Herbert and no other!
460   BEG.   'Tis a feast to see him,
        Lank as a ghost and tall, his shoulders bent,
        And long beard white with age – yet evermore,
        As if he were the only Saint on earth,
        He turns his face to heaven.
    OSW.   But why so violent
        Against this venerable Man?
    BEG.   I'll tell you:
        He has the very hardest heart on earth;
        I had as lief turn to the Friar's school
        And knock for entrance, in mid holiday.
    MAR. But to your story.
    BEG.   I was saying, Sir –
470   Well! – he has often spurned me like a toad,
        But yesterday was worse than all; – at last
        I overtook him, Sirs, my Babe and I,
        And begged a little aid for charity:
        But he was snappish as a cottage cur.
        Well then, says I – I'll out with it; at which
        I cast a look upon the Girl, and felt
        As if my heart would burst; and so I left him.
    OSW. I think, good Woman, you are the very person
        Whom, but some few days past, I saw in Eskdale,
        At Herbert's door.

480 BEG.   Ay; and if truth were known
     I have good business there.
     OSW.   I met you at the threshold,
     And he seemed angry.
     BEG.   Angry! well he might;
     And long as I can stir I'll dog him. – Yesterday,
     To serve me so, and knowing that he owes
     The best of all he has to me and mine.
     But 'tis all over now. – That good old Lady
     Has left a power of riches; and I say it,
     If there's a lawyer in the land, the knave
     Shall give me half.
     OSW. What's this? – I fear, good Woman,
     You have been insolent.
490 BEG.   And there's the Baron,
     I spied him skulking in his peasant's dress.
     OSW. How say you? in disguise? –
     MAR.   But what's your business
     With Herbert or his Daughter?
     BEG.   Daughter! truly–
     But how's the day? – I fear, my little Boy,
     We've overslept ourselves. – Sirs, have you seen him?
                                        [*offers to go*]
     MAR.   I must have more of this; – you shall not stir
     An inch, till I am answered. Know you aught
     That doth concern this Herbert?
     BEG.   You are provoked,
     And will misuse me, Sir!
                                No trifling, Woman! –
     OSW. You are as safe as in a sanctuary;
     Speak.
     MAR. Speak!
     BEG.   He is a most hard-hearted Man.
     MAR. Your life is at my mercy.
     BEG.   Do not harm me,
     And I will tell you all! – You know not, Sir,
     What strong temptations press upon the Poor.
     OSW. Speak out.

BEG.   Oh, Sir, I've been a wicked Woman.

OSW. Nay, but speak out!

BEG.   He flattered me, and said
  What harvest it would bring us both; and so,
  I parted with the Child.

MAR.   Parted with whom?

BEG. Idonea, as he calls her; but the Girl
  Is mine.

510 MAR. Yours, Woman! are you Herbert's wife?

BEG. Wife, Sir! his wife – not I; my husband, Sir,
  Was of Kirkoswald – many a snowy winter
  We've weathered out together. My poor Gilfred!
  He has been two years in his grave.

MAR.   Enough.

OSW. We've solved the riddle – Miscreant!

MAR.   Do you,
  Good Dame, repair to Liddesdale and wait
  For my return; be sure you shall have justice.

OSW. A lucky woman! – go, you have done good service.
                                        [*Aside*]

MAR. [*to himself*] Eternal praises on the power that saved
      her! –

OSW. [*gives her money*] Here's for your little boy, – and
520   when you christen him
  I'll be his Godfather.

BEG.   Oh Sir, you are merry with me.
  In grange or farm this Hundred scarcely owns
  A dog that does not know me. – These good Folks,
  For love of God, I must not pass their doors;
  But I'll be back with my best speed: for you –
  God bless and thank you both, my gentle Masters.
                                    [*Exit* BEGGAR]

MAR. [*to himself*] The cruel Viper! – Poor devoted Maid,
  Now I *do* love thee.

OSW.   I am thunderstruck.

MAR. Where is she – holla!

[*Calling to the* BEGGAR, *who returns; he looks at her
                                        stedfastly*]

                     You are Idonea's Mother? –
530   Nay, be not terrified – it does me good
      To look upon you.
      osw. [*interrupting*] In a peasant's dress
      You saw, who was it?
      beg.   Nay, I dare not speak;
      He is a man, if it should come to his ears
      I never shall be heard of more.
      osw.   Lord Clifford?
      beg. What can I do? believe me, gentle Sirs,
      I love her, though I dare not call her daughter.
      osw. Lord Clifford – did you see him talk with Herbert?
      beg. Yes, to my sorrow – under the great oak
      At Herbert's door – and when he stood beside
540   The blind Man – at the silent Girl he looked
      With such a look – it makes me tremble, Sir,
      To think of it.
      osw.   Enough! you may depart.
      mar. [*to himself*] Father! – to God himself we cannot
           give
      A holier name; and, under such a mask,
      To lead a Spirit, spotless as the blessed,
      To that abhorrèd den of brutish vice! –
      Oswald, the firm foundation of my life
      Is going from under me; these strange discoveries –
      Looked at from every point of fear or hope,
550   Duty, or love – involve, I feel, my ruin.

ACT II

Scene, *A Chamber in the Hostel* – oswald *alone,
rising from a Table on which he had been writing.*

osw. They chose *him* for their Chief! – what covert part
      He, in the preference, modest Youth, might take,
      I neither know nor care. The insult bred
      More of contempt than hatred; both are flown;
      That either e'er existed is my shame:
      'Twas a dull spark – a most unnatural fire

That died the moment the air breathed upon it.
– These fools of feeling are mere birds of winter
That haunt some barren island of the north,
560 Where, if a famishing man stretch forth his hand,
They think it is to feed them. I have left him
To solitary meditation; – now
For a few swelling phrases, and a flash
Of truth, enough to dazzle and to blind,
And he is mine for ever – here he comes.

[*Enter* MARMADUKE]

MAR. These ten years she has moved her lips all day
And never speaks!
OSW.   Who is it?
MAR.   I have seen her.
OSW. Oh! the poor tenant of that ragged homestead,
Her whom the Monster, Clifford, drove to madness.
570 MAR. I met a peasant near the spot; he told me,
These ten years she had sate all day alone
Within those empty walls.
OSW.   I too have seen her;
Chancing to pass this way some six months gone,
At midnight, I betook me to the Churchyard:
The moon shone clear, the air was still, so still
The trees were silent as the graves beneath them.
Long did I watch, and saw her pacing round
Upon the self-same spot, still round and round,
Her lips for ever moving.
MAR.   At her door
580 Rooted I stood; for, looking at the woman,
I thought I saw the skeleton of Idonea.
OSW. But the pretended Father –
MAR.   Earthly law
Measures not crimes like his.
OSW.   *We* rank not, happily,
With those who take the spirit of their rule
From that soft class of devotees who feel

Reverence for life so deeply, that they spare
The verminous brood, and cherish what they spare
While feeding on their bodies. Would that Idonea
Were present, to the end that we might hear
590   What she can urge in his defence; she loves him.
MAR. Yes, loves him; 'tis a truth that multiplies
His guilt a thousand-fold.
OSW.   'Tis most perplexing:
What must be done?
MAR.   We will conduct her hither;
These walls shall witness it – from first to last
He shall reveal himself.
OSW.   Happy are we,
Who live in these disputed tracts, that own
No law but what each man makes for himself;
Here justice has indeed a field of triumph.
MAR. Let us begone and bring her hither; – here
600   The truth shall be laid open, his guilt proved
Before her face. The rest be left to me.
OSW. You will be firm: but though we well may trust
The issue to the justice of the cause,
Caution must not be flung aside; remember,
Yours is no common life. Self-stationed here,
Upon these savage confines, we have seen you
Stand like an isthmus 'twixt two stormy seas
That oft have checked their fury at your bidding.
'Mid the deep holds of Solway's mossy waste,
610   Your single virtue has transformed a Band
Of fierce barbarians into Ministers
Of peace and order. Aged men with tears
Have blessed their steps, the fatherless retire
For shelter to their banners. But it is,
As you must needs have deeply felt, it is
In darkness and in tempest that we seek
The majesty of Him who rules the world.
Benevolence, that has not heart to use
The wholesome ministry of pain and evil,
620   Becomes at last weak and contemptible.

Your generous qualities have won due praise,
But vigorous Spirits look for something more
Than Youth's spontaneous products; and today
You will not disappoint them; and hereafter –
MAR. You are wasting words; hear me then, once for
    all:
You are a Man – and therefore, if compassion,
Which to our kind is natural as life,
Be known unto you, you will love this Woman,
Even as I do; but I should loathe the light,
630   If I could think one weak or partial feeling –
OSW. You will forgive me –
MAR.   If I ever knew
My heart, could penetrate its inmost core,
'Tis at this moment. – Oswald, I have loved
To be the friend and father of the oppressed,
A comforter of sorrow; – there is something
Which looks like a transition in my soul,
And yet it is not. – Let us lead him hither.
OSW. Stoop for a moment; 'tis an act of justice;
And where's the triumph if the delegate
640   Must fall in the execution of his office?
The deed is done – if you will have it so –
Here where we stand – that tribe of vulgar wretches
(You saw them gathering for the festival)
Rush in – the villains seize us –
MAR.   Seize!
OSW.   Yes, they –
Men who are little given to sift and weigh –
Would wreak on us the passion of the moment.
MAR. The cloud will soon disperse – farewell – but stay,
Thou wilt relate the story.
OSW.   Am I neither
To bear a part in this Man's punishment,
Nor be its witness?
650 MAR.   I had many hopes
That were most dear to me, and some will bear
To be transferred to thee.

OSW.   When I'm dishonoured!

MAR. I would preserve thee. How may this be done?

OSW. By showing that you look beyond the instant.
  A few leagues hence we shall have open ground,
  And nowhere upon earth is place so fit
  To look upon the deed. Before we enter
  The barren Moor, hangs from a beetling rock
  The shattered Castle in which Clifford oft
660 Has held infernal orgies – with the gloom,
  And very superstition of the place,
  Seasoning his wickedness. The Debauchee
  Would there perhaps have gathered the first fruits
  Of this mock Father's guilt.

[*Enter* HOST *conducting* HERBERT]

HOST.   The Baron Herbert
  Attends your pleasure.

OSW. [*to* HOST] We are ready –

                    [*to* HERBERT] Sir!
  I hope you are refreshed. – I have just written
  A notice for your Daughter, that she may know
  What is become of you. – You'll sit down and sign it;
  'Twill glad her heart to see her father's signature.

                    [*Gives the letter he had written*]

HER. Thanks for your care. [*Sits down and writes.*

                                        Exit HOST]

670 OSW. [*aside to* MARMADUKE] Perhaps it would be useful
  That you too should subscribe your name.

[MARMADUKE *overlooks* HERBERT – *then writes –*

                    examines the letter eagerly]

MAR. I cannot leave this paper. [*He puts it up, agitated*]

OSW. [*aside*]   Dastard! Come.

[MARMADUKE *goes towards* HERBERT *and supports him –*

MARMADUKE *tremblingly beckons* OSWALD *to take his place*]

MAR. [*as he quits* HERBERT] There is a palsy in his limbs
  – he shakes.

[*Exeunt* OSWALD *and* HERBERT – MARMADUKE *following*]

SCENE *changes to a Wood – a Group of* PILGRIMS *and*
IDONEA *with them.*

FIRST PIL. A grove of darker and more lofty shade
I never saw.

SEC. PIL. The music of the birds
Drops deadened from a roof so thick with leaves.

OLD PIL. This news! it made my heart leap up with
joy.

IDON. I scarcely can believe it.

OLD PIL.   Myself, I heard
The Sheriff read, in open Court, a letter
680   Which purported it was the royal pleasure
The Baron Herbert, who, as was supposed,
Had taken refuge in this neighbourhood,
Should be forthwith restored. The hearing, Lady,
Filled my dim eyes with tears. – When I returned
From Palestine, and brought with me a heart,
Though rich in heavenly, poor in earthly, comfort,
I met your Father, then a wandering Outcast:
He had a Guide, a Shepherd's boy; but grieved
He was that One so young should pass his youth
690   In such sad service; and he parted with him.
We joined our tales of wretchedness together,
And begged our daily bread from door to door.
I talk familiarly to you, sweet Lady!
For once you loved me.

IDON.   You shall back with me
And see your Friend again. The good old Man
Will be rejoiced to greet you.

OLD PIL.   It seems but yesterday
That a fierce storm o'ertook us, worn with travel,
In a deep wood remote from any town.
A cave that opened to the road presented
700   A friendly shelter, and we entered in.

IDON. And I was with you?

OLD PIL.   If indeed 'twas you –
But you were then a tottering Little-one –
We sate us down. The sky grew dark and darker:

I struck my flint, and built up a small fire
With rotten boughs and leaves, such as the winds
Of many autumns in the cave had piled.
Meanwhile the storm fell heavy on the woods;
Our little fire sent forth a cheering warmth
And we were comforted, and talked of comfort;
710   But 'twas an angry night, and o'er our heads
The thunder rolled in peals that would have made
A sleeping man uneasy in his bed.
O Lady, you have need to love your Father.
His voice – methinks I hear it now, his voice
When, after a broad flash that filled the cave,
He said to me, that he had seen his Child,
A face (no cherub's face more beautiful)
Revealed by lustre brought with it from heaven;
And it was you, dear Lady!

IDON.   God be praised,
720   That I have been his comforter till now!
And will be so through every change of fortune
And every sacrifice his peace requires. –
Let us be gone with speed, that he may hear
These joyful tidings from no lips but mine.

[*Exeunt* IDONEA *and* PILGRIMS]

SCENE, *the Area of a half-ruined Castle – on one side the*
     entrance to a dungeon – OSWALD *and* MARMADUKE
     pacing backwards and forwards.

MAR. 'Tis a wild night.

OSW.   I'd give my cloak and bonnet
For sight of a warm fire.

MAR.   The wind blows keen;
My hands are numb.

OSW.   Ha! ha! 'tis nipping cold.
                                   [*Blowing his fingers*]
I long for news of our brave Comrades; Lacy
Would drive those Scottish Rovers to their dens
730   If once they blew a horn this side the Tweed.

MAR. I think I see a second range of Towers;

This castle has another Area – come,
Let us examine it.

OSW.   'Tis a bitter night;
I hope Idonea is well housed. That horseman,
Who at full speed swept by us where the wood
Roared in the tempest, was within an ace
Of sending to his grave our precious Charge:
That would have been a vile mischance.

MAR.   It would.

OSW. Justice had been most cruelly defrauded.

MAR. Most cruelly.

740 OSW.   As up the steep we clomb,
I saw a distant fire in the north-east;
I took it for the blaze of Cheviot Beacon:
With proper speed our quarters may be gained
Tomorrow evening.   [*Looks restlessly towards the
                             mouth of the dungeon*]

MAR.   When, upon the plank,
I had led him 'cross the torrent, his voice blessed me:
You could not hear, for the foam beat the rocks
With deafening noise, – the benediction fell
Back on himself; but changed into a curse.

OSW. As well indeed it might.

MAR.   And this you deem
The fittest place?

750 OSW. [*aside*]   He is growing pitiful.

MAR. [*listening*] What an odd moaning that is! –

OSW.   Mighty odd
The wind should pipe a little, while we stand
Cooling our heels in this way! – I'll begin
And count the stars.

MAR. [*still listening*]   That dog of his, you are sure,
Could not come after us – he *must* have perished;
The torrent would have dashed an oak to splinters.
You said you did not like his looks – that he
Would trouble us; if he were here again,
I swear the sight of him would quail me more
Than twenty armies.

OSW.   How?

760 MAR.   The old blind Man,
When you had told him the mischance, was troubled
Even to the shedding of some natural tears
Into the torrent over which he hung,
Listening in vain.

OSW.   He has a tender heart!
                [OSWALD *offers to go down into the dungeon*]
MAR. How now, what mean you?

OSW.   Truly, I was going
To waken our stray Baron. Were there not
A farm or dwelling-house within five leagues,
We should deserve to wear a cap and bells,
Three good round years, for playing the fool here
In such a night as this.

MAR.   Stop, stop.

770 OSW.   Perhaps,
You'd better like we should descend together,
And lie down by his side – what say you to it?
Three of us – we should keep each other warm:
I'll answer for it that our four-legged friend
Shall not disturb us; further, I'll not engage;
Come, come, for manhood's sake!

MAR.   These drowsy shiverings,
This mortal stupor which is creeping over me,
What do they mean? were this my single body
Opposed to armies, not a nerve would tremble:

780 Why do I tremble now? – Is not the depth
Of this Man's crimes beyond the reach of thought?
And yet, in plumbing the abyss for judgement,
Something I strike upon which turns my mind
Back on herself, I think, again – my breast
Concentres all the tèrrors of the Universe:
I look at him and tremble like a child.

OSW. Is it possible?

MAR.   One thing you noticed not:
Just as we left the glen a clap of thunder
Burst on the mountains with hell-rousing force.

790   This is a time, said he, when guilt may shudder;
      But there's a Providence for them who walk
      In helplessness, when innocence is with them.
      At this audacious blasphemy, I thought
      The spirit of vengeance seemed to ride the air.
osw. Why are you not the man you were that moment?
                              [*He draws* MARMADUKE *to the dungeon*]
mar. You say he was asleep, – look at this arm,
      And tell me if 'tis fit for such a work.
      Oswald, Oswald!   [*Leans upon* OSWALD]
osw.   This is some sudden seizure!
mar. A most strange faintness, – will you hunt me out
      A draught of water?
800 osw.   Nay, to see you thus
      Moves me beyond my bearing. – I will try
      To gain the torrent's brink.   [*Exit* OSWALD]
mar. [*after a pause*]   It seems an age
      Since that Man left me. – No, I am not lost.
her. [*at the mouth of the dungeon*] Give me your hand;
         where are you, Friends? and tell me
      How goes the night.
mar.   'Tis hard to measure time
      In such a weary night, and such a place.
her. I do not hear the voice of my friend Oswald.
mar. A minute past, he went to fetch a draught
      Of water from the torrent. 'Tis, you'll say,
      A cheerless beverage.
810 her.   How good it was in you
      To stay behind! – Hearing at first no answer,
      I was alarmed.
mar.   No wonder; this is a place
      That well may put some fears into *your* heart.
her. Why so? a roofless rock had been a comfort,
      Storm-beaten and bewildered as we were;
      And in a night like this, to lend your cloaks
      To make a bed for me! – My Girl will weep
      When she is told of it.
mar.   This Daughter of yours

Is very dear to you.

HER.   Oh! but you are young;
820   Over your head twice twenty years must roll,
      With all their natural weight of sorrow and pain,
      Ere can be known to you how much a Father
      May love his Child.

MAR.   Thank you, old Man, for this!
                                                    [*Aside*]

HER. Fallen am I, and worn out, a useless Man;
      Kindly have you protected me tonight,
      And no return have I to make but prayers;
      May you in age be blest with such a daughter! –
      When from the Holy Land I had returned
      Sightless, and from my heritage was driven,
830   A wretched Outcast – but this strain of thought
      Would lead me to talk fondly.

MAR.   Do not fear;
      Your words are precious to my ears; go on.

HER. You will forgive me, but my heart runs over.
      When my old Leader slipped into the flood
      And perished, what a piercing outcry you
      Sent after him. I have loved you ever since.
      You start – where are we?

MAR.   Oh, there is no danger;
      The cold blast struck me.

HER.   'Twas a foolish question.

MAR. But when you were an Outcast? – Heaven is just;
840   Your piety would not miss its due reward;
      The little Orphan then would be your succour,
      And do good service, though she knew it not.

HER. I turned me from the dwellings of my Fathers,
      Where none but those who trampled on my rights
      Seemed to remember me. To the wide world
      I bore her, in my arms; her looks won pity;
      She was my Raven in the wilderness,
      And brought me food. Have I not cause to love her?

MAR. Yes.

HER.   More than ever Parent loved a Child?

MAR. Yes, yes.

850 HER.　　　　　I will not murmur, merciful God!
I will not murmur; blasted as I have been,
Thou hast left me ears to hear my Daughter's voice,
And arms to fold her to my heart. Submissively
Thee I adore, and find my rest in faith.

　　[*Enter* OSWALD]

OSW. Herbert! – confusion! [*aside*] Here it is, my Friend,
　　　　　　　　　　　[*Presents the Horn*]
A charming beverage for you to carouse,
This bitter night.

HER.　　　　　Ha! Oswald! ten bright crosses
I would have given, not many minutes gone,
To have heard your voice.

OSW.　　　　　Your couch, I fear, good Baron,
860 Has been but comfortless; and yet that place,
When the tempestuous wind first drove us hither,
Felt warm as a wren's nest. You'd better turn
And under covert rest till break of day,
Or till the storm abate.
　　[*To* MARMADUKE *aside*] He has restored you.
No doubt you have been nobly entertained?
But soft! – how came he forth? The Nightmare
　　Conscience
Has driven him out of harbour?

MAR.　　　　　I believe
You have guessed right.

HER.　　　　　The trees renew their murmur:
Come, let us house together.
　　　　　　　　[OSWALD *conducts him to the dungeon*]

OSW. [*returns*]　　　　　Had I not
870 Esteemed you worthy to conduct the affair
To its most fit conclusion, do you think
I would so long have struggled with my Nature,
And smothered all that's man in me? – away! –
　　　　　　　　　　　[*Looking towards the dungeon*]
This man's the property of him who best

Can feel his crimes. I have resigned a privilege;
It now becomes my duty to resume it.

MAR. Touch not a finger –

OSW.   What then must be done?

MAR. Which way soe'er I turn, I am perplexed.

OSW. Now, on my life, I grieve for you. The misery
880 Of doubt is insupportable. Pity, the facts
Did not admit of stronger evidence;
Twelve honest men, plain men, would set us right;
Their verdict would abolish these weak scruples.

MAR. Weak! I am weak – there does my torment lie,
Feeding itself.

OSW.   Verily, when he said
How his old heart would leap to hear her steps,
You thought his voice the echo of Idonea's.

MAR. And never heard a sound so terrible.

OSW. Perchance you think so now?

MAR.   I cannot do it:
890 Twice did I spring to grasp his withered throat,
When such a sudden weakness fell upon me,
I could have dropped asleep upon his breast.

OSW. Justice – is there not thunder in the word?
Shall it be law to stab the petty robber
Who aims but at our purse; and shall this Parricide –
Worse is he far, far worse (if foul dishonour
Be worse than death) to that confiding Creature
Whom he to more than filial love and duty
Hath falsely trained – shall he fulfil his purpose?
But you are fallen.

900 MAR.   Fallen should I be indeed –
Murder – perhaps asleep, blind, old, alone,
Betrayed, in darkness! Here to strike the blow –
Away! away! – [*Flings away his sword*]

OSW.   Nay, I have done with you:
We'll lead him to the Convent. He shall live,
And she shall love him. With unquestioned title
He shall be seated in his Barony,
And we too chant the praise of his good deeds.

I now perceive we do mistake our masters,
And most despise the men who best can teach us:
910   Henceforth it shall be said that bad men only
Are brave: Clifford is brave; and that old Man
Is brave.
        [*Taking* MARMADUKE'S *sword and giving it to him*]
        To Clifford's arms he would have led
His Victim – haply to this desolate house.
MAR. [*advancing to the dungeon*] It must be ended!–
OSW.   Softly; do not rouse him;
He will deny it to the last. He lies
Within the Vault, a spear's length to the left.
            [MARMADUKE *descends to the dungeon*]
[*Alone*] The Villains rose in mutiny to destroy me;
I could have quelled the Cowards, but this Stripling
Must needs step in, and save my life. The look
920   With which he gave the boon – I see it now!
The same that tempted me to loathe the gift. –
For this old venerable Grey-beard – faith
'Tis his own fault if he hath got a face
Which doth play tricks with them that look on it:
'Twas this that put it in my thoughts – that
    countenance –
His staff – his figure – Murder! – what, of whom?
We kill a worn-out horse, and who but women
Sigh at the deed? Hew down a withered tree,
And none look grave but dotards. He may live
930   To thank me for this service. Rainbow arches,
Highways of dreaming passion, have too long,
Young as he is, diverted wish and hope
From the unpretending ground we mortals tread; –
Then shatter the delusion, break it up
And set him free. What follows? I have learned
That things will work to ends the slaves o' the world
Do never dream of. I *have* been what he –
This Boy – when he comes forth with bloody hands –
Might envy, and am now, – but he shall know
What I am now –   [*Goes and listens at the dungeon*]

940   Praying or parleying? – tut!
         Is he not eyeless? He has been half-dead
         These fifteen years –
         [*Enter female* BEGGAR *with two or three of her*
            Companions]
         [*Turning abruptly*] *Ha! speak* – what Thing art thou?
         [*Recognizes her*] Heavens! my good Friend!   [*To her*]
BEG.   Forgive me, gracious Sir! –
OSW. [*to her companions*] Begone, ye Slaves, or I will
         raise a whirlwind
         And send ye dancing to the clouds, like leaves.
                                          [*They retire affrighted*]
BEG. Indeed we meant no harm; we lodge sometimes
         In this deserted Castle – *I repent me.*
         [OSWALD *goes to the dungeon – listens – returns to the*
                                          BEGGAR]
         OSW. Woman, thou hast a helpless Infant – keep
         Thy secret for its sake, or verily
950   That wretched life of thine shall be the forfeit.
BEG. I *do* repent me, Sir; I fear the curse
         Of that blind Man. 'Twas not your money, Sir, –
OSW. Begone!
BEG. [*going*] There is some wicked deed in hand: [*Aside*]
         Would I could find the old Man and his Daughter.
                                          [*Exit* BEGGAR]
         [MARMADUKE *re-enters from the dungeon*]
OSW. It is all over then; – your foolish fears
         Are hushed to sleep, by your own act and deed,
         Made quiet as he is.
MAR.   Why came you down?
         And when I felt your hand upon my arm
         And spake to you, why did you give no answer?
960   Feared you to waken him? he must have been
         In a deep sleep. I whispered to him thrice.
         There are the strangest echoes in that place!
OSW. Tut! let them gabble till the day of doom.
MAR. Scarcely, by groping, had I reached the Spot,
         When round my wrist I felt a cord drawn tight,

As if the blind Man's dog were pulling at it.

OSW. But after that?

MAR.   The features of Idonea
Lurked in his face –

OSW.   Pshaw! Never to these eyes
Will retribution show itself again
970   With aspect so inviting. Why forbid me
To share your triumph?

MAR.   Yes, her very look,
Smiling in sleep –

OSW.   A pretty feat of Fancy!

MAR. Though but a glimpse, it sent me to my prayers.

OSW. Is he alive?

MAR.   What mean you? who alive?

OSW. Herbert! since you will have it, Baron Herbert;
He who will gain his Seignory when Idonea
Hath become Clifford's harlot – is *he* living?

MAR. The old Man in that dungeon *is* alive.

OSW. Henceforth, then, will I never in camp or field
980   Obey you more. Your weakness, to the Band,
Shall be proclaimed: brave Men, they all shall hear it.
You a protector of humanity!
Avenger you of outraged innocence!

MAR. 'Twas dark – dark as the grave; yet did I see,
Saw him – his face turned toward me; and I tell thee
Idonea's filial countenance was there
To baffle me – it put me to my prayers.
Upwards I cast my eyes, and, through a crevice,
Beheld a star twinkling above my head,
990   And, by the living God, I could not do it.
                                [Sinks exhausted]

OSW. [*to himself*] Now may I perish if this turn do more
Than make me change my course.
[*To* MARMADUKE]   Dear Marmaduke,
My words were rashly spoken; I recall them:
I feel my error; shedding human blood
Is a most serious thing.

MAR.   Not I alone,

Thou too art deep in guilt.

OSW.   We have indeed
Been most presumptuous. There *is* guilt in this,
Else could so strong a mind have ever known
These trepidations? Plain it is that Heaven
1000   Has marked out this foul Wretch as one whose crimes
Must never come before a mortal judgement-seat,
Or be chastised by mortal instruments.

MAR. A thought that's worth a thousand worlds!
                      [*Goes towards the dungeon*]

OSW.   I grieve
That, in my zeal, I have caused you so much pain.

MAR. Think not of that! 'tis over – we are safe.

OSW. [*as if to himself, yet speaking aloud*] The truth is
   hideous, but how stifle it?
                      [*Turning to* MARMADUKE]
Give me your sword – nay, here are stones and
   fragments,
The least of which would beat out a man's brains;
Or you might drive your head against that wall.
1010   No! this is not the place to hear the tale:
It should be told you pinioned in your bed,
Or on some vast and solitary plain
Blown to you from a trumpet.

MAR.   Why talk thus?
Whate'er the monster brooding in your breast
I care not: fear I have none, and cannot fear –
                 [*The sound of a horn is heard*]
That horn again – 'Tis some one of our Troop;
What do they here? Listen!

OSW.   What! dogged like thieves!
   [*Enter* WALLACE *and* LACY, &c.]

LACY. You are found at last, thanks to the vagrant
   Troop
For not misleading us.

OSW. [*looking at* WALLACE] That subtle Grey-beard –
I'd rather see my father's ghost.

1020 LACY [*to* MARMADUKE] My Captain,

We come by order of the Band. Belike
You have not heard that Henry has at last
Dissolved the Barons' League, and sent abroad
His Sheriffs with fit force to reinstate
The genuine owners of such Lands and Baronies
As, in these long commotions, have been seized.
His Power is this way tending. It befits us
To stand upon our guard, and with our swords
Defend the innocent.

MAR.   Lacy! we look

1030 But at the surfaces of things; we hear
Of towns in flames, fields ravaged, young and old
Driven out in troops to want and nakedness;
Then grasp our swords and rush upon a cure
That flatters us, because it asks not thought:
The deeper malady is better hid;
The world is poisoned at the heart.

LACY.   What mean you?

WAL. [*whose eye has been fixed suspiciously upon*
   OSWALD] Ay, what is it you mean?

MAR.   Harkee, my Friends; –   [*Appearing gay*]
Were there a Man who, being weak and helpless
And most forlorn, should bribe a Mother, pressed

1040 By penury, to yield him up her Daughter,
A little Infant, and instruct the Babe,
Prattling upon his knee, to call him Father –

LACY. Why, if his heart be tender, that offence
I could forgive him.

MAR. [*going on*] And should he make the Child
An instrument of falsehood, should he teach her
To stretch her arms, and dim the gladsome light
Of infant playfulness with piteous looks
Of misery that was not –

LACY.   Troth, 'tis hard –
But in a world like ours –

MAR. [*changing his tone*] This self-same Man –

1050 Even while he printed kisses on the cheek
Of this poor Babe, and taught its innocent tongue

200 THE BORDERERS. A TRAGEDY

To lisp the name of Father – could he look
To the unnatural harvest of that time
When he should give her up, a Woman grown,
To him who bid the highest in the market
Of foul pollution –

LACY.   The whole visible world
Contains not such a Monster!

MAR.   For this purpose
Should he resolve to taint her Soul by means
Which bathe the limbs in sweat to think of them;
1060 Should he, by tales which would draw tears from iron,
Work on her nature, and so turn compassion
And gratitude to ministers of vice,
And make the spotless spirit of filial love
Prime mover in a plot to damn his Victim
Both soul and body –

WAL.   'Tis too horrible;
Oswald, what say you to it?

LACY.   Hew him down,
And fling him to the ravens.

MAR.   But his aspect,
It is so meek, his countenance so venerable.

WAL. [*with an appearance of mistrust*] But how, what say
  you, Oswald?

LACY [*at the same moment*] Stab him, were it
Before the Altar.

1070 MAR.   What, if he were sick,
Tottering upon the very verge of life,
And old, and blind –

LACY.   Blind, say you?

OSW. [*coming forward*] Are we Men,
Or own we baby Spirits? Genuine courage
Is not an accidental quality,
A thing dependent for its casual birth
On opposition and impediment.
Wisdom, if Justice speak the word, beats down
The giant's strength; and, at the voice of Justice,
Spares not the worm. The giant and the worm –

1080   She weighs them in one scale. The wiles of woman,
      And craft of age, seducing reason, first
      Made weakness a protection, and obscured
      The moral shapes of things. His tender cries
      And helpless innocence – do they protect
      The infant lamb? and shall the infirmities,
      Which have enabled this enormous Culprit
      To perpetrate his crimes, serve as a Sanctuary
      To cover him from punishment? Shame! – Justice,
      Admitting no resistance, bends alike
1090   The feeble and the strong. She needs not here
      Her bonds and chains, which make the mighty feeble.
      – We recognize in this old Man a victim
      Prepared already for the sacrifice.

LACY. By heaven, his words are reason!

OSW.   Yes, my Friends,
      His countenance is meek and venerable;
      And, by the Mass, to see him at his prayers! –
      I am of flesh and blood, and may I perish
      When my heart does not ache to think of it! –
      Poor Victim! not a virtue under heaven
1100   But what was made an engine to ensnare thee;
      But yet I trust, Idonea, thou art safe.

LACY. Idonea!

WAL.   How! what? your Idonea?

                               [*To* MARMADUKE]

MAR.   *Mine*;
      But now no longer mine. You know Lord Clifford;
      He is the Man to whom the Maiden – pure
      As beautiful, and gentle and benign,
      And in her ample heart loving even me –
      Was to be yielded up.

LACY.   Now, by the head
      Of my own child, this Man must die; my hand,
      A worthier wanting, shall itself entwine
      In his grey hairs! –

1110 MAR. [*to* LACY]   I love the Father in thee.
      You know me, Friends; I have a heart to feel,

And I have felt, more than perhaps becomes me
Or duty sanctions.

LACY.   We will have ample justice.
Who are we, Friends? Do we not live on ground
Where Souls are self-defended, free to grow
Like mountain oaks rocked by the stormy wind.
Mark the Almighty Wisdom, which decreed
This monstrous crime to be laid open – *here*,
Where Reason has an eye that she can use,
1120   And Men alone are Umpires. To the Camp
He shall be led, and there, the Country round
All gathered to the spot, in open day
Shall Nature be avenged.

OSW.   'Tis nobly thought;
His death will be a monument for ages.

MAR. [*to* LACY] I thank you for that hint. He shall be
        brought
Before the Camp, and would that best and wisest
Of every country might be present. There
His crime shall be proclaimed; and for the rest
It shall be done as Wisdom shall decide:
1130   Meanwhile, do you two hasten back and see
That all is well prepared.

WAL.   We will obey you.
[*Aside*] But softly! we must look a little nearer.

MAR. Tell where you found us. At some future time
I will explain the cause.   [*Exeunt*]

ACT III

Scene, *the door of the Hostel, a group of* PILGRIMS
    as before; IDONEA *and the* HOST *among them.*

HOST. Lady, you'll find your Father at the Convent
As I have told you: He left us yesterday
With two Companions; one of them, as seemed,
His most familiar Friend. [*Going*] There was a letter
Of which I heard them speak, but that I fancy
Has been forgotten.

IDON. [to HOST] Farewell!

1140 HOST.   Gentle pilgrims,
    St. Cuthbert speed you on your holy errand.
                 [Exeunt IDONEA and PILGRIMS]

SCENE, a desolate Moor.

OSWALD [alone].

OSW. Carry him to the Camp! Yes, to the Camp.
    Oh, Wisdom! a most wise resolve! and then,
    That half a word should blow it to the winds!
    This last device must end my work. – Methinks
    It were a pleasant pastime to construct
    A scale and table of beliefs – as thus –
    Two columns, one for passion, one for proof;
    Each rises as the other falls: and first,
1150 Passion a unit and *against* us – proof –
    Nay, we must travel in another path,
    Or we're stuck fast for ever; – passion, then,
    Shall be a unit *for* us; proof – no, passion!
    We'll not insult thy majesty by time,
    Person, and place – the where, the when, the how,
    And all particulars that dull brains require
    To constitute the spiritless shape of Fact,
    They bow to, calling the idol, Demonstration.
    A whipping to the Moralists who preach
1160 That misery is a sacred thing: for me,
    I know no cheaper engine to degrade a man,
    Nor any half so sure. This Stripling's mind
    Is shaken till the dregs float on the surface;
    And, in the storm and anguish of the heart,
    He talks of a transition in his Soul,
    And dreams that he is happy. We dissect
    The senseless body, and why not the mind? –
    These are strange sights – the mind of man, upturned,
    Is in all natures a strange spectacle;
1170 In some a hideous one – hem! shall I stop?
    No. – Thoughts and feelings will sink deep, but then
    They have no substance. Pass but a few minutes,

And something shall be done which Memory
May touch, whene'er her Vassals are at work.

[*Enter* MARMADUKE, *from behind*]

OSW. [*turning to meet him*] But listen, for my peace –
MAR.   Why, I *believe* you.
OSW. But hear the proofs –
MAR.   Ay, prove that when two peas
    Lie snugly in a pod, the pod must then
    Be larger than the peas – prove this – 'twere matter
    Worthy the hearing. Fool was I to dream
    It ever could be otherwise!
1180 OSW.   Last night
    When I returned with water from the brook,
    I overheard the Villains – every word
    Like red-hot iron burnt into my heart.
    Said one, 'It is agreed on. The blind Man
    Shall feign a sudden illness, and the Girl,
    Who on her journey must proceed alone,
    Under pretence of violence, be seized.
    She is,' continued the detested Slave,
    'She is right willing – strange if she were not! –
1190 They say Lord Clifford is a savage man;
    But, faith, to see him in his silken tunic,
    Fitting his low voice to the minstrel's harp,
    There's witchery in't. I never knew a maid
    That could withstand it. True,' continued he,
    'When we arranged the affair, she wept a little
    (Not the less welcome to my Lord for that)
    And said, "My Father he will have it so."'
MAR. I am your hearer.
OSW.   This I caught, and more
    That may not be retold to any ear.
1200 The obstinate bolt of a small iron door
    Detained them near the gateway of the Castle.
    By a dim lantern's light I saw that wreaths
    Of flowers were in their hands, as if designed
    For festive decoration; and they said,

With brutal laughter and most foul allusion,
That they should share the banquet with their Lord
And his new Favorite.

MAR.   Misery! –

OSW.   I knew
How you would be disturbed by this dire news,
And therefore chose this solitary Moor,
1210 Here to impart the tale, of which, last night,
I strove to ease my mind, when our two Comrades,
Commissioned by the Band, burst in upon us.

MAR. Last night, when moved to lift the avenging steel,
I did believe all things were shadows – yea,
Living or dead all things were bodiless,
Or but the mutual mockeries of body,
Till that same star summoned me back again.
Now I could laugh till my ribs ached. Oh Fool!
To let a creed, built in the heart of things,
1220 Dissolve before a twinkling atom! – Oswald,
I could fetch lessons out of wiser schools
Than you have entered, were it worth the pains.
Young as I am, I might go forth a teacher,
And you should see how deeply I could reason
Of love in all its shapes, beginnings, ends;
Of moral qualities in their diverse aspects;
Of actions, and their laws and tendencies.

OSW. You take it as it merits –

MAR.   One a King,
General or Cham, Sultan or Emperor,
1230 Strews twenty acres of good meadow-ground
With carcasses, in lineament and shape
And substance, nothing differing from his own,
But that they cannot stand up of themselves;
Another sits i' the sun, and by the hour
Floats kingcups in the brook – a Hero one
We call, and scorn the other as Time's spendthrift;
But have they not a world of common ground
To occupy – both fools, or wise alike,
Each in his way?

OSW.   Troth, I begin to think so.

1240 MAR. Now for the corner-stone of my philosophy:
          I would not give a denier for the man
          Who, on such provocation as this earth
          Yields, could not chuck his babe beneath the chin,
          And send it with a fillip to its grave.

OSW. Nay, you leave me behind.

MAR.   That such a One,
          So pious in demeanour! in his look
          So saintly and so pure! – Hark'ee, my Friend,
          I'll plant myself before Lord Clifford's Castle,
          A surly mastiff kennels at the gate,

1250   And he shall howl and I will laugh, a medley
          Most tunable.

OSW.   In faith, a pleasant scheme;
          But take your sword along with you, for that
          Might in such neighbourhood find seemly use. –
          But first, how wash our hands of this old Man?

MAR. Oh yes, that mole, that viper in the path;
          Plague on my memory, him I had forgotten.

OSW. You know we left him sitting – see him yonder.

MAR. Ha! ha! –

OSW.   As 'twill be but a moment's work,
          I will stroll on; you follow when 'tis done.   [*Exeunt*]

          SCENE *changes to another part of the Moor at a short
          distance* – HERBERT *is discovered seated on a stone.*

1260 HER. A sound of laughter, too! – 'tis well – I feared
          The Stranger had some pitiable sorrow
          Pressing upon his solitary heart.
          Hush! – 'tis the feeble and earth-loving wind
          That creeps along the bells of the crisp heather.
          Alas! 'tis cold – I shiver in the sunshine –
          What can this mean? There is a psalm that speaks
          Of God's parental mercies – with Idonea
          I used to sing it. – Listen! – what foot is there?
          [*Enter* MARMADUKE]

MAR. [*aside – looking at* HERBERT] And I have loved
    this Man! and *she* hath loved him!
1270   And I loved her, and she loves the Lord Clifford!
    And there it ends; – if this be not enough
    To make mankind merry for evermore,
    Then plain it is as day, that eyes were made
    For a wise purpose – verily to weep with!
                          [*Looking round*]
    A pretty prospect this, a masterpiece
    Of Nature, finished with most curious skill!
    [*To* HERBERT] Good Baron, have you ever practised
      tillage?
    Pray tell me what this land is worth by the acre?
HER. How glad I am to hear your voice! I know not
1280   Wherein I have offended you; – last night
    I found in you the kindest of Protectors;
    This morning, when I spoke of weariness,
    You from my shoulder took my scrip and threw it
    About your own; but for these two hours past
    Once only have you spoken, when the lark
    Whirred from among the fern beneath our feet,
    And I, no coward in my better days,
    Was almost terrified.
MAR.   That's excellent! –
    So, you bethought you of the many ways
1290   In which a man may come to his end, whose crimes
    Have roused all Nature up against him – pshaw! –
HER. For mercy's sake, is nobody in sight?
    No traveller, peasant, herdsman?
MAR.   Not a soul:
    Here is a tree, ragged, and bent, and bare,
    That turns its goat's-beard flakes of pea-green moss
    From the stern breathing of the rough sea-wind;
    This have we, but no other company:
    Commend me to the place. If a man should die
    And leave his body here, it were all one
1300   As he were twenty fathoms underground.
HER. Where is our common Friend?

MAR.   A ghost, methinks –
   The Spirit of a murdered man, for instance –
   Might have fine room to ramble about here,
   A grand domain to squeak and gibber in.
HER. Lost Man! if thou have any close-pent guilt
   Pressing upon thy heart, and this the hour
   Of visitation –
MAR.   A bold word from *you*!
HER. Restore him, Heaven!
MAR.   The desperate Wretch! – A Flower,
   Fairest of all flowers, was she once, but now
1310   They have-snapped her from the stem – Poh! let her lie
   Besoiled with mire, and let the houseless snail
   Feed on her leaves. You knew her well – ay, there,
   Old Man! you were a very Lynx, you knew
   The worm was in her –
HER.   Mercy! Sir, what mean you?
MAR. You have a Daughter!
HER.   Oh that she were here! –
   She hath an eye that sinks into all hearts,
   And if I have in aught offended you,
   Soon would her gentle voice make peace between us.
MAR. [*aside*] I do believe he weeps – I could weep too –
1320   There is a vein of her voice that runs through his:
   Even such a Man my fancy bodied forth
   From the first moment that I loved the Maid;
   And for his sake I loved her more: these tears –
   I did not think that aught was left in me
   Of what I have been – yes, I thank thee, Heaven!
   One happy thought has passed across my mind.
   – It may not be – I am cut off from man;
   No more shall I be man – no more shall I
   Have human feelings! – [*To* HERBERT] – Now, for a
      little more
   About your Daughter!
1330 HER.   Troops of armed men,
   Met in the roads, would bless us; little children,
   Rushing along in the full tide of play,

  Stood silent as we passed them! I have heard
  The boisterous carman, in the miry road,
  Check his loud whip and hail us with mild voice,
  And speak with milder voice to his poor beasts.
MAR. And whither were you going?
HER.   Learn, young Man, –
  To fear the virtuous, and reverence misery,
  Whether too much for patience, or, like mine,
1340 Softened till it becomes a gift of mercy.
MAR. Now, this is as it should be!
HER.   I am weak! –
  My Daughter does not know how weak I am;
  And, as thou see'st, under the arch of heaven
  Here do I stand, alone, to helplessness,
  By the good God, our common Father, doomed! –
  But I had once a spirit and an arm –
MAR. Now, for a word about your Barony:
  I fancy when you left the Holy Land,
  And came to – what's your title – eh? your claims
  Were undisputed!
1350 HER.   Like a mendicant,
  Whom no one comes to meet, I stood alone; –
  I murmured – but, remembering Him who feeds
  The pelican and ostrich of the desert,
  From my own threshold I looked up to Heaven
  And did not want glimmerings of quiet hope.
  So, from the court I passed, and down the brook,
  Led by its murmur, to the ancient oak
  I came; and when I felt its cooling shade,
  I sate me down, and cannot but believe –
1360 While in my lap I held my little Babe
  And clasped her to my heart, my heart that ached
  More with delight than grief – I heard a voice
  Such as by Cherith on Elijah called;
  It said, 'I will be with thee.' A little boy,
  A shepherd-lad, ere yet my trance was gone,
  Hailed us as if he had been sent from heaven,
  And said, with tears, that he would be our guide:

I had a better guide – that innocent Babe –
Her, who hath saved me, to this hour, from harm,
1370   From cold, from hunger, penury, and death;
To whom I owe the best of all the good
I have, or wish for, upon earth – and more
And higher far than lies within earth's bounds:
Therefore I bless her: when I think of Man,
I bless her with sad spirit, – when of God,
I bless her in the fulness of my joy!

MAR.   The name of daughter in his mouth, he prays!
With nerves so steady, that the very flies
Sit unmolested on his staff. – Innocent! –
1380   If he were innocent – then he would tremble
And be disturbed, as I am. [*Turning aside*] I have
        read
In Story, what men now alive have witnessed,
How, when the People's mind was racked with doubt,
Appeal was made to the great Judge: the Accused
With naked feet walked over burning ploughshares.
Here is a Man by Nature's hand prepared
For a like trial, but more merciful.
Why else have I been led to this bleak Waste?
Bare is it, without house or track, and destitute
1390   Of obvious shelter, as a shipless sea.
Here will I leave him – here – All-seeing God!
Such as *he* is, and sore perplexed as I am,
I will commit him to this final *Ordeal*! –
He heard a voice – a shepherd-lad came to him
And was his guide; if once, why not again,
And in this desert? If never – then the whole
Of what he says, and looks, and does, and is,
Makes up one damning falsehood. Leave him here
To cold and hunger! – Pain is of the heart,
1400   And what are a few throes of bodily suffering
If they can waken one pang of remorse?
                              [*Goes up to* HERBERT]
Old Man! my wrath is as a flame burnt out,
It cannot be rekindled. Thou art here

    Led by my hand to save thee from perdition;
    Thou wilt have time to breathe and think –
HER.   Oh, Mercy!
MAR. I know the need that all men have of mercy,
    And therefore leave thee to a righteous judgement.
HER. My Child, my blessèd Child!
MAR.   No more of that;
    Thou wilt have many guides if thou art innocent;
1410   Yea, from the utmost corners of the earth,
    That Woman will come o'er this Waste to save thee.
                    [*He pauses and looks at* HERBERT'S *staff*]
    Ha! what is here? and carved by her own hand!
                              [*Reads upon the staff*]
    'I am eyes to the blind, saith the Lord.
    He that puts his trust in me shall not fail!'
    Yes, be it so; – repent and be forgiven –
    God and that staff are now thy only guides.
                    [*He leaves* HERBERT *on the Moor*]

SCENE, *an eminence, a Beacon on the summit.*
LACY, WALLACE, LENNOX, &c. &c.

SEVERAL OF THE BAND [*confusedly*] But patience!
ONE OF THE BAND. Curses on that Traitor, Oswald! –
    Our Captain made a prey to foul device! –
LEN. [*to* WALLACE] His tool, the wandering Beggar,
        made last night
1420   A plain confession, such as leaves no doubt,
    Knowing what otherwise we know too well,
    That she revealed the truth. Stand by me now;
    For rather would I have a nest of vipers
    Between my breast-plate and my skin, than make
    Oswald my special enemy, if you
    Deny me your support.
LACY.   We have been fooled –
    But for the motive?
WAL.   Natures such as his
    Spin motives out of their own bowels, Lacy!

    I learned this when I was a Confessor.

1430   I know him well; there needs no other motive
    Than that most strange incontinence in crime
    Which haunts this Oswald. Power is life to him
    And breath and being; where he cannot govern,
    He will destroy.

LACY.   To have been trapped like moles! –
    Yes, you are right, we need not hunt for motives:
    There is no crime from which this man would shrink;
    He recks not human law; and I have noticed
    That often when the name of God is uttered,
    A sudden blankness overspreads his face.

1440 LEN. Yet, reasoner as he is, his pride has built
    Some uncouth superstition of its own.

WAL. I have seen traces of it.

LEN.   Once he headed
    A band of Pirates in the Norway seas;
    And when the King of Denmark summoned him
    To the oath of fealty, I well remember,
    'Twas a strange answer that he made; he said,
    'I hold of Spirits, and the Sun in heaven.'

LACY. He is no madman.

WAL.   A most subtle doctor
    Were that man, who could draw the line that parts

1450   Pride and her daughter, Cruelty, from Madness,
    That should be scourged, not pitied. Restless Minds,
    Such Minds as find amid their fellow-men
    No heart that loves them, none that they can love,
    Will turn perforce and seek for sympathy
    In dim relation to imagined Beings.

ONE OF THE BAND. What if he mean to offer up our
    Captain
    An expiation and a sacrifice
    To those infernal fiends!

WAL.   Now, if the event
    Should be as Lennox has foretold, then swear,

1460   My Friends, his heart shall have as many wounds
    As there are daggers here.

LACY.   What need of swearing!

ONE OF THE BAND. Let us away!

ANOTHER.   Away!

A THIRD.   Hark! how the horns
  Of those Scotch Rovers echo through the vale.

LACY. Stay you behind; and when the sun is down,
  Light up this beacon.

ONE OF THE BAND. You shall be obeyed.

                       [*They go out together*]

SCENE, *the Wood on the edge of the Moor.* MARMADUKE
  [*alone*].

MAR. Deep, deep and vast, vast beyond human thought,
  Yet calm. – I could believe, that there was here
  The only quiet heart on earth. In terror,
  Remembered terror, there is peace and rest.
    [*Enter* OSWALD]

OSW. Ha! my dear Captain.

1470 MAR.   A later meeting, Oswald,
  Would have been better timed.

OSW.   Alone, I see;
  You have done your duty. I had hopes, which now
  I feel that you will justify.

MAR.   I had fears,
  From which I have freed myself – but 'tis my wish
  To be alone, and therefore we must part.

OSW. Nay, then – I am mistaken. There's a weakness
  About you still; you talk of solitude –
  I am your friend.

MAR.   What need of this assurance
  At any time? and why given now?

OSW.   Because

1480 You are now in truth my Master; you have taught me
  What there is not another living man
  Had strength to teach; – and therefore gratitude
  Is bold, and would relieve itself by praise.

MAR. Wherefore press this on me?

OSW.   Because I feel

That you have shown, and by a signal instance,
How they who would be just must seek the rule
By diving for it into their own bosoms.
Today you have thrown off a tyranny
That lives but in the torpid acquiescence
1490   Of our emasculated souls, the tyranny
Of the world's masters, with the musty rules
By which they uphold their craft from age to age:
You have obeyed the only law that sense
Submits to recognize; the immediate law,
From the clear light of circumstances, flashed
Upon an independent Intellect.
Henceforth new prospects open on your path;
Your faculties should grow with the demand;
I still will be your friend, will cleave to you
1500   Through good and evil, obloquy and scorn,
Oft as they dare to follow on your steps.
MAR. I would be left alone.
OSW. [*exultingly*]   I know your motives!
I am not of the world's presumptuous judges,
Who damn where they can neither see nor feel,
With a hard-hearted ignorance; your struggles
I witnessed, and now hail your victory.
MAR. Spare me awhile that greeting.
OSW.   It may be,
That some there are, squeamish half-thinking cowards,
Who will turn pale upon you, call you murderer,
1510   And you will walk in solitude among them.
A mighty evil for a strong-built mind! –
Join twenty tapers of unequal height
And light them joined, and you will see the less
How 'twill burn down the taller; and they all
Shall prey upon the tallest. Solitude! –
The Eagle lives in Solitude!
MAR.   Even so,
The Sparrow so on the house-top, and I,
The weakest of God's creatures, stand resolved
To abide the issue of my act, alone.

1520 OSW. *Now* would you? and for ever? – My young
   Friend,
  As time advances either we become
  The prey or masters of our own past deeds.
  Fellowship we *must* have, willing or no;
  And if good Angels fail, slack in their duty,
  Substitutes, turn our faces where we may,
  Are still forthcoming; some which, though they bear
  Ill names, can render no ill services,
  In recompense for what themselves required.
  So meet extremes in this mysterious world,
1530 And opposites thus melt into each other.
  MAR. Time, since Man first drew breath, has never
   moved
  With such a weight upon his wings as now;
  But they will soon be lightened.
  OSW.   Ay, look up –
  Cast round you your mind's eye, and you will learn
  Fortitude is the child of Enterprise:
  Great actions move our admiration, chiefly
  Because they carry in themselves an earnest
  That we can suffer greatly.
  MAR.   Very true.
  OSW. Action is transitory – a step, a blow,
1540 The motion of a muscle – this way or that –
  'Tis done, and in the after-vacancy
  We wonder at ourselves like men betrayed:
  Suffering is permanent, obscure and dark,
  And shares the nature of infinity.
  MAR. Truth – and I feel it.
  OSW.   What! if you had bid
  Eternal farewell to unmingled joy
  And the light dancing of the thoughtless heart;
  It is the toy of fools, and little fit
  For such a world as this. The wise abjure
1550 All thoughts whose idle composition lives
  In the entire forgetfulness of pain.
  – I see I have disturbed you.

MAR.   By no means.

OSW. Compassion! – pity! – pride can do without
    them;
    And what if you should never know them more! –
    He is a puny soul who, feeling pain,
    Finds ease because another feels it too.
    If e'er I open out this heart of mine
    It shall be for a nobler end – to teach
    And not to purchase puling sympathy.
    – Nay, you are pale.

MAR.   It may be so.

1560 OSW.   Remorse –
    It cannot live with thought; think on, think on,
    And it will die. What! in this universe,
    Where the least things control the greatest, where
    The faintest breath that breathes can move a world;
    What! feel remorse, where, if a cat had sneezed,
    A leaf had fallen, the thing had never been
    Whose very shadow gnaws us to the vitals.

MAR. Now, whither are you wandering? That a man,
    So used to suit his language to the time,
1570   Should thus so widely differ from himself –
    It is most strange.

OSW.   Murder! – what's in the word! –
    I have no cases by me ready made
    To fit all deeds. Carry him to the Camp! –
    A shallow project; – you of late have seen
    More deeply, taught us that the institutes
    Of Nature, by a cunning usurpation
    Banished from human intercourse, exist
    Only in our relations to the brutes
    That make the fields their dwelling. If a snake
1580   Crawl from beneath our feet we do not ask
    A license to destroy him: our good governors
    Hedge in the life of every pest and plague
    That bears the shape of man; and for what purpose,
    But to protect themselves from extirpation? –
    This flimsy barrier you have overleaped.

MAR. My office is fulfilled – the Man is now
   Delivered to the Judge of all things.
OSW.   Dead!
MAR. I have borne my burden to its destined end.
OSW. This instant we'll return to our Companions –
1590   Oh how I long to see their faces again!
        [*Enter* IDONEA *with* PILGRIMS *who continue their
        journey*]
IDON. [*after some time*] What, Marmaduke! now thou
        art mine for ever.
     And Oswald, too! [*To* MARMADUKE] On will we to
        my Father
     With the glad tidings which this day hath brought;
     We'll go together, and, such proof received
     Of his own rights restored, his gratitude
     To God above will make him feel for ours.
OSW. I interrupt you?
IDON.   Think not so.
MAR.   Idonea,
     That I should ever live to see this moment!
IDON. Forgive me. – Oswald knows it all – he
        knows,
1600   Each word of that unhappy letter fell
     As a blood-drop from my heart.
OSW.   'Twas even so.
MAR. I have much to say, but for whose ear? – not
        thine.
IDON. Ill can I bear that look – Plead for me, Oswald!
     You are my Father's Friend.
        [*To* MARMADUKE]   Alas, you know not,
     And never *can* you know, how much he loved me.
     Twice had he been to me a father, twice
     Had given me breath, and was I not to be
     His daughter, once his daughter? could I withstand
     His pleading face, and feel his clasping arms,
1610   And hear his prayer that I would not forsake him
     In his old age –   [*Hides her face*]
     MAR.   Patience – Heaven grant me patience! –

    She weeps, she weeps – *my* brain shall burn for hours
    Ere *I* can shed a tear.
IDON.   I was a woman;
    And, balancing the hopes that are the dearest
    To womankind with duty to my Father,
    I yielded up those precious hopes, which naught
    On earth could else have wrested from me; – if erring,
    Oh let me be forgiven!
MAR.   I *do* forgive thee.
IDON. But take me to your arms – this breast, alas!
1620   It throbs, and you have a heart that does not feel it.
MAR. [*exultingly*] She is innocent.   [*He embraces her*]
OSW. [*aside*]   Were I a Moralist,
    I should make wondrous revolution here;
    It were a quaint experiment to show
    The beauty of truth –   [*Addressing them*]
             I see I interrupt you;
    I shall have business with you, Marmaduke;
    Follow me to the Hostel.   [*Exit* OSWALD]
IDON.   Marmaduke,
    This is a happy day. My Father soon
    Shall sun himself before his native doors;
    The lame, the hungry, will be welcome there.
1630   No more shall he complain of wasted strength,
    Of thoughts that fail, and a decaying heart;
    His good works will be balm and life to him.
MAR. This is most strange! – I know not what it was,
    But there was something which most plainly said
    That thou wert innocent.
IDON.   How innocent! –
    Oh, heavens! you've been deceived.
MAR.   Thou art a Woman,
    To bring perdition on the universe.
IDON. Already I've been punished to the height
    Of my offence.   [*Smiling affectionately*]
             I see you love me still,
1640   The labours of my hand are still your joy;
    Bethink you of the hour when on your shoulder

I hung this belt.
   [*Pointing to the belt on which was suspended*
      HERBERT'S *scrip*]

MAR.   Mercy of Heaven!   [*Sinks*]

IDON.   What ails you!
                                     [*Distractedly*]

MAR. The scrip that held his food, and I forgot
  To give it back again!

IDON.   What mean your words?

MAR. I know not what I said – all may be well.

IDON. That smile hath life in it!

MAR.   This road is perilous;
  I will attend you to a Hut that stands
  Near the wood's edge – rest there tonight, I pray you:
  For me, I have business, as you heard, with Oswald,
1650 But will return to you by break of day.
                                 [*Exeunt*]

ACT IV

Scene, *A desolate prospect – a ridge of rocks – a Chapel on
the summit of one – Moon behind the rocks – night
stormy – irregular sound of a bell –*
HERBERT *enters exhausted.*

HER. That Chapel-bell in mercy seemed to guide me,
  But now it mocks my steps; its fitful stroke
  Can scarcely be the work of human hands.
  Hear me, ye Men upon the cliffs, if such
  There be who pray nightly before the Altar.
  Oh that I had but strength to reach the place!
  My Child – my Child – dark – dark – I faint – this
    wind –
  These stifling blasts – God help me!
    [*Enter* ELDRED]

ELD.   Better this bare rock,
  Though it were tottering over a man's head,

1660   Than a tight case of dungeon walls for shelter
    From such rough dealing.   [*A moaning voice is heard*]
                        Ha! what sound is that?
  Trees creaking in the wind (but none are here)
  Send forth such noises – and that weary bell!
  Surely some evil Spirit abroad tonight
  Is ringing it – 'twould stop a Saint in prayer,
  And that – what is it? never was sound so like
  A human groan. Ha! what is here? Poor Man –
  Murdered! alas! speak – speak, I am your friend:
  No answer – hush – lost wretch, he lifts his hand
  And lays it to his heart – [*Kneels to him*]
1670   I pray you speak!
  What has befallen you?
HER. [*feebly*]   A stranger has done this,
  And in the arms of a stranger I must die.
ELD. Nay, think not so: come, let me raise you up:
                         [*Raises him*]
  This is a dismal place – well – that is well –
  I was too fearful – take me for your guide
  And your support – my hut is not far off.
           [*Draws him gently off the stage*]

SCENE, *a room in the Hostel* – MARMADUKE *and*
  OSWALD.

MAR. But for Idonea! – I have cause to think
  That she is innocent.
OSW.   Leave that thought awhile,
  As one of those beliefs which in their hearts
1680   Lovers lock up as pearls, though oft no better
  Than feathers clinging to their points of passion.
  This day's event has laid on me the duty
  Of opening out my story; you must hear it,
  And without further preface. – In my youth,
  Except for that abatement which is paid
  By envy as a tribute to desert,
  I was the pleasure of all hearts, the darling
  Of every tongue – as you are now. You've heard

That I embarked for Syria. On our voyage
1690   Was hatched among the crew a foul Conspiracy
Against my honour, in the which our Captain
Was, I believed, prime Agent. The wind fell;
We lay becalmed week after week, until
The water of the vessel was exhausted;
I felt a double fever in my veins,
Yet rage suppressed itself; – to a deep stillness
Did my pride tame my pride; – for many days,
On a dead sea under a burning sky,
I brooded o'er my injuries, deserted
1700   By man and nature; – if a breeze had blown,
It might have found its way into my heart,
And I had been – no matter – do you mark me?
  MAR. Quick – to the point – if any untold crime
Doth haunt your memory.
  OSW.   Patience, hear me further! –
One day in silence did we drift at noon
By a bare rock, narrow, and white, and bare;
No food was there, no drink, no grass, no shade,
No tree, nor jutting eminence, nor form
Inanimate large as the body of man,
1710   Nor any living thing whose lot of life
Might stretch beyond the measure of one moon.
To dig for water on the spot, the Captain
Landed with a small troop, myself being one:
There I reproached him with his treachery.
Imperious at all times, his temper rose;
He struck me; and that instant had I killed him,
And put an end to his insolence, but my Comrades
Rushed in between us: then did I insist
(All hated him, and I was stung to madness)
1720   That we should leave him there, alive! – we did so.
  MAR. And he was famished?
  OSW.   Naked was the spot;
Methinks I see it now – how in the sun
Its stony surface glittered like a shield;
And in that miserable place we left him,

Alone but for a swarm of minute creatures
Not one of which could help him while alive,
Or mourn him dead.

MAR.   A man by men cast off,
Left without burial! nay, not dead nor dying,
But standing, walking, stretching forth his arms,
1730   In all things like ourselves, but in the agony
With which he called for mercy; and – even so –
He was forsaken?

OSW.   There is a power in sounds:
The cries he uttered might have stopped the boat
That bore us through the water –

MAR.   You returned
Upon that dismal hearing – did you not?

OSW. Some scoffed at him with hellish mockery,
And laughed so loud it seemed that the smooth sea
Did from some distant region echo us.

MAR. We all are of one blood, our veins are filled
At the same poisonous fountain!

1740 OSW.   'Twas an island
Only by sufferance of the winds and waves,
Which with their foam could cover it at will.
I know not how he perished; but the calm,
The same dead calm, continued many days.

MAR. But his own crime had brought on him this doom,
His wickedness prepared it; these expedients
Are terrible, yet ours is not the fault.

OSW. The man was famished, and was innocent!

MAR. Impossible!

OSW.   The man had never wronged me.

1750 MAR. Banish the thought, crush it, and be at peace.
His guilt was marked – these things could never be
Were there not eyes that see, and for good ends,
Where ours are baffled.

OSW.   I had been deceived.

MAR. And from that hour the miserable man
No more was heard of?

OSW.   I had been betrayed.

MAR. And he found no deliverance!

OSW.   The Crew
Gave me a hearty welcome; they had laid
The plot to rid themselves, at any cost,
Of a tyrannic Master whom they loathed.
1760 So we pursued our voyage: when we landed,
The tale was spread abroad; my power at once
Shrunk from me; plans and schemes, and lofty hopes –
All vanished. I gave way – do you attend?

MAR. The Crew deceived you?

OSW.   Nay, command yourself.

MAR. It is a dismal night – how the wind howls!

OSW. I hid my head within a Convent, there
Lay passive as a dormouse in mid winter.
That was no life for me – I was o'erthrown,
But not destroyed.

MAR.   The proofs – you ought to have seen
1770 The guilt – have touched it – felt it at your heart –
As I have done.

OSW.   A fresh tide of Crusaders
Drove by the place of my retreat: three nights
Did constant meditation dry my blood;
Three sleepless nights I passed in sounding on,
Through words and things, a dim and perilous way;
And, wheresoe'er I turned me, I beheld
A slavery compared to which the dungeon
And clanking chains are perfect liberty.
You understand me – I was comforted;
1780 I saw that every possible shape of action
Might lead to good – I saw it and burst forth
Thirsting for some of those exploits that fill
The earth for sure redemption of lost peace.
                    [*Marking* MARMADUKE'S *countenance*]
Nay, you have had the worst. Ferocity
Subsided in a moment, like a wind
That drops down dead out of a sky it vexed.
And yet I had within me evermore
A salient spring of energy; I mounted

From action up to action with a mind
1790   That never rested – without meat or drink
Have I lived many days – my sleep was bound
To purposes of reason – not a dream
But had a continuity and substance
That waking life had never power to give.
    MAR. O wretched Human-kind! – Until the mystery
Of all this world is solved, well may we envy
The worm, that, underneath a stone whose weight
Would crush the lion's paw with mortal anguish,
Doth lodge, and feed, and coil, and sleep, in safety.
1800   Fell not the wrath of Heaven upon those traitors?
    OSW. Give not to them a thought. From Palestine
We marched to Syria: oft I left the Camp,
When all that multitude of hearts was still,
And followed on, through woods of gloomy cedar,
Into deep chasms troubled by roaring streams;
Or from the top of Lebanon surveyed
The moonlight desert, and the moonlight sea:
In these my lonely wanderings I perceived
What mighty objects do impress their forms
1810   To elevate our intellectual being;
And felt, if aught on earth deserves a curse,
'Tis that worst principle of ill which dooms
A thing so great to perish self-consumed.
    – So much for my remorse!
    MAR.   Unhappy Man!
    OSW. When from these forms I turned to contemplate
The World's opinions and her usages,
I seemed a Being who had passed alone
Into a region of futurity,
Whose natural element was freedom –
    MAR.   Stop –
I may not, cannot, follow thee.
1820 OSW.   You must.
I had been nourished by the sickly food
Of popular applause. I now perceived
That we are praised, only as men in us

Do recognize some image of themselves,
An abject counterpart of what they are,
Or the empty thing that they would wish to be.
I felt that merit has no surer test
Than obloquy; that, if we wish to serve
The world in substance, not deceive by show,
1830 We must become obnoxious to its hate,
Or fear disguised in simulated scorn.

MAR. I pity, can forgive, you; but those wretches –
That monstrous perfidy!

OSW.   Keep down your wrath.
False Shame discarded, spurious Fame despised,
Twin sisters both of Ignorance, I found
Life stretched before me smooth as some broad way
Cleared for a monarch's progress. Priests might spin
Their veil, but not for me – 'twas in fit place
Among its kindred cobwebs. I had been,
1840 And in that dream had left my native land,
One of Love's simple bondsmen – the soft chain
Was off for ever; and the men, from whom
This liberation came, you would destroy:
Join me in thanks for their blind services.

MAR. 'Tis a strange aching that, when we would curse
And cannot. – You have betrayed me – I have done –
I am content – I know that he is guiltless –
That both are guiltless, without spot or stain,
Mutually consecrated. Poor old Man!
1850 And I had heart for this, because thou lovedst
Her who from very infancy had been
Light to thy path, warmth to thy blood! – Together
                      [*Turning to* OSWALD]
We propped his steps, he leaned upon us both.

OSW. Ay, we are coupled by a chain of adamant;
Let us be fellow-labourers, then, to enlarge
Man's intellectual empire. We subsist
In slavery; all is slavery; we receive
Laws, but we ask not whence those laws have come;
We need an inward sting to goad us on.

MAR. Have you betrayed me? Speak to that.

1860 OSW.   The mask,
    Which for a season I have stooped to wear,
    Must be cast off. – Know then that I was urged,
    (For other impulse let it pass) was driven,
    To seek for sympathy, because I saw
    In you a mirror of my youthful self;
    I would have made us equal once again,
    But that was a vain hope. You have struck home,
    With a few drops of blood cut short the business;
    Therein for ever you must yield to me.

1870   But what is done will save you from the blank
    Of living without knowledge that you live:
    Now you are suffering – for the future day,
    'Tis his who will command it. – Think of my story –
    Herbert is *innocent*.

MAR. [*in a faint voice, and doubtingly*] You do but echo
    My own wild words?

OSW.   Young Man, the seed must lie
    Hid in the earth, or there can be no harvest;
    'Tis Nature's law. What I have done in darkness
    I will avow before the face of day.
    Herbert *is* innocent.

MAR.   What fiend could prompt

1880 This action? Innocent! – oh, breaking heart! –
    Alive or dead, I'll find him.   [*Exit*]

OSW.   Alive – perdition!   [*Exit*]

SCENE, *the inside of a poor Cottage.*

ELEANOR *and* IDONEA *seated.*

IDON. The storm beats hard – Mercy for poor or rich,
    Whose heads are shelterless in such a night!

A VOICE WITHOUT. Holla! to bed, good Folks, within!

ELEA.   O save us!

IDON. What can this mean?

ELEA.   Alas, for my poor husband! –
    We'll have a counting of our flocks tomorrow;
    The wolf keeps festival these stormy nights:

Be calm, sweet Lady, they are wassailers
                    [*The voices die away in the distance*]
Returning from their Feast – my heart beats so –
1890 A noise at midnight does *so* frighten me.
IDON.   Hush!   [*Listening*]
ELEA.   They are gone. On such a night, my husband,
      Dragged from his bed, was cast into a dungeon,
      Where, hid from me, he counted many years,
      A criminal in no one's eyes but theirs –
      Not even in theirs – whose brutal violence
      So dealt with him.
IDON.   I have a noble Friend
      First among youths of knightly breeding, One
      Who lives but to protect the weak or injured.
      There again!   [*Listening*]
ELEA.   'Tis my husband's foot. Good Eldred
1900 Has a kind heart; but his imprisonment
      Has made him fearful, and he'll never be
      The man he was.
IDON.   I will retire; – good night!
                                        [*She goes within*]
      [*Enter* ELDRED (*hides a bundle*)]
ELD. Not yet in bed, Eleanor! – there are stains in that
      frock which must be washed out.
ELEA. What has befallen you?
ELD. I am belated, and you must know the cause –
      [*speaking low*] that is the blood of an unhappy Man.
ELEA. Oh! we are undone for ever.
ELD. Heaven forbid that I should lift my hand against
      any man. Eleanor, I have shed tears tonight, and it
1910 comforts me to think of it.
ELEA. Where, where is he?
ELD. I have done him no harm, but – it will be forgiven
      me; it would not have been so once.
ELEA. You have not *buried* anything? You are no richer
      than when you left me?
ELD. Be at peace; I am innocent.
ELEA. Then God be thanked –

[*A short pause; she falls upon his neck*]

ELD. Tonight I met with an old Man lying stretched
upon the ground – a sad spectacle: I raised him up
1920   with the hope that we might shelter and restore
him.

ELEA. [*as if ready to run*] Where is he? You were not
able to bring him *all* the way with you; let us
return, I can help you.   [ELDRED *shakes his head*]

ELD. He did not seem to wish for life: as I was
struggling on, by the light of the moon I saw the
stains of blood upon my clothes – he waved his
hand, as if it were all useless; and I let him sink
again to the ground.

ELEA. Oh that I had been by your side!

1930 ELD. I tell you his hands and his body were cold – how
could I disturb his last moments? he strove to turn
from me as if he wished to settle into sleep.

ELEA. But, for the stains of blood –

ELD. He must have fallen, I fancy, for his head was cut;
but I think his malady was cold and hunger.

ELEA. Oh, Eldred, I shall never be able to look up at
this roof in storm or fair but I shall tremble.

ELD. Is it not enough that my ill stars have kept me
abroad tonight till this hour? I come home, and
this is my comfort!

1940 ELEA. But did he say nothing which might have set you
at ease?

ELD. I thought he grasped my hand while he was
muttering something about his Child – his Daughter
– [*starting as if he heard a noise*] What is that?

ELEA. Eldred, you are a father.

ELD. God knows what was in my heart, and will not
curse my son for my sake.

ELEA. But you prayed by him? you waited the hour of
his release?

1950 ELD. The night was wasting fast; I have no friend; I
am spited by the world – his wound terrified me –
if I had brought him along with me, and he had

died in my arms! – I am sure I heard something
breathing – and this chair!

ELEA. Oh, Eldred, you will die alone. You will have
nobody to close your eyes – no hand to grasp your
dying hand – I shall be in my grave. A curse will
attend us all.

ELD. Have you forgot your own troubles when I was in
the dungeon?

ELEA. And you left him alive?

1960 ELD. Alive! – the damps of death were upon him – he
could not have survived an hour.

ELEA. In the cold, cold night.

ELD. [*in a savage tone*] Ay, and his head was bare; I
suppose you would have had me lend my bonnet
to cover it. – You will never rest till I am brought
to a felon's end.

ELEA. Is there nothing to be done? cannot we go to the
Convent?

ELD. Ay, and say at once that I murdered him!

ELEA. Eldred, I know that ours is the only house upon
the Waste; let us take heart; this Man may be rich;
and could he be saved by our means, his gratitude
1970 may reward us.

ELD. 'Tis all in vain.

ELEA. But let us make the attempt. This old Man may
have a wife, and he may have children – let us
return to the spot; we may restore him, and his
eyes may yet open upon those that love him.

ELD. He will never open them more; even when he
spoke to me, he kept them firmly sealed as if he
had been blind.

IDON. [*rushing out*] It is, it is, my Father –

ELD. We are betrayed.   [*looking at* IDONEA]

ELEA.   His Daughter! – God have mercy!
                                [*turning to* IDONEA]

1980 IDON. [*sinking down*] Oh! lift me up and carry me to the
place.

You are safe; the whole world shall not harm you.

ELEA. This Lady is his Daughter.

ELD. [*moved*] I'll lead you to the spot.

IDON. [*springing up*] Alive! – you heard him breathe?
    quick, quick –   [*Exeunt*]

ACT V

SCENE, *a wood on the edge of the Waste.*
Enter OSWALD *and a* FORESTER.

FOR. He leaned upon the bridge that spans the glen,
    And down into the bottom cast his eye,
    That fastened there, as it would check the current.

OSW. He listened too; did you not say he listened?

FOR. As if there came such moaning from the flood

1990   As is heard often after stormy nights.

OSW. But did he utter nothing?

FOR.   See him there!

    [MARMADUKE *appearing*]

MAR. Buzz, buzz, ye black and winged freebooters;
    That is no substance which ye settle on!

FOR. His senses play him false; and see, his arms
    Outspread, as if to save himself from falling! –
    Some terrible phantom I believe is now
    Passing before him, such as God will not
    Permit to visit any but a man
    Who has been guilty of some horrid crime.

              [MARMADUKE *disappears*]

OSW. The game is up! –

2000 FOR.   If it be needful, Sir,
    I will assist you to lay hands upon him.

OSW. No, no, my Friend, you may pursue your
        business –
    'Tis a poor wretch of an unsettled mind,
    Who has a trick of straying from his keepers;
    We must be gentle. Leave him to my care.

               [*Exit* FORESTER]

    If his own eyes play false with him, these freaks
    Of fancy shall be quickly tamed by mine;

The goal is reached. My Master shall become
A shadow of myself – made by myself.

SCENE, *the edge of the Moor.*
MARMADUKE *and* ELDRED *enter from opposite sides.*

MAR. [*raising his eyes and perceiving* ELDRED] In any
2010   corner of this savage Waste
Have you, good Peasant, seen a blind old Man?
ELD. I heard —
MAR.   You heard him, where? when heard him?
ELD.   As you know,
The first hours of last night were rough with storm:
I had been out in search of a stray heifer;
Returning late, I heard a moaning sound;
Then, thinking that my fancy had deceived me,
I hurried on, when straight a second moan,
A human voice distinct, struck on my ear.
So guided, distant a few steps, I found
2020 An aged Man, and such as you describe.
MAR. You heard! – he called you to him? Of all men
The best and kindest! – but where is he? guide me,
That I may see him.
ELD.   On a ridge of rocks
A lonesome Chapel stands, deserted now:
The bell is left, which no one dares remove;
And, when the stormy wind blows o'er the peak,
It rings, as if a human hand were there
To pull the cord. I guess he must have heard it;
And it had led him towards the precipice,
2030 To climb up to the spot whence the sound came;
But he had failed through weakness. From his hand
His staff had dropped, and close upon the brink
Of a small pool of water he was laid,
As if he had stooped to drink, and so remained
Without the strength to rise.
MAR.   Well, well, he lives,
And all is safe: what said he?

ELD.   But few words:
    He only spake to me of a dear Daughter,
    Who, so he feared, would never see him more;
    And of a Stranger to him, One by whom
2040   He had been sore misused; but he forgave
    The wrong and the wrong-doer. You are troubled –
    Perhaps you are his son?
MAR.   The All-seeing knows,
    I did not think he had a living Child. –
    But whither did you carry him?
ELD.   He was torn,
    His head was bruised, and there was blood about him—
MAR. That was no work of mine.
ELD.   Nor was it mine.
MAR. But had he strength to walk? I could have borne
    him
    A thousand miles.
ELD.   I am in poverty,
    And know how busy are the tongues of men;
2050   My heart was willing, Sir, but I am one
    Whose good deeds will not stand by their own light;
    And, though it smote me more than words can tell,
    I left him.
MAR. I believe that there are phantoms,
    That in the shape of man do cross our path
    On evil instigation, to make sport
    Of our distress – and thou art one of them!
    But things substantial have so pressed on me –
ELD. My wife and children came into my mind.
MAR. Oh Monster! Monster! there are three of us,
    And we shall howl together.
                  [*After a pause, and in a feeble voice*]
2060   I am deserted
    At my worst need, my crimes have in a net
    [*Pointing to* ELDRED] Entangled this poor man. – Where
        was it? where?   [*Dragging him along*]
ELD. 'Tis needless; spare your violence. His Daughter –
MAR. Ay, in the word a thousand scorpions lodge:

This old man *had* a Daughter.

ELD.   To the spot
I hurried back with her. – Oh save me, Sir,
From such a journey! – there was a black tree,
A single tree; she thought it was her Father. –
Oh Sir, I would not see that hour again
2070   For twenty lives. The daylight dawned, and now –
Nay; hear my tale, 'tis fit that you should hear it –
As we approached, a solitary crow
Rose from the spot; – the Daughter clapped her hands,
And then I heard a shriek so terrible
                              [MARMADUKE *shrinks back*]
The startled bird quivered upon the wing.

MAR. Dead, dead! –

ELD. [*after a pause*] A dismal matter, Sir, for me,
And seems the like for you; if 'tis your wish,
I'll lead you to his Daughter; but 'twere best
That she should be prepared; I'll go before.

MAR. There will be need of preparation. [ELDRED *goes off*]

2080   ELEA. [*enters*]   Master!
Your limbs sink under you, shall I support you?

MAR. [*taking her arm*] Woman, I've lent my body to the
       service
Which now thou tak'st upon thee. God forbid
That thou shouldst ever meet a like occasion
With such a purpose in thine heart as mine was.

ELEA. Oh, why have I to do with things like these?
                                        [*Exeunt*]

SCENE *changes to the door of* ELDRED'S *cottage* –
IDONEA *seated* – *enter* ELDRED.

ELD. Your Father, Lady, from a wilful hand
Has met unkindness; so indeed he told me,
And you remember such was my report:
2090   From what has just befallen me I have cause
To fear the very worst.

IDON.   My Father is dead;

Why dost thou come to me with words like these?

ELD. A wicked Man should answer for his crimes.

IDON. Thou seest me what I am.

ELD.   It was most heinous,
   And doth call out for vengeance.

IDON.   Do not add,
   I prithee, to the harm thou'st done already.

ELD. Hereafter you will thank me for this service.
   Hard by, a Man I met, who, from plain proofs
   Of interfering Heaven, I have no doubt,
2100   Laid hands upon your Father. Fit it were
   You should prepare to meet him.

IDON.   I have nothing
   To do with others; help me to my Father –
   [*She turns and sees* MARMADUKE *leaning on*
   ELEANOR – *throws herself upon his neck, and*
   after some time]
   In joy I met thee, but a few hours past;
   And thus we meet again; one human stay
   Is left me still in thee. Nay, shake not so.

MAR. In such a wilderness – to see no thing,
   No, not the pitying moon!

IDON.   And perish so.

MAR. Without a dog to moan for him.

IDON.   Think not of it,
   But enter there and see him how he sleeps,
2110   Tranquil as he had died in his own bed.

MAR. Tranquil – why not?

IDON.   Oh, peace!

MAR.   He is at peace;
   His body is at rest: there was a plot,
   A hideous plot, against the soul of man:
   It took effect – and yet I baffled it,
   In *some* degree.

IDON.   Between us stood, I thought,
   A cup of consolation, filled from Heaven
   For both our needs; must I, and in thy presence,
   Alone partake of it? – Belovèd Marmaduke!

MAR. Give me a reason why the wisest thing
2120 That the earth owns shall never choose to die,
      But some one must be near to count his groans.
      The wounded deer retires to solitude,
      And dies in solitude: all things but man,
      All die in solitude.   [*Moving towards the cottage door*]
                        Mysterious God,
      If she had never lived I had not done it! –
IDON. Alas, the thought of such a cruel death
      Has overwhelmed him. – I must follow.
ELD.   Lady!
      You will do well; [*she goes*] unjust suspicion may
      Cleave to this Stranger: if, upon his entering,
2130 The dead Man heave a groan, or from his side
      Uplift his hand – that would be evidence.
ELEA. Shame! Eldred, shame!
MAR. [*both returning*] The dead have but one face.
                                        [*to himself*]
      And such a Man – so meek and unoffending –
      Helpless and harmless as a babe: a Man,
      By obvious signal to the world's protection,
      Solemnly dedicated – to decoy him! –
IDON. Oh, had you seen him living! –
MAR.   I (so filled
      With horror is this world) am unto thee
      The thing most precious, that it now contains:
2140 Therefore through me alone must be revealed
      By whom thy Parent was destroyed, Idonea!
      I have the proofs! –
IDON.   O miserable Father!
      Thou didst command me to bless all mankind;
      Nor to this moment, have I ever wished
      Evil to any living thing; but hear me,
      Hear me, ye Heavens! – [*kneeling*] – may vengeance
        haunt the fiend
      For this most cruel murder: let him live
      And move in terror of the elements;
      The thunder send him on his knees to prayer

2150 In the open streets, and let him think he sees,
     If e'er he entereth the house of God,
     The roof, self-moved, unsettling o'er his head;
     And let him, when he would lie down at night,
     Point to his wife the blood-drops on his pillow!

MAR. My voice was silent, but my heart hath joined
     thee.

IDON. [*leaning on* MARMADUKE] Left to the mercy of
     that savage Man!

     How could he call upon his Child! – O Friend!
                              [*Turns to* MARMADUKE]
     My faithful, true and only Comforter.

MAR. Ay, come to me and weep. [*He kisses her*]
     [*To* ELDRED]   Yes, Varlet, look,
2160 The devils at such sights do clap their hands.
                              [ELDRED *retires alarmed*]

IDON. Thy vest is torn, thy cheek is deadly pale;
     Hast thou pursued the monster?

MAR.   I have found him. –
     Oh! would that thou hadst perished in the flames!

IDON. Here art thou, then can I be desolate? –

MAR. There was a time, when this protecting hand
     Availed against the mighty; never more
     Shall blessings wait upon a deed of mine.

IDON. Wild words for me to hear, for me, an orphan,
     Committed to thy guardianship by Heaven;
2170 And, if thou hast forgiven me, let me hope,
     In this deep sorrow, trust, that I am thine
     For closer care; – here, is no malady. [*Taking his arm*]

MAR. There, *is* a malady –
     [*Striking his heart and forehead*] And here, and here,
     A mortal malady. – I am accurst:
     All nature curses me, and in my heart
     Thy curse is fixed; the truth must be laid bare.
     It must be told, and borne. I am the man,
     (Abused, betrayed, but how it matters not)
     Presumptuous above all that ever breathed,
2180 Who, casting as I thought a guilty Person

Upon Heaven's righteous judgement, did become
An instrument of Fiends. Through me, through me,
Thy Father perished.

IDON.   Perished – by what mischance?

MAR. Belovèd! – if I dared, so would I call thee –
Conflict must cease, and, in thy frozen heart,
The extremes of suffering meet in absolute peace.

[*He gives her a letter*]

IDON. [*reads*] 'Be not surprised if you hear that some
signal judgement has befallen the man who calls
himself your father; he is now with me, as his
signature will show: abstain from conjecture till
2190   you see me.

'HERBERT.

'MARMADUKE.'

The writing Oswald's; the signature my Father's:
[*Looks steadily at the paper*] And here is yours, – or
do my eyes deceive me?
You have then seen my Father?

MAR.   He has leaned
Upon this arm.

IDON.   You led him towards the Convent?

MAR. That Convent was Stone-Arthur Castle Thither
We were his guides. I on that night resolved
That he should wait thy coming till the day
Of resurrection.

2200 IDON.   Miserable Woman,
Too quickly moved, too easily giving way,
I put denial on thy suit, and hence,
With the disastrous issue of last night,
Thy perturbation, and these frantic words.
Be calm, I pray thee!

MAR.   Oswald –

IDON.   Name him not.

[*Enter female* BEGGAR]

BEG. And he is dead! – that Moor – how shall I cross it?
By night, by day, never shall I be able
To travel half a mile alone. – Good Lady!

  Forgive me! – Saints forgive me. Had I thought
  It would have come to this! –
IDON.   What brings you hither? speak!
2210 BEG. [*pointing to* MARMADUKE] This innocent
  Gentleman.
  Sweet heavens! I told him
  Such tales of your dead Father! – God is my judge,
  I thought there was no harm: but that bad Man,
  He bribed me with his gold and looked so fierce.
  Mercy! I said I know not what – oh pity me –
  I said, sweet Lady, you were not his Daughter –
  Pity me, I am haunted; – thrice this day
  My conscience made me wish to be struck blind;
  And then I would have prayed, and had no voice.
2220 IDON. [*to* MARMADUKE] Was it my Father? – no, no,
  no, for he
  Was meek and patient, feeble, old and blind,
  Helpless, and loved me dearer than his life.
  – But hear me. For *one* question, I have a heart
  That will sustain me. Did you murder him?
  MAR. No, not by stroke of arm. But learn the process:
  Proof after proof was pressed upon me; guilt
  Made evident, as seemed, by blacker guilt,
  Whose impious folds enwrapped even thee; and truth
  And innocence, embodied in his looks,
2230 His words and tones and gestures, did but serve
  With me to aggravate his crimes, and heaped
  Ruin upon the cause for which they pleaded.
  Then pity crossed the path of my resolve:
  Confounded, I looked up to Heaven, and cast,
  Idonea! thy blind Father on the Ordeal
  Of the bleak Waste – left him – and so he died! –
    [IDONEA *sinks senseless*; BEGGAR, ELEANOR, &c.,
    crowd round, and bear her off]
  Why may we speak these things, and do no more;
  Why should a thrust of the arm have such a power,
  And words that tell these things be heard in vain?
2240 *She* is not dead. Why! – if I loved this Woman,

I would take care she never woke again;
But she WILL wake, and she will weep for me,
And say no blame was mine – and so, poor fool,
Will waste her curses on another name.
                              [*He walks about distractedly*]
        [*Enter* OSWALD]
OSW. [*to himself*] Strong to o'erturn, strong also to
        build up.   [*To* MARMADUKE]
    The starts and sallies of our last encounter
    Were natural enough; but that, I trust,
    Is all gone by. You have cast off the chains
    That fettered your nobility of mind –
    Delivered heart and head!
2250   Let us to Palestine;
    This is a paltry field for enterprise.
MAR. Ay, what shall we encounter next? This issue –
    'Twas nothing more than darkness deepening darkness,
    And weakness crowned with the impotence of death! –
    Your pupil is, you see, an apt proficient. [*ironically*]
    Start not! – Here is another face hard by;
    Come, let us take a peep at both together,
    And, with a voice at which the dead will quake,
    Resound the praise of your morality –
    Of this too much.
        [*Drawing* OSWALD *towards the Cottage – stops short
            at the door*]
2260   Men are there, millions, Oswald,
    Who with bare hands would have plucked out thy
        heart
    And flung it to the dogs: but I am raised
    Above, or sunk below, all further sense
    Of provocation. Leave me, with the weight
    Of that old Man's forgiveness on thy heart,
    Pressing as heavily as it doth on mine.
    Coward I have been; know, there lies not now
    Within the compass of a mortal thought,
    A deed that I would shrink from; – but to endure,
2270 That is my destiny. May it be thine:

Thy office, thy ambition, be henceforth
To feed remorse, to welcome every sting
Of penitential anguish, yea with tears.
When seas and continents shall lie between us –
The wider space the better – we may find
In such a course fit links of sympathy,
An incommunicable rivalship
Maintained, for peaceful ends beyond our view.
          [*Confused voices – several of the band enter – rush*
                    upon OSWALD *and seize him*]
ONE OF THEM. I would have dogged him to the jaws
          of hell –
2280 OSW. Ha! is it so! – That vagrant Hag! – this comes
          Of having left a thing like her alive!   ⌊*Aside*]
SEVERAL VOICES. Dispatch him!
OSW.   If I pass beneath a rock
          And shout, and, with the echo of my voice,
          Bring down a heap of rubbish, and it crush me,
          I die without dishonour. Famished, starved,
          A Fool and Coward blended to my wish!
          [*Smiles scornfully and exultingly at* MARMADUKE]
WAL. 'Tis done! [*stabs him*]
ANOTHER OF THE BAND. The ruthless Traitor!
MAR.   A rash deed! –
          With that reproof I do resign a station
          Of which I have been proud.
WIL. [*approaching* MARMADUKE] O my poor Master!
2290 MAR. Discerning Monitor, my faithful Wilfred,
          Why art thou here?   [*Turning to* WALLACE]
                              Wallace, upon these Borders,
          Many there be those eyes will not want cause
          To weep that I am gone. Brothers in arms!
          Raise on that dreary Waste a monument
          That may record my story: nor let words –
          Few must they be, and delicate in their touch
          As light itself – be there withheld from Her
          Who, through most wicked arts, was made an orphan
          By One who would have died a thousand times,

2300   To shield her from a moment's harm. To you,
        Wallace and Wilfred, I commend the Lady,
        By lowly nature reared, as if to make her
        In all things worthier of that noble birth,
        Whose long-suspended rights are now on the eve
        Of restoration: with your tenderest care
        Watch over her, I pray – sustain her –
        SEVERAL OF THE BAND [*eagerly*]   Captain!
        MAR. No more of that; in silence hear my doom:
        A hermitage has furnished fit relief
        To some offenders; other penitents,
2310   Less patient in their wretchedness, have fallen,
        Like the old Roman, on their own sword's point.
        They had their choice: a wanderer *must I* go,
        The Spectre of that innocent Man, my guide.
        No human ear shall ever hear me speak;
        No human dwelling ever give me food,
        Or sleep, or rest; but, over waste and wild,
        In search of nothing, that this earth can give,
        But expiation, will I wander on –
        A Man by pain and thought compelled to live,
2320   Yet loathing life – till anger is appeased
        In Heaven, and Mercy gives me leave to die.

Animal Tranquillity and Decay

The little hedgerow birds,
That peck along the road, regard him not.
He travels on, and in his face, his step,
His gait, is one expression: every limb,
His look and bending figure, all bespeak
A man who does not move with pain, but moves
With thought. – He is insensibly subdued
To settled quiet: he is one by whom
All effort seems forgotten; one to whom
10   Long patience hath such mild composure given,
That patience now doth seem a thing of which
He hath no need. He is by nature led
To peace so perfect that the young behold
With envy, what the Old Man hardly feels.

[Fragment: 'Yet once again']

Yet once again do I behold the forms
Of these huge mountains, and yet once again,
Standing beneath these elms, I hear thy voice,
Beloved Derwent, that peculiar voice
Heard in the stillness of the evening air,
Half-heard and half-created.

[Fragment: The Baker's Cart]

I have seen the Baker's horse
As he had been accustomed at your door
Stop with the loaded wain, when o'er his head
Smack went the whip, and you were left, as if
You were not born to live, or there had been

No bread in all the land. Five little ones,
They at the rumbling of the distant wheels
Had all come forth, and, ere the grove of birch
Concealed the wain, into their wretched hut
10 They all returned. While in the road I stood
Pursuing with involuntary look
The wain now seen no longer, to my side
[   ] came, a pitcher in her hand
Filled from the spring; she saw what way my eyes
Were turned, and in a low and fearful voice
By misery and rumination deep
Tied to dead things, and seeking sympathy
She said: 'that waggon does not care for us' –
The words were simple, but her look and voice
20 Made up their meaning, and bespoke a mind
Which being long neglected, and denied
The common food of hope, was now become
Sick and extravagant, – by strong access
Of momentary pangs driven to that state
In which all past experience melts away,
And the rebellious heart to its own will
Fashions the laws of nature.

Inscription for a Seat by a Roadside, Half Way up a Steep Hill, Facing the South

Thou, who in youthful vigour rich, and light
With youthful thoughts, dost need no rest! O thou,
To whom alike the valley and the hill
Present a path of ease! Should e'er thine eye
Glance on this sod, and this rude tablet, stop!
'Tis a rude spot; yet here, with thankful hearts,
The foot-worn soldier and his family
Have rested, wife and babe, and boy, perchance,
Some eight years old or less, and scantly fed,
10 Garbed like his father, and already bound
To his poor father's trade! Or think of him,

Who, laden with his implements of toil,
Returns at night to some far-distant home,
And having plodded on through rain and mire
With limbs o'erlaboured, weak from feverish heat,
And chafed and fretted by December blasts,
Here pauses, thankful, he hath reached so far;
And 'mid the sheltering warmth of these bleak trees
Finds restoration. Or reflect on them,
20 Who, in the spring, to meet the warmer sun,
Crawl up this steep hillside, that needlessly
Bends double their weak frames, already bowed
By age or malady; and when at last
They gain this wished-for turf, this seat of sods,
Repose, and, well admonished, ponder here
On final rest. And if a serious thought
Should come uncalled – how soon thy motions light,
Thy balmy spirits, and thy fervid blood,
Must change to feeble, withered, cold, and dry,
30 Cherish the wholesome sadness! And where'er
The tide of life impel thee, O be prompt
To make thy present strength the staff of all,
Their staff and resting place: so shalt thou give
To youth the sweetest joy that youth can know,
And for thy future self thou shalt provide
Through every change of various life a seat,
Not built by hands, on which thy inner part,
Imperishable, many a grievous hour,
Or bleak, or sultry, may repose; yea, sleep
40 The sleep of death, and dream of blissful worlds,
Then wake in Heaven, and find the dream all true!

The Three Graves. Part I

[Part I and the first five stanzas of Part II (in brackets) are of
questionable authorship.]

Beneath this thorn when I was young,
    This thorn that blooms so sweet,
We loved to stretch our lazy limbs
    In summer's noon-tide heat.

And hither too the old man came,
    The maiden and her feer,
'Then tell me, Sexton, tell me why
    The toad has harbour here.

'The Thorn is neither dry nor dead,
10   But still it blossoms sweet;
Then tell me why all round its roots
    The dock and nettle meet.

'Why here the hemlock, &c.

'Why these three graves all side by side,
    Beneath the flowery thorn,
Stretch out so green and dark a length,
    By any foot unworn.'

There, there a ruthless mother lies
    Beneath the flowery thorn;
20 And there a barren wife is laid,
    And there a maid forlorn.

The barren wife and maid forlorn
    Did love each other dear;
The ruthless mother wrought the woe,
    And cost them many a tear.

Fair Ellen was of serious mind,
　Her temper mild and even,
And Mary, graceful as the fir
　That points the spire to heaven.

30 Young Edward he to Mary said,
　'I would you were my bride,'
And she was scarlet as he spoke,
　And turned her face to hide.

'You know my mother she is rich,
　And you have little gear;
And go and if she say not Nay,
　Then I will be your fere.'

Young Edward to the mother went,
　To him the mother said:
40 'In truth you are a comely man;
　You shall my daughter wed.'

In Mary's joy fair Eleanor
　Did bear a sister's part;
For why, though not akin in blood,
　They sisters were in heart.

Small need to tell to any man
　That ever shed a tear
What passed within the lover's heart
　The happy day so near.

50 The mother, more than mothers use,
　Rejoiced when they were by;
And all the 'course of wooing' passed
　Beneath the mother's eye.

And here within the flowering thorn
　How deep they drank of joy:
The mother fed upon the sight,
　Nor . . .

Part II

[And now the wedding day was fixed,
 The wedding-ring was bought;
60 The wedding-cake with her own hand
 The ruthless mother brought.

'And when tomorrow's sun shines forth
 The maid shall be a bride';
Thus Edward to the mother spake
 While she sate by his side.

Alone they sate within the bower:
 The mother's colour fled,
For Mary's foot was heard above –
 She decked the bridal bed.

70 And when her foot was on the stairs
 To meet her at the door,
With steady step the mother rose,
 And silent left the bower.

She stood, her back against the door,
 And when her child drew near –
'Away! away!' the mother cried,
 'Ye shall not enter here.]

'Would ye come here, ye maiden vile,
 And rob me of my mate?'
80 And on her child the mother scowled
 The ghastly leer of hate.

Fast rooted to the spot, you guess,
 The wretched maiden stood,
As pale as any ghost of night
 [ ] wanting flesh and blood.

She did not groan, she did not fall,
  She did not shed a tear,
Nor did she cry 'oh mother, why
  May I not enter here?'

90 But wildly up the stairs she ran
  As if her sense was fled,
And then her trembling limbs she threw
  Upon the bridal bed.

The mother she to Edward went
  Where he sate in the bower,
And said 'that woman is not fit
  To be your paramour.

I could, but it will make you woe,
  Of her a story tell;
100 She is my child, I'm loth to speak
  But that I know her well.

She is my child, it makes my heart
  With grief and trouble swell;
I rue the hour that gave her birth
  For never worse befell.

For she is fierce and she is proud
  And of an envious mind;
A very hypocrite she is
  And giddy as the wind.

110 And if ye go to church with her
  You'll rue the bitter smart,
For she will wrong your marriage bed
  And she will break your heart.

Oh God! to think that I have shared
  Her deadly sins so long:
She is my child, and therefore I,
  A mother, held my tongue.

She is my child, I've risked for her
    My living soul's estate,
120 I cannot say my daily prayers
    The burden is so great.

And she would scatter gold about
    Until her back was bare,
And should you swing for lust of her
    In troth she'd little care.'

Then in a softer voice she said
    And took him by the hand;
'Sweet Edward, for one kiss of yours
    I'd give my house and land.

130 And if you'll go to church with me
    And take me for your bride,
I'll make you heir of all I have,
    Nothing shall be denied.'

Then Edward started from his seat
    And he laughed loud and long;
'In truth, good mother, you are mad
    Or drunk with liquor strong.'

To him no word the mother said,
    But on her knees she fell,
140 And fetched her breath while thrice your hand
    Might toll the passing bell.

'Thou daughter now above my head,
    Whom in my womb I bore,
May every drop of thy heart's blood
    Be curst for evermore.

And cursèd be the hour when first
    I heard thee wail and cry,
And in the churchyard cursèd be
    The grave where thou shalt lie.'

150 In wrath young Edward left the hall,
   And turning round, he sees
  The mother looking up to God
   And still upon her knees.

  And Mary on the bridal bed
   Her mother's curse had heard,
  And while the cruel mother spake
   The bed beneath her stirred.

  Young Edward he to Mary went
   Where on the bed she lay;
160 'Sweet love, this is a wicked house
   Sweet love, we must away.'

  He raised her from the bridal bed
   All pale and wan with fear;
  'No dog,' quoth he, 'if he were wise,
   No dog would kennel here.'

  He led her from the bridal bed
   He led her down the stairs;
  Had sense been hers she had not dared
   To venture on her prayers.

170 The mother still was in the bower,
   And with a greedy heart
  She drank perdition on her knees
   Which never may depart.

  But when their steps were heard below
   On God she did not call,
  She did forget the God of Heaven,
   For they were in the hall.

  She started up, the servant maid
   Did see her when she rose,
180 And she hath oft declared to me
   The blood within her froze.

As Edward led his bride along
  And hurried to the door,
The ruthless mother springing forth
  Stopped midway on the floor.

What did she mean? What did she mean?
  For with a smile she cried;
'Unblest ye shall not pass my door
  The bridegroom and his bride.

190 Be blithe as lambs in April are,
  As flies when fruits are red;
Nay God forbid that thought of me
  Should haunt your marriage bed.

And let the night be given to bliss,
  The day be given to glee;
I am a woman weak and old
  Why turn a thought to me?

What can an aged mother do,
  And what have ye to dread?
200 A curse is wind, it hath no shape
  To haunt your marriage bed.'

When they were gone and out of sight
  She rent her hoary hair,
And foamed like any dog of June
  When sultry sunbeams glare.

.   .   .   .   .

And she was pinched and pricked with pins,
  And twitched with cord and wire;
And starting from her seat would cry,
  'It is a stool of fire.'

210 And she would bare her maiden breast,
 And if you looked would shew
The milk which clinging imps of hell
 And sucking daemons drew.

.   .   .   .   .

Oh cursèd mother, mother curst,
 Oh dig the grave for thee
And let the grave where thou art laid
 For ever cursèd be.

*Address to Silence

SILENCE! calm, venerable majesty:
Guardian of contemplation and of love.
Thy voice, in marvellous words of nature, speaks
Not to the ear, but to the eye of man;
Thy placid mien restores the ruffled heath
Or shattered forests, where the storm is past;
And calms the ocean wave without a shore.
Sometimes, when not a single leaf is waved;
When no mild breeze sweeps o'er the smiling vale;
10 When, in the lake, each undulation sleeps;
When heaven is full serene; and grove, and hill,
And mother earth are stript of herb and flower
By winter's hand, laying in deep repose
Whole islands; heavenly musing silence reigns.
Round Iceland's coast the frozen sea its base,
Its top the sky, lit by the polar star,
Thy throne is fixt. Thy palace, now and then,
Is to the centre shook, by falling rocks
Of glittering ice; or the enormous whale;
20 Or by the roar of Hecla's flaming mouth
Loud thundering o'er thy widely echoing realms.

Silence! I would not visit thy domains,
In north and south, for the most precious ore,

The gold and gems which Afric, Asia hold;
Or rivers wash into the eastern main:
No: Not for the sweet beauties of our earth;
Nor the proud glories of the light of day.
Sceptres and thrones, imperial crowns and stars,
Fade in the shadowy mansions of the dead,
30   Where Kings, lords, slaves, without distinction lie
Beneath thy sway.

    Thy peaceful sceptre scorns
The triumphs of the thronged metropolis,
And exclamations of the multitude.
Floods; cataracts o'er precipices huge;
The mighty sounds of Ganges and of Nile,
Have not a charm for thee; nor thunder's voice,
Nor dire convulsions, which the mountains shake.
Far, far remote from noise, thy presence dwells.
The sleeping infant, and his mother's eye;
40   The smiling picture, and the breathless bust;
The rest of ages, and the mourner's face;
The mould'ring abbey, and the quiet grave;
The lonely tower on a desart rock;
The shining valley, with the full orbed moon,
Are thy delights: With them thou art well pleased.
With thee 'tis peace: peace now; peace evermore!

Eternity of calmness is thy joy;
Immensity of space is thine abode;
The rolling planets own thy sacred power;
50   Our little years are moments of thy life;
Our little world is lost amid thy spheres.

The harmony serene of mind is thine;
And human thought, that wings its boundless way
From earth to heaven, is led through air by thee;
With solitude and thee our God resides!
Hush winds! be still: Cease flood! thy tedious voice,
The monotonous music of thy streams;

Or I must leave you, and with silence stray
To the deep forest, or the deeper grave,
60 Where neither winds nor waves disturb repose.

Yet, silence! let me once review the haunts
Of men. Once more let me enjoy the scene
Of social hearts; and view sweet friendship's smiles,
Ere I be seen no more!
    Then have thy sway,
Silence!

Lines

Left upon a Seat in a Yew-tree, which stands near the lake of
Esthwaite, on a desolate part of the shore, commanding a beauti-
ful prospect.

Nay, Traveller! rest. This lonely Yew-tree stands
Far from all human dwelling: what if here
No sparkling rivulet spread the verdant herb?
What if the bee love not these barren boughs?
Yet, if the wind breathe soft, the curling waves,
That break against the shore, shall lull thy mind
By one soft impulse saved from vacancy.
                  Who he was
That piled these stones and with the mossy sod
10 First covered, and here taught this agèd Tree
With its dark arms to form a circling bower,
I well remember. – He was one who owned
No common soul. In youth by science nursed,
And led by nature into a wild scene
Of lofty hopes, he to the world went forth
A favoured Being, knowing no desire
Which genius did not hallow; 'gainst the taint
Of dissolute tongues, and jealousy, and hate,
And scorn, – against all enemies prepared,
20 All but neglect. The world, for so it thought,
Owed him no service; wherefore he at once

With indignation turned himself away,
And with the food of pride sustained his soul
In solitude. – Stranger! these gloomy boughs
Had charms for him; and here he loved to sit,
His only visitants a straggling sheep,
The stone-chat, or the glancing sand-piper:
And on these barren rocks, with fern and heath,
And juniper and thistle, sprinkled o'er,
30 Fixing his downcast eye, he many an hour
A morbid pleasure nourished, tracing here
An emblem of his own unfruitful life:
And, lifting up his head, he then would gaze
On the more distant scene, – how lovely 'tis
Thou seest, – and he would gaze till it became
Far lovelier, and his heart could not sustain
The beauty, still more beauteous! Nor, that time,
When nature had subdued him to herself,
Would he forget those Beings to whose minds
40 Warm from the labours of benevolence
The world, and human life, appeared a scene
Of kindred loveliness: then he would sigh,
Inly disturbed, to think that others felt
What he must never feel: and so, lost Man!
On visionary views would fancy feed,
Till his eye streamed with tears. In this deep vale
He died, – this seat his only monument.

If Thou be one whose heart the holy forms
Of young imagination have kept pure,
50 Stranger! henceforth be warned; and know that pride,
Howe'er disguised in its own majesty,
Is littleness; that he who feels contempt
For any living thing, hath faculties
Which he has never used; that thought with him
Is in its infancy. The man whose eye
Is ever on himself doth look on one,
The least of Nature's works, one who might move
The wise man to that scorn which wisdom holds

Unlawful, ever. O be wiser, Thou!
60 Instructed that true knowledge leads to love;
True dignity abides with him alone
Who, in the silent hour of inward thought,
Can still suspect, and still revere himself,
In lowliness of heart.

Incipient Madness

I crossed the dreary moor
In the clear moonlight: when I reached the hut
I entered in, but all was still and dark,
Only within the ruin I beheld
At a small distance, on the dusky ground
A broken pane which glittered in the moon
And seemed akin to life. There is a mood
A settled temper of the heart, when grief,
Become an instinct, fastening on all things
10 That promise food, doth like a sucking babe
Create it where it is not. From this time
That speck of glass was dearer to my soul
Than was the moon in heaven. Another time
The winds of Autumn drove me o'er the heath
One gloomy evening: by the storm compelled
The poor man's horse that feeds along the lanes
Had hither come among these fractured walls
To weather out the night; and as I passed
While restlessly he turned from the fierce wind
20 And from the open sky, I heard, within,
The iron links with which his feet were clogged
Mix their dull clanking with the heavy noise
Of falling rain. I started from the spot
And heard the sound still following in the wind.

·   ·   ·   ·   ·

Three weeks
O'er arched by the same bramble's dusky shade
On this green bank a glow worm hung its light

And then was seen no more. Within the thorn
Whose flowery head half hides those ruined pales
30   Three seasons did a blackbird build his nest
And then he disappeared. On the green top
Of that tall ash a linnet perched himself
And sang a pleasant melancholy song
Two summers and then vanished. I alone
Remained: the winds of heaven remained. With them
My heart claimed fellowship and with the beams
Of dawn and of the setting sun that seemed
To live and linger on the mouldering walls.

.   .   .   .   .

The Farmer of Tilsbury Vale

'Tis not for the unfeeling, the falsely refined,
The squeamish in taste, and the narrow of mind,
And the small critic wielding his delicate pen,
That I sing of old Adam, the pride of old men.

He dwells in the centre of London's wide Town;
His staff is a sceptre – his grey hairs a crown;
And his bright eyes look brighter, set off by the streak
Of the unfaded rose that still blooms on his cheek.

'Mid the dews, in the sunshine of morn, – 'mid the joy
10   Of the fields, he collected that bloom, when a boy;
That countenance there fashioned, which, spite of a stain
That his life hath received, to the last will remain.

A Farmer he was; and his house far and near
Was the boast of the country for excellent cheer:
How oft have I heard in sweet Tilsbury Vale
Of the silver-rimmed horn whence he dealt his mild ale!

Yet Adam was far as the farthest from ruin,
His fields seemed to know what their Master was doing;

And turnips, and corn-land, and meadow, and lea,
20 All caught the infection – as generous as he.

Yet Adam prized little the feast and the bowl, –
The fields better suited the ease of his soul:
He strayed through the fields like an indolent wight,
The quiet of nature was Adam's delight.

For Adam was simple in thought; and the poor,
Familiar with him, made an inn of his door:
He gave them the best that he had; or, to say
What less may mislead you, they took it away.

Thus thirty smooth years did he thrive on his farm:
30 The Genius of plenty preserved him from harm:
At length, what to most is a season of sorrow,
His means are run out, – he must beg, or must borrow.

To the neighbours he went, – all were free with their
    money;
For his hive had so long been replenished with honey,
That they dreamt not of dearth; – He continued his
    rounds,
Knocked here – and knocked there, pounds still adding
    to pounds.

He paid what he could with his ill-gotten pelf,
And something, it might be, reserved for himself:
Then (what is too true) without hinting a word,
40 Turned his back on the country – and off like a bird.

You lift up your eyes! – but I guess that you frame
A judgement too harsh of the sin and the shame;
In him it was scarcely a business of art,
For this he did all in the *ease* of his heart.

To London – a sad emigration I ween –
With his grey hairs he went from the brook and the
    green;
And there, with small wealth but his legs and his hands,
As lonely he stood as a crow on the sands.

All trades, as need was, did old Adam assume, –
50 Served as stable-boy, errand-boy, porter, and groom;
But nature is gracious, necessity kind,
And, in spite of the shame that may lurk in his mind,

He seems ten birthdays younger, is green and is stout;
Twice as fast as before does his blood run about;
You would say that each hair of his beard was alive,
And his fingers are busy as bees in a hive.

For he's not like an Old Man that leisurely goes
About work that he knows, in a track that he knows;
But often his mind is compelled to demur,
60 And you guess that the more then his body must stir.

In the throng of the town like a stranger is he,
Like one whose own country's far over the sea;
And Nature, while through the great city he hies,
Full ten times a day takes his heart by surprise.

This gives him the fancy of one that is young,
More of soul in his face than of words on his tongue;
Like a maiden of twenty he trembles and sighs,
And tears of fifteen will come into his eyes.

What's a tempest to him, or the dry parching heats?
70 Yet he watches the clouds that pass over the streets;
With a look of such earnestness often will stand,
You might think he'd twelve reapers at work in the
    Strand.

Where proud Covent-garden, in desolate hours
Of snow and hoar-frost, spreads her fruits and her
    flowers,
Old Adam will smile at the pains that have made
Poor winter look fine in such strange masquerade.

'Mid coaches and chariots, a waggon of straw,
Like a magnet, the heart of old Adam can draw;
With a thousand soft pictures his memory will teem,
80 And his hearing is touched with the sounds of a dream.

Up the Haymarket hill he oft whistles his way,
Thrusts his hands in a waggon, and smells at the hay;
He thinks of the fields he so often hath mown,
And is happy as if the rich freight were his own.

But chiefly to Smithfield he loves to repair, –
If you pass by at morning, you'll meet with him there.
The breath of the cows you may see him inhale,
And his heart all the while is in Tilsbury Vale.

Now farewell, old Adam! when low thou art laid,
90 May one blade of grass spring up over thy head;
And I hope that thy grave, wheresoever it be,
Will hear the wind sigh through the leaves of a tree.

The Reverie of Poor Susan

At the corner of Wood Street, when daylight appears,
Hangs a Thrush that sings loud, it has sung for three
    years:
Poor Susan has passed by the spot, and has heard
In the silence of morning the song of the Bird.

'Tis a note of enchantment; what ails her? She sees
A mountain ascending, a vision of trees;
Bright volumes of vapour through Lothbury glide,
And a river flows on through the vale of Cheapside.

Green pastures she views in the midst of the dale,
10 Down which she so often has tripped with her pail;
And a single small cottage, a nest like a dove's,
The one only dwelling on earth that she loves.

She looks, and her heart is in heaven: but they fade,
The mist and the river, the hill and the shade:
The stream will not flow, and the hill will not rise,
And the colours have all passed away from her eyes!

A Character

I marvel how Nature could ever find space
For so many strange contrasts in one human face:
There's thought and no thought, and there's paleness
    and bloom
And bustle and sluggishness, pleasure and gloom.

There's weakness, and strength both redundant and vain;
Such strength as, if ever affliction and pain
Could pierce through a temper that's soft to disease,
Would be rational peace – a philosopher's ease.

There's indifference, alike when he fails or succeeds,
10 And attention full ten times as much as there needs;
Pride where there's no envy, there's so much of joy;
And mildness, and spirit both forward and coy.

There's freedom, and sometimes a diffident stare
Of shame scarcely seeming to know that she's there,
There's virtue, the title it surely may claim,
Yet wants heaven knows what to be worthy the name.

This picture from nature may seem to depart,
Yet the Man would at once run away with your heart;
And I for five centuries right gladly would be
20 Such an odd, such a kind happy creature as he.

A Night-Piece

— The sky is overcast
With a continuous cloud of texture close,
Heavy and wan, all whitened by the Moon,
Which through that veil is indistinctly seen,
A dull, contracted circle, yielding light
So feebly spread, that not a shadow falls,
Chequering the ground – from rock, plant, tree, or
    tower.
At length a pleasant instantaneous gleam
Startles the pensive traveller while he treads
His lonesome path, with unobserving eye
Bent earthwards; he looks up – the clouds are split
Asunder, – and above his head he sees
The clear Moon, and the glory of the heavens.
There, in a black-blue vault she sails along,
Followed by multitudes of stars, that, small
And sharp, and bright, along the dark abyss
Drive as she drives: how fast they wheel away,
Yet vanish not! – the wind is in the tree,
But they are silent; – still they roll along
Immeasurably distant; and the vault,
Built round by those white clouds, enormous clouds,
Still deepens its unfathomable depth.
At length the Vision closes; and the mind,
Not undisturbed by the delight it feels,
Which slowly settles into peaceful calm,
Is left to muse upon the solemn scene.

The Old Cumberland Beggar

The class of Beggars, to which the Old Man here described
belongs, will probably soon be extinct. It consisted of poor,
and, mostly, old and infirm persons, who confined themselves

to a stated round in their neighbourhood, and had certain
fixed days, on which, at different houses, they regularly received
alms, sometimes in money, but mostly in provisions.

I saw an aged Beggar in my walk;
And he was seated, by the highway side,
On a low structure of rude masonry
Built at the foot of a huge hill, that they
Who lead their horses down the steep rough road
May thence remount at ease. The aged Man
Had placed his staff across the broad smooth stone
That overlays the pile; and, from a bag
All white with flour, the dole of village dames,
10   He drew his scraps and fragments, one by one;
And scanned them with a fixed and serious look
Of idle computation. In the sun,
Upon the second step of that small pile,
Surrounded by those wild unpeopled hills,
He sat, and ate his food in solitude:
And ever, scattered from his palsied hand,
That, still attempting to prevent the waste,
Was baffled still, the crumbs in little showers
Fell on the ground; and the small mountain birds,
20   Not venturing yet to peck their destined meal,
Approached within the length of half his staff.

Him from my childhood have I known; and then
He was so old, he seems not older now;
He travels on, a solitary Man,
So helpless in appearance, that for him
The sauntering Horseman throws not with a slack
And careless hand his alms upon the ground,
But stops, – that he may safely lodge the coin
Within the old Man's hat; nor quits him so,
30   But still, when he has given his horse the rein,
Watches the aged Beggar with a look
Sidelong, and half-reverted. She who tends
The toll-gate, when in summer at her door

She turns her wheel, if on the road she sees
The aged Beggar coming, quits her work,
And lifts the latch for him that he may pass.
The post-boy, when his rattling wheels o'ertake
The aged Beggar in the woody lane,
Shouts to him from behind; and, if thus warned
40   The old Man does not change his course, the boy
Turns with less noisy wheels to the roadside,
And passes gently by, without a curse
Upon his lips, or anger at his heart.

He travels on, a solitary Man;
His age has no companion. On the ground
His eyes are turned, and, as he moves along,
They move along the ground; and, evermore,
Instead of common and habitual sight
Of fields with rural works, of hill and dale,
50   And the blue sky, one little span of earth
Is all his prospect. Thus, from day to day,
Bow-bent, his eyes for ever on the ground,
He plies his weary journey; seeing still,
And seldom knowing that he sees, some straw,
Some scattered leaf, or marks which, in one track,
The nails of cart or chariot-wheel have left
Impressed on the white road, – in the same line,
At distance still the same. Poor Traveller!
His staff trails with him; scarcely do his feet
60   Disturb the summer dust; he is so still
In look and motion, that the cottage curs,
Ere he has passed the door, will turn away,
Weary of barking at him. Boys and girls,
The vacant and the busy, maids and youths,
And urchins newly breeched – all pass him by:
Him even the slow-paced waggon leaves behind.

But deem not this Man useless – Statesmen! ye
Who are so restless in your wisdom, ye
Who have a broom still ready in your hands

70 To rid the world of nuisances; ye proud,
Heart-swoln, while in your pride ye contemplate
Your talents, power, or wisdom, deem him not
A burden of the earth! 'Tis Nature's law
That none, the meanest of created things,
Of forms created the most vile and brute,
The dullest or most noxious, should exist
Divorced from good – a spirit and pulse of good,
A life and soul, to every mode of being
Inseparably linked. Then be assured

80 That least of all can aught – that ever owned
The heaven-regarding eye and front sublime
Which man is born to – sink, howe'er depressed,
So low as to be scorned without a sin;
Without offence to God cast out of view;
Like the dry remnant of a garden-flower
Whose seeds are shed, or as an implement
Worn out and worthless. While from door to door,
This old Man creeps, the villagers in him
Behold a record which together binds

90 Past deeds and offices of charity,
Else unremembered, and so keeps alive
The kindly mood in hearts which lapse of years,
And that half-wisdom half-experience gives,
Make slow to feel, and by sure steps resign
To selfishness and cold oblivious cares.
Among the farms and solitary huts,
Hamlets and thinly-scattered villages,
Where'er the aged Beggar takes his rounds,
The mild necessity of use compels

100 To acts of love; and habit does the work
Of reason; yet prepares that after-joy
Which reason cherishes. And thus the soul,
By that sweet taste of pleasure unpursued,
Doth find herself insensibly disposed
To virtue and true goodness. Some there are,
By their good works exalted, lofty minds
And meditative, authors of delight

And happiness, which to the end of time
Will live, and spread, and kindle: even such minds
110 In childhood, from this solitary Being,
Or from like wanderer, haply have received
(A thing more precious far than all that books
Or the solicitudes of love can do!)
That first mild touch of sympathy and thought,
In which they found their kindred with a world
Where want and sorrow were. The easy man
Who sits at his own door, – and, like the pear
That overhangs his head from the green wall,
Feeds in the sunshine; the robust and young,
120 The prosperous and unthinking, they who live
Sheltered, and flourish in a little grove
Of their own kindred; – all behold in him
A silent monitor, which on their minds
Must needs impress a transitory thought
Of self-congratulation, to the heart
Of each recalling his peculiar boons,
His charters and exemptions; and, perchance,
Though he to no one give the fortitude
And circumspection needful to preserve
130 His present blessings, and to husband up
The respite of the season, he, at least,
And 'tis no vulgar service, makes them felt.

Yet further. – Many, I believe, there are
Who live a life of virtuous decency,
Men who can hear the Decalogue and feel
No self-reproach; who of the moral law
Established in the land where they abide
Are strict observers; and not negligent
In acts of love to those with whom they dwell,
140 Their kindred, and the children of their blood.
Praise be to such, and to their slumbers peace!
– But of the poor man ask, the abject poor;
Go, and demand of him, if there be here
In this cold abstinence from evil deeds,

And these inevitable charities,
Wherewith to satisfy the human soul?
No – man is dear to man; the poorest poor
Long for some moments in a weary life
When they can know and feel that they have been,
150 Themselves, the fathers and the dealers-out
Of some small blessings; have been kind to such
As needed kindness, for this single cause,
That we have all of us one human heart.
– Such pleasure is to one kind Being known,
My neighbour, when with punctual care, each week,
Duly as Friday comes, though pressed herself
By her own wants, she from her store of meal
Takes one unsparing handful for the scrip
Of this old Mendicant, and, from her door
160 Returning with exhilarated heart,
Sits by her fire, and builds her hope in heaven.

Then let him pass, a blessing on his head!
And while in that vast solitude to which
The tide of things has borne him, he appears
To breathe and live but for himself alone,
Unblamed, uninjured, let him bear about
The good which the benignant law of Heaven
Has hung around him: and, while life is his,
Still let him prompt the unlettered villagers
170 To tender offices and pensive thoughts.
– Then let him pass, a blessing on his head!
And, long as he can wander, let him breathe
The freshness of the valleys; let his blood
Struggle with frosty air and winter snows;
And let the chartered wind that sweeps the heath
Beat his grey locks against his withered face.
Reverence the hope whose vital anxiousness
Gives the last human interest to his heart.
May never HOUSE, misnamed of INDUSTRY,
180 Make him a captive! – for that pent-up din,
Those life-consuming sounds that clog the air,

Be his the natural silence of old age!
Let him be free of mountain solitudes;
And have around him, whether heard or not,
The pleasant melody of woodland birds.
Few are his pleasures: if his eyes have now
Been doomed so long to settle upon earth
That not without some effort they behold
The countenance of the horizontal sun,
190   Rising or setting, let the light at least
Find a free entrance to their languid orbs.
And let him, *where* and *when* he will, sit down
Beneath the trees, or on a grassy bank
Of highway side, and with the little birds
Share his chance-gathered meal; and, finally,
As in the eye of Nature he has lived,
So in the eye of Nature let him die!

[*Fragments from the Alfoxden Note-Book (1)*]

I

        there would he stand
In the still covert of some [lonesome?] rock,
Or gaze upon the moon until its light
Fell like a strain of music on his soul
And seemed to sink into his very heart.

II

        Why is it we feel
So little for each other, but for this,
That we with nature have no sympathy,
Or with such things as have no power to hold
Articulate language?

———————

And never for each other shall we feel
As we may feel, till we have sympathy
With nature in her forms inanimate,

With objects such as have no power to hold
Articulate language. In all forms of things
There is a mind

III
Of unknown modes of being which on earth,
Or in the heavens, or in the heavens and earth
Exist by mighty combinations, bound
Together by a link, and with a soul
Which makes all one.

                             To gaze
On that green hill and on those scattered trees
And feel a pleasant consciousness of life
In the impression of that loveliness
Until the sweet sensation called the mind
Into itself, by image from without
Unvisited, and all her reflex powers
Wrapped in a still dream [?of] forgetfulness.

I lived without the knowledge that I lived
Then by those beauteous forms brought back again
To lose myself again as if my life
Did ebb and flow with a strange mystery.

To My Sister

It is the first mild day of March:
Each minute sweeter than before,
The redbreast sings from the tall larch
That stands beside our door.

There is a blessing in the air,
Which seems a sense of joy to yield
To the bare trees, and mountains bare,
And grass in the green field.

My sister! ('tis a wish of mine)
10 Now that our morning meal is done,
Make haste, your morning task resign;
Come forth and feel the sun.

Edward will come with you; – and, pray,
Put on with speed your woodland dress;
And bring no book: for this one day
We'll give to idleness.

No joyless forms shall regulate
Out living calendar:
We from today, my Friend, will date
20 The opening of the year.

Love, now a universal birth,
From heart to heart is stealing,
From earth to man, from man to earth:
– It is the hour of feeling.

One moment now may give us more
Than years of toiling reason:
Our minds shall drink at every pore
The spirit of the season.

Some silent laws our hearts will make,
30 Which they shall long obey:
We for the year to come may take
Our temper from today.

And from the blessed power that rolls
About, below, above,
We'll frame the measure of our souls:
They shall be tuned to love.

Then come, my Sister! come, I pray,
With speed put on your woodland dress;
And bring no book: for this one day
40 We'll give to idleness.

Goody Blake and Harry Gill

A TRUE STORY

Oh! what's the matter? what's the matter?
What is't that ails young Harry Gill?
That evermore his teeth they chatter,
Chatter, chatter, chatter still!
Of waistcoats Harry has no lack,
Good duffle grey, and flannel fine;
He has a blanket on his back,
And coats enough to smother nine.

In March, December, and in July,
10　'Tis all the same with Harry Gill;
The neighbours tell, and tell you truly,
His teeth they chatter, chatter still.
At night, at morning, and at noon,
'Tis all the same with Harry Gill;
Beneath the sun, beneath the moon,
His teeth they chatter, chatter still!

Young Harry was a lusty drover,
And who so stout of limb as he?
His cheeks were red as ruddy clover;
20　His voice was like the voice of three.
Old Goody Blake was old and poor;
Ill fed she was, and thinly clad;
And any man who passed her door
Might see how poor a hut she had.

All day she spun in her poor dwelling:
And then her three hours' work at night,
Alas! 'twas hardly worth the telling,
It would not pay for candle-light.
Remote from sheltered village-green,
30　On a hill's northern side she dwelt,
Where from sea-blasts the hawthorns lean,
And hoary dews are slow to melt.

By the same fire to boil their pottage,
Two poor old Dames, as I have known,
Will often live in one small cottage;
But she, poor Woman! housed alone.
'Twas well enough, when summer came,
The long, warm, lightsome summer-day,
Then at her door the *canty* Dame
40 Would sit, as any linnet, gay.

But when the ice our streams did fetter,
Oh then how her old bones would shake!
You would have said, if you had met her,
'Twas a hard time for Goody Blake.
Her evenings then were dull and dead:
Sad case it was, as you may think,
For very cold to go to bed;
And then for cold not sleep a wink.

O joy for her! whene'er in winter
50 The winds at night had made a rout;
And scattered many a lusty splinter
And many a rotten bough about.
Yet never had she, well or sick,
As every man who knew her says,
A pile beforehand, turf or stick,
Enough to warm her for three days.

Now, when the frost was past enduring,
And made her poor old bones to ache,
Could any thing be more alluring
60 Than an old hedge to Goody Blake?
And, now and then, it must be said,
When her old bones were cold and chill,
She left her fire, or left her bed,
To seek the hedge of Harry Gill.

Now Harry he had long suspected
This trespass of old Goody Blake;

And vowed that she should be detected –
That he on her would vengeance take.
And oft from his warm fire he'd go,
70 And to the fields his road would take;
And there, at night, in frost and snow,
He watched to seize old Goody Blake.

And once, behind a rick of barley,
Thus looking out did Harry stand:
The moon was full and shining clearly,
And crisp with frost the stubble land.
– He hears a noise – he's all awake –
Again? – on tip-toe down the hill
He softly creeps – 'tis Goody Blake;
80 She's at the hedge of Harry Gill!

Right glad was he when he beheld her:
Stick after stick did Goody pull:
He stood behind a bush of elder,
Till she had filled her apron full.
When with her load she turned about,
The by-way back again to take;
He started forward, with a shout,
And sprang upon poor Goody Blake.

And fiercely by the arm he took her,
90 And by the arm he held her fast,
And fiercely by the arm he shook her,
And cried, 'I've caught you then at last!'
Then Goody, who had nothing said,
Her bundle from her lap let fall;
And, kneeling on the sticks, she prayed
To God that is the judge of all.

She prayed, her withered hand uprearing,
While Harry held her by the arm –
'God! who art never out of hearing,

100 O may he never more be warm!'
The cold, cold moon above her head,
Thus on her knees did Goody pray;
Young Harry heard what she had said:
And icy cold he turned away.

He went complaining all the morrow
That he was cold and very chill:
His face was gloom, his heart was sorrow,
Alas! that day for Harry Gill!
That day he wore a riding-coat,
110 But not a whit the warmer he:
Another was on Thursday brought,
And ere the Sabbath he had three.

'Twas all in vain, a useless matter,
And blankets were about him pinned;
Yet still his jaws and teeth they clatter,
Like a loose casement in the wind.
And Harry's flesh it fell away;
And all who see him say, 'tis plain,
That, live as long as live he may,
120 He never will be warm again.

No word to any man he utters,
A-bed or up, to young or old;
But ever to himself he mutters,
'Poor Harry Gill is very cold.'
A-bed or up, by night or day;
His teeth they chatter, chatter still.
Now think, ye farmers all, I pray,
Of Goody Blake and Harry Gill!

The Complaint of a Forsaken Indian Woman

[When a Northern Indian, from sickness, is unable to continue his journey with his companions, he is left behind, covered over with deer-skins, and is supplied with water, food, and fuel, if the situation of the place will afford it. He is informed of the track which his companions intend to pursue, and if he be unable to follow, or overtake them, he perishes alone in the desert, unless he should have the good fortune to fall in with some other tribes of Indians. The females are equally, or still more, exposed to the same fate. See that very interesting work Hearne's 'Journey from Hudson's Bay to the Northern Ocean'. In the high northern latitudes, as the same writer informs us, when the northern lights vary their position in the air, they make a rustling and a crackling noise, as alluded to in the following poem.]

I

Before I see another day,
Oh let my body die away!
In sleep I heard the northern gleams;
The stars, they were among my dreams;
In rustling conflict through the skies,
I heard, I saw the flashes drive,
And yet they are upon my eyes,
And yet I am alive;
Before I see another day,
10 Oh let my body die away!

II

My fire is dead: it knew no pain;
Yet is it dead, and I remain:
All stiff with ice the ashes lie;
And they are dead, and I will die.
When I was well, I wished to live,
For clothes, for warmth, for food, and fire;
But they to me no joy can give,
No pleasure now, and no desire.

Then here contented will I lie!
20 Alone, I cannot fear to die.

III
Alas! ye might have dragged me on
Another day, a single one!
Too soon I yielded to despair;
Why did ye listen to my prayer?
When ye were gone my limbs were stronger;
And oh, how grievously I rue,
That, afterwards, a little longer,
My friends, I did not follow you!
For strong and without pain I lay,
30 Dear friends, when ye were gone away.

IV
My Child! they gave thee to another,
A woman who was not thy mother.
When from my arms my Babe they took,
On me how strangely did he look!
Through his whole body something ran,
A most strange working did I see;
– As if he strove to be a man,
That he might pull the sledge for me:
And then he stretched his arms, how wild!
40 Oh mercy! like a helpless child.

V
My little joy! my little pride!
In two days more I must have died.
Then do not weep and grieve for me;
I feel I must have died with thee.
O wind, that o'er my head art flying
The way my friends their course did bend,
I should not feel the pain of dying,
Could I with thee a message send;
Too soon, my friends, ye went away;
50 For I had many things to say.

VI

I'll follow you across the snow;
Ye travel heavily and slow;
In spite of all my weary pain
I'll look upon your tents again.
– My fire is dead, and snowy white
The water which beside it stood:
The wolf has come to me tonight,
And he has stolen away my food.
For ever left alone am I;
60 Then wherefore should I fear to die?

VII

Young as I am, my course is run,
I shall not see another sun;
I cannot lift my limbs to know
If they have any life or no.
My poor forsaken Child, if I
For once could have thee close to me,
With happy heart I then would die,
And my last thought would happy be;
But thou, dear Babe, art far away,
70 Nor shall I see another day.

Her Eyes Are Wild

I

Her eyes are wild, her head is bare,
The sun has burnt her coal-black hair;
Her eyebrows have a rusty stain,
And she came far from over the main.
She has a baby on her arm,
Or else she were alone:
And underneath the hay-stack warm,
And on the greenwood stone,
She talked and sung the woods among,
10 And it was in the English tongue.

II

'Sweet babe! they say that I am mad,
But nay, my heart is far too glad;
And I am happy when I sing
Full many a sad and doleful thing:
Then, lovely baby, do not fear!
I pray thee have no fear of me;
But safe as in a cradle, here
My lovely baby! thou shalt be:
To thee I know too much I owe;
20 I cannot work thee any woe.

III

'A fire was once within my brain;
And in my head a dull, dull pain;
And fiendish faces, one, two, three,
Hung at my breast, and pulled at me;
But then there came a sight of joy;
It came at once to do me good;
I waked, and saw my little boy,
My little boy of flesh and blood;
Oh joy for me that sight to see!
30 For he was here, and only he.

IV

'Suck, little babe, oh suck again!
It cools my blood; it cools my brain;
Thy lips I feel them, baby! they
Draw from my heart the pain away.
Oh! press me with thy little hand;
It loosens something at my chest;
About that tight and deadly band
I feel thy little fingers prest.
The breeze I see is in the tree:
40 It comes to cool my babe and me.

V

'Oh! love me, love me, little boy!
Thou art thy mother's only joy;
And do not dread the waves below,
When o'er the sea-rock's edge we go;
The high crag cannot work me harm,
Nor leaping torrents when they howl;
The babe I carry on my arm,
He saves for me my precious soul;
Then happy lie; for blest am I;
50 Without me my sweet babe would die.

VI

'Then do not fear, my boy! for thee
Bold as a lion will I be;
And I will always be thy guide,
Through hollow snows and rivers wide.
I'll build an Indian bower; I know
The leaves that make the softest bed:
And, if from me thou wilt not go,
But still be true till I am dead,
My pretty thing! then thou shalt sing
60 As merry as the birds in spring.

VII

'Thy father cares not for my breast,
'Tis thine, sweet baby, there to rest;
'Tis all thine own! – and, if its hue
Be changed, that was so fair to view,
'Tis fair enough for thee, my dove!
My beauty, little child, is flown,
But thou wilt live with me in love;
And what if my poor cheek be brown?
'Tis well for me, thou canst not see
70 How pale and wan it else would be.

VIII

'Dread not their taunts, my little Life;
I am thy father's wedded wife;
And underneath the spreading tree
We two will live in honesty.
If his sweet boy he could forsake,
With me he never would have stayed:
From him no harm my babe can take;
But he, poor man! is wretched made;
And every day we two will pray
80 For him that's gone and far away.

IX

'I'll teach my boy the sweetest things:
I'll teach him how the owlet sings.
My little babe! thy lips are still,
And thou hast almost sucked thy fill.
– Where art thou gone, my own dear child?
What wicked looks are those I see?
Alas! alas! that look so wild,
It never, never came from me:
If thou art mad, my pretty lad,
90 Then I must be for ever sad.

X

'Oh! smile on me, my little lamb!
For I thy own dear mother am:
My love for thee has well been tried:
I've sought thy father far and wide.
I know the poisons of the shade;
I know the earth-nuts fit for food:
Then, pretty dear, be not afraid:
We'll find thy father in the wood.
Now laugh and be gay, to the woods away!
100 And there, my babe, we'll live for aye.'

The Idiot Boy

'Tis eight o'clock, – a clear March night,
The moon is up, – the sky is blue,
The owlet, in the moonlight air,
Shouts from nobody knows where;
He lengthens out his lonely shout,
Halloo! halloo! a long halloo!

– Why bustle thus about your door,
What means this bustle, Betty Foy?
Why are you in this mighty fret?
10 And why on horseback have you set
Him whom you love, your Idiot Boy?

Scarcely a soul is out of bed;
Good Betty, put him down again;
His lips with joy they burr at you;
But, Betty! what has he to do
With stirrup, saddle, or with rein?

But Betty's bent on her intent;
For her good neighbour, Susan Gale,
Old Susan, she who dwells alone,
20 Is sick, and makes a piteous moan,
As if her very life would fail.

There's not a house within a mile,
No hand to help them in distress;
Old Susan lies a-bed in pain,
And sorely puzzled are the twain,
For what she ails they cannot guess.

And Betty's husband's at the wood,
Where by the week he doth abide,
A woodman in the distant vale;

30   There's none to help poor Susan Gale;
      What must be done? what will betide?

      And Betty from the lane has fetched
      Her Pony, that is mild and good;
      Whether he be in joy or pain,
      Feeding at will along the lane,
      Or bringing fagots from the wood.

      And he is all in travelling trim, –
      And, by the moonlight, Betty Foy
      Has on the well-girt saddle set
40   (The like was never heard of yet)
      Him whom she loves, her Idiot Boy.

      And he must post without delay
      Across the bridge and through the dale,
      And by the church, and o'er the down,
      To bring a Doctor from the town,
      Or she will die, old Susan Gale.

      There is no need of boot or spur,
      There is no need of whip or wand;
      For Johnny has his holly-bough,
50   And with a *hurly-burly* now
      He shakes the green bough in his hand.

      And Betty o'er and o'er has told
      The Boy, who is her best delight,
      Both what to follow, what to shun,
      What do, and what to leave undone,
      How turn to left, and how to right.

      And Betty's most especial charge,
      Was, 'Johnny! Johnny! mind that you
      Come home again, nor stop at all, –
60   Come home again, whate'er befall,
      My Johnny, do, I pray you, do.'

To this did Johnny answer make,
Both with his head and with his hand,
And proudly shook the bridle too;
And then! his words were not a few,
Which Betty well could understand.

And now that Johnny is just going,
Though Betty's in a mighty flurry,
She gently pats the Pony's side,
70   On which her Idiot Boy must ride,
And seems no longer in a hurry.

But when the Pony moved his legs,
Oh! then for the poor Idiot Boy!
For joy he cannot hold the bridle,
For joy his head and heels are idle,
He's idle all for very joy.

And while the Pony moves his legs,
In Johnny's left hand you may see
The green bough motionless and dead:
80   The Moon that shines above his head
Is not more still and mute than he.

His heart it was so full of glee
That, till full fifty yards were gone,
He quite forgot his holly whip,
And all his skill in horsemanship:
Oh! happy, happy, happy John.

And while the Mother, at the door,
Stands fixed, her face with joy o'erflows,
Proud of herself, and proud of him,
90   She sees him in his travelling trim,
How quietly her Johnny goes.

The silence of her Idiot Boy,
What hopes it sends to Betty's heart!

He's at the guide-post – he turns right;
She watches till he's out of sight,
And Betty will not then depart.

Burr, burr – now Johnny's lips they burr,
As loud as any mill, or near it;
Meek as a lamb the Pony moves,
100 And Johnny makes the noise he loves,
And Betty listens, glad to hear it.

Away she hies to Susan Gale:
Her Messenger's in merry tune;
The owlets hoot, the owlets curr,
And Johnny's lips they burr, burr, burr,
As on he goes beneath the moon.

His steed and he right well agree;
For of this Pony there's a rumour,
That, should he lose his eyes and ears,
110 And should he live a thousand years,
He never will be out of humour.

But then he is a horse that thinks!
And when he thinks, his pace is slack;
Now, though he knows poor Johnny well,
Yet, for his life, he cannot tell
What he has got upon his back.

So through the moonlight lanes they go,
And far into the moonlight dale,
And by the church, and o'er the down,
120 To bring a Doctor from the town,
To comfort poor old Susan Gale.

And Betty, now at Susan's side,
Is in the middle of her story,
What speedy help her Boy will bring,
With many a most diverting thing,
Of Johnny's wit, and Johnny's glory.

And Betty, still at Susan's side,
By this time is not quite so flurried:
Demure with porringer and plate
130   She sits, as if in Susan's fate
Her life and soul were buried.

But Betty, poor good woman! she,
You plainly in her face may read it,
Could lend out of that moment's store
Five years of happiness or more
To any that might need it.

But yet I guess that now and then
With Betty all was not so well;
And to the road she turns her ears,
140   And thence full many a sound she hears,
Which she to Susan will not tell.

Poor Susan moans, poor Susan groans;
'As sure as there's a moon in heaven,'
Cries Betty, 'he'll be back again;
They'll both be here – 'tis almost ten –
Both will be here before eleven.'

Poor Susan moans, poor Susan groans;
The clock gives warning for eleven;
'Tis on the stroke – 'He must be near,'
150   Quoth Betty, 'and will soon be here,
As sure as there's a moon in heaven.'

The clock is on the stroke of twelve,
And Johnny is not yet in sight:
– The Moon's in heaven, as Betty sees,
But Betty is not quite at ease;
And Susan has a dreadful night.

And Betty, half an hour ago,
On Johnny vile reflections cast:

'A little idle sauntering Thing!'
160 With other names, an endless string;
But now that time is gone and past.

And Betty's drooping at the heart,
That happy time all past and gone,
'How can it be he is so late?
The Doctor, he has made him wait;
Susan! they'll both be here anon.'

And Susan's growing worse and worse,
And Betty's in a sad *quandary*;
And then there's nobody to say
170 If she must go, or she must stay!
– She's in a sad *quandary*.

The clock is on the stroke of one;
But neither Doctor nor his Guide
Appears along the moonlight road;
There's neither horse nor man abroad,
And Betty's still at Susan's side.

And Susan now begins to fear
Of sad mischances not a few,
That Johnny may perhaps be drowned;
180 Or lost, perhaps, and never found;
Which they must both for ever rue.

She prefaced half a hint of this
With, 'God forbid it should be true!'
At the first word that Susan said
Cried Betty, rising from the bed,
'Susan, I'd gladly stay with you.

'I must be gone, I must away:
Consider, Johnny's but half-wise;
Susan, we must take care of him,
190 If he is hurt in life or limb' –
'Oh God forbid!' poor Susan cries.

'What can I do?' says Betty, going,
'What can I do to ease your pain?
Good Susan tell me, and I'll stay;
I fear you're in a dreadful way,
But I shall soon be back again.'

'Nay, Betty, go! good Betty, go!
There's nothing that can ease my pain.'
Then off she hies; but with a prayer
200   That God poor Susan's life would spare,
Till she comes back again.

So, through the moonlight lane she goes,
And far into the moonlight dale;
And how she ran, and how she walked,
And all that to herself she talked,
Would surely be a tedious tale.

In high and low, above, below,
In great and small, in round and square,
In tree and tower was Johnny seen,
210   In bush and brake, in black and green;
'Twas Johnny, Johnny, everywhere.

And while she crossed the bridge, there came
A thought with which her heart is sore –
Johnny perhaps his horse forsook,
To hunt the moon within the brook,
And never will be heard of more.

Now is she high upon the down,
Alone amid a prospect wide;
There's neither Johnny nor his Horse
220   Among the fern or in the gorse;
There's neither Doctor nor his Guide.

'Oh saints! what is become of him?
Perhaps he's climbed into an oak,

Where he will stay till he is dead;
Or sadly he has been misled,
And joined the wandering gypsy-folk.

'Or him that wicked Pony's carried
To the dark cave, the goblin's hall;
Or in the castle he's pursuing
230   Among the ghosts his own undoing;
Or playing with the waterfall.'

At poor old Susan then she railed,
While to the town she posts away;
'If Susan had not been so ill,
Alas! I should have had him still,
My Johnny, till my dying day.'

Poor Betty, in this sad distemper,
The Doctor's self could hardly spare:
Unworthy things she talked, and wild;
240   Even he, of cattle the most mild,
The Pony had his share.

But now she's fairly in the town,
And to the Doctor's door she hies;
'Tis silence all on every side;
The town so long, the town so wide,
Is silent as the skies.

And now she's at the Doctor's door,
She lifts the knocker, rap, rap, rap;
The Doctor at the casement shows
250   His glimmering eyes that peep and doze!
And one hand rubs his old night-cap.

'Oh Doctor! Doctor! where's my Johnny?'
'I'm here, what is 't you want with me?'
'Oh Sir! you know I'm Betty Foy,
And I have lost my poor dear Boy,
You know him – him you often see;

'He's not so wise as some folks be:'
'The devil take his wisdom!' said
The Doctor, looking somewhat grim,
260 'What, Woman! should I know of him?'
And, grumbling, he went back to bed!

'O woe is me! O woe is me!
Here will I die; here will I die;
I thought to find my lost one here,
But he is neither far nor near,
Oh! what a wretched Mother I!'

She stops, she stands, she looks about;
Which way to turn she cannot tell.
Poor Betty! it would ease her pain
270 If she had heart to knock again;
– The clock strikes three – a dismal knell!

Then up along the town she hies,
No wonder if her senses fail;
This piteous news so much it shocked her,
She quite forgot to send the Doctor,
To comfort poor old Susan Gale.

And now she's high upon the down,
And she can see a mile of road:
'O cruel! I'm almost threescore;
280 Such night as this was ne'er before,
There's not a single soul abroad.'

She listens, but she cannot hear
The foot of horse, the voice of man;
The streams with softest sound are flowing,
The grass you almost hear it growing,
You hear it now, if e'er you can.

The owlets through the long blue night
Are shouting to each other still:

Fond lovers! yet not quite hob nob,
290   They lengthen out the tremulous sob,
That echoes far from hill to hill.

Poor Betty now has lost all hope,
Her thoughts àre bent on deadly sin,
A green-grown pond she just has past,
And from the brink she hurries fast,
Lest she should drown herself therein.

And now she sits her down and weeps;
Such tears she never shed before;
'Oh dear, dear Pony! my sweet joy!
300   Oh carry back my Idiot Boy!
And we will ne'er o'erload thee more.'

A thought is come into her head:
The Pony he is mild and good,
And we have always used him well;
Perhaps he's gone along the dell,
And carried Johnny to the wood.

Then up she springs as if on wings;
She thinks no more of deadly sin;
If Betty fifty ponds should see,
310   The last of all her thoughts would be
To drown herself therein.

Oh Reader! now that I might tell
What Johnny and his Horse are doing!
What they've been doing all this time,
Oh could I put it into rhyme,
A most delightful tale pursuing!

Perhaps, and no unlikely thought!
He with his Pony now doth roam
The cliffs and peaks so high that are,
320   To lay his hands upon a star,
And in his pocket bring it home.

Perhaps he's turned himself about,
His face unto his horse's tail,
And, still and mute, in wonder lost,
All silent as a horseman-ghost,
He travels slowly down the vale.

And now, perhaps, is hunting sheep,
A fierce and dreadful hunter he;
Yon valley, now so trim and green,
330   In five months' time, should he be seen,
A desert wilderness will be!

Perhaps, with head and heels on fire,
And like the very soul of evil,
He's galloping away, away,
And so will gallop on for aye,
The bane of all that dread the devil!

I to the Muses have been bound
These fourteen years, by strong indentures:
O gentle Muses! let me tell
340   But half of what to him befell;
He surely met with strange adventures.

O gentle Muses! is this kind?
Why will ye thus my suit repel?
Why of your further aid bereave me?
And can ye thus unfriended leave me;
Ye Muses! whom I love so well?

Who's yon, that, near the waterfall,
Which thunders down with headlong force,
Beneath the moon, yet shining fair,
350   As careless as if nothing were,
Sits upright on a feeding horse?

Unto his horse – there feeding free,
He seems, I think, the rein to give;

Of moon or stars he takes no heed;
Of such we in romances read:
— 'Tis Johnny! Johnny! as I live.

And that's the very Pony, too!
Where is she, where is Betty Foy?
She hardly can sustain her fears;
360   The roaring waterfall she hears,
And cannot find her Idiot Boy.

Your Pony's worth his weight in gold:
Then calm your terrors, Betty Foy!
She's coming from among the trees,
And now all full in view she sees
Him whom she loves, her Idiot Boy.

And Betty sees the Pony too:
Why stand you thus, good Betty Foy?
It is no goblin, 'tis no ghost,
370   'Tis he whom you so long have lost,
He whom you love, your Idiot Boy.

She looks again — her arms are up —
She screams — she cannot move for joy;
She darts, as with a torrent's force,
She almost has o'erturned the Horse,
And fast she holds her Idiot Boy.

And Johnny burrs, and laughs aloud;
Whether in cunning or in joy
I cannot tell; but while he laughs,
380   Betty a drunken pleasure quaffs
To hear again her Idiot Boy.

And now she's at the Pony's tail,
And now is at the Pony's head, —
On that side now, and now on this;
And, almost stifled with her bliss,
A few sad tears does Betty shed.

She kisses o'er and o'er again
Him whom she loves, her Idiot Boy;
She's happy here, is happy there,
390 She is uneasy everywhere;
Her limbs are all alive with joy.

She pats the Pony, where or when
She knows not, happy Betty Foy!
The little Pony glad may be,
But he is milder far than she,
You hardly can perceive his joy.

'Oh! Johnny, never mind the Doctor;
You've done your best, and that is all:'
She took the reins, when this was said,
400 And gently turned the Pony's head
From the loud waterfall.

By this the stars were almost gone,
The moon was setting on the hill,
So pale you scarcely looked at her:
The little birds began to stir,
Though yet their tongues were still.

The Pony, Betty, and her Boy,
Wind slowly through the woody dale;
And who is she, betimes abroad,
410 That hobbles up the steep rough road?
Who is it, but old Susan Gale?

Long time lay Susan lost in thought;
And many dreadful fears beset her,
Both for her Messenger and Nurse;
And, as her mind grew worse and worse,
Her body – it grew better.

She turned, she tossed herself in bed,
On all sides doubts and terrors met her;

Point after point did she discuss;
420 And, while her mind was fighting thus,
Her body still grew better.

'Alas! what is become of them?
These fears can never be endured;
I'll to the wood.' – The word scarce said,
Did Susan rise up from her bed,
As if by magic cured.

Away she goes up hill and down,
And to the wood at length is come;
She spies her Friends, she shouts a greeting;
430 Oh me! it is a merry meeting
As ever was in Christendom.

The owls have hardly sung their last,
While our four travellers homeward wend;
The owls have hooted all night long,
And with the owls began my song,
And with the owls must end.

For while they all were travelling home,
Cried Betty, 'Tell us, Johnny, do,
Where all this long night you have been,
440 What you have heard, what you have seen:
And, Johnny, mind you tell us true.'

Now Johnny all night long had heard
The owls in tuneful concert strive;
No doubt too he the moon had seen;
For in the moonlight he had been
From eight o'clock till five.

And thus, to Betty's question, he
Made answer, like a traveller bold,
(His very words I give to you,)

450 'The cocks did crow to-whoo, to-whoo,
And the sun did shine so cold!'
– Thus answered Johnny in his glory,
And that was all his travel's story.

The Last of the Flock

I

In distant countries have I been,
And yet I have not often seen
A healthy man, a man full grown,
Weep in the public roads, alone.
But such a one, on English ground,
And in the broad highway, I met;
Along the broad highway he came,
His cheeks with tears were wet:
Sturdy he seemed, though he was sad;
10 And in his arms a Lamb he had.

II

He saw me, and he turned aside,
As if he wished himself to hide:
And with his coat did then essay
To wipe those briny tears away.
I followed him, and said, 'My friend,
What ails you? wherefore weep you so?'
– 'Shame on me, Sir! this lusty Lamb,
He makes my tears to flow.
Today I fetched him from the rock;
20 He is the last of all my flock.

III

'When I was young, a single man,
And after youthful follies ran,
Though little given to care and thought,
Yet, so it was, an ewe I bought;
And other sheep from her I raised,

As healthy sheep as you might see;
And then I married, and was rich
As I could wish to be;
Of sheep I numbered a full score,
30 And every year increased my store.

IV

'Year after year my stock it grew;
And from this one, this single ewe,
Full fifty comely sheep I raised,
As fine a flock as ever grazed!
Upon the Quantock hills they fed;
They throve, and we at home did thrive:
– This lusty Lamb of all my store
Is all that is alive;
And now I care not if we die,
40 And perish all of poverty.

V

'Six Children, Sir! had I to feed;
Hard labour in a time of need!
My pride was tamed, and in our grief
I of the Parish asked relief.
They said, I was a wealthy man;
My sheep upon the uplands fed,
And it was fit that thence I took
Whereof to buy us bread.
"Do this: how can we give to you,"
50 They cried, "what to the poor is due?"

VI

'I sold a sheep, as they had said,
And bought my little children bread,
And they were healthy with their food;
For me – it never did me good.
A woeful time it was for me,
To see the end of all my gains,
The pretty flock which I had reared

With all my care and pains,
To see it melt like snow away –
60 For me it was a woeful day.

VII

'Another still! and still another!
A little lamb, and then its mother!
It was a vein that never stopped –
Like blood-drops from my heart they dropped.
Till thirty were not left alive
They dwindled, dwindled, one by one;
And I may say, that many a time
I wished they all were gone –
Reckless of what might come at last
70 Were but the bitter struggle past.

VIII

'To wicked deeds I was inclined,
And wicked fancies crossed my mind;
And every man I chanced to see,
I thought he knew some ill of me:
No peace, no comfort could I find,
No ease, within doors or without;
And, crazily and wearily
I went my work about;
And oft was moved to flee from home,
80 And hide my head where wild beasts roam.

IX

'Sir! 'twas a precious flock to me,
As dear as my own children be;
For daily with my growing store
I loved my children more and more.
Alas! it was an evil time;
God cursed me in my sore distress;
I prayed, yet every day I thought
I loved my children less;
And every week, and every day,
90 My flock it seemed to melt away.

X

'They dwindled, Sir, sad sight to see!
From ten to five, from five to three,
A lamb, a wether, and a ewe; –
And then at last from three to two;
And, of my fifty, yesterday
I had but only one:
And here it lies upon my arm,
Alas! and I have none; –
Today I fetched it from the rock;
100 It is the last of all my flock.'

We Are Seven

– A simple Child,
That lightly draws its breath,
And feels its life in every limb,
What should it know of death?

I met a little cottage Girl:
She was eight years old, she said;
Her hair was thick with many a curl
That clustered round her head.

She had a rustic, woodland air,
10 And she was wildly clad:
Her eyes were fair, and very fair;
– Her beauty made me glad.

'Sisters and brothers, little Maid,
How many may you be?'
'How many? Seven in all,' she said,
And wondering looked at me.

'And where are they? I pray you tell.'
She answered, 'Seven are we;
And two of us at Conway dwell,
20 And two are gone to sea.

'Two of us in the church-yard lie,
My sister and my brother;
And, in the church-yard cottage, I
Dwell near them with my mother.'

'You say that two at Conway dwell,
And two are gone to sea,
Yet ye are seven! I pray you tell,
Sweet Maid, how this may be.'

Then did the little Maid reply,
30   'Seven boys and girls are we;
Two of us in the church-yard lie,
Beneath the church-yard tree.'

'You run about, my little Maid,
Your limbs they are alive;
If two are in the church-yard laid,
Then ye are only five.'

'Their graves are green, they may be seen,'
The little Maid replied,
'Twelve steps or more from my mother's door,
40   And they are side by side.

'My stockings there I often knit,
My kerchief there I hem;
And there upon the ground I sit,
And sing a song to them.

'And often after sun-set, Sir,
When it is light and fair,
I take my little porringer,
And eat my supper there.

'The first that died was sister Jane;
50   In bed she moaning lay,
Till God released her of her pain;
And then she went away.

'So in the church-yard she was laid;
And, when the grass was dry,
Together round her grave we played,
My brother John and I.

'And when the ground was white with snow,
And I could run and slide,
My brother John was forced to go,
60 And he lies by her side.'

'How many are you, then,' said I,
'If they two are in heaven?'
Quick was the little Maid's reply,
'O Master! we are seven.'

'But they are dead; those two are dead!
Their spirits are in heaven!'
'Twas throwing words away; for still
The little Maid would have her will,
And said, 'Nay, we are seven!'

Simon Lee, the Old Huntsman

With an incident in which he was concerned.

In the sweet shire of Cardigan,
Not far from pleasant Ivor-hall,
An old Man dwells, a little man, –
'Tis said he once was tall.
Full five-and-thirty years he lived
A running huntsman merry;
And still the centre of his cheek
Is red as a ripe cherry.

No man like him the horn could sound,
10 And hill and valley rang with glee
When Echo bandied, round and round,
The halloo of Simon Lee.

In those proud days, he little cared
For husbandry or tillage;
To blither tasks did Simon rouse
The sleepers of the village.

He all the country could outrun,
Could leave both man and horse behind;
And often, ere the chase was done,
20   He reeled, and was stone-blind.
And still there's something in the world
At which his heart rejoices;
For when the chiming hounds are out,
He dearly loves their voices!

But, oh the heavy change! – bereft
Of health, strength, friends, and kindred, see!
Old Simon to the world is left
In liveried poverty.
His Master's dead, – and no one now
30   Dwells in the Hall of Ivor;
Men, dogs, and horses, all are dead;
He is the sole survivor.

And he is lean and he is sick;
His body, dwindled and awry,
Rests upon ankles swoln and thick;
His legs are thin and dry.
One prop he has, and only one,
His wife, an aged woman,
Lives with him, near the waterfall,
40   Upon the village Common.

Beside their moss-grown hut of clay,
Not twenty paces from the door,
A scrap of land they have, but they
Are poorest of the poor.
This scrap of land he from the heath
Enclosed when he was stronger;

But what to them avails the land
Which he can till no longer?

Oft, working by her Husband's side,
50   Ruth does what Simon cannot do;
For she, with scanty cause for pride,
Is stouter of the two.
And, though you with your utmost skill
From labour could not wean them,
'Tis little, very little – all
That they can do between them.

Few months of life has he in store
As he to you will tell,
For still, the more he works, the more
60   Do his weak ankles swell.
My gentle Reader, I perceive
How patiently you've waited,
And now I fear that you expect
Some tale will be related.

O Reader! had you in your mind
Such stores as silent thought can bring,
O gentle Reader! you would find
A tale in everything.
What more I have to say is short,
70   And you must kindly take it:
It is no tale; but, should you think,
Perhaps a tale you'll make it.

One summer-day I chanced to see
This old Man doing all he could
To unearth the root of an old tree,
A stump of rotten wood.
The mattock tottered in his hand;
So vain was his endeavour,
That at the root of the old tree
80   He might have worked for ever.

'You're overtasked, good Simon Lee,
Give me your tool,' to him I said;
And at the word right gladly he
Received my proffered aid.
I struck, and with a single blow
The tangled root I severed,
At which the poor old Man so long
And vainly had endeavoured.

The tears into his eyes were brought,
90 And thanks and praises seemed to run
So fast out of his heart, I thought
They never would have done.
– I've heard of hearts unkind, kind deeds
With coldness still returning;
Alas! the gratitude of men
Hath oftener left me mourning.

'*A whirl-blast from behind the hill*'

A whirl-blast from behind the hill
Rushed o'er the wood with startling sound;
Then – all at once the air was still,
And showers of hailstones pattered round.
Where leafless oaks towered high above,
I sat within an undergrove
Of tallest hollies, tall and green;
A fairer bower was never seen.
From year to year the spacious floor
10 With withered leaves is covered o'er,
And all the year the bower is green.
But see! where'er the hailstones drop
The withered leaves all skip and hop;
There's not a breeze – no breath of air –
Yet here, and there, and everywhere
Along the floor, beneath the shade
By those embowering hollies made,

The leaves in myriads jump and spring,
As if with pipes and music rare
20   Some Robin Good-fellow were there,
And all those leaves, in festive glee,
Were dancing to the minstrelsy.

The Thorn

I

'There is a Thorn – it looks so old,
In truth, you'd find it hard to say
How it could ever have been young,
It looks so old and grey.
Not higher than a two years' child
It stands erect, this aged Thorn;
No leaves it has, no prickly points;
It is a mass of knotted joints,
A wretched thing forlorn.
10   It stands erect, and like a stone
With lichens is it overgrown.

II

'Like rock or stone, it is o'ergrown,
With lichens to the very top,
And hung with heavy tufts of moss,
A melancholy crop:
Up from the earth these mosses creep,
And this poor Thorn they clasp it round
So close, you'd say that they are bent
With plain and manifest intent
20   To drag it to the ground;
And all have joined in one endeavour
To bury this poor Thorn for ever.

III

'High on a mountain's highest ridge,
Where oft the stormy winter gale

Cuts like a scythe, while through the clouds
It sweeps from vale to vale;
Not five yards from the mountain path,
This Thorn you on your left espy;
And to the left, three yards beyond,
30 You see a little muddy pond
Of water – never dry
Though but of compass small, and bare
To thirsty suns and parching air.

IV

'And, close beside this aged Thorn,
There is a fresh and lovely sight,
A beauteous heap, a hill of moss,
Just half a foot in height.
All lovely colours there you see,
All colours that were ever seen;
40 And mossy network too is there,
As if by hand of lady fair
The work had woven been;
And cups, the darlings of the eye,
So deep is their vermillion dye.

V

'Ah me! what lovely tints are there
Of olive green and scarlet bright,
In spikes, in branches, and in stars,
Green, red, and pearly white!
This heap of earth o'ergrown with moss,
50 Which close beside the Thorn you see,
So fresh in all its beauteous dyes,
Is like an infant's grave in size,
As like as like can be:
But never, never anywhere,
An infant's grave was half so fair.

VI

'Now would you see this aged Thorn,
This pond, and beauteous hill of moss,
You must take care and choose your time
The mountain when to cross.
60 For oft there sits between the heap,
So like an infant's grave in size,
And that same pond of which I spoke,
A Woman in a scarlet cloak,
And to herself she cries,
"Oh misery! oh misery!
Oh woe is me! oh misery!"

VII

'At all times of the day and night
This wretched Woman thither goes;
And she is known to every star,
70 And every wind that blows;
And there, beside the Thorn, she sits
When the blue daylight's in the skies,
And when the whirlwind's on the hill,
Or frosty air is keen and still,
And to herself she cries,
"Oh misery! oh misery!
Oh woe is me! oh misery!"'

VIII

'Now wherefore, thus, by day and night,
In rain, in tempest, and in snow,
80 Thus to the dreary mountain-top
Does this poor Woman go?
And why sits she beside the Thorn
When the blue daylight's in the sky
Or when the whirlwind's on the hill,
Or frosty air is keen and still,
And wherefore does she cry? –
O wherefore? wherefore? tell me why
Does she repeat that doleful cry?'

IX

'I cannot tell; I wish I could;
90 For the true reason no one knows:
But would you gladly view the spot,
The spot to which she goes;
The hillock like an infant's grave,
The pond – and Thorn, so old and grey;
Pass by her door – 'tis seldom shut –
And, if you see her in her hut –
Then to the spot away!
I never heard of such as dare
Approach the spot when she is there.'

X

100 'But wherefore to the mountain-top
Can this unhappy Woman go,
Whatever star is in the skies,
Whatever wind may blow?'
'Full twenty years are past and gone
Since she (her name is Martha Ray)
Gave with a maiden's true good-will
Her company to Stephen Hill;
And she was blithe and gay,
While friends and kindred all approved
110 Of him whom tenderly she loved.

XI

'And they had fixed the wedding day,
The morning that must wed them both;
But Stephen to another Maid
Had sworn another oath;
And, with this other Maid, to church
Unthinking Stephen went –
Poor Martha! on that woeful day
A pang of pitiless dismay
Into her soul was sent;
120 A fire was kindled in her breast,
Which might not burn itself to rest.

XII

'They say, full six months after this,
While yet the summer leaves were green,
She to the mountain-top would go,
And there was often seen.
What could she seek? – or wish to hide?
Her state to any eye was plain;
She was with child, and she was mad;
Yet often was she sober sad
130 From her exceeding pain.
O guilty Father – would that death
Had saved him from that breach of faith!

XIII

'Sad case for such a brain to hold
Communion with a stirring child!
Sad case, as you may think, for one
Who had a brain so wild!
Last Christmas-eve we talked of this,
And grey-haired Wilfred of the glen
Held that the unborn infant wrought
140 About its mother's heart, and brought
Her senses back again:
And, when at last her time drew near,
Her looks were calm, her senses clear.

XIV

'More know I not, I wish I did,
And it should all be told to you;
For what became of this poor child
No mortal ever knew;
Nay – if a child to her was born
No earthly tongue could ever tell;
150 And if 'twas born alive or dead,
Far less could this with proof be said;
But some remember well,
That Martha Ray about this time
Would up the mountain often climb.

XV

'And all that winter, when at night
The wind blew from the mountain-peak,
'Twas worth your while, though in the dark,
The churchyard path to seek:
For many a time and oft were heard
160 Cries coming from the mountain head:
Some plainly living voices were;
And others, I've heard many swear,
Were voices of the dead:
I cannot think, whate'er they say,
They had to do with Martha Ray.

XVI

'But that she goes to this old Thorn,
The Thorn which I described to you,
And there sits in a scarlet cloak,
I will be sworn is true.
170 For one day with my telescope,
To view the ocean wide and bright,
When to this country first I came,
Ere I had heard of Martha's name,
I climbed the mountain's height: –
A storm came on, and I could see
No object higher than my knee.

XVII

''Twas mist and rain, and storm and rain:
No screen, no fence could I discover;
And then the wind! in sooth, it was
180 A wind full ten times over.
I looked around, I thought I saw
A jutting crag, – and off I ran,
Head-foremost, through the driving rain,
The shelter of the crag to gain;
And, as I am a man,
Instead of jutting crag, I found
A Woman seated on the ground.

XVIII

'I did not speak – I saw her face;
Her face! – it was enough for me;
190 I turned about and heard her cry,
"Oh misery! oh misery!"
And there she sits, until the moon
Through half the clear blue sky will go;
And when the little breezes make
The waters of the pond to shake,
As all the country know,
She shudders, and you hear her cry,
"Oh misery! oh misery!" '

XIX

'But what's the Thorn? and what the pond?
200 And what the hill of moss to her?
And what the creeping breeze that comes
The little pond to stir?'
'I cannot tell; but some will say
She hanged her baby on the tree;
Some say she drowned it in the pond,
Which is a little step beyond:
But all and each agree,
The little Babe was buried there,
Beneath that hill of moss so fair.

XX

210 'I've heard, the moss is spotted red
With drops of that poor infant's blood;
But kill a new-born infant thus,
I do not think she could!
Some say, if to the pond you go,
And fix on it a steady view,
The shadow of a babe you trace,
A baby and a baby's face,
And that it looks at you;
Whene'er you look on it, 'tis plain
220 The baby looks at you again.

XXI

'And some had sworn an oath that she
Should be to public justice brought;
And for the little infant's bones
With spades they would have sought.
But instantly the hill of moss
Before their eyes began to stir!
And, for full fifty yards around,
The grass – it shook upon the ground!
Yet all do still aver
230 The little Babe lies buried there,
Beneath that hill of moss so fair.

XXII

'I cannot tell how this may be,
But plain it is the Thorn is bound
With heavy tufts of moss that strive
To drag it to the ground;
And this I know, full many a time,
When she was on the mountain high,
By day, and in the silent night,
When all the stars shone clear and bright,
240 That I have heard her cry,
"Oh misery! oh misery!
Oh woe is me! oh misery!" '

[*Fragments from the Alfoxden Note-Book (11)*]

I

Solemn dreams,
Dreams beautiful as the fair hues that lie
About the moon in clouds of various depth,
In many clouds about the full-orbed moon.
Why cannot they be still those barking curs
That so disturb the stillness of the moon
And make the [   ] restless?

II
> lovely as the fairy day
Which one hour after sunset the sea gains
From the bright west when, on the bare hill-top,
Scarce distant twenty paces, the sheep bleats
Unseen, and darkness covers all the vales.

Lines Written in Early Spring

I heard a thousand blended notes,
While in a grove I sate reclined,
In that sweet mood when pleasant thoughts
Bring sad thoughts to the mind.

To her fair works did Nature link
The human soul that through me ran;
And much it grieved my heart to think
What man has made of man.

Through primrose tufts, in that green bower,
10 The periwinkle trailed its wreaths;
And 'tis my faith that every flower
Enjoys the air it breathes.

The birds around me hopped and played,
Their thoughts I cannot measure: —
But the least motion which they made,
It seemed a thrill of pleasure.

The budding twigs spread out their fan,
To catch the breezy air;
And I must think, do all I can,
20 That there was pleasure there.

If this belief from heaven be sent,
If such be Nature's holy plan,
Have I not reason to lament
What man has made of man?

Anecdote for Fathers

'Retine vim istam, falsa enim dicam, si coges.' EUSEBIUS.

I have a boy of five years old;
His face is fair and fresh to see;
His limbs are cast in beauty's mould,
And dearly he loves me.

One morn we strolled on our dry walk,
Our quiet home all full in view,
And held such intermitted talk
As we are wont to do.

My thoughts on former pleasures ran;
10   I thought of Kilve's delightful shore,
Our pleasant home when spring began,
A long, long year before.

A day it was when I could bear
Some fond regrets to entertain;
With so much happiness to spare,
I could not feel a pain.

The green earth echoed to the feet
Of lambs that bounded through the glade,
From shade to sunshine, and as fleet
20   From sunshine back to shade.

Birds warbled round me – and each trace
Of inward sadness had its charm;
Kilve, thought I, was a favoured place,
And so is Liswyn farm.

My boy beside me tripped, so slim
And graceful in his rustic dress!
And, as we talked, I questioned him,
In very idleness.

'Now tell me, had you rather be,'
30   I said, and took him by the arm,
'On Kilve's smooth shore, by the green sea,
Or here at Liswyn farm?'

In careless mood he looked at me,
While still I held him by the arm,
And said, 'At Kilve I'd rather be
Than here at Liswyn farm.'

'Now, little Edward, say why so:
My little Edward, tell me why.' –
'I cannot tell, I do not know.' –
40   'Why, this is strange,' said I;

'For, here are woods, hills smooth and warm:
There surely must some reason be
Why you would change sweet Liswyn farm
For Kilve by the green sea.'

At this, my boy hung down his head,
He blushed with shame, nor made reply;
And three times to the child I said,
'Why, Edward, tell me why?'

His head he raised – there was in sight,
50   It caught his eye, he saw it plain –
Upon the house-top, glittering bright,
A broad and gilded vane.

Then did the boy his tongue unlock,
And eased his mind with this reply:
'At Kilve there was no weather-cock;
And that's the reason why.'

O dearest, dearest boy! my heart
For better lore would seldom yearn,
Could I but teach the hundredth part
60   Of what from thee I learn.

Peter Bell
A Tale

'What's in a *Name*?'

*   *   *   *   *   *

'Brutus will start a Spirit as soon as Caesar!'

TO ROBERT SOUTHEY, ESQ., P.L., ETC., ETC.

MY DEAR FRIEND,

The Tale of Peter Bell, which I now introduce to your notice, and to that of the Public, has, in its Manuscript state, nearly survived its *minority*: – for it first saw the light in the summer of 1798. During this long interval, pains have been taken at different times to make the production less unworthy of a favourable reception; or, rather, to fit it for filling *permanently* a station, however humble, in the Literature of our Country. This has, indeed, been the aim of all my endeavours in Poetry, which, you know, have been sufficiently laborious to prove that I deem the Art not lightly to be approached; and that the attainment of excellence in it may laudably be made the principal object of intellectual pursuit by any man, who, with reasonable consideration of circumstances, has faith in his own impulses.

The Poem of Peter Bell, as the Prologue will show, was composed under a belief that the Imagination not only does not require for its exercise the intervention of supernatural agency, but that, though such agency be excluded, the faculty may be called forth as imperiously, and for kindred results of pleasure, by incidents within the compass of poetic probability, in the humblest departments of daily life. Since that Prologue was written, *you* have exhibited most splendid effects of judicious daring, in the opposite and usual course. Let this acknowledgement make my peace with the lovers of the supernatural; and I am persuaded it will be admitted, that to you, as a Master in that province of the art, the following Tale, whether from

contrast or congruity, is not an unappropriate offering.
Accept it, then, as a public testimony of affectionate
admiration from one with whose name yours has been often
coupled (to use your own words) for evil and for good;
and believe me to be, with earnest wishes that life and
health may be granted you to complete the many important
works in which you are engaged, and with high respect,

Most faithfully yours,

RYDAL MOUNT,   WILLIAM WORDSWORTH.
April 7, 1819.

PROLOGUE

There's something in a flying horse,
There's something in a huge balloon;
But through the clouds I'll never float
Until I have a little Boat,
Shaped like the crescent-moon.

And now I *have* a little Boat,
In shape a very crescent-moon:
Fast through the clouds my Boat can sail;
But if perchance your faith should fail,
10 Look up – and you shall see me soon!

The woods, my Friends, are round you roaring,
Rocking and roaring like a sea;
The noise of danger's in your ears,
And ye have all a thousand fears
Both for my little Boat and me!

Meanwhile untroubled I admire
The pointed horns of my canoe;
And, did not pity touch my breast,
To see how ye are all distrest,
20 Till my ribs ached, I'd laugh at you!

Away we go, my Boat and I –
Frail man ne'er sate in such another;
Whether among the winds we strive,
Or deep into the clouds we dive,
Each is contented with the other.

Away we go – and what care we
For treasons, tumults, and for wars?
We are as calm in our delight
As is the crescent-moon so bright
30   Among the scattered stars.

Up goes my Boat among the stars
Through many a breathless field of light,
Through many a long blue field of ether,
Leaving ten thousand stars beneath her:
Up goes my little Boat so bright!

The Crab, the Scorpion, and the Bull –
We pry among them all; have shot
High o'er the red-haired race of Mars,
Covered from top to toe with scars;
40   Such company I like it not!

The towns in Saturn are decayed,
And melancholy Spectres throng them; –
The Pleiads, that appear to kiss
Each other in the vast abyss,
With joy I sail among them.

Swift Mercury resounds with mirth,
Great Jove is full of stately bowers;
But these, and all that they contain,
What are they to that tiny grain,
50   That little Earth of ours?

Then back to Earth, the dear green Earth: –
Whole ages if I here should roam,

The world for my remarks and me
Would not a whit the better be;
I've left my heart at home.

See! there she is, the matchless Earth!
There spreads the famed Pacific Ocean!
Old Andes thrusts yon craggy spear
Through the grey clouds; the Alps are here,
60 Like waters in commotion!

Yon tawny slip is Libya's sands;
That silver thread the river Dnieper;
And look, where clothed in brightest green
Is a sweet Isle, of isles the Queen;
Ye fairies, from all evil keep her!

And see the town where I was born!
Around those happy fields we span
In boyish gambols; – I was lost
Where I have been, but on this coast
70 I feel I am a man.

Never did fifty things at once
Appear so lovely, never, never; –
How tunefully the forests ring!
To hear the earth's soft murmuring
Thus could I hang for ever!

'Shame on you!' cried my little Boat,
'Was ever such a homesick Loon,
Within a living Boat to sit,
And make no better use of it;
80 A Boat twin-sister of the crescent-moon!

'Ne'er in the breast of full-grown Poet
Fluttered so faint a heart before; –
Was it the music of the spheres
That overpowered your mortal ears?
– Such din shall trouble them no more.

'These nether precincts do not lack
Charms of their own; – then come with me;
I want a comrade, and for you
There's nothing that I would not do;
90   Naught is there that you shall not see.

'Haste! and above Siberian snows
We'll sport amid the boreal morning;
Will mingle with her lustres gliding
Among the stars, the stars now hiding,
And now the stars adorning.

'I know the secrets of a land
Where human foot did never stray;
Fair is that land as evening skies,
And cool, though in the depth it lies
100   Of burning Africa.

'Or we'll into the realm of Faery,
Among the lovely shades of things;
The shadowy forms of mountains bare,
And streams, and bowers, and ladies fair,
The shades of palaces and kings!

'Or, if you thirst with hardy zeal
Less quiet regions to explore,
Prompt voyage shall to you reveal
How earth and heaven are taught to feel
110   The might of magic lore!'

'My little vagrant Form of light,
My gay and beautiful Canoe,
Well have you played your friendly part;
As kindly take what from my heart
Experience forces – then adieu!

'Temptation lurks among your words;
But, while these pleasures you're pursuing

Without impediment or let,
No wonder if you quite forget
120 What on the earth is doing.

'There was a time when all mankind
Did listen with a faith sincere
To tuneful tongues in mystery versed;
Then Poets fearlessly rehearsed
The wonders of a wild career.

'Go – (but the world's a sleepy world,
And 'tis, I fear, an age too late)
Take with you some ambitious Youth!
For, restless Wanderer! I, in truth,
130 Am all unfit to be your mate.

'Long have I loved what I behold,
The night that calms, the day that cheers;
The common growth of mother-earth
Suffices me – her tears, her mirth,
Her humblest mirth and tears.

'The dragon's wing, the magic ring,
I shall not covet for my dower,
If I along that lowly way
With sympathetic heart may stray,
140 And with a soul of power.

'These given, what more need I desire
To stir, to soothe, or elevate?
What nobler marvels than the mind
May in life's daily prospect find,
May find or there create?

'A potent wand doth Sorrow wield;
What spell so strong as guilty Fear!
Repentance is a tender Sprite;
If aught on earth have heavenly might,
150 'Tis lodged within her silent tear.

'But grant my wishes, – let us now
Descend from this ethereal height;
Then take thy way, adventurous Skiff,
More daring far than Hippogriff,
And be thy own delight!

'To the stone-table in my garden,
Loved haunt of many a summer hour,
The Squire is come: his daughter Bess
Beside him in the cool recess
160   Sits blooming like a flower.

'With these are many more convened;
They know not I have been so far; –
I see them there, in number nine,
Beneath the spreading Weymouth-pine!
I see them – there they are!

'There sits the Vicar and his Dame;
And there my good friend, Stephen Otter;
And, ere the light of evening fail,
To them I must relate the Tale
170   Of Peter Bell the Potter.'

Off flew the Boat – away she flees,
Spurning her freight with indignation!
And I, as well as I was able,
On two poor legs, toward my stone-table
Limped on with sore vexation.

'O, here he is!' cried little Bess –
She saw me at the garden-door;
'We've waited anxiously and long,'
They cried, and all around me throng,
180   Full nine of them or more!

'Reproach me not – your fears be still –
Be thankful we again have met; –

Resume, my Friends! within the shade
Your seats, and quickly shall be paid
The well-remembered debt.'

I spake with faltering voice, like one
Not wholly rescued from the pale
Of a wild dream, or worse illusion;
But straight, to cover my confusion,
190 Began the promised Tale.

PART FIRST

All by the moonlight river-side
Groaned the poor Beast – alas! in vain;
The staff was raised to loftier height,
And the blows fell with heavier weight
As Peter struck – and struck again.

'Hold!' cried the Squire, 'against the rules
Of common sense you're surely sinning;
This leap is for us all too bold;
Who Peter was, let that be told,
200 And start from the beginning.'

– 'A Potter, Sir, he was by trade,'
Said I, becoming quite collected;
'And wheresoever he appeared,
Full twenty times was Peter feared
For once that Peter was respected.

'He, two-and-thirty years or more,
Had been a wild and woodland rover;
Had heard the Atlantic surges roar
On farthest Cornwall's rocky shore,
210 And trod the cliffs of Dover.

'And he had seen Caernarvon's towers,
And well he knew the spire of Sarum;

And he had been where Lincoln bell
Flings o'er the fen that ponderous knell –
A far-renowned alarum.

'At Doncaster, at York, and Leeds,
And merry Carlisle had he been;
And all along the Lowlands fair,
All through the bonny shire of Ayr;
220 And far as Aberdeen.

'And he had been at Inverness;
And Peter, by the mountain-rills,
Had danced his round with Highland lasses;
And he had lain beside his asses
On lofty Cheviot Hills:

'And he had trudged through Yorkshire dales,
Among the rocks and winding *scars*;
Where deep and low the hamlets lie
Beneath their little patch of sky
230 And little lot of stars:

'And all along the indented coast,
Bespattered with the salt-sea foam;
Where'er a knot of houses lay
On headland, or in hollow bay; –
Sure never man like him did roam!

'As well might Peter, in the Fleet,
Have been fast bound, a begging debtor; –
He travelled here, he travelled there; –
But not the value of a hair
240 Was heart or head the better.

'He roved among the vales and streams,
In the green wood and hollow dell;
They were his dwellings night and day, –
But nature ne'er could find the way
Into the heart of Peter Bell.

'In vain, through every changeful year,
Did Nature lead him as before;
A primrose by a river's brim
A yellow primrose was to him,
250 And it was nothing more.

'Small change it made in Peter's heart
To see his gentle panniered train
With more than vernal pleasure feeding,
Where'er the tender grass was leading
Its earliest green along the lane.

'In vain, through water, earth, and air,
The soul of happy sound was spread,
When Peter on some April morn,
Beneath the broom or budding thorn,
260 Made the warm earth his lazy bed.

'At noon, when, by the forest's edge
He lay beneath the branches high,
The soft blue sky did never melt
Into his heart; he never felt
The witchery of the soft blue sky!

'On a fair prospect some have looked
And felt, as I have heard them say,
As if the moving time had been
A thing as stedfast as the scene
270 On which they gazed themselves away.

'Within the breast of Peter Bell
These silent raptures found no place;
He was a Carl as wild and rude
As ever hue-and-cry pursued,
As ever ran a felon's race.

'Of all that lead a lawless life,
Of all that love their lawless lives,

In city or in village small,
He was the wildest far of all; –
280 He had a dozen wedded wives.

'Nay, start not! – wedded wives – and twelve!
But how one wife could e'er come near him,
In simple truth I cannot tell;
For, be it said of Peter Bell,
To see him was to fear him.

'Though Nature could not touch his heart
By lovely forms, and silent weather,
And tender sounds, yet you might see
At once, that Peter Bell and she
290 Had often been together.

'A savage wildness round him hung
As of a dweller out of doors;
In his whole figure and his mien
A savage character was seen
Of mountains and of dreary moors.

'To all the unshaped half-human thoughts
Which solitary Nature feeds
'Mid summer storms or winter's ice,
Had Peter joined whatever vice
300 The cruel city breeds.

'His face was keen as is the wind
That cuts along the hawthorn-fence;
Of courage you saw little there,
But, in its stead, a medley air
Of cunning and of impudence.

'He had a dark and sidelong walk,
And long and slouching was his gait;
Beneath his looks so bare and bold,
You might perceive, his spirit cold
310 Was playing with some inward bait.

'His forehead wrinkled was and furred;
A work, one half of which was done
By thinking of his "*whens*" and "*hows*";
And half, by knitting of his brows
Beneath the glaring sun.

'There was a hardness in his cheek,
There was a hardness in his eye,
As if the man had fixed his face,
In many a solitary place,
320 Against the wind and open sky!'

———————

ONE NIGHT, (and now, my little Bess!
We've reached at last the promised Tale;)
One beautiful November night,
When the full moon was shining bright
Upon the rapid river Swale,

Along the river's winding banks
Peter was travelling all alone; –
Whether to buy or sell, or led
By pleasure running in his head,
330 To me was never known.

He trudged along through copse and brake
He trudged along o'er hill and dale;
Nor for the moon cared he a tittle,
And for the stars he cared as little,
And for the murmuring river Swale.

But, chancing to espy a path
That promised to cut short the way;
As many a wiser man hath done,
He left a trusty guide for one
340 That might his steps betray.

To a thick wood he soon is brought
Where cheerily his course he weaves,

And whistling loud may yet be heard,
Though often buried, like a bird
Darkling, among the boughs and leaves.

But quickly Peter's mood is changed,
And on he drives with cheeks that burn
In downright fury and in wrath; –
There's little sign the treacherous path
350   Will to the road return!

The path grows dim, and dimmer still;
Now up, now down, the Rover wends,
With all the sail that he can carry,
Till brought to a deserted quarry –
And there the pathway ends.

He paused – for shadows of strange shape,
Massy and black, before him lay;
But through the dark, and through the cold,
And through the yawning fissures old,
360   Did Peter boldly press his way

Right through the quarry; – and behold
A scene of soft and lovely hue!
Where blue and grey, and tender green,
Together make as sweet a scene
As ever human eye did view.

Beneath the clear blue sky he saw
A little field of meadow ground;
But field or meadow name it not;
Call it of earth a small green plot,
370   With rocks encompassed round.

The Swale flowed under the grey rocks,
But he flowed quiet and unseen; –
You need a strong and stormy gale
To bring the noises of the Swale
To that green spot, so calm and green!

And is there no one dwelling here,
No hermit with his beads and glass?
And does no little cottage look
Upon this soft and fertile nook?
380 Does no one live near this green grass?

Across the deep and quiet spot
Is Peter driving through the grass –
And now has reached the skirting trees;
When, turning round his head, he sees
A solitary Ass.

'A prize!' cries Peter – but he first
Must spy about him far and near:
There's not a single house in sight,
No woodman's hut, no cottage light –
390 Peter, you need not fear!

There's nothing to be seen but woods,
And rocks that spread a hoary gleam,
And this one Beast, that from the bed
Of the green meadow hangs his head
Over the silent stream.

His head is with a halter bound;
The halter seizing, Peter leapt
Upon the Creature's back, and plied
With ready heels his shaggy side;
400 But still the Ass his station kept.

Then Peter gave a sudden jerk,
A jerk that from a dungeon-floor
Would have pulled up an iron ring;
But still the heavy-headed Thing
Stood just as he had stood before!

Quoth Peter, leaping from his seat,
'There is some plot against me laid;'

Once more the little meadow-ground
And all the hoary cliffs around
410 He cautiously surveyed.

All, all is silent – rocks and woods,
All still and silent – far and near!
Only the Ass, with motion dull,
Upon the pivot of his skull
Turns round his long left ear.

Thought Peter, What can mean all this?
Some ugly witchcraft must be here!
– Once more the Ass, with motion dull,
Upon the pivot of his skull
420 Turned round his long left ear.

Suspicion ripened into dread;
Yet with deliberate action slow,
His staff high-raising, in the pride
Of skill, upon the sounding hide
He dealt a sturdy blow.

The poor Ass staggered with the shock;
And then, as if to take his ease,
In quiet uncomplaining mood,
Upon the spot where he had stood,
430 Dropped gently down upon his knees;

As gently on his side he fell;
And by the river's brink did lie;
And, while he lay like one that mourned,
The patient Beast on Peter turned
His shining hazel eye.

'Twas but one mild, reproachful look,
A look more tender than severe;
And straight in sorrow, not in dread,
He turned the eye-ball in his head
440 Towards the smooth river deep and clear.

Upon the Beast the sapling rings;
His lank sides heaved, his limbs they stirred;
He gave a groan, and then another,
Of that which went before the brother,
And then he gave a third.

All by the moonlight river side
He gave three miserable groans;
And not till now hath Peter seen
How gaunt the Creature is, – how lean
450 And sharp his staring bones!

With legs stretched out and stiff he lay: –
No word of kind commiseration
Fell at the sight from Peter's tongue;
With hard contempt his heart was wrung,
With hatred and vexation.

The meagre beast lay still as death;
And Peter's lips with fury quiver;
Quoth he, 'You little mulish dog,
I'll fling your carcass like a log
460 Head-foremost down the river!'

An impious oath confirmed the threat –
Whereat from the earth on which he lay
To all the echoes, south and north,
And east and west, the Ass sent forth
A long and clamorous bray!

This outcry, on the heart of Peter,
Seems like a note of joy to strike, –
Joy at the heart of Peter knocks;
But in the echo of the rocks
470 Was something Peter did not like.

Whether to cheer his coward breast,
Or that he could not break the chain,

In this serene and solemn hour,
Twined round him by demoniac power,
To the blind work he turned again.

Among the rocks and winding crags;
Among the mountains far away;
Once more the Ass did lengthen out
More ruefully a deep-drawn shout,
480 The hard dry see-saw of his horrible bray!

What is there now in Peter's heart!
Or whence the might of this strange sound?
The moon uneasy looked and dimmer,
The broad blue heavens appeared to glimmer,
And the rocks staggered all around –

From Peter's hand the sapling dropped!
Threat has he none to execute;
'If anyone should come and see
That I am here, they'll think,' quoth he,
490 'I'm helping this poor dying brute.'

He scans the Ass from limb to limb,
And ventures now to uplift his eyes;
More steady looks the moon, and clear,
More like themselves the rocks appear
And touch more quiet skies.

His scorn returns – his hate revives;
He stoops the Ass's neck to seize
With malice – that again takes flight;
For in the pool a startling sight
500 Meets him, among the inverted trees.

Is it the moon's distorted face?
The ghost-like image of a cloud?
It is a gallows there portrayed?
Is Peter of himself afraid?
Is it a coffin, – or a shroud?

A grisly idol hewn in stone?
Or imp from witch's lap let fall?
Perhaps a ring of shining fairies?
Such as pursue their feared vagaries
510 In sylvan bower, or haunted hall?

Is it a fiend that to a stake
Of fire his desperate self is tethering?
Or stubborn spirit doomed to yell
In solitary ward or cell,
Ten thousand miles from all his brethren?

Never did pulse so quickly throb,
And never heart so loudly panted;
He looks, he cannot choose but look;
Like some one reading in a book –
520 A book that is enchanted.

Ah, well-a-day for Peter Bell!
He will be turned to iron soon,
Meet Statue for the court of Fear!
His hat is up – and every hair
Bristles, and whitens in the moon!

He looks, he ponders, looks again;
He sees a motion – hears a groan;
His eyes will burst – his heart will break –
He gives a loud and frightful shriek,
530 And back he falls, as if his life were flown!

PART SECOND

We left our Hero in a trance,
Beneath the alders, near the river;
The Ass is by the river-side,
And, where the feeble breezes glide,
Upon the stream the moonbeams quiver.

A happy respite! but at length
He feels the glimmering of the moon;
Wakes with glazed eye, and feebly sighing –
To sink, perhaps, where he is lying,
540 Into a second swoon!

He lifts his head, he sees his staff;
He touches – 'tis to him a treasure!
Faint recollection seems to tell
That he is yet where mortals dwell –
A thought received with languid pleasure!

His head upon his elbow propped,
Becoming less and less perplexed,
Sky-ward he looks – to rock and wood –
And then – upon the glassy flood
550 His wandering eye is fixed.

Thought he, that is the face of one
In his last sleep securely bound!
So toward the stream his head he bent,
And downward thrust his staff, intent
The river's depth to sound.

Now – like a tempest-shattered bark,
That overwhelmed and prostrate lies,
And in a moment to the verge
Is lifted of a foaming surge –
560 Full suddenly the Ass doth rise!

His staring bones all shake with joy,
And close by Peter's side he stands:
While Peter o'er the river bends,
The little Ass his neck extends,
And fondly licks his hands.

Such life is in the Ass's eyes,
Such life is in his limbs and ears;

That Peter Bell, if he had been
The veriest coward ever seen,
570   Must now have thrown aside his fears.

The Ass looks on – and to his work
Is Peter quietly resigned;
He touches here – he touches there –
And now among the dead man's hair
His sapling Peter has entwined.

He pulls – and looks – and pulls again;
And he whom the poor Ass had lost,
The man who had been four days dead
Head-foremost from the river's bed
580   Uprises like a ghost!

And Peter draws him to dry land;
And through the brain of Peter pass
Some poignant twitches, fast and faster;
'No doubt,' quoth he, 'he is the Master
Of this poor miserable Ass!'

The meagre shadow that looks on –
What would he now? what is he doing?
His sudden fit of joy is flown, –
He on his knees hath laid him down,
590   As if he were his grief renewing;

But no – that Peter on his back
Must mount, he shows well as he can:
Thought Peter then, come weal or woe,
I'll do what he would have me do,
In pity to this poor drowned man.

With that resolve he boldly mounts
Upon the pleased and thankful Ass;
And then, without a moment's stay,
That earnest Creature turned away,
600   Leaving the body on the grass.

Intent upon his faithful watch,
The Beast four days and nights had past;
A sweeter meadow ne'er was seen,
And there the Ass four days had been,
Nor ever once did break his fast:

Yet firm his step, and stout his heart;
The mead is crossed – the quarry's mouth
Is reached; but there the trusty guide
Into a thicket turns aside,
610 And deftly ambles towards the south.

When hark a burst of doleful sound!
And Peter honestly might say,
The like came never to his ears,
Though he has been, full thirty years,
A rover – night and day!

'Tis not a plover of the moors,
'Tis not a bittern of the fen;
Nor can it be a barking fox,
Nor night-bird chambered in the rocks,
620 Nor wild-cat in a woody glen!

The Ass is startled – and stops short
Right in the middle of the thicket;
And Peter, wont to whistle loud
Whether alone or in a crowd,
Is silent as a silent cricket.

What ails you now, my little Bess?
Well may you tremble and look grave!
This cry – that rings along the wood,
This cry – that floats adown the flood,
630 Comes from the entrance of a cave:

I see a blooming Wood-boy there,
And if I had the power to say

How sorrowful the wanderer is,
Your heart would be as sad as his
Till you had kissed his tears away!

Grasping a hawthorn branch in hand,
All bright with berries ripe and red,
Into the cavern's mouth he peeps;
Thence back into the moonlight creeps;
640   Whom seeks he – whom? – the silent dead:

His father! – Him doth he require –
Him hath he sought with fruitless pains,
Among the rocks, behind the trees;
Now creeping on his hands and knees,
Now running o'er the open plains.

And hither is he come at last,
When he through such a day has gone,
By this dark cave to be distrest
Like a poor bird – her plundered nest
650   Hovering around with dolorous moan!

Of that intense and piercing cry
The listening Ass conjectures well;
Wild as it is, he there can read
Some intermingled notes that plead
With touches irresistible.

But Peter – when he saw the Ass
Not only stop but turn, and change
The cherished tenor of his pace
That lamentable cry to chase –
660   It wrought in him conviction strange;

A faith that, for the dead man's sake
And this poor slave who loved him well,
Vengeance upon his head will fall,
Some visitation worse than all
Which ever till this night befell.

Meanwhile the Ass to reach his home
Is striving stoutly as he may;
But, while he climbs the woody hill,
The cry grows weak – and weaker still;
670 And now at last it dies away.

So with his freight the Creature turns
Into a gloomy grove of beech,
Along the shade with footsteps true
Descending slowly, till the two
The open moonlight reach.

And there, along the narrow dell,
A fair smooth pathway you discern,
A length of green and open road –
As if it from a fountain flowed –
680 Winding away between the fern.

The rocks that tower on either side
Build up a wild fantastic scene;
Temples like those among the Hindoos,
And mosques, and spires, and abbey-windows,
And castles all with ivy green!

And while the Ass pursues his way,
Along this solitary dell,
As pensively his steps advance,
The mosques and spires change countenance,
690 And look at Peter Bell!

That unintelligible cry
Hath left him high in preparation, –
Convinced that he, or soon or late,
This very night will meet his fate –
And so he sits in expectation!

The strenuous Animal hath clomb
With the green path; and now he wends

Where, shining like the smoothest sea,
In undisturbed immensity
700 A level plain extends.

But whence this faintly-rustling sound
By which the journeying pair are chased?
– A withered leaf is close behind,
Light plaything for the sportive wind
Upon that solitary waste.

When Peter spied the moving thing,
It only doubled his distress;
'Where there is not a bush or tree,
The very leaves they follow me –
710 So huge hath been my wickedness!'

To a close lane they now are come,
Where, as before, the enduring Ass
Moves on without a moment's stop,
Nor once turns round his head to crop
A bramble-leaf or blade of grass.

Between the hedges as they go,
The white dust sleeps upon the lane;
And Peter, ever and anon
Back-looking, sees, upon a stone,
720 Or in the dust, a crimson stain.

A stain – as of a drop of blood
By moonlight made more faint and wan;
Ha! why these sinkings of despair?
He knows not how the blood comes there –
And Peter is a wicked man.

At length he spies a bleeding wound,
Where he had struck the Ass's head;
He sees the blood, knows what it is, –
A glimpse of sudden joy was his,
730 But then it quickly fled;

Of him whom sudden death had seized
He thought, – of thee, O faithful Ass!
And once again those ghastly pains,
Shoot to and fro through heart and reins,
And through his brain like lightning pass.

PART THIRD

I've heard of one, a gentle Soul,
Though given to sadness and to gloom,
And for the fact will vouch, – one night
It chanced that by a taper's light
740   This man was reading in his room;

Bending, as you or I might bend
At night o'er any pious book,
When sudden blackness overspread
The snow-white page on which he read,
And made the good man round him look.

The chamber walls were dark all round, –
And to his book he turned again;
– The light had left the lonely taper,
And formed itself upon the paper
750   Into large letters – bright and plain!

The godly book was in his hand –
And, on the page, more black than coal,
Appeared, set forth in strange array,
A *word* – which to his dying day
Perplexed the good man's gentle soul.

The ghostly word, thus plainly seen,
Did never from his lips depart;
But he hath said, poor gentle wight!
It brought full many a sin to light
760   Out of the bottom of his heart.

Dread Spirits! to confound the meek
Why wander from your course so far,
Disordering colour, form, and stature!
– Let good men feel the soul of nature,
And see things as they are.

Yet, potent Spirits! well I know,
How ye, that play with soul and sense,
Are not unused to trouble friends
Of goodness, for most gracious ends –
770 And this I speak in reverence!

But might I give advice to you,
Whom in my fear I love so well;
From men of pensive virtue go,
Dread Beings! and your empire show
On hearts like that of Peter Bell.

Your presence often have I felt
In darkness and the stormy night;
And with like force, if need there be,
Ye can put forth your agency
780 When earth is calm, and heaven is bright.

Then, coming from the wayward world,
That powerful world in which ye dwell,
Come, Spirits of the Mind! and try,
Tonight, beneath the moonlight sky,
What may be done with Peter Bell!

– O, would that some more skilful voice
My further labour might prevent!
Kind Listeners, that around me sit,
I feel that I am all unfit
790 For such high argument.

– I've played, I've danced, with my narration;
I loitered long ere I began:

Ye waited then on my good pleasure;
Pour out indulgence still, in measure
As liberal as ye can!

Our Travellers, ye remember well,
Are thridding a sequestered lane;
And Peter many tricks is trying,
And many anodynes applying,
800 To ease his conscience of its pain.

By this his heart is lighter far;
And, finding that he can account
So snugly for that crimson stain,
His evil spirit up again
Does like an empty bucket mount.

And Peter is a deep logician
Who hath no lack of wit mercurial;
'Blood drops – leaves rustle – yet,' quoth he,
'This poor man never, but for me,
810 Could have had Christian burial.

'And, say the best you can, 'tis plain,
That here has been some wicked dealing;
No doubt the devil in me wrought;
I'm not the man who could have thought
An Ass like this was worth the stealing!'

So from his pocket Peter takes
His shining horn tobacco-box;
And, in a light and careless way,
As men who with their purpose play,
820 Upon the lid he knocks.

Let them whose voice can stop the clouds,
Whose cunning eye can see the wind,
Tell to a curious world the cause
Why, making here a sudden pause,
The Ass turned round his head, and *grinned*.

Appalling process! I have marked
The like on heath, in lonely wood;
And, verily, have seldom met
A spectacle more hideous – yet
830   It suited Peter's present mood.

And, grinning in his turn, his teeth
He in jocose defiance showed –
When, to upset his spiteful mirth,
A murmur, pent within the earth,
In the dead earth beneath the road,

Rolled audibly! – it swept along,
A muffled noise – a rumbling sound! –
'Twas by a troop of miners made,
Plying with gunpowder their trade,
840   Some twenty fathoms underground.

Small cause of dire effect! for, surely,
If ever mortal, King or Cotter,
Believed that earth was charged to quake
And yawn for his unworthy sake,
'Twas Peter Bell the Potter.

But, as an oak in breathless air
Will stand though to the centre hewn;
Or as the weakest things, if frost
Have stiffened them, maintain their post;
850   So he, beneath the gazing moon! –

The Beast bestriding thus, he reached
A spot where, in a sheltering cove,
A little chapel stands alone,
With greenest ivy overgrown,
And tufted with an ivy grove;

Dying insensibly away
From human thoughts and purposes,

It seemed – wall, window, roof and tower –
To bow to some transforming power,
860 And blend with the surrounding trees.

As ruinous a place it was,
Thought Peter, in the shire of Fife
That served my turn, when following still
From land to land a reckless will
I married my sixth wife!

The unheeding Ass moves slowly on,
And now is passing by an inn
Brim-full of a carousing crew,
That make, with curses not a few,
870 An uproar and a drunken din.

I cannot well express the thoughts
Which Peter in those noises found; –
A stifling power compressed his frame,
While-as a swimming darkness came
Over that dull and dreary sound.

For well did Peter know the sound;
The language of those drunken joys
To him, a jovial soul, I ween,
But a few hours ago, had been
880 A gladsome and a welcome noise.

Now, turned adrift into the past,
He finds no solace in his course;
Like planet-stricken men of yore,
He trembles, smitten to the core
By strong compunction and remorse.

But, more than all, his heart is stung
To think of one, almost a child;
A sweet and playful Highland girl,
As light and beauteous as a squirrel,
890 As beauteous and as wild!

Her dwelling was a lonely house,
A cottage in a heathy dell;
And she put on her gown of green,
And left her mother at sixteen,
And followed Peter Bell.

But many good and pious thoughts
Had she; and, in the kirk to pray,
Two long Scotch miles, through rain or snow,
To kirk she had been used to go,
900 Twice every Sabbath-day.

And, when she followed Peter Bell,
It was to lead an honest life;
For he, with tongue not used to falter,
Had pledged his troth before the altar
To love her as his wedded wife.

A mother's hope is hers; – but soon
She drooped and pined like one forlorn;
From Scripture she a name did borrow;
Benoni, or the child of sorrow,
910 She called her babe unborn.

For she had learned how Peter lived,
And took it in most grievous part;
She to the very bone was worn,
And, ere that little child was born,
Died of a broken heart.

And now the Spirits of the Mind
Are busy with poor Peter Bell;
Upon the rights of visual sense
Usurping, with a prevalence
920 More terrible than magic spell.

Close by a brake of flowering furze
(Above it shivering aspens play)

He sees an unsubstantial creature,
His very self in form and feature,
Not four yards from the broad highway:

And stretched beneath the furze he sees
The Highland girl – it is no other;
And hears her crying as she cried,
The very moment that she died,
930 'My mother! oh my mother!'

The sweat pours down from Peter's face,
So grievous is his heart's contrition;
With agony his eye-balls ache
While he beholds by the furze-brake
This miserable vision!

Calm is the well-deserving brute,
His peace hath no offence betrayed;
But now, while down that slope he wends,
A voice to Peter's ear ascends,
940 Resounding from the woody glade:

The voice, though clamorous as a horn
Re-echoed by a naked rock,
Comes from that tabernacle – List!
Within, a fervent Methodist
Is preaching to no heedless flock!

'Repent! repent!' he cries aloud,
'While yet ye may find mercy; – strive
To love the Lord with all your might;
Turn to him, seek him day and night,
950 And save your souls alive!

'Repent! repent! though ye have gone,
Through paths of wickedness and woe,
After the Babylonian harlot;
And, though your sins be red as scarlet,
They shall be white as snow!'

Even as he passed the door, these words
Did plainly come to Peter's ears;
And they such joyful tidings were,
The joy was more than he could bear! –
960 He melted into tears.

Sweet tears of hope and tenderness!
And fast they fell, a plenteous shower!
His nerves, his sinews seemed to melt;
Through all his iron frame was felt
A gentle, a relaxing, power!

Each fibre of his frame was weak;
Weak all the animal within;
But, in its helplessness, grew mild
And gentle as an infant child,
970 An infant that has known no sin.

'Tis said, meek Beast! that, through Heaven's grace,
He not unmoved did notice now
The cross upon thy shoulder scored,
For lasting impress, by the Lord
To whom all human-kind shall bow;

Memorial of his touch – that day
When Jesus humbly deigned to ride,
Entering the proud Jerusalem,
By an immeasurable stream
980 Of shouting people deified!

Meanwhile the persevering Ass
Turned towards a gate that hung in view
Across a shady lane; his chest
Against the yielding gate he pressed
And quietly passed through.

And up the stony lane he goes;
No ghost more softly ever trod;

Among the stones and pebbles, he
Sets down his hoofs inaudibly,
990 As if with felt his hoofs were shod.

Along the lane the trusty Ass
Went twice two hundred yards or more,
And no one could have guessed his aim, –
Till to a lonely house he came,
And stopped beside the door.

Thought Peter, 'tis the poor man's home!
He listens – not a sound is heard
Save from the trickling household rill;
But, stepping o'er the cottage-sill,
1000 Forthwith a little Girl appeared.

She to the Meeting-house was bound
In hopes some tidings there to gather:
No glimpse it is, no doubtful gleam;
She saw – and uttered with a scream,
'My father! here's my father!'

The very word was plainly heard,
Heard plainly by the wretched Mother –
Her joy was like a deep affright:
And forth she rushed into the light,
1010 And saw it was another!

And, instantly, upon the earth,
Beneath the full moon shining bright,
Close to the Ass's feet she fell;
At the same moment Peter Bell
Dismounts in most unhappy plight.

As he beheld the Woman lie
Breathless and motionless, the mind
Of Peter sadly was confused;
But, though to such demands unused,
1020 And helpless almost as the blind,

He raised her up; and, while he held
Her body propped against his knee,
The Woman waked – and when she spied
The poor Ass standing by her side,
She moaned most bitterly.

'Oh! God be praised – my heart's at ease –
For he is dead – I know it well!'
– At this she wept a bitter flood;
And, in the best way that he could,
1030 His tale did Peter tell.

He trembles – he is pale as death;
His voice is weak with perturbation;
He turns aside his head, he pauses;
Poor Peter from a thousand causes
Is crippled sore in his narration.

At length she learned how he espied
The Ass in that small meadow-ground;
And that her Husband now lay dead,
Beside that luckless river's bed
1040 In which he had been drowned.

A piercing look the Widow cast
Upon the Beast that near her stands;
She sees 'tis he, that 'tis the same;
She calls the poor Ass by his name,
And wrings, and wrings her hands.

'O wretched loss – untimely stroke!
If he had died upon his bed!
He knew not one forewarning pain;
He never will come home again –
1050 Is dead, for ever dead!'

Beside the Woman Peter stands;
His heart is opening more and more;

A holy sense pervades his mind;
He feels what he for human-kind
Had never felt before.

At length, by Peter's arm sustained,
The Woman rises from the ground –
'Oh, mercy! something must be done,
My little Rachel, you must run, –
1060 Some willing neighbour must be found.

'Make haste – my little Rachel – do,
The first you meet with – bid him come,
Ask him to lend his horse tonight,
And this good Man, whom Heaven requite,
Will help to bring the body home.'

Away goes Rachel weeping loud; –
An Infant, waked by her distress,
Makes in the house a piteous cry;
And Peter hears the Mother sigh,
1070 'Seven are they, and all fatherless!'

And now is Peter taught to feel
That man's heart is a holy thing;
And Nature, through a world of death,
Breathes into him a second breath,
More searching than the breath of spring.

Upon a stone the Woman sits
In agony of silent grief –
From his own thoughts did Peter start;
He longs to press her to his heart,
1080 From love that cannot find relief.

But roused, as if through every limb
Had past a sudden shock of dread,
The Mother o'er the threshold flies,
And up the cottage stairs she hies,
And on the pillow lays her burning head.

And Peter turns his steps aside
Into a shade of darksome trees,
Where he sits down, he knows not how,
With his hands pressed against his brow,
1090 His elbows on his tremulous knees.

There, self-involved, does Peter sit
Until no sign of life he makes,
As if his mind were sinking deep
Through years that have been long asleep!
The trance is passed away – he wakes;

He lifts his head – and sees the Ass
Yet standing in the clear moonshine;
'When shall I be as good as thou?
Oh! would, poor beast, that I had now
1100 A heart but half as good as thine!'

But *He* – who deviously hath sought
His Father through the lonesome woods,
Hath sought, proclaiming to the ear
Of night his grief and sorrowful fear –
He comes, escaped from fields and floods; –

With weary pace is drawing nigh;
He sees the Ass – and nothing living
Had ever such a fit of joy
As hath this little orphan Boy,
1110 For he has no misgiving!

Forth to the gentle Ass he springs,
And up about his neck he climbs;
In loving words he talks to him,
He kisses, kisses face and limb, –
He kisses him a thousand times!

This Peter sees, while in the shade
He stood beside the cottage-door;

And Peter Bell, the ruffian wild,
Sobs loud, he sobs even like a child,
1120 'Oh! God, I can endure no more!'

– Here ends my Tale: for in a trice
Arrived a neighbour with his horse;
Peter went forth with him straightway;
And, with due care, ere break of day,
Together they brought back the Corse.

And many years did this poor Ass,
Whom once it was my luck to see
Cropping the shrubs of Leming-Lane,
Help by his labour to maintain
1130 The Widow and her family.

And Peter Bell, who, till that night,
Had been the wildest of his clan,
Forsook his crimes, renounced his folly,
And, after ten months' melancholy,
Became a good and honest man.

Andrew Jones

I hate that Andrew Jones: he'll breed
His children up to waste and pillage:
I wish the press-gang, or the drum
Would, with its rattling music, come –
And sweep him from the village.

I said not this, because he loves
Through the long day to swear and tipple;
But for the poor dear sake of one
To whom a foul deed he had done,
10   A friendless man, a travelling Cripple.

For this poor crawling helpless wretch
Some Horseman, who was passing by,
A penny on the ground had thrown;
But the poor Cripple was alone,
And could not stoop – no help was nigh.

Inch-thick the dust lay on the ground,
For it had long been droughty weather:
So with his staff the Cripple wrought
Among the dust, till he had brought
20   The halfpennies together.

It chanced that Andrew passed that way
Just at the time; and there he found
The Cripple in the mid-day heat
Standing alone, and at his feet
He saw the penny on the ground.

He stooped and took the penny up:
And when the Cripple nearer drew,
Quoth Andrew, 'Under half-a-crown,
What a man finds is all his own;
30   And so, my friend, good-day to you.'

And *hence* I say, that Andrew's boys
Will all be trained to waste and pillage;
And wished the press-gang, or the drum
Would, with its rattling music, come –
And sweep him from the village.

'I love upon a stormy night'

I love upon a stormy night
To hear those fits of slender song
Which through the woods and open plains,
Among the clouds or in the rains,
The loud winds bear along.

Then do I love to stand alone
By some huge rock or tree defended,
To stand like one that's blind, and catch
Of those small strains the last faint snatch
10 For human ears intended.

But sweeter when the moon shines bright
And the clear sky in calm blue weather
With rocks and woods and with the green
Of a small meadow makes a scene
Of earth and heaven together.

But sweeter then when you could hear,
Almost could hear a falling feather,
To listen to that music small
Prolonged through many a madrigal
20 For half an hour together.

But you will say how can this be?
I'll tell you, for the truth I know;
Above the ocean's foaming waves,
Through hollow woods and gloomy caves,
A thousand beings come and go.

I've heard them many and many a time,
A thing you'll say that's past conceiving,
Over the green and open lands,
And o'er the bare and yellow sands,
30 Their airy dances weaving.

'Tis not for one like me to tell
Their shape, their colour, and their size,
But they are thin and very spare,
Beings far thinner than the air,
And happier than the summer flies.

And often too by lake or grove
Have I beheld, from time to time,
A troop of tiny spirits fair,
All glistening like the moonlight air
40 Or sparkles in the frosty rime.

Oft have I seen in glade or bower
Sweet shapes upon the moonlight ground,
Some here, as little fairies small,
Some there, as human beings tall,
All dancing round and round.

'*Away, away, it is the air*'

Away, away, it is the air
That stirs among the withered leaves;
Away, away, it is not there,
Go, hunt among the harvest sheaves.
There is a bed in shape as plain
As from a hare or lion's lair
It is the bed where we have lain
In anguish and despair.

Away, and take the eagle's eyes,
10 The tiger's smell,
Ears that can hear the agonies
And murmurings of hell;
And when you there have stood
By that same bed of pain,
The groans are gone, the tears remain.
Then tell me if the thing be clear,
The difference betwixt a tear
Of water and of blood.

[Fragments from the Alfoxden Note-Book (III)]

                    and beneath the star
Of evening let the steep and lonely path
The steep path of the rocky mountain side
Among the stillness of the mountains hear
The panting of thy breath.

                    Where truth
Like some fair fabric in romantic glory
Built by the charm of sounds and symphonies
Uplifts her fair proportions at the call
Of pleasure her best minister.

                    these populous slopes
With all their groves and with their murmurous woods,
Giving a curious feeling to the mind
Of peopled solitude.

Expostulation and Reply

'Why, William, on that old grey stone,
Thus for the length of half a day,
Why, William, sit you thus alone,
And dream your time away?

'Where are your books? – that light bequeathed
To Beings else forlorn and blind!
Up! up! and drink the spirit breathed
From dead men to their kind.

'You look round on your Mother Earth,
10 As if she for no purpose bore you;
As if you were her first-born birth,
And none had lived before you!'

One morning thus, by Esthwaite lake,
When life was sweet, I knew not why,
To me my good friend Matthew spake,
And thus I made reply:

'The eye – it cannot choose but see;
We cannot bid the ear be still;
Our bodies feel, where'er they be,
20 Against or with our will.

'Nor less I deem that there are Powers
Which of themselves our minds impress;
That we can feed this mind of ours
In a wise passiveness.

'Think you, 'mid all this mighty sum
Of things for ever speaking,
That nothing of itself will come,
But we must still be seeking?

'– Then ask not wherefore, here, alone,
30 Conversing as I may,
I sit upon this old grey stone,
And dream my time away.'

The Tables Turned
An Evening Scene on the Same Subject

Up! up! my Friend, and quit your books;
Or surely you'll grow double:
Up! up! my Friend, and clear your looks;
Why all this toil and trouble?

The sun, above the mountain's head,
A freshening lustre mellow
Through all the long green fields has spread,
His first sweet evening yellow.

Books! 'tis a dull and endless strife:
10 Come, hear the woodland linnet,
How sweet his music! on my life,
There's more of wisdom in it.

And hark! how blithe the throstle sings!
He, too, is no mean preacher:
Come forth into the light of things,
Let Nature be your Teacher.

She has a world of ready wealth,
Our minds and hearts to bless –
Spontaneous wisdom breathed by health,
20 Truth breathed by cheerfulness.

One impulse from a vernal wood
May teach you more of man,
Of moral evil and of good,
Than all the sages can.

Sweet is the lore which Nature brings;
Our meddling intellect
Mis-shapes the beauteous forms of things: –
We murder to dissect.

Enough of Science and of Art;
30 Close up those barren leaves;
Come forth, and bring with you a heart
That watches and receives.

*Lines Composed a Few Miles above Tintern
Abbey, on Revisiting the Banks of the Wye
during a Tour. July 13, 1798*

Five years have past; five summers, with the length
Of five long winters! and again I hear
These waters, rolling from their mountain-springs
With a soft inland murmur. – Once again

Do I behold these steep and lofty cliffs,
That on a wild secluded scene impress
Thoughts of more deep seclusion; and connect
The landscape with the quiet of the sky.
The day is come when I again repose
10 Here, under this dark sycamore, and view
These plots of cottage-ground, these orchard-tufts,
Which at this season, with their unripe fruits,
Are clad in one green hue, and lose themselves
'Mid groves and copses. Once again I see
These hedge-rows, hardly hedge-rows, little lines
Of sportive wood run wild: these pastoral farms,
Green to the very door; and wreaths of smoke
Sent up, in silence, from among the trees!
With some uncertain notice, as might seem
20 Of vagrant dwellers in the houseless woods,
Or of some Hermit's cave, where by his fire
The Hermit sits alone.
                        These beauteous forms,
Through a long absence, have not been to me
As is a landscape to a blind man's eye:
But oft, in lonely rooms, and 'mid the din
Of towns and cities, I have owed to them
In hours of weariness, sensations sweet,
Felt in the blood, and felt along the heart;
And passing even into my purer mind,
30 With tranquil restoration: – feelings too
Of unremembered pleasure: such, perhaps,
As have no slight or trivial influence
On that best portion of a good man's life,
His little, nameless, unremembered, acts
Of kindness and of love. Nor less, I trust,
To them I may have owed another gift,
Of aspect more sublime; that blessed mood,
In which the burden of the mystery,
In which the heavy and the weary weight
40 Of all this unintelligible world,
Is lightened: – that serene and blessed mood,

In which the affections gently lead us on, –
Until, the breath of this corporeal frame
And even the motion of our human blood
Almost suspended, we are laid asleep
In body, and become a living soul:
While with an eye made quiet by the power
Of harmony, and the deep power of joy,
We see into the life of things.
                  If this
50 Be but a vain belief, yet, oh! how oft –
In darkness and amid the many shapes
Of joyless daylight; when the fretful stir
Unprofitable, and the fever of the world,
Have hung upon the beatings of my heart –
How oft, in spirit, have I turned to thee,
O sylvan Wye! thou wanderer through the woods,
How often has my spirit turned to thee!

   And now, with gleams of half-extinguished thought,
With many recognitions dim and faint,
60 And somewhat of a sad perplexity,
The picture of the mind revives again:
While here I stand, not only with the sense
Of present pleasure, but with pleasing thoughts
That in this moment there is life and food
For future years. And so I dare to hope,
Though changed, no doubt, from what I was when first
I came among these hills; when like a roe
I bounded o'er the mountains, by the sides
Of the deep rivers, and the lonely streams,
70 Wherever nature led: more like a man
Flying from something that he dreads, than one
Who sought the thing he loved. For nature then
(The coarser pleasures of my boyish days,
And their glad animal movements all gone by)
To me was all in all. – I cannot paint
What then I was. The sounding cataract
Haunted me like a passion: the tall rock,

The mountain, and the deep and gloomy wood,
Their colours and their forms, were then to me
80 An appetite; a feeling and a love,
That had no need of a remoter charm,
By thought supplied, nor any interest
Unborrowed from the eye. – That time is past,
And all its aching joys are now no more,
And all its dizzy raptures. Not for this
Faint I, nor mourn nor murmur; other gifts
Have followed; for such loss, I would believe,
Abundant recompense. For I have learned
To look on nature, not as in the hour
90 Of thoughtless youth; but hearing oftentimes
The still, sad music of humanity,
Nor harsh nor grating, though of ample power
To chasten and subdue. And I have felt
A presence that disturbs me with the joy
Of elevated thoughts; a sense sublime
Of something far more deeply interfused,
Whose dwelling is the light of setting suns,
And the round ocean and the living air,
And the blue sky, and in the mind of man:
100 A motion and a spirit, that impels
All thinking things, all objects of all thought,
And rolls through all things. Therefore am I still
A lover of the meadows and the woods,
And mountains; and of all that we behold
From this green earth; of all the mighty world
Of eye, and ear, – both what they half create,
And what perceive; well pleased to recognize
In nature and the language of the sense,
The anchor of my purest thoughts, the nurse,
110 The guide, the guardian of my heart, and soul
Of all my moral being.
                              Nor perchance,
If I were not thus taught, should I the more
Suffer my genial spirits to decay:
For thou art with me here upon the banks

Of this fair river; thou my dearest Friend,
My dear, dear Friend; and in thy voice I catch
The language of my former heart, and read
My former pleasures in the shooting lights
Of thy wild eyes. Oh! yet a little while
120 May I behold in thee what I was once,
My dear, dear Sister! and this prayer I make,
Knowing that Nature never did betray
The heart that loved her; 'tis her privilege,
Through all the years of this our life, to lead
From joy to joy: for she can so inform
The mind that is within us, so impress
With quietness and beauty, and so feed
With lofty thoughts, that neither evil tongues,
Rash judgements, nor the sneers of selfish men,
130 Nor greetings where no kindness is, nor all
The dreary intercourse of daily life,
Shall e'er prevail against us, or disturb
Our cheerful faith, that all which we behold
Is full of blessings. Therefore let the moon
Shine on thee in thy solitary walk;
And let the misty mountain-winds be free
To blow against thee: and, in after years,
When these wild ecstasies shall be matured
Into a sober pleasure; when thy mind
140 Shall be a mansion for all lovely forms,
Thy memory be as a dwelling-place
For all sweet sounds and harmonies; oh! then,
If solitude, or fear, or pain, or grief,
Should be thy portion, with what healing thoughts
Of tender joy wilt thou remember me,
And these my exhortations! Nor, perchance –
If I should be where I no more can hear
Thy voice, nor catch from thy wild eyes these gleams
Of past existence – wilt thou then forget
150 That on the banks of this delightful stream
We stood together; and that I, so long
A worshipper of Nature, hither came

Unwearied in that service: rather say
With warmer love – oh! with far deeper zeal
Of holier love. Nor wilt thou then forget,
That after many wanderings, many years
Of absence, these steep woods and lofty cliffs,
And this green pastoral landscape, were to me
More dear, both for themselves and for thy sake!

There Was a Boy

There was a Boy; ye knew him well, ye cliffs
And islands of Winander! – many a time,
At evening, when the earliest stars began
To move along the edges of the hills,
Rising or setting, would he stand alone,
Beneath the trees, or by the glimmering lake;
And there, with fingers interwoven, both hands
Pressed closely palm to palm and to his mouth
Uplifted, he, as through an instrument,
10   Blew mimic hootings to the silent owls,
That they might answer him. – And they would shout
Across the watery vale, and shout again,
Responsive to his call, – with quivering peals,
And long halloos, and screams, and echoes loud
Redoubled and redoubled; concourse wild
Of jocund din! And, when there came a pause
Of silence such as baffled his best skill:
Then, sometimes, in that silence, while he hung
Listening, a gentle shock of mild surprise
20   Has carried far into his heart the voice
Of mountain-torrents; or the visible scene
Would enter unawares into his mind
With all its solemn imagery, its rocks,
Its woods, and that uncertain heaven received
Into the bosom of the steady lake.

This boy was taken from his mates, and died
In childhood, ere he was full twelve years old.
Pre-eminent in beauty is the vale
Where he was born and bred: the churchyard hangs
30 Upon a slope above the village-school;
And, through that churchyard when my way has led
On summer-evenings, I believe, that there
A long half-hour together I have stood
Mute – looking at the grave in which he lies!

*Alcaeus to Sappho

How sweet, when crimson colours dart
Across a breast of snow,
To see that you are in the heart
That beats and throbs below!

All Heaven is in a Maiden's blush,
In which the soul doth speak,
That it was you who sent the flush
Into the Maiden's cheek!

Large stedfast eyes, eyes gently rolled,
10 In shades of changing blue,
How sweet are they, if they behold
No dearer sight than you!

And, can a lip more richly glow,
Or be more fair than this?
The world will surely answer, No!
I, Sappho! answer, Yes!

Then grant one smile, though it should mean
A thing of doubtful birth;
That I may say these eyes have seen
20 The fairest face on earth!

'*A slumber did my spirit seal*'

A slumber did my spirit seal;
    I had no human fears:
She seemed a thing that could not feel
    The touch of earthly years.

No motion has she now, no force;
    She neither hears nor sees;
Rolled round in earth's diurnal course,
    With rocks, and stones, and trees.

Influence of Natural Objects in Calling Forth and Strengthening the Imagination in Boyhood and Early Youth

FROM AN UNPUBLISHED POEM

[This extract is reprinted from *The Friend*.]

Wisdom and Spirit of the universe!
Thou Soul, that art the Eternity of thought!
And giv'st to forms and images a breath
And everlasting motion! not in vain,
By day or star-light, thus from my first dawn
Of childhood didst thou intertwine for me
The passions that build up our human soul;
Not with the mean and vulgar works of Man;
But with high objects, with enduring things,
10 With life and nature; purifying thus
The elements of feeling and of thought,
And sanctifying by such discipline
Both pain and fear, – until we recognize
A grandeur in the beatings of the heart.

Nor was this fellowship vouchsafed to me
With stinted kindness. In November days,
When vapours rolling down the valleys made
A lonely scene more lonesome; among woods
At noon; and 'mid the calm of summer nights,
20 When, by the margin of the trembling lake,
Beneath the gloomy hills, homeward I went
In solitude, such intercourse was mine:
Mine was it in the fields both day and night,
And by the waters, all the summer long.
And in the frosty season, when the sun
Was set, and, visible for many a mile,
The cottage-windows through the twilight blazed,
I heeded not the summons: happy time
It was indeed for all of us; for me
30 It was a time of rapture! Clear and loud
The village-clock tolled six – I wheeled about,
Proud and exulting like an untired horse
That cares not for his home. – All shod with steel
We hissed along the polished ice, in games
Confederate, imitative of the chase
And woodland pleasures, – the resounding horn,
The pack loud-chiming, and the hunted hare.
So through the darkness and the cold we flew,
And not a voice was idle: with the din
40 Smitten, the precipices rang aloud;
The leafless trees and every icy crag
Tinkled like iron; while far-distant hills
Into the tumult sent an alien sound
Of melancholy, not unnoticed while the stars,
Eastward, were sparkling clear, and in the west
The orange sky of evening died away.

Not seldom from the uproar I retired
Into a silent bay, or sportively
Glanced sideway, leaving the tumultuous throng,
50 To cut across the reflex of a star;
Image, that, flying still before me, gleamed

Upon the glassy plain: and oftentimes,
When we had given our bodies to the wind,
And all the shadowy banks on either side
Came sweeping through the darkness, spinning still
The rapid line of motion, then at once
Have I, reclining back upon my heels,
Stopped short; yet still the solitary cliffs
Wheeled by me – even as ˙f the earth had rolled
60   With visible motion her diurnal round!
Behind me did they stretch in solemn train,
Feebler and feebler, and I stood and watched
Till all was tranquil as a summer sea.

'*She dwelt among the untrodden ways*'

She dwelt among the untrodden ways
    Beside the springs of Dove,
A Maid whom there were none to praise
    And very few to love:

A violet by a mossy stone
    Half hidden from the eye!
– Fair as a star, when only one
    Is shining in the sky.

She lived unknown, and few could know
10   When Lucy ceased to be;
But she is in her grave, and, oh,
    The difference to me!

'*Strange fits of passion have I known*'

Strange fits of passion have I known:
And I will dare to tell,
But in the Lover's ear alone,
What once to me befell.

When she I loved looked every day
Fresh as a rose in June,
I to her cottage bent my way,
Beneath an evening moon.

Upon the moon I fixed my eye,
10 All over the wide lea;
With quickening pace my horse drew nigh
Those paths so dear to me.

And now we reached the orchard-plot;
And, as we climbed the hill,
The sinking moon to Lucy's cot
Came near, and nearer still.

In one of those sweet dreams I slept,
Kind Nature's gentlest boon!
And all the while my eyes I kept
20 On the descending moon.

My horse moved on; hoof after hoof
He raised, and never stopped:
When down behind the cottage roof,
At once, the bright moon dropped.

What fond and wayward thoughts will slide
Into a Lover's head!
'O mercy!' to myself I cried,
'If Lucy should be dead!'

Nutting

——————— It seems a day
(I speak of one from many singled out)
One of those heavenly days that cannot die;
When, in the eagerness of boyish hope,
I left our cottage-threshold, sallying forth

With a huge wallet o'er my shoulders slung,
A nutting-crook in hand; and turned my steps
Toward some far-distant wood, a Figure quaint,
Tricked out in proud disguise of cast-off weeds
10 Which for that service had been husbanded,
By exhortation of my frugal Dame –
Motley accoutrement, of power to smile
At thorns, and brakes, and brambles, – and, in truth,
More ragged than need was! O'er pathless rocks,
Through beds of matted fern, and tangled thickets,
Forcing my way, I came to one dear nook
Unvisited, where not a broken bough
Drooped with its withered leaves, ungracious sign
Of devastation; but the hazels rose
20 Tall and erect, with tempting clusters hung,
A virgin scene! – A little while I stood,
Breathing with such suppression of the heart
As joy delights in; and, with wise restraint
Voluptuous, fearless of a rival, eyed
The banquet; – or beneath the trees I sate
Among the flowers, and with the flowers I played;
A temper known to those who, after long
And weary expectation, have been blest
With sudden happiness beyond all hope.
30 Perhaps it was a bower beneath whose leaves
The violets of five seasons re-appear
And fade, unseen by any human eye;
Where fairy water-breaks do murmur on
For ever; and I saw the sparkling foam,
And – with my cheek on one of those green stones
That, fleeced with moss, under the shady trees,
Lay round me, scattered like a flock of sheep –
I heard the murmur and the murmuring sound,
In that sweet mood when pleasure loves to pay
40 Tribute to ease; and, of its joy secure,
The heart luxuriates with indifferent things,
Wasting its kindliness on stocks and stones,
And on the vacant air. Then up I rose,

And dragged to earth both branch and bough, with
    crash
And merciless ravage: and the shady nook
Of hazels, and the green and mossy bower,
Deformed and sullied, patiently gave up
Their quiet being: and, unless I now
Confound my present feelings with the past,
50 Ere from the mutilated bower I turned
Exulting, rich beyond the wealth of kings,
I felt a sense of pain when I beheld
The silent trees, and saw the intruding sky. –
Then, dearest Maiden, move along these shades
In gentleness of heart; with gentle hand
Touch – for there is a spirit in the woods.

The Danish Boy

A FRAGMENT

I

Between two sister moorland rills
There is a spot that seems to lie
Sacred to flowerets of the hills,
And sacred to the sky.
And in this smooth and open dell
There is a tempest-stricken tree;
A corner-stone by lightning cut,
The last stone of a lonely hut;
And in this dell you see
10 A thing no storm can e'er destroy,
The shadow of a Danish Boy.

II

In clouds above, the lark is heard,
But drops not here to earth for rest;
Within this lonesome nook the bird
Did never build her nest.
No beast, no bird, hath here his home;

Bees, wafted on the breezy air,
Pass high above those fragrant bells
To other flowers: – to other dells
20 Their burdens do they bear;
The Danish Boy walks here alone:
The lovely dell is all his own.

III
A Spirit of noon-day is he;
Yet seems a form of flesh and blood;
Nor piping shepherd shall he be,
Nor herd-boy of the wood.
A regal vest of fur he wears,
In colour like a raven's wing;
It fears not rain, nor wind, nor dew;
30 But in the storm 'tis fresh and blue
As budding pines in spring;
His helmet has a vernal grace,
Fresh as the bloom upon his face.

IV
A harp is from his shoulder slung;
Resting the harp upon his knee,
To words of a forgotten tongue
He suits its melody.
Of flocks upon the neighbouring hill
He is the darling and the joy;
40 And often, when no cause appears,
The mountain-ponies prick their ears,
– They hear the Danish Boy,
While in the dell he sings alone
Beside the tree and corner-stone.

V
There sits he; in his face you spy
No trace of a ferocious air,
Nor ever was a cloudless sky
So steady or so fair.

The lovely Danish Boy is blest
50 And happy in his flowery cove:
From bloody deeds his thoughts are far;
And yet he warbles songs of war,
That seem like songs of love,
For calm and gentle is his mien;
Like a dead Boy he is serene.

Ruth

When Ruth was left half desolate,
Her Father took another Mate;
And Ruth, not seven years old,
A slighted child, at her own will
Went wandering over dale and hill,
In thoughtless freedom, bold.

And she had made a pipe of straw,
And music from that pipe could draw
Like sounds of winds and floods;
10 Had built a bower upon the green,
As if she from her birth had been
An infant of the woods.

Beneath her father's roof, alone
She seemed to live; her thoughts her own;
Herself her own delight;
Pleased with herself, nor sad, nor gay;
And, passing thus the live-long day,
She grew to woman's height.

There came a Youth from Georgia's shore –
20 A military casque he wore,
With splendid feathers drest;
He brought them from the Cherokees;
The feathers nodded in the breeze,
And made a gallant crest.

From Indian blood you deem him sprung:
But no! he spake the English tongue,
And bore a soldier's name;
And, when America was free
From battle and from jeopardy,
30   He 'cross the ocean came.

With hues of genius on his cheek
In finest tones the Youth could speak:
– While he was yet a boy,
The moon, the glory of the sun,
And streams that murmur as they run,
Had been his dearest joy.

He was a lovely Youth! I guess
The panther in the wilderness
Was not so fair as he;
40   And, when he chose to sport and play,
No dolphin ever was so gay
Upon the tropic sea.

Among the Indians he had fought,
And with him many tales he brought
Of pleasure and of fear;
Such tales as told to any maid
By such a Youth, in the green shade,
Were perilous to hear.

He told of girls – a happy rout!
50   Who quit their fold with dance and shout,
Their pleasant Indian town,
To gather strawberries all day long;
Returning with a choral song
When daylight is gone down.

He spake of plants that hourly change
Their blossoms, through a boundless range
Of intermingling hues;

With budding, fading, faded flowers
They stand the wonder of the bowers
60 From morn to evening dews.

He told of the magnolia, spread
High as a cloud, high over head!
The cypress and her spire;
– Of flowers that with one scarlet gleam
Cover a hundred leagues, and seem
To set the hills on fire.

The Youth of green savannahs spake,
And many an endless, endless lake,
With all its fairy crowds
70 Of islands, that together lie
As quietly as spots of sky
Among the evening clouds.

'How pleasant,' then he said, 'it were
A fisher or a hunter there,
In sunshine or in shade
To wander with an easy mind;
And build a household fire, and find
A home in every glade!

'What days and what bright years! Ah me!
80 Our life were life indeed, with thee
So passed in quiet bliss,
And all the while,' said he, 'to know
That we were in a world of woe,
On such an earth as this!'

And then he sometimes interwove
Fond thoughts about a father's love:
'For there,' said he, 'are spun
Around the heart such tender ties,
That our own children to our eyes
90 Are dearer than the sun.

'Sweet Ruth! and could you go with me
My helpmate in the woods to be,
Our shed at night to rear;
Or run, my own adopted bride,
A sylvan huntress at my side,
And drive the flying deer!

'Beloved Ruth!' – No more he said.
The wakeful Ruth at midnight shed
A solitary tear:
100   She thought again – and did agree
With him to sail across the sea,
And drive the flying deer.

'And now, as fitting is and right,
We in the church our faith will plight,
A husband and a wife.'
Even so they did; and I may say
That to sweet Ruth that happy day
Was more than human life.
Through dream and vision did she sink,
110   Delighted all the while to think
That on those lonesome floods,
And green savannahs, she should share
His board with lawful joy, and bear
His name in the wild woods.

But, as you have before been told,
This Stripling, sportive, gay, and bold,
And, with his dancing crest,
So beautiful, through savage lands
Had roamed about, with vagrant bands
120   Of Indians in the West.

The wind, the tempest roaring high,
The tumult of a tropic sky,
Might well be dangerous food
For him, a Youth to whom was given

So much of earth – so much of heaven,
And such impetuous blood.

Whatever in those climes he found
Irregular in sight or sound
Did to his mind impart
130   A kindred impulse, seemed allied
To his own powers, and justified
The workings of his heart.

Nor less, to feed voluptuous thought,
The beauteous forms of nature wrought,
Fair trees and gorgeous flowers;
The breezes their own languor lent;
The stars had feelings, which they sent
Into those favored bowers.

Yet, in his worse pursuits, I ween
140   That sometimes there did intervene
Pure hopes of high intent:
For passions linked to forms so fair
And stately, needs must have their share
Of noble sentiment.

But ill he lived, much evil saw,
With men to whom no better law
Nor better life was known;
Deliberately, and undeceived,
Those wild men's vices he received,
150   And gave them back his own.

His genius and his moral frame
Were thus impaired, and he became
The slave of low desires:
A Man who without self-control
Would seek what the degraded soul
Unworthily admires.

And yet he with no feigned delight
Had wooed the Maiden, day and night
Had loved her, night and morn:
160 What could he less than love a Maid
Whose heart with so much nature played
So kind and so forlorn!

Sometimes, most earnestly, he said,
'O Ruth! I have been worse than dead;
False thoughts, thoughts bold and vain,
Encompassed me on every side
When I, in confidence and pride,
Had crossed the Atlantic main.

'Before me shone a glorious world –
170 Fresh as a banner bright, unfurled
To music suddenly:
I looked upon those hills and plains,
And seemed as if let loose from chains,
To live at liberty.

'No more of this; for now, by thee
Dear Ruth! more happily set free
With nobler zeal I burn;
My soul from darkness is released,
Like the whole sky when to the east
180 The morning doth return.'

Full soon that better mind was gone;
No hope, no wish remained, not one, –
They stirred him now no more;
New objects did new pleasure give,
And once again he wished to live
As lawless as before.

Meanwhile, as thus with him it fared,
They for the voyage were prepared,
And went to the sea-shore,

190 But, when they thither came, the Youth
Deserted his poor Bride, and Ruth
Could never find him more.

God help thee, Ruth! – Such pains she had,
That she in half a year was mad,
And in a prison housed;
And there, with many a doleful song
Made of wild words, her cup of wrong
She fearfully caroused.

Yet sometimes milder hours she knew,
200 Nor wanted sun, nor rain, nor dew,
Nor pastimes of the May;
– They all were with her in her cell;
And a clear brook with cheerful knell
Did o'er the pebbles play.

When Ruth three seasons thus had lain,
There came a respite to her pain;
She from her prison fled;
But of the Vagrant none took thought;
And where it liked her best she sought
210 Her shelter and her bread.

Among the fields she breathed again:
The master-current of her brain
Ran permanent and free;
And, coming to the Banks of Tone,
There did she rest; and dwell alone
Under the greenwood tree.

The engines of her pain, the tools
That shaped her sorrow, rocks and pools,
And airs that gently stir
220 The vernal leaves – she loved them still;
Nor ever taxed them with the ill
Which had been done to her.

A Barn her *winter* bed supplies;
But, till the warmth of summer skies
And summer days is gone,
(And all do in this tale agree)
She sleeps beneath the greenwood tree,
And other home hath none.

An innocent life, yet far astray!
230 And Ruth will, long before her day,
Be broken down and old:
Sore aches she needs must have! but less
Of mind, than body's wretchedness,
From damp, and rain, and cold.

If she is prest by want of food,
She from her dwelling in the wood
Repairs to a road-side;
And there she begs at one steep place
Where up and down with easy pace
240 The horsemen-travellers ride.

That oaten pipe of hers is mute,
Or thrown away; but with a flute
Her loneliness she cheers:
This flute, made of a hemlock stalk,
At evening in his homeward walk
The Quantock woodman hears.

I, too, have passed her on the hills
Setting her little water-mills
By spouts and fountains wild –
250 Such small machinery as she turned
Ere she had wept, ere she had mourned,
A young and happy Child!

Farewell! and when thy days are told,
Ill-fated Ruth, in hallowed mould
Thy corpse shall buried be,

For thee a funeral bell shall ring,
And all the congregation sing
A Christian psalm for thee.

To a Sexton

Let thy wheel-barrow alone –
Wherefore, Sexton, piling still
In thy bone-house bone on bone?
'Tis already like a hill
In a field of battle made,
Where three thousand skulls are laid;
These died in peace each with the other, –
Father, sister, friend, and brother.

Mark the spot to which I point!
10 From this platform, eight feet square,
Take not even a finger-joint:
Andrew's whole fire-side is there.
Here, alone, before thine eyes,
Simon's sickly daughter lies,
From weakness now, and pain defended,
Whom he twenty winters tended.

Look but at the gardener's pride –
How he glories, when he sees
Roses, lilies, side by side,
20 Violets in families!
By the heart of Man, his tears,
By his hopes and by his fears,
Thou, too heedless, art the Warden
Of a far superior garden.

Thus then, each to other dear,
Let them all in quiet lie,
Andrew there, and Susan here,
Neighbours in mortality.

And should I live through sun and rain
30   Seven widowed years without my Jane,
O Sexton, do not then remove her,
Let one grave hold the Loved and Lover!

Matthew

In the School of — is a tablet, on which are inscribed, in gilt
letters, the Names of the several persons who have been School-
masters there since the foundation of the School, with the time
at which they entered upon and quitted their office. Opposite
to one of those Names the Author wrote the following lines.

If Nature, for a favourite child,
In thee hath tempered so her clay,
That every hour thy heart runs wild,
Yet never once doth go astray,

Read o'er these lines; and then review
This tablet, that thus humbly rears
In such diversity of hue
Its history of two hundred years.

– When through this little wreck of fame,
10   Cipher and syllable! thine eye
Has travelled down to Matthew's name,
Pause with no common sympathy.

And, if a sleeping tear should wake,
Then be it neither checked nor stayed:
For Matthew a request I make
Which for himself he had not made.

Poor Matthew, all his frolics o'er,
Is silent as a standing pool;
Far from the chimney's merry roar,
20   And murmur of the village school.

The sighs which Matthew heaved were sighs
Of one tired out with fun and madness;
The tears which came to Matthew's eyes
Were tears of light, the dew of gladness.

Yet, sometimes, when the secret cup
Of still and serious thought went round,
It seemed as if he drank it up –
He felt with spirit so profound.

– Thou soul of God's best earthly mould!
30 Thou happy Soul! and can it be
That these two words of glittering gold
Are all that must remain of thee?

The Two April Mornings

We walked along, while bright and red
Uprose the morning sun;
And Matthew stopped, he looked, and said,
'The will of God be done!'

A village schoolmaster was he,
With hair of glittering grey;
As blithe a man as you could see
On a spring holiday.

And on that morning, through the grass,
10 And by the steaming rills,
We travelled merrily, to pass
A day among the hills.

'Our work,' said I, 'was well begun,
Then, from thy breast what thought,
Beneath so beautiful a sun,
So sad a sigh has brought?'

A second time did Matthew stop;
And fixing still his eye
Upon the eastern mountain-top,
20   To me he made reply:

'Yon cloud with that long purple cleft
Brings fresh into my mind
A day like this which I have left
Full thirty years behind.

'And just above yon slope of corn
Such colours, and no other,
Were in the sky, that April morn,
Of this the very brother.

'With rod and line I sued the sport
30   Which that sweet season gave,
And, to the churchyard come, stopped short
Beside my daughter's grave.

'Nine summers had she scarcely seen,
The pride of all the vale;
And then she sang; – she would have been
A very nightingale.

'Six feet in earth my Emma lay;
And yet I loved her more,
For so it seemed, than till that day
40   I e'er had loved before.

'And, turning from her grave, I met,
Beside the churchyard yew,
A blooming Girl, whose hair was wet
With points of morning dew.

'A basket on her head she bare;
Her brow was smooth and white:
To see a child so very fair,
It was a pure delight!

'No fountain from its rocky cave
50 E'er tripped with foot so free;
She seemed as happy as a wave
That dances on the sea.

'There came from me a sigh of pain
Which I could ill confine;
I looked at her, and looked again:
And did not wish her mine!'

Matthew is in his grave, yet now,
Methinks, I see him stand,
As at that moment, with a bough
60 Of wilding in his hand.

The Fountain

A CONVERSATION

We talked with open heart, and tongue
Affectionate and true,
A pair of friends, though I was young,
And Matthew seventy-two.

We lay beneath a spreading oak,
Beside a mossy seat;
And from the turf a fountain broke,
And gurgled at our feet.

'Now, Matthew!' said I, 'let us match
10 This water's pleasant tune
With some old border-song, or catch
That suits a summer's noon;

'Or of the church-clock and the chimes
Sing here beneath the shade,
That half-mad thing of witty rhymes
Which you last April made!'

In silence Matthew lay, and eyed
The spring beneath the tree;
And thus the dear old Man replied,
20   The grey-haired man of glee:

'No check, no stay, this Streamlet fears;
How merrily it goes!
'Twill murmur on a thousand years,
And flow as now it flows.

'And here, on this delightful day,
I cannot choose but think
How oft, a vigorous man, I lay
Beside this fountain's brink.

'My eyes are dim with childish tears,
30   My heart is idly stirred,
For the same sound is in my ears
Which in those days I heard.

'Thus fares it still in our decay:
And yet the wiser mind
Mourns less for what age takes away
Than what it leaves behind.

'The blackbird amid leafy trees,
The lark above the hill,
Let loose their carols when they please,
40   Are quiet when they will.

'With Nature never do *they* wage
A foolish strife; they see
A happy youth, and their old age
Is beautiful and free:

'But we are pressed by heavy laws;
And often, glad no more,
We wear a face of joy, because
We have been glad of yore.

'If there be one who need bemoan
50   His kindred laid in earth,
    The household hearts that were his own;
    It is the man of mirth.

    'My days, my Friend, are almost gone,
    My life has been approved,
    And many love me; but by none
    Am I enough beloved.'

    'Now both himself and me he wrongs,
    The man who thus complains!
    I live and sing my idle songs
60   Upon these happy plains;

    'And, Matthew, for thy children dead
    I'll be a son to thee!'
    At this he grasped my hand, and said,
    'Alas! that cannot be.'

    We rose up from the fountain-side;
    And down the smooth descent
    Of the green sheep-track did we glide;
    And through the wood we went;

    And, ere we came to Leonard's rock,
70   He sang those witty rhymes
    About the crazy old church-clock,
    And the bewildered chimes.

'Could I the priest's consent have gained'

Could I the priest's consent have gained
Or his who tolled thy passing bell,
Then, Matthew, had thy bones remained
Beneath this tree we loved so well.

Yet in our thorn will I suspend
Thy gift this twisted oaken staff,
And here where trunk and branches blend
Will I engrave thy epitaph.

Just as the blowing thorn began
10   To spread again its vernal shade,
This village lost as good a man
As ever handled book or spade.

Then Traveller passing o'er the green,
Thy course a single moment stay,
Though here no mouldering [heap?] be seen
To tell thee thou art kindred clay.

A schoolmaster by title known
Long Matthew penned his little flock
Within yon pile that stands alone
20   In colour like its native rock.

Learning will often dry the heart,
The very bones it will distress,
But Matthew had an idle art
Of teaching love and happiness.

The neat trim house, the cottage rude
All owed to Matthew gifts of gold,
Light pleasures every day renewed
Or blessings half a century old.

His fancy played with endless play
30   So full of mother wit was he,
He was a thousand times more gay
Than any dunce has power to be.

Yet when his hair was white as rime
And he twice thirty years had seen
Would Matthew wish from time to time
That he a graver man had been.

But nothing could his heart have bribed
To be as sad as mine is now,
As I have been while I inscribed
40 This verse beneath the hawthorn bough.

Elegy Written in the Same Place
Upon the Same Occasion

Remembering how thou didst beguile
With thy w[ild] ways our eyes and ears,
I feel more sorrow in a smile
Than in a waggon-load of tears;

I smile to hear the hunter's horn,
I smile at meadow, rock and shore,
I smile too at this silly thorn
Which blooms as sweetly as before.

I think of thee in silent love
10 And feel just like a wavering leaf,
Along my face the muscles move,
Nor know if 'tis with joy or grief,

But oft when I look up and view
Yon huts upon the mountain-side
I sigh and say, it was for you
An evil day when Matthew died.

The neat trim house, the cottage rude
All owed to Matthew gifts of gold,
Light pleasures every day renewed
20 Or blessings half a century old.

Then weep, ye Elves, a noisy race
Thoughtless as roses newly blown,
Weep Matthew with his happy face
Now lying in his grave alone.

Thou one blind Sailor, child of joy
Thy lonely tunes in sadness hum
And mourn, thou poor half-witted boy,
Born deaf and living deaf and dumb.

Mourn, Shepherd, near thy old grey stone,
30 Thou Angler by the silent flood,
And mourn when thou art all alone
Thou woodman in the lonesome wood.

Mourn sick man sitting in the shade
When summer suns have warmed the earth,
Ye saw the [   ] which Matthew made
And shook with weakness and with mirth.

Mourn reapers thirsting in a crew
Who rouse with shouts the evening vale,
Thou mower in the morning dew,
40 Thou milkmaid by thy evening pail.

Ye little girls, ye loved his name,
Come here and knit your gloves of yarn,
Ye loved him better than your dame
– The schoolmaster of fair Glencarn.

For though to many a wanton boy
Did Matthew act a father's part,
Ye tiny maids, *ye* were his joy,
Ye were the favourites of his heart.

Ye ruddy damsels past sixteen
50 Weep now that Matthew's race is run;
He wrote your love-letters, I ween
Ye kissed him when the work was done.

Ye Brothers gone to towns remote,
And ye upon the ocean tost,
Ye many a good and pious thought
And many a [   ] have lost.

Staid men may weep, from him they quaffed
Such wit as never failed to please,
While at his [   ] they laughed
60 Enough to set their hearts at ease.

Ye mothers who for jibe or jest
Have little room in heart or head,
The child that lies upon your breast
May make you think of Matthew dead.

Old women in your elbow chairs,
Who now will be your fence and shield,
When wintry blasts and cutting airs
Are busy in both house and field?

And weep thou School of fair Glencarn,
70 No more shalt thou in stormy weather
Be like a play-house in a barn
Where Punch and Hamlet play together.

Ye sheep-curs, a mirth-loving corps!
Now let your tails lie still between
Your drooping hips – you'll never more
Bark at his voice upon the green.

Remembering how thou didst beguile
With thy wild ways our eyes and ears,
I feel more sorrow in a smile
80 Than in a waggon-load of tears.

Address to the Scholars of the Village School of —

1798

I come, ye little noisy Crew,
Not long your pastime to prevent;
I heard the blessing which to you
Our common Friend and Father sent.

I kissed his cheek before he died;
And when his breath was fled,
I raised, while kneeling by his side,
His hand: – it dropped like lead.
Your hands, dear Little-ones, do all
10   That can be done, will never fall
Like his till they are dead.
By night or day, blow foul or fair,
Ne'er will the best of all your train
Play with the locks of his white hair,
Or stand between his knees again.

Here did he sit confined for hours;
But he could see the woods and plains,
Could hear the wind and mark the showers
Come streaming down the streaming panes.
20   Now stretched beneath his grass-green mound
He rests a prisoner of the ground.
He loved the breathing air,
He loved the sun, but if it rise
Or set, to him where now he lies,
Brings not a moment's care.
Alas! what idle words; but take
The Dirge which for our Master's sake
And yours, love prompted me to make.
The rhymes so homely in attire
30   With learnèd ears may ill agree,
But chanted by your Orphan Choir
Will make a touching melody.

DIRGE

Mourn, Shepherd, near thy old grey stone;
Thou Angler, by the silent flood;
And mourn when thou art all alone,
Thou Woodman, in the distant wood!

Thou one blind Sailor, rich in joy
Though blind, thy tunes in sadness hum;
And mourn, thou poor half-witted Boy!
40 Born deaf, and living deaf and dumb.

Thou drooping sick Man, bless the Guide
Who checked or turned thy headstrong youth,
As he before had sanctified
Thy infancy with heavenly truth.

Ye Striplings, light of heart and gay,
Bold settlers on some foreign shore,
Give, when your thoughts are turned this way,
A sigh to him whom we deplore.

For us who here in funeral strain
50 With one accord our voices raise,
Let sorrow overcharged with pain
Be lost in thankfulness and praise.

And when our hearts shall feel a sting
From ill we meet or good we miss,
May touches of his memory bring
Fond healing, like a mother's kiss.

BY THE SIDE OF THE GRAVE SOME YEARS AFTER

Long time his pulse hath ceased to beat;
But benefits, his gift, we trace –
Expressed in every eye we meet
60 Round this dear Vale, his native place.

To stately Hall and Cottage rude
Flowed from his life what still they hold,
Light pleasures, every day renewed;
And blessings half a century old.

Oh true of heart, of spirit gay,
Thy faults, where not already gone
From memory, prolong their stay
For charity's sweet sake alone.

Such solace find we for our loss;
70 And what beyond this thought we crave
Comes in the promise from the Cross,
Shining upon thy happy grave.

Lucy Gray; or, Solitude

Oft I had heard of Lucy Gray:
And, when I crossed the wild,
I chanced to see at break of day
The solitary child.

No mate, no comrade Lucy knew;
She dwelt on a wide moor,
– The sweetest thing that ever grew
Beside a human door!

You yet may spy the fawn at play,
10 The hare upon the green;
But the sweet face of Lucy Gray
Will never more be seen.

'Tonight will be a stormy night –
You to the town must go;
And take a lantern, Child, to light
Your mother through the snow.'

'That, Father! will I gladly do:
'Tis scarcely afternoon –
The minster-clock has just struck two,
20 And yonder is the moon!'

At this the Father raised his hook,
And snapped a faggot-band;
He plied his work; – and Lucy took
The lantern in her hand.

Not blither is the mountain roe:
With many a wanton stroke
Her feet disperse the powdery snow,
That rises up like smoke.

The storm came on before its time:
30 She wandered up and down;
And many a hill did Lucy climb:
But never reached the town.

The wretched parents all that night
Went shouting far and wide;
But there was neither sound nor sight
To serve them for a guide.

At day-break on a hill they stood
That overlooked the moor;
And thence they saw the bridge of wood,
40 A furlong from their door.

They wept – and, turning homeward, cried,
'In heaven we all shall meet;'
– When in the snow the mother spied
The print of Lucy's feet.

Then downwards from the steep hill's edge
They tracked the footmarks small;
And through the broken hawthorn hedge,
And by the long stone-wall;

And then an open field they crossed:
50 The marks were still the same;
They tracked them on, nor ever lost;
And to the bridge they came.

They followed from the snowy bank
Those footmarks, one by one,
Into the middle of the plank;
And further there were none!

– Yet some maintain that to this day
She is a living child;
That you may see sweet Lucy Gray
60   Upon the lonesome wild.

O'er rough and smooth she trips along,
And never looks behind;
And sings a solitary song
That whistles in the wind.

Written in Germany on One of the Coldest Days of the Century

The Reader must be apprised that the Stoves in North Germany
generally have the impression of a galloping horse upon them,
this being part of the Brunswick Arms.

A plague on your languages, German and Norse!
Let me have the song of the kettle;
And the tongs and the poker, instead of that horse
That gallops away with such fury and force
On this dreary dull plate of black metal.

See that Fly, – a disconsolate creature! perhaps
A child of the field or the grove;
And, sorrow for him! the dull treacherous heat
Has seduced the poor fool from his winter retreat,
10   And he creeps to the edge of my stove.

Alas! how he fumbles about the domains
Which this comfortless oven environ!
He cannot find out in what track he must crawl,
Now back to the tiles, then in search of the wall,
And now on the brink of the iron.

Stock-still there he stands like a traveller bemazed:
The best of his skill he has tried;
His feelers, methinks, I can see him put forth
To the east and the west, to the south and the north,
20 But he finds neither guide-post nor guide.

His spindles sink under him, foot, leg, and thigh!
His eyesight and hearing are lost;
Between life and death his blood freezes and thaws;
And his two pretty pinions of blue dusky gauze
Are glued to his sides by the frost.

No brother, no mate has he near him – while I
Can draw warmth from the cheek of my Love;
As blest and as glad, in this desolate gloom,
As if green summer grass were the floor of my room,
30 And woodbines were hanging above.

Yet, God is my witness, thou small helpless Thing!
Thy life I would gladly sustain
Till summer come up from the south, and with crowds
Of thy brethren a march thou shouldst sound through
        the clouds,
And back to the forests again!

A Poet's Epitaph

Art thou a Statist in the van
Of public conflicts trained and bred?
– First learn to love one living man;
Then mayst thou think upon the dead.

A Lawyer art thou? – draw not nigh!
Go, carry to some fitter place
The keenness of that practised eye,
The hardness of that sallow face.

Art thou a Man of purple cheer?
10 A rosy Man, right plump to see?
Approach; yet, Doctor, not too near,
This grave no cushion is for thee.

Or art thou one of gallant pride,
A Soldier and no man of chaff?
Welcome! – but lay thy sword aside,
And lean upon a peasant's staff.

Physician art thou? – one, all eyes,
Philosopher! – a fingering slave,
One that would peep and botanize
20 Upon his mother's grave?

Wrapt closely in thy sensual fleece,
O turn aside, – and take, I pray,
That he below may rest in peace,
Thy ever-dwindling soul, away!

A Moralist perchance appears;
Led, Heaven knows how! to this poor sod:
And he has neither eyes nor ears;
Himself his world, and his own God;

One to whose smooth-rubbed soul can cling
30 Nor form, nor feeling, great or small;
A reasoning, self-sufficing thing,
An intellectual All-in-all!

Shut close the door; press down the latch;
Sleep in thy intellectual crust;
Nor lose ten tickings of thy watch
Near this unprofitable dust.

But who is He, with modest looks,
And clad in homely russet brown?
He murmurs near the running brooks
40 A music sweeter than their own.

He is retired as noontide dew,
Or fountain in a noon-day grove;
And you must love him, ere to you
He will seem worthy of your love.

The outward shows of sky and earth,
Of hill and valley, he has viewed;
And impulses of deeper birth
Have come to him in solitude.

In common things that round us lie
50   Some random truths he can impart, –
The harvest of a quiet eye
That broods and sleeps on his own heart.

But he is weak; both Man and Boy,
Hath been an idler in the land;
Contented if he might enjoy
The things which others understand.

– Come hither in thy hour of strength;
Come, weak as is a breaking wave!
Here stretch thy body at full length;
60   Or build thy house upon this grave.

Ellen Irwin: or The Braes of Kirtle

Fair Ellen Irwin, when she sate
Upon the braes of Kirtle,
Was lovely as a Grecian maid
Adorned with wreaths of myrtle;
Young Adam Bruce beside her lay,
And there did they beguile the day
With love and gentle speeches,
Beneath the budding beeches.

From many knights and many squires
10 The Bruce had been selected;
And Gordon, fairest of them all,
By Ellen was rejected.
Sad tidings to that noble Youth!
For it may be proclaimed with truth,
If Bruce hath loved sincerely,
That Gordon loves as dearly.

But what are Gordon's form and face,
His shattered hopes and crosses,
To them, 'mid Kirtle's pleasant braes,
20 Reclined on flowers and mosses?
Alas that ever he was born!
The Gordon, couched behind a thorn,
Sees them and their caressing;
Beholds them blest and blessing.

Proud Gordon, maddened by the thoughts
That through his brain are travelling,
Rushed forth, and at the heart of Bruce
He launched a deadly javelin!
Fair Ellen saw it as it came,
30 And, starting up to meet the same,
Did with her body cover
The Youth, her chosen lover.

And, falling into Bruce's arms,
Thus died the beauteous Ellen,
Thus, from the heart of her True-love,
The mortal spear repelling.
And Bruce, as soon as he had slain
The Gordon, sailed away to Spain;
And fought with rage incessant
40 Against the Moorish crescent.

But many days, and many months,
And many years ensuing,

This wretched Knight did vainly seek
The death that he was wooing.
So, coming his last help to crave,
Heart-broken, upon Ellen's grave,
His body he extended,
And there his sorrow ended.

Now ye, who willingly have heard
50 The tale I have been telling,
May in Kirkconnel churchyard view
The grave of lovely Ellen:
By Ellen's side the Bruce is laid;
And, for the stone upon his head,
May no rude hand deface it,
And its forlorn 𝕳𝕚𝕔 𝕛𝕒𝕔𝕖𝕥!

*[Fragment: 'For let the impediment
be what it may']*

For let the impediment be what it may
His hands must clothe and nourish them, and there
From hour to hour so constantly he feels
An obligation pressing him with weight
Inevitable, that all offices
Which want this single tendency appear
Or trivial or redundant; hence remains
So little to be done which can assume
The appearance of a voluntary act,
10 That his affections in their very core
Are false, there is no freedom in his love.
Nor would he err perhaps who should assert
That this perceived necessity creates
The same constriction of the heart, the same
[   ] in those with whom he lives,
His wife and children. What then can we hope
From one who is the worst of slaves, the slave

Of his own house? The light that shines abroad,
How can it lead him to an act of love?
20 Whom can he comfort? Will the afflicted turn
Their steps to him, or will the eye of grief
And sorrow seek him? Is the name of friend
Known to the poor man? Whence is he to hear
The sweet creative voice of gratitude?

[*Fragment: Redundance*]

Not the more
Failed I to lengthen out my watch. I stood
Within the area of the frozen vale,
Mine eye subdued and quiet as the ear
Of one that listens, for even yet the scene,
Its fluctuating hues and surfaces,
And the decaying vestiges of forms,
Did to the dispossessing power of night
Impart a feeble visionary sense
Of movement and creation doubly felt

'*Three years she grew in sun and shower*'

Three years she grew in sun and shower,
Then Nature said, 'A lovelier flower
On earth was never sown;
This Child I to myself will take;
She shall be mine, and I will make
A Lady of my own.

'Myself will to my darling be
Both law and impulse: and with me
The Girl, in rock and plain,
10 In earth and heaven, in glade and bower,
Shall feel an overseeing power
To kindle or restrain.

'She shall be sportive as the fawn
That wild with glee across the lawn
Or up the mountain springs;
And hers shall be the breathing balm,
And hers the silence and the calm
Of mute insensate things.

'The floating clouds their state shall lend
20 To her; for her the willow bend;
Nor shall she fail to see
Even in the motions of the Storm
Grace that shall mould the Maiden's form
By silent sympathy.

'The stars of midnight shall be dear
To her; and she shall lean her ear
In many a secret place
Where rivulets dance their wayward round,
And beauty born of murmuring sound
30 Shall pass into her face.

'And vital feelings of delight
Shall rear her form to stately height,
Her virgin bosom swell;
Such thoughts to Lucy I will give
While she and I together live
Here in this happy dell.'

Thus Nature spake—The work was done—
How soon my Lucy's race was run!
She died, and left to me
40 This heath, this calm, and quiet scene;
The memory of what has been,
And never more will be.

The Brothers

'These Tourists, heaven preserve us! needs must live
A profitable life: some glance along,
Rapid and gay, as if the earth were air,
And they were butterflies to wheel about
Long as the summer lasted: some, as wise,
Perched on the forehead of a jutting crag,
Pencil in hand and book upon the knee,
Will look and scribble, scribble on and look,
Until a man might travel twelve stout miles,
10 Or reap an acre of his neighbour's corn.
But, for that moping Son of Idleness,
Why can he tarry *yonder*? – In our church-yard
Is neither epitaph nor monument,
Tombstone nor name – only the turf we tread
And a few natural graves.'
                  To Jane, his wife,
Thus spake the homely Priest of Ennerdale.
It was a July evening; and he sate
Upon the long stone-seat beneath the eaves
Of his old cottage, – as it chanced, that day,
20 Employed in winter's work. Upon the stone
His wife sate near him, teasing matted wool,
While, from the twin cards toothed with glittering wire,
He fed the spindle of his youngest child,
Who, in the open air, with due accord
Of busy hands and back-and-forward steps,
Her large round wheel was turning. Towards the field
In which the Parish Chapel stood alone,
Girt round with a bare ring of mossy wall,
While half an hour went by, the Priest had sent
30 Many a long look of wonder: and at last,
Risen from his seat, beside the snow-white ridge
Of carded wool which the old man had piled
He laid his implements with gentle care,
Each in the other locked; and, down the path,

That from his cottage to the church-yard led,
He took his way, impatient to accost
The Stranger, whom he saw still lingering there.

   'Twas one well known to him in former days,
A Shepherd-lad; who ere his sixteenth year
40 Had left that calling, tempted to entrust
His expectations to the fickle winds
And perilous waters; with the mariners
A fellow-mariner; – and so had fared
Through twenty seasons; but he had been reared
Among the mountains, and he in his heart
Was half a shepherd on the stormy seas.
Oft in the piping shrouds had Leonard heard
The tones of waterfalls, and inland sounds
Of caves and trees: – and, when the regular wind
50 Between the tropics filled the steady sail,
And blew with the same breath through days and weeks,
Lengthening invisibly its weary line
Along the cloudless Main, he, in those hours
Of tiresome indolence, would often hang
Over the vessel's side, and gaze and gaze;
And, while the broad blue wave and sparkling foam
Flashed round him images and hues that wrought
In union with the employment of his heart,
He, thus by feverish passion overcome,
60 Even with the organs of his bodily eye,
Below him, in the bosom of the deep,
Saw mountains; saw the forms of sheep that grazed
On verdant hills – with dwellings among trees,
And shepherds clad in the same country grey
Which he himself had worn.
                 And now, at last,
From perils manifold, with some small wealth
Acquired by traffic 'mid the Indian Isles,
To his paternal home he is returned,
With a determined purpose to resume
70 The life he had lived there; both for the sake

Of many darling pleasures, and the love
Which to an only brother he has borne
In all his hardships, since that happy time
When, whether it blew foul or fair, they two
Were brother-shepherds on their native hills.
– They were the last of all their race: and now,
When Leonard had approached his home, his heart
Failed in him; and, not venturing to inquire
Tidings of one so long and dearly loved,
80 He to the solitary church-yard turned;
That, as he knew in what particular spot
His family were laid, he thence might learn
If still his Brother lived, or to the file
Another grave was added. – He had found
Another grave, – near which a full half-hour
He had remained; but, as he gazed, there grew
Such a confusion in his memory,
That he began to doubt; and even to hope
That he had seen this heap of turf before, –
90 That it was not another grave; but one
He had forgotten. He had lost his path,
As up the vale, that afternoon, he walked
Through fields which once had been well known to him:
And oh what joy this recollection now
Sent to his heart! he lifted up his eyes,
And, looking round, imagined that he saw
Strange alteration wrought on every side
Among the woods and fields, and that the rocks,
And everlasting hills themselves were changed.

100   By this the Priest, who down the field had come,
Unseen by Leonard, at the church-yard gate
Stopped short, – and thence, at leisure, limb by limb
Perused him with a gay complacency.
Ay, thought the Vicar, smiling to himself,
'Tis one of those who needs must leave the path
Of the world's business to go wild alone:
His arms have a perpetual holiday;

The happy man will creep about the fields,
Following his fancies by the hour, to bring
110 Tears down his cheek, or solitary smiles
Into his face, until the setting sun
Write fool upon his forehead. – Planted thus
Beneath a shed that over-arched the gate
Of this rude church-yard, till the stars appeared
The good Man might have communed with himself,
But that the Stranger, who had left the grave,
Approached; he recognized the Priest at once,
And, after greetings interchanged, and given
By Leonard to the Vicar as to one
120 Unknown to him, this dialogue ensued.
    LEONARD. You live, Sir, in these dales, a quiet life:
Your years make up one peaceful family;
And who would grieve and fret, if, welcome come
And welcome gone, they are so like each other,
They cannot be remembered? Scarce a funeral
Comes to this church-yard once in eighteen months;
And yet, some changes must take place among you:
And you, who dwell here, even among these rocks,
Can trace the finger of mortality,
130 And see, that with our threescore years and ten
We are not all that perish. – I remember,
(For many years ago I passed this road)
There was a foot-way all along the fields
By the brook-side – 'tis gone – and that dark cleft!
To me it does not seem to wear the face
Which then it had!
    PRIEST.   Nay, Sir, for aught I know,
That chasm is much the same –
    LEONARD.   But, surely, yonder –
    PRIEST. Ay, there, indeed, your memory is a friend
That does not play you false. – On that tall pike
140 (It is the loneliest place of all these hills)
There were two springs which bubbled side by side,
As if they had been made that they might be
Companions for each other: the huge crag

Was rent with lightning – one hath disappeared;
The other, left behind, is flowing still.
For accidents and changes such as these,
We want not store of them; – a waterspout
Will bring down half a mountain; what a feast
For folks that wander up and down like you,
150 To see an acre's breadth of that wide cliff
One roaring cataract! a sharp May-storm
Will come with loads of January snow,
And in one night send twenty score of sheep
To feed the ravens; or a shepherd dies
By some untoward death among the rocks:
The ice breaks up and sweeps away a bridge;
A wood is felled: – and then for our own homes!
A child is born or christened, a field ploughed,
A daughter sent to service, a web spun,
160 The old house-clock is decked with a new face;
And hence, so far from wanting facts or dates
To chronicle the time, we all have here
A pair of diaries, – one serving, Sir,
For the whole dale, and one for each fire-side –
Yours was a stranger's judgement: for historians,
Commend me to these valleys!
    LEONARD.   Yet your Church-yard
Seems, if such freedom may be used with you,
To say that you are heedless of the past:
An orphan could not find his mother's grave:
170 Here's neither head nor foot-stone, plate of brass,
Cross-bones nor skull, – type of our earthly state
Nor emblem of our hopes: the dead man's home
Is but a fellow to that pasture-field.
    PRIEST. Why, there, Sir, is a thought that's new to me!
The stone-cutters, 'tis true, might beg their bread
If every English church-yard were like ours;
Yet your conclusion wanders from the truth:
We have no need of names and epitaphs;
We talk about the dead by our fire-sides.
180 And then, for our immortal part! *we* want

No symbols, Sir, to tell us that plain tale:
The thought of death sits easy on the man
Who has been born and dies among the mountains.
    LEONARD. Your Dalesmen, then, do in each other's
        thoughts
Possess a kind of second life: no doubt
You, Sir, could help me to the history
Of half these graves?
    PRIEST.   For eight-score winters past,
With what I've witnessed, and with what I've heard,
Perhaps I might; and, on a winter-evening,
190   If you were seated at my chimney's nook,
By turning o'er these hillocks one by one,
We two could travel, Sir, through a strange round;
Yet all in the broad highway of the world.
Now there's a grave – your foot is half upon it, –
It looks just like the rest; and yet that man
Died broken-hearted.
    LEONARD.   'Tis a common case.
We'll take another: who is he that lies
Beneath yon ridge, the last of those three graves?
It touches on that piece of native rock
Left in the church-yard wall.
200   PRIEST.   That's Walter Ewbank.
He had as white a head and fresh a cheek
As ever were produced by youth and age
Engendering in the blood of hale four-score.
Through five long generations had the heart
Of Walter's forefathers o'erflowed the bounds
Of their inheritance, that single cottage –
You see it yonder! and those few green fields.
They toiled and wrought, and still, from sire to son,
Each struggled, and each yielded as before
210   A little – yet a little, – and old Walter,
They left to him the family heart, and land
With other burdens than the crop it bore.
Year after year the old man still kept up
A cheerful mind, – and buffeted with bond,

Interest, and mortgages; at last he sank,
And went into his grave before his time.
Poor Walter! whether it was care that spurred him
God only knows, but to the very last
He had the lightest foot in Ennerdale:
220 His pace was never that of an old man:
I almost see him tripping down the path
With his two grandsons after him: – but you,
Unless our Landlord be your host tonight,
Have far to travel, – and on these rough paths
Even in the longest day of midsummer –
    LEONARD. But those two Orphans!
    PRIEST.   Orphans! – Such they were –
Yet not while Walter lived: – for, though their parents
Lay buried side by side as now they lie,
The old man was a father to the boys,
230 Two fathers in one father: and if tears,
Shed when he talked of them where they were not,
And hauntings from the infirmity of love,
Are aught of what makes up a mother's heart,
This old Man, in the day of his old age,
Was half a mother to them. – If you weep, Sir,
To hear a stranger talking about strangers,
Heaven bless you when you are among your kindred!
Ay – you may turn that way – it is a grave
Which will bear looking at.
    LEONARD.   These boys – I hope
They loved this good old Man? –
240   PRIEST.   They did – and truly:
But that was what we almost overlooked,
They were such darlings of each other. Yes,
Though from the cradle they had lived with Walter,
The only kinsman near them, and though he
Inclined to both by reason of his age,
With a more fond, familiar, tenderness;
They, notwithstanding, had much love to spare,
And it all went into each other's hearts.
Leonard, the elder by just eighteen months,

250   Was two years taller: 'twas a joy to see,
To hear, to meet them! – From their house the school
Is distant three short miles, and in the time
Of storm and thaw, when every water-course
And unbridged stream, such as you may have noticed
Crossing our roads at every hundred steps,
Was swoln into a noisy rivulet,
Would Leonard then, when elder boys remained
At home, go staggering through the slippery fords,
Bearing his brother on his back. I have seen him,
260   On windy days, in one of those stray brooks,
Ay, more than once I have seen him, mid-leg deep,
Their two books lying both on a dry stone,
Upon the hither side: and once I said,
As I remember, looking round these rocks
And hills on which we all of us were born,
That God who made the great book of the world
Would bless such piety –
      LEONARD.   It may be then –
      PRIEST. Never did worthier lads break English bread;
The very brightest Sunday Autumn saw,
270   With all its mealy clusters of ripe nuts,
Could never keep those boys away from church,
Or tempt them to an hour of sabbath breach.
Leonard and James! I warrant, every corner
Among these rocks, and every hollow place
That venturous foot could reach, to one or both
Was known as well as to the flowers that grow there.
Like roe-bucks they went bounding o'er the hills;
They played like two young ravens on the crags:
Then they could write, ay, and speak too, as well
280   As many of their betters – and for Leonard!
The very night before he went away,
In my own house I put into his hand
A Bible, and I'd wager house and field
That, if he be alive, he has it yet.
      LEONARD. It seems, these Brothers have not lived to be
A comfort to each other –

PRIEST. That they might
Live to such end is what both old and young
In this our valley all of us have wished,
And what, for my part, I have often prayed:
But Leonard –

290   LEONARD. Then James still is left among you!
     PRIEST. 'Tis of the elder brother I am speaking:
They had an uncle; – he was at that time
A thriving man, and trafficked on the seas:
And, but for that same uncle, to this hour
Leonard had never handled rope or shroud:
For the boy loved the life which we lead here;
And though of unripe years, a stripling only,
His soul was knit to this his native soil.
But, as I said, old Walter was too weak

300 To strive with such a torrent; when he died,
The estate and house were sold; and all their sheep,
A pretty flock, and which, for aught I know,
Had clothed the Ewbanks for a thousand years:—
Well – all was gone, and they were destitute,
And Leonard, chiefly for his Brother's sake,
Resolved to try his fortune on the seas.
Twelve years are past since we had tidings from him.
If there were one among us who had heard
That Leonard Ewbank was come home again,

310 From the Great Gavel, down by Leeza's banks,
And down the Enna, far as Egremont,
The day would be a joyous festival;
And those two bells of ours, which there you see –
Hanging in the open air – but, O good Sir!
This is sad talk – they'll never sound for him –
Living or dead. – When last we heard of him,
He was in slavery among the Moors
Upon the Barbary coast. – 'Twas not a little
That would bring down his spirit; and no doubt,

320 Before it ended in his death, the Youth
Was sadly crossed. – Poor Leonard! when we parted,
He took me by the hand, and said to me,

If e'er he should grow rich, he would return,
To live in peace upon his father's land,
And lay his bones among us.
    LEONARD.   If that day
Should come, 'twould needs be a glad day for him;
He would himself, no doubt, be happy then
As any that should meet him –
    PRIEST.   Happy! Sir –
    LEONARD. You said his kindred all were in their graves,
And that he had one Brother –
330   PRIEST.   That is but
A fellow-tale of sorrow. From his youth
James, though not sickly, yet was delicate;
And Leonard being always by his side
Had done so many offices about him,
That, though he was not of a timid nature,
Yet still the spirit of a mountain-boy
In him was somewhat checked; and, when his Brother
Was gone to sea, and he was left alone,
The little colour that he had was soon
340 Stolen from his cheek; he drooped, and pined, and pined –
    LEONARD. But these are all the graves of full-grown
      men!
    PRIEST. Ay, Sir, that passed away: we took him to us;
He was the child of all the dale – he lived
Three months with one, and six months with another;
And wanted neither food, nor clothes, nor love:
And many, many happy days were his.
But, whether blithe or sad, 'tis my belief
His absent Brother still was at his heart.
And, when he dwelt beneath our roof, we found
350 (A practise till this time unknown to him)
That often, rising from his bed at night,
He in his sleep would walk about, and sleeping
He sought his brother Leonard. – You are moved!
Forgive me, Sir: before I spoke to you,
I judged you most unkindly.
    LEONARD.   But this Youth,

How did he die at last?

    PRIEST.   One sweet May-morning,
(It will be twelve years since when Spring returns)
He had gone forth among the new-dropped lambs,
With two or three companions, whom their course
360 Of occupation led from height to height
Under a cloudless sun – till he, at length,
Through weariness, or, haply, to indulge
The humour of the moment, lagged behind.
You see yon precipice; – it wears the shape
Of a vast building made of many crags;
And in the midst is one particular rock
That rises like a column from the vale,
Whence by our shepherds it is called, THE PILLAR.
Upon its aëry summit crowned with heath,
370 The loiterer, not unnoticed by his comrades,
Lay stretched at ease; but, passing by the place
On their return, they found that he was gone.
No ill was feared; till one of them by chance
Entering, when evening was far spent, the house
Which at that time was James's home, there learned
That nobody had seen him all that day:
The morning came, and still he was unheard of:
The neighbours were alarmed, and to the brook
Some hastened; some ran to the lake: ere noon
380 They found him at the foot of that same rock
Dead, and with mangled limbs. The third day after
I buried him, poor Youth, and there he lies!

    LEONARD. And that then *is* his grave! – Before his
    death
You say that he saw many happy years?

    PRIEST. Ay, that he did –

    LEONARD.   And all went well with him? –

    PRIEST. If he had one, the Youth had twenty homes.

    LEONARD. And you believe, then, that his mind was
    easy? –

    PRIEST. Yes, long before he died, he found that time
Is a true friend to sorrow; and unless

390 His thoughts were turned on Leonard's luckless fortune,
He talked about him with a cheerful love.
    LEONARD. He could not come to an unhallowed end!
    PRIEST. Nay, God forbid! – You recollect I mentioned
A habit which disquietude and grief
Had brought upon him; and we all conjectured
That, as the day was warm, he had lain down
On the soft heath, – and, waiting for his comrades,
He there had fallen asleep; that in his sleep
He to the margin of the precipice
400 Had walked, and from the summit had fallen headlong:
And so no doubt he perished. When the Youth
Fell, in his hand he must have grasped, we think,
His shepherd's staff; for on that Pillar of rock
It had been caught mid-way; and there for years
It hung; – and mouldered there.
                    The Priest here ended –
The Stranger would have thanked him, but he felt
A gushing from his heart, that took away
The power of speech. Both left the spot in silence;
And Leonard, when they reached the church-yard gate,
410 As the Priest lifted up the latch, turned round, –
And, looking at the grave, he said, 'My Brother!'
The Vicar did not hear the words: and now,
He pointed towards his dwelling-place, entreating
That Leonard would partake his homely fare:
The other thanked him with an earnest voice;
But added, that, the evening being calm,
He would pursue his journey. So they parted.

    It was not long ere Leonard reached a grove
That overhung the road: he there stopped short,
420 And, sitting down beneath the trees, reviewed
All that the Priest had said: his early years
Were with him: – his long absence, cherished hopes,
And thoughts which had been his an hour before,
All pressed on him with such a weight, that now,
This vale, where he had been so happy, seemed

A place in which he could not bear to live:
So he relinquished all his purposes.
He travelled back to Egremont: and thence,
That night, he wrote a letter to the Priest,
430 Reminding him of what had passed between them;
And adding, with a hope to be forgiven,
That it was from the weakness of his heart
He had not dared to tell him who he was.
This done, he went on shipboard, and is now
A Seaman, a grey-headed Mariner.

To M. H.

Our walk was far among the ancient trees:
There was no road, nor any woodman's path;
But a thick umbrage – checking the wild growth
Of weed and sapling, along soft green turf
Beneath the branches – of itself had made
A track, that brought us to a slip of lawn,
And a small bed of water in the woods.
All round this pool both flocks and herds might drink
On its firm margin, even as from a well,
10 Or some stone-basin which the herdsman's hand
Had shaped for their refreshment; nor did sun,
Or wind from any quarter, ever come,
But as a blessing to this calm recess,
This glade of water and this one green field.
The spot was made by Nature for herself;
The travellers know it not, and 'twill remain
Unknown to them; but it is beautiful;
And if a man should plant his cottage near,
Should sleep beneath the shelter of its trees,
20 And blend its waters with his daily meal,
He would so love it, that in his death-hour
Its image would survive among his thoughts:
And therefore, my sweet MARY, this still Nook,
With all its beeches, we have named from You!

Hart-Leap Well

Hart-Leap Well is a small spring of water, about five miles from
Richmond in Yorkshire, and near the side of the road that leads
from Richmond to Askrigg. Its name is derived from a remark-
able Chase, the memory of which is preserved by the monu-
ments spoken of in the second Part of the following Poem, which
monuments do now exist as I have there described them.

The Knight had ridden down from Wensley Moor
With the slow motion of a summer's cloud,
And now, as he approached a vassal's door,
'Bring forth another horse!' he cried aloud.

'Another horse!' – That shout the vassal heard
And saddled his best Steed, a comely grey;
Sir Walter mounted him; he was the third
Which he had mounted on that glorious day.

Joy sparkled in the prancing courser's eyes;
10   The horse and horseman are a happy pair;
But, though Sir Walter like a falcon flies,
There is a doleful silence in the air.

A rout this morning left Sir Walter's Hall,
That as they galloped made the echoes roar;
But horse and man are vanished, one and all;
Such race, I think, was never seen before.

Sir Walter, restless as a veering wind,
Calls to the few tired dogs that yet remain:
Blanch, Swift, and Music, noblest of their kind,
20   Follow, and up the weary mountain strain.

The Knight hallooed, he cheered and chid them on
With suppliant gestures and upbraidings stern;
But breath and eyesight fail; and, one by one,
The dogs are stretched among the mountain fern.

Where is the throng, the tumult of the race?
The bugles that so joyfully were blown?
– This chase it looks not like an earthly chase;
Sir Walter and the Hart are left alone.

The poor Hart toils along the mountain-side;
30   I will not stop to tell how far he fled,
Nor will I mention by what death he died;
But now the Knight beholds him lying dead.

Dismounting, then, he leaned against a thorn;
He had no follower, dog, nor man, nor boy:
He neither cracked his whip, nor blew his horn,
But gazed upon the spoil with silent joy.

Close to the thorn on which Sir Walter leaned
Stood his dumb partner in this glorious feat;
Weak as a lamb the hour that it is yeaned;
40   And white with foam as if with cleaving sleet.

Upon his side the Hart was lying stretched:
His nostril touched a spring beneath a hill,
And with the last deep groan his breath had fetched
The waters of the spring were trembling still.

And now, too happy for repose or rest,
(Never had living man such joyful lot!)
Sir Walter walked all round, north, south, and west,
And gazed and gazed upon that darling spot.

And climbing up the hill – (it was at least
50   Four roods of sheer ascent) Sir Walter found
Three several hoof-marks which the hunted Beast
Had left imprinted on the grassy ground.

Sir Walter wiped his face, and cried, 'Till now
Such sight was never seen by human eyes:
Three leaps have borne him from this lofty brow,
Down to the very fountain where he lies.

'I'll build a pleasure-house upon this spot,
And a small arbour, made for rural joy;
'Twill be the traveller's shed, the pilgrim's cot,
60 A place of love for damsels that are coy.

'A cunning artist will I have to frame
A basin for that fountain in the dell!
And they who do make mention of the same,
From this day forth, shall call it HART-LEAP WELL.

'And, gallant Stag! to make thy praises known,
Another monument shall here be raised;
Three several pillars, each a rough-hewn stone,
And planted where thy hoofs the turf have grazed.

'And, in the summer-time when days are long,
70 I will come hither with my Paramour;
And with the dancers and the minstrel's song
We will make merry in that pleasant bower.

'Till the foundations of the mountains fail
My mansion with its arbour shall endure; –
The joy of them who till the fields of Swale,
And them who dwell among the woods of Ure!'

Then home he went, and left the Hart, stone-dead,
With breathless nostrils stretched above the spring.
– Soon did the Knight perform what he had said;
80 And far and wide the fame thereof did ring.

Ere thrice the Moon into her port had steered,
A cup of stone received the living well;
Three pillars of rude stone Sir Walter reared,
And built a house of pleasure in the dell.

And near the fountain, flowers of stature tall
With trailing plants and trees were intertwined, –
Which soon composed a little sylvan hall,
A leafy shelter from the sun and wind.

And thither, when the summer days were long,
90 Sir Walter led his wondering Paramour;
And with the dancers and the minstrel's song
Made merriment within that pleasant bower.

The Knight, Sir Walter, died in course of time,
And his bones lie in his paternal vale. –
But there is matter for a second rhyme,
And I to this would add another tale.

PART SECOND

The moving accident is not my trade;
To freeze the blood I have no ready arts:
'Tis my delight, alone in summer shade,
100 To pipe a simple song for thinking hearts.

As I from Hawes to Richmond did repair,
It chanced that I saw standing in a dell
Three aspens at three corners of a square;
And one, not four yards distant, near a well.

What this imported I could ill divine:
And, pulling now the rein my horse to stop,
I saw three pillars standing in a line, –
The last stone-pillar on a dark hill-top.

The trees were grey, with neither arms nor head;
110 Half wasted the square mound of tawny green;
So that you just might say, as then I said,
'Here in old time the hand of man hath been.'

I looked upon the hill both far and near,
More doleful place did never eye survey;
It seemed as if the spring-time came not here,
And Nature here were willing to decay.

I stood in various thoughts and fancies lost,
When one, who was in shepherd's garb attired,
Came up the hollow: – him did I accost,
120 And what this place might be I then inquired.

The Shepherd stopped, and that same story told
Which in my former rhyme I have rehearsed.
'A jolly place,' said he, 'in times of old!
But something ails it now: the spot is curst.

'You see these lifeless stumps of aspen wood –
Some say that they are beeches, others elms –
These were the bower; and here a mansion stood,
The finest palace of a hundred realms!

'The arbour does its own condition tell;
130 You see the stones, the fountain, and the stream;
But as to the great Lodge! you might as well
Hunt half a day for a forgotten dream.

'There's neither dog nor heifer, horse nor sheep,
Will wet his lips within that cup of stone;
And oftentimes, when all are fast asleep,
This water doth send forth a dolorous groan.

'Some say that here a murder has been done,
And blood cries out for blood: but, for my part,
I've guessed, when I've been sitting in the sun,
140 That it was all for that unhappy Hart.

'What thoughts must through the creature's brain have
    past!
Even from the topmost stone, upon the steep,
Are but three bounds – and look, Sir, at this last –
O Master! it has been a cruel leap.

'For thirteen hours he ran a desperate race;
And in my simple mind we cannot tell

What cause the Hart might have to love this place,
And come and make his death-bed near the well.

'Here on the grass perhaps asleep he sank,
150 Lulled by the fountain in the summer-tide;
This water was perhaps the first he drank
When he had wandered from his mother's side.

'In April here beneath the flowering thorn
He heard the birds their morning carols sing;
And he, perhaps, for aught we know, was born
Not half a furlong from that self-same spring.

'Now, here is neither grass nor pleasant shade;
The sun on drearier hollow never shone;
So will it be, as I have often said,
160 Till trees, and stones, and fountain, all are gone.'

'Grey-headed Shepherd, thou hast spoken well;
Small difference lies between thy creed and mine:
This Beast not unobserved by Nature fell;
His death was mourned by sympathy divine.

'The Being, that is in the clouds and air,
That is in the green leaves among the groves,
Maintains a deep and reverential care
For the unoffending creatures whom he loves.

'The pleasure-house is dust: – behind, before,
170 This is no common waste, no common gloom;
But Nature, in due course of time, once more
Shall here put on her beauty and her bloom.

'She leaves these objects to a slow decay,
That what we are, and have been, may be known;
But at the coming of the milder day,
These monuments shall all be overgrown.

'One lesson, Shepherd, let us two divide,
Taught both by what she shows, and what conceals;
Never to blend our pleasure or our pride
180   With sorrow of the meanest thing that feels.'

*The Voice from the Side of Etna;
or, The Mad Monk*

An Ode, in Mrs Radcliff's manner.

I heard a voice from Etna's side,
   Where o'er a Cavern's mouth,
   That fronted to the South,
A chestnut spread its umbrage wide.
A Hermit, or a Monk, the man might be,
But him I could not see:
And thus the music flowed along,
In melody most like an old Sicilian song.

There was a time when earth, and sea, and skies,
10   The bright green vale and forest's dark recess,
When all things lay before my eyes
      In steady loveliness.
But now I feel on earth's uneasy scene
      Such motions as will never cease!
      I only ask for peace –
Then wherefore must I know, that such a time has been?

A silence then ensued.
      Till from the cavern came
      A voice. It was the same:
20   And thus that mournful voice its dreary plaint renewed.
Last night, as o'er the sloping turf I trod,
      The smooth green turf to me a vision gave:
      Beneath my eyes I saw the sod,
      The roof of ROSA'S grave.

My heart has need with dreams like these to strive,
For when I waked, beneath my eyes I found
    That plot of mossy ground,
  On which so soft we sate when ROSA was alive.
  Why must the rock, and margin of the flood,
30   Why must the hills so many flowerets bear,
  Whose colours to a wounded woman's blood
    Such sad resemblance wear?

  I struck the wound – this hand of mine!
    For, oh! thou Maid divine,
    I loved to agony!
    The youth, whom thou call'dst thine,
    Did never love like me.

  It is the stormy clouds above,
    That flash so red a gleam
40   On yonder downward trickling stream;
    'Tis not the blood of her I love.
The sun torments me from his western bed!
  O let him cease for ever to diffuse
  Those crimson spectre hues!
O let me lie in peace, and be for ever dead!

  Here ceased the voice! In deep dismay,
  Down through the forest I pursued my way.
  The twilight fays came forth in dewy shoon,
    Ere I within the cabin had withdrawn,
50   The goat-herd's tent upon the open lawn.
  That night there was no moon!!

'There is an Eminence, – of these our hills'

There is an Eminence, – of these our hills
The last that parleys with the setting sun;
We can behold it from our orchard-seat;
And, when at evening we pursue our walk

Along the public way, this Peak, so high
Above us, and so distant in its height,
Is visible; and often seems to send
Its own deep quiet to restore our hearts.
The meteors make of it a favourite haunt:
10 The star of Jove, so beautiful and large
In the mid heavens, is never half so fair
As when he shines above it. 'Tis in truth
The loneliest place we have among the clouds.
And She who dwells with me, whom I have loved
With such communion, that no place on earth
Can ever be a solitude to me,
Hath to this lonely Summit given my Name.

'*It was an April morning: fresh and clear*'

It was an April morning: fresh and clear
The Rivulet, delighting in its strength,
Ran with a young man's speed; and yet the voice
Of waters which the winter had supplied
Was softened down into a vernal tone.
The spirit of enjoyment and desire,
And hopes and wishes, from all living things
Went circling, like a multitude of sounds.
The budding groves seemed eager to urge on
10 The steps of June; as if their various hues
Were only hindrances that stood between
Them and their object: but, meanwhile, prevailed
Such an entire contentment in the air
That every naked ash, and tardy tree
Yet leafless, showed as if the countenance
With which it looked on this delightful day
Were native to the summer. – Up the brook
I roamed in the confusion of my heart,
Alive to all things and forgetting all.
20 At length I to a sudden turning came
In this continuous glen, where down a rock

The Stream, so ardent in its course before,
Sent forth such sallies of glad sound, that all
Which I till then had heard, appeared the voice
Of common pleasure: beast and bird, the lamb,
The shepherd's dog, the linnet and the thrush
Vied with this waterfall, and made a song,
Which, while I listened, seemed like the wild growth
Or like some natural produce of the air,
30 That could not cease to be. Green leaves were here;
But 'twas the foliage of the rocks – the birch,
The yew, the holly, and the bright green thorn,
With hanging islands of resplendent furze:
And, on a summit, distant a short space,
By any who should look beyond the dell,
A single mountain-cottage might be seen.
I gazed and gazed, and to myself I said,
'Our thoughts at least are ours; and this wild nook,
MY EMMA, I will dedicate to thee.'
40 – Soon did the spot become my other home,
My dwelling, and my out-of-doors abode.
And, of the Shepherds who have seen me there,
To whom I sometimes in our idle talk
Have told this fancy, two or three, perhaps,
Years after we are gone and in our graves,
When they have cause to speak of this wild place,
May call it by the name of EMMA'S DELL.

Written with a Pencil upon a Stone in the
Wall of the House (an Out-House), on the
Island at Grasmere

Rude is this Edifice, and Thou hast seen
Buildings, albeit rude, that have maintained
Proportions more harmonious, and approached
To closer fellowship with ideal grace.
But take it in good part: – alas! the poor
Vitruvius of our village had no help

From the great City; never, upon leaves
Of red Morocco folio saw displayed,
In long succession, pre-existing ghosts
10 Of Beauties yet unborn – the rustic Lodge
Antique, and Cottage with verandah graced,
Nor lacking, for fit company, alcove,
Green-house, shell-grot, and moss-lined hermitage.
Thou see'st a homely Pile, yet to these walls
The heifer comes in the snow-storm, and here
The new-dropped lamb finds shelter from the wind.
And hither does one Poet sometimes row
His pinnace, a small vagrant barge, up-piled
With plenteous store of heath and withered fern,
20 (A lading which he with his sickle cuts,
Among the mountains) and beneath this roof
He makes his summer couch, and here at noon
Spreads out his limbs, while, yet unshorn, the Sheep,
Panting beneath the burden of their wool,
Lie round him, even as if they were a part
Of his own Household: nor, while from his bed
He looks, through the open door-place, toward the lake
And to the stirring breezes, does he want
Creations lovely as the work of sleep –
30 Fair sights, and visions of romantic joy!

The Idle Shepherd-Boys;
or, Dungeon-Ghyll Force.
A Pastoral

The valley rings with mirth and joy;
Among the hills the echoes play
A never never ending song,
To welcome in the May.
The magpie chatters with delight;
The mountain raven's youngling brood
Have left the mother and the nest;
And they go rambling east and west

In search of their own food;
10 Or through the glittering vapours dart
In very wantonness of heart.

Beneath a rock, upon the grass,
Two boys are sitting in the sun;
Their work, if any work they have,
Is out of mind – or done.
On pipes of sycamore they play
The fragments of a Christmas hymn;
Or with that plant which in our dale
We call stag-horn, or fox's tail,
20 Their rusty hats they trim:
And thus, as happy as the day,
Those Shepherds wear the time away.

Along the river's stony marge
The sand-lark chants a joyous song;
The thrush is busy in the wood,
And carols loud and strong.
A thousand lambs are on the rocks,
All newly born! both earth and sky
Keep jubilee, and more than all,
30 Those boys with their green coronal;
They never hear the cry,
That plaintive cry! which up the hill
Comes from the depth of Dungeon-Ghyll.

Said Walter, leaping from the ground,
'Down to the stump of yon old yew
We'll for our whistles run a race.'
– Away the shepherds flew;
They leapt – they ran – and when they came
Right opposite to Dungeon-Ghyll,
40 Seeing that he should lose the prize,
'Stop!' to his comrade Walter cries –
James stopped with no good will:

Said Walter then, exulting; 'Here
You'll find a task for half a year.

'Cross, if you dare, where I shall cross –
Come on, and tread where I shall tread.'
The other took him at his word,
And followed as he led.
It was a spot which you may see
50 If ever you to Langdale go;
Into a chasm a mighty block
Hath fallen, and made a bridge of rock:
The gulf is deep below;
And, in a basin black and small,
Receives a lofty waterfall.

With staff in hand across the cleft
The challenger pursued his march;
And now, all eyes and feet, hath gained
The middle of the arch.
60 When list! he hears a piteous moan –
Again! – his heart within him dies –
His pulse is stopped, his breath is lost,
He totters, pallid as a ghost,
And, looking down, espies
A lamb, that in the pool is pent
Within that black and frightful rent.

The lamb had slipped into the stream,
And safe without a bruise or wound
70 The cataract had borne him down
Into the gulf profound.
His dam had seen him when he fell,
She saw him down the torrent borne;
And, while with all a mother's love
She from the lofty rocks above
Sent forth a cry forlorn,
The lamb, still swimming round and round,
Made answer to that plaintive sound.

When he had learnt what thing it was,
That sent this rueful cry; I ween
80 The Boy recovered heart, and told
The sight which he had seen.
Both gladly now deferred their task;
Nor was there wanting other aid –
A Poet, one who loves the brooks
Far better than the sages' books,
By chance had thither strayed;
And there the helpless lamb he found
By those huge rocks encompassed round.

He drew it from the troubled pool,
90 And brought it forth into the light:
The Shepherds met him with his charge,
An unexpected sight!
Into their arms the lamb they took,
Whose life and limbs the flood had spared;
Then up the steep ascent they hied,
And placed him at his mother's side;
And gently did the Bard
Those idle Shepherd-boys upbraid,
And bade them better mind their trade.

The Two Thieves; or,
The Last Stage of Avarice

O now that the genius of Bewick were mine,
And the skill which he learned on the banks of the Tyne,
Then the Muses might deal with me just as they chose,
For I'd take my last leave both of verse and of prose.

What feats would I work with my magical hand!
Book-learning and books should be banished the land:
And, for hunger and thirst and such troublesome calls,
Every ale-house should then have a feast on its walls.

The traveller would hang his wet clothes on a chair;
10 Let them smoke, let them burn, not a straw would he
      care!
For the Prodigal Son, Joseph's Dream and his sheaves,
Oh, what would they be to my tale of two Thieves?

The One, yet unbreeched, is not three birthdays old,
His Grandsire that age more than thirty times told;
There are ninety good seasons of fair and foul weather
Between them, and both go a-pilfering together.

With chips is the carpenter strewing his floor?
Is a cart-load of turf at an old woman's door?
Old Daniel his hand to the treasure will slide!
20 And his Grandson's as busy at work by his side.

Old Daniel begins; he stops short – and his eye,
Through the lost look of dotage, is cunning and sly:
'Tis a look which at this time is hardly his own,
But tells a plain tale of the days that are flown.

He once had a heart which was moved by the wires
Of manifold pleasures and many desires:
And what if he cherished his purse? 'Twas no more
Than treading a path trod by thousands before.

'Twas a path trod by thousands; but Daniel is one
30 Who went something farther than others have gone,
And now with old Daniel you see how it fares;
You see to what end he has brought his grey hairs.

The pair sally forth hand in hand: ere the sun
Has peered o'er the beeches, their work is begun:
And yet, into whatever sin they may fall,
This child but half knows it, and that not at all.

They hunt through the streets with deliberate tread,
And each, in his turn, becomes leader or led;

And, wherever they carry their plots and their wiles,
40 Every face in the village is dimpled with smiles.

Neither checked by the rich nor the needy they roam;
For the grey-headed Sire has a daughter at home,
Who will gladly repair all the damage that's done;
And three, were it asked, would be rendered for one.

Old Man! whom so oft I with pity have eyed,
I love thee, and love the sweet Boy at thy side:
Long yet may'st thou live! for a teacher we see
That lifts up the veil of our nature in thee.

'A narrow girdle of rough stones and crags'

A narrow girdle of rough stones and crags,
A rude and natural causeway, interposed
Between the water and a winding slope
Of copse and thicket, leaves the eastern shore
Of Grasmere safe in its own privacy:
And there myself and two beloved Friends,
One calm September morning, ere the mist
Had altogether yielded to the sun,
Sauntered on this retired and difficult way.
10 — Ill suits the road with one in haste; but we
Played with our time; and, as we strolled along,
It was our occupation to observe
Such objects as the waves had tossed ashore –
Feather, or leaf, or weed, or withered bough,
Each on the other heaped, along the line
Of the dry wreck. And, in our vacant mood,
Not seldom did we stop to watch some tuft
Of dandelion seed or thistle's beard,
That skimmed the surface of the dead calm lake,
20 Suddenly halting now – a lifeless stand!
And starting off again with freak as sudden;
In all its sportive wanderings, all the while,

Making report of an invisible breeze
That was its wings, its chariot, and its horse,
Its playmate, rather say, its moving soul.
— And often, trifling with a privilege
Alike indulged to all, we paused, one now,
And now the other, to point out, perchance
To pluck, some flower or water-weed, too fair
30   Either to be divided from the place
On which it grew, or to be left alone
To its own beauty. Many such there are,
Fair ferns and flowers, and chiefly that tall fern,
So stately, of the Queen Osmunda named;
Plant lovelier, in its own retired abode
On Grasmere's beach, than Naiad by the side
Of Grecian brook, or Lady of the Mere,
Sole-sitting by the shores of old romance.
— So fared we that bright morning: from the fields,
40   Meanwhile, a noise was heard, the busy mirth
Of reapers, men and women, boys and girls.
Delighted much to listen to those sounds,
And feeding thus our fancies, we advanced
Along the indented shore; when suddenly,
Through a thin veil of glittering haze was seen
Before us, on a point of jutting land,
The tall and upright figure of a Man
Attired in peasant's garb, who stood alone,
Angling beside the margin of the lake.
50   'Improvident and reckless,' we exclaimed,
'The Man must be, who thus can lose a day
Of the mid harvest, when the labourer's hire
Is ample, and some little might be stored
Wherewith to cheer him in the winter time.'
Thus talking of that Peasant, we approached
Close to the spot where with his rod and line
He stood alone; whereat he turned his head
To greet us — and we saw a Man worn down
By sickness, gaunt and lean, with sunken cheeks
60   And wasted limbs, his legs so long and lean

That for my single self I looked at them,
Forgetful of the body they sustained. –
Too weak to labour in the harvest field,
The Man was using his best skill to gain
A pittance from the dead unfeeling lake
That knew not of his wants. I will not say
What thoughts immediately were ours, nor how
The happy idleness of that sweet morn,
With all its lovely images, was changed
70 To serious musing and to self-reproach.
Nor did we fail to see within ourselves
What need there is to be reserved in speech,
And temper all our thoughts with charity.
– Therefore, unwilling to forget that day,
My Friend, Myself, and She who then received
The same admonishment, have called the place
By a memorial name, uncouth indeed
As e'er by mariner was given to bay
Or foreland, on a new-discovered coast;
80 And POINT RASH-JUDGEMENT is the name it bears.

*On Seeing Some Tourists of the Lakes Pass by
Reading; a Practice Very Common*

What waste in the labour of Chariot and Steed!
For this came ye hither? is this your delight?
There are twenty-four letters, and those ye can read;
But Nature's ten thousand are Blanks in your sight.
Then throw by your Books, and the study begin;
Or sleep, and be blameless, and wake at Your Inn!

Written with a Slate Pencil upon a Stone, the Largest of a Heap Lying near a Deserted Quarry, upon One of the Islands at Rydal

Stranger! this hillock of mis-shapen stones
Is not a Ruin spared or made by time,
Nor, as perchance thou rashly deem'st, the Cairn
Of some old British Chief: 'tis nothing more
Than the rude embryo of a little Dome
Or Pleasure-house, once destined to be built
Among the birch-trees of this rocky isle.
But, as it chanced, Sir William having learned
That from the shore a full-grown man might wade,
10 And make himself a freeman of this spot
At any hour he chose, the prudent Knight
Desisted, and the quarry and the mound
Are monuments of his unfinished task.
The block on which these lines are traced, perhaps,
Was once selected as the corner-stone
Of that intended Pile, which would have been
Some quaint odd plaything of elaborate skill,
So that, I guess, the linnet and the thrush,
And other little builders who dwell here,
20 Had wondered at the work. But blame him not,
For old Sir William was a gentle Knight,
Bred in this vale, to which he appertained
With all his ancestry. Then peace to him,
And for the outrage which he had devised
Entire forgiveness! – But if thou art one
On fire with thy impatience to become
An inmate of these mountains, – if, disturbed
By beautiful conceptions, thou hast hewn
Out of the quiet rock the elements
30 Of thy trim Mansion destined soon to blaze
In snow-white splendour, – think again; and, taught
By old Sir William and his quarry, leave

Thy fragments to the bramble and the rose;
There let the vernal slow-worm sun himself,
And let the redbreast hop from stone to stone.

The Oak and the Broom
A Pastoral

I

His simple truths did Andrew glean
Beside the babbling rills;
A careful student he had been
Among the woods and hills.
One winter's night, when through the trees
The wind was roaring, on his knees
His youngest born did Andrew hold:
And while the rest, a ruddy choir,
Were seated round their blazing fire,
10   This Tale the Shepherd told.

II

'I saw a crag, a lofty stone
As ever tempest beat!
Out of its head an Oak had grown,
A Broom out of its feet.
The time was March, a cheerful noon –
The thaw-wind, with the breath of June,
Breathed gently from the warm south-west:
When, in a voice sedate with age,
This Oak, a giant and a sage,
20   His Neighbour thus addressed: –

III

' "Eight weary weeks, through rock and clay,
Along this mountain's edge,
The Frost hath wrought both night and day,
Wedge driving after wedge.
Look up! and think, above your head

What trouble, surely, will be bred;
Last night I heard a crash – 'tis true,
The splinters took another road –
I see them yonder – what a load
30 For such a Thing as you!

IV

' "You are preparing as before,
To deck your slender shape;
And yet, just three years back – no more –
You had a strange escape:
Down from yon cliff a fragment broke;
It thundered down, with fire and smoke,
And hitherward pursued its way;
This ponderous block was caught by me,
And o'er your head, as you may see,
40 'Tis hanging to this day!

V

' "If breeze or bird to this rough steep
Your kind's first seed did bear;
The breeze had better been asleep,
The bird caught in a snare:
For you and your green twigs decoy
The little witless shepherd-boy
To come and slumber in your bower;
And, trust me, on some sultry noon,
Both you and he, Heaven knows how soon!
50 Will perish in one hour.

VI

' "From me this friendly warning take" –
The Broom began to doze,
And thus, to keep herself awake,
Did gently interpose:
"My thanks for your discourse are due;
That more than what you say is true,
I know, and I have known it long;

Frail is the bond by which we hold
Our being, whether young or old,
60 Wise, foolish, weak, or strong.

VII

' "Disasters, do the best we can,
Will reach both great and small;
And he is oft the wisest man,
Who is not wise at all.
For me, why should I wish to roam?
This spot is my paternal home,
It is my pleasant heritage;
My father many a happy year
Spread here his careless blossoms, here
70 Attained a good old age.

VIII

' "Even such as his may be my lot.
What cause have I to haunt
My heart with terrors? Am I not
In truth a favoured plant!
On me such bounty Summer pours,
That I am covered o'er with flowers;
And, when the Frost is in the sky,
My branches are so fresh and gay
That you might look at me and say,
80 This Plant can never die.

IX

' "The butterfly, all green and gold,
To me hath often flown,
Here in my blossoms to behold
Wings lovely as his own.
When grass is chill with rain or dew,
Beneath my shade, the mother-ewe
Lies with her infant lamb; I see
The love they to each other make,
And the sweet joy which they partake,
90 It is a joy to me."

X

'Her voice was blithe, her heart was light;
The Broom might have pursued
Her speech, until the stars of night
Their journey had renewed;
But in the branches of the oak
Two ravens now began to croak
Their nuptial song, a gladsome air;
And to her own green bower the breeze
That instant brought two stripling bees
100 To rest, or murmur there.

XI

'One night, my Children! from the north
There came a furious blast;
At break of day I ventured forth,
And near the cliff I passed.
The storm had fallen upon the Oak,
And struck him with a mighty stroke,
And whirled, and whirled him far away;
And, in one hospitable cleft,
The little careless Broom was left
110 To live for many a day.'

The Waterfall and the Eglantine

I

'Begone, thou fond presumptuous Elf,'
Exclaimed an angry Voice,
'Nor dare to thrust thy foolish self
Between me and my choice!'
A small Cascade fresh swoln with snows
Thus threatened a poor Briar-rose,
That, all bespattered with his foam,
And dancing high and dancing low,
Was living, as a child might know,
10 In an unhappy home.

II

'Dost thou presume my course to block?
Off, off! or, puny Thing!
I'll hurl thee headlong with the rock
To which thy fibres cling.'
The Flood was tyrannous and strong;
The patient Briar suffered long,
Nor did he utter groan or sigh,
Hoping the danger would be past;
But, seeing no relief, at last,
20 He ventured to reply.

III

'Ah!' said the Briar, 'blame me not;
Why should we dwell in strife?
We who in this sequestered spot
Once lived a happy life!
You stirred me on my rocky bed –
What pleasure through my veins you spread
The summer long, from day to day,
My leaves you freshened and bedewed;
Nor was it common gratitude
30 That did your cares repay.

IV

'When spring came on with bud and bell,
Among these rocks did I
Before you hang my wreaths to tell
That gentle days were nigh!
And in the sultry summer hours,
I sheltered you with leaves and flowers;
And in my leaves – now shed and gone,
The linnet lodged, and for us two
Chanted his pretty songs, when you
40 Had little voice or none.

V
'But now proud thoughts are in your breast –
What grief is mine you see,
Ah! would you think, even yet how blest
Together we might be!
Though of both leaf and flower bereft,
Some ornaments to me are left –
Rich store of scarlet hips is mine,
With which I, in my humble way,
Would deck you many a winter day,
50 A happy Eglantine!'

VI
What more he said I cannot tell,
The Torrent down the rocky dell
Came thundering loud and fast;
I listened, nor aught else could hear;
The Briar quaked – and much I fear
Those accents were his last.

Song for the Wandering Jew

Though the torrents from their fountains
Roar down many a craggy steep,
Yet they find among the mountains
Resting-places calm and deep.

Clouds that love through air to hasten,
Ere the storm its fury stills,
Helmet-like themselves will fasten
On the heads of towering hills.

What, if through the frozen centre
10 Of the Alps the Chamois bound,
Yet he has a home to enter
In some nook of chosen ground:

And the Sea-horse, though the ocean
Yield him no domestic cave,
Slumbers without sense of motion,
Couched upon the rocking wave.

If on windy days the Raven
Gambol like a dancing skiff,
Not the less she loves her haven
20   In the bosom of the cliff.

The fleet Ostrich, till day closes,
Vagrant over desert sands,
Brooding on her eggs reposes
When chill night that care demands.

Day and night my toils redouble,
Never nearer to the goal;
Night and day, I feel the trouble
Of the Wanderer in my soul.

''Tis said, that some have died for love'

'Tis said, that some have died for love:
And here and there a church-yard grave is found
In the cold north's unhallowed ground,
Because the wretched man himself had slain,
His love was such a grievous pain.
And there is one whom I five years have known;
He dwells alone
Upon Helvellyn's side:
He loved – the pretty Barbara died;
10   And thus he makes his moan:
Three years had Barbara in her grave been laid
When thus his moan he made:

'Oh, move, thou Cottage, from behind that oak!
Or let the aged tree uprooted lie,
That in some other way yon smoke
May mount into the sky!
The clouds pass on; they from the heavens depart:
I look – the sky is empty space;
I know not what I trace;
20 But when I cease to look, my hand is on my heart.

'O! what a weight is in these shades! Ye leaves,
That murmur once so dear, when will it cease?
Your sound my heart of rest bereaves,
It robs my heart of peace.
Thou Thrush, that singest loud – and loud and free,
Into yon row of willows flit,
Upon that alder sit;
Or sing another song, or choose another tree.

'Roll back, sweet Rill! back to thy mountain-bounds,
30 And there for ever be thy waters chained!
For thou dost haunt the air with sounds
That cannot be sustained;
If still beneath that pine-tree's ragged bough
Headlong yon waterfall must come,
Oh let it then be dumb!
Be anything, sweet Rill, but that which thou art now.

'Thou Eglantine, so bright with sunny showers,
Proud as a rainbow spanning half the vale,
Thou one fair shrub, oh! shed thy flowers,
40 And stir not in the gale.
For thus to see thee nodding in the air,
To see thy arch thus stretch and bend,
Thus rise and thus descend, –
Disturbs me till the sight is more than I can bear.'

The Man who makes this feverish complaint
Is one of giant stature, who could dance

Equipped from head to foot in iron mail.
Ah gentle Love! if ever thought was thine
To store up kindred hours for me, thy face
50 Turn from me, gentle Love! nor let me walk
Within the sound of Emma's voice, nor know
Such happiness as I have known today.

For the Spot Where the Hermitage Stood on St Herbert's Island, Derwent-Water

If thou in the dear love of some one Friend
Hast been so happy that thou know'st what thoughts
Will sometimes in the happiness of love
Make the heart sink, then wilt thou reverence
This quiet spot; and, Stranger! not unmoved
Wilt thou behold this shapeless heap of stones,
The desolate ruins of St Herbert's Cell.
Here stood his threshold; here was spread the roof
That sheltered him, a self-secluded Man,
10 After long exercise in social cares
And offices humane, intent to adore
The Deity, with undistracted mind,
And meditate on everlasting things,
In utter solitude. – But he had left
A Fellow-labourer, whom the good Man loved
As his own soul. And, when with eye upraised
To heaven he knelt before the crucifix,
While o'er the lake the cataract of Lodore
Pealed to his orisons, and when he paced
20 Along the beach of this small isle and thought
Of his Companion, he would pray that both
(Now that their earthly duties were fulfilled)
Might die in the same moment. Nor in vain
So prayed he: – as our chronicles report,
Though here the Hermit numbered his last day
Far from St Cuthbert his belovèd Friend,
Those holy Men both died in the same hour.

The Seven Sisters
or, The Solitude of Binnorie

I

Seven Daughters had Lord Archibald,
All children of one mother:
You could not say in one short day
What love they bore each other.
A garland, of seven lilies, wrought!
Seven Sisters that together dwell;
But he, bold Knight as ever fought,
Their Father, took of them no thought,
He loved the wars so well.
10   Sing, mournfully, oh! mournfully,
The solitude of Binnorie!

II

Fresh blows the wind, a western wind,
And from the shores of Erin,
Across the wave, a Rover brave
To Binnorie is steering:
Right onward to the Scottish strand
The gallant ship is borne;
The warriors leap upon the land,
And hark! the Leader of the band
20   Hath blown his bugle horn.
Sing, mournfully, oh! mournfully,
The solitude of Binnorie.

III

Beside a grotto of their own,
With boughs above them closing,
The Seven are laid, and in the shade
They lie like fawns reposing.
But now, upstarting with affright
At noise of man and steed,
Away they fly to left, to right –

30 Of your fair household, Father-knight,
Methinks you take small heed!
Sing, mournfully, oh! mournfully,
The solitude of Binnorie.

IV
Away the seven fair Campbells fly,
And, over hill and hollow,
With menace proud, and insult loud,
The youthful Rovers follow.
Cried they, 'Your Father loves to roam:
Enough for him to find
40 The empty house when he comes home;
For us your yellow ringlets comb,
For us be fair and kind!'
Sing, mournfully, oh! mournfully,
The solitude of Binnorie.

V
Some close behind, some side by side,
Like clouds in stormy weather;
They run, and cry, 'Nay, let us die,
And let us die together.'
A lake was near; the shore was steep;
50 There never foot had been;
They ran, and with a desperate leap
Together plunged into the deep,
Nor evermore were seen.
Sing, mournfully, oh! mournfully,
The solitude of Binnorie.

VI
The stream that flows out of the lake,
As through the glen it rambles,
Repeats a moan o'er moss and stone,
For those seven lovely Campbells.
60 Seven little Islands, green and bare,
Have risen from out the deep:

The fishers say, those sisters fair
By faeries all are buried there,
And there together sleep.
Sing, mournfully, oh! mournfully,
The solitude of Binnorie.

To Joanna

Amid the smoke of cities did you pass
The time of early youth; and there you learned,
From years of quiet industry, to love
The living Beings by your own fire-side,
With such a strong devotion, that your heart
Is slow to meet the sympathies of them
Who look upon the hills with tenderness,
And make dear friendships with the streams and groves.
Yet we, who are transgressors in this kind,
10 Dwelling retired in our simplicity
Among the woods and fields, we love you well,
Joanna! and I guess, since you have been
So distant from us now for two long years,
That you will gladly listen to discourse,
However trivial, if you thence be taught
That they, with whom you once were happy, talk
Familiarly of you and of old times.

    While I was seated, now some ten days past,
Beneath those lofty firs, that overtop
20 Their ancient neighbour, the old steeple-tower,
The Vicar from his gloomy house hard by
Came forth to greet me; and when he had asked,
'How fares Joanna, that wild-hearted Maid!
And when will she return to us?' he paused;
And, after short exchange of village news,
He with grave looks demanded, for what cause,
Reviving obsolete idolatry,
I, like a Runic Priest, in characters

Of formidable size had chiselled out
30 Some uncouth name upon the native rock,
Above the Rotha, by the forest-side.
– Now, by those dear immunities of heart
Engendered between malice and true love,
I was not loth to be so catechised,
And this was my reply: – 'As it befell,
One summer morning we had walked abroad
At break of day, Joanna and myself.
– 'Twas that delightful season when the broom,
Full-flowered, and visible on every steep,
40 Along the copses runs in veins of gold.
Our pathway led us on to Rotha's banks;
And when we came in front of that tall rock
That eastward looks, I there stopped short – and stood
Tracing the lofty barrier with my eye
From base to summit; such delight I found
To note in shrub and tree, in stone and flower,
That intermixture of delicious hues,
Along so vast a surface, all at once,
In one impression, by connecting force
50 Of their own beauty, imaged in the heart.
– When I had gazed perhaps two minutes' space,
Joanna, looking in my eyes, beheld
That ravishment of mine, and laughed aloud.
The Rock, like something starting from a sleep,
Took up the Lady's voice, and laughed again;
That ancient Woman seated on Helm-crag
Was ready with her cavern; Hammar-scar,
And the tall Steep of Silver-how, sent forth
A noise of laughter; southern Loughrigg heard,
60 And Fairfield answered with a mountain tone;
Helvellyn far into the clear blue sky
Carried the Lady's voice, – old Skiddaw blew
His speaking-trumpet; – back out of the clouds
Of Glaramara southward came the voice;
And Kirkstone tossed it from his misty head.
– Now whether (said I to our cordial Friend,

Who in the hey-day of astonishment
Smiled in my face) this were in simple truth
A work accomplished by the brotherhood
70 Of ancient mountains, or my ear was touched
With dreams and visionary impulses
To me alone imparted, sure I am
That there was a loud uproar in the hills.
And, while we both were listening, to my side
The fair Joanna drew, as if she wished
To shelter from some object of her fear.
– And hence, long afterwards, when eighteen moons
Were wasted, as I chanced to walk alone
Beneath this rock, at sunrise, on a calm
80 And silent morning, I sat down, and there,
In memory of affections old and true,
I chiselled out in those rude characters
Joanna's name deep in the living stone: –
And I, and all who dwell by my fireside,
Have called the lovely rock, JOANNA'S ROCK.'

NOTE. – In Cumberland and Westmoreland are several In-
scriptions, upon the native rock, which, from the wasting of time,
and the rudeness of the workmanship, have been mistaken for
Runic. They are, without doubt, Roman.

The Rotha, mentioned in this poem, is the River which,
flowing through the lakes of Grasmere and Rydal, falls into
Wynandermere. On Helm-crag, that impressive single moun-
tain at the head of the Vale of Grasmere, is a rock which from
most points of view bears a striking resemblance to an old
Woman cowering. Close by this rock is one of those fissures or
caverns, which in the language of the country are called dun-
geons. Most of the mountains here mentioned immediately
surround the Vale of Grasmere; of the others, some are at a
considerable distance, but they belong to the same cluster.

'When, to the attractions of the busy world'

When, to the attractions of the busy world,
Preferring studious leisure, I had chosen
A habitation in this peaceful Vale,
Sharp season followed of continual storm
In deepest winter; and, from week to week,
Pathway, and lane, and public road, were clogged
With frequent showers of snow. Upon a hill
At a short distance from my cottage, stands
A stately Fir-grove, whither I was wont
10 To hasten, for I found, beneath the roof
Of that perennial shade, a cloistral place
Of refuge, with an unincumbered floor.
Here, in safe covert, on the shallow snow,
And, sometimes, on a speck of visible earth,
The redbreast near me hopped; nor was I loth
To sympathize with vulgar coppice birds
That, for protection from the nipping blast,
Hither repaired. – A single beech-tree grew
Within this grove of firs! and, on the fork
20 Of that one beech, appeared a thrush's nest;
A last year's nest, conspicuously built
At such small elevation from the ground
As gave sure sign that they, who in that house
Of nature and of love had made their home
Amid the fir-trees, all the summer long
Dwelt in a tranquil spot. And oftentimes
A few sheep, stragglers from some mountain-flock,
Would watch my motions with suspicious stare,
From the remotest outskirts of the grove, –
30 Some nook where they had made their final stand,
Huddling together from two fears – the fear
Of me and of the storm. Full many an hour
Here did I lose. But in this grove the trees
Had been so thickly planted, and had thriven
In such perplexed and intricate array,

That vainly did I seek, beneath their stems
A length of open space, where to and fro
My feet might move without concern or care;
And, baffled thus, though earth from day to day
40   Was fettered, and the air by storm disturbed,
I ceased the shelter to frequent, – and prized,
Less than I wished to prize, that calm recess.

    The snows dissolved, and genial Spring returned
To clothe the fields with verdure. Other haunts
Meanwhile were mine; till, one bright April day,
By chance retiring from the glare of noon
To this forsaken covert, there I found
A hoary pathway traced between the trees,
And winding on with such an easy line
50   Along a natural opening, that I stood
Much wondering how I could have sought in vain
For what was now so obvious. To abide,
For an allotted interval of ease,
Under my cottage-roof, had gladly come
From the wild sea a cherished Visitant;
And with the sight of this same path – begun,
Begun and ended, in the shady grove,
Pleasant conviction flashed upon my mind
That, to this opportune recess allured,
60   He had surveyed it with a finer eye,
A heart more wakeful; and had worn the track
By pacing here, unwearied and alone,
In that habitual restlessness of foot
That haunts the Sailor measuring o'er and o'er
His short domain upon the vessel's deck,
While she pursues her course through the dreary sea.

    When thou hadst quitted Esthwaite's pleasant shore,
And taken thy first leave of those green hills
And rocks that were the play-ground of thy youth,
70   Year followed year, my Brother! and we two,

Conversing not, knew little in what mould
Each other's mind was fashioned; and at length,
When once again we met in Grasmere Vale,
Between us there was little other bond
Than common feelings of fraternal love.
But thou, a School-boy, to the sea hadst carried
Undying recollections; Nature there
Was with thee; she, who loved us both, she still
Was with thee; and even so didst thou become
80 A *silent* Poet; from the solitude
Of the vast sea didst bring a watchful heart
Still couchant, an inevitable ear,
And an eye practised like a blind man's touch.
– Back to the joyless Ocean thou art gone;
Nor from this vestige of thy musing hours
Could I withhold thy honoured name, – and now
I love the fir-grove with a perfect love.
Thither do I withdraw when cloudless suns
Shine hot, or wind blows troublesome and strong;
90 And there I sit at evening, when the steep
Of Silver-how, and Grasmere's peaceful lake,
And one green island, gleam between the stems
Of the dark firs, a visionary scene!
And, while I gaze upon the spectacle
Of clouded splendour, on this dream-like sight
Of solemn loveliness, I think on thee,
My Brother, and on all which thou hast lost.
Nor seldom, if I rightly guess, while Thou,
Muttering the verses which I muttered first
100 Among the mountains, through the midnight watch
Art pacing thoughtfully the vessel's deck
In some far region, here, while o'er my head,
At every impulse of the moving breeze,
The fir-grove murmurs with a sea-like sound,
Alone I tread this path; – for aught I know,
Timing my steps to thine; and, with a store
Of undistinguishable sympathies,
Mingling most earnest wishes for the day

When we, and others whom we love, shall meet
110 A second time, in Grasmere's happy Vale.

NOTE. – This wish was not granted; the lamented Person not
long after perished by shipwreck, in discharge of his duty as
Commander of the Honourable East India Company's Vessel,
the Earl of Abergavenny.

The Childless Father

'Up, Timothy, up with your staff and away!
Not a soul in the village this morning will stay;
The hare has just started from Hamilton's grounds,
And Skiddaw is glad with the cry of the hounds.'

– Of coats and of jackets grey, scarlet, and green,
On the slopes of the pastures all colours were seen;
With their comely blue aprons, and caps white as snow,
The girls on the hills made a holiday show.

Fresh sprigs of green box-wood, not six months before,
10 Filled the funeral basin at Timothy's door;
A coffin through Timothy's threshold had past;
One Child did it bear, and that Child was his last.

Now fast up the dell came the noise and the fray,
The horse and the horn, and the hark! hark away!
Old Timothy took up his staff, and he shut
With a leisurely motion the door of his hut.

Perhaps to himself at that moment he said;
'The key I must take, for my Ellen is dead.'
But of this in my ears not a word did he speak;
20 And he went to the chase with a tear on his cheek.

The Pet–Lamb
A Pastoral

The dew was falling fast, the stars began to blink;
I heard a voice; it said, 'Drink, pretty creature, drink!'
And, looking o'er the hedge, before me I espied
A snow-white mountain-lamb with a Maiden at its side.

Nor sheep nor kine were near; the lamb was all alone,
And by a slender cord was tethered to a stone;
With one knee on the grass did the little Maiden kneel,
While to that mountain-lamb she gave its evening meal.

The lamb, while from her hand he thus his supper took,
10   Seemed to feast with head and ears; and his tail with
      pleasure shook.
'Drink, pretty creature, drink,' she said in such a tone
That I almost received her heart into my own.

'Twas little Barbara Lewthwaite, a child of beauty rare!
I watched them with delight, they were a lovely pair.
Now with her empty can the Maiden turned away:
But ere ten yards were gone her footsteps did she stay.

Right towards the lamb she looked; and from a shady
      place
I unobserved could see the workings of her face:
If Nature to her tongue could measured numbers bring,
20   Thus, thought I, to her lamb that little Maid might sing:

'What ails thee, young One? what? Why pull so at thy
      cord?
Is it not well with thee? well both for bed and board?
Thy plot of grass is soft, and green as grass can be;
Rest, little young One, rest; what is't that aileth thee?

'What is it thou wouldst seek? What is wanting to thy
   heart?
Thy limbs, are they not strong? And beautiful thou art:
This grass is tender grass; these flowers they have no
   peers;
And that green corn all day is rustling in thy ears!

'If the sun be shining hot, do but stretch thy woollen
   chain,
30 This beech is standing by, its covert thou canst gain;
For rain and mountain-storms! the like thou need'st not
   fear,
The rain and storm are things that scarcely can come
   here.

'Rest, little young One, rest; thou hast forgot the day
When my father found thee first in places far away;
Many flocks were on the hills, but thou wert owned by
   none,
And thy mother from thy side for evermore was gone.

'He took thee in his arms, and in pity brought thee
   home:
A blessèd day for thee! then whither wouldst thou roam?
A faithful nurse thou hast; the dam that did thee yean
40 Upon the mountain-tops no kinder could have been.

'Thou know'st that twice a day I have brought thee in
   this can
Fresh water from the brook, as clear as ever ran;
And twice in the day, when the ground is wet with dew,
I bring thee draughts of milk, warm milk it is and new.

'Thy limbs will shortly be twice as stout as they are now,
Then I'll yoke thee to my cart like a pony in the plough;
My playmate thou shalt be; and when the wind is cold
Our hearth shall be thy bed, our house shall be thy fold.

'It will not, will not rest! – Poor creature, can it be
50 That 'tis thy mother's heart which is working so in thee?
Things that I know not of belike to thee are dear,
And dreams of things which thou canst neither see nor
hear.

'Alas, the mountain-tops that look so green and fair!
I've heard of fearful winds and darkness that come there;
The little brooks that seem all pastime and all play,
When they are angry, roar like lions for their prey.

'Here thou need'st not dread the raven in the sky;
Night and day thou art safe, – our cottage is hard by.
Why bleat so after me? Why pull so at thy chain?
60 Sleep – and at break of day I will come to thee again!'

– As homeward through the lane I went with lazy feet,
  This song to myself did I oftentimes repeat;
And it seemed, as I retraced the ballad line by line,
That but half of it was hers, and one half of it was *mine*.

Again, and once again, did I repeat the song;
'Nay,' said I, 'more than half to the damsel must belong,
For she looked with such a look, and she spake with
    such a tone,
That I almost received her heart into my own.'

Rural Architecture

There's George Fisher, Charles Fleming, and Reginald
    Shore,
Three rosy-cheeked school-boys, the highest not more
Than the height of a counsellor's bag;
To the top of GREAT HOW did it please them to climb:
And there they built up, without mortar or lime,
A Man on the peak of the crag.

They built him of stones gathered up as they lay:
They built him and christened him all in one day,
An urchin both vigorous and hale;
10   And so without scruple they called him Ralph Jones.
Now Ralph is renowned for the length of his bones;
The Magog of Legberthwaite dale.

Just half a week after, the wind sallied forth,
And, in anger or merriment, out of the north,
Coming on with a terrible pother,
From the peak of the crag blew the giant away.
And what did these school-boys? – The very next day
They went and they built up another.

– Some little I've seen of blind boisterous works
20   By Christian disturbers more savage than Turks,
Spirits busy to do and undo:
At remembrance whereof my blood sometimes will flag;
Then, light-hearted Boys, to the top of the crag;
And I'll build up a giant with you.

Michael
A Pastoral Poem

If from the public way you turn your steps
Up the tumultuous brook of Green-head Ghyll,
You will suppose that with an upright path
Your feet must struggle; in such bold ascent
The pastoral mountains front you, face to face.
But, courage! for around that boisterous brook
The mountains have all opened out themselves,
And made a hidden valley of their own.
No habitation can be seen; but they
10   Who journey thither find themselves alone
With a few sheep, with rocks and stones, and kites
That overhead are sailing in the sky.
It is in truth an utter solitude;
Nor should I have made mention of this Dell

But for one object which you might pass by,
Might see and notice not. Beside the brook
Appears a straggling heap of unhewn stones!
And to that simple object appertains
A story — unenriched with strange events,
20   Yet not unfit, I deem, for the fireside,
Or for the summer shade. It was the first
Of those domestic tales that spake to me
Of Shepherds, dwellers in the valleys, men
Whom I already loved; — not verily
For their own sakes, but for the fields and hills
Where was their occupation and abode.
And hence this Tale, while I was yet a Boy
Careless of books, yet having felt the power
Of Nature, by the gentle agency
30   Of natural objects, led me on to feel
For passions that were not my own, and think
(At random and imperfectly indeed)
On man, the heart of man, and human life.
Therefore, although it be a history
Homely and rude, I will relate the same
For the delight of a few natural hearts;
And, with yet fonder feeling, for the sake
Of youthful Poets, who among these hills
Will be my second self when I am gone.

40   Upon the forest-side in Grasmere Vale
There dwelt a Shepherd, Michael was his name;
An old man, stout of heart, and strong of limb.
His bodily frame had been from youth to age
Of an unusual strength: his mind was keen,
Intense, and frugal, apt for all affairs,
And in his shepherd's calling he was prompt
And watchful more than ordinary men.
Hence had he learned the meaning of all winds,
Of blasts of every tone; and, oftentimes,
50   When others heeded not, he heard the South
Make subterraneous music, like the noise

Of bagpipers on distant Highland hills.
The Shepherd, at such warning, of his flock
Bethought him, and he to himself would say,
'The winds are now devising work for me!'
And, truly, at all times, the storm, that drives
The traveller to a shelter, summoned him
Up to the mountains: he had been alone
Amid the heart of many thousand mists,
60 That came to him, and left him, on the heights.
So lived he till his eightieth year was past.
And grossly that man errs, who should suppose
That the green valleys, and the streams and rocks,
Were things indifferent to the Shepherd's thoughts.
Fields, where with cheerful spirits he had breathed
The common air; hills, which with vigorous step
He had so often climbed; which had impressed
So many incidents upon his mind
Of hardship, skill or courage, joy or fear;
70 Which, like a book, preserved the memory
Of the dumb animals, whom he had saved,
Had fed or sheltered, linking to such acts
The certainty of honourable gain;
Those fields, those hills – what could they less? had laid
Strong hold on his affections, were to him
A pleasurable feeling of blind love,
The pleasure which there is in life itself.

His days had not been passed in singleness.
His Helpmate was a comely matron, old –
80 Though younger than himself full twenty years.
She was a woman of a stirring life,
Whose heart was in her house: two wheels she had
Of antique form; this large, for spinning wool;
That small, for flax; and if one wheel had rest,
It was because the other was at work.
The Pair had but one inmate in their house,
An only Child, who had been born to them
When Michael, telling o'er his years, began

To deem that he was old, – in shepherd's phrase,
90 With one foot in the grave. This only Son,
With two brave sheep-dogs tried in many a storm,
The one of an inestimable worth,
Made all their household. I may truly say,
That they were as a proverb in the vale
For endless industry. When day was gone,
And from their occupations out of doors
The Son and Father were come home, even then,
Their labour did not cease; unless when all
Turned to the cleanly supper-board, and there,
100 Each with a mess of pottage and skimmed milk,
Sat round the basket piled with oaten cakes,
And their plain home-made cheese. Yet when the meal
Was ended, Luke (for so the Son was named)
And his old Father both betook themselves
To such convenient work as might employ
Their hands by the fire-side; perhaps to card
Wool for the Housewife's spindle, or repair
Some injury done to sickle, flail, or scythe,
Or other implement of house or field.

110   Down from the ceiling, by the chimney's edge,
That in our ancient uncouth country style
With huge and black projection overbrowed
Large space beneath, as duly as the light
Of day grew dim the Housewife hung a lamp;
An aged utensil, which had performed
Service beyond all others of its kind.
Early at evening did it burn – and late,
Surviving comrade of uncounted hours,
Which, going by from year to year, had found,
120 And left the couple neither gay perhaps
Nor cheerful, yet with objects and with hopes,
Living a life of eager industry.
And now, when Luke had reached his eighteenth year,
There by the light of this old lamp they sate,
Father and Son, while far into the night

The Housewife plied her own peculiar work,
Making the cottage through the silent hours
Murmur as with the sound of summer flies.
This light was famous in its neighbourhood,
130   And was a public symbol of the life
That thrifty Pair had lived. For, as it chanced,
Their cottage on a plot of rising ground
Stood single, with large prospect, north and south,
High into Easedale, up to Dunmail-Raise,
And westward to the village near the lake;
And from this constant light, so regular
And so far seen, the House itself, by all
Who dwelt within the limits of the vale,
Both old and young, was named THE EVENING STAR.

140   Thus living on through such a length of years,
The Shepherd, if he loved himself, must needs
Have loved his Helpmate; but to Michael's heart
This son of his old age was yet more dear —
Less from instinctive tenderness, the same
Fond spirit that blindly works in the blood of all —
Than that a child, more than all other gifts
That earth can offer to declining man,
Brings hope with it, and forward-looking thoughts,
And stirrings of inquietude, when they
150   By tendency of nature needs must fail.
Exceeding was the love he bare to him,
His heart and his heart's joy! For often-times
Old Michael, while he was a babe in arms,
Had done him female service, not alone
For pastime and delight, as is the use
Of fathers, but with patient mind enforced
To acts of tenderness; and he had rocked
His cradle, as with a woman's gentle hand.

And, in a later time, ere yet the Boy
160   Had put on boy's attire, did Michael love,
Albeit of a stern unbending mind,

To have the Young-one in his sight, when he
Wrought in the field, or on his shepherd's stool
Sate with a fettered sheep before him stretched
Under the large old oak, that near his door
Stood single, and, from matchless depth of shade,
Chosen for the Shearer's covert from the sun,
Thence in our rustic dialect was called
The CLIPPING TREE, a name which yet it bears.
170 There, while they two were sitting in the shade,
With others round them, earnest all and blithe,
Would Michael exercise his heart with looks
Of fond correction and reproof bestowed
Upon the Child, if he disturbed the sheep
By catching at their legs, or with his shouts
Scared them, while they lay still beneath the shears.

And when by Heaven's good grace the boy grew up
A healthy Lad, and carried in his cheek
Two steady roses that were five years old;
180 Then Michael from a winter coppice cut
With his own hand a sapling, which he hooped
With iron, making it throughout in all
Due requisites a perfect shepherd's staff,
And gave it to the Boy; wherewith equipt
He as a watchman oftentimes was placed
At gate or gap, to stem or turn the flock;
And, to his office prematurely called,
There stood the urchin, as you will divine,
Something between a hindrance and a help;
190 And for this cause not always, I believe,
Receiving from his Father hire of praise;
Though naught was left undone which staff, or voice,
Or looks, or threatening gestures, could perform.

But soon as Luke, full ten years old, could stand
Against the mountain blasts; and to the heights,
Not fearing toil, nor length of weary ways,
He with his Father daily went, and they

Were as companions, why should I relate
That objects which the Shepherd loved before
200 Were dearer now? that from the Boy there came
Feelings and emanations – things which were
Light to the sun and music to the wind;
And that the old Man's heart seemed born again?

Thus in his Father's sight the Boy grew up:
And now, when he had reached his eighteenth year,
He was his comfort and his daily hope.

While in this sort the simple household lived
From day to day, to Michael's ear there came
Distressful tidings. Long before the time
210 Of which I speak, the Shepherd had been bound
In surety for his brother's son, a man
Of an industrious life, and ample means;
But unforeseen misfortunes suddenly
Had prest upon him; and old Michael now
Was summoned to discharge the forfeiture,
A grievous penalty, but little less
Than half his substance. This unlooked-for claim,
At the first hearing, for a moment took
More hope out of his life than he supposed
220 That any old man ever could have lost.
As soon as he had armed himself with strength
To look his trouble in the face, it seemed
The Shepherd's sole resource to sell at once
A portion of his patrimonial fields.
Such was his first resolve; he thought again,
And his heart failed him. 'Isabel,' said he,
Two evenings after he had heard the news,
'I have been toiling more than seventy years,
And in the open sunshine of God's love
230 Have we all lived; yet if these fields of ours
Should pass into a stranger's hand, I think
That I could not lie quiet in my grave.
Our lot is a hard lot; the sun himself

Has scarcely been more diligent than I;
And I have lived to be a fool at last
To my own family. An evil man
That was, and made an evil choice, if he
Were false to us; and if he were not false,
There are ten thousand to whom loss like this
240 Had been no sorrow. I forgive him; – but
'Twere better to be dumb than to talk thus.

   'When I began, my purpose was to speak
Of remedies and of a cheerful hope.
Our Luke shall leave us, Isabel; the land
Shall not go from us, and it shall be free;
He shall possess it, free as is the wind
That passes over it. We have, thou know'st,
Another kinsman – he will be our friend
In this distress. He is a prosperous man,
250 Thriving in trade – and Luke to him shall go,
And with his kinsman's help and his own thrift
He quickly will repair this loss, and then
He may return to us. If here he stay,
What can be done? Where every one is poor,
What can be gained?'
                 At this the old Man paused,
And Isabel sat silent, for her mind
Was busy, looking back into past times.
There's Richard Bateman, thought she to herself,
He was a parish-boy – at the church-door
260 They made a gathering for him, shillings, pence,
And halfpennies, wherewith the neighbours bought
A basket, which they filled with pedlar's wares;
And, with this basket on his arm, the lad
Went up to London, found a master there,
Who, out of many, chose the trusty boy
To go and overlook his merchandise
Beyond the seas; where he grew wondrous rich,
And left estates and monies to the poor,
And, at his birth-place, built a chapel floored

270 With marble, which he sent from foreign lands.
These thoughts, and many others of like sort,
Passed quickly through the mind of Isabel,
And her face brightened. The old Man was glad,
And thus resumed: – 'Well, Isabel! this scheme
These two days, has been meat and drink to me.
Far more than we have lost is left us yet.
– We have enough – I wish indeed that I
Were younger; – but this hope is a good hope.
Make ready Luke's best garments, of the best
280 Buy for him more, and let us send him forth
Tomorrow, or the next day, or tonight:
– If he *could* go, the Boy should go tonight.'

Here Michael ceased, and to the fields went forth
With a light heart. The Housewife for five days
Was restless morn and night, and all day long
Wrought on with her best fingers to prepare
Things needful for the journey of her son.
But Isabel was glad when Sunday came
To stop her in her work: for, when she lay
290 By Michael's side, she through the last two nights
Heard him, how he was troubled in his sleep:
And when they rose at morning she could see
That all his hopes were gone. That day at noon
She said to Luke, while they two by themselves
Were sitting at the door, 'Thou must not go:
We have no other Child but thee to lose,
None to remember – do not go away,
For if thou leave thy Father he will die.'
The Youth made answer with a jocund voice;
300 And Isabel, when she had told her fears,
Recovered heart. That evening her best fare
Did she bring forth, and all together sat
Like happy people round a Christmas fire.

With daylight Isabel resumed her work;
And all the ensuing week the house appeared

As cheerful as a grove in Spring: at length
The expected letter from their kinsman came,
With kind assurances that he would do
His utmost for the welfare of the Boy;
310 To which, requests were added, that forthwith
He might be sent to him. Ten times or more
The letter was read over; Isabel
Went forth to show it to the neighbours round;
Nor was there at that time on English land
A prouder heart than Luke's. When Isabel
Had to her house returned, the old Man said,
'He shall depart tomorrow.' To this word
The Housewife answered, talking much of things
Which, if at such short notice he should go,
320 Would surely be forgotten. But at length
She gave consent, and Michael was at ease.

Near the tumultuous brook of Green-head Ghyll,
In that deep valley, Michael had designed
To build a Sheep-fold; and, before he heard
The tidings of his melancholy loss,
For this same purpose he had gathered up
A heap of stones, which by the streamlet's edge
Lay thrown together, ready for the work.
With Luke that evening thitherward he walked:
330 And soon as they had reached the place he stopped,
And thus the old Man spake to him: – 'My Son,
Tomorrow thou wilt leave me: with full heart
I look upon thee, for thou art the same
That wert a promise to me ere thy birth,
And all thy life hast been my daily joy.
I will relate to thee some little part
Of our two histories; 'twill do thee good
When thou art from me, even if I should touch
On things thou canst not know of. – After thou
340 First cam'st into the world – as oft befalls
To new-born infants – thou didst sleep away
Two days, and blessings from thy Father's tongue

Then fell upon thee. Day by day passed on,
And still I loved thee with increasing love.
Never to living ear came sweeter sounds
Than when I heard thee by our own fire-side
First uttering, without words, a natural tune;
While thou, a feeding babe, didst in thy joy
Sing at thy Mother's breast. Month followed month,
350 And in the open fields my life was passed
And on the mountains; else I think that thou
Hadst been brought up upon thy Father's knees.
But we were playmates, Luke: among these hills,
As well thou knowest, in us the old and young
Have played together, nor with me didst thou
Lack any pleasure which a boy can know.'
Luke had a manly heart; but at these words
He sobbed aloud. The old Man grasped his hand,
And said, 'Nay, do not take it so – I see
360 That these are things of which I need not speak.
– Even to the utmost I have been to thee
A kind and a good Father: and herein
I but repay a gift which I myself
Received at others' hands; for, though now old
Beyond the common life of man, I still
Remember them who loved me in my youth.
Both of them sleep together: here they lived,
As all their Forefathers had done; and when
At length their time was come, they were not loth
370 To give their bodies to the family mould.
I wished that thou should'st live the life they lived:
But 'tis a long time to look back, my Son,
And see so little gain from threescore years.
These fields were burdened when they came to me;
Till I was forty years of age, not more
Than half of my inheritance was mine.
I toiled and toiled; God blessed me in my work,
And till these three weeks past the land was free.
– It looks as if it never could endure
380 Another Master. Heaven forgive me, Luke,

If I judge ill for thee, but it seems good
That thou shouldst go.'
      At this the old Man paused;
Then, pointing to the stones near which they stood,
Thus, after a short silence, he resumed:
'This was a work for us; and now, my Son,
It is a work for me. But, lay one stone –
Here, lay it for me, Luke, with thine own hands.
Nay, Boy, be of good hope; – we both may live
To see a better day. At eighty-four
390 I still am strong and hale; – do thou thy part;
I will do mine. – I will begin again
With many tasks that were resigned to thee:
Up to the heights, and in among the storms,
Will I without thee go again, and do
All works which I was wont to do alone,
Before I knew thy face. – Heaven bless thee, Boy!
Thy heart these two weeks has been beating fast
With many hopes; it should be so – yes – yes –
I knew that thou couldst never have a wish
400 To leave me, Luke: thou hast been bound to me
Only by links of love: when thou art gone,
What will be left to us! – But, I forget
My purposes. Lay now the corner-stone,
As I requested; and hereafter, Luke,
When thou art gone away, should evil men
Be thy companions, think of me, my Son,
And of this moment; hither turn thy thoughts,
And God will strengthen thee: amid all fear
And all temptation, Luke, I pray that thou
410 May'st bear in mind the life thy Fathers lived,
Who, being innocent, did for that cause
Bestir them in good deeds. Now, fare thee well –
When thou return'st, thou in this place wilt see
A work which is not here: a covenant
'Twill be between us; but, whatever fate
Befall thee, I shall love thee to the last,
And bear thy memory with me to the grave.'

The Shepherd ended here; and Luke stooped down,
And, as his Father had requested, laid
420 The first stone of the Sheep-fold. At the sight
The old Man's grief broke from him; to his heart
He pressed his Son, he kissèd him and wept;
And to the house together they returned.
– Hushed was that House in peace, or seeming peace,
Ere the night fell: – with morrow's dawn the Boy
Began his journey, and when he had reached
The public way, he put on a bold face;
And all the neighbours, as he passed their doors,
Came forth with wishes and with farewell prayers,
430 That followed him till he was out of sight.

A good report did from their Kinsman come,
Of Luke and his well-doing: and the Boy
Wrote loving letters, full of wondrous news,
Which, as the Housewife phrased it, were throughout
'The prettiest letters that were ever seen.'
Both parents read them with rejoicing hearts.
So, many months passed on: and once again
The Shepherd went about his daily work
With confident and cheerful thoughts; and now
440 Sometimes when he could find a leisure hour
He to that valley took his way, and there
Wrought at the Sheep-fold. Meantime Luke began
To slacken in his duty; and, at length,
He in the dissolute city gave himself
To evil courses: ignominy and shame
Fell on him, so that he was driven at last
To seek a hiding-place beyond the seas.

There is a comfort in the strength of love;
'Twill make a thing endurable, which else
450 Would overset the brain, or break the heart:
I have conversed with more than one who well
Remember the old Man, and what he was
Years after he had heard this heavy news.

His bodily frame had been from youth to age
Of an unusual strength. Among the rocks
He went, and still looked up to sun and cloud,
And listened to the wind; and, as before,
Performed all kinds of labour for his sheep,
And for the land, his small inheritance.
460 And to that hollow dell from time to time
Did he repair, to build the Fold of which
His flock had need. 'Tis not forgotten yet
The pity which was then in every heart
For the old Man – and 'tis believed by all
That many and many a day he thither went,
And never lifted up a single stone.

There, by the Sheep-fold, sometimes was he seen
Sitting alone, or with his faithful Dog,
Then old, beside him, lying at his feet.
470 The length of full seven years, from time to time,
He at the building of this Sheep-fold wrought,
And left the work unfinished when he died.
Three years, or little more, did Isabel
Survive her Husband: at her death the estate
Was sold, and went into a stranger's hand.
The Cottage which was named the EVENING STAR
Is gone – the ploughshare has been through the ground
On which it stood; great changes have been wrought
In all the neighbourhood: – yet the oak is left
480 That grew beside their door; and the remains
Of the unfinished Sheep-fold may be seen
Beside the boisterous brook of Green-head Ghyll.

[*Fragments from the 'Christabel' Note-book*]

I
Thou issuest from a fissure in the rock
Compact into one individual stream,
A small short stream not longer than the blade

Of a child's coral, then, upon the face
Of the steep crag diffused, thou dost flow down
Wide, weak and glimmering, and so thin withal
Thy course is like the brushing of a breeze
Upon a calm smooth lake. A few bold drops
Are there, these starting regularly forth
10 Strike somewhere on the rocks and stones beneath
And are thy voice, for thou wert silent else.

II
                    The leaves stir not,
They all are steady as the cloudless sky;
How deep the Quiet: all is motionless,
As if the life of the vast world was hushed
Into a breathless dream.

III
Oh 'tis a joy divine on summer days
When not a breeze is stirring, not a cloud,
To sit within some solitary wood,
Far in some lonely wood, and hear no sound
Which the heart does not make, or else so fit[s]
To its own temper that in external things
No longer seem internal difference
All melts away, and things that are without
Live in our minds as in their native home.

IV
The clouds are standing still in the mid heavens;
A perfect quietness is in the air;
The ear hears not; and yet, I know not how,
More than the other senses does it hold
A manifest communion with the heart.

V
The sl[ender] dandelion bows his head
With graceful [motion?]; touched by the same breeze
The low geranium shivers wantonly.

Child art thou of the mountains, infant [stream?]
A Brother of the stormy breeze; these flowers
Are they not all thy neighbours? yet with thee
Do they maintain no visible fellowship,
Nor can I say that aught which they possess,
Of garb or colour is a gift of thine.

VI

There is creation in the eye,
Nor less in all the other senses; powers
They are that colour, model, and combine
The things perceived with such an absolute
Essential energy that we may say
That those most godlike faculties of ours
At one and the same moment are the mind
And the mind's minister. In many a walk
At evening or by moonlight, or reclined
10   At midday upon beds of forest moss,
Have we to Nature and her impulses
Of our whole being made free gift, and when
Our trance had left us, oft have we, by aid
Of the impressions which it left behind,
Looked inward on ourselves, and learned, perhaps,
Something of what we are. Nor in those hours
Did we destroy [   ]
The original impression of delight,
But by such retrospect it was recalled
To yet a second and a second life,
20   While in this excitation of the [mind?]
A vivid pulse of sentiment and thought
Beat palpably within us, and all shades
Of consciousness were ours.

VII

Long had I stood and looked into the west,
Where clouds and mountain tops and gleams of light,
Children of glory all [   ]
Made one society and seemed to be

Of the same nature; long I stood and looked,
But when my thoughts began to fail, I turned
Towards a grove, a spot which well I knew,
For oftentimes its sympathies had fallen
Like a refreshing dew upon my heart;
10 I stretch[ed] myself beneath the shade
And soon the stirring and inquisitive mind
Was laid asleep; the godlike senses gave
Short impulses of life that seemed to tell
Of our existence, and then passed away.

VIII
The moon is in the East, I see her not:
But to the summit of the arch of heaven
She whitens o'er the azure of the sky
With thin and milky gleams of visible light.

[*Fragment: A Somersetshire Tragedy*]

Ill fared it now with his poor wife, I ween
That in her hut she could no more remain;
Oft in the early morning she was seen
Ere Robert to his work had crossed the green,
She roamed from house to house the weary day
And when the housewife's evening hearth was clean
She lingered still and if you chanced to say,
'Robert his supper needs,' her colour passed away.

[*Fragment: 'Witness thou'*]

Witness thou
The dear companion of my lonely walk,
My hope, my joy, my sister, and my friend,
Or something dearer still, if reason knows
A dearer thought, or in the heart of love
There be a dearer name.

[*Fragment from Dove Cottage Manuscript 44 (1)*]

I have been here in the Moon-light,
I have been here in the Day,
I have been here in the Dark Night,
And the Stream was still roaring away.

Motto Intended for Poems on the Naming of Places

Some minds have room alone for pageant stories,
Some for strong passion fleshed in action strong;
Others find tales and endless allegories
By river margins, and green woods among.

The Affliction of Margaret —

I

Where art thou, my beloved Son,
Where art thou, worse to me than dead?
Oh find me, prosperous or undone!
Or, if the grave be now thy bed,
Why am I ignorant of the same
That I may rest; and neither blame
Nor sorrow may attend thy name?

II

Seven years, alas! to have received
No tidings of an only child;
10 To have despaired, have hoped, believed,
And been for evermore beguiled;
Sometimes with thoughts of very bliss!
I catch at them, and then I miss;
Was ever darkness like to this?

III
He was among the prime in worth,
An object beauteous to behold;
Well born, well bred; I sent him forth
Ingenuous, innocent, and bold:
If things ensued that wanted grace,
20   As hath been said, they were not base;
And never blush was on my face.

IV
Ah! little doth the young-one dream,
When full of play and childish cares,
What power is in his wildest scream,
Heard by his mother unawares!
He knows it not, he cannot guess:
Years to a mother bring distress;
But do not make her love the less.

V
Neglect me! no, I suffered long
30   From that ill thought; and, being blind,
Said, 'Pride shall help me in my wrong:
Kind mother have I been, as kind
As ever breathed:' and that is true;
I've wet my path with tears like dew,
Weeping for him when no one knew.

VI
My Son, if thou be humbled, poor,
Hopeless of honour and of gain,
Oh! do not dread thy mother's door;
Think not of me with grief and pain:
40   I now can see with better eyes;
And worldly grandeur I despise,
And fortune with her gifts and lies.

VII

Alas! the fowls of heaven have wings,
And blasts of heaven will aid their flight;
They mount – how short a voyage brings
The wanderers back to their delight!
Chains tie us down by land and sea;
And wishes, vain as mine, may be
All that is left to comfort thee.

VIII

50 Perhaps some dungeon hears thee groan,
Maimed, mangled by inhuman men;
Or thou upon a desert thrown
Inheritest the lion's den;
Or hast been summoned to the deep,
Thou, thou and all thy mates, to keep
An incommunicable sleep.

IX

I look for ghosts; but none will force
Their way to me: 'tis falsely said
That there was ever intercourse
60 Between the living and the dead;
For, surely, then I should have sight
Of him I wait for day and night,
With love and longings infinite.

X

My apprehensions come in crowds;
I dread the rustling of the grass;
The very shadows of the clouds
Have power to shake me as they pass:
I question things and do not find
One that will answer to my mind;
70 And all the world appears unkind.

XI

Beyond participation lie
My troubles, and beyond relief:
If any chance to heave a sigh,
They pity me, and not my grief.
Then come to me, my Son, or send
Some tidings that my woes may end;
I have no other earthly friend!

The Forsaken

The peace which others seek they find;
The heaviest storms not longest last;
Heaven grants even to the guiltiest mind
An amnesty for what is past;
When will my sentence be reversed?
I only pray to know the worst;
And wish as if my heart would burst.

O weary struggle! silent years
Tell seemingly no doubtful tale;
10   And yet they leave it short, and fears
And hopes are strong and will prevail.
My calmest faith escapes not pain;
And, feeling that the hope is vain,
I think that he will come again.

The Orchard Pathway

Orchard Pathway, to and fro,
Ever with thee, did I go,
Weaving Verses, a huge store!
These, and many hundreds more,
And, in memory of the same,
This little lot shall bear *Thy Name!*

'*I travelled among unknown men*'

I travelled among unknown men,
    In lands beyond the sea;
Nor, England! did I know till then
    What love I bore to thee.

'Tis past, that melancholy dream!
    Nor will I quit thy shore
A second time; for still I seem
    To love thee more and more.

Among thy mountains did I feel
10   The joy of my desire;
And she I cherished turned her wheel
    Beside an English fire.

Thy mornings showed, thy nights concealed,
    The bowers where Lucy played;
And thine too is the last green field
    That Lucy's eyes surveyed.

Repentance
A Pastoral Ballad

The fields which with covetous spirit we sold,
Those beautiful fields, the delight of the day,
Would have brought us more good than a burden of gold,
Could we but have been as contented as they.

When the troublesome Tempter beset us, said I,
'Let him come, with his purse proudly grasped in his
    hand;
But, Allan, be true to me, Allan, – we'll die
Before he shall go with an inch of the land!'

There dwelt we, as happy as birds in their bowers;
10 Unfettered as bees that in gardens abide;
We could do what we liked with the land, it was ours;
And for us the brook murmured that ran by its side.

But now we are strangers, go early or late;
And often, like one overburdened with sin,
With my hand on the latch of the half-opened gate,
I look at the fields, but I cannot go in!

When I walk by the hedge on a bright summer's day,
Or sit in the shade of my grandfather's tree,
A stern face it puts on, as if ready to say,
20 'What ails you, that you must come creeping to me!'

With our pastures about us, we could not be sad;
Our comfort was near if we ever were crost;
But the comfort, the blessings, and wealth that we had,
We slighted them all, – and our birthright was lost.

Oh, ill-judging sire of an innocent son
Who must now be a wanderer! but peace to that strain!
Think of evening's repose when our labour was done,
The sabbath's return; and its leisure's soft chain!

And in sickness, if night had been sparing of sleep,
30 How cheerful, at sunrise, the hill where I stood,
Looking down on the kine, and our treasure of sheep
That besprinkled the field; 'twas like youth in my blood!

Now I cleave to the house, and am dull as a snail;
And, oftentimes, hear the church-bell with a sigh,
That follows the thought – We've no land in the vale,
Save six feet of earth where our forefathers lie!

The Manciple's Tale – [A Modernization]

THE MANCIPLE FROM *The Prologue.*

A Manciple there was, one of a Temple
Of whom all caterers might take example
Wisely to purchase stores, whate'er the amount,
Whether he paid, or took them on account.
So well on every bargain did he wait,
He was beforehand aye in good estate.
Now is not that of God a full fair grace
That one man's natural sense should so surpass
The wisdom of a heap of learned men?

10   Of masters he had more than three times ten
That were in law expert and curious,
Of which there was a dozen in that house
Fit to be steward over land and rent
For any Lord in England, competent
Each one to make him live upon his own
In debtless honour, were his wits not flown;
Or sparely live, even to his heart's desire;
Men who could give good help to a whole Shire
In any urgent case that might befall,
20   Yet could this Manciple outwit them all.

THE MANCIPLE'S TALE

When Phoebus took delight on earth to dwell
Among mankind, as ancient stories tell,
He was the blithest bachelor, I trow,
Of all this world, and the best archer too.
He slew the serpent Python as he lay
Sleeping against the sun upon a day,
And many another worthy noble deed
Wrought with his bow as men the same may read.
He played, all music played on earthly ground,
10   And 'twas a melody to hear the sound

Of his clear voice, so sweetly would he sing.
Certes Amphion, that old Theban king
Who walled a city with his minstrelsy,
Was never heard to sing so sweet as he.
Therewith this Phoebus was the seemliest man
That is or hath been since the world began.
His features to describe I need not strive;
For in this world is none so fair alive.
He was moreover, full of gentleness,
20   Of honour and of perfect worthiness.

This Phoebus, flower in forest and in court,
This comely Bachelor for his disport
And eke in token of his victory earned
Of Python, as is from the story learned,
Was wont to carry in his hand a bow.
Now had this Phoebus in his house a Crow
Which in a cage he fostered many a day
And taught to speak as men will teach a jay.
White was this Crow as is a snow-white Swan,
30   And counterfeit the speech of every man
He could, when he had mind to tell a tale;
Besides, in all this world no Nightingale
Could ring out of his heart so blithe a peal;
No, not a hundred thousandth part as well.

Now had this Phoebus in his house a Wife
Whom he loved better than he loved his life;
And, night and day, he strove with diligence
To please her, and to do her reverence,
Save only, for 'tis truth, the noble Elf
40   Was jealous, and would keep her to himself.
For he was loth a laughing stock to be,
And so is every wight in like degree;
But all for naught, for it availeth naught,
A good Wife that is pure in deed and thought
Should not be kept in watch and ward, – and, do
The best you may, you cannot keep a Shrew.

It will not be – vain labour is it wholly;
Lordings! this hold I for an arrant folly
Labour to waste in custody of wives;
50 And so old Clerks have written in their lives.

But to my purpose as I first began.
This worthy Phoebus doeth all he can
To please her, weening that through such delight
And of his government and manhood's right
No man should ever put him from her grace,
But Man's best plans, God knoweth, in no case
Shall compass to constrain a thing which nature
Hath naturally implanted in a creature.

Take any bird and put it in a cage
60 And wait upon this bird as nurse or page
To feed it tenderly with meat and drink
And every dainty whereof thou canst think,
And also keep it cleanly as thou may;
Although the cage of gold be never so gay
Yet hath this bird by twenty thousand fold
Rather in forest that is wild and cold
Go feed on worms and such like wretchedness,
For ever will this Bird do more or less
To escape out of his cage whene'er he may;
70 His liberty the Bird desireth aye.

Go take a Cat and nourish her with milk
And tender flesh, and make her couch of silk,
And let her see a mouse go by the wall,
Anon she waiveth milk and flesh and all
And every dainty which is in that house,
Such appetite hath she to eat the mouse.
Behold the domination here of kind,
Appetite drives discretion from her mind.

A she-wolf also in her kind is base;
80 Meets she the sorriest wolf in field or chase

Him will she take – what matters his estate
In time when she hath liking to a mate?

Examples all for men that are untrue.
With women I have nothing now to do:
For men have still a wayward appetite
With lower things to seek for their delight
Than with their wives, albeit women fair
Never so true, never so debonair.
All flesh is so newfangled, plague upon't
90 That are we pleased with aught on whose clear front
Virtue is stampt, 'tis but for a brief while.

This Phoebus, he that thought upon no guile,
Deceived was for all his jollity;
For under him another one had she,
One of small note and little thought upon,
Naught worth to Phoebus in comparison.
The more harm is, it happeneth often so
Of which there cometh mickle harm and woe.

And so befell as soon as Phoebus went
100 From home, his wife hath for her Lemman sent,
Her Lemman, certes that's a knavish speech;
Forgive it me and that I you beseech.

Plato the wise hath said, as ye may read,
The word must needs be suited to the deed;
No doubtful meanings in a tale should lurk,
The word must aye be cousin to the work;
I am a bold blunt man, I speak out plain
There is no difference truly, not a grain,
Between a wife that is of high degree
110 (If of her body she dishonest be)
And every low-born wench no more than this
(If it so be that both have done amiss)
That, as the gentle is in state above,
She shall be called his Lady and his Love

And that the other a poor woman is
She shall be called his harlot and his miss.
And yet, in very truth, mine own dear brother,
Men lay as low that one as lies that other.
Right so betwixt a haughty tyrant chief
120 And a rough outlaw or an errant thief,
The same I say, no difference I hold,
(To Alexander was this sentence told)
But, for the Tyrant is of greater might
By force of multitudes to slay downright
And burn both house and home, and make all plain,
Lo! therefore Captain is he called; again
Since the other heads a scanty company
And may not do so great a harm as he,
Or lay upon the land such heavy grief
130 Men christen him an Outlaw or a Thief.

But I'm no man of texts and instances,
Therefore I will not give you much of these
But with my tale go on as I was bent.

When Phoebus' wife had for her Lemman sent
In their loose dalliance they anon engage;
This white Crow, that hung alway in the cage,
Beheld the shame, and did not say one word;
But soon as home was come Phoebus, the Lord,
The Crow sang Cuckow, Cuckow, Cuckow, 'How!
140 What, Bird,' quoth Phoebus, 'what song singst thou now,
Wert thou not wont to sing as did rejoice
My inmost heart, so merrily thy voice
Greeted my ear, alas, what song is this?'
'So help me Gods, I do not sing amiss,
Phoebus,' quoth he, 'for all thy worthiness,
For all thy beauty and all thy gentleness,
For all thy song and all thy minstrelsy,
For all thy waiting, hoodwinked is thine eye
By one we know not whom, we know not what,
150 A man to thee no better than a gnat,

For I full plainly as I hope for life
Saw him in guilty converse with thy wife.'

    What would you more, the Crow when [he] him told
By serious tokens and words stout and bold
How that his wife had played a wanton game
To his abasement, and exceeding shame,
And told him oft he saw it with his eyes,
Then Phoebus turned away in woeful guise
Him thought his heart would burst in two with sorrow,
160 His bow he bent, and set therein an arrow,
And in his anger he his wife did slay;
This is the effect, there is no more to say.
For grief of which he brake his minstrelsy
Both lute and harp, guitar and psaltery,
And also brake his arrows and his bow
And after that thus spake he to the Crow.

    'Thou Traitor! with thy scorpion tongue,' quoth he,
'To my confusion am I brought by thee.
Why was I born, why have I yet a life
170 O wife, O gem of pleasure, O dear wife,
That wert to me so stedfast and so true,
Now dead thou liest with face pale of hue
Full innocent, that durst I swear, I wis.
O thou rash hand that wrought so far amiss,
O reckless outrage, O disordered wit
That unadvisèd didst the guiltless smite,
What in my false suspicion have I done,
Why through mistrust was I thus wrought upon?

    'Let every Man beware and keep aloof
180 From rashness, and trust only to strong proof;
Smite not too soon before ye have learnt why,
And be advised well and stedfastly,
Ere ye to any execution bring
Yourselves from wrath or surmise of a thing.
Alas! a thousand folk hath ire laid low

Fully undone and brought to utter woe,
Alas for sorrow I myself will slay.'

And to the Crow, 'O vile wretch,' did he say,
'Now will I thee requite for thy false tale.
190 Whilom thou sang like any Nightingale,
Henceforth, false thief, thy song from thee is gone
And vanished thy white feathers, every one.
In all thy life thou nevermore shalt speak.
Thus on a traitor I men's wrongs do wreak.
Thou and thy offspring ever shall be black,
Never again sweet noises shall ye make,
But ever cry against the storm and rain
In token that through thee my Wife is slain.'

And to the Crow he sprang and that anon
200 And plucking his white feathers left not one
And made him black, and took from him his song,
And eke his speech, and out of doors him flung
Unto perdition, whither let him go
And for this very reason, you must know,
Black is the colour now of every Crow.

Lordings, by this example you I pray
Beware and take good heed of what you say,
Nor ever tell a man in all your life
That he hath got a false and slippery wife;
210 His deadly hatred till his life's last day
You will provoke. Dan Solomon, Clerks say,
For keeping well the tongue hath rules good store,
But I'm no textman, as I said before,
Nathless this teaching had I from my Dame.
My son, think of the Crow in God's good name.
My son, full often times hath mickle speech
Brought many a man to ruin, as Clerks teach,
But 'tis not often words bring harm to men
Spoken advisedly, and now and then.
220 My son be like the wise man who restrains

His tongue at all times, save when taking pains
To speak of God in honour, and in prayer.
'Tis the first virtue, and the one most rare,
My son, to keep the tongue with proper care.
Wouldst thou be told what a rash tongue can do,
Right as a sword cutteth an arm in two
So can a tongue, my child, a friendship sever,
Parted in two to be disjoined for ever.
A babbler is to God abominable.
230 Read Solomon so wise and honourable,
Read Seneca, the Psalms of David read,
Speak not, dear son, but beckon with thy head,
Make show that thou wert deaf if any prater
Do in thy hearing touch a perilous matter;
The Fleming taught, and learn it if thou list,
That little babbling causeth mickle rest.
My son, if thou no wicked word have said
Then need'st thou have no fear to be betrayed,
But who misspeaks, whatever may befall,
240 Cannot by any means his word recall.
Thing that is said, *is* said, goes forth anon,
Howe'er we grieve repenting, it is gone,
The tale-bearer's his slave to whom he said
The thing for which he now is fitly paid.
My son, beware, and be not Author new
Of tidings, whether they be false or true.
Where'er thou travel, among high or low,
Keep well thy tongue, and think upon the Crow.

The Prioress' Tale – [A Modernization]

'Call up him who left half told
The story of Cambuscan bold.'

In the following Poem no further deviation from the original
has been made than was necessary for the fluent reading and
instant understanding of the Author: so much, however, is the
language altered since Chaucer's time, especially in pronuncia-
tion, that much was to be removed, and its place supplied with

as little incongruity as possible. The ancient accent has been
retained in a few conjunctions, as *also* and *alway*, from a con-
viction that such sprinklings of antiquity would be admitted,
by persons of taste, to have a graceful accordance with the sub-
ject. The fierce bigotry of the Prioress forms a fine background
for her tenderhearted sympathies with the Mother and Child;
and the mode in which the story is told amply atones for the
extravagance of the miracle.

I

'O Lord, our Lord! how wondrously,' (quoth she)
'Thy name in this large world is spread abroad!
For not alone by men of dignity
Thy worship is performed and precious laud;
But by the mouths of children, gracious God!
Thy goodness is set forth; they when they lie
Upon the breast Thy name do glorify.

II

'Wherefore in praise, the worthiest that I may,
Jesu! of Thee, and the white Lily-flower
10   Which did Thee bear, and is a Maid for aye,
To tell a story I will use my power;
Not that I may increase her honour's dower,
For she herself is honour, and the root
Of goodness, next her Son, our soul's best boot.

III

'O Mother Maid! O Maid and Mother free!
O bush unburnt! burning in Moses' sight!
That down didst ravish from the Deity,
Through humbleness, the spirit that did alight
Upon thy heart, whence, through that glory's might,
20   Conceivèd was the Father's sapience,
Help me to tell it in thy reverence!

IV

'Lady! thy goodness, thy magnificence,
Thy virtue, and thy great humility,

Surpass all science and all utterance;
For sometimes, Lady! ere men pray to thee
Thou goest before in thy benignity,
The light to us vouchsafing of thy prayer,
To be our guide unto thy Son so dear.

V

'My knowledge is so weak, O blissful Queen!
30   To tell abroad thy mighty worthiness,
That I the weight of it may not sustain;
But as a child of twelvemonths old or less,
That laboureth his language to express,
Even so fare I; and therefore, I thee pray,
Guide thou my song which I of thee shall say.

VI

'There was in Asia, in a mighty town,
'Mong Christian folk, a street where Jews might be,
Assigned to them and given them for their own
By a great Lord, for gain and usury,
40   Hateful to Christ and to His company;
And through this street who list might ride and wend;
Free was it, and unbarred at either end.

VII

'A little school of Christian people stood
Down at the farther end, in which there were
A nest of children come of Christian blood,
That learnèd in that school from year to year
Such sort of doctrine as men usèd there,
That is to say, to sing and read alsò,
As little children in their childhood do.

VIII

50   'Among these children was a Widow's son,
A little scholar, scarcely seven years old,
Who day by day unto this school hath gone,
And eke, when he the image did behold

Of Jesu's Mother, as he had been told,
This Child was wont to kneel adown and say
Ave Marie, as he goeth by the way.

IX

'This Widow thus her little Son hath taught
Our blissful Lady, Jesu's Mother dear,
To worship aye, and he forgat it not;
60 For simple infant hath a ready ear.
Sweet is the holiness of youth: and hence,
Calling to mind this matter when I may,
Saint Nicholas in my presence standeth aye,
For he so young to Christ did reverence.

X

'This little Child, while in the school he sate
His Primer conning with an earnest cheer,
The whilst the rest their anthem-book repeat
The *Alma Redemptoris* did he hear;
And as he durst he drew him near and near,
70 And hearkened to the words and to the note,
Till the first verse he learned it all by rote.

XI

'This Latin knew he nothing what it said,
For he too tender was of age to know;
But to his comrade he repaired, and prayed
That he the meaning of this song would show,
And unto him declare why men sing so;
This oftentimes, that he might be at ease,
This child did him beseech on his bare knees.

XII

'His Schoolfellow, who elder was than he,
80 Answered him thus: – "This song, I have heard say,
Was fashioned for our blissful Lady free;
Her to salute, and also her to pray
To be our help upon our dying day:

If there is more in this, I know it not;
Song do I learn, – small grammar I have got."

XIII

' "And is this song fashioned in reverence
Of Jesu's Mother?" said this Innocent;
"Now, certès, I will use my diligence
To con it all ere Christmas-tide be spent;
90   Although I for my Primer shall be shent,
And shall be beaten three times in an hour,
Our Lady I will praise with all my power."

XIV

'His Schoolfellow, whom he had so besought,
As they went homeward taught him privily
And then he sang it well and fearlessly,
From word to word according to the note:
Twice in a day it passèd through his throat;
Homeward and schoolward whensoe'er he went,
On Jesu's Mother fixed was his intent.

XV

100 'Through all the Jewry (this before said I)
This little Child, as he came to and fro,
Full merrily then would he sing and cry,
O *Alma Redemptoris*! high and low:
The sweetness of Christ's Mother piercèd so
His heart, that her to praise, to her to pray,
He cannot stop his singing by the way.

XVI

'The Serpent, Satan, our first foe, that hath
His wasp's nest in Jew's heart, upswelled – "O woe,
O Hebrew people!" said he in his wrath,
110 "Is it an honest thing? Shall this be so?
That such a Boy where'er he lists shall go
In your despite, and sing his hymns and saws,
Which is against the reverence of our laws!"

XVII

'From that day forward have the Jews conspired
Out of the world this Innocent to chase;
And to this end a Homicide they hired,
That in an alley had a privy place,
And, as the Child 'gan to the school to pace,
This cruel Jew him seized, and held him fast
120 And cut his throat, and in a pit him cast.

XVIII

'I say that him into a pit they threw,
A loathsome pit, whence noisome scents exhale;
O cursèd folk! away, ye Herods new!
What may your ill intentions you avail?
Murder will out; certès it will not fail;
Know, that the honour of high God may spread,
The blood cries out on your accursèd deed.

XIX

'O Martyr 'stablished in virginity!
Now may'st thou sing for aye before the throne,
130 Following the Lamb celestial,' quoth she,
'Of which the great Evangelist, Saint John,
In Patmos wrote, who saith of them that go
Before the Lamb singing continually,
That never fleshly woman they did know.

XX

'Now this poor Widow waiteth all that night
After her little Child, and he came not;
For which, by earliest glimpse of morning light,
With face all pale with dread and busy thought,
She at the School and elsewhere him hath sought,
140 Until thus far she learned, that he had been
In the Jews' street, and there he last was seen.

XXI

'With Mother's pity in her breast enclosed
She goeth, as she were half out of her mind,

To every place wherein she hath supposed
By likelihood her little Son to find;
And ever on Christ's Mother meek and kind
She cried, till to the Jewry she was brought,
And him among the accursèd Jews she sought.

XXII
'She asketh, and she piteously doth pray
150 To every Jew that dwelleth in that place
To tell her if her child had passed that way;
They all said – Nay; but Jesu of His grace
Gave to her thought, that in a little space
She for her Son in that same spot did cry
Where he was cast into a pit hard by.

XXIII
'O Thou great God that dost perform Thy laud
By mouths of Innocents, lo! here Thy might;
This gem of chastity, this emerald,
And eke of martyrdom this ruby bright,
160 There, where with mangled throat he lay upright,
The *Alma Redemptoris* 'gan to sing
So loud, that with his voice the place did ring.

XXIV
'The Christian folk that through the Jewry went
Come to the spot in wonder at the thing;
And hastily they for the Provost sent;
Immediately he came, not tarrying,
And praiseth Christ that is our heavenly King,
And eke his Mother, honour of Mankind:
Which done, he bade that they the Jews should bind.

XXV
170 'This Child with pitetous lamentation then
Was taken up, singing his song alwày;
And with procession great and pomp of men
To the next Abbey him they bare away;

His Mother swooning by the body lay:
And scarcely could the people that were near
Remove this second Rachel from the bier.

XXVI
'Torment and shameful death to every one
This Provost doth for those bad Jews prepare
That of this murder wist, and that anon:
180 Such wickedness his judgements cannot spare;
Who will do evil, evil shall he bear;
Them therefore with wild horses did he draw,
And after that he hung them by the law.

XXVII
'Upon his bier this Innocent doth lie
Before the altar while the Mass doth last:
The Abbot with his convent's company
Then sped themselves to bury him full fast;
And, when they holy water on him cast,
Yet spake this Child when sprinkled was the water;
190 And sang, O *Alma Redemptoris Mater*!

XXVIII
'This Abbot, for he was a holy man,
As all Monks are, or surely ought to be,
In supplication to the Child began
Thus saying, "O dear Child! I summon thee
In virtue of the holy Trinity
Tell me the cause why thou dost sing this hymn,
Since that thy throat is cut, as it doth seem."

XXIX
' "My throat is cut unto the bone, I trow,"
Said this young Child, "and by the law of kind
200 I should have died, yea many hours ago;
But Jesus Christ, as in the books ye find,
Will that His glory last, and be in mind;
And, for the worship of His Mother dear,
Yet may I sing, O *Alma*! loud and clear.

XXX
' "This well of mercy, Jesu's Mother sweet,
After my knowledge I have loved alwày;
And in the hour when I my death did meet
To me she came, and thus to me did say,
'Thou in thy dying sing this holy lay,'
210 As ye have heard; and soon as I had sung
Methought she laid a grain upon my tongue.

XXXI
' "Wherefore I sing, nor can from song refrain,
In honour of that blissful Maiden free,
Till from my tongue off-taken is the grain;
And after that thus said she unto me;
'My little Child, then will I come for thee
Soon as the grain from off thy tongue they take:
Be not dismayed, I will not thee forsake!' "

XXXII
'This holy Monk, this Abbot – him mean I,
220 Touched then his tongue, and took away the grain;
And he gave up the ghost full peacefully;
And, when the Abbot had this wonder seen,
His salt tears trickled down like showers of rain;
And on his face he dropped upon the ground,
And still he lay as if he had been bound.

XXXIII
'Eke the whole Convent on the pavement lay,
Weeping and praising Jesu's Mother dear;
And after that they rose, and took their way,
And lifted up this Martyr from the bier,
230 And in a tomb of precious marble clear
Enclosed his uncorrupted body sweet. –
Where'er he be, God grant us him to meet!

XXXIV
'Young Hew of Lincoln! in like sort laid low
By cursèd Jews – thing well and widely known,

For it was done a little while ago –
Pray also thou for us, while here we tarry
Weak sinful folk, that God, with pitying eye,
In mercy would his mercy multiply
On us, for reverence of his Mother Mary!'

The Cuckoo and the Nightingale –
[A Modernization]

I

The God of Love – ah, *benedicite*!
How mighty and how great a Lord is he!
For he of low hearts can make high, of high
He can make low, and unto death bring nigh;
And hard hearts he can make them kind and free.

II

Within a little time, as hath been found,
He can make sick folk whole and fresh and sound:
Them who are whole in body and in mind,
He can make sick, – bind can he and unbind
10   All that he will have bound, or have unbound.

III

To tell his might my wit may not suffice;
Foolish men he can make them out of wise; –
For he may do all that he will devise;
Loose livers he can make abate their vice,
And proud hearts can make tremble in a trice.

IV

In brief, the whole of what he will, he may;
Against him dare not any wight say nay;
To humble or afflict whome'er he will,
To gladden or to grieve, he hath like skill;
20   But most his might he sheds on the eve of May.

V

For every true heart, gentle heart and free,
That with him is, or thinketh so to be,
Now against May shall have some stirring – whether
To joy, or be it to some mourning; never
At other time, methinks, in like degree.

VI

For now when they may hear the small birds' song,
And see the budding leaves the branches throng,
This unto their remembrance doth bring
All kinds of pleasure mixed with sorrowing;
30 And longing of sweet thoughts that ever long.

VII

And of that longing heaviness doth come,
Whence oft great sickness grows of heart and home;
Sick are they all for lack of their desire;
And thus in May their hearts are set on fire,
So that they burn forth in great martyrdom.

VIII

In sooth, I speak from feeling, what though now
Old am I, and to genial pleasure slow;
Yet have I felt of sickness through the May,
Both hot and cold, and heart-aches every day, –
40 How hard, alas! to bear, I only know.

IX

Such shaking doth the fever in me keep
Through all this May that I have little sleep;
And also 'tis not likely unto me,
That any living heart should sleepy be
In which Love's dart its fiery point doth steep.

X

But tossing lately on a sleepless bed,
I of a token thought which Lovers heed;

How among them it was a common tale,
That it was good to hear the Nightingale,
50   Ere the vile Cuckoo's note be utterèd.

XI

And then I thought anon as it was day,
I gladly would go somewhere to essay
If I perchance a Nightingale might hear,
For yet had I heard none, of all that year,
And it was then the third night of the May.

XII

And soon as I a glimpse of day espied,
No longer would I in my bed abide,
But straightway to a wood that was hard by,
Forth did I go, alone and fearlessly,
60   And held the pathway down by a brook-side;

XIII

Till to a lawn I came all white and green,
I in so fair a one had never been.
The ground was green, with daisy powdered over;
Tall were the flowers, the grove a lofty cover,
All green and white; and nothing else was seen.

XIV

There sate I down among the fair fresh flowers,
And saw the birds come tripping from their bowers,
Where they had rested them all night; and they,
Who were so joyful at the light of day,
70   Began to honour May with all their powers.

XV

Well did they know that service all by rote,
And there was many and many a lovely note,
Some, singing loud, as if they had complained;
Some with their notes another manner feigned;
And some did sing all out with the full throat.

XVI

They pruned themselves, and made themselves right gay,
Dancing and leaping light upon the spray;
And ever two and two together were,
The same as they had chosen for the year,
80 Upon Saint Valentine's returning day.

XVII

Meanwhile the stream, whose bank I sate upon,
Was making such a noise as it ran on
Accordant to the sweet Birds' harmony;
Methought that it was the best melody
Which ever to man's ear a passage won.

XVIII

And for delight, but how I never wot,
I in a slumber and a swoon was caught,
Not all asleep and yet not waking wholly;
And as I lay, the Cuckoo, bird unholy,
90 Broke silence, or I heard him in my thought.

XIX

And that was right upon a tree fast by,
And who was then ill satisfied but I?
Now, God, quoth I, that died upon the rood,
From thee and thy base throat, keep all that's good,
Full little joy have I now of thy cry.

XX

And, as I with the Cuckoo thus 'gan chide,
In the next bush that was me fast beside,
I heard the lusty Nightingale so sing,
That her clear voice made a loud rioting,
100 Echoing thorough all the green wood wide.

XXI

Ah! good sweet Nightingale! for my heart's cheer,
Hence hast thou stayed a little while too long;

For we have had the sorry Cuckoo here,
And she hath been before thee with her song;
Evil light on her! she hath done me wrong.

XXII

But hear you now a wondrous thing, I pray;
As long as in that swooning-fit I lay,
Methought I wist right well what these birds meant,
And had good knowing both of their intent,
110 And of their speech, and all that they would say..

XXIII

The Nightingale thus in my hearing spake: –
Good Cuckoo, seek some other bush or brake,
And, prithee, let us that can sing dwell here;
For every wight eschews thy song to hear,
Such uncouth singing verily dost thou make.

XXIV

What! quoth she then, what is't that ails thee now?
It seems to me I sing as well as thou;
For mine's a song that is both true and plain, –
Although I cannot quaver so in vain
120 As thou dost in thy throat, I wot not how.

XXV

All men may understanding have of me,
But, Nightingale, so may they not of thee;
For thou hast many a foolish and quaint cry: –
Thou say'st OSEE, OSEE, then how may I
Have knowledge, I thee pray, what this may be?

XXVI

Ah, fool! quoth she, wist thou not what it is?
Oft as I say OSEE, OSEE, I wis,
Then mean I, that I should be wonderous fain
That shamefully they one and all were slain,
130 Whoever against Love mean aught amiss.

XXVII

And also would I that they all were dead,
Who do not think in love their life to lead;
For who is loth the God of Love to obey,
Is only fit to die, I dare well say,
And for that cause OSEE I cry; take heed!

XXVIII

Ay, quoth the Cuckoo, that is a quaint law,
That all must love or die; but I withdraw,
And take my leave of all such company,
For mine intent it neither is to die,
140 Nor ever while I live Love's yoke to draw.

XXIX

For lovers, of all folk that be alive,
The most disquiet have and least do thrive;
Most feeling have of sorrow, woe and care,
And the least welfare cometh to their share;
What need is there against the truth to strive?

XXX

What! quoth she, thou art all out of thy mind,
That in thy churlishness a cause canst find
To speak of Love's true Servants in this mood;
For in this world no service is so good
150 To every wight that gentle is of kind.

XXXI

For thereof comes all goodness and all worth;
All gentiless and honour thence come forth;
Thence worship comes, content and true heart's pleasure,
And full-assured trust, joy without measure,
And jollity, fresh cheerfulness, and mirth;

XXXII

And bounty, lowliness, and courtesy,
And seemliness, and faithful company,

And dread of shame that will not do amiss;
For he that faithfully Love's servant is,
160 Rather than be disgraced, would choose to die.

XXXIII
And that the very truth it is which I
Now say – in such belief I'll live and die;
And Cuckoo, do thou so, by my advice.
Then, quoth she, let me never hope for bliss,
If with that counsel I do e'er comply.

XXXIV
Good Nightingale! thou speakest wondrous fair,
Yet for all that, the truth is found elsewhere;
For Love in young folk is but rage, I wis;
And Love in old folk a great dotage is;
170 Who most it useth, him 'twill most impair.

XXXV
For thereof come all contraries to gladness;
Thence sickness comes, and overwhelming sadness,
Mistrust and jealousy, despite, debate,
Dishonour, shame, envy importunate,
Pride, anger, mischief, poverty, and madness.

XXXVI
Loving is aye an office of despair,
And one thing is therein which is not fair;
For whoso gets of love a little bliss,
Unless it alway stay with him, I wis
180 He may full soon go with an old man's hair.

XXXVII
And, therefore, Nightingale! do thou keep nigh,
For trust me well, in spite of thy quaint cry,
If long time from thy mate thou be, or far,
Thou'lt be as others that forsaken are;
Then shalt thou raise a clamour as do I.

XXXVIII

Fie, quoth she, on thy name, Bird ill beseen!
The God of Love afflict thee with all teen,
For thou art worse than mad a thousand fold;
For many a one hath virtues manifold,
190   Who had been naught, if Love had never been.

XXXIX

For evermore his servants Love amendeth,
And he from every blemish them defendeth;
And maketh them to burn, as in a fire,
In loyalty, and worshipful desire,
And, when it likes him, joy enough them sendeth.

XL

Thou Nightingale! the Cuckoo said, be still,
For Love no reason hath but his own will; –
For to the untrue he oft gives ease and joy;
True lovers doth so bitterly annoy,
200   He lets them perish through that grievous ill.

XLI

With such a master would I never be;
For he, in sooth, is blind, and may not see,
And knows not when he hurts and when he heals;
Within this court full seldom Truth avails,
So diverse in his wilfulness is he.

XLII

Then of the Nightingale did I take note,
How from her inmost heart a sigh she brought,
And said, Alas! that ever I was born,
Not one word have I now, I am so forlorn, –
210   And with that word, she into tears burst out.

XLIII

Alas, alas! my very heart will break,
Quoth she, to hear this churlish bird thus speak

Of Love, and of his holy services;
Now, God of Love! thou help me in some wise,
That vengeance on this Cuckoo I may wreak.

XLIV

And so methought I started up anon,
And to the brook I ran and got a stone,
Which at the Cuckoo hardily I cast,
And he for dread did fly away full fast;
220   And glad, in sooth, was I when he was gone.

XLV

And as he flew, the Cuckoo, ever and aye,
Kept crying, 'Farewell! – farewell, Popinjay!'
As if in scornful mockery of me;
And on I hunted him from tree to tree,
Till he was far, all out of sight, away.

XLVI

Then straightway came the Nightingale to me,
And said, Forsooth, my friend, do I thank thee,
That thou wert near to rescue me; and now,
Unto the God of Love I make a vow,
230   That all this May I will thy songstress be.

XLVII

Well satisfied, I thanked her, and she said,
By this mishap no longer be dismayed,
Though thou the Cuckoo heard, ere thou heard'st me;
Yet if I live it shall amended be,
When next May comes, if I am not afraid.

XLVIII

And one thing will I counsel thee alsó,
The Cuckoo trust not thou, nor his Love's saw;
All that she said is an outrageous lie.
Nay, nothing shall me bring thereto, quoth I,
240   For Love, and it hath done me mighty woe.

XLIX

Yea, hath it? use, quoth she, this medicine;
This May-time, every day before thou dine,
Go look on the fresh daisy; then say I,
Although for pain thou mayst be like to die,
Thou wilt be eased, and less wilt droop and pine.

L

And mind always that thou be good and true,
And I will sing one song, of many new,
For love of thee, as loud as I may cry;
And then did she begin this song full high,
250   'Beshrew all them that are in love untrue.'

LI

And soon as she had sung it to the end,
Now farewell, quoth she, for I hence must wend;
And, God of Love, that can right well and may,
Send unto thee as mickle joy this day,
As ever he to Lover yet did send.

LII

Thus takes the Nightingale her leave of me;
I pray to God with her always to be,
And joy of love to send her evermore;
And shield us from the Cuckoo and her lore,
260   For there is not so false a bird as she.

LIII

Forth then she flew, the gentle Nightingale,
To all the Birds that lodged within that dale,
And gathered each and all into one place;
And them besought to hear her doleful case,
And thus it was that she began her tale.

LIV

The Cuckoo – 'tis not well that I should hide
How she and I did each the other chide,

And without ceasing, since it was daylight;
And now I pray you all to do me right
270 Of that false Bird whom Love can not abide.

LV

Then spake one Bird, and full assent all gave;
This matter asketh counsel good as grave,
For birds we are – all here together brought;
And, in good sooth, the Cuckoo here is not;
And therefore we a Parliament will have.

LVI

And thereat shall the Eagle be our Lord,
And other Peers whose names are on record;
A summons to the Cuckoo shall be sent,
And judgement there be given; or that intent
280 Failing, we finally shall make accord.

LVII

And all this shall be done, without a nay,
The morrow after Saint Valentine's day,
Under a maple that is well beseen,
Before the chamber-window of the Queen,
At Woodstock, on the meadow green and gay.

LVIII

She thankèd them; and then her leave she took,
And flew into a hawthorn by that brook;
And there she sate and sung – upon that tree –
'For term of life Love shall have hold of me' –
290 So loudly, that I with that song awoke.

Unlearned Book and rude, as well I know,
For beauty thou hast none, nor eloquence,
Who did on thee the hardiness bestow
To appear before my Lady? but a sense
Thou surely hast of her benevolence,
Whereof her hourly bearing proof doth give;
For of all good she is the best alive.

Alas, poor Book! for thy unworthiness,
To show to her some pleasant meanings writ
300 In winning words, since through her gentiless,
Thee she accepts as for her service fit!
Oh! it repents me I have neither wit
Nor leisure unto thee more worth to give;
For of all good she is the best alive.

Beseech her meekly with all lowliness,
Though I be far from her I reverence,
To think upon my truth and stedfastness,
And to abridge my sorrow's violence,
Caused by the wish, as knows your sapience,
310 She of her liking proof to me would give;
For of all good she is the best alive.

L'ENVOY

Pleasure's Aurora, Day of gladsomeness!
Luna by night, with heavenly influence
Illumined! root of beauty and goodnesse,
Write, and allay, by your beneficence,
My sighs breathed forth in silence, – comfort give!
Since of all good, you are the best alive.
EXPLICIT

Troilus and Cresida – [A Modernization]

Next morning Troilus began to clear
His eyes from sleep, at the first break of day,
And unto Pandarus, his own Brother dear,
For love of God, full piteously did say,
We must the Palace see of Cresida;
For since we yet may have no other feast,
Let us behold her Palace at the least!

And therewithal to cover his intent
A cause he found into the Town to go,

10 And they right forth to Cresid's Palace went;
But, Lord, this simple Troilus was woe,
Him thought his sorrowful heart would break in two;
For when he saw her doors fast bolted all,
Well nigh for sorrow down he 'gan to fall.

Therewith when this true Lover 'gan behold,
How shut was every window of the place,
Like frost he thought his heart was icy cold;
For which, with changèd, pale, and deadly face,
Without word uttered, forth he 'gan to pace;
20 And on his purpose bent so fast to ride,
That no wight his continuance espied.

Then said he thus, – O Palace desolate!
O house of houses, once so richly dight!
O Palace empty and disconsolate!
Thou lamp of which extinguished is the light;
O Palace whilom day that now art night,
Thou ought'st to fall and I to die; since she
Is gone who held us both in sovereignty.

O, of all houses once the crownèd boast!
30 Palace illumined with the sun of bliss;
O ring of which the ruby now is lost,
O cause of woe, that cause has been of bliss:
Yet, since I may no better, would I kiss
Thy cold doors; but I dare not for this rout;
Farewell, thou shrine of which the Saint is out!

Therewith he cast on Pandarus an eye,
With changèd face, and piteous to behold;
And when he might his time aright espy,
Aye as he rode, to Pandarus he told
40 Both his new sorrow and his joys of old,
So piteously, and with so dead a hue,
That every wight might on his sorrow rue.

Forth from the spot he rideth up and down,
And everything to his rememberànce
Came as he rode by places of the town
Where he had felt such perfect pleasure once.
Lo, yonder saw I mine own Lady dance,
And in that Temple she with her bright eyes,
My Lady dear, first bound me captive-wise.

50 And yonder with joy-smitten heart have I
Heard my own Cresid's laugh; and once at play
I yonder saw her eke full blissfully;
And yonder once she unto me 'gan say –
Now, my sweet Troilus, love me well, I pray!
And there so graciously did me behold,
That hers unto the death my heart I hold.

And at the corner of that self-same house
Heard I my most beloved Lady dear,
So womanly, with voice melodious
60 Singing so well, so goodly, and so clear,
That in my soul methinks I yet do hear
The blissful sound; and in that very place
My Lady first me took unto her grace.

O blissful God of Love! then thus he cried,
When I the process have in memory,
How thou hast wearied me on every side,
Men thence a book might make, a history;
What need to seek a conquest over me,
Since I am wholly at thy will? what joy
70 Hast thou thy own liege subjects to destroy?

Dread Lord! so fearful when provoked, thine ire
Well hast thou wreaked on me by pain and grief;
Now mercy, Lord! thou know'st well I desire
Thy grace above all pleasures first and chief;
And live and die I will in thy belief;
For which I ask for guerdon but one boon,
That Cresida again thou send me soon.

Constrain her heart as quickly to return,
As thou dost mine with longing her to see,
80 Then know I well that she would not sojourn.
Now, blissful Lord, so cruel do not be
Unto the blood of Troy, I pray of thee,
As Juno was unto the Theban blood,
From whence to Thebes came griefs in multitude.

And after this he to the gate did go
Whence Cresid rode, as if in haste she was;
And up and down there went, and to and fro,
And to himself full oft he said, alas!
From hence my hope and solace forth did pass.
90 O would the blissful God now for his joy,
I might her see again coming to Troy!

And up to yonder hill was I her guide;
Alas, and there I took of her my leave;
Yonder I saw her to her Father ride,
For very grief of which my heart shall cleave; —
And hither home I came when it was eve;
And here I dwell an outcast from all joy,
And shall, unless I see her soon in Troy.

And of himself did he imagine oft,
100 That he was blighted, pale, and waxen less
Than he was wont; and that in whispers soft
Men said, what may it be, can no one guess
Why Troilus hath all this heaviness?
All which he of himself conceited wholly
Out of his weakness and his melancholy.

Another time he took into his head,
That every wight, who in the way passed by,
Had of him ruth, and fancied that they said,
I am right sorry Troilus will die:
110 And thus a day or two drove wearily;
As ye have heard; such life 'gan he to lead
As one that standeth betwixt hope and dread.

For which it pleased him in his songs to show
The occasion of his woe, as best he might;
And made a fitting song, of words but few,
Somewhat his woeful heart to make more light;
And when he was removed from all men's sight,
With a soft voice, he of his Lady dear,
That absent was, 'gan sing as ye may hear.

120   O star, of which I lost have all the light,
With a sore heart well ought I to bewail,
That ever dark in torment, night by night,
Toward my death with wind I steer and sail;
For which upon the tenth night if thou fail
With thy bright beams to guide me but one hour,
My ship and me Charybdis will devour.

As soon as he this song had thus sung through,
He fell again into his sorrows old;
And every night, as was his wont to do,
130   Troilus stood the bright moon to behold;
And all his trouble to the moon he told,
And said: I wis, when thou art horned anew,
I shall be glad if all the world be true.

Thy horns were old as now upon that morrow,
When hence did journey my bright Lady dear,
That cause is of my torment and my sorrow;
For which, oh, gentle Luna, bright and clear,
For love of God, run fast about thy sphere;
For when thy horns begin once more to spring,
140   Then shall she come, that with her bliss may bring.

The day is more, and longer every night
Than they were wont to be – for he thought so;
And that the sun did take his course not right,
By longer way than he was wont to go;
And said, I am in constant dread I trow,
That Phäeton his son is yet alive,
His too fond father's car amiss to drive.

Upon the walls fast also would he walk,
To the end that he the Grecian host might see;
150 And ever thus he to himself would talk: –
Lo! yonder is my own bright Lady free;
Or yonder is it that the tents must be;
And thence does come this air which is so sweet,
That in my soul I feel the joy of it.

And certainly this wind, that more and more
By moments thus increaseth in my face,
Is of my Lady's sighs heavy and sore;
I prove it thus; for in no other space
Of all this town, save only in this place,
160 Feel I a wind, that soundeth so like pain;
It saith, Alas, why severed are we twain?

A weary while in pain he tosseth thus,
Till fully past and gone was the ninth night;
And ever at his side stood Pandarus,
Who busily made use of all his might
To comfort him, and make his heart more light;
Giving him always hope, that she the morrow
Of the tenth day will come, and end his sorrow.

*Written in a Grotto

O Moon! if e'er I joyed when thy soft light
Danced to the murmuring rill on Lomond's wave,
Or sighed for thy sweet presence some dark night,
When thou wert hidden in thy monthly grave:
If e'er, on wings which active fancy gave,
I sought thy golden vales with daring flight,
Then, stretched at ease in some sequestered cave,
Gazed on thy lovely Nymphs with fond delight,
Thy Nymphs with more than earthly beauty bright!
10 If e'er thy beam, as Smyrna's shepherds tell,
Soft as the gentle kiss of amorous maid

On the closed eyes of young ENDYMION fell,
That he might wake to clasp thee in the shade;
Each night, while I recline within this cell,
Guide hither, O sweet MOON! the maid I love so well!

To a Young Lady Who Had Been Reproached for Taking Long Walks in the Country

Dear Child of Nature, let them rail!
– There is a nest in a green dale,
A harbour and a hold;
Where thou, a Wife and Friend, shalt see
Thy own heart-stirring days, and be
A light to young and old.

There, healthy as a shepherd boy,
And treading among flowers of joy
Which at no season fade,
10   Thou, while thy babes around thee cling,
Shalt show us how divine a thing
A Woman may be made.

Thy thoughts and feelings shall not die,
Nor leave thee, when grey hairs are nigh,
A melancholy slave;
But an old age serene and bright,
And lovely as a Lapland night,
Shall lead thee to thy grave.

Louisa
After Accompanying Her on a Mountain Excursion

I met Louisa in the shade,
And, having seen that lovely Maid,

Why should I fear to say
That, nymph-like, she is fleet and strong,
And down the rocks can leap along
Like rivulets in May?

And she hath smiles to earth unknown;
Smiles, that with motion of their own
Do spread, and sink, and rise;
10 That come and go with endless play,
And ever, as they pass away,
Are hidden in her eyes.

She loves her fire, her cottage-home;
Yet o'er the moorland will she roam
In weather rough and bleak;
And, when against the wind she strains,
Oh! might I kiss the mountain rains
That sparkle on her cheek.

Take all that's mine 'beneath the moon,'
20 If I with her but half a noon
May sit beneath the walls
Of some old cave, or mossy nook,
When up she winds along the brook
To hunt the waterfalls.

The Sailor's Mother

One morning (raw it was and wet –
A foggy day in winter time)
A Woman on the road I met,
Not old, though something past her prime:
Majestic in her person, tall and straight;
And like a Roman matron's was her mien and gait.

The ancient spirit is not dead;
Old times, thought I, are breathing there;
Proud was I that my country bred

10 Such strength, a dignity so fair:
    She begged an alms, like one in poor estate;
    I looked at her again, nor did my pride abate.

    When from these lofty thoughts I woke,
    'What is it,' said I, 'that you bear,
    Beneath the covert of your Cloak,
    Protected from this cold damp air?'
    She answered, soon as she the question heard,
    'A simple burden, Sir, a little Singing-bird.'

    And, thus continuing, she said,
20 'I had a Son, who many a day
    Sailed on the seas, but he is dead;
    In Denmark he was cast away:
    And I have travelled weary miles to see
    If aught which he had owned might still remain for me.

    'The bird and cage they both were his:
    'Twas my Son's bird; and neat and trim
    He kept it: many voyages
    The singing-bird had gone with him;
    When last he sailed, he left the bird behind;
30 From bodings, as might be, that hung upon his mind.

    'He to a fellow-lodger's care
    Had left it, to be watched and fed,
    And pipe its song in safety; – there
    I found it when my Son was dead;
    And now, God help me for my little wit!
    I bear it with me, Sir; – he took so much delight in it.'

Alice Fell;
or, Poverty

The post-boy drove with fierce career,
For threatening clouds the moon had drowned;
When, as we hurried on, my ear
Was smitten with a startling sound.

As if the wind blew many ways,
I heard the sound, – and more and more;
It seemed to follow with the chaise,
And still I heard it as before.

At length I to the boy called out;
10   He stopped his horses at the word,
But neither cry, nor voice, nor shout,
Nor aught else like it, could be heard.

The boy then smacked his whip, and fast
The horses scampered through the rain;
But, hearing soon upon the blast
The cry, I bade him halt again.

Forthwith alighting on the ground,
'Whence comes,' said I, 'this piteous moan?'
And there a little Girl I found,
20   Sitting behind the chaise, alone.

'My cloak!' no other word she spake,
But loud and bitterly she wept,
As if her innocent heart would break;
And down from off her seat she leapt.

'What ails you, child?' – she sobbed, 'Look here!'
I saw it in the wheel entangled,
A weather-beaten rag as e'er
From any garden scare-crow dangled.

There, twisted between nave and spoke,
30   It hung, nor could at once be freed;
But our joint pains unloosed the cloak,
A miserable rag indeed!

'And whither are you going, child,
Tonight along these lonesome ways?'
'To Durham,' answered she, half wild –
'Then come with me into the chaise.'

Insensible to all relief
Sat the poor girl, and forth did send
Sob after sob, as if her grief
40   Could never, never have an end.

'My child, in Durham do you dwell?'
She checked herself in her distress,
And said, 'My name is Alice Fell;
I'm fatherless and motherless.

'And I to Durham, Sir, belong.'
Again, as if the thought would choke
Her very heart, her grief grew strong;
And all was for her tattered cloak!

The chaise drove on; our journey's end
50   Was nigh; and, sitting by my side,
As if she had lost her only friend
She wept, nor would be pacified.

Up to the tavern-door we post;
Of Alice and her grief I told;
And I gave money to the host,
To buy a new cloak for the old.

'And let it be of duffil grey,
As warm a cloak as man can sell!'
Proud creature was she the next day,
60   The little orphan, Alice Fell!

Beggars

She had a tall man's height or more;
Her face from summer's noontide heat
No bonnet shaded, but she wore
A mantle, to her very feet
Descending with a graceful flow,
And on her head a cap as white as new-fallen snow.

Her skin was of Egyptian brown:
Haughty, as if her eye had seen
Its own light to a distance thrown,
10 She towered, fit person for a Queen
To lead those ancient Amazonian files;
Or ruling Bandit's wife among the Grecian isles.

Advancing, forth she stretched her hand
And begged an alms with doleful plea
That ceased not; on our English land
Such woes, I knew, could never be;
And yet a boon I gave her, for the creature
Was beautiful to see – a weed of glorious feature.

I left her, and pursued my way;
20 And soon before me did espy
A pair of little Boys at play,
Chasing a crimson butterfly;
The taller followed with his hat in hand,
Wreathed round with yellow flowers the gayest of the land.

The other wore a rimless crown
With leaves of laurel stuck about;
And, while both followed up and down,
Each whooping with a merry shout,
In their fraternal features I could trace
30 Unquestionable lines of that wild Suppliant's face.

Yet *they*, so blithe of heart, seemed fit
For finest tasks of earth or air:
Wings let them have, and they might flit
Precursors to Aurora's car,
Scattering fresh flowers; though happier far, I ween,
To hunt their fluttering game o'er rock and level green.

They dart across my path – but lo,
Each ready with a plaintive whine!
Said I, 'not half an hour ago
40 Your Mother has had alms of mine.'
'That cannot be,' one answered – 'she is dead:' –
I looked reproof – they saw – but neither hung his head.

'She has been dead, Sir, many a day.' –
'Hush, boys! you're telling me a lie;
It was your Mother, as I say!'
And, in the twinkling of an eye,
'Come! come!' cried one, and without more ado,
Off to some other play the joyous Vagrants flew!

To a Butterfly

Stay near me – do not take thy flight!
A little longer stay in sight!
Much converse do I find in thee,
Historian of my infancy!
Float near me; do not yet depart!
Dead times revive in thee:
Thou bring'st, gay creature as thou art!
A solemn image to my heart,
My father's family!

10 Oh! pleasant, pleasant were the days,
The time, when, in our childish plays,
My sister Emmeline and I
Together chased the butterfly!

A very hunter did I rush
Upon the prey: – with leaps and springs
I followed on from brake to bush;
But she, God love her! feared to brush
The dust from off its wings.

The Emigrant Mother

Once in a lonely hamlet I sojourned
In which a Lady driven from France did dwell;
The big and lesser griefs with which she mourned,
In friendship she to me would often tell.

This Lady, dwelling upon British ground,
Where she was childless, daily would repair
To a poor neighbouring cottage; as I found,
For sake of a young Child whose home was there.

Once having seen her clasp with fond embrace
10　This Child, I chanted to myself a lay,
Endeavouring, in our English tongue, to trace
Such things as she unto the Babe might say:
And thus, from what I heard and knew, or guessed,
My song the workings of her heart expressed.

I
'Dear Babe, thou daughter of another,
One moment let me be thy mother!
An infant's face and looks are thine
And sure a mother's heart is mine:
Thy own dear mother's far away,
20　At labour in the harvest field:
Thy little sister is at play; –
What warmth, what comfort would it yield
To my poor heart, if thou wouldst be
One little hour a child to me!

II

'Across the waters I am come,
And I have left a babe at home:
A long, long way of land and sea!
Come to me – I'm no enemy:
I am the same who at thy side
30 Sate yesterday, and made a nest
For thee, sweet Baby! – thou hast tried,
Thou know'st the pillow of my breast;
Good, good art thou: – alas! to me
Far more than I can be to thee.

III

'Here, little Darling, dost thou lie;
An infant thou, a mother I!
Mine wilt thou be, thou hast no fears;
Mine art thou – spite of these my tears.
Alas! before I left the spot,
40 My baby and its dwelling-place,
The nurse said to me, "Tears should not
Be shed upon an infant's face,
It was unlucky" – no, no, no;
No truth is in them who say so!

IV

'My own dear Little-one will sigh,
Sweet Babe! and they will let him die.
"He pines," they'll say, "it is his doom,
And you may see his hour is come."
Oh! had he but thy cheerful smiles,
50 Limbs stout as thine, and lips as gay,
Thy looks, thy cunning, and thy wiles,
And countenance like a summer's day,
They would have hopes of him; – and then
I should behold his face again!

V

' 'Tis gone – like dreams that we forget;
There was a smile or two – yet – yet

I can remember them, I see
The smiles, worth all the world to me.
Dear Baby! I must lay thee down;
60   Thou troublest me with strange alarms;
Smiles hast thou, bright ones of thy own;
I cannot keep thee in my arms;
For they confound me; – where – where is
That last, that sweetest smile of his?

VI

'Oh! how I love thee! – we will stay
Together here this one half day.
My sister's child, who bears my name,
From France to sheltering England came;
She with her mother crossed the sea;
70   The babe and mother near me dwell:
Yet does my yearning heart to thee
Turn rather, though I love her well:
Rest, little Stranger, rest thee here!
Never was any child more dear!

VII

'– I cannot help it; ill intent
I've none, my pretty Innocent!
I weep – I know they do thee wrong,
These tears – and my poor idle tongue.
Oh, what a kiss was that! my cheek
80   How cold it is! but thou art good;
Thine eyes are on me – they would speak,
I think, to help me if they could.
Blessings upon that soft, warm face,
My heart again is in its place!

VIII

'While thou art mine, my little Love,
This cannot be a sorrowful grove;
Contentment, hope, and mother's glee,
I seem to find them all in thee:

Here's grass to play with, here are flowers;
90 I'll call thee by my darling's name;
Thou hast, I think, a look of ours,
Thy features seem to me the same;
His little sister thou shalt be;
And, when once more my home I see,
I'll tell him many tales of Thee.'

To the Cuckoo

O blithe New-comer! I have heard,
I hear thee and rejoice.
O Cuckoo! shall I call thee Bird,
Or but a wandering Voice?

While I am lying on the grass
Thy twofold shout I hear,
From hill to hill it seems to pass,
At once far off, and near.

Though babbling only to the Vale,
10 Of sunshine and of flowers,
Thou bringest unto me a tale
Of visionary hours.

Thrice welcome, darling of the Spring!
Even yet thou art to me
No bird, but an invisible thing,
A voice, a mystery;

The same whom in my schoolboy days
I listened to; that Cry
Which made me look a thousand ways
20 In bush, and tree, and sky.

To seek thee did I often rove
Through woods and on the green;

And thou wert still a hope, a love;
Still longed for, never seen.

And I can listen to thee yet;
Can lie upon the plain
And listen, till I do beget
That golden time again.

O blessèd Bird! the earth we pace
30 Again appears to be
An unsubstantial, faery place;
That is fit home for Thee!

'*My heart leaps up when I behold*'

My heart leaps up when I behold
    A rainbow in the sky:
So was it when my life began;
So is it now I am a man;
So be it when I shall grow old,
    Or let me die!
The Child is father of the Man;
And I could wish my days to be
Bound each to each by natural piety.

To H.C., Six Years Old

O thou! whose fancies from afar are brought;
Who of thy words dost make a mock apparel,
And fittest to unutterable thought
The breeze-like motion and the self-born carol;
Thou faery voyager! that dost float
In such clear water, that thy boat
May rather seem
To brood on air than on an earthly stream;
Suspended in a stream as clear as sky,

10 Where earth and heaven do make one imagery;
O blessèd vision! happy child!
Thou art so exquisitely wild,
I think of thee with many fears
For what may be thy lot in future years.

I thought of times when Pain might be thy guest,
Lord of thy house and hospitality;
And Grief, uneasy lover! never rest
But when she sate within the touch of thee.
O too industrious folly!
20 O vain and causeless melancholy!
Nature will either end thee quite;
Or, lengthening out thy season of delight,
Preserve for thee, by individual right,
A young lamb's heart among the full-grown flocks.
What hast thou to do with sorrow,
Or the injuries of tomorrow?
Thou art a dew-drop, which the morn brings forth,
Ill fitted to sustain unkindly shocks,
Or to be trailed along the soiling earth;
30 A gem that glitters while it lives,
And no forewarning gives;
But, at the touch of wrong, without a strife
Slips in a moment out of life.

Ode:

Intimations of Immortality from Recollections of Early Childhood

The Child is Father of the Man;
And I could wish my days to be
Bound each to each by natural piety.

I

There was a time when meadow, grove, and stream,
The earth, and every common sight,
      To me did seem
      Apparelled in celestial light,

The glory and the freshness of a dream.
It is not now as it hath been of yore; –
     Turn wheresoe'er I may,
      By night or day,
The things which I have seen I now can see no more.

    II

10   The Rainbow comes and goes,
        And lovely is the Rose;
        The Moon doth with delight
Look round her when the heavens are bare;
       Waters on a starry night
       Are beautiful and fair;
   The sunshine is a glorious birth;
   But yet I know, where'er I go,
That there hath past away a glory from the earth.

    III
Now, while the birds thus sing a joyous song,
20   And while the young lambs bound
      As to the tabor's sound,
To me alone there came a thought of grief:
A timely utterance gave that thought relief,
     And I again am strong:
The cataracts blow their trumpets from the steep;
No more shall grief of mine the season wrong;
I hear the Echoes through the mountains throng,
The Winds come to me from the fields of sleep,
     And all the earth is gay;
30   Land and sea
      Give themselves up to jollity,
      And with the heart of May
     Doth every Beast keep holiday; –
      Thou Child of Joy,
Shout round me, let me hear thy shouts, thou happy
       Shepherd-boy!

IV

Ye blessèd Creatures, I have heard the call
   Ye to each other make; I see
The heavens laugh with you in your jubilee;
   My heart is at your festival,
40   My head hath its coronal,
The fulness of your bliss, I feel – I feel it all.
     Oh evil day! if I were sullen
     While Earth herself is adorning,
       This sweet May-morning,
     And the Children are culling
       On every side,
     In a thousand valleys far and wide,
     Fresh flowers; while the sun shines warm,
And the Babe leaps up on his Mother's arm: –
50   I hear, I hear, with joy I hear!
     – But there's a Tree, of many, one,
A single Field which I have looked upon,
Both of them speak of something that is gone:
     The Pansy at my feet
     Doth the same tale repeat:
Whither is fled the visionary gleam?
Where is it now, the glory and the dream?

V

Our birth is but a sleep and a forgetting:
The Soul that rises with us, our life's Star,
60   Hath had elsewhere its setting,
       And cometh from afar:
     Not in entire forgetfulness,
     And not in utter nakedness,
But trailing clouds of glory do we come
     From God, who is our home:
Heaven lies about us in our infancy!
Shades of the prison-house begin to close
     Upon the growing Boy,
       But He
70 Beholds the light, and whence it flows,

He sees it in his joy;
The Youth, who daily farther from the east
    Must travel, still is Nature's Priest,
    And by the vision splendid
    Is on his way attended;
At length the Man perceives it die away,
And fade into the light of common day.

VI

Earth fills her lap with pleasures of her own;
Yearnings she hath in her own natural kind,
80 And, even with something of a Mother's mind,
    And no unworthy aim,
    The homely Nurse doth all she can
To make her Foster-child, her Inmate Man,
    Forget the glories he hath known,
And that imperial palace whence he came.

VII

Behold the Child among his new-born blisses,
A six years' Darling of a pigmy size!
See, where 'mid work of his own hand he lies,
Fretted by sallies of his mother's kisses,
90 With light upon him from his father's eyes!
See, at his feet, some little plan or chart,
Some fragment from his dream of human life,
Shaped by himself with newly-learnèd art;
    A wedding or a festival,
    A mourning or a funeral;
      And this hath now his heart,
    And unto this he frames his song:
      Then will he fit his tongue
To dialogues of business, love, or strife;
100   But it will not be long
    Ere this be thrown aside,
    And with new joy and pride
The little Actor cons another part;
Filling from time to time his 'humorous stage'
With all the Persons, down to palsied Age,

That Life brings with her in her equipage;
    As if his whole vocation
    Were endless imitation.

VIII

Thou, whose exterior semblance doth belie
110   Thy Soul's immensity;
Thou best Philosopher, who yet dost keep
Thy heritage, thou Eye among the blind,
That, deaf and silent, read'st the eternal deep,
Haunted for ever by the eternal mind, –
    Mighty Prophet! Seer blest!
    On whom those truths do rest,
Which we are toiling all our lives to find,
In darkness lost, the darkness of the grave;
Thou, over whom thy Immortality
120 Broods like the Day, a Master o'er a Slave,
A Presence which is not to be put by;
Thou little Child, yet glorious in the might
Of heaven-born freedom on thy being's height,
Why with such earnest pains dost thou provoke
The years to bring the inevitable yoke,
Thus blindly with thy blessedness at strife?
Full soon thy Soul shall have her earthly freight,
And custom lie upon thee with a weight,
Heavy as frost, and deep almost as life!

IX

130   O joy! that in our embers
    Is something that doth live,
    That nature yet remembers
    What was so fugitive!
The thought of our past years in me doth breed
Perpetual benediction: not indeed
For that which is most worthy to be blest;
Delight and liberty, the simple creed
Of Childhood, whether busy or at rest,
With new-fledged hope still fluttering in his breast: –

140   Not for these I raise
        The song of thanks and praise;
      But for those obstinate questionings
      Of sense and outward things,
      Fallings from us, vanishings;
      Blank misgivings of a Creature
Moving about in worlds not realized,
High instincts before which our mortal Nature
Did tremble like a guilty Thing surprised:
      But for those first affections,
150   Those shadowy recollections,
       Which, be they what they may,
Are yet the fountain light of all our day,
Are yet a master light of all our seeing;
      Uphold us, cherish, and have power to make
Our noisy years seem moments in the being
Of the eternal Silence: truths that wake,
        To perish never;
Which neither listlessness, nor mad endeavour,
        Nor Man nor Boy,
160 Nor all that is at enmity with joy,
Can utterly abolish or destroy!
       Hence in a season of calm weather
       Though inland far we be,
Our Souls have sight of that immortal sea
       Which brought us hither,
      Can in a moment travel thither,
And see the Children sport upon the shore,
And hear the mighty waters rolling evermore.

X
Then sing, ye Birds, sing, sing a joyous song!
170   And let the young Lambs bound
       As to the tabor's sound!
We in thought will join your throng,
       Ye that pipe and ye that play,
       Ye that through your hearts today
       Feel the gladness of the May!

What though the radiance which was once so bright
Be now for ever taken from my sight,
    Though nothing can bring back the hour
Of splendour in the grass, of glory in the flower;
180   We will grieve not, rather find
      Strength in what remains behind;
      In the primal sympathy
      Which having been must ever be;
      In the soothing thoughts that spring
      Out of human suffering;
      In the faith that looks through death,
In years that bring the philosophic mind.

XI

And O, ye Fountains, Meadows, Hills, and Groves,
Forebode not any severing of our loves!
190 Yet in my heart of hearts I feel your might;
I only have relinquished one delight
To live beneath your more habitual sway.
I love the Brooks which down their channels fret,
Even more than when I tripped lightly as they;
The innocent brightness of a new-born Day
      Is lovely yet;
The Clouds that gather round the setting sun
Do take a sober colouring from an eye
That hath kept watch o'er man's mortality;
200 Another race hath been, and other palms are won.
Thanks to the human heart by which we live,
Thanks to its tenderness, its joys, and fears,
To me the meanest flower that blows can give
Thoughts that do often lie too deep for tears.

The Sparrow's Nest

Behold, within the leafy shade,
Those bright blue eggs together laid!
On me the chance-discovered sight

Gleamed like a vision of delight.
I started – seeming to espy
The home and sheltered bed,
The Sparrow's dwelling, which, hard by
My Father's house, in wet or dry
My sister Emmeline and I
10   Together visited.

She looked at it and seemed to fear it;
Dreading, though wishing, to be near it:
Such heart was in her, being then
A little Prattler among men.
The Blessing of my later years
Was with me when a boy:
She gave me eyes, she gave me ears;
And humble cares, and delicate fears;
A heart, the fountain of sweet tears;
20   And love, and thought, and joy.

To a Sky-Lark

Up with me! up with me into the clouds!
    For thy song, Lark, is strong;
Up with me, up with me into the clouds!
    Singing, singing,
With clouds and sky about thee ringing,
    Lift me, guide me till I find
That spot which seems so to thy mind!

I have walked through wildernesses dreary,
And today my heart is weary;
10 Had I now the wings of a Faery,
Up to thee would I fly.
There is madness about thee, and joy divine
In that song of thine;
Lift me, guide me high and high
To thy banqueting place in the sky.
        Joyous as morning,

Thou art laughing and scorning;
Thou hast a nest for thy love and thy rest,
And, though little troubled with sloth,
20   Drunken Lark! thou wouldst be loth
To be such a traveller as I.
Happy, happy Liver,
With a soul as strong as a mountain river
Pouring out praise to the almighty Giver,
Joy and jollity be with us both!

Alas! my journey, rugged and uneven,
Through prickly moors or dusty ways must wind;
But hearing thee, or others of thy kind,
As full of gladness and as free of heaven,
30 I, with my fate contented, will plod on,
And hope for higher raptures, when life's day is done.

'Among all lovely things my Love had been'
[The Glow-Worm]

Among all lovely things my Love had been;
Had noted well the stars, all flowers that grew
About her home; but she had never seen
A Glow-worm, never one, and this I knew.

While riding near her home one stormy night
A single Glow-worm did I chance to espy;
I gave a fervent welcome to the sight,
And from my Horse I leapt; great joy had I.

Upon a leaf the Glow-worm did I lay,
10 To bear it with me through the stormy night:
And, as before, it shone without dismay;
Albeit putting forth a fainter light.

When to the Dwelling of my Love I came,
I went into the Orchard quietly;
And left the Glow-worm, blessing it by name,
Laid safely by itself, beneath a Tree.

The whole next day, I hoped, and hoped with fear;
At night the Glow-worm shone beneath the Tree:
I led my Lucy to the spot, 'Look here!'
20 Oh! joy it was for her, and joy for me!

Written in March While Resting on the Bridge at the Foot of Brother's Water

The Cock is crowing,
The stream is flowing,
The small birds twitter,
The lake doth glitter,
The green field sleeps in the sun;
  The oldest and youngest
  Are at work with the strongest;
  The cattle are grazing,
  Their heads never raising;
10 There are forty feeding like one!

Like an army defeated
The snow hath retreated,
And now doth fare ill
On the top of the bare hill;
The Ploughboy is whooping – anon – anon:
  There's joy in the mountains;
  There's life in the fountains;
  Small clouds are sailing,
  Blue sky prevailing;
20 The rain is over and gone!

The Green Linnet

Beneath these fruit-tree boughs that shed
Their snow-white blossoms on my head,
With brightest sunshine round me spread
    Of spring's unclouded weather,
In this sequestered nook how sweet
To sit upon my orchard-seat!
And birds and flowers once more to greet,
    My last year's friends together.

One have I marked, the happiest guest
10 In all this covert of the blest:
Hail to Thee, far above the rest
    In joy of voice and pinion!
Thou, Linnet! in thy green array,
Presiding Spirit here today,
Dost lead the revels of the May;
    And this is thy dominion.

While birds, and butterflies, and flowers,
Make all one band of paramours,
Thou, ranging up and down the bowers,
20   Art sole in thy employment:
A Life, a Presence like the Air,
Scattering thy gladness without care,
Too blest with anyone to pair;
    Thyself thy own enjoyment.

Amid yon tuft of hazel trees,
That twinkle to the gusty breeze,
Behold him perched in ecstasies,
    Yet seeming still to hover;
There! where the flutter of his wings
30 Upon his back and body flings
Shadows and sunny glimmerings,
    That cover him all over.

My dazzled sight he oft deceives,
A Brother of the dancing leaves;
Then flits, and from the cottage-eaves
    Pours forth his song in gushes;
As if by that exulting strain
He mocked and treated with disdain
The voiceless Form he chose to feign,
40   While fluttering in the bushes.

To the Daisy

'Her divine skill taught me this,
That from every thing I saw
I could some instruction draw,
And raise pleasure to the height
Through the meanest object's sight.
By the murmur of a spring,
Or the least bough's rustelling;
By a Daisy whose leaves spread
Shut when Titan goes to bed;
Or a shady bush or tree;
She could more infuse in me
Than all Nature's beauties can
In some other wiser man.'   G. WITHER

In youth from rock to rock I went,
From hill to hill in discontent
Of pleasure high and turbulent,
    Most pleased when most uneasy;
But now my own delights I make, –
My thirst at every rill can slake,
And gladly Nature's love partake,
    Of Thee, sweet Daisy!

Thee Winter in the garland wears
10 That thinly decks his few grey hairs;
Spring parts the clouds with softest airs,
    That she may sun thee;
Whole Summer-fields are thine by right;

And Autumn, melancholy Wight!
Doth in thy crimson head delight
   When rains are on thee.

In shoals and bands, a morrice train,
Thou greet'st the traveller in the lane;
Pleased at his greeting thee again;
20   Yet nothing daunted,
Nor grieved if thou be set at naught:
And oft alone in nooks remote
We meet thee, like a pleasant thought,
   When such are wanted.

Be violets in their secret mews
The flowers the wanton Zephyrs choose;
Proud be the rose, with rains and dews
   Her head impearling,
Thou liv'st with less ambitious aim,
30 Yet hast not gone without thy fame;
Thou art indeed by many a claim
   The Poet's darling.

If to a rock from rains he fly,
Or, some bright day of April sky,
Imprisoned by hot sunshine lie
   Near the green holly,
And wearily at length should fare;
He needs but look about, and there
Thou art! – a friend at hand, to scare
40   His melancholy.

A hundred times, by rock or bower,
Ere thus I have lain couched an hour,
Have I derived from thy sweet power
   Some apprehension;
Some steady love; some brief delight;
Some memory that had taken flight;
Some chime of fancy wrong or right;
   Or stray invention.

If stately passions in me burn,
50 And one chance look to Thee should turn,
I drink out of an humbler urn
   A lowlier pleasure;
The homely sympathy that heeds
The common life our nature breeds;
A wisdom fitted to the needs
   Of hearts at leisure.

Fresh-smitten by the morning ray,
When thou art up, alert and gay,
Then, cheerful Flower! my spirits play
60   With kindred gladness:
And when, at dusk, by dews opprest
Thou sink'st, the image of thy rest
Hath often eased my pensive breast
   Of careful sadness.

And all day long I number yet,
All seasons through, another debt,
Which I, wherever thou art met,
   To thee am owing;
An instinct call it, a blind sense;
70 A happy, genial influence,
Coming one knows not how, nor whence,
   Nor whither going.

Child of the Year! that round dost run
Thy pleasant course, – when day's begun
As ready to salute the sun
   As lark or leveret,
Thy long-lost praise thou shalt regain;
Nor be less dear to future men
Than in old time; – thou not in vain
80   Art Nature's favourite.

To the Daisy

Bright Flower! whose home is everywhere,
Bold in maternal Nature's care,
And all the long year through the heir
    Of joy and sorrow;
Methinks that there abides in thee
Some concord with humanity,
Given to no other flower I see
    The forest thorough!

Is it that Man is soon deprest?
10 A thoughtless Thing! who, once unblest,
Does little on his memory rest,
    Or on his reason,
And Thou wouldst teach him how to find
A shelter under every wind,
A hope for times that are unkind
    And every season?

Thou wander'st the wide world about,
Unchecked by pride or scrupulous doubt,
With friends to greet thee, or without,
20   Yet pleased and willing;
Meek, yielding to the occasion's call,
And all things suffering from all,
Thy function apostolical
    In peace fulfilling.

To the Same Flower [The Daisy]

With little here to do or see
Of things that in the great world be,
Daisy! again I talk to thee,
  For thou art worthy,

Thou unassuming Common-place
Of Nature, with that homely face,
And yet with something of a grace,
   Which Love makes for thee!

Oft on the dappled turf at ease
10 I sit, and play with similes,
Loose types of things through all degrees,
   Thoughts of thy raising:
And many a fond and idle name
I give to thee, for praise or blame,
As is the humour of the game,
   While I am gazing.

A nun demure of lowly port;
Or sprightly maiden, of Love's court,
In thy simplicity the sport
20   Of all temptations;
A queen in crown of rubies drest;
A starveling in a scanty vest;
Are all, as seems to suit thee best,
   Thy appellations.

A little Cyclops with one eye
Staring to threaten and defy,
That thought comes next – and instantly
   The freak is over,
The shape will vanish – and behold
30 A silver shield with boss of gold,
That spreads itself, some faery bold
   In fight to cover!

I see thee glittering from afar –
And then thou art a pretty star;
Not quite so fair as many are
   In heaven above thee!
Yet like a star, with glittering crest,
Self-poised in air thou seem'st to rest; –

May peace come never to his nest,
40   Who shall reprove thee!

Bright *Flower*! for by that name at last,
When all my reveries are past,
I call thee, and to that cleave fast,
    Sweet silent creature!
That breath'st with me in sun and air,
Do thou, as thou art wont, repair
My heart with gladness, and a share
    Of thy meek nature!

The Redbreast Chasing the Butterfly

Art thou the bird whom Man loves best,
The pious bird with the scarlet breast,
    Our little English Robin;
The bird that comes about our doors
When Autumn-winds are sobbing?
Art thou the Peter of Norway Boors?
    Their Thomas in Finland,
    And Russia far inland?
The bird, that by some name or other
10   All men who know thee call their brother,
The darling of children and men?
Could Father Adam open his eyes
And see this sight beneath the skies,
He'd wish to close them again.
– If the Butterfly knew but his friend,
Hither his flight he would bend;
And find his way to me,
Under the branches of the tree:
In and out, he darts about;
20   Can this be the bird, to man so good,
That, after their bewildering,
Covered with leaves the little children,
    So painfully in the wood?

What ailed thee, Robin, that thou couldst pursue
    A beautiful creature,
That is gentle by nature?
Beneath the summer sky
From flower to flower let him fly;
'Tis all that he wishes to do.
30 The cheerer Thou of our in-door sadness,
He is the friend of our summer gladness:
What hinders, then, that ye should be
Playmates in the sunny weather,
And fly about in the air together!
His beautiful wings in crimson are drest,
A crimson as bright as thine own:
Wouldst thou be happy in thy nest,
O pious Bird! whom man loves best,
Love him, or leave him alone!

To a Butterfly

I've watched you now a full half-hour,
Self-poised upon that yellow flower;
And, little Butterfly! indeed
I know not if you sleep or feed.
How motionless! – not frozen seas
More motionless! and then
What joy awaits you, when the breeze
Hath found you out among the trees,
And calls you forth again!

10 This plot of orchard-ground is ours;
My trees they are, my Sister's flowers;
Here rest your wings when they are weary;
Here lodge as in a sanctuary!
Come often to us, fear no wrong;
Sit near us on the bough!
We'll talk of sunshine and of song,

And summer days, when we were young;
Sweet childish days, that were as long
As twenty days are now.

[*Fragments from Dove Cottage Manuscript 44 (11)*]

These Chairs they have no words to utter,
No fire is in the grate to stir or flutter,
The ceiling and floor are mute as a stone,
My chamber is hushed and still,
    And I am alone,
    Happy and alone.

Oh who would be afraid of life,
The passion the sorrow and the strife,
    When he may be
10   Sheltered so easily?
May lie in peace on his bed
Happy as they who are dead.

Half an hour afterwards
I have thoughts that are fed by the sun.
    The things which I see
    Are welcome to me,
    Welcome every one:
I do not wish to lie
    Dead, dead,
Dead without any company;
20   Here alone on my bed,
With thoughts that are fed by the Sun,
And hopes that are welcome every one,
    Happy am I.

O Life, there is about thee
A deep delicious peace,
I would not be without thee,

Stay, oh stay!
Yet be thou ever as now,
Sweetness and breath with the quiet of death,
30 Be but thou ever as now,
    Peace, peace, peace.

The Tinker

Who leads a happy life
If it's not the merry Tinker?
Not too old to have a Wife;
Not too much a thinker:
Through the meadows, over stiles,
Where there are no measured miles,
Day by day he finds his way
Among the lonely houses:
Right before the Farmer's door
10 Down he sits; his brows he knits;
Then his hammer he rouses;
Batter! batter! batter!
He begins to clatter;
And while the work is going on
Right good ale he bouzes;
And, when it is done, away he is gone;
    And, in his scarlet coat,
    With a merry note,
    He sings the sun to bed;
20 And, without making a pother,
Finds some place or other
For his own careless head.

When in the woods the little Fowls
Begin their merry-making,
Again the jolly Tinker bowls
Forth with small leave-taking:
Through the valley, up the hill;
He can't go wrong, go where he will:

   Tricks he has twenty,
30 And pastimes in plenty;
He's the terror of boys in the midst of their noise;
   When the market Maiden,
   Bringing home her lading,
   Hath passed him in a nook,
   With his outlandish look,
   And visage grim and sooty,
   Bumming, bumming, bumming,
   What is that that's coming?
   Silly Maid as ever was!
40 She thinks that she and all she has
   Will be the Tinker's booty;
   At the pretty Maiden's dread
   The Tinker shakes his head,
   Laughing, laughing, laughing,
As if he would laugh himself dead.
   And thus, with work or none,
   The Tinker lives in fun,
   With a light soul to cover him;
   And sorrow and care blow over him,
50 Whether he's up or a-bed.

Foresight

That is work of waste and ruin –
Do as Charles and I are doing!
Strawberry-blossoms, one and all,
We must spare them – here are many:
Look at it – the flower is small,
Small and low, though fair as any:
Do not touch it! summers two
I am older, Anne, than you.

Pull the primrose, sister Anne!
10 Pull as many as you can.
 – Here are daisies, take your fill;

Pansies, and the cuckoo-flower:
Of the lofty daffodil
Make your bed, or make your bower;
Fill your lap, and fill your bosom;
Only spare the strawberry-blossom!

Primroses, the Spring may love them –
Summer knows but little of them:
Violets, a barren kind,
20 Withered on the ground must lie;
Daisies leave no fruit behind
When the pretty flowerets die;
Pluck them, and another year
As many will be blowing here.

God has given a kindlier power
To the favoured strawberry-flower.
Hither soon as spring is fled
You and Charles and I will walk;
Lurking berries, ripe and red,
30 Then will hang on every stalk,
Each within its leafy bower;
And for that promise spare the flower!

To the Small Celandine

Pansies, lilies, kingcups, daisies,
Let them live upon their praises;
Long as there's a sun that sets,
Primroses will have their glory;
Long as there are violets,
They will have a place in story:
There's a flower that shall be mine,
'Tis the little Celandine.

Eyes of some men travel far
10 For the finding of a star;

Up and down the heavens they go,
Men that keep a mighty rout!
I'm as great as they, I trow,
Since the day I found thee out,
Little Flower! – I'll make a stir,
Like a sage astronomer.

Modest, yet withal an Elf
Bold, and lavish of thyself;
Since we needs must first have met
20 I have seen thee, high and low,
Thirty years or more, and yet
'Twas a face I did not know;
Thou hast now, go where I may,
Fifty greetings in a day.

Ere a leaf is on a bush,
In the time before the thrush
Has a thought about her nest,
Thou wilt come with half a call,
Spreading out thy glossy breast
30 Like a careless Prodigal;
Telling tales about the sun,
When we've little warmth, or none.

Poets, vain men in their mood!
Travel with the multitude:
Never heed them; I aver
That they all are wanton wooers;
But the thrifty cottager,
Who stirs little out of doors,
Joys to spy thee near her home;
40 Spring is coming, Thou art come!

Comfort have thou of thy merit,
Kindly, unassuming Spirit!
Careless of thy neighbourhood,
Thou dost show thy pleasant face

On the moor, and in the wood,
In the lane; – there's not a place,
Howsoever mean it be,
But 'tis good enough for thee.

Ill befall the yellow flowers,
50 Children of the flaring hours!
Buttercups, that will be seen,
Whether we will see or no;
Others, too, of lofty mien;
They have done as worldlings do,
Taken praise that should be thine,
Little, humble Celandine.

Prophet of delight and mirth,
Ill-requited upon earth;
Herald of a mighty band,
60 Of a joyous train ensuing,
Serving at my heart's command,
Tasks that are no tasks renewing,
I will sing, as doth behove,
Hymns in praise of what I love!

*The Barberry-Tree

Late on a breezy vernal eve
  When breezes wheeled their whirling flight;
I wandered forth; and I believe
  I never saw so sweet a sight.

It nodded in the breeze
  It rustled in mine ear;
Fairest of blossomed trees
  In hill or valley, far or near:

No tree that grew in hill or vale
10   Such blithesome blossoms e'er displayed:

They laughed and danced upon the gale;
   They seemed as they could never fade:
As they could never fade they seemed;
   And still they danced, now high, now low;
In very joy their colours gleamed:
   But whether it be thus or no;
That while they danced upon the wind
They felt a joy like humankind:
That this blithe breeze which cheerly sung
20 While the merry boughs he swung;
Did in that moment, while the bough
   Whispered to his gladsome singing:
Feel the pleasures that even now
   In my breast are springing:
And whether, as I said before,
   These golden blossoms dancing high,
   These breezes piping through the sky
Have in themselves of joy a store:
And mingling breath and murmured motion
30 Like eddies of the gusty ocean,
Do in their leafy morris bear
Mirth and gladness through the air:
As up and down the branches toss,
And above and beneath and across
The breezes brush on lusty pinion
Sportive struggling for dominion:
If living sympathy be theirs
   And leaves and airs,
The piping breeze and dancing tree
40 Are all alive and glad as we:
Whether this be truth or no
I cannot tell, I do not know;
Nay – whether now I reason well,
I do not know, I cannot tell.
But this I know, and will declare,
   Rightly and surely *this* I know;
That never here, that never there,
      Around me, aloft, or alow;

Nor here nor there, nor anywhere
50   Saw I a scene so very fair.
And on this food of thought I fed
Till moments, minutes, hours had fled:
And had not sudden the church-chimes
    Rung out the well-known peal I love;
I had forgotten Peter Grimes,
    His nuts and cyder in the apple-grove:
I say, and I aver it true,
    That had I not the warning heard
      Which told how late it grew,
60   (And I to Grimes had pledged my word;)

In that most happy mood of mind
    There like a Statue had I stood, till now:
        And when my trance was ended
        And on my way I tended,
    Still, so it was, I know not how,
But passed it not away, that piping wind:

For as I went, in sober sooth
    It seemed to go along with me;
I tell you now the very truth,
70   It seemed part of myself to be:
That in my inner self I had
Those whispering sounds which made me glad.
Now if you feel a wish dear Jones!
    To see these branches dancing so;
Lest you in vain should stir your bones,
    I will advise you when to go:
That is, if you should wish to see
This piping, skipping Barberry:
(For so they call the shrub I mean,
80   Whose blossomed branches thus are seen,
      Uptossing their leafy shrouds
        As if they were fain to spring
          On the whirl-zephyr's wing,
          Up to the clouds.)

If Jacob Jones, you have at heart
   To hear this sound and see this sight:
[?This] advice I do impart,
   [?That] Jacob, you don't go by night;
[?It's] possible the shrub so green
90   [?And so] low, may not well be seen:
[?Nor Jaco]b, would I have you go
When the blithe winds forbear to blow;
I think it may be safely then averred
   The piping leaves will not be heard.
     But when the wind rushes
     Through brakes and through bushes;
And around, and within, and without,
     Makes a roar and a rout;
      Then may you see
100   The Barberry-tree;
      With all its yellow flowers
      And interwoven bowers:
      Toss in merry madness
      Every bough of gladness:
And dance to and fro to the loud-singing breeze,
The blithest of gales, and the maddest of trees:
     And then like me
   Even from the blossoms of the Barberry,
     Mayst thou a store of thought lay by
110   For present time and long futurity:
     And teach to fellow-men a lore
     They never learned before;
The manly strain of natural poesy.

To the Same Flower [*The Small Celandine*]

Pleasures newly found are sweet
When they lie about our feet:
February last, my heart
First at sight of thee was glad;
All unheard of as thou art,

Thou must needs, I think, have had,
Celandine! and long ago,
Praise of which I nothing know.

I have not a doubt but he,
10 Whosoe'er the man might be,
Who the first with pointed rays
(Workman worthy to be sainted)
Set the sign-board in a blaze,
When the rising sun he painted,
Took the fancy from a glance
At thy glittering countenance.

Soon as gentle breezes bring
News of winter's vanishing,
And the children build their bowers,
20 Sticking 'kerchief-plots of mould
All about with full-blown flowers,
Thick as sheep in shepherd's fold!
With the proudest thou art there,
Mantling in the tiny square.

Often have I sighed to measure
By myself a lonely pleasure,
Sighed to think, I read a book
Only read, perhaps, by me;
Yet I long could overlook
30 Thy bright coronet and Thee,
And thy arch and wily ways,
And thy store of other praise.

Blithe of heart, from week to week
Thou dost play at hide-and-seek;
While the patient primrose sits
Like a beggar in the cold,
Thou, a flower of wiser wits,
Slip'st into thy sheltering hold;
Liveliest of the vernal train
40 When ye all are out again.

Drawn by what peculiar spell,
By what charm of sight or smell,
Does the dim-eyed curious Bee,
Labouring for her waxen cells,
Fondly settle upon Thee
Prized above all buds and bells
Opening daily at thy side,
By the season multiplied?

Thou art not beyond the moon,
50 But a thing 'beneath our shoon':
Let the bold Discoverer thrid
In his bark the polar sea;
Rear who will a pyramid;
Praise it is enough for me,
If there be but three or four
Who will love my little Flower.

Resolution and Independence

I
There was a roaring in the wind all night;
The rain came heavily and fell in floods;
But now the sun is rising calm and bright;
The birds are singing in the distant woods;
Over his own sweet voice the Stock-dove broods;
The Jay makes answer as the Magpie chatters;
And all the air is filled with pleasant noise of waters.

II
All things that love the sun are out of doors;
The sky rejoices in the morning's birth;
10 The grass is bright with rain-drops; – on the moors
The hare is running races in her mirth;
And with her feet she from the plashy earth
Raises a mist; that, glittering in the sun,
Runs with her all the way, wherever she doth run.

III

I was a Traveller then upon the moor;
I saw the hare that raced about with joy;
I heard the woods and distant waters roar;
Or heard them not, as happy as a boy:
The pleasant season did my heart employ:
20 My old remembrances went from me wholly;
And all the ways of men, so vain and melancholy.

IV

But, as it sometimes chanceth, from the might
Of joy in minds that can no further go,
As high as we have mounted in delight
In our dejection do we sink as low;
To me that morning did it happen so;
And fears and fancies thick upon me came;
Dim sadness – and blind thoughts, I knew not, nor
    could name.

V

I heard the sky-lark warbling in the sky;
30 And I bethought me of the playful hare:
Even such a happy Child of earth am I;
Even as these blissful creatures do I fare;
Far from the world I walk, and from all care;
But there may come another day to me –
Solitude, pain of heart, distress, and poverty.

VI

My whole life I have lived in pleasant thought,
As if life's business were a summer mood;
As if all needful things would come unsought
To genial faith, still rich in genial good;
40 But how can He expect that others should
Build for him, sow for him, and at his call
Love him, who for himself will take no heed at all?

VII

I thought of Chatterton, the marvellous Boy,
The sleepless Soul that perished in his pride;
Of Him who walked in glory and in joy
Following his plough, along the mountain-side:
By our own spirits are we deified:
We Poets in our youth begin in gladness;
But thereof come in the end despondency and madness.

VIII

50 Now, whether it were by peculiar grace,
A leading from above, a something given,
Yet it befell, that, in this lonely place,
When I with these untoward thoughts had striven,
Beside a pool bare to the eye of heaven
I saw a Man before me unawares:
The oldest man he seemed that ever wore grey hairs.

IX

As a huge stone is sometimes seen to lie
Couched on the bald top of an eminence;
Wonder to all who do the same espy,
60 By what means it could thither come, and whence;
So that it seems a thing endued with sense:
Like a sea-beast crawled forth, that on a shelf
Of rock or sand reposeth, there to sun itself;

X

Such seemed this Man, not all alive nor dead,
Nor all asleep – in his extreme old age:
His body was bent double, feet and head
Coming together in life's pilgrimage;
As if some dire constraint of pain, or rage
Of sickness felt by him in times long past,
70 A more than human weight upon his frame had cast.

XI

Himself he propped, limbs, body, and pale face,
Upon a long grey staff of shaven wood:

And, still as I drew near with gentle pace,
Upon the margin of that moorish flood
Motionless as a cloud the old Man stood,
That heareth not the loud winds when they call;
And moveth all together, if it move at all.

XII

At length, himself unsettling, he the pond
Stirred with his staff, and fixedly did look
80   Upon the muddy water, which he conned,
As if he had been reading in a book:
And now a stranger's privilege I took;
And, drawing to his side, to him did say,
'This morning gives us promise of a glorious day.'

XIII

A gentle answer did the old Man make,
In courteous speech which forth he slowly drew:
And him with further words I thus bespake,
'What occupation do you there pursue?
This is a lonesome place for one like you.'
90   Ere he replied, a flash of mild surprise
Broke from the sable orbs of his yet-vivid eyes.

XIV

His words came feebly, from a feeble chest,
But each in solemn order followed each,
With something of a lofty utterance drest –
Choice word and measured phrase, above the reach
Of ordinary men; a stately speech;
Such as grave Livers do in Scotland use,
Religious men, who give to God and man their dues.

XV

He told, that to these waters he had come
100 To gather leeches, being old and poor:
Employment hazardous and wearisome!
And he had many hardships to endure:

From pond to pond he roamed, from moor to moor;
Housing, with God's good help, by choice or chance;
And in this way he gained an honest maintenance.

XVI

The old Man still stood talking by my side;
But now his voice to me was like a stream
Scarce heard; nor word from word could I divide;
And the whole body of the Man did seem
110 Like one whom I had met with in a dream;
Or like a man from some far region sent,
To give me human strength, by apt admonishment.

XVII

My former thoughts returned: the fear that kills;
And hope that is unwilling to be fed;
Cold, pain, and labour, and all fleshly ills;
And mighty Poets in their misery dead.
– Perplexed, and longing to be comforted,
My question eagerly did I renew,
'How is it that you live, and what is it you do?'

XVIII

120 He with a smile did then his words repeat;
And said that, gathering leeches, far and wide
He travelled; stirring thus about his feet
The waters of the pools where they abide.
'Once I could meet with them on every side;
But they have dwindled long by slow decay;
Yet still I persevere, and find them where I may.'

XIX

While he was talking thus, the lonely place,
The old Man's shape, and speech – all troubled me:
In my mind's eye I seemed to see him pace
130 About the weary moors continually,
Wandering about alone and silently.
While I these thoughts within myself pursued,
He, having made a pause, the same discourse renewed.

XX

And soon with this he other matter blended,
Cheerfully uttered, with demeanour kind,
But stately in the main; and when he ended,
I could have laughed myself to scorn to find
In that decrepit Man so firm a mind.
'God,' said I, 'be my help and stay secure;
140 I'll think of the Leech-gatherer on the lonely moor!'

Travelling

This is the spot: – how mildly does the sun
Shine in between the fading leaves! the air
In the habitual silence of this wood
Is more than silent; and this bed of heath –
Where shall we find so sweet a resting-place?
Come, let me see thee sink into a dream
Of quiet thoughts, protracted till thine eye
Be calm as water when the winds are gone
And no one can tell whither. My sweet Friend,
10 We two have had such happy hours together
That my heart melts in me to think of it.

Stanzas
Written in my Pocket-Copy of Thomson's 'Castle of Indolence'

Within our happy Castle there dwelt One
Whom without blame I may not overlook;
For never sun on living creature shone
Who more devout enjoyment with us took:
Here on his hours he hung as on a book,
On his own time here would he float away,
As doth a fly upon a summer brook;
But go tomorrow, or belike today,
Seek for him, – he is fled; and whither none can say.

10   Thus often would he leave our peaceful home,
And find elsewhere his business or delight;
Out of our Valley's limits did he roam:
Full many a time, upon a stormy night,
His voice came to us from the neighbouring height:
Oft could we see him driving full in view
At mid-day when the sun was shining bright;
What ill was on him, what he had to do,
A mighty wonder bred among our quiet crew.

Ah! piteous sight it was to see this Man
20   When he came back to us, a withered flower, –
Or like a sinful creature, pale and wan.
Down would he sit; and without strength or power
Look at the common grass from hour to hour:
And oftentimes, how long I fear to say,
Where apple-trees in blossom made a bower,
Retired in that sunshiny shade he lay;
And, like a naked Indian, slept himself away.

Great wonder to our gentle tribe it was
Whenever from our Valley he withdrew;
30   For happier soul no living creature has
Than he had, being here the long day through.
Some thought he was a lover, and did woo:
Some thought far worse of him, and judged him wrong;
But verse was what he had been wedded to;
And his own mind did like a tempest strong
Come to him thus, and drove the weary Wight along.

With him there often walked in friendly guise,
Or lay upon the moss by brook or tree,
A noticeable Man with large grey eyes,
40   And a pale face that seemed undoubtedly
As if a blooming face it ought to be;
Heavy his low-hung lip did oft appear,
Deprest by weight of musing Phantasy;
Profound his forehead was, though not severe;
Yet some did think that he had little business here:

Sweet heaven forefend! his was a lawful right;
Noisy he was, and gamesome as a boy;
His limbs would toss about him with delight,
Like branches when strong winds the trees annoy.
50 Nor lacked his calmer hours device or toy
To banish listlessness and irksome care;
He would have taught you how you might employ
Yourself; and many did to him repair, –
And certes not in vain; he had inventions rare.

Expedients, too, of simplest sort he tried:
Long blades of grass, plucked round him as he lay,
Made, to his ear attentively applied,
A pipe on which the wind would deftly play;
Glasses he had, that little things display,
60 The beetle panoplied in gems and gold,
A mailèd angel on a battle-day;
The mysteries that cups of flowers enfold,
And all the gorgeous sights which fairies do behold.

He would entice that other Man to hear
His music, and to view his imagery:
And, sooth, these two were each to the other dear:
No livelier love in such a place could be:
There did they dwell – from earthly labour free,
As happy spirits as were ever seen;
70 If but a bird, to keep them company,
Or butterfly sate down, they were, I ween,
As pleased as if the same had been a Maiden-queen.

1801

I grieved for Buonaparté, with a vain
And an unthinking grief! The tenderest mood
Of that Man's mind – what can it be? what food
Fed his first hopes? what knowledge could *he* gain?
'Tis not in battles that from youth we train

The Governor who must be wise and good,
And temper with the sternness of the brain
Thoughts motherly, and meek as womanhood.
Wisdom doth live with children round her knees:
10 Books, leisure, perfect freedom, and the talk
Man holds with week-day man in the hourly walk
Of the mind's business: these are the degrees
By which true Sway doth mount; this is the stalk
True Power doth grow on; and her rights are these.

'Methought I saw the footsteps of a throne'

Methought I saw the footsteps of a throne
Which mists and vapours from mine eyes did shroud –
Nor view of who might sit thereon allowed;
But all the steps and ground about were strown
With sights the ruefullest that flesh and bone
Ever put on; a miserable crowd,
Sick, hale, old, young, who cried before that cloud,
'Thou art our king, O Death! to thee we groan.'
Those steps I clomb; the mists before me gave
10 Smooth way; and I beheld the face of one
Sleeping alone within a mossy cave,
With her face up to heaven; that seemed to have
Pleasing remembrance of a thought foregone;
A lovely Beauty in a summer grave!

'Great men have been among us; hands that penned'

Great men have been among us; hands that penned
And tongues that uttered wisdom – better none:
The later Sidney, Marvell, Harrington,
Young Vane, and others who called Milton friend.
These moralists could act and comprehend:
They knew how genuine glory was put on;

Taught us how rightfully a nation shone
In splendour: what strength was, that would not bend
But in magnanimous meekness. France, 'tis strange,
10   Hath brought forth no such souls as we had then.
Perpetual emptiness! unceasing change!
No single volume paramount, no code,
No master spirit, no determined road;
But equally a want of books and men!

'England! the time is come when thou shouldst wean'

England! the time is come when thou shouldst wean
Thy heart from its emasculating food;
The truth should now be better understood;
Old things have been unsettled; we have seen
Fair seed-time, better harvest might have been
But for thy trespasses; and, at this day,
If for Greece, Egypt, India, Africa,
Aught good were destined, thou wouldst step between.
England! all nations in this charge agree:
10   But worse, more ignorant in love and hate,
Far – far more abject, is thine Enemy:
Therefore the wise pray for thee, though the freight
Of thy offences be a heavy weight:
Oh grief that Earth's best hopes rest all with Thee!

'It is not to be thought of that the Flood'

It is not to be thought of that the Flood
Of British freedom, which, to the open sea
Of the world's praise, from dark antiquity
Hath flowed, 'with pomp of waters, unwithstood,'
Roused though it be full often to a mood
Which spurns the check of salutary bands,
That this most famous Stream in bogs and sands

Should perish; and to evil and to good
Be lost for ever. In our halls is hung
10 Armoury of the invincible Knights of old:
We must be free or die, who speak the tongue
That Shakespeare spake; the faith and morals hold
Which Milton held. – In everything we are sprung
Of Earth's first blood, have titles manifold.

'*There is a bondage worse, far worse, to bear*'

There is a bondage worse, far worse, to bear
Than his who breathes, by roof, and floor, and wall,
Pent in, a Tyrant's solitary Thrall:
'Tis his who walks about in the open air,
One of a Nation who, henceforth, must wear
Their fetters in their souls. For who could be,
Who, even the best, in such condition, free
From self-reproach, reproach that he must share
With Human-nature? Never be it ours
10 To see the sun how brightly it will shine,
And know that noble feelings, manly powers,
Instead of gathering strength, must droop and pine;
And earth with all her pleasant fruits and flowers
Fade, and participate in man's decline.

'*When I have borne in memory what has tamed*'

When I have borne in memory what has tamed
Great Nations, how ennobling thoughts depart
When men change swords for ledgers, and desert
The student's bower for gold, some fears unnamed
I had, my Country! – am I to be blamed?
Now, when I think of thee, and what thou art,
Verily, in the bottom of my heart,
Of those unfilial fears I am ashamed.
For dearly must we prize thee; we who find

10   In thee a bulwark for the cause of men;
      And I by my affection was beguiled:
      What wonder if a Poet now and then,
      Among the many movements of his mind,
      Felt for thee as a lover or a child!

To Sleep

      O gentle Sleep! do they belong to thee,
      These twinklings of oblivion? Thou dost love
      To sit in meekness, like the brooding Dove,
      A captive never wishing to be free.
      This tiresome night, O Sleep! thou art to me
      A Fly, that up and down himself doth shove
      Upon a fretful rivulet, now above,
      Now on the water vexed with mockery.
      I have no pain that calls for patience, no;
10   Hence am I cross and peevish as a child:
      Am pleased by fits to have thee for my foe,
      Yet ever willing to be reconciled:
      O gentle Creature! do not use me so,
      But once and deeply let me be beguiled.

To Sleep

      A flock of sheep that leisurely pass by,
      One after one; the sound of rain, and bees
      Murmuring; the fall of rivers, winds and seas,
      Smooth fields, white sheets of water, and pure sky;
      I have thought of all by turns, and yet do lie
      Sleepless! and soon the small birds' melodies
      Must hear, first uttered from my orchard trees;
      And the first cuckoo's melancholy cry.
      Even thus last night, and two nights more, I lay,
10   And could not win thee, Sleep! by any stealth:
      So do not let me wear tonight away:

Without Thee what is all the morning's wealth?
Come, blessed barrier between day and day,
Dear mother of fresh thoughts and joyous health!

To Sleep

Fond words have oft been spoken to thee, Sleep!
And thou hast had thy store of tenderest names;
The very sweetest, Fancy culls or frames,
When thankfulness of heart is strong and deep!
Dear Bosom-child we call thee, that dost steep
In rich reward all suffering; Balm that tames
All anguish; Saint that evil thoughts and aims
Takest away, and into souls dost creep,
Like to a breeze from heaven. Shall I alone,
10   I surely not a man ungently made,
Call thee worst Tyrant by which Flesh is crost?
Perverse, self-willed to own and to disown,
Mere slave of them who never for thee prayed,
Still last to come where thou art wanted most!

' "*Beloved Vale!*" I said, "*when I shall con*" '

'Beloved Vale!' I said, 'when I shall con
Those many records of my childish years,
Remembrance of myself and of my peers
Will press me down: to think of what is gone
Will be an awful thought, if life have one.'
But, when into the Vale I came, no fears
Distressed me; from mine eyes escaped no tears;
Deep thought, or dread remembrance, had I none.
By doubts and thousand petty fancies crost
10   I stood, of simple shame the blushing Thrall;
So narrow seemed the brooks, the fields so small!
A Juggler's balls old Time about him tossed;
I looked, I stared, I smiled, I laughed; and all
The weight of sadness was in wonder lost.

'Brook! whose society the Poet seeks'

Brook! whose society the Poet seeks,
Intent his wasted spirits to renew;
And whom the curious Painter doth pursue
Through rocky passes, among flowery creeks,
And tracks thee dancing down thy water-breaks;
If wish were mine some type of thee to view,
Thee, and not thee thyself, I would not do
Like Grecian Artists, give thee human cheeks,
Channels for tears; no Naiad shouldst thou be, –
10   Have neither limbs, feet, feathers, joints nor hairs:
It seems the Eternal Soul is clothed in thee
With purer robes than those of flesh and blood,
And hath bestowed on thee a safer good;
Unwearied joy, and life without its cares.

'What if our numbers barely could defy'

What if our numbers barely could defy
The arithmetic of babes, must foreign hordes,
Slaves, vile as ever were befooled by words,
Striking through English breasts the anarchy
Of Terror, bear us to the ground, and tie
Our hands behind our backs with felon cords?
Yields everything to discipline of swords?
Is man as good as man, none low, none high? –
Nor discipline nor valour can withstand
10   The shock, nor quell the inevitable rout,
When in some great extremity breaks out
A people, on their own beloved Land
Risen, like one man, to combat in the sight
Of a just God for liberty and right.

'*There is a little unpretending Rill*'

There is a little unpretending Rill
Of limpid water, humbler far than aught
That ever among Men or Naiads sought
Notice or name! – It quivers down the hill,
Furrowing its shallow way with dubious will;
Yet to my mind this scanty Stream is brought
Oftener than Ganges or the Nile; a thought
Of private recollection sweet and still!
Months perish with their moons; year treads on year;
10 But, faithful Emma! thou with me canst say
That, while ten thousand pleasures disappear,
And flies their memory fast almost as they;
The immortal Spirit of one happy day
Lingers beside that Rill, in vision clear.

'*I find it written of* SIMONIDES'

I find it written of SIMONIDES
That, travelling in strange countries, once he found
A corpse that lay exposed upon the ground,
For which, with pains, he caused due obsequies
To be performed, and paid all holy fees.
Soon after, this man's ghost unto him came,
And told him not to sail, as was his aim,
On board a ship then ready for the seas.
SIMONIDES, admonished by the ghost,
10 Remained behind: the ship the following day
Set sail, was wrecked, and all on board were lost.
Thus was the tenderest Poet that could be,
Who sang in ancient Greece his moving lay,
Saved out of many by his piety.

'*How sweet it is, when mother Fancy rocks*'

How sweet it is, when mother Fancy rocks
The wayward brain, to saunter through a wood!
An old place, full of many a lovely brood,
Tall trees, green arbours, and ground-flowers in flocks;
And wild rose tip-toe upon hawthorn stocks,
Like a bold Girl, who plays her agile pranks
At Wakes and Fairs with wandering Mountebanks, –
When she stands cresting the Clown's head, and mocks
The crowd beneath her. Verily I think,
10 Such place to me is sometimes like a dream
Or map of the whole world: thoughts, link by link,
Enter through ears and eyesight, with such gleam
Of all things, that at last in fear I shrink,
And leap at once from the delicious stream.

Personal Talk

I

I am not One who much or oft delight
To season my fireside with personal talk, –
Of friends, who live within an easy walk,
Or neighbours, daily, weekly, in my sight:
And, for my chance-acquaintance, ladies bright,
Sons, mothers, maidens withering on the stalk,
These all wear out of me, like Forms, with chalk
Painted on rich men's floors, for one feast-night.
Better than such discourse doth silence long,
10 Long, barren silence, square with my desire;
To sit without emotion, hope, or aim,
In the loved presence of my cottage-fire,
And listen to the flapping of the flame,
Or kettle whispering its faint undersong.

II

'Yet life,' you say, 'is life; we have seen and see,
And with a living pleasure we describe;
And fits of sprightly malice do but bribe
The languid mind into activity.
Sound sense, and love itself, and mirth and glee
20 Are fostered by the comment and the gibe.'
Even be it so: yet still among your tribe,
Our daily world's true Worldlings, rank not me!
Children are blest, and powerful; their world lies
More justly balanced; partly at their feet,
And part far from them: – sweetest melodies
Are those that are by distance made more sweet;
Whose mind is but the mind of his own eyes,
He is a Slave; the meanest we can meet!

III

Wings have we, – and as far as we can go
30 We may find pleasure: wilderness and wood,
Blank ocean and mere sky, support that mood
Which with the lofty sanctifies the low.
Dreams, books, are each a world; and books, we know,
Are a substantial world, both pure and good:
Round these, with tendrils strong as flesh and blood,
Our pastime and our happiness will grow.
There find I personal themes, a plenteous store,
Matter wherein right voluble I am,
To which I listen with a ready ear;
40 Two shall be named, pre-eminently dear, –
The gentle Lady married to the Moor;
And heavenly Una with her milk-white Lamb.

IV

Nor can I not believe but that hereby
Great gains are mine; for thus I live remote
From evil-speaking; rancour, never sought,
Comes to me not; malignant truth, or lie.
Hence have I genial seasons, hence have I

Smooth passions, smooth discourse, and joyous thought:
And thus from day to day my little boat
50 Rocks in its harbour, lodging peaceably.
Blessings be with them – and eternal praise,
Who gave us nobler loves, and nobler cares –
The Poets, who on earth have made us heirs
Of truth and pure delight by heavenly lays!
Oh! might my name be numbered among theirs,
Then gladly would I end my mortal days.

'Pelion and Ossa flourish side by side'

Pelion and Ossa flourish side by side,
Together in immortal books enrolled:
His ancient dower Olympus hath not sold;
And that inspiring Hill, which 'did divide
Into two ample horns his forehead wide,'
Shines with poetic radiance as of old;
While not an English Mountain we behold
By the celestial Muses glorified.
Yet round our sea-girt shore they rise in crowds:
10 What was the great Parnassus' self to Thee,
Mount Skiddaw? In his natural sovereignty
Our British Hill is nobler far; he shrouds
His double front among Atlantic clouds,
And pours forth streams more sweet than Castaly.

'The world is too much with us; late and soon'

The world is too much with us; late and soon,
Getting and spending, we lay waste our powers:
Little we see in Nature that is ours;
We have given our hearts away, a sordid boon!
This Sea that bares her bosom to the moon;
The winds that will be howling at all hours,
And are up-gathered now like sleeping flowers;

For this, for everything, we are out of tune;
It moves us not. – Great God! I'd rather be
10 A Pagan suckled in a creed outworn;
So might I, standing on this pleasant lea,
Have glimpses that would make me less forlorn;
Have sight of Proteus rising from the sea;
Or hear old Triton blow his wreathèd horn.

To the Memory of Raisley Calvert

Calvert! it must not be unheard by them
Who may respect my name, that I to thee
Owed many years of early liberty.
This care was thine when sickness did condemn
Thy youth to hopeless wasting, root and stem –
That I, if frugal and severe, might stray
Where'er I liked; and finally array
My temples with the Muse's diadem.
Hence, if in freedom I have loved the truth;
10 If there be aught of pure, or good, or great,
In my past verse; or shall be, in the lays
Of higher mood, which now I meditate; –
It gladdens me, O worthy, short-lived, Youth!
To think how much of this will be thy praise.

'Where lies the Land to which yon Ship must go?'

Where lies the Land to which yon Ship must go?
Fresh as a lark mounting at break of day,
Festively she puts forth in trim array;
Is she for tropic suns, or polar snow?
What boots the inquiry? – Neither friend nor foe
She cares for; let her travel where she may,
She finds familiar names, a beaten way
Ever before her, and a wind to blow.
Yet still I ask, what haven is her mark?

10 And, almost as it was when ships were rare,
 (From time to time, like Pilgrims, here and there
 Crossing the waters) doubt, and something dark,
 Of the old Sea some reverential fear,
 Is with me at thy farewell, joyous Bark!

"*With how sad steps, O Moon, thou climb'st the sky*"'

'With how sad steps, O Moon, thou climb'st the sky,
How silently, and with how wan a face!'
Where art thou? Thou so often seen on high
Running among the clouds a Wood-nymph's race!
Unhappy Nuns, whose common breath's a sigh
Which they would stifle, move at such a pace!
The northern Wind, to call thee to the chase,
Must blow tonight his bugle horn. Had I
The power of Merlin, Goddess! this should be:
10 And all the stars, fast as the clouds were riven,
Should sally forth, to keep thee company,
Hurrying and sparkling through the clear blue heaven;
But, Cynthia! should to thee the palm be given,
Queen both for beauty and for majesty.

'*With Ships the sea was sprinkled far and nigh*'

With Ships the sea was sprinkled far and nigh,
Like stars in heaven, and joyously it showed;
Some lying fast at anchor in the road,
Some veering up and down, one knew not why.
A goodly Vessel did I then espy
Come like a giant from a haven broad;
And lustily along the bay she strode,
Her tackling rich, and of apparel high.
This Ship was naught to me, nor I to her,
10 Yet I pursued her with a Lover's look;

This Ship to all the rest did I prefer:
When will she turn, and whither? She will brook
No tarrying; where She comes the winds must stir:
On went She, and due north her journey took.

'It is no Spirit who from heaven hath flown'

It is no Spirit who from heaven hath flown,
And is descending on his embassy;
Nor Traveller gone from earth the heavens to espy!
'Tis Hesperus – there he stands with glittering crown,
First admonition that the sun is down!
For yet it is broad day-light: clouds pass by;
A few are near him still – and now the sky,
He hath it to himself – 'tis all his own.
O most ambitious Star! an inquest wrought
10   Within me when I recognized thy light;
A moment I was startled at the sight:
And, while I gazed, there came to me a thought
That I might step beyond my natural race
As thou seem'st now to do; might one day trace
Some ground not mine; and, strong her strength above,
My Soul, an Apparition in the place,
Tread there with steps that no one shall reprove!

On the Extinction of the Venetian Republic

Once did She hold the gorgeous east in fee;
And was the safeguard of the west: the worth
Of Venice did not fall below her birth,
Venice, the eldest Child of Liberty.
She was a maiden City, bright and free;
No guile seduced, no force could violate;
And, when she took unto herself a Mate,
She must espouse the everlasting Sea.
And what if she had seen those glories fade,

10 Those titles vanish, and that strength decay;
    Yet shall some tribute of regret be paid
    When her long life hath reached its final day:
    Men are we, and must grieve when even the Shade
    Of that which once was great, is passed away.

A Farewell

Farewell, thou little Nook of mountain-ground,
Thou rocky corner in the lowest stair
Of that magnificent temple which doth bound
One side of our whole vale with grandeur rare;
Sweet garden-orchard, eminently fair,
The loveliest spot that man hath ever found,
Farewell! – we leave thee to Heaven's peaceful care,
Thee, and the Cottage which thou dost surround.

Our boat is safely anchored by the shore,
10 And there will safely ride when we are gone;
The flowering shrubs that deck our humble door
Will prosper, though untended and alone:
Fields, goods, and far-off chattels we have none:
These narrow bounds contain our private store
Of things earth makes, and sun doth shine upon;
Here are they in our sight – we have no more.

Sunshine and shower be with you, bud and bell!
For two months now in vain we shall be sought;
We leave you here in solitude to dwell
20 With these our latest gifts of tender thought;
Thou, like the morning, in thy saffron coat,
Bright gowan, and marsh-marigold, farewell!
Whom from the borders of the Lake we brought,
And placed together near our rocky Well.

We go for One to whom ye will be dear;
And she will prize this Bower, this Indian shed,

Our own contrivance, Building without peer!
– A gentle Maid, whose heart is lowly bred,
Whose pleasures are in wild fields gatherèd,
30 With joyousness, and with a thoughtful cheer,
Will come to you; to you herself will wed;
And love the blessed life that we lead here.

Dear Spot! which we have watched with tender heed,
Bringing thee chosen plants and blossoms blown
Among the distant mountains, flower and weed,
Which thou hast taken to thee as thy own,
Making all kindness registered and known;
Thou for our sakes, though Nature's child indeed,
Fair in thyself and beautiful alone,
40 Hast taken gifts which thou dost little need.

And O most constant, yet most fickle Place,
That hast thy wayward moods, as thou dost show
To them who look not daily on thy face;
Who, being loved, in love no bounds dost know,
And say'st, when we forsake thee, 'Let them go!'
Thou easy-hearted Thing, with thy wild race
Of weeds and flowers, till we return be slow,
And travel with the year at a soft pace.

Help us to tell Her tales of years gone by,
50 And this sweet spring, the best beloved and best;
Joy will be flown in its mortality;
Something must stay to tell us of the rest.
Here, thronged with primroses, the steep rock's breast
Glittered at evening like a starry sky;
And in this bush our sparrow built her nest,
Of which I sang one song that will not die.

O happy Garden! whose seclusion deep
Hath been so friendly to industrious hours;
And to soft slumbers, that did gently steep
60 Our spirits, carrying with them dreams of flowers,

And wild notes warbled among leafy bowers;
Two burning months let summer overleap,
And, coming back with Her who will be ours,
Into thy bosom we again shall creep.

'The sun has long been set'

This *Impromptu* appeared, many years ago, among the Author's
poems, from which, in subsequent editions, it was excluded. It
is reprinted at the request of the Friend in whose presence the
lines were thrown off.

The sun has long been set,
   The stars are out by twos and threes,
The little birds are piping yet
   Among the bushes and trees;
There's a cuckoo, and one or two thrushes,
And a far-off wind that rushes,
And a sound of water that gushes,
And the cuckoo's sovereign cry
Fills all the hollow of the sky.
10   Who would go 'parading'
In London, and 'masquerading,'
On such a night of June
With that beautiful soft half-moon,
And all these innocent blisses?
On such a night as this is!

Composed Upon Westminster Bridge, September 3, 1802

Earth has not anything to show more fair:
Dull would he be of soul who could pass by
A sight so touching in its majesty:
This City now doth, like a garment, wear
The beauty of the morning; silent, bare,
Ships, towers, domes, theatres, and temples lie

Open unto the fields, and to the sky;
All bright and glittering in the smokeless air.
Never did sun more beautifully steep
10   In his first splendour, valley, rock, or hill;
Ne'er saw I, never felt, a calm so deep!
The river glideth at his own sweet will:
Dear God! the very houses seem asleep;
And all that mighty heart is lying still!

Composed near Calais, on the Road
Leading to Ardres, August 7, 1802

Jones! as from Calais southward you and I
Went pacing side by side, this public Way
Streamed with the pomp of a too-credulous day,
When faith was pledged to new-born Liberty:
A homeless sound of joy was in the sky:
From hour to hour the antiquated Earth
Beat like the heart of Man: songs, garlands, mirth,
Banners, and happy faces, far and nigh!
And now, sole register that these things were,
10   Two solitary greetings have I heard,
'*Good morrow, Citizen!*' a hollow word,
As if a dead man spake it! Yet despair
Touches me not, though pensive as a bird
Whose vernal coverts winter hath laid bare.

Calais, August, 1802

Is it a reed that's shaken by the wind,
Or what is it that ye go forth to see?
Lords, lawyers, statesmen, squires of low degree,
Men known, and men unknown, sick, lame, and blind,
Post forward all, like creatures of one kind,
With first-fruit offerings crowd to bend the knee
In France, before the new-born Majesty.

'Tis ever thus. Ye men of prostrate mind,
A seemly reverence may be paid to power;
10 But that's a loyal virtue, never sown
In haste, nor springing with a transient shower:
When truth, when sense, when liberty were flown,
What hardship had it been to wait an hour?
Shame on you, feeble Heads, to slavery prone!

Composed by the Sea-Side, near Calais, August, 1802

Fair Star of evening, Splendour of the west,
Star of my Country! – on the horizon's brink
Thou hangest, stooping, as might seem, to sink
On England's bosom; yet well pleased to rest,
Meanwhile, and be to her a glorious crest
Conspicuous to the Nations. Thou, I think,
Shouldst be my Country's emblem; and shouldst wink,
Bright Star! with laughter on her banners, drest
In thy fresh beauty. There! that dusky spot
10 Beneath thee, that is England; there she lies.
Blessings be on you both! one hope, one lot,
One life, one glory! – I, with many a fear
For my dear Country, many heartfelt sighs,
Among men who do not love her, linger here.

'It is a beauteous evening, calm and free'

It is a beauteous evening, calm and free,
The holy time is quiet as a Nun
Breathless with adoration; the broad sun
Is sinking down in its tranquillity;
The gentleness of heaven broods o'er the Sea:
Listen! the mighty Being is awake,
And doth with his eternal motion make
A sound like thunder – everlastingly.

Dear Child! dear Girl! that walkest with me here,
10   If thou appear untouched by solemn thought,
Thy nature is not therefore less divine:
Thou liest in Abraham's bosom all the year;
And worshipp'st at the Temple's inner shrine,
God being with thee when we know it not.

To Toussaint l'Ouverture

Toussaint, the most unhappy man of men!
Whether the whistling Rustic tend his plough
Within thy hearing, or thy head be now
Pillowed in some deep dungeon's earless den; –
O miserable Chieftain! where and when
Wilt thou find patience! Yet die not; do thou
Wear rather in thy bonds a cheerful brow:
Though fallen thyself, never to rise again,
Live, and take comfort. Thou hast left behind
10   Powers that will work for thee; air, earth, and skies;
There's not a breathing of the common wind
That will forget thee; thou hast great allies;
Thy friends are exultations, agonies,
And love, and man's unconquerable mind.

Calais, August 15, 1802

Festivals have I seen that were not names:
This is young Buonaparté's natal day,
And his is henceforth an established sway –
Consul for life. With worship France proclaims
Her approbation, and with pomps and games.
Heaven grant that other Cities may be gay!
Calais is not: and I have bent my way
To the sea-coast, noting that each man frames
His business as he likes. Far other show
10   My youth here witnessed, in a prouder time;

The senselessness of joy was then sublime!
Happy is he, who, caring not for Pope,
Consul, or King, can sound himself to know
The destiny of Man, and live in hope.

September 1, 1802

Among the capricious acts of tyranny that disgraced those times,
was the chasing of all Negroes from France by decree of the
government: we had a Fellow-passenger who was one of the
expelled.

We had a female Passenger who came
From Calais with us, spotless in array, –
A white-robed Negro, like a lady gay,
Yet downcast as a woman fearing blame;
Meek, destitute, as seemed, of hope or aim
She sate, from notice turning not away,
But on all proffered intercourse did lay
A weight of languid speech, or to the same
No sign of answer made by word or face:
10 Yet still her eyes retained their tropic fire,
That, burning independent of the mind,
Joined with the lustre of her rich attire
To mock the Outcast – O ye Heavens, be kind!
And feel, thou Earth, for this afflicted Race!

Composed in the Valley near Dover,
on the Day of Landing

Here, on our native soil, we breathe once more.
The cock that crows, the smoke that curls, that sound
Of bells; – those boys who in yon meadow-ground
In white-sleeved shirts are playing; and the roar
Of the waves breaking on the chalky shore; –
All, all are English. Oft have I looked round
With joy in Kent's green vales; but never found

Myself so satisfied in heart before.
Europe is yet in bonds; but let that pass,
10 Thought for another moment. Thou art free,
My Country! and 'tis joy enough and pride
For one hour's perfect bliss, to tread the grass
Of England once again, and hear and see,
With such a dear Companion at my side.

September, 1802. Near Dover

Inland, within a hollow vale, I stood;
And saw, while sea was calm and air was clear,
The coast of France – the coast of France how near!
Drawn almost into frightful neighbourhood.
I shrunk; for verily the barrier flood
Was like a lake, or river bright and fair,
A span of waters; yet what power is there!
What mightiness for evil and for good!
Even so doth God protect us if we be
10 Virtuous and wise. Winds blow, and waters roll,
Strength to the brave, and Power, and Deity;
Yet in themselves are nothing! One decree
Spake laws to *them*, and said that by the soul
Only, the Nations shall be great and free.

London, 1802

Milton! thou shouldst be living at this hour:
England hath need of thee: she is a fen
Of stagnant waters: altar, sword, and pen,
Fireside, the heroic wealth of hall and bower,
Have forfeited their ancient English dower
Of inward happiness. We are selfish men;
Oh! raise us up, return to us again;
And give us manners, virtue, freedom, power.
Thy soul was like a Star, and dwelt apart:

10   Thou hadst a voice whose sound was like the sea:
      Pure as the naked heavens, majestic, free,
      So didst thou travel on life's common way,
      In cheerful godliness; and yet thy heart
      The lowliest duties on herself did lay.

Written in London, September, 1802

      O Friend! I know not which way I must look
      For comfort, being, as I am, opprest,
      To think that now our life is only drest
      For show; mean handy-work of craftsman, cook,
      Or groom! – We must run glittering like a brook
      In the open sunshine, or we are unblest:
      The wealthiest man among us is the best:
      No grandeur now in nature or in book
      Delights us. Rapine, avarice, expense,
10   This is idolatry; and these we adore:
      Plain living and high thinking are no more:
      The homely beauty of the good old cause
      Is gone; our peace, our fearful innocence,
      And pure religion breathing household laws.

Composed after a Journey across the Hambleton Hills, Yorkshire

      Dark and more dark the shades of evening fell;
      The wished-for point was reached – but at an hour
      When little could be gained from that rich dower
      Of prospect, whereof many thousands tell.
      Yet did the glowing west with marvellous power
      Salute us; there stood Indian citadel,
      Temple of Greece, and minster with its tower
      Substantially expressed – a place for bell
      Or clock to toll from! Many a tempting isle,
10   With groves that never were imagined, lay

'Mid seas how stedfast! objects all for the eye
Of silent rapture; but we felt the while
We should forget them; they are of the sky,
And from our earthly memory fade away.

'Those words were uttered as in pensive mood'

– 'they are of the sky,
And from our earthly memory fade away.'

Those words were uttered as in pensive mood
We turned, departing from that solemn sight:
A contrast and reproach to gross delight,
And life's unspiritual pleasures daily wooed!
But now upon this thought I cannot brood;
It is unstable as a dream of night;
Nor will I praise a cloud, however bright,
Disparaging Man's gifts, and proper food.
Grove, isle, with every shape of sky-built dome,
10 Though clad in colours beautiful and pure,
Find in the heart of man no natural home:
The immortal Mind craves objects that endure:
These cleave to it; from these it cannot roam,
Nor they from it: their fellowship is secure.

[Translation of Ariosto]

Orlando who great length of time had been
Enamoured of the fair Angelica
And left for her beyond the Indian seas
In Media, Tartary and lands between
Infinite trophies to endure for aye,
Now to the west with her had bent his way
Where underneath the lofty Pyrenees
With might of French and Germans, Charlemagne
Had pitched his tents upon the open plain.

10   To make Marsilius and king Agramont
Each for his senseless daring smite his head,
The one for having out of Afric led
As many as could carry spear or lance,
The other for pushing all Spain militant
To overthrow the beauteous realm of France;
Thus in fit time Orlando reached the tents
But of his coming quickly he repents.

For there to him was his fair Lady lost,
Taken away! how frail our judgements are
20   She who from western unto eastern coast
[   ] with so long a war
Was taken from him now 'mid such a band
Of his own friends and in his native land,
Not one sword drawn to help the thing or bar!
'Twas the sage Emperor wishing much to slake
A burning feud who did the Lady take.

For quarrels had sprung lately and yet were
Twixt Count Orlando and Rinaldo; wroth
Were the two kinsmen, for that beauty rare
30   With amorous desire had moved them both.
The Emperor Charles who looked with little favour
On such contention, to make fast the aid
The two Knights owed him took away the Maid
And to Duke Namo he in wardship gave her,

Promising her to him who of the two
During that contest on that mighty day,
The greatest host of Infidels should slay
And most excelling feats in battle do;
But the baptized, who looked not for such fate,
40   On that day's conflict fled their foes before;
The Duke a prisoner was with many more
And the Pavillion was left desolate.

Wherein the Lady (as it were in thrall
Remaining there to be the Victor's prize)

Mounted, to meet such chance as might befall,
Her courser and at length away she flies.
[Presaging?] Fortune would the Christian faith
Disown that day, into a wood she hies,
Where she a knight on foot encountered hath
50 Who was approaching on a narrow path.

Helmet on head and cuirass on his back,
Sword by his side and on his arm his shield,
He ran more lightly on the forest track
Than swain half naked racing in the field;
Never did Shepherdess when she hath spied
A snake turn round so quickly in her fear
As drew Angelica the rein aside
When she beheld the knight approaching near.

This was that doughty Paladin, the Son
60 Of Amon Lord of Montalban in France,
From whom his steed Bayardo by strange chance
Had slipped not long before and loose had run.
Soon as he to the Lady turned his eyes,
Though distant, he that mien angelical
And that fair countenance did recognize,
Whereby his knightly heart was held in thrall.

The affrighted Lady turned her Horse around
And drove him with loose bridle through the wood,
Nor e'er in rough or smooth did she take thought
70 If safer way or better might be found;
But pale and trembling, taking her of naught
She left the horse to find what way he could;
Now up now down along the forest fast
She drove and to a river came at last.

There was Ferráno on the river brink
All overspread with dust and faint with heat;
Who thither from the fight had come to drink
And to repose himself in this retreat;

And there though loth was he compelled to stay;
80　His helmet while with thirst he drank amain
　　Had slipped into the river where it lay,
　　Nor [could?] he yet recover it again.

Sonnet Translated from the Italian of Milton

Written during his travels

A plain youth, Lady, and a simple lover,
　Since of myself a last leave I must take,
　To you devoutly of my heart I make
An humble gift, and doing this I proffer
A heart that is intrepid, slow to waver,
　Gracious in thought, discreet, good, prompt, awake,
　If the great earth should to her centre shake,
Armed in itself, and adamant all over;
Not more secure from envy, chance, desire,
10　And vulgar hopes and fears that vex the earth,
　Than wedded to high valour, wit, and worth,
　To the sweet Muses, and the sounding lyre:
Weak only will you find it in that part
Where Love incurably hath fixed his dart.

*Cantata, from Metastasio

LAURA, farewell my LAURA!
　'Tis come, that hour distressing;
How shall I live, my blessing,
　So far from thee?
Sorrow will still pursue me,
　No good will e'er come to me;
And thou, who knowst if ever
　Thou wilt remember me?

Let, at least, in the footing
10　Of my peace that is departed,

Some thoughts heavy-hearted
  Thy pursuivants be:
Though far off, still in union,
  I will be thy companion;
And thou, who knowst if ever
  Thou wilt remember me!

[*Translations from Metastasio*]

I

To the grove, the meadow, the well
I will go with the flock I love;
At the well, in the meadow, the grove,
LAURA will find with me,
Whatever shed or cell
Shall to us a covert be
That there, with pleasure and glee,
Innocence will dwell.

II

The Swallow, that hath lost
  His mate and lover,
  Flies from coast to coast,
  All the country over;
  Nor finds rest on earth beneath him
  Pastime in heaven above;
Crystal fountain, sunny river
  Seeks no more, forsakes the daylight,
  And, in his lonesome life, he ever
  Remembers his first love.

III

Oh! blessed all bliss above,
  Innocent shepherdesses,
  Whom in love no law distresses,
  Who have no law but love.
Could I, as ye may do,

Who, concealed, adore him,
Tell what love I have for him;
   Blessed were I too
   All bliss above.

IV

I will be that fond Mother
   Who her Babe doth threaten
   Yet is it never beaten
   Never at all.
She lifts her hand to strike it
   But the blow intended
   By Love is suspended
   When it would fall.

V

Gentle Zephyr,
   If you pass her by,
   Tell her you're a sigh;
   But tell her not from whom.

Limpid Streamlet,
   If you meet her ever,
   Say, with your best endeavour,
   That swoln with tears you come;
   But tell her not of whom.

'*Nuns fret not at their convent's narrow room*'

Nuns fret not at their convent's narrow room;
And hermits are contented with their cells;
And students with their pensive citadels;
Maids at the wheel, the weaver at his loom,
Sit blithe and happy; bees that soar for bloom,
High as the highest Peak of Furness-fells,
Will murmur by the hour in foxglove bells:
In truth the prison, unto which we doom

Ourselves, no prison is: and hence for me,
10 In sundry moods, 'twas pastime to be bound
Within the Sonnet's scanty plot of ground;
Pleased if some Souls (for such there needs must be)
Who have felt the weight of too much liberty,
Should find brief solace there, as I have found.

[*Translation of the Sestet of a Sonnet by Tasso*]

Camoëns, he the accomplished and the good,
Gave to thy fame a more illustrious flight
Than that brave vessel, though she sailed so far;
Through him her course along the Austral flood
Is known to all beneath the polar star,
Through him the Antipodes in thy name delight.

At the Grave of Burns, 1803
Seven Years after his Death

I shiver, Spirit fierce and bold,
At thought of what I now behold:
As vapours breathed from dungeons cold
       Strike pleasure dead,
So sadness comes from out the mould
       Where Burns is laid.

And have I then thy bones so near,
And thou forbidden to appear?
As if it were thyself that's here
10   I shrink with pain;
And both my wishes and my fear
       Alike are vain.

Off weight – nor press on weight! – away
Dark thoughts! – they came, but not to stay;

With chastened feelings would I pay
    The tribute due
To him, and aught that hides his clay
    From mortal view.

Fresh as the flower, whose modest worth
20 He sang, his genius 'glinted' forth,
Rose like a star that touching earth,
    For so it seems,
Doth glorify its humble birth
    With matchless beams.

The piercing eye, the thoughtful brow,
The struggling heart, where be they now? –
Full soon the Aspirant of the plough,
    The prompt, the brave,
Slept, with the obscurest, in the low
30   And silent grave.

I mourned with thousands, but as one
More deeply grieved, for He was gone
Whose light I hailed when first it shone,
    And showed my youth
How Verse may build a princely throne
    On humble truth.

Alas! where'er the current tends,
Regret pursues and with it blends, –
Huge Criffel's hoary top ascends
40   By Skiddaw seen, –
Neighbours we were, and loving friends
    We might have been;

True friends though diversely inclined;
But heart with heart and mind with mind,
Where the main fibres are entwined,
    Through Nature's skill,
May even by contraries be joined
    More closely still.

The tear will start, and let it flow;
50   Thou 'poor Inhabitant below,'
At this dread moment – even so –
    Might we together
Have sate and talked where gowans blow,
    Or on wild heather.

What treasures would have then been placed
Within my reach; of knowledge graced
By fancy what a rich repast!
    But why go on? –
Oh! spare to sweep, thou mournful blast,
60   His grave grass-grown.

There, too, a Son, his joy and pride,
(Not three weeks past the Stripling died,)
Lies gathered to his Father's side,
    Soul-moving sight!
Yet one to which is not denied
    Some sad delight.

For *he* is safe, a quiet bed
Hath early found among the dead,
Harboured where none can be misled,
70   Wronged, or distrest;
And surely here it may be said
    That such are blest.

And oh for Thee, by pitying grace
Checked oft-times in a devious race,
May He who halloweth the place
    Where Man is laid
Receive thy Spirit in the embrace
    For which it prayed!

Sighing I turned away; but ere
80 Night fell I heard, or seemed to hear,

Music that sorrow comes not near,
    A ritual hymn,
Chanted in love that casts out fear
    By Seraphim.

Thoughts Suggested the Day Following,
on the Banks of Nith, near the Poet's Residence

Too frail to keep the lofty vow
That must have followed when his brow
Was wreathed – 'The Vision' tells us how –
    With holly spray,
He faltered, drifted to and fro,
    And passed away.

Well might such thoughts, dear Sister, throng
Our minds when, lingering all too long,
Over the grave of Burns we hung
10   In social grief –
Indulged as if it were a wrong
    To seek relief.

But, leaving each unquiet theme
Where gentlest judgements may misdeem,
And prompt to welcome every gleam
    Of good and fair,
Let us beside the limpid Stream
    Breathe hopeful air.

Enough of sorrow, wreck, and blight;
20   Think rather of those moments bright
When to the consciousness of right
    His course was true,
When Wisdom prospered in his sight
    And virtue grew.

Yes, freely let our hearts expand,
Freely as in youth's season bland,
When side by side, his Book in hand,
    We wont to stray,
Our pleasure varying at command
30   Of each sweet Lay.

How oft inspired must he have trod
These pathways, yon far-stretching road!
There lurks his home; in that Abode,
    With mirth elate,
Or in his nobly-pensive mood,
    The Rustic sate.

Proud thoughts that Image overawes,
Before it humbly let us pause,
And ask of Nature from what cause
40   And by what rules
She trained her Burns to win applause
    That shames the Schools.

Through busiest street and loneliest glen
Are felt the flashes of his pen;
He rules 'mid winter snows, and when
    Bees fill their hives;
Deep in the general heart of men
    His power survives.

What need of fields in some far clime
50   Where Heroes, Sages, Bards sublime,
And all that fetched the flowing rhyme
    From genuine springs,
Shall dwell together till old Time
    Folds up his wings?

Sweet Mercy! to the gates of Heaven
This Minstrel lead, his sins forgiven;

The rueful conflict, the heart riven
   With vain endeavour,
And memory of Earth's bitter leaven,
60   Effaced for ever.

But why to Him confine the prayer,
When kindred thoughts and yearnings bear
On the frail heart the purest share
   With all that live? –
The best of what we do and are,
   Just God, forgive!

Address to Kilchurn Castle, upon Loch Awe

'From the top of the hill a most impressive scene opened upon
our view, – a ruined Castle on an Island (for an Island the flood
had made it) at some distance from the shore, backed by a Cove
of the Mountain Cruachan, down which came a foaming
stream. The Castle occupied every foot of the Island that was
visible to us, appearing to rise out of the water, – mists rested
upon the mountain side, with spots of sunshine; there was a
mild desolation in the low grounds, a solemn grandeur in the
mountains, and the Castle was wild, yet stately – not dismantled
of turrets – nor the walls broken down, though obviously a
ruin.' – *Extract from the Journal of my Companion.*

Child of loud-throated War! the mountain Stream
Roars in thy hearing; but thy hour of rest
Is come, and thou art silent in thy age;
Save when the wind sweeps by and sounds are caught
Ambiguous, neither wholly thine nor theirs.
Oh! there is life that breathes not; Powers there are
That touch each other to the quick in modes
Which the gross world no sense hath to perceive,
No soul to dream of. What art Thou, from care
10 Cast off – abandoned by thy rugged Sire,
Nor by soft Peace adopted; though, in place
And in dimension, such that thou mightst seem
But a mere footstool to yon sovereign Lord,

Huge Cruachan, (a thing that meaner hills
Might crush, nor know that it had suffered harm;)
Yet he, not loth, in favour of thy claims
To reverence, suspends his own; submitting
All that the God of Nature hath conferred,
All that he holds in common with the stars,
20 To the memorial majesty of Time
Impersonated in thy calm decay!

Take, then, thy seat, Vicegerent unreproved!
Now, while a farewell gleam of evening light
Is fondly lingering on thy shattered front,
Do thou, in turn, be paramount; and rule
Over the pomp and beauty of a scene
Whose mountains, torrents, lake, and woods, unite
To pay thee homage; and with these are joined,
In willing admiration and respect,
30 Two Hearts, which in thy presence might be called
Youthful as Spring. – Shade of departed Power,
Skeleton of unfleshed humanity,
The chronicle were welcome that should call
Into the compass of distinct regard
The toils and struggles of thy infant years!
Yon foaming flood seems motionless as ice;
Its dizzy turbulence eludes the eye,
Frozen by distance; so, majestic Pile,
To the perception of this Age, appear
40 Thy fierce beginnings, softened and subdued
And quieted in character – the strife,
The pride, the fury uncontrollable,
Lost on the aërial heights of the Crusades!

Sonnet Composed at — Castle

Degenerate Douglas! oh, the unworthy Lord!
Whom mere despite of heart could so far please,
And love of havoc, (for with such disease

Fame taxes him,) that he could send forth word
To level with the dust a noble horde,
A brotherhood of venerable Trees,
Leaving an ancient dome, and towers like these,
Beggared and outraged! – Many hearts deplored
The fate of those old Trees; and oft with pain
10 The traveller, at this day, will stop and gaze
On wrongs, which Nature scarcely seems to heed:
For sheltered places, bosoms, nooks, and bays,
And the pure mountains, and the gentle Tweed,
And the green silent pastures, yet remain.

'Fly, some kind Harbinger, to Grasmere-dale!'

Fly, some kind Harbinger, to Grasmere-dale!
Say that we come, and come by this day's light;
Fly upon swiftest wing round field and height,
But chiefly let one Cottage hear the tale;
There let a mystery of joy prevail,
The kitten frolic, like a gamesome sprite,
And Rover whine, as at a second sight
Of near-approaching good that shall not fail:
And from that Infant's face let joy appear;
10 Yea, let our Mary's one companion child –
That hath her six weeks' solitude beguiled
With intimations manifold and dear,
While we have wandered over wood and wild –
Smile on his Mother now with bolder cheer.

To the Men of Kent. October, 1803

Vanguard of Liberty, ye men of Kent,
Ye children of a Soil that doth advance
Her haughty brow against the coast of France,
Now is the time to prove your hardiment!
To France be words of invitation sent!

They from their fields can see the countenance
Of your fierce war, may ken the glittering lance
And hear you shouting forth your brave intent.
Left single, in bold parley, ye, of yore,
10   Did from the Norman win a gallant wreath;
Confirmed the charters that were yours before; –
No parleying now! In Britain is one breath;
We all are with you now from shore to shore: –
Ye men of Kent, 'tis victory or death!

Anticipation. October, 1803

Shout, for a mighty Victory is won!
On British ground the Invaders are laid low;
The breath of Heaven has drifted them like snow,
And left them lying in the silent sun,
Never to rise again! – the work is done.
Come forth, ye old men, now in peaceful show
And greet your sons! drums beat and trumpets blow!
Make merry, wives! ye little children, stun
Your grandames' ears with pleasure of your noise!
10   Clap, infants, clap your hands! Divine must be
That triumph, when the very worst, the pain,
And even the prospect of our brethren slain,
Hath something in it which the heart enjoys: –
In glory will they sleep and endless sanctity.

Sonnet in the Pass of Killicranky

An invasion being expected, October, 1803.

Six thousand veterans practised in war's game,
Tried men, at Killicranky were arrayed
Against an equal host that wore the plaid,
Shepherds and herdsmen. – Like a whirlwind came
The Highlanders, the slaughter spread like flame;
And Garry, thundering down his mountain-road,

Was stopped, and could not breathe beneath the load
Of the dead bodies. – 'Twas a day of shame
For them whom precept and the pedantry
10 Of cold mechanic battle do enslave.
O for a single hour of that Dundee,
Who on that day the word of onset gave!
Like conquest would the Men of England see;
And her Foes find a like inglorious grave.

Lines on the Expected Invasion 1803

Come ye – who, if (which Heaven avert!) the Land
Were with herself at strife, would take your stand,
Like gallant Falkland, by the Monarch's side,
And, like Montrose, make Loyalty your pride –
Come ye – who, not less zealous, might display
Banners at enmity with regal sway,
And, like the Pyms and Miltons of that day,
Think that a State would live in sounder health
If Kingship bowed its head to Commonwealth –
10 Ye too – whom no discreditable fear
Would keep, perhaps with many a fruitless tear,
Uncertain what to choose and how to steer –
And ye – who might mistake for sober sense
And wise reserve the plea of indolence –
Come ye – whate'er your creed – O waken all,
Whate'er your temper, at your Country's call;
Resolving (this a free-born Nation can)
To have one Soul, and perish to a man,
Or save this honoured Land from every Lord
20 But British reason and the British sword.

October, 1803

One might believe that natural miseries
Had blasted France, and made of it a land
Unfit for men; and that in one great band

Her sons were bursting forth, to dwell at ease.
But 'tis a chosen soil, where sun and breeze
Shed gentle favours: rural works are there,
And ordinary business without care;
Spot rich in all things that can soothe and please!
How piteous then that there should be such dearth
10   Of knowledge; that whole myriads should unite
To work against themselves such fell despite:
Should come in phrensy and in drunken mirth,
Impatient to put out the only light
Of Liberty that yet remains on earth!

October, 1803

These times strike monied worldlings with dismay:
Even rich men, brave by nature, taint the air
With words of apprehension and despair:
While tens of thousands, thinking on the affray,
Men unto whom sufficient for the day
And minds not stinted or untilled are given,
Sound, healthy, children of the God of heaven,
Are cheerful as the rising sun in May.
What do we gather hence but firmer faith
10   That every gift of noble origin
Is breathed upon by Hope's perpetual breath;
That virtue and the faculties within
Are vital, – and that riches are akin
To fear, to change, to cowardice, and death?

October, 1803

When, looking on the present face of things,
I see one man, of men the meanest too!
Raised up to sway the world, to do, undo,
With mighty Nations for his underlings,
The great events with which old story rings

Seem vain and hollow; I find nothing great:
Nothing is left which I can venerate;
So that a doubt almost within me springs
Of Providence, such emptiness at length
10 Seems at the heart of all things. But, great God!
I measure back the steps which I have trod;
And tremble, seeing whence proceeds the strength
Of such poor Instruments, with thoughts sublime
I tremble at the sorrow of the time.

To a Highland Girl
(*at Inversneyde, upon Loch Lomond*)

Sweet Highland Girl, a very shower
Of beauty is thy earthly dower!
Twice seven consenting years have shed
Their utmost bounty on thy head:
And these grey rocks; that household lawn;
Those trees, a veil just half withdrawn;
This fall of water that doth make
A murmur near the silent lake;
This little bay; a quiet road
10 That holds in shelter thy Abode –
In truth together do ye seem
Like something fashioned in a dream;
Such Forms as from their covert peep
When earthly cares are laid asleep!
But, O fair Creature! in the light
Of common day, so heavenly bright,
I bless Thee, Vision as thou art,
I bless thee with a human heart;
God shield thee to thy latest years!
20 Thee, neither know I, nor thy peers;
And yet my eyes are filled with tears.

With earnest feeling I shall pray
For thee when I am far away:
For never saw I mien, or face,

In which more plainly I could trace
Benignity and home-bred sense
Ripening in perfect innocence.
Here scattered, like a random seed,
Remote from men, Thou dost not need
30 The embarrassed look of shy distress,
And maidenly shamefacedness:
Thou wear'st upon thy forehead clear
The freedom of a Mountaineer:
A face with gladness overspread!
Soft smiles, by human kindness bred!
And seemliness complete, that sways
Thy courtesies, about thee plays;
With no restraint, but such as springs
From quick and eager visitings
40 Of thoughts that lie beyond the reach
Of thy few words of English speech:
A bondage sweetly brooked, a strife
That gives thy gestures grace and life!
So have I, not unmoved in mind,
Seen birds of tempest-loving kind –
Thus beating up against the wind.

What hand but would a garland cull
For thee who art so beautiful?
O happy pleasure! here to dwell
50 Beside thee in some heathy dell;
Adopt your homely ways, and dress,
A Shepherd, thou a Shepherdess!
But I could frame a wish for thee
More like a grave reality:
Thou art to me but as a wave
Of the wild sea; and I would have
Some claim upon thee, if I could,
Though but of common neighbourhood.
What joy to hear thee, and to see!
60 Thy elder Brother I would be,
Thy Father – anything to thee!

Now thanks to Heaven! that of its grace
Hath led me to this lonely place.
Joy have I had; and going hence
I bear away my recompense.
In spots like these it is we prize
Our Memory, feel that she hath eyes:
Then, why should I be loth to stir?
I feel this place was made for her;
70 To give new pleasure like the past,
Continued long as life shall last.
Nor am I loth, though pleased at heart,
Sweet Highland Girl! from thee to part;
For I, methinks, till I grow old,
As fair before me shall behold,
As I do now, the cabin small,
The lake, the bay, the waterfall;
And Thee, the Spirit of them all!

Yarrow Unvisited

See the various Poems the scene of which is laid upon the banks
of the Yarrow; in particular, the exquisite Ballad of Hamilton
beginning
'Busk ye, busk ye, my bonny, bonny Bride,
Busk ye, busk ye, my winsome Marrow!' –

From Stirling castle we had seen
The mazy Forth unravelled;
Had trod the banks of Clyde, and Tay,
And with the Tweed had travelled;
And when we came to Clovenford,
Then said my '*winsome Marrow*,'
'Whate'er betide, we'll turn aside,
And see the Braes of Yarrow.'

'Let Yarrow folk, *frae* Selkirk town,
10 Who have been buying, selling,

Go back to Yarrow, 'tis their own;
Each maiden to her dwelling!
On Yarrow's banks let herons feed,
Hares couch, and rabbits burrow!
But we will downward with the Tweed,
Nor turn aside to Yarrow.

'There's Galla Water, Leader Haughs,
Both lying right before us;
And Dryborough, where with chiming Tweed
20 The lintwhites sing in chorus;
There's pleasant Tiviot-dale, a land
Made blithe with plough and harrow:
Why throw away a needful day
To go in search of Yarrow?

'What's Yarrow but a river bare,
That glides the dark hills under?
There are a thousand such elsewhere
As worthy of your wonder.'
– Strange words they seemed of slight and scorn;
30 My True-love sighed for sorrow;
And looked me in the face, to think
I thus could speak of Yarrow!

'Oh! green,' said I, 'are Yarrow's holms,
And sweet is Yarrow flowing!
Fair hangs the apple frae the rock,
But we will leave it growing.
O'er hilly path, and open Strath,
We'll wander Scotland thorough;
But, though so near, we will not turn
40 Into the dale of Yarrow.

'Let beeves and home-bred kine partake
The sweets of Burn-mill meadow;
The swan on still St Mary's Lake
Float double, swan and shadow!

We will not see them; will not go,
Today, nor yet tomorrow;
Enough if in our hearts we know
There's such a place as Yarrow.

'Be Yarrow stream unseen, unknown!
50 It must, or we shall rue it:
We have a vision of our own;
Ah! why should we undo it?
The treasured dreams of times long past,
We'll keep them, winsome Marrow!
For when we're there, although 'tis fair,
'Twill be another Yarrow!

'If Care with freezing years should come,
And wandering seem but folly, –
Should we be loth to stir from home,
60 And yet be melancholy;
Should life be dull, and spirits low,
'Twill soothe us in our sorrow,
That earth hath something yet to show,
The bonny holms of Yarrow!'

At Applethwaite, near Keswick

Beaumont! it was thy wish that I should rear
A seemly Cottage in this sunny Dell,
On favoured ground, thy gift, where I might dwell
In neighbourhood with One to me most dear,
That undivided we from year to year
Might work in our high Calling – a bright hope
To which our fancies, mingling, gave free scope
Till checked by some necessities severe.
And should these slacken, honoured BEAUMONT! still
10 Even then we may perhaps in vain implore
Leave of our fate thy wishes to fulfil.

Whether this boon be granted us or not,
Old Skiddaw will look down upon the Spot
With pride, the Muses love it evermore.

'She was a Phantom of delight'

She was a Phantom of delight
When first she gleamed upon my sight;
A lovely Apparition, sent
To be a moment's ornament;
Her eyes as stars of Twilight fair;
Like Twilight's, too, her dusky hair;
But all things else about her drawn
From May-time and the cheerful Dawn;
A dancing Shape, an Image gay,
10 To haunt, to startle, and way-lay.

I saw her upon nearer view,
A Spirit, yet a Woman too!
Her household motions light and free,
And steps of virgin-liberty;
A countenance in which did meet
Sweet records, promises as sweet;
A Creature not too bright or good
For human nature's daily food;
For transient sorrows, simple wiles,
20 Praise, blame, love, kisses, tears, and smiles.

And now I see with eye serene
The very pulse of the machine;
A Being breathing thoughtful breath,
A Traveller between life and death;
The reason firm, the temperate will,
Endurance, foresight, strength, and skill;
A perfect Woman, nobly planned,
To warn, to comfort, and command;
And yet a Spirit still, and bright
30 With something of angelic light.

The Small Celandine

There is a Flower, the lesser Celandine,
That shrinks, like many more, from cold and rain;
And, the first moment that the sun may shine,
Bright as the sun himself, 'tis out again!

When hailstones have been falling, swarm on swarm,
Or blasts the green field and the trees distrest,
Oft have I seen it muffled up from harm,
In close self-shelter, like a Thing at rest.

But lately, one rough day, this Flower I passed
10 And recognized it, though an altered form,
Now standing forth an offering to the blast,
And buffeted at will by rain and storm.

I stopped, and said with inly-muttered voice,
'It doth not love the shower, nor seek the cold:
This neither is its courage nor its choice,
But its necessity in being old.

'The sunshine may not cheer it, nor the dew;
It cannot help itself in its decay;
Stiff in its members, withered, changed of hue.'
20 And, in my spleen, I smiled that it was grey.

To be a Prodigal's Favourite – then, worse truth,
A Miser's Pensioner – behold our lot!
O Man, that from thy fair and shining youth
Age might but take the things Youth needed not!

[*Fragment: 'Along the mazes of this song I go'*]

Along the mazes of this song I go
As inward motions of the wandering thought
Lead me, or outward circumstance impels.
Thus do I urge a never-ending way
Year after year, with many a sleep between,
Through joy and sorrow; if my lot be joy
More joyful if it be with sorrow soothed.

Ode to Duty

'Jam non consilio bonus, sed more eò perductus, ut non tantum
rectè facere possim, sed nisi rectè facere non possim.'

Stern Daughter of the Voice of God!
O Duty! if that name thou love
Who art a light to guide, a rod
To check the erring, and reprove;
Thou, who art victory and law
When empty terrors overawe;
From vain temptations dost set free;
And calm'st the weary strife of frail humanity!

There are who ask not if thine eye
10   Be on them; who, in love and truth,
Where no misgiving is, rely
Upon the genial sense of youth:
Glad Hearts! without reproach or blot;
Who do thy work, and know it not:
Oh! if through confidence misplaced
They fail, thy saving arms, dread Power! around them
        cast.

Serene will be our days and bright,
And happy will our nature be,
When love is an unerring light,

20   And joy its own security.
And they a blissful course may hold
Even now, who, not unwisely bold,
Live in the spirit of this creed;
Yet seek thy firm support, according to their need.

I, loving freedom, and untried;
No sport of every random gust,
Yet being to myself a guide,
Too blindly have reposed my trust:
And oft, when in my heart was heard
30   Thy timely mandate, I deferred
The task, in smoother walks to stray;
But thee I now would serve more strictly, if I may.

Through no disturbance of my soul,
Or strong compunction in me wrought,
I supplicate for thy control;
But in the quietness of thought:
Me this unchartered freedom tires;
I feel the weight of chance-desires:
My hopes no more must change their name,
40   I long for a repose that ever is the same.

[Yet not the less would I throughout
Still act according to the voice
Of my own wish; and feel past doubt.
That my submissiveness was choice:
Not seeking in the school of pride
For 'precepts over dignified',
Denial and restraint I prize
No farther than they breed a second Will more wise.]

Stern Lawgiver! yet thou dost wear
50   The Godhead's most benignant grace;
Nor know we anything so fair
As is the smile upon thy face:
Flowers laugh before thee on their beds

And fragrance in thy footing treads;
Thou dost preserve the stars from wrong;
And the most ancient heavens, through Thee, are fresh
    and strong.

To humbler functions, awful Power!
I call thee: I myself commend
Unto thy guidance from this hour;
60   Oh, let my weakness have an end!
Give unto me, made lowly wise,
The spirit of self-sacrifice;
The confidence of reason give;
And in the light of truth thy Bondman let me live!

The Matron of Jedborough and Her Husband

At Jedborough, my companion and I went into private lodgings
for a few days; and the following Verses were called forth by
the character and domestic situation of our Hostess.

Age! twine thy brows with fresh spring flowers,
And call a train of laughing Hours;
And bid them dance, and bid them sing;
And thou, too, mingle in the ring!
Take to thy heart a new delight;
If not, make merry in despite
That there is One who scorns thy power: –
But dance! for under Jedborough Tower
A Matron dwells who, though she bears
10   The weight of more than seventy years,
Lives in the light of youthful glee,
And she will dance and sing with thee.

   Nay! start not at that Figure – there!
Him who is rooted to his chair!
Look at him – look again! for he
Hath long been of thy family.
With legs that move not, if they can,
And useless arms, a trunk of man,

He sits, and with a vacant eye;
20 A sight to make a stranger sigh!
Deaf, drooping, that is now his doom:
His world is in this single room:
Is this a place for mirthful cheer?
Can merry-making enter here?

    The joyous Woman is the Mate
Of him in that forlorn estate!
He breathes a subterraneous damp;
But bright as Vesper shines her lamp:
He is as mute as Jedborough Tower:
30 She jocund as it was of yore,
With all its bravery on; in times
When all alive with merry chimes,
Upon a sun-bright morn of May,
It roused the Vale to holiday.

    I praise thee, Matron! and thy due
Is praise, heroic praise, and true!
With admiration I behold
Thy gladness unsubdued and bold:
Thy looks, thy gestures, all present
40 The picture of a life well spent:
This do I see; and something more;
A strength unthought of heretofore!
Delighted am I for thy sake;
And yet a higher joy partake:
Our Human-nature throws away
Its second twilight, and looks gay;
A land of promise and of pride
Unfolding, wide as life is wide.

    Ah! see her helpless Charge! enclosed
50 Within himself as seems, composed;
To fear of loss, and hope of gain,
The strife of happiness and pain,

Utterly dead! yet in the guise
Of little infants, when their eyes
Begin to follow to and fro
The persons that before them go,
He tracks her motions, quick or slow.
Her buoyant spirit can prevail
Where common cheerfulness would fail;
60   She strikes upon him with the heat
Of July suns; he feels it sweet;
An animal delight though dim!
'Tis all that now remains for him!

The more I looked, I wondered more –
And, while I scanned them o'er and o'er,
Some inward trouble suddenly
Broke from the Matron's strong black eye –
A remnant of uneasy light,
A flash of something over-bright!
70   Nor long this mystery did detain
My thoughts; – she told in pensive strain
That she had borne a heavy yoke,
Been stricken by a twofold stroke;
Ill health of body; and had pined
Beneath worse ailments of the mind.

So be it! – but let praise ascend
To Him who is our lord and friend!
Who from disease and suffering
Hath called for thee a second spring;
80   Repaid thee for that sore distress
By no untimely joyousness;
Which makes of thine a blissful state;
And cheers thy melancholy Mate!

The Blind Highland Boy
A Tale Told by the Fire-side, after Returning
to the Vale of Grasmere

Now we are tired of boisterous joy,
Have romped enough, my little Boy!
Jane hangs her head upon my breast,
And you shall bring your stool and rest;
  This corner is your own.

There! take your seat, and let me see
That you can listen quietly:
And, as I promised, I will tell
That strange adventure which befell
10 A poor blind Highland Boy.

A *Highland* Boy! – why call him so?
Because, my Darlings, ye must know
That, under hills which rise like towers,
Far higher hills than these of ours!
  He from his birth had lived.

He ne'er had seen one earthly sight;
The sun, the day; the stars, the night;
Or tree, or butterfly, or flower,
Or fish in stream, or bird in bower,
20 Or woman, man, or child.

And yet he neither drooped nor pined,
Nor had a melancholy mind;
For God took pity on the Boy,
And was his friend; and gave him joy
  Of which we nothing know.

His Mother, too, no doubt, above
Her other children him did love:

For, was she here, or was she there,
She thought of him with constant care,
30   And more than mother's love.

And proud she was of heart, when clad
In crimson stockings, tartan plaid,
And bonnet with a feather gay,
To Kirk he on the sabbath day
      Went hand in hand with her.

A dog, too, had he; not for need,
But one to play with and to feed;
Which would have led him, if bereft
Of company or friends, and left
40   Without a better guide.

And then the bagpipes he could blow –
And thus from house to house would go;
And all were pleased to hear and see,
For none made sweeter melody
      Than did the poor blind Boy.

Yet he had many a restless dream;
Both when he heard the eagles scream,
And when he heard the torrents roar,
And heard the water beat the shore
50   Near which their cottage stood.

Beside a lake their cottage stood,
Not small like ours, a peaceful flood;
But one of mighty size, and strange;
That, rough or smooth, is full of change,
      And stirring in its bed.

For to this lake, by night and day,
The great Sea-water finds its way
Through long, long windings of the hills
And drinks up all the pretty rills
60   And rivers large and strong:

Then hurries back the road it came –
Returns, on errand still the same;
This did it when the earth was new;
And this for evermore will do,
    As long as earth shall last.

And, with the coming of the tide,
Come boats and ships that safely ride
Between the woods and lofty rocks;
And to the shepherds with their flocks
70   Bring tales of distant lands.

And of those tales, whate'er they were,
The blind Boy always had his share;
Whether of mighty towns, or vales
With warmer suns and softer gales,
    Or wonders of the Deep.

Yet more it pleased him, more it stirred,
When from the water-side he heard
The shouting, and the jolly cheers;
The bustle of the mariners
80   In stillness or in storm.

But what do his desires avail?
For He must never handle sail;
Nor mount the mast, nor row, nor float
In sailor's ship, or fisher's boat,
    Upon the rocking waves.

His Mother often thought, and said,
What sin would be upon her head
If she should suffer this: 'My Son,
Whate'er you do, leave this undone;
90   The danger is so great.'

Thus lived he by Loch Leven's side
Still sounding with the sounding tide,

And heard the billows leap and dance,
Without a shadow of mischance,
        Till he was ten years old.

When one day (and now mark me well,
Ye soon shall know how this befell)
He in a vessel of his own
On the swift flood is hurrying down,
100   Down to the mighty Sea.

In such a vessel never more
May human creature leave the shore!
If this or that way he should stir,
Woe to the poor blind Mariner!
        For death will be his doom.

But say what bears him? – Ye have seen
The Indian's bow, his arrows keen,
Rare beasts, and birds with plumage bright;
Gifts which, for wonder or delight,
110   Are brought in ships from far.

Such gifts had those seafaring men
Spread round that haven in the glen;
Each hut, perchance, might have its own
And to the Boy they all were known –
        He knew and prized them all.

The rarest was a Turtle-shell
Which he, poor Child, had studied well;
A shell of ample size, and light
As the pearly car of Amphitrite,
120   That sportive dolphins drew.

And, as a Coracle that braves
On Vaga's breast the fretful waves,
This shell upon the deep would swim,
And gaily lift its fearless brim
        Above the tossing surge.

And this the little blind Boy knew;
And he a story strange yet true
Had heard, how in a shell like this
An English Boy, O thought of bliss!
130   Had stoutly launched from shore;

Launched from the margin of a bay
Among the Indian isles, where lay
His father's ship, and had sailed far –
To join that gallant ship of war,
       In his delightful shell.

Our Highland Boy oft visited
The house that held this prize; and, led
By choice or chance, did thither come
One day when no one was at home,
140   And found the door unbarred.

While there he sate, alone and blind,
That story flashed upon his mind; –
A bold thought roused him, and he took
The shell from out its secret nook,
       And bore it on his head.

He launched his vessel, – and in pride
Of spirit, from Loch Leven's side,
Stepped into it – his thoughts all free
As the light breezes that with glee
150   Sang through the adventurer's hair.

A while he stood upon his feet;
He felt the motion – took his seat;
Still better pleased as more and more
The tide retreated from the shore,
       And sucked, and sucked him in.

And there he is in face of Heaven.
How rapidly the Child is driven!

The fourth part of a mile, I ween,
He thus had gone, ere he was seen
160   By any human eye.

But when he was first seen, oh me
What shrieking and what misery!
For many saw; among the rest
His Mother, she who loved him best,
      She saw her poor blind Boy.

But for the child, the sightless Boy,
It is the triumph of his joy!
The bravest traveller in balloon,
Mounting as if to reach the moon,
170   Was never half so blessed.

And let him, let him go his way,
Alone, and innocent, and gay!
For, if good Angels love to wait
On the forlorn unfortunate,
      This Child will take no harm.

But now the passionate lament,
Which from the crowd on shore was sent,
The cries which broke from old and young
In Gaelic, or the English tongue,
180   Are stifled – all is still.

And quickly with a silent crew
A boat is ready to pursue;
And from the shore their course they take,
And swiftly down the running lake
      They follow the blind Boy.

But soon they move with softer pace;
So have ye seen the fowler chase
On Grasmere's clear unruffled breast
A youngling of the wild-duck's nest
190   With deftly-lifted oar;

Or as the wily sailors crept
To seize (while on the Deep it slept)
The hapless creature which did dwell
Erewhile within the dancing shell,
    They steal upon their prey.

With sound the least that can be made,
They follow, more and more afraid,
More cautious as they draw more near;
But in his darkness he can hear,
200   And guesses their intent.

'*Lei-gha* – *Lei-gha*' – he then cried out,
'*Lei-gha* – *Lei-gha*' – with eager shout;
Thus did he cry, and thus did pray,
And what he meant was 'Keep away,
    And leave me to myself!'

Alas! and when he felt their hands –
You've often heard of magic wands,
That with a motion overthrow
A palace of the proudest show,
210   Or melt it into air;

So all his dreams – that inward light
With which his soul had shone so bright –
All vanished; – 'twas a heartfelt cross
To him, a heavy, bitter loss,
    As he had ever known.

But hark! a gratulating voice,
With which the very hills rejoice:
'Tis from the crowd, who tremblingly
Have watched the event, and now can see
220   That he is safe at last.

And then, when he was brought to land,
Full sure they were a happy band,

Which, gathering round, did on the banks
Of that great Water give God thanks,
    And welcomed the poor Child.

And in the general joy of heart
The blind Boy's little dog took part;
He leapt about, and oft did kiss
His master's hands in sign of bliss,
230   With sound like lamentation.

But most of all, his Mother dear,
She who had fainted with her fear,
Rejoiced when waking she espies
The Child; when she can trust her eyes,
    And touches the blind Boy.

She led him home, and wept amain,
When he was in the house again:
Tears flowed in torrents from her eyes;
She kissed him – how could she chastise?
240   She was too happy far.

Thus, after he had fondly braved
The perilous Deep, the Boy was saved;
And, though his fancies had been wild,
Yet he was pleased and reconciled
    To live in peace on shore.

And in the lonely Highland dell
Still do they keep the Turtle-shell;
And long the story will repeat
Of the blind Boy's adventurous feat,
250   And how he was preserved.

NOTE. – It is recorded in Dampier's Voyages, that a boy, son of
the captain of a Man-of-War, seated himself in a Turtle-shell,
and floated in it from the shore to his father's ship, which lay
at anchor at the distance of half a mile. In deference to the

opinion of a Friend, I have substituted such a shell for the less
elegant vessel in which my blind Voyager did actually entrust
himself to the dangerous current of Loch Leven, as was related
to me by an eye-witness.

Admonition

Intended particularly for the perusal of those who may have
happened to be enamoured of some beautiful place of Retreat,
in the Country of the Lakes.

Well mayst thou halt – and gaze with brightening eye!
The lovely Cottage in the guardian nook
Hath stirred thee deeply; with its own dear brook,
Its own small pasture, almost its own sky!
But covet not the Abode; – forbear to sigh,
As many do, repining while they look;
Intruders – who would tear from Nature's book
This precious leaf, with harsh impiety.
Think what the Home must be if it were thine,
10 Even thine, though few thy wants! – Roof, window,
    door,
The very flowers are sacred to the Poor,
The roses to the porch which they entwine:
Yea, all, that now enchants thee, from the day
On which it should be touched, would melt away.

'Who fancied what a pretty sight'

Who fancied what a pretty sight
This Rock would be if edged around
With living snow-drops? circlet bright!
How glorious to this orchard-ground!
Who loved the little Rock, and set
Upon its head this coronet?

Was it the humour of a child?
Or rather of some gentle maid,
Whose brows, the day that she was styled
10   The shepherd-queen, were thus arrayed?
Of man mature, or matron sage?
Or old man toying with his age!

I asked – 'twas whispered; the device
To each and all might well belong:
It is the Spirit of Paradise
That prompts such work, a Spirit strong,
That gives to all the self-same bent
Where life is wise and innocent.

'I wandered lonely as a cloud'

I wandered lonely as a cloud
That floats on high o'er vales and hills,
When all at once I saw a crowd,
A host, of golden daffodils;
Beside the lake, beneath the trees,
Fluttering and dancing in the breeze.

Continuous as the stars that shine
And twinkle on the milky way,
They stretched in never-ending line
10   Along the margin of a bay:
Ten thousand saw I at a glance,
Tossing their heads in sprightly dance.

The waves beside them danced; but they
Out-did the sparkling waves in glee:
A poet could not but be gay,
In such a jocund company:
I gazed – and gazed – but little thought
What wealth the show to me had brought:

For oft, when on my couch I lie
20   In vacant or in pensive mood,
They flash upon that inward eye
Which is the bliss of solitude;
And then my heart with pleasure fills,
And dances with the daffodils.

Address to My Infant Daughter, Dora
on Being Reminded That She Was a Month Old
That Day, September 16

————Hast thou then survived –
Mild Offspring of infirm humanity,
Meek Infant! among all forlornest things
The most forlorn – one life of that bright star,
The second glory of the Heavens? – Thou hast;
Already hast survived that great decay,
That transformation through the wide earth felt,
And by all nations. In that Being's sight
From whom the Race of human kind proceed,
10   A thousand years are but as yesterday;
And one day's narrow circuit is to Him
Not less capacious than a thousand years.
But what is time? What outward glory? Neither
A measure is of Thee, whose claims extend
Through 'heaven's eternal year.' – Yet hail to Thee,
Frail, feeble, Monthling! – by that name, methinks,
Thy scanty breathing-time is portioned out
Not idly. – Hadst thou been of Indian birth,
Couched on a casual bed of moss and leaves,
20   And rudely canopied by leafy boughs,
Or to the churlish elements exposed
On the blank plains, – the coldness of the night,
Or the night's darkness, or its cheerful face
Of beauty, by the changing moon adorned,
Would, with imperious admonition, then

Have scored thine age, and punctually timed
Thine infant history, on the minds of those
Who might have wandered with thee. – Mother's love,
Nor less than mother's love in other breasts,
30 Will, among us warm-clad and warmly housed,
Do for thee what the finger of the heavens
Doth all too often harshly execute
For thy unblest coevals, amid wilds
Where fancy hath small liberty to grace
The affections, to exalt them or refine;
And the maternal sympathy itself,
Though strong, is, in the main, a joyless tie
Of naked instinct, wound about the heart.
Happier, far happier is thy lot and ours!
40 Even now – to solemnize thy helpless state,
And to enliven in the mind's regard
Thy passive beauty – parallels have risen,
Resemblances, or contrasts, that connect,
Within the region of a father's thoughts,
Thee and thy mate and sister of the sky.
And first; – thy sinless progress, through a world
By sorrow darkened and by care disturbed,
Apt likeness bears to hers, through gathered clouds
Moving untouched in silver purity,
50 And cheering oft-times their reluctant gloom.
Fair are ye both, and both are free from stain:
But thou, how leisurely thou fill'st thy horn
With brightness! leaving her to post along,
And range about, disquieted in change,
And still impatient of the shape she wears.
Once up, once down the hill, one journey, Babe,
That will suffice thee; and it seems that now
Thou hast foreknowledge that such task is thine;
Thou travellest so contentedly, and sleep'st
60 In such a heedless peace. Alas! full soon
Hath this conception, grateful to behold,
Changed countenance, like an object sullied o'er
By breathing mist; and thine appears to be

A mournful labour, while to her is given
Hope, and a renovation without end.
– That smile forbids the thought; for on thy face
Smiles are beginning, like the beams of dawn,
To shoot and circulate; smiles have there been seen;
Tranquil assurances that Heaven supports
70   The feeble motions of thy life, and cheers
Thy loneliness: or shall those smiles be called
Feelers of love, put forth as if to explore
This untried world, and to prepare thy way
Through a strait passage intricate and dim?
Such are they; and the same are tokens, signs,
Which, when the appointed season hath arrived,
Joy, as her holiest language, shall adopt;
And Reason's godlike Power be proud to own.

Yew-Trees

There is a Yew-tree, pride of Lorton Vale,
Which to this day stands single, in the midst
Of its own darkness, as it stood of yore:
Not loth to furnish weapons for the bands
Of Umfraville or Percy ere they marched
To Scotland's heaths; or those that crossed the sea
And drew their sounding bows at Azincour,
Perhaps at earlier Crecy, or Poictiers.
Of vast circumference and gloom profound
10   This solitary Tree! a living thing
Produced too slowly ever to decay;
Of form and aspect too magnificent
To be destroyed. But worthier still of note
Are those fraternal Four of Borrowdale,
Joined in one solemn and capacious grove;
Huge trunks! and each particular trunk a growth
Of intertwisted fibres serpentine
Up-coiling, and inveterately convolved;
Nor uninformed with Phantasy, and looks

20   That threaten the profane; – a pillared shade,
      Upon whose grassless floor of red-brown hue,
      By sheddings from the pining umbrage tinged
      Perennially – beneath whose sable roof
      Of boughs, as if for festal purpose, decked
      With unrejoicing berries – ghostly Shapes
      May meet at noontide; Fear and trembling Hope,
      Silence and Foresight; Death the Skeleton
      And Time the Shadow; – there to celebrate,
      As in a natural temple scattered o'er
30   With altars undisturbed of mossy stone,
      United worship; or in mute repose
      To lie, and listen to the mountain flood
      Murmuring from Glaramara's inmost caves.

Vaudracour and Julia

The following tale was written as an Episode, in a work from
which its length may perhaps exclude it. The facts are true; no
invention as to these has been exercised, as none was needed.

  O happy time of youthful lovers (thus
  My story may begin) O balmy time,
  In which a love-knot on a lady's brow
  Is fairer than the fairest star in heaven!
  To such inheritance of blessed fancy
  (Fancy that sports more desperately with minds
  Than ever fortune hath been known to do)
  The high-born Vaudracour was brought, by years
  Whose progress had a little overstepped
10   His stripling prime. A town of small repute,
      Among the vine-clad mountains of Auvergne,
      Was the Youth's birth-place. There he wooed a Maid
      Who heard the heart-felt music of his suit
      With answering vows. Plebeian was the stock,
      Plebeian, though ingenuous, the stock,
      From which her graces and her honours sprung:

And hence the father of the enamoured Youth,
With haughty indignation, spurned the thought
Of such alliance. – From their cradles up,
20   With but a step between their several homes,
Twins had they been in pleasure; after strife
And petty quarrels, had grown fond again;
Each other's advocate, each other's stay;
And, in their happiest moments, not content,
If more divided than a sportive pair
Of sea-fowl, conscious both that they are hovering
Within the eddy of a common blast,
Or hidden only by the concave depth
Of neighbouring billows from each other's sight.

30   Thus, not without concurrence of an age
Unknown to memory, was an earnest given
By ready nature for a life of love,
For endless constancy, and placid truth;
But whatsoe'er of such rare treasure lay
Reserved, had fate permitted, for support
Of their maturer years, his present mind
Was under fascination; – he beheld
A vision, and adored the thing he saw.
Arabian fiction never filled the world
40   With half the wonders that were wrought for him.
Earth breathed in one great presence of the spring;
Life turned the meanest of her implements,
Before his eyes, to price above all gold;
The house she dwelt in was a sainted shrine;
Her chamber-window did surpass in glory
The portals of the dawn; all paradise
Could, by the simple opening of a door,
Let itself in upon him: – pathways, walks,
Swarmed with enchantment, till his spirit sank,
50   Surcharged, within him, overblest to move
Beneath a sun that wakes a weary world
To its dull round of ordinary cares;
A man too happy for mortality!

So passed the time, till whether through effect
Of some unguarded moment that dissolved
Virtuous restraint – ah, speak it, think it, not!
Deem rather that the fervent Youth, who saw
So many bars between his present state
And the dear haven where he wished to be
60   In honourable wedlock with his Love,
Was in his judgement tempted to decline
To perilous weakness, and entrust his cause
To nature for a happy end of all;
Deem that by such fond hope the Youth was swayed,
And bear with their transgression, when I add
That Julia, wanting yet the name of wife,
Carried about her for a secret grief
The promise of a mother.
                              To conceal
The threatened shame, the parents of the Maid
70   Found means to hurry her away by night,
And unforewarned, that in some distant spot
She might remain shrouded in privacy,
Until the babe was born. When morning came,
The Lover, thus bereft, stung with his loss,
And all uncertain whither he should turn,
Chafed like a wild beast in the toils; but soon
Discovering traces of the fugitives,
Their steps he followed to the Maid's retreat.
Easily may the sequel be divined –
80   Walks to and fro – watchings at every hour;
And the fair Captive, who, whene'er she may,
Is busy at her casement as the swallow
Fluttering its pinions, almost within reach,
About the pendent nest, did thus espy
Her Lover! – thence a stolen interview,
Accomplished under friendly shade of night.

I pass the raptures of the pair; – such theme
Is, by innumerable poets, touched
In more delightful verse than skill of mine

90 Could fashion; chiefly by that darling bard
  Who told of Juliet and her Romeo,
  And of the lark's note heard before its time,
  And of the streaks that laced the severing clouds
  In the unrelenting east. – Through all her courts
  The vacant city slept; the busy winds,
  That keep no certain intervals of rest,
  Moved not; meanwhile the galaxy displayed
  Her fires, that like mysterious pulses beat
  Aloft; – momentous but uneasy bliss!
100 To their full hearts the universe seemed hung
  On that brief meeting's slender filament!

   They parted; and the generous Vaudracour
  Reached speedily the native threshold, bent
  On making (so the Lovers had agreed)
  A sacrifice of birthright to attain
  A final portion from his father's hand;
  Which granted, Bride and Bridegroom then would flee
  To some remote and solitary place,
  Shady as night, and beautiful as heaven,
110 Where they may live, with no one to behold
  Their happiness, or to disturb their love.
  But *now* of this no whisper; not the less,
  If ever an obtrusive word were dropped
  Touching the matter of his passion, still,
  In his stern father's hearing, Vaudracour
  Persisted openly that death alone
  Should abrogate his human privilege
  Divine, of swearing everlasting truth,
  Upon the altar, to the Maid he loved.

120 'You shall be baffled in your mad intent
  If there be justice in the court of France,'
  Muttered the Father. – From these words the Youth
  Conceived a terror; and, by night or day,
  Stirred nowhere without weapons, that full soon
  Found dreadful provocation: for at night,

When to his chamber he retired, attempt
Was made to seize him by three armèd men,
Acting, in furtherance of the father's will,
Under a private signet of the State.
130 One the rash Youth's ungovernable hand
Slew, and as quickly to a second gave
A perilous wound – he shuddered to behold
The breathless corse; then peacefully resigned
His person to the law, was lodged in prison,
And wore the fetters of a criminal.

Have you observed a tuft of wingèd seed
That, from the dandelion's naked stalk,
Mounted aloft, is suffered not to use
Its natural gifts for purposes of rest,
140 Driven by the autumnal whirlwind to and fro
Through the wide element? or have you marked
The heavier substance of a leaf-clad bough,
Within the vortex of a foaming flood,
Tormented? by such aid you may conceive
The perturbation that ensued; – ah, no!
Desperate the Maid – the Youth is stained with blood;
Unmatchable on earth is their disquiet!
Yet as the troubled seed and tortured bough
Is Man, subjected to despotic sway.

150 For him, by private influence with the Court,
Was pardon gained, and liberty procured;
But not without exaction of a pledge,
Which liberty and love dispersed in air.
He flew to her from whom they would divide him –
He clove to her who could not give him peace –
Yea, his first word of greeting was, – 'All right
Is gone from me; my lately-towering hopes,
To the least fibre of their lowest root,
Are withered; thou no longer canst be mine,
160 I thine – the conscience-stricken must not woo

The unruffled Innocent, – I see thy face,
Behold thee, and my misery is complete!'

'One, are we not?' exclaimed the Maiden – 'One,
For innocence and youth, for weal and woe?'
Then with the father's name she coupled words
Of vehement indignation; but the Youth
Checked her with filial meekness; for no thought
Uncharitable crossed his mind, no sense
Of hasty anger, rising in the eclipse
170 Of true domestic loyalty, did e'er
Find place within his bosom. – Once again
The persevering wedge of tyranny
Achieved their separation: and once more
Were they united, – to be yet again
Disparted, pitiable lot! But here
A portion of the tale may well be left
In silence, though my memory could add
Much how the Youth, in scanty space of time,
Was traversed from without; much, too, of thoughts
180 That occupied his days in solitude
Under privation and restraint; and what,
Through dark and shapeless fear of things to come,
And what, through strong compunction for the past,
He suffered – breaking down in heart and mind!

Doomed to a third and last captivity,
His freedom he recovered on the eve
Of Julia's travail. When the babe was born,
Its presence tempted him to cherish schemes
Of future happiness. 'You shall return,
190 Julia,' said he, 'and to your father's house
Go with the child. – You have been wretched; yet
The silver shower, whose reckless burden weighs
Too heavily upon the lily's head,
Oft leaves a saving moisture at its root.
Malice, beholding you, will melt away.
Go! – 'tis a town where both of us were born;

None will reproach you, for our truth is known;
And if, amid those once-bright bowers, our fate
Remain unpitied, pity is not in man.
200   With ornaments – the prettiest, nature yields
Or art can fashion, shall you deck our boy,
And feed his countenance with your own sweet looks
Till no one can resist him. – Now, even now,
I see him sporting on the sunny lawn;
My father from the window sees him too;
Startled, as if some new-created thing
Enriched the earth, or Faery of the woods
Bounded before him; – but the unweeting Child
Shall by his beauty win his grandsire's heart
210   So that it shall be softened, and our loves
End happily, as they began!'

                    These gleams
Appeared but seldom; oftener was he seen
Propping a pale and melancholy face
Upon the Mother's bosom; resting thus
His head upon one breast, while from the other
The Babe was drawing in its quiet food.
– That pillow is no longer to be thine,
Fond Youth! that mournful solace now must pass
Into the list of things that cannot be!
220   Unwedded Julia, terror-smitten, hears
The sentence, by her mother's lip pronounced,
That dooms her to a convent. – Who shall tell,
Who dares report, the tidings to the lord
Of her affections? so they blindly asked
Who knew not to what quiet depths a weight
Of agony had pressed the Sufferer down:
The word, by others dreaded, he can hear
Composed and silent, without visible sign
Of even the least emotion. Noting this,
230   When the impatient object of his love
Upbraided him with slackness, he returned
No answer, only took the mother's hand

And kissed it; seemingly devoid of pain,
Or care, that what so tenderly he pressed
Was a dependant on the obdurate heart
Of one who came to disunite their lives
For ever – sad alternative! preferred,
By the unbending Parents of the Maid,
To secret 'spousals meanly disavowed.
– So be it!

240   In the city he remained
A season after Julia had withdrawn
To those religious walls. He, too, departs –
Who with him? – even the senseless Little-one.
With that sole charge he passed the city-gates,
For the last time, attendant by the side
Of a close chair, a litter, or sedan,
In which the Babe was carried. To a hill,
That rose a brief league distant from the town,
The dwellers in that house where he had lodged
250 Accompanied his steps, by anxious love
Impelled; – they parted from him there, and stood
Watching below till he had disappeared
On the hill top. His eyes he scarcely took,
Throughout that journey, from the vehicle
(Slow-moving ark of all his hopes!) that veiled
The tender infant: and at every inn,
And under every hospitable tree
At which the bearers halted or reposed,
Laid him with timid care upon his knees,
260 And looked, as mothers ne'er were known to look,
Upon the nursling which his arms embraced.

    This was the manner in which Vaudracour
Departed with his infant; and thus reached
His father's house, where to the innocent child
Admittance was denied. The young man spake
No word of indignation or reproof,
But of his father begged, a last request,

That a retreat might be assigned to him,
Where in forgotten quiet he might dwell,
270 With such allowance as his wants required;
For wishes he had none. To a lodge that stood
Deep in a forest, with leave given, at the age
Of four-and-twenty summers he withdrew;
And thither took with him his motherless Babe,
And one domestic for their common needs,
An aged woman. It consoled him here
To attend upon the orphan, and perform
Obsequious service to the precious child,
Which, after a short time, by some mistake
280 Or indiscretion of the Father, died. –
The Tale I follow to its last recess
Of suffering or of peace, I know not which:
Theirs be the blame who caused the woe, not mine!

From this time forth he never shared a smile
With mortal creature. An Inhabitant
Of that same town, in which the pair had left
So lively a remembrance of their griefs,
By chance of business, coming within reach
Of his retirement, to the forest lodge
290 Repaired, but only found the matron there,
Who told him that his pains were thrown away,
For that her Master never uttered word
To living thing – not even to her. – Behold!
While they were speaking, Vaudracour approached;
But, seeing someone near, as on the latch
Of the garden-gate his hand was laid, he shrunk –
And, like a shadow, glided out of view.
Shocked at his savage aspect, from the place
The visitor retired.

Thus lived the Youth
300 Cut off from all intelligence with man,
And shunning even the light of common day;
Nor could the voice of Freedom, which through France

Full speedily resounded, public hope,
Or personal memory of his own deep wrongs,
Rouse him: but in those solitary shades
His days he wasted, an imbecile mind!

[*Fragment: 'There was a spot'*]

There was a spot,
My favourite station when the winds were up,
Three knots of fir-trees, small and circular,
Which with smooth space of open plain between
Stood single, for the delicate eye of taste
Too formally arranged. Right opposite
The central clump I loved to stand and hear
The wind come on and touch the several groves
Each after each, and thence in the dark night
10 Elicit all proportions of sweet sounds
As from an instrument. 'The strains are passed,'
Thus often to myself I said, 'the sounds
Even while they are approaching are gone by,
And now they are more distant, more and more.
O listen, listen, how they wind away
Still heard they wind away, heard yet and yet,
While the last touch they leave upon the sense
Is sweeter than whate'er was heard before,
And seems to say that they can never die.'

The Kitten and Falling Leaves

That way look, my Infant, lo!
What a pretty baby-show!
See the Kitten on the wall,
Sporting with the leaves that fall,
Withered leaves – one – two – and three –
From the lofty elder-tree!
Through the calm and frosty air
Of this morning bright and fair,

Eddying round and round they sink
10 Softly, slowly: one might think,
From the motions that are made,
Every little leaf conveyed
Sylph or Faery hither tending, –
To this lower world descending,
Each invisible and mute,
In his wavering parachute.
– But the Kitten, how she starts,
Crouches, stretches, paws, and darts!
First at one, and then its fellow
20 Just as light and just as yellow;
There are many now – now one –
Now they stop and there are none:
What intenseness of desire
In her upward eye of fire!
With a tiger-leap half-way
Now she meets the coming prey,
Lets it go as fast, and then
Has it in her power again:
Now she works with three or four,
30 Like an Indian conjurer;
Quick as he in feats of art,
Far beyond in joy of heart.
Were her antics played in the eye
Of a thousand standers-by,
Clapping hands with shout and stare,
What would little Tabby care
For the plaudits of the crowd?
Over happy to be proud,
Over wealthy in the treasure
40 Of her own exceeding pleasure!

'Tis a pretty baby-treat;
Nor, I deem, for me unmeet;
Here, for neither Babe nor me,
Other playmate can I see.
Of the countless living things,

That with stir of feet and wings
(In the sun or under shade,
Upon bough or grassy blade)
And with busy revellings,
50 Chirp and song, and murmurings,
Made this orchard's narrow space,
And this vale, so blithe a place;
Multitudes are swept away
Never more to breathe the day:
Some are sleeping; some in bands
Travelled into distant lands;
Others slunk to moor and wood,
Far from human neighbourhood;
And, among the Kinds that keep
60 With us closer fellowship,
With us openly abide,
All have laid their mirth aside.

Where is he, that giddy Sprite,
Blue-cap, with his colours bright,
Who was blest as bird could be,
Feeding in the apple-tree;
Made such wanton spoil and rout,
Turning blossoms inside out:
Hung – head pointing towards the ground –
70 Fluttered, perched, into a round
Bound himself, and then unbound;
Lithest, gaudiest Harlequin!
Prettiest tumbler ever seen!
Light of heart and light of limb;
What is now become of Him?
Lambs, that through the mountains went
Frisking, bleating merriment,
When the year was in its prime,
They are sobered by this time.
80 If you look to vale or hill,
If you listen, all is still,
Save a little neighbouring rill,

That from out the rocky ground
Strikes a solitary sound.
Vainly glitter hill and plain,
And the air is calm in vain;
Vainly Morning spreads the lure
Of a sky serene and pure;
Creature none can she decoy
90   Into open sign of joy:
Is it that they have a fear
Of the dreary season near?
Or that other pleasures be
Sweeter even than gaiety?

Yet, whate'er enjoyments dwell
In the impenetrable cell
Of the silent heart which Nature
Furnishes to every creature;
Whatsoe'er we feel and know
100   Too sedate for outward show,
Such a light of gladness breaks,
Pretty Kitten! from thy freaks, –
Spreads with such a living grace
O'er my little Dora's face;
Yes, the sight so stirs and charms
Thee, Baby, laughing in my arms,
That almost I could repine
That your transports are not mine,
That I do not wholly fare
110   Even as ye do, thoughtless pair!
And I will have my careless season
Spite of melancholy reason,
Will walk through life in such a way
That, when time brings on decay,
Now and then I may possess
Hours of perfect gladsomeness.
– Pleased by any random toy;
By a kitten's busy joy,
Or an infant's laughing eye

120 Sharing in the ecstasy;
I would fare like that or this,
Find my wisdom in my bliss;
Keep the sprightly soul awake,
And have faculties to take,
Even from things by sorrow wrought,
Matter for a jocund thought,
Spite of care, and spite of grief,
To gambol with Life's falling Leaf.

*French Revolution As It Appeared
to Enthusiasts at Its Commencement.
Reprinted from 'The Friend'*

Oh! pleasant exercise of hope and joy!
For mighty were the auxiliars which then stood
Upon our side, we who were strong in love!
Bliss was it in that dawn to be alive,
But to be young was very heaven! – Oh! times,
In which the meagre, stale, forbidding ways
Of custom, law, and statute, took at once
The attraction of a country in romance!
When Reason seemed the most to assert her rights,
10 When most intent on making of herself
A prime Enchantress – to assist the work,
Which then was going forward in her name!
Not favoured spots alone, but the whole earth,
The beauty wore of promise, that which sets
(As at some moment might not be unfelt
Among the bowers of paradise itself)
The budding rose above the rose full blown.
What temper at the prospect did not wake
To happiness unthought of? The inert
20 Were roused, and lively natures rapt away!
They who had fed their childhood upon dreams,
The playfellows of fancy, who had made

All powers of swiftness, subtlety, and strength
Their ministers, – who in lordly wise had stirred
Among the grandest objects of the sense,
And dealt with whatsoever they found there
As if they had within some lurking right
To wield it; – they, too, who, of gentle mood,
Had watched all gentle motions, and to these
30 Had fitted their own thoughts, schemers more mild,
And in the region of their peaceful selves; –
Now was it that both found, the meek and lofty
Did both find, helpers to their heart's desire,
And stuff at hand, plastic as they could wish;
Were called upon to exercise their skill,
Not in Utopia, subterranean fields,
Or some secreted island, Heaven knows where!
But in the very world, which is the world
Of all of us, – the place where in the end
40 We find our happiness, or not at all!

[*Inscription for the Moss-Hut at Dove Cottage*]

No whimsy of the purse is here,
No Pleasure-House forlorn;
Use, Comfort, do this roof endear;
A tributary Shed to cheer
The little Cottage that is near,
To help it and adorn.

The Simplon Pass

    — Brook and road
Were fellow-travellers in this gloomy Pass,
And with them did we journey several hours
At a slow step. The immeasurable height
Of woods decaying, never to be decayed,
The stationary blasts of waterfalls,
And in the narrow rent, at every turn,

Winds thwarting winds bewildered and forlorn,
The torrents shooting from the clear blue sky,
10 The rocks that muttered close upon our ears,
Black drizzling crags that spake by the wayside
As if a voice were in them, the sick sight
And giddy prospect of the raving stream,
The unfettered clouds and region of the heavens,
Tumult and peace, the darkness and the light –
Were all like workings of one mind, the features
Of the same face, blossoms upon one tree,
Characters of the great Apocalypse,
The types and symbols of Eternity,
20 Of first, and last, and midst, and without end.

The King of Sweden

The Voice of song from distant lands shall call
To that great King; shall hail the crownèd Youth
Who, taking counsel of unbending Truth,
By one example hath set forth to all
How they with dignity may stand; or fall,
If fall they must. Now, whither doth it tend?
And what to him and his shall be the end?
That thought is one which neither can appal
Nor cheer him; for the illustrious Swede hath done
10 The thing which ought to be; is raised *above*
All consequences: work he hath begun
Of fortitude, and piety, and love,
Which all his glorious ancestors approve:
The heroes bless him, him their rightful son.

Glen-Almain; Or, The Narrow Glen

In this still place, remote from men,
Sleeps Ossian, in the NARROW GLEN;
In this still place, where murmurs on

But one meek streamlet, only one:
He sang of battles, and the breath
Of stormy war, and violent death;
And should, methinks, when all was past,
Have rightfully been laid at last
Where rocks were rudely heaped, and rent
10 As by a spirit turbulent;
Where sights were rough, and sounds were wild,
And everything unreconciled;
In some complaining, dim retreat,
For fear and melancholy meet;
But this is calm; there cannot be
A more entire tranquillity.

   Does then the Bard sleep here indeed?
Or is it but a groundless creed?
What matters it? – I blame them not
20 Whose Fancy in this lonely Spot
Was moved; and in such way expressed
Their notion of its perfect rest.
A convent, even a hermit's cell,
Would break the silence of this Dell:
It is not quiet, is not ease;
But something deeper far than these:
The separation that is here
Is of the grave; and of austere
Yet happy feelings of the dead:
30 And, therefore, was it rightly said
That Ossian, last of all his race!
Lies buried in this lonely place.

Elegiac Stanzas Suggested by a Picture of
Peele Castle, in a Storm, Painted by
Sir George Beaumont

I was thy neighbour once, thou rugged Pile!
Four summer weeks I dwelt in sight of thee:

I saw thee every day; and all the while
Thy Form was sleeping on a glassy sea.

So pure the sky, so quiet was the air!
So like, so very like, was day to day!
Whene'er I looked, thy Image still was there;
It trembled, but it never passed away.

How perfect was the calm! it seemed no sleep;
10 No mood, which season takes away, or brings:
I could have fancied that the mighty Deep
Was even the gentlest of all gentle Things.

Ah! THEN, if mine had been the Painter's hand,
To express what then I saw; and add the gleam,
The light that never was, on sea or land,
The consecration, and the Poet's dream;

I would have planted thee, thou hoary Pile
Amid a world how different from this!
Beside a sea that could not cease to smile;
20 On tranquil land, beneath a sky of bliss.

Thou shouldst have seemed a treasure-house divine
Of peaceful years; a chronicle of heaven; –
Of all the sunbeams that did ever shine
The very sweetest had to thee been given.

A Picture had it been of lasting ease,
Elysian quiet, without toil or strife;
No motion but the moving tide, a breeze,
Or merely silent Nature's breathing life.

Such, in the fond illusion of my heart,
30 Such Picture would I at that time have made:
And seen the soul of truth in every part,
A stedfast peace that might not be betrayed.

So once it would have been, – 'tis so no more;
I have submitted to a new control:
A power is gone, which nothing can restore;
A deep distress hath humanized my Soul.

Not for a moment could I now behold
A smiling sea, and be what I have been:
The feeling of my loss will ne'er be old;
40 This, which I know, I speak with mind serene.

Then, Beaumont, Friend! who would have been the
    Friend,
If he had lived, of Him whom I deplore,
This work of thine I blame not, but commend;
This sea in anger, and that dismal shore.

O 'tis a passionate Work! – yet wise and well,
Well chosen is the spirit that is here;
That Hulk which labours in the deadly swell,
This rueful sky, this pageantry of fear!

And this huge Castle, standing here sublime,
50 I love to see the look with which it braves,
Cased in the unfeeling armour of old time,
The lightning, the fierce wind, and trampling waves.

Farewell, farewell the heart that lives alone,
Housed in a dream, at distance from the Kind!
Such happiness, wherever it be known,
Is to be pitied; for 'tis surely blind.

But welcome fortitude, and patient cheer,
And frequent sights of what is to be borne!
Such sights, or worse, as are before me here. –
60 Not without hope we suffer and we mourn.

'*Distressful gift! this Book receives*'

Distressful gift! this Book receives
Upon its melancholy leaves,
This poor ill-fated Book:
I wrote, and when I reached the end
Started to think that thou, my Friend,
Upon the words which I had penned
Must never, never look.

Alas, alas, it is a Tale
Of Thee thyself; fond heart and frail!
10 The sadly-tuneful line
The written words that seem to throng
The dismal page, the sound, the song,
The murmur all to thee belong,
Too surely they are thine.

And so I write what neither Thou
Must look upon, nor others now,
Their tears would flow too fast;
Some solace thus I strive to gain,
Making a kind of secret chain,
20 If so I may, betwixt us twain
In memory of the past.

Oft have I handled, often eyed,
This volume with delight and pride,
The written page and white;
Oft have I turned them o'er and o'er,
One after one and score by score,
All filled or to be filled with store
Of verse for his delight.

He framed the Book which now I see,
30 This book that rests upon my knee,
He framed with dear intent;

To travel with him night and day,
And in his private hearing say
Refreshing things, whatever way
His weary Vessel went.

And now – upon the written leaf
With heart oppressed by pain and grief
I look, but, gracious God,
Oh grant that I may never find
40 Worse matter or a heavier mind,
Grant this, and let me be resigned
Beneath thy chastening rod.

To the Daisy

Sweet Flower! belike one day to have
A place upon thy Poet's grave,
I welcome thee once more:
But He, who was on land, at sea,
My Brother, too, in loving thee,
Although he loved more silently,
Sleeps by his native shore.

Ah! hopeful, hopeful was the day
When to that Ship he bent his way,
10 To govern and to guide:
His wish was gained: a little time
Would bring him back in manhood's prime
And free for life, these hills to climb;
With all his wants supplied.

And full of hope day followed day
While that stout Ship at anchor lay
Beside the shores of Wight;
The May had then made all things green;
And, floating there, in pomp serene,
20 That Ship was goodly to be seen,
His pride and his delight!

Yet then, when called ashore, he sought
The tender peace of rural thought:
In more than happy mood
To your abodes, bright daisy Flowers!
He then would steal at leisure hours,
And loved you glittering in your bowers,
A starry multitude.

But hark the word! – the ship is gone; –
30 Returns from her long course: – anon
Sets sail: – in season due,
Once more on English earth they stand:
But, when a third time from the land
They parted, sorrow was at hand
For Him and for his crew.

Ill-fated Vessel! – ghastly shock!
– At length delivered from the rock,
The deep she hath regained;
And through the stormy night they steer;
40 Labouring for life, in hope and fear,
To reach a safer shore – how near,
Yet not to be attained!

'Silence!' the brave Commander cried;
To that calm word a shriek replied,
It was the last death-shriek.
– A few (my soul oft sees that sight)
Survive upon the tall mast's height;
But one dear remnant of the night –
For Him in vain I seek.

50 Six weeks beneath the moving sea
He lay in slumber quietly;
Unforced by wind or wave
To quit the Ship for which he died,
(All claims of duty satisfied);
And there they found him at her side;
And bore him to the grave.

Vain service! yet not vainly done
For this, if other end were none,
That He, who had been cast
60 Upon a way of life unmeet
For such a gentle Soul and sweet,
Should find an undisturbed retreat
Near what he loved, at last –

That neighbourhood of grove and field
To Him a resting-place should yield,
A meek man and a brave!
The birds shall sing and ocean make
A mournful murmur for *his* sake;
And Thou, sweet Flower, shalt sleep and wake
70 Upon his senseless grave.

Stepping Westward

While my Fellow-traveller and I were walking by the side of
Loch Ketterine, one fine evening after sunset, in our road to a
Hut where, in the course of our Tour, we had been hospitably
entertained some weeks before, we met, in one of the loneliest
parts of that solitary region, two well-dressed Women, one of
whom said to us, by way of greeting, 'What, you are stepping
westward?'

'*What, you are stepping westward?*' – 'Yea.'
– 'Twould be a *wildish* destiny,
If we, who thus together roam
In a strange Land, and far from home,
Were in this place the guests of Chance:
Yet who would stop, or fear to advance,
Though home or shelter he had none,
With such a sky to lead him on?

The dewy ground was dark and cold;
10 Behind, all gloomy to behold;
And stepping westward seemed to be

A kind of *heavenly* destiny:
I liked the greeting; 'twas a sound
Of something without place or bound;
And seemed to give me spiritual right
To travel through that region bright.

The voice was soft, and she who spake
Was walking by her native lake:
The salutation had to me
20   The very sound of courtesy:
Its power was felt; and while my eye
Was fixed upon the glowing Sky,
The echo of the voice enwrought
A human sweetness with the thought
Of travelling through the world that lay
Before me in my endless way.

Elegiac Verses
in Memory of My Brother, John Wordsworth

Commander of the E. I. Company's ship, the Earl of Aber-
gavenny, in which he perished by calamitous shipwreck, Feb.
6th, 1805. Composed near the Mountain track, that leads from
Grasmere through Grisdale Hawes, where it descends towards
Patterdale.

I
The Sheep-boy whistled loud, and lo!
That instant, startled by the shock,
The Buzzard mounted from the rock
Deliberate and slow:
Lord of the air, he took his flight;
Oh! could he on that woeful night
Have lent his wing, my Brother dear,
For one poor moment's space to Thee,
And all who struggled with the Sea,
10   When safety was so near.

II

Thus in the weakness of my heart
I spoke (but let that pang be still)
When rising from the rock at will,
I saw the Bird depart.
And let me calmly bless the Power
That meets me in this unknown Flower,
Affecting type of him I mourn!
With calmness suffer and believe,
And grieve, and know that I must grieve,
20 Not cheerless, though forlorn.

III

Here did we stop; and here looked round
While each into himself descends,
For that last thought of parting Friends
That is not to be found.
Hidden was Grasmere Vale from sight,
Our home and his, his heart's delight,
His quiet heart's selected home.
But time before him melts away,
And he hath feeling of a day
30 Of blessedness to come.

IV

Full soon in sorrow did I weep,
Taught that the mutual hope was dust,
In sorrow, but for higher trust,
How miserably deep!
All vanished in a single word,
A breath, a sound, and scarcely heard.
Sea – Ship – drowned – Shipwreck – so it came,
The meek, the brave, the good, was gone;
He who had been our living John
40 Was nothing but a name.

V

That was indeed a parting! oh,
Glad am I, glad that it is past;
For there were some on whom it cast
Unutterable woe.
But they as well as I have gains; –
From many a humble source, to pains
Like these, there comes a mild release;
Even here I feel it, even this Plant
Is in its beauty ministrant
50   To comfort and to peace.

VI

He would have loved thy modest grace,
Meek Flower! To Him I would have said,
'It grows upon its native bed
Beside our Parting-place;
There, cleaving to the ground, it lies
With multitude of purple eyes,
Spangling a cushion green like moss;
But we will see it, joyful tide!
Some day, to see it in its pride,
60   The mountain will we cross.'

VII

– Brother and friend, if verse of mine
Have power to make thy virtues known,
Here let a monumental Stone
Stand – sacred as a Shrine;
And to the few who pass this way,
Traveller or Shepherd, let it say,
Long as these mighty rocks endure, –
Oh do not Thou too fondly brood,
Although deserving of all good,
70   On any earthly hope, however pure!

Fidelity

A barking sound the Shepherd hears,
A cry as of a dog or fox;
He halts – and searches with his eyes
Among the scattered rocks:
And now at distance can discern
A stirring in a brake of fern;
And instantly a dog is seen,
Glancing through that covert green.

The Dog is not of mountain breed;
10 Its motions, too, are wild and shy;
With something, as the Shepherd thinks,
Unusual in its cry:
Nor is there anyone in sight
All round, in hollow or on height;
Nor shout, nor whistle strikes his ear;
What is the creature doing here?

It was a cove, a huge recess,
That keeps, till June, December's snow;
A lofty precipice in front,
20 A silent tarn below!
Far in the bosom of Helvellyn,
Remote from public road or dwelling,
Pathway, or cultivated land;
From trace of human foot or hand.

There sometimes doth a leaping fish
Send through the tarn a lonely cheer;
The crags repeat the raven's croak,
In symphony austere;
Thither the rainbow comes – the cloud –
30 And mists that spread the flying shroud;
And sunbeams; and the sounding blast,
That, if it could, would hurry past;
But that enormous barrier holds it fast.

Not free from boding thoughts, a while
The Shepherd stood; then makes his way
O'er rocks and stones, following the Dog
As quickly as he may;
Nor far had gone before he found
A human skeleton on the ground;
40   The appalled Discoverer with a sigh
Looks round, to learn the history.

From those abrupt and perilous rocks
The Man had fallen, that place of fear!
At length upon the Shepherd's mind
It breaks, and all is clear:
He instantly recalled the name,
And who he was, and whence he came;
Remembered, too, the very day
On which the Traveller passed this way.

50   But hear a wonder, for whose sake
This lamentable tale I tell!
A lasting monument of words
This wonder merits well.
The Dog, which still was hovering nigh,
Repeating the same timid cry,
This Dog, had been through three months' space
A dweller in that savage place.

Yes, proof was plain that, since the day
When this ill-fated Traveller died,
60   The Dog had watched about the spot,
Or by his master's side:
How nourished here through such long time
He knows, Who gave that love sublime;
And gave that strength of feeling, great
Above all human estimate!

Incident Characteristic of a Favourite Dog

On his morning rounds the Master
Goes to learn how all things fare;
Searches pasture after pasture,
Sheep and cattle eyes with care;
And, for silence or for talk,
He hath comrades in his walk;
Four dogs, each pair of different breed,
Distinguished two for scent, and two for speed.

See a hare before him started!
10   – Off they fly in earnest chase;
Every dog is eager-hearted,
All the four are in the race:
And the hare whom they pursue,
Knows from instinct what to do;
Her hope is near: no turn she makes;
But, like an arrow, to the river takes.

Deep the river was, and crusted
Thinly by a one night's frost;
But the nimble Hare hath trusted
20   To the ice, and safely crost;
She hath crost, and without heed
All are following at full speed,
When, lo! the ice, so thinly spread,
Breaks – and the greyhound, DART, is over-head!

Better fate have PRINCE and SWALLOW –
See them cleaving to the sport!
MUSIC has no heart to follow,
Little MUSIC, she stops short.
She hath neither wish nor heart,
30   Hers is now another part:
A loving creature she, and brave!
And fondly strives her struggling friend to save.

From the brink her paws she stretches,
Very hands as you would say!
And afflicting moans she fetches,
As he breaks the ice away.
For herself she hath no fears, –
Him alone she sees and hears, –
Makes efforts with complainings; nor gives o'er
40   Until her fellow sinks to re-appear no more.

Tribute to the Memory of the Same Dog

Lie here, without a record of thy worth,
Beneath a covering of the common earth!
It is not from unwillingness to praise,
Or want of love, that here no Stone we raise;
More thou deserv'st; but *this* man gives to man,
Brother to brother, *this* is all we can.
Yet they to whom thy virtues made thee dear
Shall find thee through all changes of the year:
This Oak points out thy grave; the silent tree
10   Will gladly stand a monument of thee.

    We grieved for thee, and wished thy end were past;
And willingly have laid thee here at last:
For thou hadst lived till everything that cheers
In thee had yielded to the weight of years;
Extreme old age had wasted thee away,
And left thee but a glimmering of the day;
Thy ears were deaf, and feeble were thy knees, –
I saw thee stagger in the summer breeze,
Too weak to stand against its sportive breath,
20   And ready for the gentlest stroke of death.
It came, and we were glad; yet tears were shed;
Both man and woman wept when thou wert dead;
Not only for a thousand thoughts that were,
Old household thoughts, in which thou hadst thy share;
But for some precious boons vouchsafed to thee,

Found scarcely anywhere in like degree!
For love, that comes wherever life and sense
Are given by God, in thee was most intense;
A chain of heart, a feeling of the mind,
30 A tender sympathy, which did thee bind
Not only to us Men, but to thy Kind:
Yea, for thy fellow-brutes in thee we saw
A soul of love, love's intellectual law: –
Hence, if we wept, it was not done in shame;
Our tears from passion and from reason came,
And, therefore, shalt thou be an honoured name!

From the Italian of Michelangelo

Yes! hope may with my strong desire keep pace,
And I be undeluded, unbetrayed;
For if of our affections none finds grace
In sight of Heaven, then, wherefore hath God made
The world which we inhabit? Better plea
Love cannot have, than that in loving thee
Glory to that eternal Peace is paid,
Who such divinity to thee imparts
As hallows and makes pure all gentle hearts.
10 His hope is treacherous only whose love dies
With beauty, which is varying every hour;
But, in chaste hearts uninfluenced by the power
Of outward change, there blooms a deathless flower,
That breathes on earth the air of paradise.

Rob Roy's Grave

The history of Rob Roy is sufficiently known; his grave is near
the head of Loch Ketterine, in one of those small pinfold-
like Burial-grounds, of neglected and desolate appearance, which
the traveller meets with in the Highlands of Scotland.

A famous man is Robin Hood,
The English ballad-singer's joy!

And Scotland has a thief as good,
An outlaw of as daring mood;
She has her brave ROB ROY!
Then clear the weeds from off his Grave,
And let us chant a passing stave,
In honour of that Hero brave!

Heaven gave Rob Roy a dauntless heart
10 And wondrous length and strength of arm:
Nor craved he more to quell his foes,
　　Or keep his friends from harm.

Yet was Rob Roy as *wise* as brave;
Forgive me if the phrase be strong; –
A Poet worthy of Rob Roy
　　Must scorn a timid song.

Say, then, that he was wise as brave;
As wise in thought as bold in deed:
For in the principles of things
20 　　*He* sought his moral creed.

Said generous Rob, 'What need of books?
Burn all the statutes and their shelves:
They stir us up against our kind;
　　And worse, against ourselves.

'We have a passion – make a law,
Too false to guide us or control!
And for the law itself we fight
　　In bitterness of soul.

'And, puzzled, blinded thus, we lose
30 Distinctions that are plain and few:
These find I graven on my heart:
　　That tells me what to do.

'The creatures see of flood and field,
And those that travel on the wind!
With them no strife can last; they live
   In peace, and peace of mind.

'For why? – because the good old rule
Sufficeth them, the simple plan,
That they should take, who have the power,
40   And they should keep who can.

'A lesson that is quickly learned,
A signal this which all can see!
Thus nothing here provokes the strong
   To wanton cruelty.

'All freakishness of mind is checked;
He tamed, who foolishly aspires;
While to the measure of his might
   Each fashions his desires.

'All kinds, and creatures, stand and fall
50 By strength of prowess or of wit:
'Tis God's Appointment who must sway,
   And who is to submit.

'Since, then, the rule of right is plain,
And longest life is but a day;
To have my ends, maintain my rights,
I'll take the shortest way.'

And thus among these rocks he lived,
Through summer heat and winter snow:
The Eagle, he was lord above,
60   And Rob was lord below.

So was it – *would*, at least, have been
But through untowardness of fate;
For Polity was then too strong –
   He came an age too late;

Or shall we say an age too soon?
For, were the bold Man living *now*,
How might he flourish in his pride,
   With buds on every bough!

Then rents and factors, rights of chase,
70 Sheriffs, and lairds and their domains,
Would all have seemed but paltry things,
   Not worth a moment's pains.

Rob Roy had never lingered here,
To these few meagre Vales confined;
But thought how wide the world, the times
   How fairly to his mind!

And to his Sword he would have said,
'Do Thou my sovereign will enact
From land to land through half the earth!
80   Judge thou of law and fact!

' 'Tis fit that we should do our part,
Becoming, that mankind should learn
That we are not to be surpassed
   In fatherly concern.

'Of old things all are over old,
Of good things none are good enough: –
We'll show that we can help to frame
   A world of other stuff.

'I, too, will have my kings that take
90 From me the sign of life and death:
Kingdoms shall shift about, like clouds,
   Obedient to my breath.'

And, if the word had been fulfilled,
As *might* have been, then, thought of joy!
France would have had her present Boast,
   And we our own Rob Roy!

Oh! say not so; compare them not;
I would not wrong thee, Champion brave!
Would wrong thee nowhere; least of all
100   Here standing by thy grave.

For Thou, although with some wild thoughts,
Wild Chieftain of a savage Clan!
Hadst this to boast of; thou didst love
    The *liberty* of man.

And, had it been thy lot to live
With us who now behold the light,
Thou wouldst have nobly stirred thyself,
    And battled for the Right.

For thou wert still the poor man's stay,
110   The poor man's heart, the poor man's hand;
And all the oppressed, who wanted strength,
    Had thine at their command.

Bear witness many a pensive sigh
Of thoughtful Herdsman when he strays
Alone upon Loch Veol's heights,
    And by Loch Lomond's braes.

And, far and near, through vale and hill,
Are faces that attest the same;
The proud heart flashing through the eyes,
120   At sound of ROB ROY's name.

To the Sons of Burns, after Visiting the Grave of Their Father

'The Poet's grave is in a corner of the churchyard. We looked at it with melancholy and painful reflections, repeating to each other his own verses – "Is there a man whose judgement clear," etc.' – *Extract from the Journal of my Fellow-traveller.*

'Mid crowded obelisks and urns
I sought the untimely grave of Burns;
Sons of the Bard, my heart still mourns
    With sorrow true;
And more would grieve, but that it turns
    Trembling to you!

Through twilight shades of good and ill
Ye now are panting up life's hill,
And more than common strength and skill
10   Must ye display;
If ye would give the better will
    Its lawful sway.

Hath Nature strung your nerves to bear
Intemperance with less harm, beware!
But if the Poet's wit ye share,
    Like him can speed
The social hour – of tenfold care
    There will be need;

For honest men delight will take
20   To spare your failings for his sake,
Will flatter you, – and fool and rake
    Your steps pursue;
And of your Father's name will make
    A snare for you.

Far from their noisy haunts retire,
And add your voices to the choir
That sanctify the cottage fire
    With service meet;
There seek the genius of your Sire,
30   His spirit greet;

Or where, 'mid 'lonely heights and hows,'
He paid to Nature tuneful vows;
Or wiped his honourable brows

Bedewed with toil,
While reapers strove, or busy ploughs
   Upturned the soil;

His judgement with benignant ray
Shall guide, his fancy cheer, your way;
But ne'er to a seductive lay
40   Let faith be given;
Nor deem that 'light which leads astray,
   Is light from Heaven.'

Let no mean hope your souls enslave;
Be independent, generous, brave;
Your Father such example gave,
   And such revere;
But be admonished by his grave,
   And think, and fear!

The Solitary Reaper

Behold her, single in the field,
Yon solitary Highland Lass!
Reaping and singing by herself;
Stop here, or gently pass!
Alone she cuts and binds the grain,
And sings a melancholy strain;
O listen! for the Vale profound
Is overflowing with the sound.

No Nightingale did ever chaunt
10 More welcome notes to weary bands
Of travellers in some shady haunt,
Among Arabian sands:
A voice so thrilling ne'er was heard
In spring-time from the Cuckoo-bird,
Breaking the silence of the seas
Among the farthest Hebrides.

Will no one tell me what she sings? –
Perhaps the plaintive numbers flow
For old, unhappy, far-off things,
20 And battles long ago:
Or is it some more humble lay,
Familiar matter of today?
Some natural sorrow, loss, or pain,
That has been, and may be again?

Whate'er the theme, the Maiden sang
As if her song could have no ending;
I saw her singing at her work,
And o'er the sickle bending; –
I listened, motionless and still;
30 And, as I mounted up the hill,
The music in my heart I bore,
Long after it was heard no more.

*From the Italian of Michelangelo.
To the Supreme Being*

The prayers I make will then be sweet indeed
If Thou the spirit give by which I pray:
My unassisted heart is barren clay,
That of its native self can nothing feed:
Of good and pious works Thou art the seed,
That quickens only where Thou say'st it may:
Unless Thou show to us thine own true way
No man can find it: Father! Thou must lead.
Do Thou, then, breathe those thoughts into my mind
10 By which such virtue may in me be bred
That in thy holy footsteps I may tread;
The fetters of my tongue do Thou unbind,
That I may have the power to sing of Thee,
And sound thy praises everlastingly.

From the Italian of Michelangelo

No mortal object did these eyes behold
When first they met the placid light of thine,
And my Soul felt her destiny divine,
And hope of endless peace in me grew bold:
Heaven-born, the Soul a heavenward course must hold;
Beyond the visible world she soars to seek
(For what delights the sense is false and weak)
Ideal Form, the universal mould.
The wise man, I affirm, can find no rest
10   In that which perishes: nor will he lend
His heart to aught which doth on time depend.
'Tis sense, unbridled will, and not true love,
That kills the soul: love betters what is best,
Even here below, but more in heaven above.

*From the Italian of Michelangelo

Well-nigh the voyage now is overpast,
And my frail bark, through troubled seas and rude,
Draws near that common haven where at last
Of every action, be it evil or good,
Must due account be rendered. Well I know
How vain will then appear that favoured art,
Sole Idol long and Monarch of my heart,
For all is vain that man desires below.
And now remorseful thoughts the past upbraid,
10   And fear of twofold death my soul alarms,
That which must come, and that beyond the grave;
Picture and Sculpture lose their feeble charms,
And to that Love Divine I turn for aid,
Who from the Cross extends His arms to save.

From the Italian of Michelangelo

Rid of a vexing and a heavy load
Eternal Lord! and from the world set free,
Like a frail Bark, weary I turn to Thee,
From frightful storms into a quiet road.
On much repentance grace will be bestowed:
The nails, the thorns, and thy two hands, thy face,
Benign, meek, lacerated, offers grace
To sinners whom their sins oppress and goad.
Let not thy justice view, O light divine,
10 My fault and keep it from thy sacred ear,
And do not that way turn thine arm severe;
Cleanse with thy blood my sins: to this incline
More readily, the more my years require
Prompt aid, forgiveness speedy and entire.

Character of the Happy Warrior

Who is the happy Warrior? Who is he
That every man in arms should wish to be?
– It is the generous Spirit, who, when brought
Among the tasks of real life, hath wrought
Upon the plan that pleased his boyish thought:
Whose high endeavours are an inward light
That makes the path before him always bright:
Who, with a natural instinct to discern
What knowledge can perform, is diligent to learn;
10 Abides by this resolve, and stops not there,
But makes his moral being his prime care;
Who, doomed to go in company with Pain,
And Fear, and Bloodshed, miserable train!
Turns his necessity to glorious gain;
In face of these doth exercise a power
Which is our human nature's highest dower;
Controls them and subdues, transmutes, bereaves

Of their bad influence, and their good receives:
By objects, which might force the soul to abate
20 Her feeling, rendered more compassionate;
Is placable – because occasions rise
So often that demand such sacrifice;
More skilful in self-knowledge, even more pure,
As tempted more; more able to endure,
As more exposed to suffering and distress;
Thence, also, more alive to tenderness.
– 'Tis he whose law is reason; who depends
Upon that law as on the best of friends;
Whence, in a state where men are tempted still
30 To evil for a guard against worse ill,
And what in quality or act is best
Doth seldom on a right foundation rest,
He labours good on good to fix, and owes
To virtue every triumph that he knows:
– Who, if he rise to station of command,
Rises by open means; and there will stand
On honourable terms, or else retire,
And in himself possess his own desire;
Who comprehends his trust, and to the same
40 Keeps faithful with a singleness of aim;
And therefore does not stoop, nor lie in wait
For wealth, or honours, or for worldly state;
Whom they must follow; on whose head must fall,
Like showers of manna, if they come at all:
Whose powers shed round him in the common strife,
Or mild concerns of ordinary life,
A constant influence, a peculiar grace;
But who, if he be called upon to face
Some awful moment to which Heaven has joined
50 Great issues, good or bad for human kind,
Is happy as a Lover; and attired
With sudden brightness, like a Man inspired;
And, through the heat of conflict, keeps the law
In calmness made, and sees what he foresaw;
Or if an unexpected call succeed,

Come when it will, is equal to the need:
– He who, though thus endued as with a sense
And faculty for storm and turbulence,
Is yet a Soul whose master-bias leans
60 To homefelt pleasures and to gentle scenes;
Sweet images! which, whereso'er he be,
Are at his heart; and such fidelity
It is his darling passion to approve;
More brave for this, that he hath much to love: –
'Tis, finally, the Man, who, lifted high,
Conspicuous object in a Nation's eye,
Or left unthought-of in obscurity, –
Who, with a toward or untoward lot,
Prosperous or adverse, to his wish or not –
70 Plays, in the many games of life, that one
Where what he most doth value must be won:
Whom neither shape of danger can dismay,
Nor thought of tender happiness betray;
Who, not content that former worth stand fast,
Looks forward, persevering to the last,
From well to better, daily self-surpast:
Who, whether praise of him must walk the earth
For ever, and to noble deeds give birth,
Or he must fall, to sleep without his fame,
80 And leave a dead unprofitable name –
Finds comfort in himself and in his cause;
And, while the mortal mist is gathering, draws
His breath in confidence of Heaven's applause:
This is the happy Warrior; this is He
That every Man in arms should wish to be.

*The Cottager to Her Infant by My Sister

[The last two stanzas are by William Wordsworth]

The days are cold, the nights are long,
The north-wind sings a doleful song;
Then hush again upon my breast;

All merry things are now at rest,
   Save thee, my pretty Love!

The kitten sleeps upon the hearth,
The crickets long have ceased their mirth;
There's nothing stirring in the house
Save one *wee*, hungry, nibbling mouse,
10   Then why so busy thou?

Nay! start not at that sparkling light;
'Tis but the moon that shines so bright
On the window pane bedropped with rain:
Then, little Darling! sleep again,
   And wake when it is day.

Ah! if I were a lady gay
I should not grieve with thee to play;
Right gladly would I lie awake
Thy lively spirits to partake
20   And ask no better cheer.

But, babe, there's none to work for me,
And I must rise to industry;
Soon as the cock begin to crow
Thy mother to the fold must go
    To tend the sheep and kine.

[*Translations from Michelangelo. A Fragment*]

And sweet it is to see in summer time
   The daring goats upon a rocky hill
Climb here and there, still browzing as they climb,
   While, far below, on rugged pipe and shrill
The master vents his pain; or homely rhyme
   He chaunts; now changing place, now standing still;
While his beloved, cold of heart and stern!
   Looks from the shade in sober unconcern.

Nor less another sight do I admire,
10   The rural family round their hut of clay;
Some spread the table, and some light the fire
    Beneath the household Rock, in open day;
The ass's colt with panniers some attire;
    Some tend the bristly hogs with fondling play;
This with delighted heart the Old Man sees,
    Sits out of doors, and suns himself at ease.

The outward image speaks the inner mind,
    Peace without hatred, which no care can fret;
Entire contentment in their plough they find,
20   Nor home return until the sun be set:
No bolts they have, their houses are resigned
    To Fortune – let her take what she can get:
A hearty meal then crowns the happy day,
    And sound sleep follows on a bed of hay.

In that condition Envy is unknown,
    And Haughtiness was never there a guest;
They only crave some meadow overgrown
    With herbage that is greener than the rest;
The plough's a sovereign treasure of their own;
30   The glittering share, the gem they dream the best;
A pair of panniers serve them for buffette;
    Trenchers and porringers, for golden plate.

Michelangelo in Reply to the Passage upon His Statue of Night Sleeping

Night Speaks.
Grateful is Sleep, my life in stone bound fast
More grateful still: while wrong and shame shall last,
On me can time no happier state bestow

Than to be left unconscious of the woe.
Ah then, lest you awaken me, speak low.

Grateful is Sleep, more grateful still to be
Of marble; for while shameless wrong and woe
Prevail 'tis best to neither hear nor see:
Then wake me not, I pray you. Hush, speak low.

[*Translation: Come, gentle Sleep*]

Come, gentle Sleep, Death's image though thou art,
Come share my couch nor speedily depart;
How sweet thus living without life to lie,
Thus without death how sweet it is to die.

The Waggoner

'In Cairo's crowded streets
The impatient Merchant, wondering, waits in vain,
And Mecca saddens at the long delay.'   THOMSON.

TO CHARLES LAMB, ESQ.

MY DEAR FRIEND,

When I sent you, a few weeks ago, the Tale of Peter Bell,
you asked 'why THE WAGGONER was not added?' – To say the
truth, – from the higher tone of imagination, and the deeper
touches of passion aimed at in the former, I apprehended this
little Piece could not accompany it without disadvantage. In the
year 1806, if I am not mistaken, THE WAGGONER was read to
you in manuscript, and, as you have remembered it for so long a
time, I am the more encouraged to hope that, since the localities
on which the Poem partly depends did not prevent its being
interesting to you, it may prove acceptable to others. Being
therefore in some measure the cause of its present appearance,
you must allow me the gratification of inscribing it to you; in
acknowledgement of the pleasure I have derived from your
Writings, and of the high esteem with which

                              I am very truly yours,
RYDAL MOUNT, *May 20, 1819*
                    WILLIAM WORDSWORTH.

CANTO FIRST

'Tis spent – this burning day of June!
Soft darkness o'er its latest gleams is stealing;
The buzzing dor-hawk, round and round, is wheeling, –
That solitary bird
Is all that can be heard
In silence deeper far than that of deepest noon!

Confiding Glow-worms, 'tis a night
Propitious to your earth-born light!
But, where the scattered stars are seen
10   In hazy straits the clouds between,
Each, in his station twinkling not,
Seems changed into a pallid spot.
The mountains against heaven's grave weight
Rise up, and grow to wondrous height.
The air, as in a lion's den,
Is close and hot; – and now and then
Comes a tired and sultry breeze
With a haunting and a panting,
Like the stifling of disease;
20   But the dews allay the heat,
And the silence makes it sweet.

Hush, there is someone on the stir!
'Tis Benjamin the Waggoner;
Who long hath trod this toilsome way,
Companion of the night and day.
That far-off tinkling's drowsy cheer,
Mixed with a faint yet grating sound
In a moment lost and found,
The Wain announces – by whose side
30   Along the banks of Rydal Mere
He paces on, a trusty Guide, –
Listen! you can scarcely hear!
Hither he his course is bending; –
Now he leaves the lower ground,
And up the craggy hill ascending

Many a stop and stay he makes,
Many a breathing-fit he takes; –
Steep the way and wearisome,
Yet all the while his whip is dumb!

40   The Horses have worked with right good-will,
And so have gained the top of the hill;
He was patient, they were strong,
And now they smoothly glide along,
Recovering breath, and pleased to win
The praises of mild Benjamin.
Heaven shield him from mishap and snare!
But why so early with this prayer?
Is it for threatenings in the sky?
Or for some other danger nigh?

50   No; none is near him yet, though he
Be one of much infirmity;
For at the bottom of the brow,
Where once the DOVE and OLIVE-BOUGH
Offered a greeting of good ale
To all who entered Grasmere Vale;
And called on him who must depart
To leave it with a jovial heart;
There, where the DOVE and OLIVE-BOUGH
Once hung, a Poet harbours now,

60   A simple water-drinking Bard;
Why need our Hero then (though frail
His best resolves) be on his guard?
He marches by, secure and bold;
Yet while he thinks on times of old,
It seems that all looks wondrous cold;
He shrugs his shoulders, shakes his head,
And, for the honest folk within,
It is a doubt with Benjamin
Whether they be alive or dead!

70   *Here* is no danger, – none at all!
Beyond his wish he walks secure;

But pass a mile – and *then* for trial, –
Then for the pride of self-denial;
If he resist that tempting door,
Which with such friendly voice will call;
If he resist those casement panes,
And that bright gleam which thence will fall
Upon his Leaders' bells and manes,
Inviting him with cheerful lure:
80 For still, though all be dark elsewhere,
Some shining notice will be *there*,
Of open house and ready fare.

    The place to Benjamin right well
Is known, and by as strong a spell
As used to be that sign of love
And hope – the OLIVE-BOUGH and DOVE;
He knows it to his cost, good Man!
Who does not know the famous SWAN?
Object uncouth! and yet our boast,
90 For it was painted by the Host;
His own conceit the figure planned,
'Twas coloured all by his own hand;
And that frail Child of thirsty clay,
Of whom I sing this rustic lay,
Could tell with self-dissatisfaction
Quaint stories of the bird's attraction!

    Well! that is past – and in despite
Of open door and shining light.
And now the conqueror essays
100 The long ascent of Dunmail-raise;
And with his team is gentle here
As when he clomb from Rydal Mere;
His whip they do not dread – his voice
They only hear it to rejoice.
To stand or go is at *their* pleasure;
Their efforts and their time they measure

By generous pride within the breast;
And, while they strain, and while they rest,
He thus pursues his thoughts at leisure.

110   Now am I fairly safe tonight –
And with proud cause my heart is light:
I trespassed lately worse than ever –
But Heaven has blest a good endeavour;
And, to my soul's content, I find
The evil One is left behind.
Yes, let my master fume and fret,
Here am I – with my horses yet!
My jolly team, he finds that ye
Will work for nobody but me!
120   Full proof of this the Country gained;
It knows how ye were vexed and strained,
And forced unworthy stripes to bear,
When trusted to another's care.
Here was it – on this rugged slope,
Which now ye climb with heart and hope,
I saw you, between rage and fear,
Plunge, and fling back a spiteful ear,
And ever more and more confused,
As ye were more and more abused:
130   As chance would have it, passing by
I saw you in that jeopardy:
A word from me was like a charm;
Ye pulled together with one mind;
And your huge burden, safe from harm,
Moved like a vessel in the wind!
– Yes, without me, up hills so high
'Tis vain to strive for mastery.
Then grieve not, jolly team! though tough
The road we travel, steep, and rough;
140   Though Rydal-heights and Dunmail-raise,
And all their fellow banks and braes,
Full often make you stretch and strain,
And halt for breath and halt again,

Yet to their sturdiness 'tis owing
That side by side we still are going!

 While Benjamin in earnest mood
His meditations thus pursued,
A storm, which had been smothered long,
Was growing inwardly more strong;
150 And, in its struggles to get free,
Was busily employed as he.
The thunder had begun to growl –
He heard not, too intent of soul;
The air was now without a breath –
He marked not that 'twas still as death.
But soon large rain-drops on his head
Fell with the weight of drops of lead; –
He starts – and takes, at the admonition,
A sage survey of his condition.
160 The road is black before his eyes,
Glimmering faintly where it lies;
Black is the sky – and every hill,
Up to the sky, is blacker still –
Sky, hill, and dale, one dismal room,
Hung round and overhung with gloom;
Save that above a single height
Is to be seen a lurid light,
Above Helm-crag – a streak half dead,
A burning of portentous red;
170 And near that lurid light, full well
The ASTROLOGER, sage Sidrophel,
Where at his desk and book he sits,
Puzzling aloft his curious wits;
He whose domain is held in common
With no one but the ANCIENT WOMAN,
Cowering beside her rifted cell,
As if intent on magic spell; –
Dread pair that, spite of wind and weather,
Still sit upon Helm-crag together!

180   The ASTROLOGER was not unseen
       By solitary Benjamin;
       But total darkness came anon,
       And he and everything was gone:
       And suddenly a ruffling breeze,
       (That would have rocked the sounding trees
       Had aught of sylvan growth been there)
       Swept through the Hollow long and bare:
       The rain rushed down – the road was battered,
       As with the force of billows shattered;
190   The horses are dismayed, nor know
       Whether they should stand or go;
       And Benjamin is groping near them,
       Sees nothing, and can scarcely hear them.
       He is astounded, – wonder not, –
       With such a charge in such a spot;
       Astounded in the mountain gap
       With thunder-peals, clap after clap,
       Close-treading on the silent flashes –
       And somewhere, as he thinks, by crashes
200   Among the rocks; with weight of rain,
       And sullen motions long and slow,
       That to a dreary distance go –
       Till, breaking in upon the dying strain,
       A rending o'er his head begins the fray again.

           Meanwhile, uncertain what to do,
       And oftentimes compelled to halt,
       The horses cautiously pursue
       Their way, without mishap or fault;
       And now have reached that pile of stones,
210   Heaped over brave King Dunmail's bones,
       He who had once supreme command,
       Last king of rocky Cumberland;
       His bones, and those of all his Power,
       Slain here in a disastrous hour!

           When, passing through this narrow strait,
       Stony, and dark, and desolate,

Benjamin can faintly hear
A voice that comes from someone near,
A female voice: – 'Whoe'er you be,
220 Stop,' it exclaimed, 'and pity me!'
And, less in pity than in wonder,
Amid the darkness and the thunder,
The Waggoner, with prompt command,
Summons his horses to a stand.

While, with increasing agitation,
The Woman urged her supplication,
In rueful words, with sobs between –
The voice of tears that fell unseen;
There came a flash – a startling glare,
230 And all Seat-Sandal was laid bare!
'Tis not a time for nice suggestion,
And Benjamin, without a question,
Taking her for some way-worn rover,
Said, 'Mount, and get you under cover!'

Another voice, in tone as hoarse
As a swoln brook with rugged course,
Cried out, 'Good brother, why so fast?
I've had a glimpse of you – *avast*!
Or, since it suits you to be civil,
240 Take her at once – for good and evil!'

'It is my Husband,' softly said
The Woman, as if half afraid:
By this time she was snug within,
Through help of honest Benjamin;
She and her Babe, which to her breast
With thankfulness the Mother pressed;
And now the same strong voice more near
Said cordially, 'My Friend, what cheer?
Rough doings these! as God's my judge,
250 The sky owes somebody a grudge!
We've had in half an hour or less
A twelvemonth's terror and distress!'

Then Benjamin entreats the Man
Would mount, too, quickly as he can:
The Sailor – Sailor now no more,
But such he had been heretofore –
To courteous Benjamin replied,
'Go you your way, and mind not me;
For I must have, whate'er betide,
260 My Ass and fifty things beside, –
Go, and I'll follow speedily!'

The Waggon moves – and with its load
Descends along the sloping road;
And the rough Sailor instantly
Turns to a little tent hard by:
For when, at closing-in of day,
The family had come that way,
Green pasture and the soft warm air
Tempted them to settle there. –
270 Green is the grass for beast to graze,
Around the stones of Dunmail-raise!

The Sailor gathers up his bed,
Takes down the canvas overhead;
And, after farewell to the place,
A parting word – though not of grace,
Pursues, with Ass and all his store,
The way the Waggon went before.

CANTO SECOND

If Wythburn's modest House of prayer,
As lowly as the lowliest dwelling,
Had, with its belfry's humble stock,
A little pair that hang in air,
Been mistress also of a clock,
(And one, too, not in crazy plight)
Twelve strokes that clock would have been telling
Under the brow of old Helvellyn –

Its bead-roll of midnight,
10 Then, when the Hero of my tale
Was passing by, and, down the vale
(The vale now silent, hushed, I ween,
As if a storm had never been)
Proceeding with a mind at ease;
While the old Familiar of the seas,
Intent to use his utmost haste,
Gained ground upon the Waggon fast,
And gives another lusty cheer;
For, spite of rumbling of the wheels,
20 A welcome greeting he can hear; –
It is a fiddle in its glee
Dinning from the CHERRY TREE!

Thence the sound – the light is there –
As Benjamin is now aware,
Who, to his inward thoughts confined,
Had almost reached the festive door,
When, startled by the Sailor's roar,
He hears a sound and sees the light,
And in a moment calls to mind
30 That 'tis the village MERRY-NIGHT!

Although before in no dejection,
At this insidious recollection
His heart with sudden joy is filled, –
His ears are by the music thrilled,
His eyes take pleasure in the road
Glittering before him bright and broad;
And Benjamin is wet and cold,
And there are reasons manifold
That make the good, towards which he's yearning,
40 Look fairly like a lawful earning.

Nor has thought time to come and go,
To vibrate between yes and no;
For, cries the Sailor, 'Glorious chance

That blew us hither! – let him dance,
Who can or will! – my honest soul,
Our treat shall be a friendly bowl!'
He draws him to the door – 'Come in,
Come, come,' cries he to Benjamin!
And Benjamin – ah, woe is me!
50   Gave the word – the horses heard
And halted, though reluctantly.

'Blithe souls and lightsome hearts have we,
Feasting at the CHERRY TREE!'
This was the outside proclamation,
This was the inside salutation;
What bustling – jostling – high and low!
A universal overflow!
What tankards foaming from the tap!
What store of cakes in every lap!
60   What thumping – stumping – overhead!
The thunder had not been more busy:
With such a stir you would have said,
This little place may well be dizzy!
'Tis who can dance with greatest vigour –
'Tis what can be most prompt and eager;
As if it heard the fiddle's call,
The pewter clatters on the wall;
The very bacon shows its feeling,
Swinging from the smoky ceiling!

70   A steaming bowl, a blazing fire,
What greater good can heart desire?
'Twere worth a wise man's while to try
The utmost anger of the sky:
To *seek* for thoughts of a gloomy cast,
If such the bright amends at last.
Now should you say I judge amiss,
The CHERRY TREE shows proof of this;
For soon, of all the happy there,
Our Travellers are the happiest pair;

80　All care with Benjamin is gone –
　　A Caesar past the Rubicon!
　　He thinks not of his long, long, strife; –
　　The Sailor, Man by nature gay,
　　Hath no resolves to throw away;
　　And he hath now forgot his Wife,
　　Hath quite forgotten her – or may be
　　Thinks her the luckiest soul on earth,
　　Within that warm and peaceful berth,
　　　　Under cover,
90　　　Terror over,
　　Sleeping by her sleeping Baby. '

　　　With bowl that sped from hand to hand,
　　The gladdest of the gladsome band,
　　Amid their own delight and fun,
　　They hear – when every dance is done,
　　When every whirling bout is o'er –
　　The fiddle's *squeak* – that call to bliss,
　　Ever followed by a kiss;
　　They envy not the happy lot,
100　But enjoy their own the more!

　　　While thus our jocund Travellers fare,
　　Up springs the Sailor from his chair –
　　Limps (for I might have told before
　　That he was lame) across the floor –
　　Is gone – returns – and with a prize;
　　With what? – a Ship of lusty size;
　　A gallant stately Man-of-war,
　　Fixed on a smoothly-sliding car.
　　Surprise to all, but most surprise
110　To Benjamin, who rubs his eyes,
　　Not knowing that he had befriended
　　A Man so gloriously attended!

　　　'This,' cries the Sailor, 'a Third-rate is –
　　Stand back, and you shall see her gratis!

This was the Flag-ship at the Nile,
The VANGUARD – you may smirk and smile,
But, pretty Maid, if you look near,
You'll find you've much in little here!
A nobler ship did never swim,
120 And you shall see her in full trim:
I'll set, my friends, to do you honour,
Set every inch of sail upon her.'
So said, so done; and masts, sails, yards,
He names them all; and interlards
His speech with uncouth terms of art,
Accomplished in the showman's part;
And then, as from a sudden check,
Cries out – ' 'Tis there, the quarter-deck
On which brave Admiral Nelson stood –
130 A sight that would have roused your blood! –
One eye he had, which, bright as ten,
Burned like a fire among his men;
Let this be land, and that be sea,
Here lay the French – and *thus* came we!'

Hushed was by this the fiddle's sound,
The dancers all were gathered round,
And, such the stillness of the house,
You might have heard a nibbling mouse;
While, borrowing helps where'er he may,
140 The Sailor through the story runs
Of ships to ships and guns to guns;
And does his utmost to display
The dismal conflict, and the might
And terror of that marvellous night!
'A bowl, a bowl of double measure,'
Cries Benjamin, 'a draught of length,
To Nelson, England's pride and treasure,
Her bulwark and her tower of strength!'
When Benjamin had seized the bowl,
150 The mastiff, from beneath the waggon,
Where he lay, watchful as a dragon,

Rattled his chain; – 'twas all in vain,
For Benjamin, triumphant soul!
He heard the monitory growl;
Heard – and in opposition quaffed
A deep, determined, desperate draught!
Nor did the battered Tar forget,
Or flinch from what he deemed his debt:
Then, like a hero crowned with laurel,
160 Back to her place the ship he led;
Wheeled her back in full apparel;
And so, flag flying at mast head,
Re-yoked her to the Ass: – anon,
Cries Benjamin, 'We must be gone.'
Thus, after two hours' hearty stay,
Again behold them on their way!

CANTO THIRD

Right gladly had the horses stirred,
When they the wished-for greeting heard,
The whip's loud notice from the door,
That they were free to move once more.
You think, those doings must have bred
In them disheartening doubts and dread;
No, not a horse of all the eight,
Although it be a moonless night,
Fears either for himself or freight;
10 For this they know (and let it hide,
In part, the offences of their guide)
That Benjamin, with clouded brains,
Is worth the best with all their pains;
And, if they had a prayer to make,
The prayer would be that they may take
With him whatever comes in course,
The better fortune or the worse;
That no one else may have business near them,
And, drunk or sober, he may steer them.

20   So forth in dauntless mood they fare,
      And with them goes the guardian pair.

         Now, heroes, for the true commotion,
      The triumph of your late devotion!
      Can aught on earth impede delight,
      Still mounting to a higher height;
      And higher still – a greedy flight!
      Can any low-born care pursue her,
      Can any mortal clog come to her?
      No notion have they – not a thought,
30   That is from joyless regions brought!
      And, while they coast the silent lake,
      Their inspiration I partake;
      Share their empyreal spirits – yea,
      With their enraptured vision, see –
      O fancy – what a jubilee!
      What shifting pictures – clad in gleams
      Of colour bright as feverish dreams!
      Earth, spangled sky, and lake serene,
      Involved and restless all – a scene
40   Pregnant with mutual exaltation,
      Rich change, and multiplied creation!
      This sight to me the Muse imparts; –
      And then, what kindness in their hearts!
      What tears of rapture, what vow-making,
      Profound entreaties, and hand-shaking!
      What solemn, vacant, interlacing,
      As if they'd fall asleep embracing!
      Then, in the turbulence of glee,
      And in the excess of amity,
50   Says Benjamin, 'That Ass of thine,
      He spoils thy sport, and hinders mine:
      If he were tethered to the waggon,
      He'd drag as well what he is dragging;
      And we, as brother should with brother,
      Might trudge it alongside each other!'

Forthwith, obedient to command,
The horses made a quiet stand;
And to the waggon's skirts was tied
The Creature, by the Mastiff's side,
60 The Mastiff wondering, and perplext
With dread of what will happen next;
And thinking it but sorry cheer,
To have such company so near!

This new arrangement made, the Wain
Through the still night proceeds again;
No Moon hath risen her light to lend;
But indistinctly may be kenned
The VANGUARD, following close behind,
Sails spread, as if to catch the wind!

70 'Thy wife and child are snug and warm,
Thy ship will travel without harm;
I like,' said Benjamin, 'her shape and stature:
And this of mine – this bulky creature
Of which I have the steering – this,
Seen fairly, is not much amiss!
We want your streamers, friend, you know;
But, altogether as we go,
We make a kind of handsome show!
Among these hills, from first to last,
80 We've weathered many a furious blast;
Hard passage forcing on, with head
Against the storm, and canvas spread.
I hate a boaster; but to thee
Will say't, who know'st both land and sea,
The unluckiest hulk that stems the brine
Is hardly worse beset than mine,
When cross-winds on her quarter beat;
And, fairly lifted from my feet,
I stagger onward – heaven knows how;
90 But not so pleasantly as now:
Poor pilot I, by snows confounded,

And many a foundrous pit surrounded!
Yet here we are, by night and day
Grinding through rough and smooth our way;
Through foul and fair our task fulfilling;
And long shall be so yet – God willing!'

'Ay,' said the Tar, 'through fair and foul –
But save us from yon screeching owl!'
That instant was begun a fray
100 Which called their thoughts another way:
The Mastiff, ill-conditioned carl!
What must he do but growl and snarl,
Still more and more dissatisfied
With the meek comrade at his side!
Till, not incensed though put to proof,
The Ass, uplifting a hind hoof,
Salutes the Mastiff on the head;
And so were better manners bred,
And all was calmed and quieted.

110 'Yon screech-owl,' says the Sailor, turning
Back to his former cause of mourning,
'Yon owl! – pray God that all be well!'
'Tis worse than any funeral bell;
As sure as I've the gift of sight,
We shall be meeting ghosts tonight!'
– Said Benjamin, 'This whip shall lay
A thousand, if they cross our way.
I know that Wanton's noisy station,
I know him and his occupation;
120 The jolly bird hath learned his cheer
Upon the banks of Windermere;
Where a tribe of them make merry,
Mocking the Man that keeps the ferry;
Hallooing from an open throat,
Like travellers shouting for a boat.
– The tricks he learned at Windermere
This vagrant owl is playing here –

That is the worst of his employment:
He's at the top of his enjoyment!'

130   This explanation stilled the alarm,
Cured the foreboder like a charm;
This, and the manner, and the voice,
Summoned the Sailor to rejoice;
His heart is up – he fears no evil
From life or death, from man or devil;
He wheels – and, making many stops,
Brandished his crutch against the mountain tops;
And, while he talked of blows and scars,
Benjamin, among the stars,
140 Beheld a dancing – and a glancing;
Such retreating and advancing
As, I ween, was never seen
In bloodiest battle since the days of Mars!

CANTO FOURTH

Thus they, with freaks of proud delight,
Beguile the remnant of the night;
And many a snatch of jovial song
Regales them as they wind along;
While to the music, from on high,
The echoes make a glad reply. –
But the sage Muse the revel heeds
No farther than her story needs;
Nor will she servilely attend
10 The loitering journey to its end.
– Blithe spirits of her own impel
The Muse, who scents the morning air,
To take of this transported pair
A brief and unreproved farewell;
To quit the slow-paced waggon's side,
And wander down yon hawthorn dell,
With murmuring Greta for her guide.
– There doth she ken the awful form

Of Raven-crag – black as a storm –
20 Glimmering through the twilight pale;
And Ghimmer-crag, his tall twin brother,
Each peering forth to meet the other: –
And, while she roves through St John's Vale,
Along the smooth unpathwayed plain,
By sheep-track or through cottage lane,
Where no disturbance comes to intrude
Upon the pensive solitude,
Her unsuspecting eye, perchance,
With the rude shepherd's favoured glance,
30 Beholds the faeries in array,
Whose party-coloured garments gay
The silent company betray:
Red, green, and blue; a moment's sight!
For Skiddaw-top with rosy light
Is touched – and all the band take flight.
– Fly also, Muse! and from the dell
Mount to the ridge of Nathdale Fell;
Thence, look thou forth o'er wood and lawn
Hoar with the frost-like dews of dawn;
40 Across yon meadowy bottom look,
Where close fogs hide their parent brook;
And see, beyond that hamlet small,
The ruined towers of Threlkeld-hall,
Lurking in a double shade,
By trees and lingering twilight made!
There, at Blencathara's rugged feet,
Sir Lancelot gave a safe retreat
To noble Clifford; from annoy
Concealed the persecuted boy,
50 Well pleased in rustic garb to feed
His flock, and pipe on shepherd's reed
Among this multitude of hills,
Crags, woodlands, waterfalls, and rills;
Which soon the morning shall enfold,
From east to west, in ample vest
Of massy gloom and radiance bold.

The mists, that o'er the streamlet's bed
Hung low, begin to rise and spread;
Even while I speak, their skirts of grey
60 Are smitten by a silver ray;
And lo! – up Castrigg's naked steep
(Where, smoothly urged, the vapours sweep
Along – and scatter and divide,
Like fleecy clouds self-multiplied)
The stately waggon is ascending,
With faithful Benjamin attending,
Apparent now beside his team –
Now lost amid a glittering stream:
And with him goes his Sailor-friend,
70 By this time near their journey's end;
And, after their high-minded riot,
Sickening into thoughtful quiet;
As if the morning's pleasant hour
Had for their joys a killing power.
And, sooth, for Benjamin a vein
Is opened of still deeper pain,
As if his heart by notes were stung
From out the lowly hedge-rows flung;
As if the warbler lost in light
80 Reproved his soarings of the night,
In strains of rapture pure and holy
Upbraided his distempered folly.

Drooping is he, his step is dull;
But the horses stretch and pull;
With increasing vigour climb,
Eager to repair lost time;
Whether, by their own desert,
Knowing what cause there is for shame,
They are labouring to avert
90 As much as may be of the blame,
Which, they foresee, must soon alight
Upon *his* head, whom, in despite
Of all his failings, they love best;

Whether for him they are distrest;
Or, by length of fasting roused,
Are impatient to be housed:
Up against the hill they strain
Tugging at the iron chain,
Tugging all with might and main,
100 Last and foremost, every horse
To the utmost of his force!
And the smoke and respiration,
Rising like an exhalation,
Blend with the mist – a moving shroud
To form, an undissolving cloud;
Which, with slant ray, the merry sun
Takes delight to play upon.
Never golden-haired Apollo,
Pleased some favourite chief to follow
110 Through accidents of peace or war,
In a perilous moment threw
Around the object of his care
Veil of such celestial hue;
Interposed so bright a screen –
Him and his enemies between!

Alas! what boots it? – who can hide,
When the malicious Fates are bent
On working out an ill intent?
Can destiny be turned aside?
120 No – sad progress of my story!
Benjamin, this outward glory
Cannot shield thee from thy Master,
Who from Keswick has pricked forth,
Sour and surly as the north;
And, in fear of some disaster,
Comes to give what help he may,
And to hear what thou canst say;
If, as needs he must forbode,
Thou hast been loitering on the road!
130 His fears, his doubts, may now take flight –

The wished-for object is in sight;
Yet, trust the Muse, it rather hath
Stirred him up to livelier wrath;
Which he stifles, moody man!
With all the patience that he can;
To the end that, at your meeting,
He may give thee decent greeting.

There he is – resolved to stop,
Till the waggon gains the top;
140 But stop he cannot – must advance:
Him Benjamin, with lucky glance,
Espies – and instantly is ready,
Self-collected, poised, and steady:
And, to be the better seen,
Issues from his radiant shroud,
From his close-attending cloud,
With careless air and open mien.
Erect his port, and firm his going;
So struts yon cock that now is crowing;
150 And the morning light in grace
Strikes upon his lifted face,
Hurrying the pallid hue away
That might his trespasses betray.
But what can all avail to clear him,
Or what need of explanation,
Parley or interrogation?
For the Master sees, alas!
That unhappy Figure near him,
Limping o'er the dewy grass,
160 Where the road it fringes, sweet,
Soft and cool to way-worn feet;
And, O indignity! an Ass,
By his noble Mastiff's side,
Tethered to the waggon's tail:
And the ship, in all her pride,
Following after in full sail!
Not to speak of babe and mother;

Who, contented with each other,
And snug as birds in leafy arbour,
170 Find, within, a blessed harbour!
    With eager eyes the Master pries;
Looks in and out, and through and through;
Says nothing – till at last he spies
A wound upon the Mastiff's head,
A wound, where plainly might be read
What feats an Ass's hoof can do!
But drop the rest: – this aggravation,
This complicated provocation,
A hoard of grievances unsealed;
180 All past forgiveness it repealed;
And thus, and through distempered blood
On both sides, Benjamin the good,
The patient, and the tender-hearted,
Was from his team and waggon parted;
When duty of that day was o'er,
Laid down his whip – and served no more. –
Nor could the waggon long survive,
When Benjamin had ceased to drive:
It lingered on; – guide after guide
190 Ambitiously the office tried;
But each unmanageable hill
Called for *his* patience and *his* skill; –
And sure it is, that through this night,
And what the morning brought to light,
Two losses had we to sustain,
We lost both WAGGONER and WAIN!

Accept, O Friend, for praise or blame,
The gift of this adventurous song;
A record which I dared to frame,
200 Though timid scruples checked me long;
They checked me – and I left the theme
Untouched; – in spite of many a gleam
Of fancy which thereon was shed,
Like pleasant sunbeams shifting still

Upon the side of a distant hill:
But Nature might not be gainsaid;
For what I have and what I miss
I sing of these; – it makes my bliss!
Nor is it I who play the part,
210 But a shy spirit in my heart,
That comes and goes – will sometimes leap
From hiding-places ten years deep;
Or haunts me with familiar face,
Returning, like a ghost unlaid,
Until the debt I owe be paid.
Forgive me, then; for I had been
On friendly terms with this Machine:
In him, while he was wont to trace
Our roads, through many a long year's space,
220 A living almanack had we;
We had a speaking diary,
That in this uneventful place,
Gave to the days a mark and name
By which we knew them when they came.
– Yes, I, and all about me here,
Through all the changes of the year,
Had seen him through the mountains go,
In pomp of mist or pomp of snow,
Majestically huge and slow:
230 Or, with a milder grace adorning
The landscape of a summer's morning;
While Grasmere smoothed her liquid plain
The moving image to detain;
And mighty Fairfield, with a chime
Of echoes, to his march kept time;
When little other business stirred,
And little other sound was heard;
In that delicious hour of balm,
Stillness, solitude, and calm,
240 While yet the valley is arrayed,
On this side with a sober shade;
On that is prodigally bright –

Crag, lawn, and wood – with rosy light.
– But most of all, thou lordly Wain!
I wish to have thee here again,
When windows flap and chimney roars,
And all is dismal out of doors;
And, sitting by my fire, I see
Eight sorry carts, no less a train!
250 Unworthy successors of thee,
Come straggling through the wind and rain:
And oft, as they pass slowly on,
Beneath my windows, one by one,
See, perched upon the naked height
The summit of a cumbrous freight,
A single traveller – and there
Another; then perhaps a pair –
The lame, the sickly, and the old;
Men, women, heartless with the cold;
260 And babes in wet and starveling plight;
Which once, be weather as it might,
Had still a nest within a nest,
Thy shelter – and their mother's breast!
Then most of all, then far the most,
Do I regret what we have lost;
Am grieved for that unhappy sin
Which robbed us of good Benjamin; –
And of his stately Charge, which none
Could keep alive when He was gone!

Power of Music

An Orpheus! an Orpheus! yes, Faith may grow bold,
And take to herself all the wonders of old; –
Near the stately Pantheon you'll meet with the same
In the street that from Oxford hath borrowed its name.

His station is there; and he works on the crowd,
He sways them with harmony merry and loud;

He fills with his power all their hearts to the brim –
Was aught ever heard like his fiddle and him?

What an eager assembly! what an empire is this!
10   The weary have life, and the hungry have bliss;
The mourner is cheered, and the anxious have rest;
And the guilt-burdened soul is no longer opprest.

As the Moon brightens round her the clouds of the
      night,
So He, where he stands, is a centre of light;
It gleams on the face, there, of dusky-browed Jack,
And the pale-visaged Baker's, with basket on back.

That errand-bound 'Prentice was passing in haste –
What matter! he's caught – and his time runs to waste;
The Newsman is stopped, though he stops on the fret;
20   And the half-breathless Lamplighter – he's in the net!

The Porter sits down on the weight which he bore;
The Lass with her barrow wheels hither her store; –
If a thief could be here he might pilfer at ease;
She sees the Musician, 'tis all that she sees!

He stands, backed by the wall; – he abates not his din;
His hat gives him vigour, with boons dropping in,
From the old and the young, from the poorest; and
      there!
The one-pennied Boy has his penny to spare.

O blest are the hearers, and proud be the hand
30   Of the pleasure it spreads through so thankful a band;
I am glad for him, blind as he is! – all the while
If they speak 'tis to praise, and they praise with a smile.

That tall Man, a giant in bulk and in height,
Not an inch of his body is free from delight;
Can he keep himself still, if he would? oh, not he!
The music stirs in him like wind through a tree.

Mark that Cripple who leans on his crutch; like a tower
That long has leaned forward, leans hour after hour! –
That Mother, whose spirit in fetters is bound,
40 While she dandles the Babe in her arms to the sound.

Now, coaches and chariots! roar on like a stream;
Here are twenty souls happy as souls in a dream:
They are deaf to your murmurs – they care not for you,
Nor what ye are flying, nor what ye pursue!

Stray Pleasures

' – *Pleasure is spread through the earth*
In stray gifts to be claimed by whoever shall find.'

By their floating mill,
That lies dead and still,
Behold yon Prisoners three,
The Miller with two Dames, on the breast of the
Thames!
The platform is small, but gives room for them all;
And they're dancing merrily.

From the shore come the notes
To their mill where it floats,
To their house and their mill tethered fast:
10 To the small wooden isle where, their work to beguile,
They from morning to even take whatever is given; –
And many a blithe day they have past.

In sight of the spires,
All alive with the fires
Of the sun going down to his rest,
In the broad open eye of the solitary sky,
They dance, – there are three, as jocund as free,
While they dance on the calm river's breast.

      Man and Maidens wheel,
20   They themselves make the reel,
And their music's a prey which they seize;
It plays not for them, – what matter? 'tis theirs;
And if they had care, it has scattered their cares
While they dance, crying, 'Long as ye please!'

      They dance not for me,
      Yet mine is their glee!
Thus pleasure is spread through the earth
In stray gifts to be claimed by whoever shall find;
Thus a rich loving-kindness, redundantly kind,
30 Moves all nature to gladness and mirth.

      The showers of the spring
      Rouse the birds, and they sing;
If the wind do but stir for his proper delight,
Each leaf, that and this, his neighbour will kiss;
Each wave, one and t'other, speeds after his brother;
They are happy, for that is their right!

Star-Gazers

What crowd is this? what have we here! we must not
    pass it by;
A Telescope upon its frame, and pointed to the sky:
Long is it as a barber's pole, or mast of little boat,
Some little pleasure-skiff, that doth on Thames's waters
    float.

The Show-man chooses well his place, 'tis Leicester's
    busy Square;
And is as happy in his night, for the heavens are blue
    and fair;
Calm, though impatient, is the crowd; each stands ready
    with the fee,
And envies him that's looking; – what an insight must
    it be!

Yet, Show-man, where can lie the cause? Shall thy
   Implement have blame,
10 A boaster that, when he is tried, fails, and is put to
   shame?
Or is it good as others are, and be their eyes in fault?
Their eyes, or minds? or, finally, is yon resplendent
   vault?

Is nothing of that radiant pomp so good as we have
   here?
Or gives a thing but small delight that never can be
   dear?
The silver moon with all her vales, and hills of
   mightiest fame,
Doth she betray us when they're seen? or are they but a
   name?

Or is it rather that Conceit rapacious is and strong,
And bounty never yields so much but it seems to do
   her wrong?
Or is it that, when human Souls a journey long have
   had
20 And are returned into themselves, they cannot but be
   sad?

Or must we be constrained to think that these
   Spectators rude,
Poor in estate, of manners base, men of the multitude,
Have souls which never yet have risen, and therefore
   prostrate lie?
No, no, this cannot be; – men thirst for power and
   majesty!

Does, then, a deep and earnest thought the blissful
   mind employ
Of him who gazes, or has gazed? a grave and steady joy,
That doth reject all show of pride, admits no outward
   sign,
Because not of this noisy world, but silent and divine!

Whatever be the cause, 'tis sure that they who pry and
    pore
30 Seem to meet with little gain, seem less happy than
    before:
One after One they take their turn, nor have I one
    espied
That doth not slackly go away, as if dissatisfied.

'*Yes, it was the mountain Echo*'

Yes, it was the mountain Echo,
Solitary, clear, profound,
Answering to the shouting Cuckoo,
Giving to her sound for sound!

Unsolicited reply
To a babbling wanderer sent;
Like her ordinary cry,
Like – but oh, how different!

Hears not also mortal Life?
10 Hear not we, unthinking Creatures!
Slaves of folly, love, or strife –
Voices of two different natures?

Have not *we* too? – yes, we have
Answers, and we know not whence;
Echoes from beyond the grave,
Recognized intelligence!

Such rebounds our inward ear
Catches sometimes from afar –
Listen, ponder, hold them dear;
20 For of God, – of God they are.

The Recluse. Part First. Book First.
Home at Grasmere

Once to the verge of yon steep barrier came
A roving School-boy; what the Adventurer's age
Hath now escaped his memory – but the hour,
One of a golden summer holiday,
He well remembers, though the year be gone.
Alone and devious from afar he came;
And, with a sudden influx overpowered
At sight of this seclusion, he forgot
His haste, for hasty had his footsteps been
10   As boyish his pursuits; and, sighing said,
'What happy fortune were it here to live!
And, if a thought of dying, if a thought
Of mortal separation, could intrude
With paradise before him, here to die!'
No Prophet was he, had not even a hope,
Scarcely a wish, but one bright pleasing thought,
A fancy in the heart of what might be
The lot of Others, never could be his.

   The Station whence he looked was soft and green,
20   Not giddy yet aërial, with a depth
Of Vale below, a height of hills above.
For rest of body, perfect was the Spot,
All that luxurious nature could desire,
But stirring to the Spirit; who could gaze
And not feel motions there? He thought of clouds
That sail on winds; of Breezes that delight
To play on water, or in endless chase
Pursue each other through the yielding plain
Of grass or corn, over and through and through,
30   In billow after billow, evermore
Disporting. Nor unmindful was the Boy
Of sunbeams, shadows, butterflies and birds;
Of fluttering Sylphs, and softly-gliding Fays,

Genii, and winged Angels that are Lords
Without restraint, of all which they behold.
The illusion strengthening as he gazed, he felt
That such unfettered liberty was his,
Such power and joy; but only for this end,
To flit from field to rock, from rock to field,
40   From shore to island, and from isle to shore,
From open ground to covert, from a bed
Of meadow-flowers into a tuft of wood;
From high to low, from low to high, yet still
Within the bound of this high Concave; here
Must be his Home, this Valley be his World.

    Since that day forth the place to him – *to me*
(For I who live to register the truth
Was that same young and happy Being) became
As beautiful to thought, as it had been,
50   When present, to the bodily sense; a haunt
Of pure affections, shedding upon joy
A brighter joy; and through such damp and gloom
Of the gay mind, as ofttimes splenetic Youth
Mistakes for sorrow darting beams of light
That no self-cherished sadness could withstand:
And now 'tis mine, perchance for life, dear Vale,
Beloved Grasmere (let the Wandering Streams
Take up, the cloud-capt hills repeat, the Name),
One of thy lowly Dwellings is my Home.

60   And was the cost so great? and could it seem
An act of courage, and the thing itself
A conquest? who must bear the blame? sage Man
Thy prudence, thy experience – thy desires,
Thy apprehensions – blush thou for them all.

    Yes, the realities of life so cold,
So cowardly, so ready to betray,
So stinted in the measure of their grace
As we pronounce them doing them much wrong

Have been to me more bountiful than hope,
70 Less timid than desire – but that is passed.

On Nature's invitation do I come
By Reason sanctioned – Can the choice mislead
That made the calmest, fairest spot of earth,
With all its unappropriated good,
My own; and not mine only, for with me
Entrenched, say rather peacefully embowered,
Under yon Orchard, in yon humble Cot,
A younger Orphan of a Home extinct,
The only Daughter of my Parents, dwells.

80 Aye, think on that, my Heart, and cease to stir,
Pause upon that and let the breathing frame
No longer breathe, but all be satisfied.
– Oh if such silence be not thanks to God
For what hath been bestowed, then where, where then
Shall gratitude find rest? Mine eyes did ne'er
Fix on a lovely object nor my mind
Take pleasure in the midst of happy thoughts,
But either She whom now I have, who now
Divides with me this loved Abode, was there,
90 Or not far off. Where'er my footsteps turned,
Her Voice was like a hidden Bird that sang,
The thought of her was like a flash of light,
Or an *unseen* companionship, a breath
Or fragrance independent of the wind.
In all my goings, in the new and old
Of all my meditations, and in this
Favourite of all, in this the most of all.
– What Being, therefore, since the birth of Man
Had ever more abundant cause to speak
100 Thanks, and if favours of the heavenly Muse
Make him more thankful, then to call on verse
To aid him, and in Song resound his joy.
The boon is absolute; surpassing grace
To me hath been vouchsafed; among the bowers

Of blissful Eden this was neither given
Nor could be given, possession of the good
Which had been sighed for, ancient thought fulfilled
And dear Imaginations realized,
Up to their highest measure, yea and more.

110   Embrace me then, ye Hills, and close me in,
Now in the clear and open day I feel
Your guardianship; I take it to my heart;
'Tis like the solemn shelter of the night.
But I would call thee beautiful, for mild,
And soft, and gay, and beautiful thou art,
Dear Valley, having in thy face a smile
Though peaceful, full of gladness. Thou art pleased,
Pleased with thy crags, and woody steeps, thy Lake,
Its one green Island and its winding shores;
120   The multitude of little rocky hills,
Thy Church and Cottages of mountain stone
Clustered like stars some few, but single most,
And lurking dimly in their shy retreats,
Or glancing at each other cheerful looks,
Like separated stars with clouds between.
What want we? have we not perpetual streams,
Warm woods, and sunny hills, and fresh green fields,
And mountains not less green, and flocks, and herds,
And thickets full of songsters, and the voice
130   Of lordly birds, an unexpected sound
Heard now and then from morn to latest eve,
Admonishing the man who walks below
Of solitude and silence in the sky?
These have we, and a thousand nooks of earth
Have also these, but *no* where else is found,
Nowhere (or is it fancy?) *can* be found
The one sensation that is here; 'tis here,
Here as it found its way into my heart
In childhood, here as it abides by day,
140   By night, here only; or in chosen minds
That take it with them hence, where'er they go.

'Tis, but I cannot name it, 'tis the sense
Of majesty, and beauty, and repose,
A blended holiness of earth and sky,
Something that makes this individual Spot,
This small Abiding-place of many Men,
A termination, and a last retreat,
A Centre, come from wheresoe'er you will,
A Whole without dependence or defect,
150 Made for itself, and happy in itself,
Perfect Contentment, Unity entire.

Bleak season was it, turbulent and bleak,
When hitherward we journeyed, side by side
Through burst of sunshine and through flying showers;
Paced the long Vales, how long they were, and yet
How fast that length of way was left behind,
Wensley's rich Vale and Sedbergh's naked heights.
The frosty wind, as if to make amends
For its keen breath, was aiding to our steps
160 And drove us onward like two ships at sea,
Or like two Birds, companions in mid-air,
Parted and re-united by the blast.
Stern was the face of Nature; we rejoiced
In that stern countenance, for our Souls thence drew
A feeling of their strength. The naked Trees,
The icy brooks, as on we passed, appeared
To question us. 'Whence come ye? to what end?'
They seemed to say; 'What would ye,' said the shower,
'Wild Wanderers, whither through my dark domain?'
170 The sunbeam said, 'Be happy.' When this Vale
We entered, bright and solemn was the sky
That faced us with a passionate welcoming,
And led us to our threshold. Daylight failed
Insensibly, and round us gently fell
Composing darkness, with a quiet load
Of full contentment, in a little Shed
Disturbed, uneasy in itself as seemed,
And wondering at its new inhabitants.

It loves us now, this Vale so beautiful
180 Begins to love us! By a sullen storm,
Two months unwearied of severest storm,
It put the temper of our minds to proof
And found us faithful through the gloom, and heard
The Poet mutter his prelusive songs
With cheerful heart, an unknown voice of joy
Among the silence of the woods and hills;
Silent to any gladsomeness of sound
With all their Shepherds.
                            But the gates of Spring
Are opened; churlish Winter hath given leave
190 That she should entertain for this one day,
Perhaps for many genial days to come,
His guests, and make them jocund. They are pleased,
But most of all the Birds that haunt the flood
With the mild summons; inmates though they be
Of Winter's household, they keep festival
This day, who drooped, or seemed to droop, so long;
They show their pleasure, and shall I do less?
Happier of happy though I be, like them
I cannot take possession of the sky,
200 Mount with a thoughtless impulse, and wheel there,
One of a mighty multitude, whose way
Is a perpetual harmony, and dance
Magnificent. Behold, how with a grace
Of ceaseless motion, that might scarcely seem
Inferior to angelical, they prolong
Their curious pastime, shaping in mid-air,
And sometimes with ambitious wing that soars
High as the level of the mountain tops,
A circuit ampler than the lake beneath,
210 Their own domain; – but ever, while intent
On tracing and retracing that large round,
Their jubilant activity evolves
Hundreds of curves and circlets, to and fro,
Upwards and downwards, progress intricate
Yet unperplexed, as if one spirit swayed

Their indefatigable flight. 'Tis done;
Ten times and more I fancied it had ceased.
But lo! the vanished company again
Ascending, they approach – I hear their wings
220 Faint, faint at first; and then an eager sound
Passed in a moment – and as faint again!
They tempt the sun to sport among their plumes;
Tempt the smooth water, or the gleaming ice,
To show them a fair image, – 'tis themselves,
Their own fair forms, upon the glimmering plain,
Painted more soft and fair as they descend,
Almost to touch, – then up again aloft,
Up with a sally and a flash of speed,
As if they scorned both resting-place and rest!

230　　This day is a thanksgiving, 'tis a day
Of glad emotion and deep quietness;
Not upon me alone hath been bestowed,
Me rich in many onward-looking thoughts,
The penetrating bliss; oh surely these
Have felt it, not the happy Choirs of Spring,
Her own peculiar family of love
That sport among green leaves, a blither train.

　　　　But two are missing – two, a lonely pair
Of milk-white Swans, wherefore are they not seen
240 Partaking this day's pleasure? From afar
They came, to sojourn here in solitude,
Choosing this Valley, they who had the choice
Of the whole world. We saw them day by day,
Through those two months of unrelenting storm,
Conspicuous at the centre of the Lake
Their safe retreat; we knew them well, I guess
That the whole Valley knew them; but to us
They were more dear than may be well believed,
Not only for their beauty, and their still
250 And placid way of life and constant love
Inseparable, not for these alone,

But that their state so much resembled ours,
They having also chosen this abode;
They strangers, and we strangers; they a pair,
And we a solitary pair like them.
They should not have departed; many days
Did I look forth in vain, nor on the wing
Could see them, nor in that small open space
Of blue unfrozen water, where they lodged,
260 And lived so long in quiet, side by side.
Shall we behold them, consecrated friends,
Faithful Companions, yet another year
Surviving, they for us, and we for them,
And neither pair be broken? Nay perchance
It is too late already for such hope,
The Dalesmen may have aimed the deadly tube,
And parted them; or haply both are gone
One death, and that were mercy given to both.
Recall my song the ungenerous thought; forgive,
270 Thrice favoured Region, the conjecture harsh
Of such inhospitable penalty
Inflicted upon confidence so pure.
Ah, if I wished to follow where the sight
Of all that is before my eyes, the voice
Which speaks from a presiding Spirit here,
Would lead me – I should whisper to myself;
They who are dwellers in this holy place
Must needs themselves be hallowed, they require
No benediction from the Stranger's lips,
280 For they are blest already; none would give
The greeting 'peace be with you' unto them
For peace they have, it cannot but be theirs,
And mercy, and forbearance – Nay – not these,
Their healing offices a pure good-will
Precludes, and charity beyond the bounds
Of charity – an overflowing love;
Not for the Creature only, but for all
That is around them, love for everything
Which in this happy Region they behold!

290   Thus do we soothe ourselves, and when the thought
Is passed we blame it not for having come.
– What if I floated down a pleasant Stream
And now am landed, and the motion gone,
Shall I reprove myself? Ah no, the Stream
Is flowing, and will never cease to flow,
And I shall float upon that Stream again.
By such forgetfulness the Soul becomes,
Words cannot say, how beautiful: then hail,
Hail to the visible Presence, hail to thee,
300 Delightful Valley, habitation fair!
And to whatever else of outward form
Can give us inward help, can purify,
And elevate, and harmonize, and soothe,
And steal away, and for a while deceive
And lap in pleasing rest, and bear us on
Without desire in full complacency,
Contemplating perfection absolute
And entertained as in a placid sleep.

    But not betrayed by tenderness of mind
310 That feared, or wholly overlooked the truth,
Did we come hither, with romantic hope
To find in midst of so much loveliness,
Love, perfect love; of so much majesty
A like majestic frame of mind in those
Who here abide, the persons like the place.
Not from such hope, or aught of such belief
Hath issued any portion of the joy
Which I have felt this day. An awful voice,
'Tis true, hath in my walks been often heard,
320 Sent from the mountains or the sheltered fields,
Shout after shout – reiterated whoop
In manner of a bird that takes delight
In answering to itself; or like a hound
Single at chase among the lonely woods,
His yell repeating; yet it was in truth
A human voice – a Spirit of coming night,

How solemn when the sky is dark, and earth
Not dark, nor yet enlightened, but by snow
Made visible, amid a noise of winds
330 And bleatings manifold of mountain sheep,
Which in that iteration recognize
Their summons, and are gathering round for food,
Devoured with keenness ere to grove or bank
Or rocky *bield* with patience they retire.

    That very voice, which, in some timid mood
Of superstitious fancy, might have seemed
Awful as ever stray Demoniac uttered,
His steps to govern in the Wilderness;
Or as the Norman Curfew's regular beat,
340 To hearths when first they darkened at the knell:
That Shepherd's voice, it may have reached mine ear
Debased and under profanation, made
The ready Organ of articulate sounds
From ribaldry, impiety, or wrath
Issuing when shame hath ceased to check the brawls
Of some abused Festivity – so be it.
I came not dreaming of unruffled life,
Untainted manners; born among the hills,
Bred also there, I wanted not a scale
350 To regulate my hopes; pleased with the good,
I shrink not from the evil with disgust,
Or with immoderate pain. I look for Man,
The common Creature of the brotherhood,
Differing but little from the Man elsewhere,
For selfishness, and envy, and revenge,
Ill neighbourhood – pity that this should be,
Flattery and double-dealing, strife and wrong.

    Yet is it something gained, it is in truth
A mighty gain, that Labour here preserves
360 His rosy face, a Servant only here
Of the fire-side or of the open field,
A Freeman, therefore, sound and unimpaired;

That extreme penury is here unknown
And cold and hunger's abject wretchedness,
Mortal to body and the heaven-born mind;
That they who want, are not too great a weight
For those who can relieve; here may the heart
Breathe in the air of fellow-suffering
Dreadless, as in a kind of fresher breeze
370   Of her own native element, the hand
Be ready and unwearied without plea
From tasks too frequent, or beyond its power
For languor or indifference or despair.
And as these lofty barriers break the force
Of winds, this deep Vale, – as it doth in part
Conceal us from the Storm, – so here abides
A power and a protection for the mind,
Dispensed indeed to other solitudes,
Favoured by noble privilege like this,
380   Where kindred independence of estate
Is prevalent, where he who tills the field,
He, happy Man! is Master of the field,
And treads the mountains which his Fathers trod.

    Not less than half-way up *yon* Mountain's side
Behold a dusky spot, a grove of Firs
That seems still smaller than it is; this grove
Is haunted – by what ghost? a gentle Spirit
Of memory faithful to the call of love;
For, as reports the Dame, whose fire sends up
390   Yon curling smoke from the grey cot below,
The trees (her first-born Child being then a babe)
Were planted by her husband and herself,
That ranging o'er the high and houseless ground
Their sheep might neither want (from perilous storms
Of winter, nor from summer's sultry heat)
A friendly covert. 'And they knew it well,'
Said she, 'for thither as the trees grew up,
We to the patient creatures carried food
In times of heavy snow.' She then began

400 In fond obedience to her private thoughts
To speak of her dead Husband: is there not
An art, a music, and a strain of words
That shall be life, the acknowledged voice of life,
Shall speak of what is done among the fields,
Done truly there, or felt, of solid good
And real evil, yet be sweet withal,
More grateful, more harmonious than the breath,
The idle breath of softest pipe attuned
To pastoral fancies? Is there such a stream
410 Pure and unsullied, flowing from the heart
With motions of true dignity and grace?
Or must we seek that stream where Man is not?
Methinks I could repeat in tuneful verse
Delicious as the gentlest breeze that sounds
Through that aërial fir-grove, could preserve
Some portion of its human history
As gathered from the Matron's lips, and tell
Of tears that have been shed at sight of it
And moving dialogues between this Pair,
420 Who in their prime of wedlock, with joint hands
Did plant the grove, now flourishing, while they
No longer flourish, he entirely gone,
She withering in her loneliness. Be this
A task above my skill: the silent mind
Has her own treasures, and I think of these,
Love what I see, and honour humankind.

No, we are not alone, we do not stand,
My Sister, here misplaced and desolate,
Loving what no one cares for but ourselves;
430 We shall not scatter through the plains and rocks
Of this fair Vale, and o'er its spacious heights
Unprofitable kindliness, bestowed
On objects unaccustomed to the gifts
Of feeling, which were cheerless and forlorn
But few weeks past, and would be so again
Were we not here; we do not tend a lamp

Whose lustre we alone participate,
Which shines dependent upon us alone,
Mortal though bright, a dying, dying flame.
440 Look where we will, some human hand has been
Before us with its offering; not a tree
Sprinkles these little pastures but the same
Hath furnished matter for a thought; perchance
For someone serves as a familiar friend.
Joy spreads and sorrow spreads; and this whole Vale,
Home of untutored Shepherds as it is,
Swarms with sensation, as with gleams of sunshine,
Shadows or breezes, scents or sounds. Nor deem
These feelings, though subservient more than ours
450 To every day's demand for daily bread
And borrowing more their spirit, and their shape
From self-respecting interests, deem them not
Unworthy therefore, and unhallowed – no,
They lift the animal being, do themselves
By Nature's kind and ever-present aid
Refine the selfishness from which they spring,
Redeem by love the individual sense
Of anxiousness with which they are combined.
And thus it is that fitly they become
460 Associates in the joy of purest minds
They blend therewith congenially: meanwhile
Calmly they breathe their own undying life
Through this their mountain sanctuary; long,
Oh long may it remain inviolate,
Diffusing health and sober cheerfulness
And giving to the moments as they pass
Their little boons of animating thought
That sweeten labour, make it seen and felt
To be no arbitrary weight imposed,
470 But a glad function natural to Man.

Fair proof of this, Newcomer though I be,
Already have I gained. The inward frame
Though slowly opening, opens every day

With process not unlike to that which cheers
A pensive Stranger journeying at his leisure
Through some Helvetian Dell, when low-hung mists
Break up, and are beginning to recede;
How pleased he is where thin and thinner grows
The veil, or where it parts at once, to spy
480 The dark pines thrusting forth their spiky heads;
To watch the spreading lawns with cattle grazed,
Then to be greeted by the scattered huts,
As they shine out; and *see* the streams whose murmur
Had soothed his ear while they were hidden: how
        pleased
To have about him, which way e'er he goes,
Something on every side concealed from view,
In every quarter something visible,
Half-seen or wholly, lost and found again,
Alternate progress and impediment
490 And yet a growing prospect in the main.

    Such pleasure now is mine, albeit forced,
Herein less happy than the Traveller
To cast from time to time a painful look
Upon unwelcome things which unawares
Reveal themselves; not therefore is my heart
Depressed nor does it fear what is to come,
But confident, enriched at every glance.
The more I see the more delight my mind
Receives, or by reflexion can create.
500 Truth justifies herself, and as she dwells
With Hope, who would not follow where she leads?

    Nor let me pass unheeded other loves
Where no fear is, and humbler sympathies.
Already hath sprung up within my heart
A liking for the small grey horse that bears
The paralytic Man, and for the brute
In Scripture sanctified – the patient brute
On which the cripple, in the Quarry maimed,

Rides to and fro: I know them and their ways.
510 The famous Sheep-dog, first in all the Vale
Though yet to me a Stranger, will not be
A Stranger long; nor will the blind man's guide,
Meek and neglected thing, of no renown!
Soon will peep forth the primrose; ere it fades
Friends shall I have at dawn, blackbird and thrush
To rouse me, and a hundred Warblers more;
And if those Eagles to their ancient Hold
Return, Helvellyn's Eagles! with the Pair
From my own door I shall be free to claim
520 Acquaintance as they sweep from cloud to cloud.
The Owl that gives the name to Owlet-Crag
Have I heard whooping, and he soon will be
A chosen one of my regards. See there.
The Heifer in yon little Croft belongs
To one who holds it dear; with duteous care
She reared it, and in speaking of her charge
I heard her scatter some endearing words
Domestic, and in spirit motherly
She being herself a Mother, happy Beast
530 If the caresses of a human voice
Can make it so, and care of human hands.

    And ye as happy under Nature's care,
Strangers to me and all men, or at least
Strangers to all particular amity,
All intercourse of knowledge or of love
That parts the individual from his kind,
Whether in large communities ye keep
From year to year, not shunning Man's abode,
A settled residence, or be from far,
540 Wild creatures, and of many homes, that come
The gift of winds, and whom the winds again
Take from us at your pleasure; yet shall ye
Not want, for this, your own subordinate place
In my affections. Witness the delight
With which erewhile I saw that multitude

Wheel through the sky, and see them now at rest,
Yet not at rest, upon the glassy lake.
They *cannot* rest, they gambol like young whelps;
Active as lambs, and overcome with joy,
550 They try all frolic motions; flutter, plunge
And beat the passive water with their wings.
Too distant are they for plain view, but lo!
Those little fountains, sparkling in the sun,
Betray their occupation, rising up,
First one and then another silver spout,
As one or other takes the fit of glee,
Fountains and spouts, yet somewhat in the guise
Of plaything fire-works, that on festal nights
Sparkle about the feet of wanton boys.
560 – How vast the compass of this theatre,
Yet nothing to be seen but lovely pomp
And silent majesty; the birch-tree woods
Are hung with thousand thousand diamond drops
Of melted hoar-frost, every tiny knot
In the bare twigs, each little budding-place
Cased with its several bead, what myriads there
Upon one tree, while all the distant grove
That rises to the summit of the steep
Shows like a mountain built of silver light:
570 See yonder the same pageant, and again
Behold the universal imagery
Inverted, all its sun-bright features touched
As with the varnish, and the gloss of dreams;
Dreamlike the blending also of the whole
Harmonious landscape; all along the shore
The boundary lost, the line invisible
That parts the image from reality;
And the clear hills, as high as they ascend
Heavenward, so deep piercing the lake below.
580 Admonished of the days of love to come
The raven croaks, and fills the upper air
With a strange sound of genial harmony;
And in and all about that playful band,

Incapable although they be of rest
And in their fashion very rioters,
There is a stillness; and they seem to make
Calm revelry in that their calm abode.
Them leaving to their joyous hours I pass,
Pass with a thought the life of the whole year
590   That is to come: the throng of woodland flowers,
And lilies that will dance upon the waves.

    Say boldly then that solitude is not
Where these things are: he truly is alone,
He of the multitude whose eyes are doomed
To hold a vacant commerce day by day
With objects wanting life – repelling love;
He by the vast Metropolis immured,
Where pity shrinks from unremitting calls,
Where numbers overwhelm humanity,
600   And neighbourhood serves rather to divide
Than to unite. What sighs more deep than his,
Whose nobler will hath long been sacrificed;
Who must inhabit, under a black sky,
A City where, if indifference to disgust
Yield not, to scorn, or sorrow, living Men
Are ofttimes to their fellow-men no more
Than to the Forest Hermit are the leaves
That hang aloft in myriads, nay, far less,
For they protect his walk from sun and shower,
610   Swell his devotion with their voice in storms
And whisper while the stars twinkle among them
His lullaby. From crowded streets remote
Far from the living and dead wilderness
Of the thronged World, Society is here
A true Community – a genuine frame
Of many into one incorporate.
That must be looked for here; paternal sway,
One household, under God, for high and low,
One family and one mansion; to themselves
620   Appropriate, and divided from the world

As if it were a cave, a multitude
Human and brute, possessors undisturbed
Of this Recess, their legislative Hall,
Their Temple and their glorious Dwelling-place.

    Dismissing therefore all Arcadian dreams,
All golden fancies of the golden Age,
The bright array of shadowy thoughts from times
That were before all time, or are to be
Ere time expire, the pageantry that stirs
630 And will be stirring when our eyes are fixed
On lovely objects and we wish to part
With all remembrance of a jarring world,
– Take we at once this one sufficient hope,
What need of more? that we shall neither droop
Nor pine for want of pleasure in the life
Scattered about us, nor through dearth of aught
That keeps in health the insatiable mind;
– That we shall have for knowledge and for love
Abundance, and that, feeling as we do
640 How goodly, how exceeding fair, how pure
From all reproach is yon ethereal vault
And this deep Vale, its earthly counterpart,
By which, and under which, we are enclosed
To breathe in peace; we shall moreover find
(If sound, and what we ought to be ourselves
If rightly we observe and justly weigh)
The Inmates not unworthy of their home
The Dwellers of their Dwelling.
                       And if this
Were otherwise, we have within ourselves
650 Enough to fill the present day with joy
And overspread the future years with hope,
Our beautiful and quiet home, enriched
Already with a Stranger whom we love
Deeply, a Stranger of our Father's House,
A never-resting Pilgrim of the Sea,
Who finds at last an hour to his content

Beneath our roof. And others whom we love
Will seek us also, Sisters of our hearts
And One, like them, a Brother of our hearts,
660   Philosopher and Poet in whose sight
These Mountains will rejoice with open joy
– Such is our wealth; O Vale of Peace, we are
And must be, with God's will, a happy Band.

Yet 'tis not to enjoy that we exist,
For that end only; something must be done.
I must not walk in unreproved delight
These narrow bounds, and think of nothing more,
No duty that looks further, and no care.
Each Being has *his* office, lowly some
670   And common, yet all worthy if fulfilled
With zeal, acknowledgement that with the gift
Keeps pace, a harvest answering to the seed.
Of ill-advised Ambition, and of Pride
I would stand clear, but yet to me I feel
That an internal brightness is vouchsafed
That must not die, that must not pass away.
Why does this inward lustre fondly seek
And gladly blend with outward fellowship?
Why do *they* shine around me whom I love?
680   Why do they teach me whom I thus revere?
Strange question, yet it answers not itself.
That humble Roof embowered among the trees,
That calm fire-side, it is not even in them,
Blest as they are, to furnish a reply
That satisfies and ends in perfect rest.
Possessions have I that are solely mine,
Something within which yet is shared by none,
Not even the nearest to me and most dear,
Something which power and effort may impart,
690   I would impart it, I would spread it wide,
Immortal in the world which is to come.
Forgive me if I add another claim
And would not wholly perish even in this,

Lie down and be forgotten in the dust,
I and the modest Partners of my days
Making a silent company in death.
Love, Knowledge, all my manifold delights
All buried with me without monument
Or profit unto any but ourselves.
700 It must not be, if I, divinely taught,
Be privileged to speak as I have felt
Of what in man is human or divine.

While yet an innocent Little-one, with a heart
That doubtless wanted not its tender moods,
I breathed (for this I better recollect)
Among wild appetites and blind desires,
Motions of savage instinct my delight
And exaltation. Nothing at that time
So welcome, no temptation half so dear
710 As that which urged me to a daring feat.
Deep pools, tall trees, black chasms and dizzy crags,
And tottering towers, I loved to stand and read
Their looks forbidding, read and disobey,
Sometimes in act, and evermore in thought.
With impulses that scarcely were by these
Surpassed in strength, I heard of danger, met
Or sought with courage; enterprise forlorn
By one, sole keeper of his own intent,
Or by a resolute few who for the sake
720 Of glory fronted multitudes in arms.
Yea to this hour I cannot read a tale
Of two brave Vessels matched in deadly fight
And fighting to the death, but I am pleased
More than a wise man ought to be. I wish,
Fret, burn, and struggle, and in soul am there;
But me hath Nature tamed and bade to seek
For other agitations or be calm;
Hath dealt with me as with a turbulent Stream,
Some nursling of the mountains, whom she leads
730 Through quiet meadows after he has learnt

His strength and had his triumph and his joy,
His desperate course of tumult and of glee.
That which in stealth by Nature was performed
Hath Reason sanctioned: her deliberate Voice
Hath said, 'Be mild and cleave to gentle things,
Thy glory and thy happiness be there.
Nor fear, though thou confide in me, a want
Of aspirations that *have* been – of foes
To wrestle with, and victory to complete,
740 Bounds to be leapt, darkness to be explored,
All that inflamed thy infant heart, the love,
The longing, the contempt, the undaunted quest,
All shall survive though changed their office, all
Shall live – it is not in their power to die.'

Then farewell to the Warrior's schemes, farewell
The forwardness of Soul which looks that way
Upon a less incitement than the cause
Of Liberty endangered, and farewell
That other hope, long mine, the hope to fill
750 The heroic trumpet with the Muse's breath!
Yet in this peaceful Vale we will not spend
Unheard-of days, though loving peaceful thoughts.
A Voice shall speak, and what will be the Theme?
On Man, on Nature, and on Human Life
Musing in Solitude

Water Fowl

'Let me be allowed the aid of verse to describe the evolutions
which these visitants sometimes perform, on a fine day towards
the close of winter.' – *Extract from the Author's Book on the
Lakes.*

Mark how the feathered tenants of the flood,
With grace of motion that might scarcely seem
Inferior to angelical, prolong
Their curious pastime! shaping in mid air

(And sometimes with ambitious wing that soars
High as the level of the mountain-tops)
A circuit ampler than the lake beneath –
Their own domain; but ever, while intent
On tracing and retracing that large round,
10 Their jubilant activity evolves
Hundreds of curves and circlets, to and fro,
Upward and downward, progress intricate
Yet unperplexed, as if one spirit swayed
Their indefatigable flight. 'Tis done –
Ten times, or more, I fancied it had ceased;
But lo! the vanished company again
Ascending; they approach – I hear their wings,
Faint, faint at first; and then an eager sound,
Past in a moment – and as faint again!
20 They tempt the sun to sport amid their plumes;
They tempt the water, or the gleaming ice,
To show them a fair image; 'tis themselves,
Their own fair forms, upon the glimmering plain,
Painted more soft and fair as they descend
Almost to touch; – then up again aloft,
Up with a sally and a flash of speed,
As if they scorned both resting-place and rest!

To the Evening Star over Grasmere Water

The Lake is thine,
The mountains too are thine, some clouds there are,
Some little feeble stars, but all is thine,
Thou, thou art king, and sole proprietor.

A moon among her stars, a mighty vale,
Fresh as the freshest field, scooped out, and green
As is the greenest billow of the sea.

The multitude of little rocky hills,
Rocky or green, that do like islands rise
10 From the flat meadow lonely there.

.   .   .   .   .

Embowering mountains, and the dome of Heaven
And waters in the midst, a Second Heaven.

To the Spade of a Friend
(*An Agriculturist*)

Composed while we were labouring together in his pleasure-
ground.

Spade! with which Wilkinson hath tilled his lands,
And shaped these pleasant walks by Emont's side,
Thou art a tool of honour in my hands;
I press thee, through the yielding soil, with pride.

Rare master has it been thy lot to know;
Long hast Thou served a man to reason true;
Whose life combines the best of high and low,
The labouring many and the resting few;

Health, meekness, ardour, quietness secure,
10 And industry of body and of mind;
And elegant enjoyments, that are pure
As nature is; – too pure to be refined.

Here often hast Thou heard the Poet sing
In concord with his river murmuring by;
Or in some silent field, while timid spring
Is yet uncheered by other minstrelsy.

Who shall inherit Thee when death has laid
Low in the darksome cell thine own dear lord?
That man will have a trophy, humble Spade!
20 A trophy nobler than a conqueror's sword.

If he be one that feels, with skill to part
False praise from true, or, greater from the less,
Thee will he welcome to his hand and heart,
Thou monument of peaceful happiness!

He will not dread with Thee a toilsome day –
Thee his loved servant, his inspiring mate!
And, when thou art past service, worn away,
No dull oblivious nook shall hide thy fate.

His thrift thy uselessness will never scorn;
30 An *heir-loom* in his cottage wilt thou be: –
High will he hang thee up, well pleased to adorn
His rustic chimney with the last of Thee!

[*Fragment: 'The rains at length have ceased, the winds are stilled'*]

The rains at length have ceased, the winds are stilled,
The stars shine brightly between clouds at rest,
And as a cavern is with darkness filled,
The vale is by a mighty sound possessed.

Lines

Composed at Grasmere, during a walk one Evening, after a
stormy day, the Author having just read in a Newspaper that
the dissolution of Mr Fox was hourly expected.

Loud is the Vale! the Voice is up
With which she speaks when storms are gone,
A mighty unison of streams!
Of all her Voices, One!

Loud is the Vale; – this inland Depth
In peace is roaring like the Sea;
Yon star upon the mountain-top
Is listening quietly.

Sad was I, even to pain deprest,
10 Importunate and heavy load!
The Comforter hath found me here,
Upon this lonely road;

And many thousands now are sad –
Wait the fulfilment of their fear;
For he must die who is their stay,
Their glory disappear.

A Power is passing from the earth
To breathless Nature's dark abyss;
But when the great and good depart
20 What is it more than this –

That Man, who is from God sent forth,
Doth yet again to God return? –
Such ebb and flow must ever be,
Then wherefore should we mourn?

The Horn of Egremont Castle

Ere the Brothers through the gateway
Issued forth with old and young,
To the Horn Sir Eustace pointed
Which for ages there had hung.
Horn it was which none could sound,
No one upon living ground,
Save He who came as rightful Heir
To Egremont's Domains and Castle fair.

Heirs from times of earliest record
10 Had the House of Lucie born,
Who of right had held the Lordship
Claimed by proof upon the Horn:
Each at the appointed hour
Tried the Horn, – it owned his power;

He was acknowledged: and the blast,
Which good Sir Eustace sounded, was the last.

With his lance Sir Eustace pointed,
And to Hubert thus said he,
'What I speak this Horn shall witness
20 For thy better memory.
Hear, then, and neglect me not!
At this time, and on this spot,
The words are uttered from my heart,
As my last earnest prayer ere we depart.

'On good service we are going
Life to risk by sea and land,
In which course if Christ our Saviour
Do my sinful soul demand,
Hither come thou back straightway,
30 Hubert, if alive that day;
Return, and sound the Horn, that we
May have a living House still left in thee!'

'Fear not,' quickly answered Hubert;
'As I am thy Father's son,
What thou askest, noble Brother,
With God's favour shall be done.'
So were both right well content:
Forth they from the Castle went,
And at the head of their Array
40 To Palestine the Brothers took their way.

Side by side they fought (the Lucies
Were a line for valour famed)
And where'er their strokes alighted,
There the Saracens were tamed.
Whence, then, could it come – the thought –
By what evil spirit brought?
Oh! can a brave Man wish to take
His Brother's life, for Lands' and Castle's sake?

'Sir!' the Ruffians said to Hubert,
50   'Deep he lies in Jordan flood.'
Stricken by this ill assurance,
Pale and trembling Hubert stood.
'Take your earnings.' – Oh! that I
Could have *seen* my Brother die!
It was a pang that vexed him then;
And oft returned, again, and yet again.

Months passed on, and no Sir Eustace!
Nor of him were tidings heard.
Wherefore, bold as day, the Murderer
60   Back again to England steered.
To his Castle Hubert sped;
Nothing has he now to dread.
But silent and by stealth he came,
And at an hour which nobody could name.

None could tell if it were night-time,
Night or day, at even or morn;
No one's eye had seen him enter,
No one's ear had heard the Horn.
But bold Hubert lives in glee:
70   Months and years went smilingly;
With plenty was his table spread;
And bright the Lady is who shares his bed.

Likewise he had sons and daughters;
And, as good men do, he sate
At his board by these surrounded,
Flourishing in fair estate.
And while thus in open day
Once he sate, as old books say,
A blast was uttered from the Horn,
80   Where by the Castle-gate it hung forlorn.

'Tis the breath of good Sir Eustace!
He is come to claim his right:

Ancient castle, woods, and mountains
Hear the challenge with delight.
Hubert! though the blast be blown
He is helpless and alone:
Thou hast a dungeon, speak the word!
And there he may be lodged, and thou be Lord.

Speak! – astounded Hubert cannot;
90 And, if power to speak he had,
All are daunted, all the household
Smitten to the heart, and sad.
'Tis Sir Eustace; if it be
Living man, it must be he!
Thus Hubert thought in his dismay,
And by a postern-gate he slunk away.

Long, and long was he unheard of:
To his Brother then he came,
Made confession, asked forgiveness,
100 Asked it by a brother's name,
And by all the saints in heaven;
And of Eustace was forgiven:
Then in a convent went to hide
His melancholy head, and there he died.

But Sir Eustace, whom good angels
Had preserved from murderers' hands,
And from Pagan chains had rescued,
Lived with honour on his lands.
Sons he had, saw sons of theirs:
110 And through ages, heirs of heirs,
A long posterity renowned,
Sounded the Horn which they alone could sound.

Thought of a Briton on the Subjugation of Switzerland

Two Voices are there; one is of the sea,
One of the mountains; each a mighty Voice:
In both from age to age thou didst rejoice,
They were thy chosen music, Liberty!
There came a Tyrant, and with holy glee
Thou fought'st against him; but hast vainly striven:
Thou from thy Alpine holds at length art driven,
Where not a torrent murmurs heard by thee.
Of one deep bliss thine ear hath been bereft:
10   Then cleave, O cleave to that which still is left;
For, high-souled Maid, what sorrow would it be
That Mountain floods should thunder as before,
And Ocean bellow from his rocky shore,
And neither awful Voice be heard by thee!

November, 1806

Another year! – another deadly blow!
Another mighty Empire overthrown!
And We are left, or shall be left, alone;
The last that dare to struggle with the Foe.
'Tis well! from this day forward we shall know
That in ourselves our safety must be sought;
That by our own right hands it must be wrought;
That we must stand unpropped, or be laid low.
O dastard whom such foretaste doth not cheer!
10   We shall exult, if they who rule the land
Be men who hold its many blessings dear,
Wise, upright, valiant; not a servile band,
Who are to judge of danger which they fear,
And honour which they do not understand.

Song at the Feast of Brougham Castle
upon the Restoration of Lord Clifford,
the Shepherd, to the Estates and Honours of
His Ancestors

High in the breathless Hall the Minstrel sate,
And Emont's murmur mingled with the Song. –
The words of ancient time I thus translate,
A festal strain that hath been silent long: –

   'From town to town, from tower to tower,
   The red rose is a gladsome flower.
   Her thirty years of winter past,
   The red rose is revived at last;
   She lifts her head for endless spring,
10   For everlasting blossoming:
   Both roses flourish, red and white:
   In love and sisterly delight
   The two that were at strife are blended,
   And all old troubles now are ended. –
   Joy! joy to both! but most to her
   Who is the flower of Lancaster!
   Behold her how She smiles today
   On this great throng, this bright array!
   Fair greeting doth she send to all
20   From every corner of the hall;
   But chiefly from above the board
   Where sits in state our rightful Lord,
   A Clifford to his own restored!

   'They came with banner, spear, and shield;
   And it was proved in Bosworth-field.
   Not long the Avenger was withstood –
   Earth helped him with the cry of blood:
   St George was for us, and the might
   Of blessed Angels crowned the right.

30   Loud voice the Land has uttered forth,
We loudest in the faithful north:
Our fields rejoice, our mountains ring,
Our streams proclaim a welcoming;
Our strong-abodes and castles see
The glory of their loyalty.

'How glad is Skipton at this hour –
Though lonely, a deserted Tower;
Knight, squire, and yeoman, page and groom:
We have them at the feast of Brough'm.
40   How glad Pendragon – though the sleep
Of years be on her! – She shall reap
A taste of this great pleasure, viewing
As in a dream her own renewing.
Rejoiced is Brough, right glad, I deem,
Beside her little humble stream;
And she that keepeth watch and ward
Her statelier Eden's course to guard;
They both are happy at this hour,
Though each is but a lonely Tower: –
50   But here is perfect joy and pride
For one fair House by Emont's side,
This day, distinguished without peer,
To see her Master and to cheer –
Him, and his Lady-mother dear!

'Oh! it was a time forlorn
When the fatherless was born –
Give her wings that she may fly,
Or she sees her infant die!
Swords that are with slaughter wild
60   Hunt the Mother and the Child.
Who will take them from the light?
– Yonder is a man in sight –
Yonder is a house – but where?
No, they must not enter there.
To the caves, and to the brooks,

To the clouds of heaven she looks;
She is speechless, but her eyes
Pray in ghostly agonies.
Blissful Mary, Mother mild,
70   Maid and Mother undefiled,
Save a Mother and her Child!

'Now Who is he that bounds with joy
On Carrock's side, a Shepherd-boy?
No thoughts hath he but thoughts that pass
Light as the wind along the grass.
Can this be He who hither came
In secret, like a smothered flame?
O'er whom such thankful tears were shed
For shelter, and a poor man's bread!
80   God loves the Child; and God hath willed
That those dear words should be fulfilled,
The Lady's words, when forced away,
The last she to her Babe did say:
"My own, my own, thy Fellow-guest
I may not be; but rest thee, rest,
For lowly shepherd's life is best!"

'Alas! when evil men are strong
No life is good, no pleasure long.
The Boy must part from Mosedale's groves,
90   And leave Blencathara's rugged coves,
And quit the flowers that summer brings
To Glenderamakin's lofty springs;
Must vanish, and his careless cheer
Be turned to heaviness and fear.
– Give Sir Lancelot Threlkeld praise!
Hear it, good man, old in days!
Thou tree of covert and of rest
For this young Bird that is distrest;
Among thy branches safe he lay,
100   And he was free to sport and play,
When falcons were abroad for prey.

'A recreant harp, that sings of fear
And heaviness in Clifford's ear!
I said, when evil men are strong,
No life is good, no pleasure long,
A weak and cowardly untruth!
Our Clifford was a happy Youth,
And thankful through a weary time,
That brought him up to manhood's prime.
110   — Again he wanders forth at will,
And tends a flock from hill to hill:
His garb is humble; ne'er was seen
Such garb with such a noble mien;
Among the shepherd-grooms no mate
Hath he, a Child of strength and state!
Yet lacks not friends for simple glee,
Nor yet for higher sympathy.
To his side the fallow-deer
Came, and rested without fear;
120   The eagle, lord of land and sea,
Stooped down to pay him fealty;
And both the undying fish that swim
Through Bowscale-tarn did wait on him;
The pair were servants of his eye
In their immortality;
And glancing, gleaming, dark or bright,
Moved to and fro, for his delight.
He knew the rocks which Angels haunt
Upon the mountains visitant;
130   He hath kenned them taking wing:
And into caves where Faeries sing
He hath entered; and been told
By Voices how men lived of old.
Among the heavens his eye can see
The face of thing that is to be;
And, if that men report him right,
His tongue could whisper words of might.
— Now another day is come,
Fitter hope, and nobler doom;

140   He hath thrown aside his crook,
         And hath buried deep his book;
         Armour rusting in his halls
         On the blood of Clifford calls; –
         "Quell the Scot," exclaims the Lance –
         Bear me to the heart of France,
         Is the longing of the Shield –
         Tell thy name, thou trembling Field;
         Field of death, where'er thou be,
         Groan thou with our victory!
150   Happy day, and mighty hour,
         When our Shepherd, in his power,
         Mailed and horsed, with lance and sword,
         To his ancestors restored
         Like a re-appearing Star,
         Like a glory from afar,
         First shall head the flock of war!'

         Alas! the impassioned minstrel did not know
         How, by Heaven's grace, this Clifford's heart was
             framed:
         How he, long forced in humble walks to go,
160   Was softened into feeling, soothed, and tamed.

         Love had he found in huts where poor men lie;
         His daily teachers had been woods and rills,
         The silence that is in the starry sky,
         The sleep that is among the lonely hills.

         In him the savage virtue of the Race,
         Revenge, and all ferocious thoughts were dead:
         Nor did he change; but kept in lofty place
         The wisdom which adversity had bred.

         Glad were the vales, and every cottage-hearth;
170   The Shepherd-lord was honoured more and more;
         And, ages after he was laid in earth,
         'The good Lord Clifford' was the name he bore.

'Though narrow be that old Man's cares, and near'

– 'gives to airy nothing
A local habitation and a name.'

Though narrow be that old Man's cares, and near,
The poor old Man is greater than he seems:
For he hath waking empire, wide as dreams;
An ample sovereignty of eye and ear.
Rich are his walks with supernatural cheer;
The region of his inner spirit teems
With vital sounds and monitory gleams
Of high astonishment and pleasing fear.
He the seven birds hath seen, that never part,
10 Seen the SEVEN WHISTLERS in their nightly rounds,
And counted them: and oftentimes will start –
For overhead are sweeping GABRIEL'S HOUNDS,
Doomed, with their impious Lord, the flying Hart
To chase for ever, on aërial grounds!

A Complaint

There is a change – and I am poor;
Your love hath been, nor long ago,
A fountain at my fond heart's door,
Whose only business was to flow;
And flow it did; not taking heed
Of its own bounty, or my need.

What happy moments did I count!
Blest was I then all bliss above!
Now, for that consecrated fount
10 Of murmuring, sparkling, living love,
What have I? shall I dare to tell?
A comfortless and hidden well.

A well of love – it may be deep –
I trust it is, – and never dry:
What matter? if the waters sleep
In silence and obscurity.
– Such change, and at the very door
Of my fond heart, hath made me poor.

Song for the Spinning Wheel–
Founded upon a Belief Prevalent among the
Pastoral Vales of Westmoreland

Swiftly turn the murmuring wheel!
Night has brought the welcome hour,
When the weary fingers feel
Help, as if from faery power;
Dewy night o'ershades the ground;
Turn the swift wheel round and round!

Now, beneath the starry sky,
Couch the widely-scattered sheep; –
Ply the pleasant labour, ply!
10 For the spindle, while they sleep,
Runs with speed more smooth and fine,
Gathering up a trustier line.

Short-lived likings may be bred
By a glance from fickle eyes;
But true love is like the thread
Which the kindly wool supplies,
When the flocks are all at rest,
Sleeping on the mountain's breast.

'Through Cumbrian wilds, in many a mountain cove'

Through Cumbrian wilds, in many a mountain cove,
The pastoral muse laments the wheel – no more
Engaged, near blazing hearth on clean-swept floor,
In tasks which guardian angels might approve,
Friendly the weight of leisure to remove,
And to beguile the lassitude of ease;
Gracious to all the dear dependencies
Of house and field, – to plenty, peace, and love.
There too did *Fancy* prize the murmuring wheel;
10   For sympathies, inexplicably fine,
Instilled a confidence – how sweet to feel!
That ever in the night calm, when the sheep
Upon their grassy beds lay couched in sleep,
The quickening spindle drew a trustier line.

A Prophecy February, 1807

High deeds, O Germans, are to come from you!
Thus in your books the record shall be found,
'A watchword was pronounced, a potent sound –
ARMINIUS! – all the people quaked like dew
Stirred by the breeze; they rose, a Nation, true,
True to herself – the mighty Germany,
She of the Danube and the Northern Sea,
She rose, and off at once the yoke she threw.
All power was given her in the dreadful trance;
10   Those new-born Kings she withered like a flame.'
– Woe to them all! but heaviest woe and shame
To that Bavarian who could first advance
His banner in accursed league with France,
First open traitor to the German name!

'O Nightingale! thou surely art'

O Nightingale! thou surely art
A creature of a 'fiery heart': –
These notes of thine – they pierce and pierce;
Tumultuous harmony and fierce!
Thou sing'st as if the God of wine
Had helped thee to a Valentine;
A song in mockery and despite
Of shades, and dews, and silent night;
And steady bliss, and all the loves
10 Now sleeping in these peaceful groves.

I heard a Stock-dove sing or say
His homely tale, this very day;
His voice was buried among trees,
Yet to be come-at by the breeze:
He did not cease; but cooed – and cooed;
And somewhat pensively he wooed:
He sang of love, with quiet blending,
Slow to begin, and never ending;
Of serious faith, and inward glee;
20 That was the song – the song for me!

To Lady Beaumont

Lady! the songs of Spring were in the grove
While I was shaping beds for winter flowers;
While I was planting green unfading bowers,
And shrubs – to hang upon the warm alcove,
And sheltering wall; and still, as Fancy wove
The dream, to time and nature's blended powers
I gave this paradise for winter hours,
A labyrinth, Lady! which your feet shall rove.
Yes! when the sun of life more feebly shines,
10 Becoming thoughts, I trust, of solemn gloom

Or of high gladness you shall hither bring;
And these perennial bowers and murmuring pines
Be gracious as the music and the bloom
And all the mighty ravishment of spring.

Gypsies

Yet are they here the same unbroken knot
Of human Beings, in the self-same spot!
   Men, women, children, yea the frame
   Of the whole spectacle the same!
Only their fire seems bolder, yielding light,
Now deep and red, the colouring of night;
   That on their Gypsy-faces falls,
   Their bed of straw and blanket-walls.
– Twelve hours, twelve bounteous hours are gone, while I
10 Have been a traveller under open sky,
   Much witnessing of change and cheer,
   Yet as I left I find them here!
The weary Sun betook himself to rest; –
Then issued Vesper from the fulgent west,
   Outshining like a visible God
   The glorious path in which he trod.
And now, ascending, after one dark hour
And one night's diminution of her power,
   Behold the mighty Moon! this way
20   She looks as if at them – but they
Regard not her: – oh better wrong and strife
(By nature transient) than this torpid life;
   Life which the very stars reprove
   As on their silent tasks they move!
Yet, witness all that stirs in heaven or earth!
In scorn I speak not; – they are what their birth
   And breeding suffer them to be;
   Wild outcasts of society!

To Thomas Clarkson, on the Final Passing of the Bill for the Abolition of the Slave Trade. March, 1807

Clarkson! it was an obstinate hill to climb:
How toilsome – nay, how dire – it was, by thee
Is known; by none, perhaps, so feelingly:
But thou, who, starting in thy fervent prime,
Didst first lead forth that enterprise sublime,
Hast heard the constant Voice its charge repeat,
Which, out of thy young heart's oracular seat,
First roused thee. – O true yoke-fellow of Time,
Duty's intrepid liegeman, see, the palm
10 Is won, and by all Nations shall be worn!
The blood-stained Writing is for ever torn;
And thou henceforth wilt have a good man's calm,
A great man's happiness; thy zeal shall find
Repose at length, firm friend of human kind!

To the Poet, John Dyer

Bard of the Fleece, whose skilful genius made
That work a living landscape fair and bright;
Nor hallowed less with musical delight
Than those soft scenes through which thy childhood
    strayed,
Those southern tracts of Cambria, 'deep embayed,
With green hills fenced, with ocean's murmur lulled;'
Though hasty Fame hath many a chaplet culled
For worthless brows, while in the pensive shade
Of cold neglect she leaves thy head ungraced,
10 Yet pure and powerful minds, hearts meek and still,
A grateful few, shall love thy modest Lay,
Long as the shepherd's bleating flock shall stray
O'er naked Snowdon's wide aërial waste;
Long as the thrush shall pipe on Grongar Hill!

'Grief, thou hast lost an ever ready friend'

Grief, thou hast lost an ever ready friend
Now that the cottage Spinning-wheel is mute;
And Care – a comforter that best could suit
Her froward mood, and softliest reprehend;
And Love – a charmer's voice, that used to lend,
More efficaciously than aught that flows
From harp or lute, kind influence to compose
The throbbing pulse – else troubled without end:
Even Joy could tell, Joy craving truce and rest
10 From her own overflow, what power sedate
On those revolving motions did await
Assiduously – to soothe her aching breast;
And, to a point of just relief, abate
The mantling triumphs of a day too blest.

'Mark the concentred hazels that enclose'

Mark the concentred hazels that enclose
Yon old grey Stone, protected from the ray
Of noontide suns: – and even the beams that play
And glance, while wantonly the rough wind blows,
Are seldom free to touch the moss that grows
Upon that roof, amid embowering gloom,
The very image framing of a Tomb,
In which some ancient Chieftain finds repose
Among the lonely mountains. – Live, ye trees!
10 And thou, grey Stone, the pensive likeness keep
Of a dark chamber where the Mighty sleep:
For more than Fancy to the influence bends
When solitary Nature condescends
To mimic Time's forlorn humanities.

'The Shepherd, looking eastward, softly said'

The Shepherd, looking eastward, softly said,
'Bright is thy veil, O Moon, as thou art bright!'
Forthwith, that little cloud, in ether spread
And penetrated all with tender light,
She cast away, and showed her fulgent head
Uncovered; dazzling the Beholder's sight
As if to vindicate her beauty's right,
Her beauty thoughtlessly disparagèd.
Meanwhile that veil, removed or thrown aside,
10   Went floating from her, darkening as it went;
And a huge mass, to bury or to hide,
Approached this glory of the firmament;
Who meekly yields, and is obscured – content
With one calm triumph of a modest pride.

'Weak is the will of Man, his judgement blind'

'Weak is the will of Man, his judgement blind;
Remembrance persecutes, and Hope betrays;
Heavy is woe; – and joy, for human-kind,
A mournful thing, so transient is the blaze!'
Thus might *he* paint our lot of mortal days
Who wants the glorious faculty assigned
To elevate the more-than-reasoning Mind,
And colour life's dark cloud with orient rays.
Imagination is that sacred power,
10   Imagination lofty and refined:
'Tis hers to pluck the amaranthine flower
Of Faith, and round the Sufferer's temples bind
Wreaths that endure affliction's heaviest shower,
And do not shrink from sorrow's keenest wind.

Composed by the Side of Grasmere Lake

Clouds, lingering yet, extend in solid bars
Through the grey west; and lo! these waters, steeled
By breezeless air to smoothest polish, yield
A vivid repetition of the stars;
Jove, Venus, and the ruddy crest of Mars
Amid his fellows beauteously revealed
At happy distance from earth's groaning field,
Where ruthless mortals wage incessant wars.
Is it a mirror? – or the nether Sphere
10 Opening to view the abyss in which she feeds
Her own calm fires? – But list! a voice is near;
Great Pan himself low-whispering through the reeds,
'Be thankful, thou; for, if unholy deeds
Ravage the world, tranquillity is here!'

The Force of Prayer; or,
The Founding of Bolton Priory
A Tradition

'𝔚𝔥𝔞𝔱 𝔦𝔰 𝔤𝔬𝔬𝔡 𝔣𝔬𝔯 𝔞 𝔟𝔬𝔬𝔱𝔩𝔢𝔰𝔰 𝔟𝔢𝔫𝔢?'
With these dark words begins my Tale;
And their meaning is, whence can comfort spring
When Prayer is of no avail?

'𝔚𝔥𝔞𝔱 𝔦𝔰 𝔤𝔬𝔬𝔡 𝔣𝔬𝔯 𝔞 𝔟𝔬𝔬𝔱𝔩𝔢𝔰𝔰 𝔟𝔢𝔫𝔢?'
The Falconer to the Lady said;
And she made answer 'ENDLESS SORROW!'
For she knew that her Son was dead.

She knew it by the Falconer's words,
10 And from the look of the Falconer's eye;
And from the love which was in her soul
For her youthful Romilly.

– Young Romilly through Barden woods
Is ranging high and low;
And holds a greyhound in a leash,
To let slip upon buck or doe.

The pair have reached that fearful chasm,
How tempting to bestride!
For lordly Wharf is there pent in
20 With rocks on either side.

The striding-place is called THE STRID,
A name which it took of yore:
A thousand years hath it borne that name,
And shall a thousand more.

And hither is young Romilly come,
And what may now forbid
That he, perhaps for the hundredth time,
Shall bound across THE STRID?

He sprang in glee, – for what cared he
30 That the river was strong, and the rocks were steep? –
But the greyhound in the leash hung back,
And checked him in his leap.

The Boy is in the arms of Wharf,
And strangled by a merciless force;
For never more was young Romilly seen
Till he rose a lifeless corse.

Now there is stillness in the vale,
And long, unspeaking, sorrow:
Wharf shall be to pitying hearts
40 A name more sad than Yarrow.

If for a Lover the Lady wept,
A solace she might borrow
From death, and from the passion of death: –
Old Wharf might heal her sorrow.

She weeps not for the wedding-day
Which was to be tomorrow:
Her hope was a further-looking hope,
And hers is a mother's sorrow.

He was a tree that stood alone,
50 And proudly did its branches wave;
And the root of this delightful tree
Was in her husband's grave!

Long, long in darkness did she sit,
And her first words were, 'Let there be
In Bolton, on the field of Wharf,
A stately Priory!'

The stately Priory was reared;
And Wharf, as he moved along,
To matins joined a mournful voice,
60 Nor failed at even-song.

And the Lady prayed in heaviness
That looked not for relief!
But slowly did her succour come,
And a patience to her grief.

Oh! there is never sorrow of heart
That shall lack a timely end,
If but to God we turn, and ask
Of Him to be our friend!

The White Doe of Rylstone; or,
The Fate of the Nortons

ADVERTISEMENT

During the Summer of 1807 I visited, for the first time, the
beautiful country that surrounds Bolton Priory in Yorkshire;
and the Poem of the WHITE DOE, founded upon a Tradition
connected with that place, was composed at the close of the
same year.

DEDICATION

In trellised shed with clustering roses gay,
And, MARY! oft beside our blazing fire,
When years of wedded life were as a day
Whose current answers to the heart's desire,
Did we together read in Spenser's Lay
How Una, sad of soul – in sad attire,
The gentle Una, of celestial birth,
To seek her Knight went wandering o'er the earth.

Ah, then, Belovèd! pleasing was the smart,
10 And the tear precious in compassion shed
For Her, who, pierced by sorrow's thrilling dart,
Did meekly bear the pang unmerited;
Meek as that emblem of her lowly heart
The milk-white Lamb which in a line she led, –
And faithful, loyal in her innocence,
Like the brave Lion slain in her defence.

Notes could we hear as of a faery shell
Attuned to words with sacred wisdom fraught;
Free Fancy prized each specious miracle,
20 And all its finer inspiration caught;
Till in the bosom of our rustic Cell,
We by a lamentable change were taught
That 'bliss with mortal Man may not abide:'
How nearly joy and sorrow are allied!

For us the stream of fiction ceased to flow,
For us the voice of melody was mute.
– But, as soft gales dissolve the dreary snow,
And give the timid herbage leave to shoot,
Heaven's breathing influence failed not to bestow
30 A timely promise of unlooked-for fruit,
Fair fruit of pleasure and serene content
From blossoms wild of fancies innocent.

It soothed us – it beguiled us – then, to hear
Once more of troubles wrought by magic spell;
And griefs whose aery motion comes not near
The pangs that tempt the Spirit to rebel:
Then, with mild Una in her sober cheer,
High over hill and low adown the dell
Again we wandered, willing to partake
40   All that she suffered for her dear Lord's sake.

Then, too, this Song *of mine* once more could please,
Where anguish, strange as dreams of restless sleep,
Is tempered and allayed by sympathies
Aloft ascending, and descending deep,
Even to the inferior Kinds; whom forest-trees
Protect from beating sunbeams, and the sweep
Of the sharp winds; – fair Creatures! – to whom
    Heaven
A calm and sinless life, with love, hath given.

This tragic Story cheered us; for it speaks
50   Of female patience winning firm repose;
And, of the recompense that conscience seeks,
A bright, encouraging, example shows;
Needful when o'er wide realms the tempest breaks,
Needful amid life's ordinary woes; –
Hence, not for them unfitted who would bless
A happy hour with holier happiness.

He serves the Muses erringly and ill,
Whose aim is pleasure light and fugitive:
O, that my mind were equal to fulfil
60   The comprehensive mandate which they give –
Vain aspiration of an earnest will!
Yet in this moral Strain a power may live,
Belovèd Wife! such solace to impart
As it hath yielded to thy tender heart.
RYDAL MOUNT, WESTMORELAND, *April* 20, 1815

'Action is transitory – a step, a blow,
The motion of a muscle – this way or that –
'Tis done; and in the after-vacancy
We wonder at ourselves like men betrayed:
Suffering is permanent, obscure and dark,
And has the nature of infinity.
Yet through that darkness (infinite though it seem
And irremoveable) gracious openings lie,
By which the soul – with patient steps of thought
Now toiling, wafted now on wings of prayer –
May pass in hope, and, though from mortal bonds
Yet undelivered, rise with sure ascent
Even to the fountain-head of peace divine.'

'They that deny a God destroy Man's nobility: for certainly
Man is of kinn to the Beast by his Body, and if he be not of
kinn to God by his Spirit, he is a base ignoble Creature. It
destroys likewise Magnanimity, and the raising of humane
Nature: for take an example of a Dogg, and mark what a
generosity and courage he will put on, when he finds himself
maintained by a Man, who to him is instead of a God, or
Melior Natura. Which courage is manifestly such, as that
Creature without that confidence of a better Nature than his
own could never attain. So Man, when he resteth and assureth
himself upon Divine protection and favour, gathereth a force
and faith which human Nature in itself could not obtain.'

LORD BACON

CANTO FIRST

From Bolton's old monastic tower
The bells ring loud with gladsome power;
The sun shines bright; the fields are gay
With people in their best array
Of stole and doublet, hood and scarf,
Along the banks of crystal Wharf,
Through the Vale retired and lowly,
Trooping to that summons holy.
And, up among the moorlands, see
10   What sprinklings of blithe company!

Of lasses and of shepherd grooms,
That down the steep hills force their way,
Like cattle through the budded brooms;
Path, or no path, what care they?
And thus in joyous mood they hie
To Bolton's mouldering Priory.

What would they there? – full fifty years
That sumptuous Pile, with all its peers,
Too harshly hath been doomed to taste
20   The bitterness of wrong and waste:
Its courts are ravaged; but the tower
Is standing with a voice of power,
That ancient voice which wont to call
To mass or some high festival;
And in the shattered fabric's heart
Remaineth one protected part;
A Chapel, like a wild-bird's nest,
Closely embowered and trimly drest;
And thither young and old repair,
30   This Sabbath-day, for praise and prayer.

Fast the church-yard fills; – anon
Look again, and they all are gone;
The cluster round the porch, and the folk
Who sate in the shade of the Prior's Oak!
And scarcely have they disappeared
Ere the prelusive hymn is heard: –
With one consent the people rejoice,
Filling the church with a lofty voice!
They sing a service which they feel:
40   For 'tis the sunrise now of zeal;
Of a pure faith the vernal prime –
In great Eliza's golden time.

A moment ends the fervent din,
And all is hushed, without and within;
For though the priest, more tranquilly,

Recites the holy liturgy,
The only voice which you can hear
Is the river murmuring near.
– When soft! – the dusky trees between,
50 And down the path through the open green,
Where is no living thing to be seen;
And through yon gateway, where is found,
Beneath the arch with ivy bound,
Free entrance to the church-yard ground –
Comes gliding in with lovely gleam,
Comes gliding in serene and slow,
Soft and silent as a dream,
A solitary Doe!
White she is as lily of June,
60 And beauteous as the silver moon
When out of sight the clouds are driven
And she is left alone in heaven;
Or like a ship some gentle day
In sunshine sailing far away,
A glittering ship, that hath the plain
Of ocean for her own domain.

Lie silent in your graves, ye dead!
Lie quiet in your church-yard bed!
Ye living, tend your holy cares;
70 Ye multitude, pursue your prayers;
And blame not me if my heart and sight
Are occupied with one delight!
'Tis a work for sabbath hours
If I with this bright Creature go:
Whether she be of forest bowers,
From the bowers of earth below;
Or a Spirit for one day given,
A pledge of grace from purest heaven.

What harmonious pensive changes
80 Wait upon her as she ranges
Round and through this Pile of state

Overthrown and desolate!
Now a step or two her way
Leads through space of open day,
Where the enamoured sunny light
Brightens her that was so bright;
Now doth a delicate shadow fall,
Falls upon her like a breath,
From some lofty arch or wall,
90 As she passes underneath:
Now some gloomy nook partakes
Of the glory that she makes, –
High-ribbed vault of stone, or cell,
With perfect cunning framed as well
Of stone, and ivy, and the spread
Of the elder's bushy head;
Some jealous and forbidding cell,
That doth the living stars repel,
And where no flower hath leave to dwell.

100   The presence of this wandering Doe
Fills many a damp obscure recess
With lustre of a saintly show;
And, reappearing, she no less
Sheds on the flowers that round her blow
A more than sunny liveliness.
But say, among these holy places,
Which thus assiduously she paces,
Comes she with a votary's task,
Rite to perform, or boon to ask?
110 Fair Pilgrim! harbours she a sense
Of sorrow, or of reverence?
Can she be grieved for choir or shrine,
Crushed as if by wrath divine?
For what survives of house where God
Was worshipped, or where Man abode;
For old magnificence undone;
Or for the gentler work begun
By Nature, softening and concealing,

And busy with a hand of healing?
120 Mourns she for lordly chamber's hearth
That to the sapling ash gives birth;
For dormitory's length laid bare
Where the wild rose blossoms fair;
Or altar, whence the cross was rent,
Now rich with mossy ornament?
– She sees a warrior carved in stone,
Among the thick weeds, stretched alone;
A warrior, with his shield of pride
Cleaving humbly to his side,
130 And hands in resignation prest,
Palm to palm, on his tranquil breast;
As little she regards the sight
As a common creature might:
If she be doomed to inward care,
Or service, it must lie elsewhere.
– But hers are eyes serenely bright,
And on she moves – with pace how light!
Nor spares to stoop her head, and taste
The dewy turf with flowers bestrown;
140 And thus she fares, until at last
Beside the ridge of a grassy grave
In quietness she lays her down;
Gentle as a weary wave
Sinks, when the summer breeze hath died,
Against an anchored vessel's side;
Even so, without distress, doth she
Lie down in peace, and lovingly.

The day is placid in its going,
To a lingering motion bound,
150 Like the crystal stream now flowing
With its softest summer sound:
So the balmy minutes pass,
While this radiant Creature lies
Couched upon the dewy grass,
Pensively with downcast eyes.

– But now again the people raise
With awful cheer a voice of praise;
It is the last, the parting song;
And from the temple forth they throng,
160 And quickly spread themselves abroad,
While each pursues his several road.
But some – a variegated band
Of middle-aged, and old, and young,
And little children by the hand
Upon their leading mothers hung –
With mute obeisance gladly paid
Turn towards the spot, where, full in view,
The white Doe, to her service true,
Her sabbath couch has made.

170   It was a solitary mound;
Which two spears' length of level ground
Did from all other graves divide:
As if in some respect of pride;
Or melancholy's sickly mood,
Still shy of human neighbourhood;
Or guilt, that humbly would express
A penitential loneliness.

    'Look, there she is, my Child! draw near;
She fears not, wherefore should we fear?
180 She means no harm;' – but still the Boy,
To whom the words were softly said,
Hung back, and smiled, and blushed for joy,
A shame-faced blush of glowing red!
Again the Mother whispered low,
'Now you have seen the famous Doe;
From Rylstone she hath found her way
Over the hills this sabbath day;
Her work, whate'er it be, is done,
And she will depart when we are gone;
190 Thus doth she keep, from year to year,
Her sabbath morning, foul or fair.'

Bright was the Creature, as in dreams
The Boy had seen her, yea, more bright;
But is she truly what she seems?
He asks with insecure delight,
Asks of himself, and doubts, – and still
The doubt returns against his will:
Though he, and all the standers-by,
Could tell a tragic history
200 Of facts divulged, wherein appear
Substantial motive, reason clear,
Why thus the milk-white Doe is found
Couchant beside that lonely mound;
And why she duly loves to pace
The circuit of this hallowed place.
Nor to the Child's inquiring mind
Is such perplexity confined:
For, spite of sober Truth that sees
A world of fixed remembrances
210 Which to this mystery belong,
If, undeceived, my skill can trace
The characters of every face,
There lack not strange delusion here,
Conjecture vague, and idle fear,
And superstitious fancies strong,
Which do the gentle Creature wrong.

That bearded, staff-supported Sire –
Who in his boyhood often fed
Full cheerily on convent-bread
220 And heard old tales by the convent-fire,
And to his grave will go with scars,
Relics of long and distant wars –
That Old Man, studious to expound
The spectacle, is mounting high
To days of dim antiquity;
When Lady Aäliza mourned
Her Son, and felt in her despair
The pang of unavailing prayer;

Her Son in Wharf's abysses drowned,
230 The noble Boy of Egremound.
From which affliction – when the grace
Of God had in her heart found place –
A pious structure, fair to see,
Rose up, this stately Priory!
The Lady's work; – but now laid low;
To the grief of her soul that doth come and go,
In the beautiful form of this innocent Doe:
Which, though seemingly doomed in its breast to
    sustain
A softened remembrance of sorrow and pain,
240 Is spotless, and holy, and gentle, and bright;
And glides o'er the earth like an angel of light.

Pass, pass who will, yon chantry door;
And, through the chink in the fractured floor
Look down, and see a griesly sight;
A vault where the bodies are buried upright!
There, face by face, and hand by hand,
The Claphams and Mauleverers stand;
And, in his place, among son and sire,
Is John de Clapham, that fierce Esquire,
250 A valiant man, and a name of dread
In the ruthless wars of the White and Red;
Who dragged Earl Pembroke from Banbury church
And smote off his head on the stones of the porch!
Look down among them, if you dare;
Oft does the White Doe loiter there,
Prying into the darksome rent;
Nor can it be with good intent:
So thinks that Dame of haughty air,
Who hath a Page her book to hold,
260 And wears a frontlet edged with gold.
Harsh thoughts with her high mood agree –
Who counts among her ancestry
Earl Pembroke, slain so impiously!

That slender Youth, a scholar pale,
From Oxford come to his native vale,
He also hath his own conceit:
It is, thinks he, the gracious Fairy,
Who loved the Shepherd-lord to meet
In his wanderings solitary:
270 Wild notes she in his hearing sang,
A song of Nature's hidden powers;
That whistled like the wind, and rang
Among the rocks and holly bowers.
'Twas said that She all shapes could wear;
And oftentimes before him stood,
Amid the trees of some thick wood,
In semblance of a lady fair;
And taught him signs, and showed him sights,
In Craven's dens, on Cumbrian heights;
280 When under cloud of fear he lay,
A shepherd clad in homely grey;
Nor left him at his later day.
And hence, when he, with spear and shield,
Rode full of years to Flodden-field,
His eye could see the hidden spring,
And how the current was to flow;
The fatal end of Scotland's King,
And all that hopeless overthrow.
But not in wars did he delight,
290 *This* Clifford wished for worthier might;
Nor in broad pomp, or courtly state;
Him his own thoughts did elevate, –
Most happy in the shy recess
Of Barden's lowly quietness.
And choice of studious friends had he
Of Bolton's dear fraternity;
Who, standing on this old church tower,
In many a calm propitious hour,
Perused, with him, the starry sky;
300 Or, in their cells, with him did pry
For other lore, – by keen desire

Urged to close toil with chemic fire;
In quest belike of transmutations
Rich as the mine's most bright creations.
But they and their good works are fled,
And all is now disquieted –
And peace is none, for living or dead!

Ah, pensive Scholar, think not so,
But look again at the radiant Doe!
310 What quiet watch she seems to keep,
Alone, beside that grassy heap!
Why mention other thoughts unmeet
For vision so composed and sweet?
While stand the people in a ring,
Gazing, doubting, questioning;
Yea, many overcome in spite
Of recollections clear and bright;
Which yet do unto some impart
An undisturbed repose of heart.
320 And all the assembly own a law
Of orderly respect and awe;
But see – they vanish one by one,
And last, the Doe herself is gone.

Harp! we have been full long beguiled
By vague thoughts, lured by fancies wild;
To which, with no reluctant strings,
Thou hast attuned thy murmurings;
And now before this Pile we stand
In solitude, and utter peace:
330 But, Harp! thy murmurs may not cease –
A Spirit, with his angelic wings,
In soft and breeze-like visitings,
Has touched thee – and a Spirit's hand:
A voice is with us – a command
To chant, in strains of heavenly glory,
A tale of tears, a mortal story!

CANTO SECOND

The Harp in lowliness obeyed;
And first we sang of the green-wood shade
And a solitary Maid;
340 Beginning, where the song must end,
With her, and with her sylvan Friend;
The Friend, who stood before her sight,
Her only unextinguished light;
Her last companion in a dearth
Of love, upon a hopeless earth.

For She it was – this Maid, who wrought
Meekly, with foreboding thought,
In vermeil colours and in gold
An unblest work; which, standing by,
350 Her Father did with joy behold, –
Exulting in its imagery;
A Banner, fashioned to fulfil
Too perfectly his headstrong will:
For on this Banner had her hand
Embroidered (such her Sire's command)
The sacred Cross; and figured there
The five dear wounds our Lord did bear;
Full soon to be uplifted high,
And float in rueful company!

360 It was the time when England's Queen
Twelve years had reigned, a Sovereign dread;
Nor yet the restless crown had been
Disturbed upon her virgin head;
But now the inly-working North
Was ripe to send its thousands forth,
A potent vassalage, to fight
In Percy's and in Neville's right,
Two Earls fast leagued in discontent,
Who gave their wishes open vent;
370 And boldly urged a general plea,

The rites of ancient piety
To be triumphantly restored,
By the stern justice of the sword!
And that same Banner on whose breast
The blameless Lady had exprest
Memorials chosen to give life
And sunshine to a dangerous strife;
That Banner, waiting for the Call,
Stood quietly in Rylstone-hall.

380   It came; and Francis Norton said,
'O Father! rise not in this fray –
The hairs are white upon your head;
Dear Father, hear me when I say
It is for you too late a day!
Bethink you of your own good name:
A just and gracious queen have we,
A pure religion, and the claim
Of peace on our humanity. –
'Tis meet that I endure your scorn;
390   I am your son, your eldest born;
But not for lordship or for land,
My Father, do I clasp your knees;
The Banner touch not, stay your hand,
This multitude of men disband,
And live at home in blameless ease;
For these my brethren's sake, for me;
And, most of all, for Emily!'

Tumultuous noises filled the hall;
And scarcely could the Father hear
400   That name – pronounced with a dying fall –
The name of his only Daughter dear,
As on the banner which stood near
He glanced a look of holy pride,
And his moist eyes were glorified;
Then did he seize the staff, and say:
'Thou, Richard, bear'st thy father's name,

Keep thou this ensign till the day
When I of thee require the same:
Thy place be on my better hand; –
410 And seven as true as thou, I see,
Will cleave to this good cause and me.'
He spake, and eight brave sons straightway
All followed him, a gallant band!

Thus, with his sons, when forth he came
The sight was hailed with loud acclaim
And din of arms and minstrelsy,
From all his warlike tenantry,
All horsed and harnessed with him to ride, –
A voice to which the hills replied!

420 But Francis, in the vacant hall,
Stood silent under dreary weight, –
A phantasm, in which roof and wall
Shook, tottered, swam before his sight;
A phantasm like a dream of night!
Thus overwhelmed, and desolate,
He found his way to a postern-gate;
And, when he waked, his languid eye
Was on the calm and silent sky;
With air about him breathing sweet,
430 And earth's green grass beneath his feet;
Nor did he fail ere long to hear
A sound of military cheer,
Faint – but it reached that sheltered spot;
He heard, and it disturbed him not.

There stood he, leaning on a lance
Which he had grasped unknowingly,
Had blindly grasped in that strong trance,
That dimness of heart-agony;
There stood he, cleansed from the despair
440 And sorrow of his fruitless prayer.
The past he calmly hath reviewed:

But where will be the fortitude
Of this brave man, when he shall see
That Form beneath the spreading tree,
And know that it is Emily?

    He saw her where in open view
She sate beneath the spreading yew –
Her head upon her lap, concealing
In solitude her bitter feeling:
450 'Might ever son *command* a sire,
The act were justified today.'
This to himself – and to the Maid,
Whom now he had approached, he said –
'Gone are they, – they have their desire;
And I with thee one hour will stay,
To give thee comfort if I may.'

    She heard, but looked not up, nor spake;
And sorrow moved him to partake
Her silence; then his thoughts turned round,
460 And fervent words a passage found.

    'Gone are they, bravely, though misled;
With a dear Father at their head!
The Sons obey a natural lord;
The Father had given solemn word
To noble Percy; and a force
Still stronger, bends him to this course.
This said, our tears today may fall
As at an innocent funeral.
In deep and awful channel runs
470 This sympathy of Sire and Sons;
Untried our Brothers have been loved
With heart by simple nature moved;
And now their faithfulness is proved:
For faithful we must call them, bearing
That soul of conscientious daring.
– There were they all in circle – there

Stood Richard, Ambrose, Christopher,
John with a sword that will not fail,
And Marmaduke in fearless mail,
480 And those bright Twins were side by side;
And there, by fresh hopes beautified,
Stood He, whose arm yet lacks the power
Of man, our youngest, fairest flower!
I, by the right of eldest born,
And in a second father's place,
Presumed to grapple with their scorn,
And meet their pity face to face;
Yea, trusting in God's holy aid,
I to my Father knelt and prayed;
490 And one, the pensive Marmaduke,
Methought, was yielding inwardly,
And would have laid his purpose by,
But for a glance of his Father's eye,
Which I myself could scarcely brook.

     'Then be we, each and all, forgiven!
Thou, chiefly thou, my Sister dear,
Whose pangs are registered in heaven –
The stifled sigh, the hidden tear,
And smiles, that dared to take their place,
500 Meek filial smiles, upon thy face,
As that unhallowed Banner grew
Beneath a loving old Man's view.
Thy part is done – thy painful part;
Be thou then satisfied in heart!
A further, though far easier, task
Than thine hath been, my duties ask;
With theirs my efforts cannot blend,
I cannot for such cause contend;
Their aims I utterly forswear;
510 But I in body will be there.
Unarmed and naked will I go,
Be at their side, come weal or woe:
On kind occasions I may wait,

See, hear, obstruct, or mitigate.
Bare breast I take and an empty hand.' –
Therewith he threw away the lance,
Which he had grasped in that strong trance;
Spurned it, like something that would stand
Between him and the pure intent
520 Of love on which his soul was bent.

'For thee, for thee, is left the sense
Of trial past without offence
To God or man; such innocence,
Such consolation, and the excess
Of an unmerited distress;
In that thy very strength must lie.
– O Sister, I could prophesy!
The time is come that rings the knell
Of all we loved, and loved so well:
530 Hope nothing, if I thus may speak
To thee, a woman, and thence weak:
Hope nothing, I repeat; for we
Are doomed to perish utterly:
'Tis meet that thou with me divide
The thought while I am by thy side,
Acknowledging a grace in this,
A comfort in the dark abyss.
But look not for me when I am gone,
And be no farther wrought upon:
540 Farewell all wishes, all debate,
All prayers for this cause, or for that!
Weep, if that aid thee; but depend
Upon no help of outward friend;
Espouse thy doom at once, and cleave
To fortitude without reprieve.
For we must fall, both we and ours –
This Mansion and these pleasant bowers,
Walks, pools, and arbours, homestead, hall –
Our fate is theirs, will reach them all;

550 The young horse must forsake his manger,
    And learn to glory in a Stranger;
    The hawk forget his perch; the hound
    Be parted from his ancient ground:
    The blast will sweep us all away –
    One desolation, one decay!
    And even this Creature!' which words saying,
    He pointed to a lovely Doe,
    A few steps distant, feeding, straying;
    Fair creature, and more white than snow!
560 'Even she will to her peaceful woods
    Return, and to her murmuring floods,
    And be in heart and soul the same
    She was before she hither came;
    Ere she had learned to love us all,
    Herself beloved in Rylstone-hall.
    – But thou, my Sister, doomed to be
    The last leaf on a blasted tree;
    If not in vain we breathed the breath
    Together of a purer faith;
570 If hand in hand we have been led,
    And thou, (O happy thought this day!)
    Not seldom foremost in the way;
    If on one thought our minds have fed,
    And we have in one meaning read;
    If, when at home our private weal
    Hath suffered from the shock of zeal,
    Together we have learned to prize
    Forbearance and self-sacrifice;
    If we like combatants have fared,
580 And for this issue been prepared;
    If thou art beautiful, and youth
    And thought endue thee with all truth –
    Be strong; – be worthy of the grace
    Of God, and fill thy destined place:
    A Soul, by force of sorrows high,
    Uplifted to the purest sky
    Of undisturbed humanity!'

He ended, – or she heard no more;
He led her from the yew-tree shade,
590   And at the mansion's silent door,
He kissed the consecrated Maid;
And down the valley then pursued,
Alone, the armèd Multitude.

CANTO THIRD

Now joy for you who from the towers
Of Brancepeth look in doubt and fear,
Telling melancholy hours!
Proclaim it, let your Masters hear
That Norton with his band is near!
The watchmen from their station high
600   Pronounced the word, – and the Earls descry,
Well-pleased, the armèd Company
Marching down the banks of Were.

Said fearless Norton to the pair
Gone forth to greet him on the plain –
'This meeting, noble Lords! looks fair,
I bring with me a goodly train;
Their hearts are with you: hill and dale
Have helped us: Ure we crossed, and Swale,
And horse and harness followed – see
610   The best part of their Yeomanry!
– Stand forth, my Sons! – these eight are mine
Whom to this service I commend;
Which way soe'er our fate incline,
These will be faithful to the end;
They are my all' – voice failed him here –
'My all save one, a Daughter dear!
Whom I have left, Love's mildest birth,
The meekest Child on this blessed earth.
I had – but these are by my side,
620   These Eight, and this is a day of pride!
The time is ripe. With festive din

Lo! how the people are flocking in, –
Like hungry fowl to the feeder's hand
When snow lies heavy upon the land.'

He spake bare truth; for far and near
From every side came noisy swarms
Of Peasants in their homely gear;
And, mixed with these, to Brancepeth came
Grave Gentry of estate and name,
630 And Captains known for worth in arms;
And prayed the Earls in self-defence
To rise, and prove their innocence. –
'Rise, noble Earls, put forth your might
For holy Church, and the People's right!'

The Norton fixed, at this demand,
His eye upon Northumberland,
And said; 'The Minds of Men will own
No loyal rest while England's Crown
Remains without an Heir, the bait
640 Of strife and factions desperate;
Who, paying deadly hate in kind
Through all things else, in this can find
A mutual hope, a common mind;
And plot, and pant to overwhelm
All ancient honour in the realm.
– Brave Earls! to whose heroic veins
Our noblest blood is given in trust,
To you a suffering State complains,
And ye must raise her from the dust.
650 With wishes of still bolder scope
On you we look, with dearest hope;
Even for our Altars – for the prize
In Heaven, of life that never dies;
For the old and holy Church we mourn,
And must in joy to her return.
Behold!' – and from his Son whose stand
Was on his right, from that guardian hand

He took the Banner, and unfurled
The precious folds – 'behold,' said he,
660 'The ransom of a sinful world;
Let this your preservation be;
The wounds of hands and feet and side,
And the sacred Cross on which Jesus died!
– This bring I from an ancient hearth,
These Records wrought in pledge of love
By hands of no ignoble birth,
A Maid o'er whom the blessed Dove
Vouchsafed in gentleness to brood
While she the holy work pursued.'

670 'Uplift the Standard!' was the cry
From all the listeners that stood round,
'Plant it, – by this we live or die.'
The Norton ceased not for that sound,
But said; 'The prayer which ye have heard,
Much injured Earls! by these preferred,
Is offered to the Saints, the sigh
Of tens of thousands, secretly.'
'Uplift it!' cried once more the Band,
And then a thoughtful pause ensued:
680 'Uplift it!' said Northumberland –
Whereat, from all the multitude
Who saw the Banner reared on high
In all its dread emblazonry,
A voice of uttermost joy brake out:
The transport was rolled down the river of Were,
And Durham, the time-honoured Durham, did hear,
And the towers of Saint Cuthbert were stirred by the
    shout!

Now was the North in arms: – they shine
In warlike trim from Tweed to Tyne,
690 At Percy's voice: and Neville sees
His Followers gathering in from Tees,
From Were, and all the little rills
Concealed among the forkèd hills –

Seven hundred Knights, Retainers all
Of Neville, at their Master's call
Had sate together in Raby Hall!
Such strength that Earldom held of yore;
Nor wanted at this time rich store
Of well-appointed chivalry.
700 – Not loth the sleepy lance to wield,
And greet the old paternal shield,
They heard the summons; – and, furthermore,
Horsemen and Foot of each degree,
Unbound by pledge of fealty,
Appeared, with free and open hate
Of novelties in Church and State;
Knight, burgher, yeoman, and esquire,
And Romish priest, in priest's attire.
And thus, in arms, a zealous Band
710 Proceeding under joint command,
To Durham first their course they bear;
And in Saint Cuthbert's ancient seat
Sang mass, – and tore the book of prayer, –
And trod the Bible beneath their feet.

      Thence marching southward smooth and free
'They mustered their host at Wetherby,
Full sixteen thousand fair to see;'
The Choicest Warriors of the North!
But none for beauty and for worth
720 Like those eight Sons – who, in a ring,
(Ripe men, or blooming in life's spring)
Each with a lance, erect and tall,
A falchion, and a buckler small,
Stood by their Sire, on Clifford-moor,
To guard the Standard which he bore.
On foot they girt their Father round;
And so will keep the appointed ground
Where'er their march: no steed will he
Henceforth bestride; – triumphantly,
730 He stands upon the grassy sod,

Trusting himself to the earth, and God.
Rare sight to embolden and inspire!
Proud was the field of Sons and Sire;
Of him the most; and, sooth to say,
No shape of man in all the array
So graced the sunshine of that day.
The monumental pomp of age
Was with this goodly Personage;
A stature undepressed in size,
740   Unbent, which rather seemed to rise,
In open victory o'er the weight
Of seventy years, to loftier height;
Magnific limbs of withered state;
A face to fear and venerate;
Eyes dark and strong; and on his head
Bright locks of silver hair, thick spread,
Which a brown morion half-concealed,
Light as a hunter's of the field;
And thus, with girdle round his waist,
750   Whereon the Banner-staff might rest
At need, he stood, advancing high
The glittering, floating Pageantry.

       Who sees him? – thousands see, and One
With unparticipated gaze;
Who, 'mong those thousands, friend hath none,
And treads in solitary ways.
He, following wheresoe'er he might,
Hath watched the Banner from afar,
As shepherds watch a lonely star,
760   Or mariners the distant light
That guides them through a stormy night.
And now, upon a chosen plot
Of rising ground, yon heathy spot!
He takes alone his far-off stand,
With breast unmailed, unweaponed hand.
Bold is his aspect; but his eye
Is pregnant with anxiety,

While, like a tutelary Power,
He there stands fixed from hour to hour:
770   Yet sometimes in more humble guise
Upon the turf-clad height he lies
Stretched, herdsman-like, as if to bask
In sunshine were his only task,
Or by his mantle's help to find
A shelter from the nipping wind:
And thus, with short oblivion blest,
His weary spirits gather rest.
Again he lifts his eyes; and lo!
The pageant glancing to and fro;
780   And hope is wakened by the sight,
He thence may learn, ere fall of night,
Which way the tide is doomed to flow.

     To London were the Chieftains bent;
But what avails the bold intent?
A Royal army is gone forth
To quell the RISING OF THE NORTH;
They march with Dudley at their head,
And, in seven days' space, will to York be led! –
Can such a mighty Host be raised
790   Thus suddenly, and brought so near?
The Earls upon each other gazed,
And Neville's cheek grew pale with fear;
For, with a high and valiant name,
He bore a heart of timid frame;
And bold if both had been, yet they
'Against so many may not stay.'
Back therefore will they hie to seize
A strong Hold on the banks of Tees;
There wait a favourable hour,
800   Until Lord Dacre with his power
From Naworth come; and Howard's aid
Be with them openly displayed.

     While through the Host, from man to man,
A rumour of this purpose ran,

The Standard trusting to the care
Of him who heretofore did bear
That charge, impatient Norton sought
The Chieftains to unfold his thought,
And thus abruptly spake; – 'We yield
810 (And can it be?) an unfought field! –
How oft has strength, the strength of heaven,
To few triumphantly been given!
Still do our very children boast
Of mitred Thurston – what a Host
He conquered! – Saw we not the Plain
(And flying shall behold again)
Where faith was proved? – while to battle moved
The Standard, on the Sacred Wain
That bore it, compassed round by a bold
820 Fraternity of Barons old;
And with those grey-haired champions stood,
Under the saintly ensigns three,
The infant Heir of Mowbray's blood –
All confident of victory! –
Shall Percy blush, then, for his name?
Must Westmorland be asked with shame
Whose were the numbers, where the loss,
In that other day of Neville's Cross?
When the Prior of Durham with holy hand
830 Raised, as the Vision gave command,
Saint Cuthbert's Relic – far and near
Kenned on the point of a lofty spear;
While the Monks prayed in Maiden's Bower
To God descending in his power.
Less would not at our need be due
To us, who war against the Untrue; –
The delegates of Heaven we rise,
Convoked the impious to chastise:
We, we, the sanctities of old
840 Would re-establish and uphold:
Be warned' – His zeal the Chiefs confounded,
But word was given, and the trumpet sounded:

Back through the melancholy Host
Went Norton, and resumed his post.
Alas! thought he, and have I borne
This Banner raised with joyful pride,
This hope of all posterity,
By those dread symbols sanctified;
Thus to become at once the scorn
850 Of babbling winds as they go by,
A spot of shame to the sun's bright eye,
To the light clouds a mockery!
– 'Even these poor eight of mine would stem –'
Half to himself, and half to them
He spake – 'would stem, or quell, a force
Ten times their number, man and horse;
This by their own unaided might,
Without their father in their sight,
Without the Cause for which they fight;
860 A Cause, which on a needful day
Would breed us thousands brave as they.'
– So speaking, he his reverend head
Raised toward that Imagery once more:
But the familiar prospect shed
Despondency unfelt before:
A shock of intimations vain,
Dismay, and superstitious pain,
Fell on him, with the sudden thought
Of her by whom the work was wrought: –
870 Oh wherefore was her countenance bright
With love divine and gentle light?
She would not, could not, disobey,
But her Faith leaned another way.
Ill tears she wept; I saw them fall,
I overheard her as she spake
Sad words to that mute Animal,
The White Doe, in the hawthorn brake;
She steeped, but not for Jesu's sake,
This Cross in tears: by her, and One
880 Unworthier far we are undone –

Her recreant Brother – he prevailed
Over that tender Spirit – assailed
Too oft alas! by her whose head
In the cold grave hath long been laid:
She first, in reason's dawn beguiled
Her docile, unsuspecting Child:
Far back – far back my mind must go
To reach the well-spring of this woe!

While thus he brooded, music sweet
890 Of border tunes was played to cheer
The footsteps of a quick retreat;
But Norton lingered in the rear,
Stung with sharp thoughts; and ere the last
From his distracted brain was cast,
Before his Father, Francis stood,
And spake in firm and earnest mood.

'Though here I bend a suppliant knee
In reverence, and unarmed, I bear
In your indignant thoughts my share;
900 Am grieved this backward march to see
So careless and disorderly.
I scorn your Chiefs – men who would lead,
And yet want courage at their need:
Then look at them with open eyes!
Deserve they further sacrifice? –
If – when they shrink, nor dare oppose
In open field their gathering foes,
(And fast, from this decisive day,
Yon multitude must melt away;)
910 If now I ask a grace not claimed
While ground was left for hope; unblamed
Be an endeavour that can do
No injury to them or you.
My Father! I would help to find
A place of shelter, till the rage
Of cruel men do like the wind

Exhaust itself and sink to rest;
Be Brother now to Brother joined!
Admit me in the equipage
920   Of your misfortunes, that at least,
Whatever fate remain behind,
I may bear witness in my breast
To your nobility of mind!'

'Thou Enemy, my bane and blight!
Oh! bold to fight the Coward's fight
Against all good' – but why declare,
At length, the issue of a prayer
Which love had prompted, yielding scope
Too free to one bright moment's hope?
930   Suffice it that the Son, who strove
With fruitless effort to allay
That passion, prudently gave way;
Nor did he turn aside to prove
His Brothers' wisdom or their love –
But calmly from the spot withdrew;
His best endeavours to renew,
Should e'er a kindlier time ensue.

CANTO FOURTH

'Tis night: in silence looking down,
The Moon from cloudless ether sees
940   A Camp, and a beleaguered Town,
And Castle like a stately crown
On the steep rocks of winding Tees; –
And southward far, with moor between,
Hill-top, and flood, and forest green,
The bright Moon sees that valley small
Where Rylstone's old sequestered Hall
A venerable image yields
Of quiet to the neighbouring fields;
While from one pillared chimney breathes
950   The smoke, and mounts in silver wreaths.

– The courts are hushed; – for timely sleep
The greyhounds to their kennel creep;
The peacock in the broad ash-tree
Aloft is roosted for the night,
He who in proud prosperity
Of colours manifold and bright
Walked round, affronting the daylight;
And higher still, above the bower
Where he is perched, from yon lone Tower
960 The hall-clock in the clear moonshine
With glittering finger points at nine.

    Ah! who could think that sadness here
Hath any sway? or pain, or fear?
A soft and lulling sound is heard
Of streams inaudible by day;
The garden pool's dark surface, stirred
By the night insects in their play,
Breaks into dimples small and bright;
A thousand, thousand rings of light
970 That shape themselves and disappear
Almost as soon as seen: – and lo!
Not distant far, the milk-white Doe –
The same who quietly was feeding
On the green herb, and nothing heeding,
When Francis, uttering to the Maid
His last words in the yew-tree shade,
Involved whate'er by love was brought
Out of his heart, or crossed his thought,
Or chance presented to his eye,
980 In one sad sweep of destiny –
The same fair Creature, who hath found
Her way into forbidden ground;
Where now – within this spacious plot
For pleasure made, a goodly spot,
With lawns and beds of flowers, and shades
Of trellis-work in long arcades,
And cirque and crescent framed by wall

Of close-clipt foliage green and tall,
Converging walks, and fountains gay,
990 And terraces in trim array –
Beneath yon cypress spiring high,
With pine and cedar spreading wide
Their darksome boughs on either side,
In open moonlight doth she lie;
Happy as others of her kind,
That, far from human neighbourhood,
Range unrestricted as the wind,
Through park, or chase, or savage wood.

But see the consecrated Maid
1000 Emerging from a cedar shade
To open moonshine, where the Doe
Beneath the cypress-spire is laid;
Like a patch of April snow –
Upon a bed of herbage green,
Lingering in a woody glade
Or behind a rocky screen –
Lonely relic! which, if seen
By the shepherd, is passed by
With an inattentive eye.
1010 Nor more regard doth She bestow
Upon the uncomplaining Doe
Now couched at ease, though oft this day
Not unperplexed nor free from pain,
When she had tried, and tried in vain,
Approaching in her gentle way,
To win some look of love, or gain
Encouragement to sport or play;
Attempts which still the heart-sick Maid
Rejected, or with slight repaid.

1020 Yet Emily is soothed; – the breeze
Came fraught with kindly sympathies.
As she approached yon rustic Shed
Hung with late-flowering woodbine, spread

Along the walls and overhead,
The fragrance of the breathing flowers
Revived a memory of those hours
When here, in this remote alcove,
(While from the pendent woodbine came
Like odours, sweet as if the same)
1030 A fondly-anxious Mother strove
To teach her salutary fears
And mysteries above her years.
Yes, she is soothed: an Image faint,
And yet not faint – a presence bright
Returns to her – that blessèd Saint
Who with mild looks and language mild
Instructed here her darling Child,
While yet a prattler on the knee,
To worship in simplicity
1040 The invisible God, and take for guide
The faith reformed and purified.

    'Tis flown – the Vision, and the sense
Of that beguiling influence;
'But oh! thou Angel from above,
Mute Spirit of maternal love,
That stood'st before my eyes, more clear
Than ghosts are fabled to appear
Sent upon embassies of fear;
As thou thy presence hast to me
1050 Vouchsafed, in radiant ministry
Descend on Francis; nor forbear
To greet him with a voice, and say; –
"If hope be a rejected stay,
Do thou, my Christian Son, beware
Of that most lamentable snare,
The self-reliance of despair!" '

    Then within the embowered retreat
Where she had found a grateful seat
Perturbed she issues. She will go!

1060 Herself will follow to the war,
  And clasp her Father's knees; – ah, no!
  She meets the insuperable bar,
  The injunction by her Brother laid;
  His parting charge – but ill obeyed –
  That interdicted all debate,
  All prayer for this cause or for that;
  All efforts that would turn aside
  The headstrong current of their fate:
  Her duty is to stand and wait;
1070 In resignation to abide
  The shock, AND FINALLY SECURE
  O'ER PAIN AND GRIEF A TRIUMPH PURE.
  – She feels it, and her pangs are checked.
  But now, as silently she paced
  The turf, and thought by thought was chased,
  Came One who, with sedate respect,
  Approached, and, greeting her, thus spake;
  'An old man's privilege I take:
  Dark is the time – a woeful day!
1080 Dear daughter of affliction, say
  How can I serve you? point the way.'

  'Rights have you, and may well be bold:
  You with my Father have grown old
  In friendship – strive – for his sake go –
  Turn from us all the coming woe:
  This would I beg; but on my mind
  A passive stillness is enjoined.
  On you, if room for mortal aid
  Be left, is no restriction laid;
1090 You not forbidden to recline
  With hope upon the Will divine.'

  'Hope,' said the old Man, 'must abide
  With all of us, whate'er betide.
  In Craven's Wilds is many a den,
  To shelter persecuted men:

Far under ground is many a cave,
Where they might lie as in the grave,
Until this storm hath ceased to rave:
Or let them cross the River Tweed,
1100 And be at once from peril freed!'
'Ah tempt me not!' she faintly sighed;
'I will not counsel nor exhort,
With my condition satisfied;
But you, at least, may make report
Of what befalls; – be this your task –
This may be done; – 'tis all I ask!'

She spake – and from the Lady's sight
The Sire, unconscious of his age,
Departed promptly as a Page
1110 Bound on some errand of delight.
– The noble Francis – wise as brave,
Thought he, may want not skill to save.
With hopes in tenderness concealed,
Unarmed he followed to the field;
Him will I seek: the insurgent Powers
Are now besieging Barnard's Towers, –
'Grant that the Moon which shines this night
May guide them in a prudent flight!'

But quick the turns of chance and change,
1120 And knowledge has a narrow range;
Whence idle fears, and needless pain,
And wishes blind, and efforts vain. –
The Moon may shine, but cannot be
Their guide in flight – already she
Hath witnessed their captivity.
She saw the desperate assault
Upon that hostile castle made; –
But dark and dismal is the vault
Where Norton and his sons are laid!
1130 Disastrous issue! – he had said
'This night yon faithless Towers must yield,

Or we for ever quit the field.
– Neville is utterly dismayed,
For promise fails of Howard's aid;
And Dacre to our call replies
That *he* is unprepared to rise.
My heart is sick; – this weary pause
Must needs be fatal to our cause.
The breach is open – on the wall,
1140 This night, – the Banner shall be planted!'
– 'Twas done: his Sons were with him – all;
They belt him round with hearts undaunted
And others follow; – Sire and Son
Leap down into the court; – ' 'Tis won' –
They shout aloud – but Heaven decreed
That with their joyful shout should close
The triumph of a desperate deed
Which struck with terror friends and foes!
The friend shrinks back – the foe recoils
1150 From Norton and his filial band;
But they, now caught within the toils,
Against a thousand cannot stand; –
The foe from numbers courage drew,
And overpowered that gallant few.
'A rescue for the Standard!' cried
The Father from within the walls;
But, see, the sacred Standard falls! –
Confusion through the Camp spread wide:
Some fled; and some their fears detained:
1160 But ere the Moon had sunk to rest
In her pale chambers of the west,
Of that rash levy naught remained.

CANTO FIFTH

High on a point of rugged ground
Among the wastes of Rylstone Fell,
Above the loftiest ridge or mound
Where foresters or shepherds dwell,

An edifice of warlike frame
Stands single – Norton Tower its name –
It fronts all quarters, and looks round
1170 O'er path and road, and plain and dell,
Dark moor, and gleam of pool and stream
Upon a prospect without bound.

   The summit of this bold ascent –
Though bleak and bare, and seldom free
As Pendle-hill or Pennygent
From wind, or frost, or vapours wet –
Had often heard the sound of glee
When there the youthful Nortons met,
To practise games and archery:
1180 How proud and happy they! the crowd
Of Lookers-on how pleased and proud!
And from the scorching noon-tide sun,
From showers, or when the prize was won,
They to the Tower withdrew, and there
Would mirth run round, with generous fare;
And the stern old Lord of Rylstone-hall
Was happiest, proudest, of them all!

   But now, his Child, with anguish pale,
Upon the height walks to and fro;
1190 'Tis well that she hath heard the tale,
Received the bitterness of woe:
For she *had* hoped, had hoped and feared,
Such rights did feeble nature claim;
And oft her steps had hither steered,
Though not unconscious of self-blame;
For she her brother's charge revered,
His farewell words; and by the same,
Yea, by her brother's very name,
Had, in her solitude, been cheered.

1200   Beside the lonely watch-tower stood
That grey-haired Man of gentle blood,

Who with her Father had grown old
In friendship; rival hunters they,
And fellow warriors in their day;
To Rylstone he the tidings brought;
Then on this height the Maid had sought,
And, gently as he could, had told
The end of that dire Tragedy,
Which it had been his lot to see.

1210   To him the Lady turned; 'You said
That Francis lives, *he* is not dead?'

'Your noble brother hath been spared;
To take his life they have not dared;
On him and on his high endeavour
The light of praise shall shine for ever!
Nor did he (such Heaven's will) in vain
His solitary course maintain;
Not vainly struggled in the might
Of duty, seeing with clear sight;
1220 He was their comfort to the last,
Their joy till every pang was past.

'I witnessed when to York they came –
What, Lady, if their feet were tied;
They might deserve a good Man's blame;
But marks of infamy and shame—
These were their triumph, these their pride;
Nor wanted 'mid the pressing crowd
Deep feeling, that found utterance loud,
"Lo, Francis comes," there were who cried,
1230 "A Prisoner once, but now set free!
'Tis well, for he the worst defied
Through force of natural piety;
He rose not in this quarrel, he,
For concord's sake and England's good,
Suit to his Brothers often made
With tears, and of his Father prayed –

And when he had in vain withstood
Their purpose – then did he divide,
He parted from them; but at their side
1240 Now walks in unanimity.
Then peace to cruelty and scorn,
While to the prison they are borne,
Peace, peace to all indignity!"

'And so in Prison were they laid –
Oh hear me, hear me, gentle Maid,
For I am come with power to bless,
By scattering gleams, through your distress,
Of a redeeming happiness.
Me did a reverent pity move
1250 And privilege of ancient love;
And, in your service, making bold,
Entrance I gained to that strong-hold.

'Your Father gave me cordial greeting;
But to his purposes, that burned
Within him, instantly returned:
He was commanding and entreating,
And said – "We need not stop, my Son!
Thoughts press, and time is hurrying on" –
And so to Francis he renewed
1260 His words, more calmly thus pursued.

' "Might this our enterprise have sped,
Change wide and deep the Land had seen,
A renovation from the dead,
A spring-tide of immortal green:
The darksome altars would have blazed
Like stars when clouds are rolled away;
Salvation to all eyes that gazed,
Once more the Rood had been upraised
To spread its arms, and stand for aye.
1270 Then, then – had I survived to see
New life in Bolton Priory;

The voice restored, the eye of Truth
Re-opened that inspired my youth;
To see her in her pomp arrayed –
This Banner (for such vow I made)
Should on the consecrated breast
Of that same Temple have found rest:
I would myself have hung it high,
Fit offering of glad victory!

1280 ' "A shadow of such thought remains
To cheer this sad and pensive time;
A solemn fancy yet sustains
One feeble Being – bids me climb
Even to the last – one effort more
To attest my Faith, if not restore.

' "Hear then," said he, "while I impart,
My Son, the last wish of my heart.
The Banner strive thou to regain;
And, if the endeavour prove not vain,
1290 Bear it – to whom if not to thee
Shall I this lonely thought consign? –
Bear it to Bolton Priory,
And lay it on Saint Mary's shrine;
To wither in the sun and breeze
'Mid those decaying sanctities.
There let at least the gift be laid,
The testimony there displayed;
Bold proof that with no selfish aim,
But for lost Faith and Christ's dear name,
1300 I helmeted a brow though white,
And took a place in all men's sight;
Yea, offered up this noble Brood,
This fair unrivalled Brotherhood,
And turned away from thee, my Son!
And left – but be the rest unsaid,
The name untouched, the tear unshed; –
My wish is known, and I have done:

Now promise, grant this one request,
This dying prayer, and be thou blest!"

1310   'Then Francis answered – "Trust thy Son,
For, with God's will, it shall be done!" –

'The pledge obtained, the solemn word
Thus scarcely given, a noise was heard,
And Officers appeared in state
To lead the prisoners to their fate.
They rose, oh! wherefore should I fear
To tell, or, Lady, you to hear?
They rose – embraces none were given –
They stood like trees when earth and heaven
1320 Are calm; they knew each other's worth,
And reverently the Band went forth.
They met, when they had reached the door,
One with profane and harsh intent
Placed there – that he might go before
And, with that rueful Banner borne
Aloft in sign of taunting scorn,
Conduct them to their punishment:
So cruel Sussex, unrestrained
By human feeling, had ordained.
1330 The unhappy Banner Francis saw,
And, with a look of calm command
Inspiring universal awe,
He took it from the soldier's hand;
And all the people that stood round
Confirmed the deed in peace profound.
– High transport did the Father shed
Upon his Son – and they were led,
Led on, and yielded up their breath;
Together died, a happy death! –
1340 But Francis, soon as he had braved
That insult, and the Banner saved,
Athwart the unresisting tide
Of the spectators occupied

In admiration or dismay,
Bore instantly his Charge away.'

These things, which thus had in the sight
And hearing passed of Him who stood
With Emily, on the Watch-tower height,
In Rylstone's woeful neighbourhood,
1350 He told; and oftentimes with voice
Of power to comfort or rejoice;
For deepest sorrows that aspire,
Go high, no transport ever higher.
'Yes – God is rich in mercy,' said
The old Man to the silent Maid,
'Yet, Lady! shines, through this black night,
One star of aspect heavenly bright;
Your brother lives – he lives – is come
Perhaps already to his home;
1360 Then let us leave this dreary place.'
She yielded, and with gentle pace,
Though without one uplifted look,
To Rylstone-hall her way she took.

CANTO SIXTH

Why comes not Francis? – From the doleful City
He fled, – and, in his flight, could hear
The death-sounds of the Minster-bell:
That sullen stroke pronounced farewell
To Marmaduke, cut off from pity!
To Ambrose that! and then a knell
1370 For him, the sweet half-opened Flower!
For all – all dying in one hour!
– Why comes not Francis? Thoughts of love
Should bear him to his Sister dear
With the fleet motion of a dove;
Yea, like a heavenly messenger
Of speediest wing, should he appear.
Why comes he not? – for westward fast

Along the plain of York he passed;
Reckless of what impels or leads,
1380 Unchecked he hurries on; – nor heeds
The sorrow, through the Villages,
Spread by triumphant cruelties
Of vengeful military force,
And punishment without remorse.
He marked not, heard not, as he fled;
All but the suffering heart was dead
For him abandoned to blank awe,
To vacancy, and horror strong:
And the first object which he saw,
1390 With conscious sight, as he swept along –
It was the Banner in his hand!
He felt – and made a sudden stand.

He looked about like one betrayed:
What hath he done? what promise made?
Oh weak, weak moment! to what end
Can such a vain oblation tend,
And he the Bearer? – Can he go
Carrying this instrument of woe,
And find, find anywhere, a right
1400 To excuse him in his Country's sight?
No; will not all men deem the change
A downward course, perverse and strange?
Here is it; – but how? when? must she,
The unoffending Emily,
Again this piteous object see?

Such conflict long did he maintain,
Nor liberty nor rest could gain:
His own life into danger brought
By this sad burden – even that thought,
1410 Exciting self-suspicion strong,
Swayed the brave man to his wrong.
And how – unless it were the sense
Of all-disposing Providence,

Its will unquestionably shown –
How has the Banner clung so fast
To a palsied, and unconscious hand;
Clung to the hand to which it passed
Without impediment? And why
But that Heaven's purpose might be known
1420 Doth now no hindrance meet his eye,
No intervention, to withstand
Fulfilment of a Father's prayer
Breathed to a Son forgiven, and blest
When all resentments were at rest,
And life in death laid the heart bare? –
Then, like a spectre sweeping by,
Rushed through his mind the prophecy
Of utter desolation made
To Emily in the yew-tree shade:
1430 He sighed, submitting will and power
To the stern embrace of that grasping hour.
'No choice is left, the deed is mine –
Dead are they, dead! – and I will go,
And, for their sakes, come weal or woe,
Will lay the Relic on the shrine.'

So forward with a steady will
He went, and traversed plain and hill;
And up the vale of Wharf his way
Pursued; – and, at the dawn of day,
1440 Attained a summit whence his eyes
Could see the Tower of Bolton rise.
There Francis for a moment's space
Made halt – but hark! a noise behind
Of horsemen at an eager pace!
He heard, and with misgiving mind.
– 'Tis Sir George Bowes who leads the Band:
They come, by cruel Sussex sent;
Who, when the Nortons from the hand
Of death had drunk their punishment,
1450 Bethought him, angry and ashamed,

How Francis, with the Banner claimed
As his own charge, had disappeared,
By all the standers-by revered.
His whole bold carriage (which had quelled
Thus far the Opposer, and repelled
All censure, enterprise so bright
That even bad men had vainly striven
Against that overcoming light)
Was then reviewed, and prompt word given,
1460 That to what place soever fled
He should be seized, alive or dead.

The troop of horse have gained the height
Where Francis stood in open sight.
They hem him round – 'Behold the proof,'
They cried, 'the Ensign in his hand!
He did not arm, he walked aloof!
For why? – to save his Father's land;
Worst Traitor of them all is he,
A Traitor dark and cowardly!'

1470 'I am no Traitor,' Francis said,
'Though this unhappy freight I bear;
And must not part with. But beware; –
Err not, by hasty zeal misled,
Nor do a suffering Spirit wrong,
Whose self-reproaches are too strong!'
At this he from the beaten road
Retreated towards a brake of thorn,
That like a place of vantage showed;
And there stood bravely, though forlorn.
1480 In self-defence with warlike brow
He stood, – nor weaponless was now;
He from a Soldier's hand had snatched
A spear, – and, so protected, watched
The Assailants, turning round and round;
But from behind with treacherous wound
A Spearman brought him to the ground.

The guardian lance, as Francis fell,
Dropped from him; but his other hand
The Banner clenched; till, from out the Band,
1490 One, the most eager for the prize,
Rushed in; and – while, O grief to tell!
A glimmering sense still left, with eyes
Unclosed the noble Francis lay –
Seized it, as hunters seize their prey;
But not before the warm life-blood
Had tinged more deeply, as it flowed,
The wounds the broidered Banner showed,
Thy fatal work, O Maiden, innocent as good!

Proudly the Horsemen bore away
1500 The Standard; and where Francis lay
There was he left alone, unwept,
And for two days unnoticed slept.
For at that time bewildering fear
Possessed the country, far and near;
But, on the third day, passing by
One of the Norton Tenantry
Espied the uncovered Corse; the Man
Shrunk as he recognized the face,
And to the nearest homesteads ran
1510 And called the people to the place.
– How desolate is Rylstone-hall!
This was the instant thought of all;
And if the lonely Lady there
Should be; to her they cannot bear
This weight of anguish and despair.
So, when upon sad thoughts had prest
Thoughts sadder still, they deemed it best
That, if the Priest should yield assent
And no one hinder their intent,
1520 Then, they, for Christian pity's sake,
In holy ground a grave would make;
And straightway buried he should be
In the Church-yard of the Priory.

Apart, some little space, was made
The grave where Francis must be laid.
In no confusion or neglect
This did they, – but in pure respect
That he was born of gentle blood;
And that there was no neighbourhood
1530 Of kindred for him in that ground:
So to the Church-yard they are bound,
Bearing the body on a bier;
And psalms they sing – a holy sound
That hill and vale with sadness hear.

But Emily hath raised her head,
And is again disquieted;
She must behold! – so many gone,
Where is the solitary One?
And forth from Rylstone-hall stepped she, –
1540 To seek her Brother forth she went,
And tremblingly her course she bent
Toward Bolton's ruined Priory.
She comes, and in the vale hath heard
The funeral dirge; – she sees the knot
Of people, sees them in one spot –
And darting like a wounded bird
She reached the grave, and with her breast
Upon the ground received the rest, –
The consummation, the whole ruth
1550 And sorrow of this final truth!

CANTO SEVENTH

'Powers there are
That touch each other to the quick – in modes
Which the gross world no sense hath to perceive,
No soul to dream of.'

Thou Spirit, whose angelic hand
Was to the harp a strong command,

Called the submissive strings to wake
In glory for this Maiden's sake,
Say, Spirit! whither hath she fled
To hide her poor afflicted head?
What mighty forest in its gloom
Enfolds her? – is a rifted tomb
Within the wilderness her seat?
1560 Some island which the wild waves beat –
Is that the Sufferer's last retreat?
Or some aspiring rock, that shrouds
Its perilous front in mists and clouds?
High-climbing rock, low sunless dale,
Sea, desert, what do these avail?
Oh take her anguish and her fears
Into a deep recess of years!

'Tis done; – despoil and desolation
O'er Rylstone's fair domain have blown;
1570 Pools, terraces, and walks are sown
With weeds; the bowers are overthrown,
Or have given way to slow mutation,
While, in their ancient habitation
The Norton name hath been unknown.
The lordly Mansion of its pride
Is stripped; the ravage hath spread wide
Through park and field, a perishing
That mocks the gladness of the Spring!
And, with this silent gloom agreeing,
1580 Appears a joyless human Being,
Of aspect such as if the waste
Were under her dominion placed.
Upon a primrose bank, her throne
Of quietness, she sits alone;
Among the ruins of a wood,
Erewhile a covert bright and green,
And where full many a brave tree stood,
That used to spread its boughs, and ring
With the sweet birds' carolling.

1590 Behold her, like a virgin Queen,
  Neglecting in imperial state
  These outward images of fate,
  And carrying inward a serene
  And perfect sway, through many a thought
  Of chance and change, that hath been brought
  To the subjection of a holy,
  Though stern and rigorous, melancholy!
  The like authority, with grace
  Of awfulness, is in her face, –
1600 There hath she fixed it; yet it seems
  To o'ershadow by no native right
  That face, which cannot lose the gleams,
  Lose utterly the tender gleams,
  Of gentleness and meek delight,
  And loving-kindness ever bright:
  Such is her sovereign mien: – her dress
  (A vest with woollen cincture tied,
  A hood of mountain-wool undyed)
  Is homely, – fashioned to express
1610 A wandering Pilgrim's humbleness.

  And she *hath* wandered, long and far,
  Beneath the light of sun and star;
  Hath roamed in trouble and in grief,
  Driven forward like a withered leaf,
  Yea, like a ship at random blown
  To distant places and unknown.
  But now she dares to seek a haven
  Among her native wilds of Craven;
  Hath seen again her Father's roof,
1620 And put her fortitude to proof;
  The mighty sorrow hath been borne,
  And she is thoroughly forlorn:
  Her soul doth in itself stand fast,
  Sustained by memory of the past
  And strength of Reason; held above
  The infirmities of mortal love;

Undaunted, lofty, calm, and stable,
And awfully impenetrable.

And so – beneath a mouldered tree,
1630 A self-surviving leafless oak
By unregarded age from stroke
Of ravage saved – sate Emily.
There did she rest, with head reclined,
Herself most like a stately flower,
(Such have I seen) whom chance of birth
Hath separated from its kind,
To live and die in a shady bower,
Single on the gladsome earth.

When, with a noise like distant thunder,
1640 A troop of deer came sweeping by;
And, suddenly, behold a wonder!
For One, among those rushing deer,
A single One, in mid career
Hath stopped, and fixed her large full eye
Upon the Lady Emily;
A Doe most beautiful, clear-white,
A radiant creature, silver-bright!

Thus checked, a little while it stayed;
A little thoughtful pause it made;
1650 And then advanced with stealth-like pace,
Drew softly near her, and more near –
Looked round – but saw no cause for fear;
So to her feet the Creature came,
And laid its head upon her knee,
And looked into the Lady's face,
A look of pure benignity,
And fond unclouded memory.
It is, thought Emily, the same,
The very Doe of other years! –
1660 The pleading look the Lady viewed,
And, by her gushing thoughts subdued,

She melted into tears –
A flood of tears that flowed apace
Upon the happy Creature's face.

    Oh, moment ever blest! O Pair
Beloved of Heaven, Heaven's chosen care,
This was for you a precious greeting;
And may it prove a fruitful meeting!
Joined are they, and the sylvan Doe
1670 Can she depart? can she forego
The Lady, once her playful peer,
And now her sainted Mistress dear?
And will not Emily receive
This lovely chronicler of things
Long past, delights and sorrowings?
Lone Sufferer! will not she believe
The promise in that speaking face;
And welcome, as a gift of grace,
The saddest thought the Creature brings?

1680   That day, the first of a re-union
Which was to teem with high communion,
That day of balmy April weather,
They tarried in the wood together.
And when, ere fall of evening dew,
She from her sylvan haunt withdrew,
The White Doe tracked with faithful pace
The Lady to her dwelling-place;
That nook where, on paternal ground,
A habitation she had found,
1690 The Master of whose humble board
Once owned her Father for his Lord;
A hut, by tufted trees defended,
Where Rylstone brook with Wharf is blended.

    When Emily by morning light
Went forth, the Doe stood there in sight.
She shrunk: – with one frail shock of pain

Received and followed by a prayer,
She saw the Creature once again;
Shun will she not, she feels, will bear; –
1700 But, wheresoever she looked round,
All now was trouble-haunted ground;
And therefore now she deems it good
Once more this restless neighbourhood
To leave. – Unwooed, yet unforbidden,
The White Doe followed up the vale,
Up to another cottage, hidden
In the deep fork of Amerdale;
And there may Emily restore
Herself, in spots unseen before.
1710 – Why tell of mossy rock, or tree,
By lurking Dernbrook's pathless side,
Haunts of a strengthening amity
That calmed her, cheered, and fortified?
For she hath ventured now to read
Of time, and place, and thought, and deed –
Endless history that lies
In her silent Follower's eyes;
Who with a power like human reason
Discerns the favourable season,
1720 Skilled to approach or to retire, –
From looks conceiving her desire;
From look, deportment, voice, or mien,
That vary to the heart within.
If she too passionately wreathed
Her arms, or over-deeply breathed,
Walked quick or slowly, every mood
In its degree was understood;
Then well may their accord be true,
And kindliest intercourse ensue.
1730 – Oh! surely 'twas a gentle rousing
When she by sudden glimpse espied
The White Doe on the mountain browsing,
Or in the meadow wandered wide!
How pleased, when down the Straggler sank

Beside her, on some sunny bank!
How soothed, when in thick bower enclosed,
They, like a nested pair, reposed!
Fair Vision! when it crossed the Maid
Within some rocky cavern laid,
1740 The dark cave's portal gliding by,
White as whitest cloud on high
Floating through the azure sky.
– What now is left for pain or fear?
That Presence, dearer and more dear,
While they, side by side, were straying,
And the shepherd's pipe was playing,
Did now a very gladness yield
At morning to the dewy field,
And with a deeper peace endued
1750 The hour of moonlight solitude.

    With her Companion, in such frame
Of mind, to Rylstone back she came;
And, ranging through the wasted groves,
Received the memory of old loves,
Undisturbed and undistrest,
Into a soul which now was blest
With a soft spring-day of holy,
Mild, and grateful, melancholy:
Not sunless gloom or unenlightened,
1760 But by tender fancies brightened.

    When the bells of Rylstone played
Their sabbath music – 'God us ayde!'
That was the sound they seemed to speak;
Inscriptive legend which I ween
May on these holy bells be seen,
That legend and her Grandsire's name;
And oftentimes the Lady meek
Had in her childhood read the same;
Words which she slighted at that day;
1770 But now, when such sad change was wrought,

And of that lonely name she thought,
The bells of Rylstone seemed to say,
While she sate listening in the shade,
With vocal music, '𝕲𝖔𝖉 𝖚𝖘 𝖆𝖞𝖉𝖊;'
And all the hills were glad to bear
Their part in this effectual prayer.

    Nor lacked she Reason's firmest power;
But with the White Doe at her side
Up would she climb to Norton Tower,
1780 And thence look round her far and wide,
Her fate there measuring; – all is stilled, –
The weak One hath subdued her heart;
Behold the prophecy fulfilled,
Fulfilled, and she sustains her part!
But here her Brother's words have failed;
Here hath a milder doom prevailed;
That she, of him and all bereft,
Hath yet this faithful Partner left;
This one Associate that disproves
1790 His words, remains for her, and loves.
If tears are shed, they do not fall
For loss of him – for one, or all;
Yet, sometimes, sometimes doth she weep
Moved gently in her soul's soft sleep;
A few tears down her cheek descend
For this her last and living Friend.

    Bless, tender Hearts, their mutual lot,
And bless for both this savage spot;
Which Emily doth sacred hold
1800 For reasons dear and manifold –
Here hath she, here before her sight,
Close to the summit of this height,
The grassy rock-encircled Pound
In which the Creature first was found.
So beautiful the timid Thrall
(A spotless Youngling white as foam)

Her youngest Brother brought it home;
The youngest, then a lusty boy,
Bore it, or led, to Rylstone-hall
1810 With heart brimful of pride and joy!

But most to Bolton's sacred Pile,
On favouring nights, she loved to go;
There ranged through cloister, court, and aisle,
Attended by the soft-paced Doe;
Nor feared she in the still moonshine
To look upon Saint Mary's shrine;
Nor on the lonely turf that showed
Where Francis slept in his last abode.
For that she came; there oft she sate
1820 Forlorn, but not disconsolate:
And, when she from the abyss returned
Of thought, she neither shrunk nor mourned;
Was happy that she lived to greet
Her mute Companion as it lay
In love and pity at her feet;
How happy in its turn to meet
The recognition! the mild glance
Beamed from that gracious countenance;
Communication, like the ray
1830 Of a new morning, to the nature
And prospects of the inferior Creature!

A mortal Song we sing, by dower
Encouraged of celestial power;
Power which the viewless Spirit shed
By whom we were first visited;
Whose voice we heard, whose hand and wings
Swept like a breeze the conscious strings,
When, left in solitude, erewhile
We stood before this ruined Pile,
1840 And, quitting unsubstantial dreams,
Sang in this Presence kindred themes;
Distress and desolation spread

Through human hearts, and pleasure dead, –
Dead – but to live again on earth,
A second and yet nobler birth;
Dire overthrow, and yet how high
The re-ascent in sanctity!
From fair to fairer; day by day
A more divine and loftier way!
1850 Even such this blessèd Pilgrim trod,
By sorrow lifted towards her God;
Uplifted to the purest sky
Of undisturbed mortality.
Her own thoughts loved she; and could bend
A dear look to her lowly Friend;
There stopped; her thirst was satisfied
With what this innocent spring supplied:
Her sanction inwardly she bore,
And stood apart from human cares:
1860 But to the world returned no more,
Although with no unwilling mind
Help did she give at need, and joined
The Wharfdale peasants in their prayers.
At length, thus faintly, faintly tied
To earth, she was set free, and died.
Thy soul, exalted Emily,
Maid of the blasted family,
Rose to the God from whom it came!
– In Rylstone Church her mortal frame
1870 Was buried by her Mother's side.

Most glorious sunset! and a ray
Survives – the twilight of this day –
In that fair Creature whom the fields
Support, and whom the forest shields;
Who, having filled a holy place,
Partakes, in her degree, Heaven's grace;
And bears a memory and a mind
Raised far above the law of kind;
Haunting the spots with lonely cheer

1880 Which her dear Mistress once held dear:
    Loves most what Emily loved most –
    The enclosure of this church-yard ground;
    Here wanders like a gliding ghost,
    And every sabbath here is found;
    Comes with the people when the bells
    Are heard among the moorland dells,
    Finds entrance through yon arch, where way
    Lies open on the sabbath-day;
    Here walks amid the mournful waste
1890 Of prostrate altars, shrines defaced,
    And floors encumbered with rich show
    Of fret-work imagery laid low;
    Paces softly, or makes halt,
    By fractured cell, or tomb, or vault;
    By plate of monumental brass
    Dim-gleaming among weeds and grass,
    And sculptured Forms of Warriors brave:
    But chiefly by that single grave,
    That one sequestered hillock green,
1900 The pensive visitant is seen.
    There doth the gentle Creature lie
    With those adversities unmoved;
    Calm spectacle, by earth and sky
    In their benignity approved!
    And aye, methinks, this hoary Pile,
    Subdued by outrage and decay,
    Looks down upon her with a smile,
    A gracious smile, that seems to say –
    'Thou, thou are not a Child of Time,
1910 But Daughter of the Eternal Prime!'

Sonnet on Milton

    Amid the dark control of lawless sway
    Ambition's rivalry, fanatic hate,
    And various ills that shook the unsettled State,

The dauntless Bard pursued his studious way,
Not more his lofty genius to display
Than raise and dignify our mortal date,
And sing the blessings which the Just await
That Man might hence in humble hope obey.
Thus on a rock in Norway's bleak domain
10 Nature impels the stately Pine to grow;
Still he preserves his firm majestic [reign?]
And restless Ocean dashes all below.

[St Paul's]

Pressed with conflicting thoughts of love and fear
I parted from thee, Friend, and took my way
Through the great City, pacing with an eye
Downcast, ear sleeping, and feet masterless
That were sufficient guide unto themselves,
And step by step went pensively. Now, mark!
Not how my trouble was entirely hushed,
(That might not be) but how, by sudden gift,
Gift of Imagination's holy power,
10 My Soul in her uneasiness received
An anchor of stability. – It chanced
That while I thus was pacing, I raised up
My heavy eyes and instantly beheld,
Saw at a glance in that familiar spot
A visionary scene – a length of street
Laid open in its morning quietness,
Deep, hollow, unobstructed, vacant, smooth,
And white with winter's purest white, as fair,
As fresh and spotless as he ever sheds
20 On field or mountain. Moving Form was none
Save here and there a shadowy Passenger
Slow, shadowy, silent, dusky, and beyond
And high above this winding length of street,
This moveless and unpeopled avenue,
Pure, silent, solemn, beautiful, was seen

The huge majestic Temple of St Paul
In awful sequestration, through a veil,
Through its own sacred veil of falling snow.

The Tuft of Primroses

Once more I welcome Thee, and Thou, fair Plant,
Fair Primrose, hast put forth thy radiant Flowers
All eager to be welcomed once again.
O pity if the faithful Spring beguiled
By her accustomed hopes had come to breathe
Upon the bosom of this barren crag
And found thee not; but Thou art here, revived
And beautiful as ever like a Queen
Smiling from thy imperishable throne,
10 And so shall keep for ages yet untold
Frail as Thou art, if the prophetic Muse
Be rightly trusted, so shalt Thou maintain
Conspicuously thy solitary state
In splendour unimpaired. For Thou art safe
From most adventurous bound of mountain sheep
By keenest hunger pressed, and from approach
Of the wild Goat still bolder, nor more cause,
Though in that sunny and obtrusive crag,
Hast thou to dread the desolating grasp
20 Of Child or Schoolboy, and though hand perchance
Of taller Passenger might want not power
To win thee, yet a thought would intervene
Though Thou be tempting, and that thought of love
Would hold him back, checked in the first conceit
And impulse of such rapine. A benign,
A good and friendly Spirit Thee hath watched
Thus far, and shall continue to preserve
Less for thy beauty's sake, though that might claim
All favour, than for pleasure which Thou shed'st
30 Down-looking and far-looking all day long
From that thy sunny and obtrusive seat

Upon the Travellers that do hourly climb
This steep, new gladness yielding to the glad,
And genial promises to those who droop
Sick, poor, or weary, or disconsolate,
Brightening at once the winter of their souls.

I have a Friend, whom Seasons as they passed
All pleased: they in her bosom damped no joy
And from her light step took no liberty,
40   When suddenly as lightning from a cloud
Came danger with disease; came suddenly
And lingered long, and this commanding Hill
Which with its rocky chambers heretofore
Had been to her a range of dear resort,
The palace of her freedom, now, sad change,
Was interdicted ground, a place of fear
For her, a melancholy Hill for us
Constrained to think and ponder for her sake.

Fair primrose, lonely and distinguished Flower
50   Well worthy of that honourable place
That holds thy beauty up to public view,
For ever parted from all neighbourhood,
In a calm course of meditative years,
Oft have I hailed thee with serene delight;
This greeting is far more – it is the voice
Of a surpassing joyance. She herself
With her own eyes shall bless thee, ere Thou fade
The Prisoner shall come forth, and all the toil
And labours of this sharp ascent shall melt
60   Before thy mild assurances, and pain
And weakness shall pass from her like a sleep
Chased by a bright glimpse of the morning Sun.

Farewell, yet turning from thee, happy Flower,
With these dear thoughts, not therefore are old claims
Unrecognized, nor have I languid sense
Of what thy reappearance would have been

Without this further joy, have been to me
In its pure self. For often when I pass
This way, while thou art in thy winter sleep,
70 Or the rank Summer hides thee from my view
Even then I think of thee. Alas how much,
Since I beheld and loved thee first, how much
Is gone, though thou be left. I would not speak
Of best Friends dead, or other deep heart-loss
Bewailed with weeping, but by River sides
And in broad fields how many gentle loves,
How many mute memorials passed away.
Stately herself, though of a lowly kind
That little Flower remains and has survived
80 The lofty band of Firs that overtopped
Their ancient neighbour the old Steeple Tower,
That consecrated File which had so oft
Swung in the blast, mingling their solemn strain
Of music with the one determined voice
From the slow funeral bell, a symphony
Most awful and affecting to the ear
Of him who passed beneath: or had dealt forth
Soft murmurs like the cooing of a Dove
Ere first distinguishably heard, and cast
90 Their dancing shadows on the flowery turf
While through the Churchyard tripped the bridal train
In festive Ribbands decked, and those same trees
By moonlight in their stillness and repose
Deepened the silence of a hundred graves.
Ah what a welcome! when from absence long
Returning, on the centre of the Vale
I looked a first glad look, and saw them not.
Was it a dream? the aerial grove, no more
Right in the centre of the lovely Vale
100 Suspended like a stationary cloud,
Had vanished like a cloud – yet say not so
For here and there a straggling Tree was left
To mourn in blanc and monumental grief,
To pine and wither for its fellows gone.

– Ill word that laid them low – unfeeling Heart
Had He who could endure that they should fall,
Who spared not them, nor spared that Sycamore high,
The universal glory of the Vale,
And did not spare the little avenue
110 Of lightly stirring Ash-trees that sufficed
To dim the glare of Summer, and to blunt
The strong Wind turned into a gentle breeze
Whose freshness cheered the pavèd walk beneath,
That ancient walk, which from the Vicar's door
Led to the Church-yard gate. Then, Grasmere, then
Thy sabbath mornings had a holy grace,
That incommunicable sanctity
Which Time and nature only can bestow
When from his plain abode the rustic Priest
120 Did issue forth glistening in best attire,
And down that consecrated vista paced
Towards the Churchyard where his ready Flock
Were gathered round in sunshine or in shade;
While Trees and mountains echoed to the Voice
Of the glad bells, and all the murmuring streams
United their Soft chorus with the Song.

Now stands the Steeple naked and forlorn
And from the Haven, the 'last Central Home',
130 To which all change conducts the Thought, looks round
Upon the changes of this peaceful Vale.
What sees the old grey Tower, through high or low
Of his domain, that calls for more regret
Than yon small Cottage? there it is aloft
And nearest to the flying clouds of three
Perched each above the other on the side
Of the vale's northern outlet – from below
And from afar – yet say not from afar
For all things in this little world of ours
Are in one bosom of close neighbourhood.
140 The hoary steeple now beholds that roof
Laid open to the glare of Common day,

And marks five graves beneath his feet, in which
Divided by a breadth of smooth green space
From nearer neighbourhood they who were erewhile
The Inmates of that Cottage are at rest.
Death to the happy House in which they dwelt
Had given a long reprieve of forty years.
Suddenly then they disappeared – not twice
Had Summer scorched the fields, not twice had fallen
150   The first white snow upon Helvellyn's top
Before the greedy visiting was closed
And the long-privileged House left empty, swept
As by a plague; yet no rapacious plague
Had been among them, all was gentle death,
One after one with intervals of peace,
A consummation, and a harmony
Sweet, perfect, to be wished for, save that here
Was something sounding to our mortal sense
Like harshness, that the old grey headed sire,
160   The oldest, he was taken last, survived
When the dear Partner of his manhood's prime,
His Son, and Daughter, then a blooming Wife,
And little smiling Grandchild were no more.
(Methinks that Emma hears the murmuring song
And the pure Ether of her Maiden soul
Is overcast, and thy maternal eyes,
Mary, are wet, but not with tears of grief.)
'Twas but a little patience and his term
Of solitude was spent – the aged One
170   Our very first in Eminence of years
The Patriarch of the Vale; a busy Hand
Yea more, a burning palm, a flashing eye
A restless foot, a head that beat at nights
Upon its pillow with a thousand schemes,
A Planter, and a Rearer from the Seed,
Builder had been but scanty means forbad.
A Man of Hope, a forward-looking Mind
Even to the last, he and his cheerful throng
Of open schemes, and all his inward hoard

180 Of unsunned griefs, too many and too keen,
Fell with the body into gentle sleep
In one blest moment, and the family
By yet a higher privilege once more
Were gathered to each other.
                                        Yet I own,
Though I can look on their associate graves
With nothing but still thoughts, that I repine,
It costs me something like a pain to feel
That after them so many of their works
Which round that Dwelling covertly preserved
190 The History of their unambitious lives
Have perished, and so soon! the Cottage-Court
Spread with blue gravel from the torrent's side
And gay with shrubs, the garden, bed and walk
His own creation; that embattled Host
Of garish tulips, fruit-trees choice and rare
And roses of all colours, which he sought
Most curiously, as generously dispersed
Their kinds, to beautify his neighbours' grounds,
Trees of the forest, too, a stately fence
200 Planted for shelter in his manhood's prime,
And small Flowers watered by his wrinkled hand,
That all are ravaged – that his Daughter's bower
Is creeping into shapelessness, self lost
In the wild wood, like a neglected image
Or Fancy which hath ceased to be recalled.
The jasmine, her own charge, which she had trained
To climb the wall, and of one flowery spray
Had made an Inmate, luring it from sun
And breeze, and from its fellows, to pervade
210 The inside of her chamber with its sweet,
I grieve to see that jasmine on the ground
Stretching its desolate length, mourn that these works
Of love and diligence and innocent care
Are sullied and disgraced; or that a gulf
Hath swallowed them which renders nothing back
That they so quickly in a cave are hidden

Which cannot be unlocked; upon their bloom
That a perpetual winter should have fallen.
Meanwhile the little Primrose of the rock
220 Remains, in sacred beauty, without taint
Of injury or decay, lives to proclaim
Her charter in the blaze of noon; salutes
Not unobserved the Early Shepherd-Swain
Or Labourer plodding at the accustomed hour
Home to his distant hearth, and will be seen
Long as the fullness of her bloom endures,
Once with an instantaneous cheer of mind
By stranger in late travel; as I myself
Have often seen her, when the last lone Thrush
230 Hath ceased his Vesper hymn, piercing the gloom
Of Twilight with the vigour of a star;
Or rather say, hung from the shadowy Rock
Like the broad Moon, with lustre somewhat dimmed
Lovely and bright, and as the Moon secure.

Oh for some band of guardian spirits prompt
As were those human Ministers of old
Who daily, nightly, under various names
With various service stood or walked their rounds
Through the wide Forest, to protect from harm
240 The wild Beast with her young, and from the touch
Of waste the green-leaved thicket to defend,
Her secret couching-place, and stately tree
Her canopy, and berry-bearing shrub
And grassy lawn, their pasture's pleasant range,
Continual and firm peace from outrage safe
And all annoyance, till the Sovereign comes
Heading his train, and through that franchise high
Urges the chase with clamorous Hound and horn.
O grant some wardenship of spirits pure
250 As duteous in their office to maintain
Inviolate for nobler purposes,
These individual precincts, to protect
Here, if here only, from despoil and wrong

All growth of nature and all frame of Art
By, and in which the blissful pleasures live.
Have not the incumbent Mountains looks of awe
In which their mandate may be read, the streams
A Voice that pleads, beseeches, and implores?
In vain: the deafness of the world is here
260 Even here, and all too many of the haunts
Which Fancy most delights in, and the best
And dearest resting-places of the heart
Vanish beneath an unrelenting doom.

What impulse drove the Hermit to his Cell,
And what detained him there till life was spent
Fast anchored in the desart? Not alone
Dread of the persecuting sword, remorse,
Wrongs unredressed, and insults unavenged
And unavengeable, defeated pride,
270 Prosperity subverted, maddening want,
Love with despair or grief in agony.
Not always from intolerable pangs
He fled; but compassed round by pleasure sighed
For independent quiet, craving peace,
The central feeling of all happiness,
Not as a refuge from distress or pain
A breathing time, vacation, or a truce,
But for its absolute self, a life of peace,
Stability without regret or fear,
280 That hath been, is, and shall be evermore.
Therefore on few external things his heart
Was set, and those his own, or if not his
Subsisting under nature's steadfast law.
What other yearnings was the master tie
Of the monastic brotherhood, upon rock
Aërial or in Green secluded Vale
One after one collected from afar
An undissolving fellowship? What but this
The universal instinct of repose
290 The longing for confirmed tranquillity

In small and great, in humble and sublime,
The life where hope and memory are as one,
Earth quiet and unchanged, the human soul
Consistent in self-rule, and heaven revealed
To meditation in that quietness.

Thus tempted, thus inspired, St Basil left
(Man as he was of noble blood, high born,
High stationed, and elaborately taught)
The vain felicities of Athens, left
300 Her throng of Sophists glorying in their snares,
Her Poets, and conflicting Orators,
Abandoned Alexandria's splendid Halls,
Antioch and Cesarea, and withdrew
To his delicious Pontic solitude,
Remembering with deep thankfulness meanwhile
Those exhortations of a female voice
Pathetically urged, his Sister's voice,
Macrina, pious Maid, most beautiful
And in the gentleness of woman wise,
310 By whom admonished, He, while yet a youth
And a triumphant Scholar, had dismissed
That loftiness and to the way inclined
Of virtue, self-restraint and privacy,
Virtue severe and absolute Restraint,
Which, when he chose, erelong he found the same
Beyond the utmost of its promise, rich
In dignity, sincere content, and joy.

Mark! for the Picture to this hour remains,
With what luxuriant fondness he portrays
320 The lineaments and image of that spot
In which upon a Mount, sylvan and high,
And at the boldest jutting in its side,
His cell was fixed, a Mount with towering Hills
Girt round, and valleys intricate and deep,
Which, leaving one blind entrance to a plain
Of fertile meadow-ground that lay beneath

Fronting the cell, had from all quarters else
Forbidden all approach; by rocks abrupt,
Or rampart as effectual of huge woods
330 Neither austere nor gloomy to behold
But in gay prospect lifting to the Sun
Majestic beds of diverse foliage, fruits
And thousand laughing blossoms; and the plain
Stretched out beneath the high-perched cell was bright
With herbs and flowers and tufts of flowering plants,
The choicest which the lavish East pours forth,
And sober-headed cypress interspersed,
And graced with presence of a famous stream
The Rapid Iris, journeying from remote
340 Armenian Mountains to his Euxine bourne,
Sole Traveller by the guarded mount; and He
To enter there had leapt with thunderous voice
Down a steep rock, and through the secret place,
Not without many a lesser bound advanced
Self-cheered with song to keep his onward course
Like a belated Pilgrim.
                                    'Come, O Friend,'
Thus did St Basil fervently break forth,
Thus call upon the man he held most dear:
'Come Nazianzen to these fortunate Isles,
350 This blest Arcadia, to these purer fields
Than those which Pagan superstition feigned
For mansions of the happy dead – O come
To this Enduring Paradise, these walks
Of Contemplation, piety and love,
Coverts serene of blessed mortality.
What if the Roses and the flowers of Kings,
Princes and Emperors, and the crowns and palms
Of all the great are blasted, or decay;
What if the meanest of their subjects, each
360 Within the narrow region of his cares,
Tremble beneath a sad uncertainty?
There is a privilege to plead, there is;
Renounce, and thou shalt find that privilege here.

No loss lamenting, no privation felt,
Disturbed by no vicissitudes, unscared
By civil faction, by religious broils
Unplagued, forgetting and forgotten here
Mayst thou possess thy own invisible nest
Like one of those small birds that round us chaunt
370 In multitudes; their warbling will be thine,
And freedom to unite thy voice with theirs
When they at morn or dewy evening praise
High heaven in sweet and solemn services.
Here mayst thou dedicate thyself to God,
And acceptably fill the votive hours
Not only as these Creatures of the grove
That need no rule, and live but to enjoy;
Not only lifted often to the calm
Of that entire beatitude in which
380 The Angels serve, but when thou must descend
From the pure vision, and thy soul admit
A salutary glow of hope and fear,
Searching in patience and humility
Among the written mysteries of faith
The will divine; or when thou wouldst assume
The burden and the seasonable yoke
Befitting our frail nature, wouldst be tamed
By vigils, abstinence and prayer with tears,
What place so fit? – a deeper solitude
390 Thebais or the Syrian Wilderness
Contains not in its dry and barren round.
For not a human form is seen this way
Unless some straggling Hunter led by chance;
Him, if the graver duties be performed,
Or overwrought with study if the mind
Be haunted by a vain disquietude
And gladly would be taken from itself;
Or if it be the time when thoughts are blithe,
Him mayst thou follow to the hills, or mount
400 Alone, as fancy prompts, equipped with bow
And shafts and quiver, not for perilous aim

At the gaunt wolf, the lion or the Pard, –
These lurk not in our bounds, but Deer and Goat
And other kinds as peaceable are there
In readiness for inoffensive chase.
The River also owns his harmless tribes,
And tempts thee to like sport; labour itself
Is pastime here; for generous is the sun,
And cool airs blowing from the mountain top
410 Refresh the brow of him who in plain field
Or garden presses his industrious spade.
Or if a different exercise thou choose
And from boon nature rather wouldst receive
Food for the day, behold the fruits that hang
In the primaeval woods; the Wells and Springs
Have each a living garland of green herbs
From which they to the rifling hand will yield
Ungrudgingly supply that never fails,
Bestowed as freely as their waters pure,
To deck thy temperate board.'

420   From theme to theme
Transported in this sort by fervent zeal
That stopped not here, the venerable man
Holy and great his invitation breathed –
And Nazianzen fashioned a reply
Ingenious and rhetorical, with taunts
Of wit and gay good-humoured ridicule
Directed both against the life itself
And that strong passion for those fortunate Isles
For the Arcadia of a golden dream.

430 But in his inward council-seat, his soul
Was moved, was rapt and filled with seriousness,
Nor was it long ere broken loose from ties
Of the world's business he the call obeyed.
And Amphilochius came, and numbers more,
Men of all tempers, qualities, estates,
Came with one spirit, like a troop of fowl
That single or in clusters, at a sign
Given by their leader, settle on the breast

Of some broad pool, green field, or loftiest tree
440   In harmony and undisturbed repose;
Or as a brood of eager younglings flock
Delighted, to the mother's outspread wings
And shelter there in unity and love.

        An intellectual Champion of the faith,
Accomplished above all who then appeared
Or, haply, since victoriously have stood
In opposition to the desperate course
Of Pagan rites or impious heresies,
St Basil, after lapse of years, went forth
450   To a station of authority and power
Upon an urgent summons, and resigned,
Ah! not without regret, the heavenly Mount,
The sheltering valley, and his loved Compeers.
He parted from them, but their common life,
If neither first nor singular, at least
More beautiful than any of like frame
That hitherto had been conceived, a life
To which by written institutes and rules
He gave a solid being, did not fail
460   Nor die with him, and hung through many an age
In bright remembrance, like a shining cloud
O'er the vast regions of the western Church;
Whence those communities of holy men,
That spread so far, to shrouded quietness
Devoted, and of saintly Virgins pure.

        Fallen, in a thousand vales the stately Towers
And branching windows gorgeously arrayed
And aisles and roofs magnificent that thrilled
With hallelujahs, and the strong-ribbed vaults
470   Are crushed; and buried under weeds and earth
The cloistral avenues – they that heard the voice
Of Rhone or Loire or some sequestered brook
Soft murmuring among woods and olive bowers
And tilth and vineyard, and the Piles that rose

On British lawns by Severn, Thames, or Tweed,
And saw their pomp reflected in the stream,
As Tintern saw; and, to this day beholds
Her faded image in the depths of Wye;
Of solemn port smitten but unsubdued
480 She stands; nor less tenacious of her rights
Stands Fountains Abbey, glorious in decay,
Before the pious Traveller's lifted eye
Threatening to outlive the ravages of Time
And bear the cross till Christ shall come again.
So cleave they to the earth in monument
Of Revelation, nor in memory less
Of nature's pure religion, as in line
Uninterrupted it hath travelled down
From the first man who heard a howling storm
490 Or knew a troubled thought or vain desire,
Or in the very sunshine of his joy
Was saddened at a perishable bliss
Or languished idly under fond regrets
That would not be subdued . . . [Methinks I hear,
Not from these woods, but from some merry grove
That lies I know not where, the spritely blast
Of the clear bugle, and from thicket green
Of hollies sparkling in an April sun
Forth, in a moment, issues to the glade
500 A Troop of green-clad Foresters in arms
Blithe Outlaws with their Chieftain: Would they rouse
The Stag, dislodge the Hart; or will they keep
Their oath in presence of Maid Marian sworn
And with a cloud of shafts this day confound
The royal Officers? Let them on, and yield
Even at their pleasure to the boisterous drift
Of pastime or adventure – let them on
I love them better when at ease]
                              'And is thy doom
510 Pronounced' (I said, a stripling at that time
Who with a Fellow-pilgrim had been driven
Through madding France before a joyous gale

And to the solemn haven of Chartreuse
Repaired for timely rest) 'and are we twain
The last, perchance the very last, of men
Who shall be welcomed here, whose limbs shall find
Repose within these modest cells, whose hearts
Receive a comfort from these awful spires?
Alas! for what I see, the flash of arms,
520 O Sorrow! and yon military glare;
And hark, those Voices! let us hide in gloom
Profoundest of St Bruno's wood – these sighs
These whispers that pursue or meet me, whence
[   ] are they but a common [   ]
From the two Sister streams of Life and Death,
Or are they by the parting Genius sent
Unheard till now and to be heard no more'?

Yes, I was moved and to this hour am moved;
What Man would bring to nothing if he might
530 A natural power or element? and who,
If the ability were his, would dare
To kill a species of insensate life,
Or to the bird of meanest wing would say,
Thou and thy kind must perish? Even so
So consecrated, almost, might he deem
That power, that organ, that transcendent frame
Of social being. – 'Stay your impious hand':
Such was the vain injunction of that hour
By Nature uttered from her Alpine throne:
540 'O leave in quiet this embodied dream
This substance by which mortal men have clothed,
Humanly clothed, the ghostliness of things
In silence visible and perpetual calm,
Let this one Temple last – be this one spot
Of Earth devoted to Eternity.' –
I heard or seemed to hear, and thus the Voice
Proceeded: 'Honour to the Patriot's zeal
Glory and life to new-born liberty –
All hail ye mighty Passions of the Time,

550 The vengeance and the transport and the hope,
But spare, if past and future be the wings
On whose support harmoniously conjoined
Moves the great Spirit of human knowledge, spare
This House, these courts of mystery, where a step
Between the Portals of the shadowy rocks
Leaves far behind the vanities of life;
Where, if a peasant enter or a king,
One holy thought, a single holy thought
Has power to initiate. Let it be redeemed
560 With all its blameless priesthood for the sake
Of Heaven-descended truth; and humbler claim
Of these majestic floods, my noblest boast,
These shining cliffs, pure as their home, the sky,
These forests unapproachable by death
That shall endure as long as Man endures
To think, to hope, to worship and to feel;
To struggle, – to be lost within himself
In trepidation, – from the dim abyss
To look with bodily eyes, and be consoled.'
570 Such repetition of that [   ]
My thoughts demanded; now an humbler task
Awaits us for the unwearied Song will lead
Into a lonely Vale the mild abode
Of female Votaries – No.[   ] plain
Blank as the Arabian wilderness defends
This chosen spot nor is it [   ]
By rocks like those of Caucasus or Alps
Shapes untransmuted of successive worlds,
Nor can it boast a massy structure huge
580 Founded and built by hands with arch and towers,
Pillar and pinnacle and glittering spire
Sublime as if in Emulation reared
Of the eternal Architect – these signs
These tokens, admonitions to recall,
Curbs to restrain, or stays to lean upon,
Such food to nourish or appease the Soul
The gentle Beings who found harbour here

Required not – Them a lowly Edifice
Embraced by [?] grounds that did not aim
590 To overshadow but to screen and hide,
Contented; and an unassuming brook
Working between these hills its careless way
Through meadow, chestnut woods and olive-bowers
And tilth and vineyard.
cetera desunt

To the Clouds

Army of Clouds! ye wingèd Host in troops
Ascending from behind the motionless brow
Of that tall rock, as from a hidden world,
Oh whither with such eagerness of speed?
What seek ye, or what shun ye? of the gale
Companions, fear ye to be left behind,
Or racing o'er your blue ethereal field
Contend ye with each other? of the sea
Children, thus post ye over vale and height
10 To sink upon your mother's lap – and rest?
Or were ye rightlier hailed, when first mine eyes
Beheld in your impetuous march the likeness
Of a wide army pressing on to meet
Or overtake some unknown enemy? –
But your smooth motions suit a peaceful aim;
And Fancy, not less aptly pleased, compares
Your squadrons to an endless flight of birds
Aërial, upon due migration bound
To milder climes; or rather do ye urge
20 In caravan your hasty pilgrimage
To pause at last on more aspiring heights
Than these, and utter your devotion there
With thunderous voice? Or are ye jubilant,
And would ye, tracking your proud lord the Sun,
Be present at his setting; or the pomp
Of Persian mornings would ye fill, and stand
Poising your splendours high above the heads

Of worshippers kneeling to their up-risen God?
Whence, whence, ye Clouds! this eagerness of speed?
30   Speak, silent creatures. – They are gone, are fled,
Buried together in yon gloomy mass
That loads the middle heaven; and clear and bright
And vacant doth the region which they thronged
Appear; a calm descent of sky conducting
Down to the unapproachable abyss,
Down to that hidden gulf from which they rose
To vanish – fleet as days and months and years,
Fleet as the generations of mankind,
Power, glory, empire, as the world itself,
40   The lingering world, when time hath ceased to be.
But the winds roar, shaking the rooted trees,
And see! a bright precursor to a train
Perchance as numerous, overpeers the rock
That sullenly refuses to partake
Of the wild impulse. From a fount of life
Invisible, the long procession moves
Luminous or gloomy, welcome to the vale
Which they are entering, welcome to mine eye
That sees them, to my soul that owns in them,
50   And in the bosom of the firmament
O'er which they move, wherein they are contained,
A type of her capacious self and all
Her restless progeny.
              A humble walk
Here is my body doomed to tread, this path,
A little hoary line and faintly traced,
Work, shall we call it, of the shepherd's foot
Or of his flock? – joint vestige of them both.
I pace it unrepining, for my thoughts
Admit no bondage and my words have wings.
60   Where is the Orphean lyre, or Druid harp,
To accompany the verse? The mountain blast
Shall be our *hand* of music; he shall sweep
The rocks, and quivering trees, and billowy lake,
And search the fibres of the caves, and they

Shall answer, for our song is of the Clouds,
And the wind loves them; and the gentle gales –
Which by their aid re-clothe the naked lawn
With annual verdure, and revive the woods,
And moisten the parched lips of thirsty flowers –
70 Love them; and every idle breeze of air
Bends to the favourite burden. Moon and stars
Keep their most solemn vigils when the Clouds
Watch also, shifting peaceably their place
Like bands of ministering Spirits, or when they lie,
As if some Protean art the change had wrought,
In listless quiet o'er the ethereal deep
Scattered, a Cyclades of various shapes
And all degrees of beauty. O ye Lightnings!
Ye are their perilous offspring; and the Sun –
80 Source inexhaustible of life and joy,
And type of man's far-darting reason, therefore
In old time worshipped as the god of verse,
A blazing intellectual deity –
Loves his own glory in their looks, and showers
Upon that unsubstantial brotherhood
Visions with all but beatific light
Enriched – too transient were they not renewed
From age to age, and did not, while we gaze
In silent rapture, credulous desire
90 Nourish the hope that memory lacks not power
To keep the treasure unimpaired. Vain thought!
Yet why repine, created as we are
For joy and rest, albeit to find them only
Lodged in the bosom of eternal things?

Elegiac Stanzas Composed in the Churchyard of Grasmere

Who weeps for strangers? Many wept
    For George and Sarah Green;
Wept for that pair's unhappy fate,
    Whose graves may here be seen.

By night, upon these stormy fells,
   Did wife and husband roam;
Six little ones at home had left,
   And could not find that home.

For *any* dwelling-place of man
10   As vainly did they seek.
He perished; and a voice was heard –
   The widow's lonely shriek.

Not many steps, and she was left
   A body without life –
A few short steps were the chain that bound
   The husband to the wife.

Now do those sternly-featured hills
   Look gently on this grave;
And quiet *now* are the depths of air,
20   As a sea without a wave.

But deeper lies the heart of peace
   In quiet more profound;
The heart of quietness is here
   Within this churchyard bound.

And from all agony of mind
   It keeps them safe, and far
From fear and grief, and from all need
   Of sun or guiding star.

O darkness of the grave! how deep,
30   After that living night –
That last and dreary living one
   Of sorrow and affright!

O sacred marriage-bed of death,
   That keeps them side by side
In bond of peace, in bond of love,
   That may not be untied!

[*Pelayo*]

A few bold Patriots, Reliques of the Fight
That crushed the Gothic sovereignty of Spain,
Beneath Pelayo's guidance urged their flight.
And when their steps had measured [   ] Plain,
Crossed Deva's [   ] flood and [   ] snow-clad height,
And wound through depth of many a sunless Vale
On which the noontide dew lay wet and pale,
And now had reached Auseva's rugged breast,
The Leader turned, and from a jutting rock
10   Calm as a Shepherd beckoning to his flock
            The little band addrest –
'Stop, Christian Warriors, faithful and undaunted,
Here, if the Saints and pitying Angels bless
The efforts of the brave in their distress,
Not vainly shall your Standard here be planted!
With swords to guard our Virtue are we come
To these Asturian wilds, a proud retreat!
Where Friends surround us in their ancient seat,
An inextinguishable people's home.
20   Aloft while here we haven, night and day
Shall multiply our host and strengthen our array.
Till we, like bursting clouds, descend and quell
            The astounded Infidel.
Meanwhile till Heaven, O patient Warriors, call
On Valour to the onset, yon wide Cave,
Whose dark throat opens like a ready grave
For desperate Fugitives, to us shall be
      A Legislative Hall
Cheered by the gladsome voice of Liberty;
30   And to that Sanctuary dark
         Will we entrust the holy Ark,
         The Covenant of the faith
         That saves the soul from death
And shall uphold our frail and mortal hands
Till we, or men as brave, the favoured bands

Of our exalted countrymen, regain
For lordship without end, the fields of universal Spain.'

    Thus spake Pelayo on his chosen hill.
And shall at this late [?hour] the Heavens belie
40   The heroic prophecy
And put to shame the great Diviner's skill?
The Power which issuing like a slender rill
From those high places waxed by slow degrees
Swoln with access of many Sovereignties
And gained a River's strength and rolled a mighty wave.
    The stream which in Pelayo's cave
Upon the illustrious Mountain took its birth
    Hath disappeared from earth;
A foreign Tyrant speaks his impious will,
50   And Spain hath owned the monarch which he gave.
Most horrible attempt, unthought of hour
Of human shame and black indignity.
Alas, not unprovoked these Tempests lower,
Not uninvited this malignity.
Full long relinquishing a precious dower
By Gothic virtue won, secured by oath
Of King and people pledged in mutual troth,
The Spaniard hath approached on servile knee
The native Ruler all too willingly.
60   Full many an age in that degenerate Land
The rightful Master hath betrayed his trust;
Earthward the imperial flower was bent
    In mortal languishment.
This knew the Spoiler whose victorious hand
Hath snapped the enfeebled stalk and laid its head in
    dust.

Composed While the Author Was Engaged in Writing a Tract, Occasioned by the Convention of Cintra

Not 'mid the World's vain objects that enslave
The free-born Soul – that World whose vaunted skill
In selfish interest perverts the will,
Whose factions lead astray the wise and brave –
Not there; but in dark wood and rocky cave,
And hollow vale which foaming torrents fill
With omnipresent murmur as they rave
Down their steep beds, that never shall be still:
Here, mighty Nature! in this school sublime
10 I weigh the hopes and fears of suffering Spain;
For her consult the auguries of time,
And through the human heart explore my way;
And look and listen – gathering, whence I may,
Triumph, and thoughts no bondage can restrain.

Composed at the Same Time and on the Same Occasion

I dropped my pen; and listened to the Wind
That sang of trees up-torn and vessels tost –
A midnight harmony; and wholly lost
To the general sense of men by chains confined
Of business, care, or pleasure; or resigned
To timely sleep. Thought I, the impassioned strain,
Which, without aid of numbers, I sustain,
Like acceptation from the World will find.
Yet some with apprehensive ear shall drink
10 A dirge devoutly breathed o'er sorrows past;
And to the attendant promise will give heed –
The prophecy, – like that of this wild blast,
Which, while it makes the heart with sadness shrink,
Tells also of bright calms that shall succeed.

1810

Ah! where is Palafox? Nor tongue nor pen
Reports of him, his dwelling or his grave!
Does yet the unheard-of vessel ride the wave?
Or is she swallowed up, remote from ken
Of pitying human-nature? Once again
Methinks that we shall hail thee, Champion brave,
Redeemed to baffle that imperial Slave,
And through all Europe cheer desponding men
With new-born hope. Unbounded is the might
10 Of martyrdom, and fortitude, and right.
Hark, how thy Country triumphs! – Smilingly
The Eternal looks upon her sword that gleams,
Like his own lightning, over mountains high,
On rampart, and the banks of all her streams.

'Hail, Zaragoza! If with unwet eye'

Hail, Zaragoza! If with unwet eye
We can approach, thy sorrow to behold,
Yet is the heart not pitiless nor cold;
Such spectacle demands not tear or sigh.
These desolate remains are trophies high
Of more than martial courage in the breast
Of peaceful civic virtue: they attest
Thy matchless worth to all posterity.
Blood flowed before thy sight without remorse;
10 Disease consumed thy vitals; War upheaved
The ground beneath thee with volcanic force:
Dread trials! yet encountered and sustained
Till not a wreck of help or hope remained,
And law was from necessity received.

'*Is there a power that can sustain and cheer*'

Is there a power that can sustain and cheer
The captive chieftain, by a tyrant's doom
Forced to descend into his destined tomb –
A dungeon dark! where he must waste the year,
And lie cut off from all his heart holds dear;
What time his injured country is a stage
Whereon deliberate Valour and the rage
Of righteous Vengeance side by side appear,
Filling from morn to night the heroic scene
10 With deeds of hope and everlasting praise: –
Say can he think of this with mind serene
And silent fetters? Yes, if visions bright
Shine on his soul, reflected from the days
When he himself was tried in open light.

'*Avaunt all specious pliancy of mind*'

Avaunt all specious pliancy of mind
In men of low degree, all smooth pretence!
I better like a blunt indifference,
And self-respecting slowness, disinclined
To win me at first sight: and be there joined
Patience and temperance with this high reserve,
Honour that knows the path and will not swerve;
Affections which, if put to proof, are kind;
And piety towards God. Such men of old
10 Were England's native growth; and, throughout Spain,
(Thanks to high God) forests of such remain:
Then for that Country let our hopes be bold;
For matched with these shall policy prove vain,
Her arts, her strength, her iron, and her gold.

The French and the Spanish Guerillas

Hunger, and sultry heat, and nipping blast
From bleak hill-top, and length of march by night
Through heavy swamp, or over snow-clad height –
These hardships ill-sustained, these dangers past,
The roving Spanish Bands are reached at last,
Charged, and dispersed like foam: but as a flight
Of scattered quails by signs do reunite,
So these, – and, heard of once again, are chased
With combinations of long-practised art
10   And newly-kindled hope; but they are fled –
Gone are they, viewless as the buried dead:
Where now? – Their sword is at the Foeman's heart!
And thus from year to year his walk they thwart,
And hang like dreams around his guilty bed.

'*Say, what is Honour? – 'Tis the finest sense*'

Say, what is Honour? – 'Tis the finest sense
Of *justice* which the human mind can frame,
Intent each lurking frailty to disclaim,
And guard the way of life from all offence
Suffered or done. When lawless violence
Invades a Realm, so pressed that in the scale
Of perilous war her weightiest armies fail,
Honour is hopeful elevation, – whence
Glory, and triumph. Yet with politic skill
10   Endangered States may yield to terms unjust;
Stoop their proud heads, but not unto the dust –
A Foe's most favourite purpose to fulfil:
Happy occasions oft by self-mistrust
Are forfeited; but infamy doth kill.

'Call not the royal Swede unfortunate'

Call not the royal Swede unfortunate,
Who never did to Fortune bend the knee;
Who slighted fear; rejected stedfastly
Temptation; and whose kingly name and state
Have 'perished by his choice, and not his fate!'
Hence lives He, to his inner self endeared;
And hence, wherever virtue is revered,
He sits a more exalted Potentate,
Throned in the hearts of men. Should Heaven ordain
10 That this great Servant of a righteous cause
Must still have sad or vexing thoughts to endure,
Yet may a sympathizing spirit pause,
Admonished by these truths, and quench all pain
In thankful joy and gratulation pure.

'Look now on that Adventurer who hath paid'

Look now on that Adventurer who hath paid
His vows to Fortune; who, in cruel slight
Of virtuous hope, of liberty, and right,
Hath followed wheresoe'er a way was made
By the blind Goddess, – ruthless, undismayed;
And so hath gained at length a prosperous height,
Round which the elements of worldly might
Beneath his haughty feet, like clouds, are laid.
O joyless power that stands by lawless force!
10 Curses are *his* dire portion, scorn, and hate,
Internal darkness and unquiet breath;
And, if old judgements keep their sacred course,
Him from that height shall Heaven precipitate
By violent and ignominious death.

'Brave Schill! by death delivered, take thy flight'

Brave Schill! by death delivered, take thy flight
From Prussia's timid region. Go, and rest
With heroes, 'mid the islands of the Blest,
Or in the fields of empyrean light.
A meteor wert thou crossing a dark night:
Yet shall thy name, conspicuous and sublime,
Stand in the spacious firmament of time,
Fixed as a star: such glory is thy right.
Alas! it may not be: for earthly fame
10 Is Fortune's frail dependant; yet there lives
A Judge, who, as man claims by merit, gives;
To whose all-pondering mind a noble aim,
Faithfully kept, is as a noble deed;
In whose pure sight all virtue doth succeed.

'Alas! what boots the long laborious quest'

Alas! what boots the long laborious quest
Of moral prudence, sought through good and ill;
Or pains abstruse – to elevate the will,
And lead us on to that transcendent rest
Where every passion shall the sway attest
Of Reason, seated on her sovereign hill;
What is it but a vain and curious skill,
If sapient Germany must lie deprest,
Beneath the brutal sword? – Her haughty Schools
10 Shall blush; and may not we with sorrow say,
A few strong instincts and a few plain rules,
Among the herdsmen of the Alps, have wrought
More for mankind at this unhappy day
Than all the pride of intellect and thought?

'*And is it among rude untutored Dales*'

And is it among rude untutored Dales,
There, and there only, that the heart is true?
And, rising to repel or to subdue,
Is it by rocks and woods that man prevails?
Ah no! though Nature's dread protection fails,
There is a bulwark in the soul. This knew
Iberian Burghers when the sword they drew
In Zaragoza, naked to the gales
Of fiercely-breathing war. The truth was felt
10 By Palafox, and many a brave compeer,
Like him of noble birth and noble mind;
By ladies, meek-eyed women without fear;
And wanderers of the street, to whom is dealt
The bread which without industry they find.

Feelings of the Tyrolese

The Land we from our fathers had in trust,
And to our children will transmit, or die:
This is our maxim, this our piety;
And God and Nature say that it is just.
That which we *would* perform in arms – we must!
We read the dictate in the infant's eye;
In the wife's smile; and in the placid sky;
And, at our feet, amid the silent dust
Of them that were before us. – Sing aloud
10 Old songs, the precious music of the heart!
Give, herds and flocks, your voices to the wind!
While we go forth, a self-devoted crowd,
With weapons grasped in fearless hands, to assert
Our virtue, and to vindicate mankind.

'*O'er the wide earth, on mountain and on plain*'

O'er the wide earth, on mountain and on plain,
Dwells in the affections and the soul of man
A Godhead, like the universal PAN;
But more exalted, with a brighter train:
And shall his bounty be dispensed in vain,
Showered equally on city and on field,
And neither hope nor stedfast promise yield
In these usurping times of fear and pain?
Such doom awaits us. Nay, forbid it Heaven!
10 We know the arduous strife, the eternal laws
To which the triumph of all good is given,
High sacrifice, and labour without pause,
Even to the death: – else wherefore should the eye
Of man converse with immortality?

[*Passage from John Wilson's* The Angler's Tent]

The placid lake that rested far below
Softly embosoming another sky,
Still as we gazed assumed a lovelier glow,
And seemed to send us looks of amity.

'*Advance – come forth from thy Tyrolean ground*'

Advance – come forth from thy Tyrolean ground,
Dear Liberty! stern Nymph of soul untamed;
Sweet Nymph, O rightly of the mountains named!
Through the long chain of Alps from mound to mound
And o'er the eternal snows, like Echo, bound;
Like Echo, when the hunter train at dawn

Have roused her from her sleep: and forest-lawn,
Cliffs, woods and caves, her viewless steps resound
And babble of her pastime! – On, dread Power!
10   With such invisible motion speed thy flight,
Through hanging clouds, from craggy height to height,
Through the green vales and through the herdsman's
     bower –
That all the Alps may gladden in thy might,
Here, there, and in all places at one hour.

Hofer

Of mortal parents is the Hero born
By whom the undaunted Tyrolese are led?
Or is it Tell's great Spirit, from the dead
Returned to animate an age forlorn?
He comes like Phoebus through the gates of morn
When dreary darkness is discomfited,
Yet mark his modest state! upon his head,
That simple crest, a heron's plume, is worn.
O Liberty! they stagger at the shock
10   From van to rear – and with one mind would flee,
But half their host is buried: – rock on rock
Descends: – beneath this godlike Warrior, see!
Hills, torrents, woods, embodied to bemock
The Tyrant, and confound his cruelty.

On the Final Submission of the Tyrolese

It was a *moral* end for which they fought;
Else how, when mighty Thrones were put to shame,
Could they, poor Shepherds, have preserved an aim,
A resolution, or enlivening thought?
Nor hath that moral good been *vainly* sought;
For in their magnanimity and fame
Powers have they left, an impulse, and a claim

Which neither can be overturned nor bought.
Sleep, Warriors, sleep! among your hills repose!
10 We know that ye, beneath the stern control
Of awful prudence, keep the unvanquished soul:
And when, impatient of her guilt and woes,
Europe breaks forth; then, Shepherds! shall ye rise
For perfect triumph o'er your Enemies.

Epitaph Translated from Chiabrera

Not without heavy grief of heart did He
On whom the duty fell (for at that time
The father sojourned in a distant land)
Deposit in the hollow of this tomb
A brother's Child, most tenderly beloved!
FRANCESCO was the name the Youth had borne,
POZZOBONNELLI his illustrious house;
And, when beneath this stone the Corse was laid,
The eyes of all Savona streamed with tears.
10 Alas! the twentieth April of his life
Had scarcely flowered: and at this early time,
By genuine virtue he inspired a hope
That greatly cheered his country: to his kin
He promised comfort; and the flattering thoughts
His friends had in their fondness entertained,
He suffered not to languish or decay.
Now is there not good reason to break forth
Into a passionate lament? – O Soul!
Short while a Pilgrim in our nether world,
20 Do thou enjoy the calm empyreal air;
And round this earthly tomb let roses rise,
An everlasting spring! in memory
Of that delightful fragrance which was once
From thy mild manners quietly exhaled.

Epitaph Translated from Chiabrera

Destined to war from very infancy
Was I, Roberto Dati, and I took
In Malta the white symbol of the Cross:
Nor in life's vigorous season did I shun
Hazard or toil; among the sands was seen
Of Lybia; and not seldom, on the banks
Of wide Hungarian Danube, 'twas my lot
To hear the sanguinary trumpet sounded.
So lived I, and repined not at such fate:
10 This only grieves me, for it seems a wrong,
That stripped of arms I to my end am brought
On the soft down of my paternal home.
Yet haply Arno shall be spared all cause
To blush for me. Thou, loiter not nor halt
In thy appointed way, and bear in mind
How fleeting and how frail is human life!

Epitaph Translated from Chiabrera

Pause, courteous Spirit! – Baldi supplicates
That Thou, with no reluctant voice, for him
Here laid in mortal darkness, wouldst prefer
A prayer to the Redeemer of the world.
This to the dead by sacred right belongs;
All else is nothing. – Did occasion suit
To tell his worth, the marble of this tomb
Would ill suffice: for Plato's lore sublime,
And all the wisdom of the Stagyrite,
10 Enriched and beautified his studious mind:
With Archimedes also he conversed
As with a chosen friend; nor did he leave
Those laureat wreaths ungathered which the Nymphs
Twine near their loved Permessus. – Finally,
Himself above each lower thought uplifting,

His ears he closed to listen to the songs
Which Sion's Kings did consecrate of old;
And his Permessus found on Lebanon.
A blessèd Man! who of protracted days
20 Made not, as thousands do, a vulgar sleep;
But truly did *He* live his life. Urbino,
Take pride in him! – O Passenger, farewell!

Epitaph Translated from Chiabrera

There never breathed a man who, when his life
Was closing, might not of that life relate
Toils long and hard. – The warrior will report
Of wounds, and bright swords flashing in the field,
And blast of trumpets. He who hath been doomed
To bow his forehead in the courts of kings,
Will tell of fraud and never-ceasing hate,
Envy and heart-inquietude, derived
From intricate cabals of treacherous friends.
10 I, who on shipboard lived from earliest youth,
Could represent the countenance horrible
Of the vexed waters, and the indignant rage
Of Auster and Boötes.. Fifty years
Over the well-steered galleys did I rule: –
From huge Pelorus to the Atlantic pillars,
Rises no mountain to mine eyes unknown;
And the broad gulfs I traversed oft and oft.
Of every cloud which in the heavens might stir
I knew the force; and hence the rough sea's pride
20 Availed not to my Vessel's overthrow.
What noble pomp and frequent have not I
On regal decks beheld! yet in the end
I learned that one poor moment can suffice
To equalize the lofty and the low.
We sail the sea of life – a *Calm* One finds,
And One a *Tempest* – and, the voyage o'er,
Death is the quiet haven of us all.

If more of my condition ye would know,
Savona was my birthplace, and I sprang
30 Of noble parents: seventy years and three
Lived I – then yielded to a slow disease.

Epitaph Translated from Chiabrera

O Thou who movest onward with a mind
Intent upon thy way, pause, though in haste!
'Twill be no fruitless moment. I was born
Within Savona's walls, of gentle blood.
On Tiber's banks my youth was dedicate
To sacred studies; and the Roman Shepherd
Gave to my charge Urbino's numerous flock.
Well did I watch, much laboured, nor had power
To escape from many and strange indignities;
10 Was smitten by the great ones of the world,
But did not fall; for Virtue braves all shocks,
Upon herself resting immoveably.
Me did a kindlier fortune then invite
To serve the glorious Henry, King of France,
And in his hands I saw a high reward
Stretched out for my acceptance, – but Death came.
Now, Reader, learn from this my fate, how false,
How treacherous to her promise, is the world;
And trust in God – to whose eternal doom
20 Must bend the sceptred Potentates of earth.

Epitaph Translated from Chiabrera

Perhaps some needful service of the State
Drew TITUS from the depth of studious bowers,
And doomed him to contend in faithless courts,
Where gold determines between right and wrong.
Yet did at length his loyalty of heart,
And his pure native genius, lead him back

To wait upon the bright and gracious Muses,
Whom he had early loved. And not in vain
Such course he held! Bologna's learned schools
10 Were gladdened by the Sage's voice, and hung
With fondness on those sweet Nestorian strains.
There pleasure crowned his days; and all his thoughts
A roseate fragrance breathed. – O human life,
That never art secure from dolorous change!
Behold a high injunction suddenly
To Arno's side hath brought him, and he charmed
A Tuscan audience: but full soon was called
To the perpetual silence of the grave.
Mourn, Italy, the loss of him who stood
20 A Champion stedfast and invincible,
To quell the rage of literary War!

[*Epitaph on Tasso Translated from Chiabrera*]

Torquato Tasso rests within this tomb;
This figure weeping from her inmost heart
Is Poesy; from such impassioned grief
Let everyone conclude what this Man was.

Epitaph Translated from Chiabrera

Weep not, belovèd Friends! nor let the air
For me with sighs be troubled. Not from life
Have I been taken; this is genuine life
And this alone – the life which now I live
In peace eternal; where desire and joy
Together move in fellowship without end. –
Francesco Ceni willed that, after death,
His tombstone thus should speak for him. And surely
Small cause there is for that fond wish of ours
10 Long to continue in this world; a world
That keeps not faith, nor yet can point a hope
To good, whereof itself is destitute.

Epitaph Translated from Chiabrera

True is it that Ambrosio Salinero
With an untoward fate was long involved
In odious litigation; and full long,
Fate harder still! had he to endure assaults
Of racking malady. And true it is
That not the less a frank courageous heart
And buoyant spirit triumphed over pain;
And he was strong to follow in the steps
Of the fair Muses. Not a covert path
10 Leads to the dear Parnassian forest's shade,
That might from him be hidden; not a track
Mounts to pellucid Hippocrene, but he
Had traced its windings. – This Savona knows,
Yet no sepulchral honors to her Son
She paid, for in our age the heart is ruled
Only by gold. And now a simple stone
Inscribed with this memorial here is raised
By his bereft, his lonely, Chiabrera.
Think not, O Passenger! who read'st the lines
20 That an exceeding love hath dazzled me;
No – he was One whose memory ought to spread
Where'er Permessus bears an honoured name,
And live as long as its pure stream shall flow.

Epitaph Translated from Chiabrera

O flower of all that springs from gentle blood,
And all that generous nurture breeds to make
Youth amiable; O friend so true of soul
To fair Aglaia; by what envy moved,
Lelius! has death cut short thy brilliant day
In its sweet opening? and what dire mishap
Has from Savona torn her best delight?
For thee she mourns, nor e'er will cease to mourn;

And, should the out-pourings of her eyes suffice not
10　For her heart's grief, she will entreat Sebeto
Not to withhold his bounteous aid, Sebeto
Who saw thee, on his margin, yield to death,
In the chaste arms of thy belovèd Love!
What profit riches? what does youth avail?
Dust are our hopes; – I, weeping bitterly,
Penned these sad lines, nor can forbear to pray
That every gentle Spirit hither led
May read them not without some bitter tears.

[*Epitaph Translated from Chiabrera*]

O Lelius, beauteous flower of gentleness,
The fair Aglaia's friend above all friends;
O darling of the fascinating Loves,
By what dire envy moved did Death uproot
Thy days ere yet full blown and what ill chance
Hath robbed Savona of her noblest grace?
She weeps for thee and shall for ever weep,
And if the fountain of her tears should fail
She would implore Sebeto to supply
10　Her need: Sebeto, sympathizing stream,
Who on his margin saw thee close thine eyes
On the chaste bosom of thy Lady dear.
Ah, what do riches, what does youth avail?
Dust are our hopes, I weeping did inscribe
In bitterness thy monument and pray
Of every gentle spirit bitterly
To read the record with as copious tears.

'*The martial courage of a day is vain*'

The martial courage of a day is vain,
An empty noise of death the battle's roar,
If vital hope be wanting to restore,

Or fortitude be wanting to sustain,
Armies or kingdoms. We have heard a strain
Of triumph, how the labouring Danube bore
A weight of hostile corses: drenched with gore
Were the wide fields, the hamlets heaped with slain.
Yet see (the mighty tumult overpast)
10   Austria a Daughter of her Throne hath sold!
And her Tyrolean Champion we behold
Murdered, like one ashore by shipwreck cast,
Murdered without relief. Oh! blind as bold,
To think that such assurance can stand fast!

Indignation of a High-Minded Spaniard 1810

We can endure that He should waste our lands,
Despoil our temples, and by sword and flame
Return us to the dust from which we came;
Such food a Tyrant's appetite demands:
And we can brook the thought that by his hands
Spain may be overpowered, and he possess,
For his delight, a solemn wilderness
Where all the brave lie dead. But, when of bands
Which he will break for us he dares to speak,
10   Of benefits, and of a future day
When our enlightened minds shall bless his sway;
Then, the strained heart of fortitude proves weak;
Our groans, our blushes, our pale cheeks declare
That he has power to inflict what we lack strength to
      bear.

'In due observance of an ancient rite'

In due observance of an ancient rite,
The rude Biscayans, when their children lie
Dead in the sinless time of infancy,
Attire the peaceful corse in vestments white;
And, in like sign of cloudless triumph bright,

They bind the unoffending creature's brows
With happy garlands of the pure white rose:
Then do a festal company unite
In choral song; and, while the uplifted cross
10 Of Jesus goes before, the child is borne
Uncovered to his grave: 'tis closed, – her loss
The Mother *then* mourns, as she needs must mourn;
But soon, through Christian faith, is grief subdued:
And joy returns, to brighten fortitude.

Feelings of a Noble Biscayan at One of Those Funerals 1810

Yet, yet, Biscayans! we must meet our Foes
With firmer soul, yet labour to regain
Our ancient freedom; else 'twere worse than vain
To gather round the bier these festal shows.
A garland fashioned of the pure white rose
Becomes not one whose father is a slave:
Oh, bear the infant covered to his grave!
These venerable mountains now enclose
A people sunk in apathy and fear.
10 If this endure, farewell, for us, all good!
The awful light of heavenly innocence
Will fail to illuminate the infant's bier;
And guilt and shame, from which is no defence,
Descend on all that issues from our blood.

The Oak of Guernica

The ancient oak of Guernica, says Laborde in his account of
Biscay, is a most venerable natural monument. Ferdinand and
Isabella, in the year 1476, after hearing Mass in the church of
Santa Maria de la Antigua, repaired to this tree, under which
they swore to the Biscayans to maintain their *fueros* (privileges).
What other interest belongs to it in the minds of this people
will appear from the following

SUPPOSED ADDRESS TO THE SAME. 1810

Oak of Guernica! Tree of holier power
Than that which in Dodona did enshrine
(So faith too fondly deemed) a voice divine
Heard from the depths of its aërial bower –
How canst thou flourish at this blighting hour?
What hope, what joy can sunshine bring to thee,
Or the soft breezes from the Atlantic sea,
The dews of morn, or April's tender shower?
Stroke merciful and welcome would that be
10 Which should extend thy branches on the ground,
If never more within their shady round
Those lofty-minded Lawgivers shall meet,
Peasant and lord, in their appointed seat,
Guardians of Biscay's ancient liberty.

1810

O'erweening Statesmen have full long relied
On fleets and armies, and external wealth:
But from *within* proceeds a Nation's health;
Which shall not fail, though poor men cleave with pride
To the paternal floor; or turn aside,
In the thronged city, from the walks of gain,
As being all unworthy to detain
A Soul by contemplation sanctified.
There are who cannot languish in this strife,
10 Spaniards of every rank, by whom the good
Of such high course was felt and understood;
Who to their Country's cause have bound a life
Erewhile, by solemn consecration, given
To labour, and to prayer, to nature, and to heaven.

On a Celebrated Event in Ancient History

A Roman Master stands on Grecian ground,
And to the people at the Isthmian Games
Assembled, He, by a herald's voice, proclaims
THE LIBERTY OF GREECE: – the words rebound
Until all voices in one voice are drowned;
Glad acclamation by which air was rent!
And birds, high flying in the element,
Dropped to the earth, astonished at the sound!
Yet were the thoughtful grieved; and still that voice
10   Haunts, with sad echoes, musing Fancy's ear:
Ah! that a *Conqueror's* words should be so dear:
Ah! that a *boon* could shed such rapturous joys!
A gift of that which is not to be given
By all the blended powers of Earth and Heaven.

Upon the Same Event

When, far and wide, swift as the beams of morn
The tidings passed of servitude repealed,
And of that joy which shook the Isthmian Field,
The rough Aetolians smiled with bitter scorn.
''Tis known,' cried they, 'that he, who would adorn
His envied temples with the Isthmian crown,
Must either win, through effort of his own,
The prize, or be content to see it worn
By more deserving brows. – Yet so ye prop,
10   Sons of the brave who fought at Marathon,
Your feeble spirits! Greece her head hath bowed,
As if the wreath of liberty thereon
Would fix itself as smoothly as a cloud,
Which, at Jove's will, descends on Pelion's top.'

Upon the Sight of a Beautiful Picture,

Painted by Sir G. H. Beaumont, Bart.

Praised by the Art whose subtle power could stay
Yon cloud, and fix it in that glorious shape;
Nor would permit the thin smoke to escape,
Nor those bright sunbeams to forsake the day;
Which stopped that band of travellers on their way,
Ere they were lost within the shady wood;
And showed the Bark upon the glassy flood
For ever anchored in her sheltering bay.
Soul-soothing Art! whom Morning, Noontide, Even,
10 Do serve with all their changeful pageantry;
Thou, with ambition modest yet sublime,
Here, for the sight of mortal man, hast given
To one brief moment caught from fleeting time
The appropriate calm of blest eternity.

Epistle to Sir George Howland Beaumont, BART.

From the South-west Coast of Cumberland. – 1811.

Far from our home by Grasmere's quiet Lake,
From the Vale's peace which all her fields partake,
Here on the bleakest point of Cumbria's shore
We sojourn stunned by Ocean's ceaseless roar;
While, day by day, grim neighbour! huge Black Comb
Frowns deepening visibly his native gloom,
Unless, perchance rejecting in despite
What on the Plain *we* have of warmth and light,
In his own storms he hides himself from sight.
10 Rough is the time; and thoughts, that would be free
From heaviness, oft fly, dear Friend, to thee;
Turn from a spot where neither sheltered road
Nor hedge-row screen invites my steps abroad;
Where one poor Plane-tree, having as it might
Attained a stature twice a tall man's height,

Hopeless of further growth, and brown and sere
Through half the summer, stands with top cut sheer,
Like an unshifting weathercock which proves
How cold the quarter that the wind best loves,
20 Or like a Sentinel that, evermore
Darkening the window, ill defends the door
Of this unfinished house – a Fortress bare,
Where strength has been the Builder's only care;
Whose rugged walls may still for years demand
The final polish of the Plasterer's hand.
– This Dwelling's Inmate more than three weeks' space
And oft a Prisoner in the cheerless place,
I – of whose touch the fiddle would complain,
Whose breath would labour at the flute in vain,
30 In music all unversed, nor blessed with skill
A bridge to copy, or to paint a mill,
Tired of my books, a scanty company!
And tired of listening to the boisterous sea –
Pace between door and window muttering rhyme,
An old resource to cheat a froward time!
Though these dull hours (mine is it, or their shame?)
Would tempt me to renounce that humble aim.
– But if there be a Muse who, free to take
Her seat upon Olympus, doth forsake
40 Those heights (like Phoebus when his golden locks
He veiled, attendant on Thessalian flocks)
And, in disguise, a Milkmaid with her pail
Trips down the pathways of some winding dale;
Or, like a Mermaid, warbles on the shores
To fishers mending nets beside their doors;
Or, Pilgrim-like, on forest moss reclined,
Gives plaintive ditties to the heedless wind,
Or listens to its play among the boughs
Above her head and so forgets her vows –
50 If such a Visitant of Earth there be
And she would deign this day to smile on me
And aid my verse, content with local bounds
Of natural beauty and life's daily rounds,

Thoughts, chances, sights, or doings, which we tell
Without reserve to those whom we love well –
Then haply, Beaumont! words in current clear
Will flow, and on a welcome page appear
Duly before thy sight, unless they perish here.

What shall I treat of? News from Mona's Isle?
60   Such have we, but unvaried in its style;
No tales of Runagates fresh landed, whence
And wherefore fugitive or on what pretence;
Of feasts, or scandal, eddying like the wind
Most restlessly alive when most confined.
Ask not of me, whose tongue can best appease
The mighty tumults of the HOUSE OF KEYS;
The last year's cup whose Ram or Heifer gained,
What slopes are planted, or what mosses drained:
An eye of fancy only can I cast
70   On that proud pageant now at hand or past,
When full five hundred boats in trim array,
With nets and sails outspread and streamers gay,
And chanted hymns and stiller voice of prayer,
For the old Manx-harvest to the Deep repair,
Soon as the herring-shoals at distance shine
Like beds of moonlight shifting on the brine.

Mona from our Abode is daily seen,
But with a wilderness of waves between;
And by conjecture only can we speak
80   Of aught transacted there in bay or creek;
No tidings reach us thence from town or field,
Only faint news her mountain sunbeams yield,
And some we gather from the misty air,
And some the hovering clouds, our telegraph, declare.
But these poetic mysteries I withhold;
For Fancy hath her fits both hot and cold,
And should the colder fit with You be on
When You might read, my credit would be gone.

    Let more substantial themes the pen engage,
90 And nearer interests culled from the opening stage
Of our migration. – Ere the welcome dawn
Had from the east her silver star withdrawn,
The Wain stood ready, at our Cottage-door,
Thoughtfully freighted with a various store;
And long or ere the uprising of the Sun
O'er dew-damped dust our journey was begun,
A needful journey, under favouring skies,
Through peopled Vales; yet something in the guise
Of those old Patriarchs when from well to well
100 They roamed through Wastes where now the tented
      Arabs dwell.

    Say first, to whom did we the charge confide,
Who promptly undertook the Wain to guide
Up many a sharply-twining road and down,
And over many a wide hill's craggy crown,
Through the quick turns of many a hollow nook,
And the rough bed of many an unbridged brook?
A blooming Lass – who in her better hand
Bore a light switch, her sceptre of command
When, yet a slender Girl, she often led,
110 Skilful and bold, the horse and burdened *sled*
From the peat-yielding Moss on Gowdar's head.
What could go wrong with such a Charioteer
For goods and chattels, or those Infants dear,
A Pair who smilingly sat side by side,
Our hope confirming that the salt-sea tide,
Whose free embraces we were bound to seek,
Would their lost strength restore and freshen the pale
      cheek?
Such hope did either Parent entertain
Pacing behind along the silent lane.

120   Blithe hopes and happy musings soon took flight,
For lo! an uncouth melancholy sight –
On a green bank a creature stood forlorn

Just half protruded to the light of morn,
Its hinder part concealed by hedge-row thorn.
The Figure called to mind a beast of prey
Stript of its frightful powers by slow decay,
And, though no longer upon rapine bent,
Dim memory keeping of its old intent.
We started, looked again with anxious eyes,
130 And in that griesly object recognize
The Curate's Dog – his long-tried friend, for they,
As well we knew, together had grown grey.
The Master died, his drooping servant's grief
Found at the Widow's feet some sad relief;
Yet still he lived in pining discontent,
Sadness which no indulgence could prevent;
Hence whole day wanderings, broken nightly sleeps
And lonesome watch that out of doors he keeps;
Not oftentimes, I trust, as we, poor brute!
140 Espied him on his legs sustained, blank, mute,
And of all visible motion destitute,
So that the very heaving of his breath
Seemed stopt, though by some other power than death.
Long as we gazed upon the form and face,
A mild domestic pity kept its place,
Unscared by thronging fancies of strange hue
That haunted us in spite of what we knew.
Even now I sometimes think of him as lost
In second-sight appearances, or crost
150 By spectral shapes of guilt, or to the ground,
On which he stood, by spells unnatural bound,
Like a gaunt shaggy Porter forced to wait
In days of old romance at Archimago's gate.

Advancing Summer, Nature's law fulfilled,
The choristers in every grove had stilled;
But we, we lacked not music of our own,
For lightsome Fanny had thus early thrown,
'Mid the gay prattle of those infant tongues,
Some notes prelusive, from the round of songs

160   With which, more zealous than the liveliest bird
       That in wild Arden's brakes was ever heard,
       Her work and her work's partners she can cheer,
       The whole day long, and all days of the year.

       Thus gladdened from our own dear Vale we pass
       And soon approach Diana's Looking-glass!
       To Loughrigg-tarn, round, clear and bright as heaven,
       Such name Italian fancy would have given,
       Ere on its banks the few grey cabins rose
       That yet disturb not its concealed repose
170   More than the feeblest wind that idly blows.

       Ah, Beaumont! when an opening in the road
       Stopped me at once by charm of what it showed,
       The encircling region vividly exprest
       Within the mirror's depth, a world at rest –
       Sky streaked with purple, grove and craggy *bield*,
       And the smooth green of many a pendent field,
       And, quieted and soothed, a torrent small,
       A little daring would-be waterfall,
       One chimney smoking and its azure wreath,
180   Associate all in the calm Pool beneath,
       With here and there a faint imperfect gleam
       Of water-lilies veiled in misty steam –
       What wonder at this hour of stillness deep,
       A shadowy link 'tween wakefulness and sleep,
       When Nature's self, amid such blending, seems
       To render visible her own soft dreams,
       If, mixed with what appeared of rock, lawn, wood,
       Fondly embosomed in the tranquil flood,
       A glimpse I caught of that Abode, by Thee
190   Designed to rise in humble privacy,
       A lowly Dwelling, here to be outspread,
       Like a small Hamlet, with its bashful head
       Half hid in native trees. Alas 'tis not,
       Nor ever was; I sighed, and left the spot
       Unconscious of its own untoward lot,

And thought in silence, with regret too keen,
Of unexperienced joys that might have been;
Of neighbourhood and intermingling arts,
And golden summer days uniting cheerful hearts.
200 But time, irrevocable time, is flown,
And let us utter thanks for blessings sown
And reaped – what hath been, and what is, our own.

   Not far we travelled ere a shout of glee,
Startling us all, dispersed my reverie;
Such shout as many a sportive echo meeting
Oft-times from Alpine *chalets* sends a greeting.
Whence the blithe hail? behold a Peasant stand
On high, a kerchief waving in her hand!
Not unexpectant that by early day
210 Our little Band would thrid this mountain way,
Before her cottage on the bright hill side
She hath advanced with hope to be descried.
Right gladly answering signals we displayed,
Moving along a tract of morning shade,
And vocal wishes sent of like good will
To our kind Friend high on the sunny hill –
Luminous region, fair as if the prime
Were tempting all astir to look aloft or climb;
Only the centre of the shining cot
220 With door left open makes a gloomy spot,
Emblem of those dark corners sometimes found
Within the happiest breast on earthly ground.

   Rich prospect left behind of stream and vale,
And mountain-tops, a barren ridge we scale;
Descend and reach, in Yewdale's depths, a plain
With haycocks studded, striped with yellowing grain –
An area level as a Lake and spread
Under a rock too steep for man to tread,
Where sheltered from the north and bleak north-west
230 Aloft the Raven hangs a visible nest,
Fearless of all assaults that would her brood molest.

Hot sunbeams fill the steaming vale; but hark,
At our approach, a jealous watch-dog's bark,
Noise that brings forth no liveried Page of state,
But the whole household, that our coming wait.
With Young and Old warm greetings we exchange,
And jocund smiles, and toward the lowly Grange
Press forward by the teasing dogs unscared.
Entering, we find the morning meal prepared:
240   So down we sit, though not till each had cast
Pleased looks around the delicate repast –
Rich cream, and snow-white eggs fresh from the nest,
With amber honey from the mountain's breast;
Strawberries from lane or woodland, offering wild
Of children's industry, in hillocks piled;
Cakes for the nonce, and butter fit to lie
Upon a lordly dish; frank hospitality
Where simple art with bounteous nature vied,
And cottage comfort shunned not seemly pride.

250   Kind Hostess! Handmaid also of the feast,
If thou be lovelier than the kindling East,
Words by thy presence unrestrained may speak
Of a perpetual dawn from brow and cheek
Instinct with light whose sweetest promise lies,
Never retiring, in thy large dark eyes,
Dark but to every gentle feeling true,
As if their lustre flowed from ether's purest blue.

Let me not ask what tears may have been wept
By those bright eyes, what weary vigils kept,
260   Beside that hearth what sighs may have been heaved
For wounds inflicted, nor what toil relieved
By fortitude and patience, and the grace
Of heaven in pity visiting the place.
Not unadvisedly those secret springs
I leave unsearched: enough that memory clings,
Here as elsewhere, to notices that make
Their own significance for hearts awake,

To rural incidents, whose genial powers
Filled with delight three summer morning hours.

270   More could my pen report of grave or gay
That through our gypsy travel cheered the way;
But, bursting forth above the waves, the Sun
Laughs at my pains, and seems to say, 'Be done.'
Yet, Beaumont, thou wilt not, I trust, reprove
This humble offering made by Truth to Love,
Nor chide the Muse that stooped to break a spell
Which might have else been on me yet: —

FAREWELL.

Departure from the Vale of Grasmere. August, 1803

The gentlest Shade that walked Elysian plains
Might sometimes covet dissoluble chains;
Even for the tenants of the zone that lies
Beyond the stars, celestial Paradise,
Methinks 'twould heighten joy, to overleap
At will the crystal battlements, and peep
Into some other region, though less fair,
To see how things are made and managed there.
Change for the worse might please, incursion bold
10   Into the tracts of darkness and of cold;
O'er Limbo lake with aëry flight to steer,
And on the verge of Chaos hang in fear.
Such animation often do I find,
Power in my breast, wings growing in my mind,
Then, when some rock or hill is overpast,
Perchance without one look behind me cast,
Some barrier with which Nature, from the birth
Of things, has fenced this fairest spot on earth.
O pleasant transit, Grasmere! to resign
20   Such happy fields, abodes so calm as thine;
Not like an outcast with himself at strife;

The slave of business, time, or care for life,
But moved by choice; or, if constrained in part,
Yet still with Nature's freedom at the heart; –
To cull contentment upon wildest shores,
And luxuries extract from bleakest moors;
With prompt embrace all beauty to enfold,
And having rights in all that we behold.
– Then why these lingering steps? – A bright adieu,
30 For a brief absence, proves that love is true;
Ne'er can the way be irksome or forlorn
That winds into itself for sweet return.

View from the Top of Black Comb

This Height a ministering Angel might select:
For from the summit of BLACK COMB (dread name
Derived from clouds and storms!) the amplest range
Of unobstructed prospect may be seen
That British ground commands: – low dusky tracts,
Where Trent is nursed, far southward! Cambrian hills
To the south-west, a multitudinous show;
And, in a line of eye-sight linked with these,
The hoary peaks of Scotland that give birth
10 To Tiviot's stream, to Annan, Tweed, and Clyde: –
Crowding the quarter whence the sun comes forth
Gigantic mountains rough with crags; beneath,
Right at the imperial station's western base,
Main ocean, breaking audibly, and stretched
Far into silent regions blue and pale; –
And visibly engirding Mona's Isle
That, as we left the plain, before our sight
Stood like a lofty mount, uplifting slowly
(Above the convex of the watery globe)
20 Into clear view the cultured fields that streak
Her habitable shores, but now appears
A dwindled object, and submits to lie
At the spectator's feet. – Yon azure ridge,

Is it a perishable cloud? Or there
Do we behold the line of Erin's coast?
Land sometimes by the roving shepherd-swain
(Like the bright confines of another world)
Not doubtfully perceived. – Look homeward now!
In depth, in height, in circuit, how serene
30 The spectacle, how pure! – Of Nature's works,
In earth, and air, and earth-embracing sea,
A revelation infinite it seems;
Display august of man's inheritance,
Of Britain's calm felicity and power!

Written with a Slate Pencil on a Stone, on the Side of the Mountain of Black Comb

Stay, bold Adventurer; rest awhile thy limbs
On this commodious Seat! for much remains
Of hard ascent before thou reach the top
Of this huge Eminence, – from blackness named,
And, to far-travelled storms of sea and land,
A favourite spot of tournament and war!
But thee may no such boisterous visitants
Molest; may gentle breezes fan thy brow;
And neither cloud conceal, nor misty air
10 Bedim, the grand terraqueous spectacle,
From centre to circumference, unveiled!
Know, if thou grudge not to prolong thy rest,
That on the summit whither thou art bound,
A geographic Labourer pitched his tent,
With books supplied and instruments of art,
To measure height and distance; lonely task,
Week after week pursued! – To him was given
Full many a glimpse (but sparingly bestowed
On timid man) of Nature's processes
20 Upon the exalted hills. He made report
That once, while there he plied his studious work
Within that canvas Dwelling, colours, lines,

And the whole surface of the out-spread map,
Became invisible: for all around
Had darkness fallen – unthreatened, unproclaimed –
As if the golden day itself had been
Extinguished in a moment; total gloom,
In which he sate alone, with unclosed eyes,
Upon the blinded mountain's silent top!

Inscription in the Grounds of Coleorton, the Seat of Sir George Beaumont, BART., Leicestershire

The embowering rose, the acacia, and the pine,
Will not unwillingly their place resign;
If but the Cedar thrive that near them stands,
Planted by Beaumont's and by Wordsworth's hands.
One wooed the silent Art with studious pains:
These groves have heard the Other's pensive strains;
Devoted thus, their spirits did unite
By interchange of knowledge and delight.
May Nature's kindliest powers sustain the Tree,
10 And Love protect it from all injury!
And when its potent branches, wide out-thrown,
Darken the brow of this memorial Stone,
Here may some Painter sit in future days,
Some future Poet meditate his lays;
Not mindless of that distant age renowned
When Inspiration hovered o'er this ground,
The haunt of him who sang how spear and shield
In civil conflict met on Bosworth-field;
And of that famous Youth, full soon removed
20 From earth, perhaps by Shakespeare's self approved,
Fletcher's Associate, Jonson's Friend beloved.

Written at the Request of Sir George Beaumont, BART., and in His Name, for an Urn, Placed by Him at the Termination of a Newly-Planted Avenue, in the Same Grounds

Ye Lime-trees, ranged before this hallowed Urn,
Shoot forth with lively power at Spring's return;
And be not slow a stately growth to rear
Of pillars, branching off from year to year,
Till they have learned to frame a darksome aisle; –
That may recall to mind that awful Pile
Where Reynolds, 'mid our country's noblest dead,
In the last sanctity of fame is laid.
– There, though by right the excelling Painter sleep
10 Where Death and Glory a joint sabbath keep,
Yet not the less his Spirit would hold dear
Self-hidden praise, and Friendship's private tear:
Hence, on my patrimonial grounds, have I
Raised this frail tribute to his memory;
From youth a zealous follower of the Art
That he professed; attached to him in heart;
Admiring, loving, and with grief and pride
Feeling what England lost when Reynolds died.

Inscription in a Garden of the Same [Coleorton]

Oft is the medal faithful to its trust
When temples, columns, towers, are laid in dust;
And 'tis a common ordinance of fate
That things obscure and small outlive the great:
Hence, when yon mansion and the flowery trim
Of this fair garden, and its alleys dim,
And all its stately trees, are passed away,
This little Niche, unconscious of decay,

Perchance may still survive. And be it known
10 That it was scooped within the living stone, –
Not by the sluggish and ungrateful pains
Of labourer plodding for his daily gains,
But by an industry that wrought in love;
With help from female hands, that proudly strove
To aid the work, what time these walks and bowers
Were shaped to cheer dark winter's lonely hours.

For a Seat in the Groves of Coleorton

Beneath yon eastern ridge, the craggy bound,
Rugged and high, of Charnwood's forest ground,
Stand yet, but, Stranger! hidden from thy view,
The ivied Ruins of forlorn GRACE DIEU;
Erst a religious House, which day and night
With hymns resounded, and the chanted rite:
And when those rites had ceased, the Spot gave birth
To honourable Men of various worth:
There, on the margin of a streamlet wild,
10 Did Francis Beaumont sport, an eager child;
There, under shadow of the neighbouring rocks,
Sang youthful tales of shepherds and their flocks;
Unconscious prelude to heroic themes,
Heart-breaking tears, and melancholy dreams
Of slighted love, and scorn, and jealous rage,
With which his genius shook the buskined stage.
Communities are lost, and Empires die,
And things of holy use unhallowed lie;
They perish; – but the Intellect can raise,
20 From airy words alone, a Pile that ne'er decays.

1811

Here pause: the poet claims at least this praise,
That virtuous Liberty hath been the scope
Of his pure song, which did not shrink from hope

In the worst moment of these evil days;
From hope, the paramount *duty* that Heaven lays,
For its own honour, on man's suffering heart.
Never may from our souls one truth depart –
That an accursed thing it is to gaze
On prosperous tyrants with a dazzled eye;
10   Nor – touched with due abhorrence of *their* guilt
For whose dire ends tears flow, and blood is spilt,
And justice labours in extremity –
Forget thy weakness, upon which is built,
O wretched man, the throne of tyranny!

1811

The power of Armies is a visible thing,
Formal, and circumscribed in time and space;
But who the limits of that power shall trace
Which a brave People into light can bring
Or hide, at will, – for freedom combating
By just revenge inflamed? No foot may chase,
No eye can follow, to a fatal place
That power, that spirit, whether on the wing
Like the strong wind, or sleeping like the wind
10   Within its awful caves. – From year to year
Springs this indigenous produce far and near;
No craft this subtle element can bind,
Rising like water from the soil, to find
In every nook a lip that it may cheer.

Spanish Guerillas 1811

They seek, are sought; to daily battle led,
Shrink not, though far outnumbered by their Foes,
For they have learnt to open and to close
The ridges of grim war; and at their head
Are captains such as erst their country bred

Or fostered, self-supported chiefs, – like those
Whom hardy Rome was fearful to oppose;
Whose desperate shock the Carthaginian fled.
In One who lived unknown a shepherd's life
10 Redoubted Viriathus breathes again;
And Mina, nourished in the studious shade,
With that great Leader vies, who, sick of strife
And bloodshed, longed in quiet to be laid
In some green island of the western main.

'*The fairest, brightest, hues of ether fade*'

The fairest, brightest, hues of ether fade;
The sweetest notes must terminate and die;
O Friend! thy flute has breathed a harmony
Softly resounded through this rocky glade;
Such strains of rapture as the Genius played
In his still haunt on Bagdad's summit high;
He who stood visible to Mirza's eye,
Never before to human sight betrayed.
Lo, in the vale, the mists of evening spread!
10 The visionary Arches are not there,
Nor the green Islands, nor the shining Seas;
Yet sacred is to me this Mountain's head,
Whence I have risen, uplifted on the breeze
Of harmony, above all earthly care.

'*Even as a dragon's eye that feels the stress*'

Even as a dragon's eye that feels the stress
Of a bedimming sleep, or as a lamp
Sullenly glaring through sepulchral damp,
So burns yon Taper 'mid a black recess
Of mountains, silent, dreary, motionless:
The lake below reflects it not; the sky
Muffled in clouds, affords no company

To mitigate and cheer its loneliness.
Yet, round the body of that joyless Thing
10 Which sends so far its melancholy light,
Perhaps are seated in domestic ring
A gay society with faces bright,
Conversing, reading, laughing; – or they sing,
While hearts and voices in the song unite.

'*Hail, Twilight, sovereign of one peaceful hour!*'

Hail, Twilight, sovereign of one peaceful hour!
Not dull art Thou as undiscerning Night;
But studious only to remove from sight
Day's mutable distinctions. – Ancient Power!
Thus did the waters gleam, the mountains lower,
To the rude Briton, when, in wolf-skin vest
Here roving wild, he laid him down to rest
On the bare rock, or through a leafy bower
Looked ere his eyes were closed. By him was seen
10 The self-same Vision which we now behold,
At thy meek bidding, shadowy Power! brought forth;
These mighty barriers, and the gulf between;
The flood, the stars, – a spectacle as old
As the beginning of the heavens and earth!

Composed on the Eve of the Marriage of a Friend in the Vale of Grasmere, 1812

What need of clamorous bells, or ribands gay,
These humble nuptials to proclaim or grace?
Angels of love, look down upon the place;
Shed on the chosen vale a sun-bright day!
Yet no proud gladness would the Bride display
Even for such promise: – serious is her face,
Modest her mien; and she, whose thoughts keep pace
With gentleness, in that becoming way

Will thank you. Faultless does the Maid appear;
10 No disproportion in her soul, no strife:
But, when the closer view of wedded life
Hath shown that nothing human can be clear
From frailty, for that insight may the Wife
To her indulgent Lord become more dear.

Epitaph

Six months to six years added he remained
Upon this sinful earth, by sin unstained:
O blessèd Lord! whose mercy then removed
A Child whom every eye that looked on loved;
Support us, teach us calmly to resign
What we possessed, and now is wholly thine!

Characteristics of a Child Three Years Old

Loving she is, and tractable, though wild;
And Innocence hath privilege in her
To dignify arch looks and laughing eyes;
And feats of cunning; and the pretty round
Of trespasses, affected to provoke
Mock-chastisement and partnership in play.
And, as a faggot sparkles on the hearth,
Not less if unattended and alone
Than when both young and old sit gathered round
10 And take delight in its activity;
Even so this happy Creature of herself
Is all-sufficient; solitude to her
Is blithe society, who fills the air
With gladness and involuntary songs.
Light are her sallies as the tripping fawn's
Forth-startled from the fern where she lay couched;
Unthought-of, unexpected, as the stir
Of the soft breeze ruffling the meadow-flowers,

Or from before it chasing wantonly
20 The many-coloured images imprest
Upon the bosom of a placid lake.

[*Fragment from Dove Cottage Manuscript 69*]

As when, upon the smooth pacific deep
Dense fogs, to sight impervious, have withheld
A gallant vessel from some bold Emprize
Day after day deferred, till anxious hope
Yields to despair, if chance a sudden breeze
Spring up and dissipate the veil, all hearts
Throb at the change, and every sail is spread
To speed her course along the dazzling waves
For recompense of glorious conquest soon
10 To be achieved upon the astonished foe.

'*Come ye that are disturbed, this steady voice*'

Come ye that are disturbed, this steady voice
Of streams, the stillness and the stiller sound
Shall awe you into peace, this gleaming lake
These glistening Cottages and hoary fields
And in the midst above and underneath
Shadowy recesses, bosoms, gloomy Holds
Viewless, impenetrable, infinite
And tranquil as the abyss of deepest sleep
Or that dark world the untroubled home of death.
10 Lo in the west a solemn sight, behold
Upon yon craggy barrier's lofty ridge
A Pageantry of darksome trees that stand
Single in their aërial solitude,
Stand motionless in solitary calm
Yet greeted gently by the moving clouds
That pass and pass, and ever are to come
Varying their colours slowly in the light

Of an invisible moon. Cloud follows cloud
As thought [succeeds?] to thought, but now ensues
20 A pause – the long procession seems to end,
No straggler left behind – not one appears,
The breeze that was in heaven hath died away
And all things are immoveably composed
Save here and there an uncomplying Star
That twinkles in its station self-disturbed.

Maternal Grief

Departed Child! I could forget thee once
Though at my bosom nursed; this woeful gain
Thy dissolution brings, that in my soul
Is present and perpetually abides
A shadow, never, never to be displaced
By the returning substance, seen or touched,
Seen by mine eyes, or clasped in my embrace.
Absence and death how differ they! and how
Shall I admit that nothing can restore
10 What one short sigh so easily removed? –
Death, life, and sleep, reality and thought,
Assist me, God, their boundaries to know,
O teach me calm submission to thy Will!

The Child she mourned had overstepped the pale
Of Infancy, but still did breathe the air
That sanctifies its confines, and partook
Reflected beams of that celestial light
To all the Little-ones on sinful earth
Not unvouchsafed – a light that warmed and cheered
20 Those several qualities of heart and mind
Which, in her own blest nature, rooted deep,
Daily before the Mother's watchful eye,
And not hers only, their peculiar charms
Unfolded, – beauty, for its present self,
And for its promises to future years,
With not unfrequent rapture fondly hailed.

Have you espied upon a dewy lawn
A pair of Leverets each provoking each
To a continuance of their fearless sport,
30 Two separate Creatures in their several gifts
Abounding, but so fashioned that, in all
That Nature prompts them to display, their looks,
Their starts of motion and their fits of rest,
An undistinguishable style appears
And character of gladness, as if Spring
Lodged in their innocent bosoms, and the spirit
Of the rejoicing morning were their own?

Such union, in the lovely Girl maintained
And her twin Brother, had the parent seen,
40 Ere, pouncing like a ravenous bird of prey,
Death in a moment parted them, and left
The Mother, in her turns of anguish, worse
Than desolate; for oft-times from the sound
Of the survivor's sweetest voice (dear child,
He knew it not) and from his happiest looks,
Did she extract the food of self-reproach,
As one that lived ungrateful for the stay
By heaven afforded to uphold her maimed
And tottering spirit. And full oft the Boy,
50 Now first acquainted with distress and grief,
Shrunk from his Mother's presence, shunned with fear
Her sad approach, and stole away to find,
In his known haunts of joy where'er he might,
A more congenial object. But, as time
Softened her pangs and reconciled the child
To what he saw, he gradually returned,
Like a scared Bird encouraged to renew
A broken intercourse; and, while his eyes
Were yet with pensive fear and gentle awe
60 Turned upon her who bore him, she would stoop
To imprint a kiss that lacked not power to spread
Faint colour over both their pallid cheeks,
And stilled his tremulous lip. Thus they were calmed

And cheered; and now together breathe fresh air
In open fields; and when the glare of day
Is gone, and twilight to the Mother's wish
Befriends the observance, readily they join
In walks whose boundary is the lost One's grave,
Which he with flowers hath planted, finding there
70 Amusement, where the Mother does not miss
Dear consolation, kneeling on the turf
In prayer, yet blending with that solemn rite
Of pious faith the vanities of grief;
For such, by pitying Angels and by Spirits
Transferred to regions upon which the clouds
Of our weak nature rest not, must be deemed
Those willing tears, and unforbidden sighs,
And all those tokens of a cherished sorrow,
Which, soothed and sweetened by the grace of Heaven
80 As now it is, seems to her own fond heart
Immortal as the love that gave it being.

November, 1813

Now that all hearts are glad, all faces bright,
Our aged Sovereign sits, to the ebb and flow
Of states and kingdoms, to their joy or woe,
Insensible. He sits deprived of sight,
And lamentably wrapped in twofold night,
Whom no weak hopes deceived; whose mind ensued,
Through perilous war, with regal fortitude,
Peace that should claim respect from lawless Might.
Dread King of Kings, vouchsafe a ray divine
10 To his forlorn condition! let thy grace
Upon his inner soul in mercy shine;
Permit his heart to kindle, and to embrace
(Though it were only for a moment's space)
The triumphs of this hour; for they are THINE!

'*If thou indeed derive thy light from Heaven*'

If thou indeed derive thy light from Heaven,
Then, to the measure of that heaven-born light,
Shine, Poet! in thy place, and be content: –
The stars pre-eminent in magnitude,
And they that from the zenith dart their beams,
(Visible though they be to half the earth,
Though half a sphere be conscious of their brightness)
Are yet of no diviner origin,
No purer essence, than the one that burns,
10 Like an untended watch-fire, on the ridge
Of some dark mountain; or than those which seem
Humbly to hang, like twinkling winter lamps,
Among the branches of the leafless trees;
All are the undying offspring of one Sire:
Then, to the measure of the light vouchsafed,
Shine, Poet! in thy place, and be content.

'*Surprised by joy – impatient as the Wind*'

Surprised by joy – impatient as the Wind
I turned to share the transport – Oh! with whom
But Thee, deep buried in the silent tomb,
That spot which no vicissitude can find?
Love, faithful love, recalled thee to my mind –
But how could I forget thee? Through what power,
Even for the least division of an hour,
Have I been so beguiled as to be blind
To my most grievous loss! – That thought's return
10 Was the worst pang that sorrow ever bore,
Save one, one only, when I stood forlorn,
Knowing my heart's best treasure was no more;
That neither present time, nor years unborn
Could to my sight that heavenly face restore.

Appendices

Preface to Lyrical Ballads, with Pastoral and Other Poems (*1802*)

The first Volume of these Poems has already been submitted to general perusal. It was published, as an experiment, which, I hoped, might be of some use to ascertain, how far, by fitting to metrical arrangement a selection of the real language of men in a state of vivid sensation, that sort of pleasure and that quantity of pleasure may be imparted, which a Poet may rationally endeavour to impart.

I had formed no very inaccurate estimate of the probable effect of those Poems: I flattered myself that they who should be pleased with them would read them with more than common pleasure: and, on the other hand, I was well aware, that by those who should dislike them they would be read with more than common dislike. The result has differed from my expectation in this only, that I have pleased a greater number, than I ventured to hope I should please.

For the sake of variety, and from a consciousness of my own weakness, I was induced to request the assistance of a Friend, who furnished me with the Poems of the ANCIENT MARINER, the FOSTER-MOTHER'S TALE, the NIGHTINGALE, and the Poem entitled LOVE. I should not, however, have requested this assistance, had I not believed that the Poems of my Friend would in a great measure have the same tendency as my own, and that, though there would be found a difference, there would be found no discordance in the colours of our style; as our opinions on the subject of poetry do almost entirely coincide.

Several of my Friends are anxious for the success of these Poems from a belief, that, if the views with which they were composed were indeed realized, a class of Poetry would be produced, well adapted to interest mankind permanently, and not unimportant in the multiplicity, and in the quality of its moral relations: and on this account they have advised me to prefix a systematic defence of the theory upon which the poems were written. But I was unwilling to undertake the task, because I knew that on this occasion the Reader would look coldly upon my arguments, since I might be suspected of having been principally influenced by the selfish and foolish hope of *reasoning* him into an approbation of these particular Poems: and I was still more unwilling to undertake the task, because, adequately to display my opinions, and fully to enforce my arguments, would require a space wholly disproportionate to the nature of a preface. For to treat the subject with the clearness and coherence, of which I believe it susceptible, it would be necessary to give a full account of the present state of the public taste in this country, and to determine how far this taste is healthy or depraved; which, again, could not be determined, without pointing out, in what manner language and the human mind act and re-act on each other, and without retracing the revolutions, not of literature alone, but likewise of society itself. I have therefore altogether declined to enter regularly upon this defence; yet I am sensible, that there would be some impropriety in abruptly obtruding upon the Public, without a few words of introduction, Poems so materially different from those upon which general approbation is at present bestowed.

It is supposed, that by the act of writing in verse an Author makes a formal engagement that he will gratify certain known habits of association; that he not only thus apprises the Reader that certain classes of ideas and expressions will be found in his book, but that others will be carefully excluded. This exponent or symbol held forth by metrical language must in different eras of literature have excited very different expectations: for example, in the age of Catullus, Terence, and Lucretius, and that of Statius or Claudian; and in our own country, in the age of Shakespeare and Beaumont and Fletcher, and that of Donne and Cowley, or Dryden, or Pope. I will not take upon me to determine the exact import of the promise which by the act of writing in verse an Author, in the present day, makes to his

Reader; but I am certain, it will appear to many persons that I have not fulfilled the terms of an engagement thus voluntarily contracted. They who have been accustomed to the gaudiness and inane phraseology of many modern writers, if they persist in reading this book to its conclusion, will, no doubt, frequently have to struggle with feelings of strangeness and awkwardness: they will look round for poetry, and will be induced to inquire by what species of courtesy these attempts can be permitted to assume that title. I hope therefore the Reader will not censure me, if I attempt to state what I have proposed to myself to perform; and also (as far as the limits of a preface will permit) to explain some of the chief reasons which have determined me in the choice of my purpose: that at least he may be spared any unpleasant feeling of disappointment, and that I myself may be protected from the most dishonourable accusation which can be brought against an Author, namely, that of an indolence which prevents him from endeavouring to ascertain what is his duty, or, when his duty is ascertained, prevents him from performing it.

The principal object, then, which I proposed to myself in these Poems was to choose incidents and situations from common life, and to relate or describe them, throughout, as far as was possible, in a selection of language really used by men; and, at the same time, to throw over them a certain colouring of imagination, whereby ordinary things should be presented to the mind in an unusual way; and, further, and above all, to make these incidents and situations interesting by tracing in them, truly though not ostentatiously, the primary laws of our nature: chiefly, as far as regards the manner in which we associate ideas in a state of excitement. Low and rustic life was generally chosen, because in that condition, the essential passions of the heart find a better soil in which they can attain their maturity, are less under restraint, and speak a plainer and more emphatic language; because in that condition of life our elementary feelings co-exist in a state of greater simplicity, and, consequently, may be more accurately contemplated, and more forcibly communicated; because the manners of rural life germinate from those elementary feelings; and, from the necessary character of rural occupations, are more easily comprehended; and are more durable; and lastly, because in that condition the passions of men are incorporated with the beautiful and permanent forms of nature. The language, too, of these men is adopted (purified indeed from what appear to be its real defects, from all lasting and rational causes of dislike or disgust) because such men hourly communicate with the best objects from which the best part of language is originally derived; and because, from their rank in society and the sameness and narrow circle of their intercourse, being less under the influence of social vanity, they convey their feelings and notions in simple and unelaborated expressions. Accordingly, such a language, arising out of repeated experience and regular feelings, is a more permanent, and a far more philosophical language, than that which is frequently substituted for it by Poets, who think that they are conferring honour upon themselves and their art, in proportion as they separate themselves from the sympathies of men, and indulge in arbitrary and capricious habits of expression, in order to furnish food for fickle tastes, and fickle appetites, of their own creation. [It is worthwhile here to observe that the affecting parts of Chaucer are almost always expressed in language pure and universally intelligible even to this day. – W.]

I cannot, however, be insensible of the present outcry against the triviality and meanness both of thought and language, which some of my contemporaries have occasionally introduced into their metrical compositions; and I acknowledge that this defect, where it exists, is more dishonourable to the Writer's own character than false refinement or arbitrary innovation, though I should contend at the same time that it is far less pernicious in the sum of its consequences. From such verses the Poems in these volumes will be found distinguished at least by one mark of difference, that each of them has a worthy *purpose*. Not that I mean to say, that I always began to write with a distinct purpose formally conceived; but I believe that my habits of meditation have so formed my feelings, as that my descriptions of such objects as strongly excite those feelings, will be found to carry along with them a *purpose*. If in this opinion I am mistaken, I can have little right to the name of a Poet. For all good poetry is the spontaneous overflow of powerful feelings: but though this be true, Poems to which any value can be attached, were never produced on any variety of subjects but by a man, who being possessed of more than usual organic sensibility, had also thought long and deeply. For our continued influxes of feeling are modified and directed by our thoughts, which are indeed the representatives of all our past feelings; and, as by contemplating the relation of these general representatives to each other we discover what is really important to men, so, by the repetition and continuance of this act, our feelings will be connected with important subjects, till at length, if we be originally possessed of much sensibility, such habits of mind will be produced, that, by obeying blindly and mechanically the impulses of those habits, we shall describe objects, and utter sentiments, of such a nature and in such connexion with each other, that the understanding of the being to whom we address ourselves, if he be in a healthful state of association, must necessarily be in some degree enlightened, and his affections ameliorated.

I have said that each of these poems has a purpose. I have also informed my Reader what this purpose will be found principally to be: namely, to illustrate the manner in which our feelings and ideas are associated in a state of excitement. But, speaking in language somewhat more appropriate, it is to follow the fluxes and refluxes of the mind when agitated by the great and simple affections of our nature. This object I have endeavoured in these short essays to attain by various means; by tracing the maternal passion through many of its more subtle windings, as in the poems of the IDIOT BOY and the MAD MOTHER; by accompanying the last struggles of a human being, at the approach of death, cleaving in solitude to life and society, as in the Poem of the FORSAKEN INDIAN; by showing, as in the Stanzas entitled WE ARE SEVEN, the perplexity and obscurity which in childhood attend our notion of death, or rather our utter inability to admit that notion; or by displaying the strength of fraternal, or to speak more philosophically, of moral attachment when early associated with the great and beautiful objects of nature, as in THE BROTHERS; or, as in the Incident of SIMON LEE, by placing my Reader in the way of receiving from ordinary moral sensations another and more salutary impression than we are accustomed to receive from them. It has also been part of my general purpose to attempt to sketch characters under the influence of less impassioned feelings, as in the TWO APRIL MORNINGS, THE FOUNTAIN, THE OLD MAN TRAVELLING, THE TWO THIEVES, &c. characters of which the elements are simple, belonging rather to nature than to manners, such as exist now, and will probably always exist, and which from their constitution may be distinctly and profitably contemplated. I will not abuse the indulgence of my Reader by dwelling longer upon this subject; but it is proper that I should mention one other circumstance which distinguishes these Poems from the popular Poetry of the day; it is this, that the feeling therein developed gives importance to the action and situation, and not the action and situation to the feeling. My meaning will be rendered perfectly intelligible by referring my Reader to the Poems entitled POOR SUSAN and the CHILDLESS FATHER, particularly to the last Stanza of the latter Poem.

I will not suffer a sense of false modesty to prevent me from asserting, that I point my Reader's attention to this mark of distinction, far less for the sake of these particular Poems than from the general importance of the subject. The subject is indeed important! For the human mind is capable of being excited without the application of gross and violent stimulants; and he must have a very faint perception of its beauty and dignity who does not know this, and who does not further know, that one being is elevated above another, in proportion as he possesses this capability. It has therefore appeared to me, that to endeavour to produce or enlarge this capability is one of the best services in which, at any period, a Writer can be engaged; but this service, escellent at all times, is expecially so at the present day. For a multitude of causes, unknown to former times, are now acting with a combined force to blunt the discriminating powers of the mind, and unfitting it for all voluntary exertion to reduce it to a state of almost savage torpor. The most effective of these causes are the great national events which are daily taking place, and the increasing accumulation of men in cities, where the uniformity of their occupations produces a craving for extraordinary incident, which the rapid communication of intelligence hourly gratifies. To this tendency of life and manners the literature and theatrical exhibitions of the country have conformed themselves. The invaluable works of our elder writers, I had almost said the works of Shakespeare and Milton, are driven into neglect by frantic novels, sickly and stupid German Tragedies, and deluges of idle and extravagant stories in verse. – When I think upon this degrading thirst after outrageous stimulation, I am almost ashamed to have spoken of the feeble effort with which I have endeavoured to counteract it; and, reflecting upon the magnitude of the general evil, I should be oppressed with no dishonourable melancholy, had I not a deep impression of certain inherent and indestructible qualities of the human mind, and likewise of certain powers in the great and permanent objects that act upon it, which are equally inherent and indestructible; and did I not further add to this impression a belief, that the time is approaching when the evil will be systematically opposed, by men of greater powers, and with far more distinguished success.

Having dwelt thus long on the subjects and aim of these Poems, I shall request the Reader's permission to apprise him of a few circumstances relating to their *style*, in order, among other reasons, that I may not be censured for not having performed what I never attempted. The Reader will find that personifications of abstract ideas rarely occur in these volumes; and, I hope, are utterly rejected as an ordinary device to elevate the style, and raise it above prose. I have proposed to myself to imitate, and, as far as is possible, to adopt the very language of men; and assuredly such personifications do not make any natural or regular part of that language. They are, indeed, a figure of speech occasionally prompted by passion, and I have made use of them as such; but I have endeavoured utterly to reject them as a mechanical device of style, or as a family language which Writers in metre seem to lay claim to by prescription. I have wished to keep my Reader in the company of flesh and blood, persuaded that by so doing I shall interest him. I am, however, well aware that others who pursue a different track may interest him likewise; I do not interfere with their claim,

I only wish to prefer a different claim of my own. There will also be found in these volumes little of what is usually called poetic diction; I have taken as much pains to avoid it as others ordinarily take to produce it; this I have done for the reason already alleged, to bring my language near to the language of men, and further, because the pleasure which I have proposed to myself to impart is of a kind very different from that which is supposed by many persons to be the proper object of poetry. I do not know how without being culpably particular I can give my Reader a more exact notion of the style in which I wished these poems to be written than by informing him that I have at all times endeavoured to look steadily at my subject; consequently, I hope that there is in these Poems little falsehood of description, and that my ideas are expressed in language fitted to their respective importance. Something I must have gained by this practise, as it is friendly to one property of all good poetry, namely good sense; but it has necessarily cut me off from a large portion of phrases and figures of speech which from father to son have long been regarded as the common inheritance of Poets. I have also thought it expedient to restrict myself still further, having abstained from the use of many expressions, in themselves proper and beautiful, but which have been foolishly repeated by bad Poets, till such feelings of disgust are connected with them as it is scarcely possible by any art of association to overpower.

If in a poem there should be found a series of lines, or even a single line, in which the language, though naturally arranged, and according to the strict laws of metre, does not differ from that of prose, there is a numerous class of critics, who, when they stumble upon these prosaisms, as they call them, imagine that they have made a notable discovery, and exult over the Poet as over a man ignorant of his own profession. Now these men would establish a canon of criticism which the Reader will conclude he must utterly reject, if he wishes to be pleased with these volumes. And it would be a most easy task to prove to him, that not only the language of a large portion of every good poem, even of the most elevated character, must necessarily, except with reference to the metre, in no respect differ from that of good prose, but likewise that some of the most interesting parts of the best poems will be found to be strictly the language of prose, when prose is well written. The truth of this assertion might be demonstrated by innumerable passages from almost all the poetical writings, even of Milton himself. I have not space for much quotation; but, to illustrate the subject in a general manner, I will here adduce a short composition of Gray, who was at the head of those who by their reasonings have attempted to widen the space of separation betwixt Prose and Metrical composition, and was more than any other man curiously elaborate in the structure of his own poetic diction.

> In vain to me the smiling mornings shine,
> And reddening Phoebus lifts his golden fire:
> The birds in vain their amorous descant join,
> Or cheerful fields resume their green attire:
> These ears, alas! for other notes repine;
> *A different object do these eyes require;*
> *My lonely anguish melts no heart but mine;*
> *And in my breast the imperfect joys expire;*
> Yet morning smiles the busy race to cheer,
> And new-born pleasure brings to happier men;
> The fields to all their wonted tribute bear;
> To warm their little loves the birds complain.
> *I fruitless mourn to him that cannot hear*
> *And weep the more because I weep in vain.*

It will easily be perceived that the only part of this Sonnet which is of any value is the lines printed in Italics: it is equally obvious, that, except in the rhyme, and in the use of the single word 'fruitless' for fruitlessly, which is so far a defect, the language of these lines does in no respect differ from that of prose.

By the foregoing quotation I have shown that the language of Prose may yet be well adapted to Poetry; and I have previously asserted that a large portion of the language of every good poem can in no respect differ from that of good Prose. I will go further. I do not doubt that it may be safely affirmed, that there neither is, nor can be, any essential difference between the language of prose and metrical composition. We are fond of tracing the resemblance between Poetry and Painting, and, accordingly, we call them Sisters: but where shall we find bonds of connexion sufficiently strict to typify the affinity betwixt metrical and prose composition? They both speak by and to the same organs; the bodies in which both of them are clothed may be said to be of the same substance, their affections are kindred and almost identical, not necessarily differing even in degree; Poetry [I here use the word 'Poetry' (though against my own judgement) as opposed to the word Prose, and synonymous with metrical composition. But much confusion has been introduced into criticism by this contradistinction of Poetry and Prose, instead of the more philosophical one of Poetry and Matter of Fact, or Science. The only strict antithesis to Prose is Metre; nor is this, in truth, a *strict* antithesis; because lines and passages of metre so naturally occur in writing prose, that it would be scarcely possible to avoid them, even were it desirable. – W.] sheds no tears 'such as Angels weep,' but natural and human tears; she can boast of no celestial Ichor that distinguishes her vital juices from those of prose; the same human blood circulates through the veins of them both.

If it be affirmed that rhyme and metrical arrangement of themselves constitute a distinction which overturns what I have been saying on the strict affinity of metrical language with that of prose, and paves the way for other artificial distinctions which the mind voluntarily admits, I answer that the [*added 1802*: language of such Poetry as I am recommending is, as far as is possible, a selection of the language really spoken by men; that this selection, wherever it is made with true taste and feeling, will of itself form a distinction far greater than would at first be imagined, and will entirely separate the composition from the vulgarity and meanness of ordinary life; and, if metre be superadded thereto, I believe that a dissimilitude will be produced altogether sufficient for the gratification of a rational mind. What other distinction would we have? Whence is it to come? And where is it to exist? Not, surely, where the Poet speaks through the mouths of his characters: it cannot be necessary here, either for elevation of style, or any of its supposed ornaments; for, if the Poet's subject be judiciously chosen, it will naturally, and upon fit occasion, lead him to passions the language of which, if selected truly and judiciously, must necessarily be dignified and variegated, and alive with metaphors and figures. I forbear to speak of an incongruity which would shock the intelligent Reader, should the Poet interweave any foreign splendour of his own with that which the passion naturally suggests: it is sufficient to say that such addition is unnecessary. And, surely, it is more probable that those passages, which with propriety abound with metaphors and figures, will have their due effect, if, upon other occasions where the passions are of a milder character, the style also be subdued and temperate.

But, as the pleasure which I hope to give by the Poems I now present to the Reader must depend entirely on just notions upon this subject, and, as it is in itself of the highest importance to our taste and moral feelings, I cannot content myself with these detached remarks. And if, in what I am about to say, it shall appear to some that my labour is unnecessary, and that I am like a man fighting a battle without enemies, I would remind such persons that, whatever may be the language outwardly holden by men, a practical faith in the opinions which I am wishing to establish is almost unknown. If my conclusions are admitted, and carried as far as they must be carried if admitted at all, our judgements concerning the works of the greatest Poets both ancient and modern will be far different from what they are at present, both when we praise, and when we censure: and our moral feelings influencing, and influenced by these judgements will, I believe, be corrected and purified.

Taking up the subject, then, upon general grounds, I ask what is meant by the word Poet? What is a Poet? To whom does he address himself? And what language is to be expected from him? He is a man speaking to men: a man, it is true, endued with more lively sensibility, more enthusiasm and tenderness, who has a greater knowledge of human nature, and a more comprehensive soul, than are supposed to be common among mankind; a man pleased with his own passions and volitions, and who rejoices more than other men in the spirit of life that is in him; delighting to contemplate similar volitions and passions as manifested in the goings-on of the Universe, and habitually impelled to create them where he does not find them. To these qualities he has added a disposition to be affected more than other men by absent things as if they were present; an ability of conjuring up in himself passions, which are indeed far from being the same as those produced by real events, yet (especially in those parts of the general sympathy which are pleasing and delightful) do more nearly resemble the passions produced by real events, than anything which, from the motions of their own minds merely, other men are accustomed to feel in themselves; whence, and from practise, he has acquired a greater readiness and power in expressing what he thinks and feels, and especially those thoughts and feelings which, by his own choice, or from the structure of his own mind, arise in him without immediate external excitement.

But, whatever portion of this faculty we may suppose even the greatest Poet to possess, there cannot be a doubt but that the language which it will suggest to him, must, in liveliness and truth, fall far short of that which is uttered by men in real life, under the actual pressure of those passions, certain shadows of which the Poet thus produces, or feels to be produced, in himself. However exalted a notion we would wish to cherish of the character of a Poet, it is obvious that, while he describes and imitates passions, his situation is altogether slavish and mechanical, compared with the freedom and power of real and substantial action and suffering. So that it will be the wish of the Poet to bring his feelings near to those of the persons whose feelings he describes, nay, for short spaces of time perhaps, to let himself slip into an entire delusion, and even confound and identify his own feelings with theirs; modifying only the language which is thus suggested to him, by a consideration that he describes for a particular purpose, that of giving pleasure. Here, then, he will apply the principle on which I have so much insisted, namely, that of selection; on this he will depend for removing what would otherwise be painful or disgusting in the passion; he will feel that there is no necessity to trick out or to elevate nature: and, the more industriously he applies this principle, the deeper will be his faith that no words, which his fancy or imagination can suggest, will be to be compared with those which are the emanations of reality and truth.

But it may be said by those who do not object to the general

spirit of these remarks, that, as it is impossible for the Poet to pro-
duce upon all occasions language as exquisitely fitted for the
passion as that which the real passion itself suggests, it is proper
that he should consider himself as in the situation of a translator,
who deems himself justified when he substitutes excellences of
another kind for those which are unattainable by him; and
endeavours occasionally to surpass his original, in order to make
some amends for the general inferiority to which he feels that
he must submit. But this would be to encourage idleness and
unmanly despair. Further, it is the language of men who speak
of what they do not understand; who talk of Poetry as of a matter
of amusement and idle pleasure; who will converse with us as
gravely about a *taste* for Poetry, as they express it, as if it were a
thing as indifferent as a taste for Rope-dancing, or Frontiniac
or Sherry. Aristotle, I have been told, hath said, that Poetry
is the most philosophic of all writing: it is so: its object is truth,
not individual and local, but general, and operative; not standing
upon external testimony, but carried alive into the heart by
passion; truth which is its own testimony, which gives strength
and divinity to the tribunal to which it appeals, and receives them
from the same tribunal. Poetry is the image of man and nature.
The obstacles which stand in the way of the fidelity of the Bio-
grapher and Historian, and of their consequent utility, are in-
calculably greater than those which are to be encountered by the
Poet who has an adequate notion of the dignity of his art. The
Poet writes under one restriction only, namely, that of the
necessity of giving immediate pleasure to a human Being pos-
sessed of that information which may be expected from him,
not as a lawyer, a physician, a mariner, an astronomer or a natural
philosopher, but as a Man. Except this one restriction, there is
no object standing between the Poet and the image of things;
between this, and the Biographer and Historian there are a
thousand.

Nor let this necessity of producing immediate pleasure be
considered as a degradation of the Poet's art. It is far otherwise.
It is an acknowledgement of the beauty of the universe, an
acknowledgement the more sincere, because it is not formal, but
indirect; it is a task light and easy to him who looks at the world

in the spirit of love: further, it is a homage paid to the native and naked dignity of man, to the grand elementary principle of pleasure, by which he knows, and feels, and lives, and moves. We have no sympathy but what is propagated by pleasure: I would not be misunderstood; but wherever we sympathize with pain it will be found that the sympathy is produced and carried on by subtle combinations with pleasure. We have no knowledge, that is, no general principles drawn from the contemplation of particular facts, but what has been built up by pleasure, and exists in us by pleasure alone. The Man of Science, the Chemist and Mathematician, whatever difficulties and disgusts they may have had to struggle with, know and feel this. However painful may be the objects with which the Anatomist's knowledge is connected, he feels that his knowledge is pleasure; and where he has no pleasure he has no knowledge. What then does the Poet? He considers man and the objects that surround him as acting and re-acting upon each other, so as to produce an infinite complexity of pain and pleasure; he considers man in his own nature and in his ordinary life as contemplating this with a certain quantity of immediate knowledge, with certain convictions, intuitions, and deductions which by habit become of the nature of intuitions; he considers him as looking upon this complex scene of ideas and sensations, and finding everywhere objects that immediately excite in him sympathies which, from the necessities of his nature, are accompanied by an overbalance of enjoyment.

To this knowledge which all men carry about with them, and to these sympathies in which without any other discipline than that of our daily life we are fitted to take delight, the Poet principally directs his attention. He considers man and nature as essentially adapted to each other, and the mind of man as naturally the mirror of the fairest and most interesting qualities of nature. And thus the Poet, prompted by this feeling of pleasure which accompanies him through the whole course of his studies, converses with general nature with affections akin to those, which, through labour and length of time, the Man of Science has raised up in himself, by conversing with those particular parts of nature which are the objects of his studies. The knowledge both of the Poet and the Man of Science is pleasure; but the knowledge of the one cleaves to us as a necessary part of our existence, our natural and unalienable inheritance; the other is a personal and individual acquisition, slow to come to us, and by no habitual and direct sympathy connecting us with our fellow-beings. The Man of Science seeks truth as a remote and unknown benefactor; he cherishes and loves it in his solitude: the Poet, singing a song in which all human beings join with him, rejoices in the presence of truth as our visible friend and hourly companion. Poetry is the breath and finer spirit of all knowledge; it is the impassioned expression which is in the countenance of all Science. Emphatically may it be said of the Poet, as Shakespeare hath said of man, 'that he looks before and after.' He is the rock of defence of human nature; an upholder and preserver, carrying everywhere with him relationship and love. In spite of difference of soil and climate, of language and manners, of laws and customs, in spite of things silently gone out of mind and things violently destroyed, the Poet binds together by passion and knowledge the vast empire of human society, as it is spread over the whole earth, and over all time. The objects of the Poet's thoughts are everywhere; though the eyes and senses of man are, it is true, his favourite guides, yet he will follow wheresoever he can find an atmosphere of sensation in which to move his wings. Poetry is the first and last of all knowledge – it is as immortal as the heart of man. If the labours of Men of Science should ever create any material revolution, direct or indirect, in our condition, and in the impressions which we habitually receive, the Poet will sleep then no more than at present, but he will be ready to follow the steps of the Man of Science, not only in those general indirect effects, but he will be at his side, carrying sensation into the midst of the objects of the Science itself. The remotest discoveries of the Chemist, the Botanist, or Mineralogist, will be as proper objects of the Poet's art as any upon which it can be employed, if the time should ever come when these things shall be familiar to us, and the relations under which they are contemplated by the followers of these respective Sciences shall be manifestly and palpably material to us as enjoying and suffering beings. If the time should ever come when what is now called Science, thus familiarized to men, shall be ready to put on, as it were, a form of flesh and blood, the Poet will lend his divine spirit to aid the transfiguration, and will welcome the Being thus produced, as a dear and genuine inmate of the household of man. – It is not, then, to be supposed that anyone, who holds that sublime notion of Poetry which I have attempted to convey, will break in upon the sanctity and truth of his pictures by transitory and accidental ornaments, and endeavour to excite admiration of himself by arts, the necessity of which must manifestly depend upon the assumed meanness of his subject.

What I have thus far said applies to Poetry in general; but especially to those parts of composition where the Poet speaks through the mouths of his characters; and upon this point it appears to have such weight that I will conclude, there are few persons of good sense, who would not allow that the dramatic parts of composition are defective, in proportion as they deviate from the real language of nature, and are coloured by a diction of the Poet's own, either peculiar to him as an individual Poet, or belonging simply to Poets in general, to a body of men who, from the circumstance of their compositions being in metre, it is expected will employ a particular language.

It is not, then, in the dramatic parts of composition that we look for this distinction of language; but still it may be proper and necessary where the Poet speaks to us in his own person and character. To this I answer by referring my Reader to the description which I have before given of a Poet. Among the qualities which I have enumerated as principally conducing to form a Poet, is implied nothing differing in kind from other men, but only in degree. The sum of what I have there said is, that the Poet is chiefly distinguished from other men by a greater promptness to think and feel without immediate external excitement, and a greater power in expressing such thoughts and feelings as are produced in him in that manner. But these passions and thoughts and feelings are the general passions and thoughts and feelings of men. And with what are they connected? Undoubtedly with our moral sentiments and animal sensations, and with the causes which excite these; with the operations of the elements and the appearances of the visible universe; with storm and sunshine, with the revolutions of the seasons, with cold and heat, with loss of friends and kindred, with injuries and resentments, gratitude and hope, with fear and sorrow. These, and the like, are the sensations and objects which the Poet describes, as they are the sensations of other men, and the objects which interest them. The Poet thinks and feels in the spirit of the passions of men. How, then, can his language differ in any material degree from that of all other men who feel vividly and see clearly? It might be *proved* that it is impossible. But supposing that this were not the case, the Poet might then be allowed to use a peculiar language, when expressing his feelings for his own gratification, or that of men like himself. But Poets do not write for Poets alone, but for men. Unless therefore we are advocates for that admiration which depends upon ignorance, and that pleasure which arises from hearing what we do not understand, the Poet must descend from this supposed height, and, in order to excite rational sympathy, he must express himself as other men express themselves. To this it may be added, that while he is only selecting from the real language of men, or, which amounts to the same thing, composing accurately in the spirit of such selection, he is treading upon safe ground, and we know what we are to expect from him. Our feelings are the same with respect to metre; for, as it may be proper to remind the Reader, *end of 1802 addition*] the distinction of metre is regular and uniform, and not like that which is produced by what is usually called poetic diction, arbitrary, and subject to infinite caprices upon which no calculation whatever can be made. In the one case, the Reader is utterly at the mercy of the Poet respecting what imagery or diction he may choose to connect with the passion, whereas, in the other, the metre obeys certain laws, to which the Poet and Reader both willingly submit because they are certain, and because no interference is made by them with the passion but such as the concurring testimony of ages has shown to heighten and improve the pleasure which co-exists with it.

It will now be proper to answer an obvious question, namely, why, professing these opinions, have I written in verse? To this, in addition to such answer as is included in what I have already said, I reply in the first place, because, however I may have restricted myself, there is still left open to me what confessedly constitutes the most valuable object of all writing whether in prose or verse, the great and universal passions of men, the most general and interesting of their occupations, and the entire world of nature, from which I am at liberty to supply myself with endless combinations of forms and imagery. Now, supposing for a moment that whatever is interesting in these objects may be as vividly described in prose, why am I to be condemned, if to such description I have endeavoured to superadd the charm which, by the consent of all nations, is acknowledged to exist in metrical language? To this, by such as are unconvinced by what I have already said, it may be answered, that a very small part of the pleasure given by Poetry depends upon the metre, and that it is injudicious to write in metre, unless it be accompanied with the other artificial distinctions of style with which metre is usually accompanied, and that by such deviation more will be lost from the shock which will be thereby given to the Reader's associations, than will be counterbalanced by any pleasure which he can derive from the general power of numbers. In answer to those who still contend for the necessity of accompanying metre with certain appropriate colours of style in order to the accomplishment of its appropriate end, and who also, in my opinion, greatly underrate the power of metre in itself, it might perhaps, as far as relates to these Poems, have been almost sufficient to observe, that poems are extant, written upon more humble subjects, and in a more naked and simple style than I have aimed at, which poems have continued to give pleasure from generation to generation. Now, if nakedness and simplicity be a defect, the fact here mentioned affords a strong presumption that poems somewhat less naked and simple are capable of affording pleasure at the present day; and, what I wished *chiefly* to attempt, at present, was to justify myself for having written under the impression of this belief.

But I might point out various causes why, when the style is manly, and the subject of some importance, words metrically arranged will long continue to impart such a pleasure to mankind as he who is sensible of the extent of that pleasure will be desirous to impart. The end of Poetry is to produce excitement in co-existence with an over-balance of pleasure. Now, by the supposition, excitement is an unusual and irregular state of the mind; ideas and feelings do not in that state succeed each other in accustomed order. But, if the words by which this excitement is produced are in themselves powerful, or the images and feelings have an undue proportion of pain connected with them, there is some danger that the excitement may be carried beyond its proper bounds. Now the co-presence of something regular, something to which the mind has been accustomed in various moods and in a less excited state, cannot but have great efficacy in tempering and restraining the passion by an intertexture of ordinary feeling, and of feeling not strictly and necessarily connected with the passion. This is unquestionably true, and hence, though the opinion will at first appear paradoxical, from the tendency of metre to divest language in a certain degree of its reality, and thus to throw a sort of half consciousness of unsubstantial existence over the whole composition, there can be little doubt but that more pathetic situations and sentiments, that is, those which have a greater proportion of pain connected with them, may be endured in metrical composition, especially in rhyme, than in prose. The metre of the old ballads is very artless; yet they contain many passages which would illustrate this opinion, and, I hope, if the following Poems be attentively perused, similar instances will be found in them. This opinion may be further illustrated by appealing to the Reader's own experience of the reluctance with which he comes to the re-perusal of the distressful parts of Clarissa Harlowe, or the Gamester. While Shakespeare's writings, in the most pathetic scenes, never act upon us as pathetic beyond the bounds of pleasure – an effect which, in a much greater degree than might at first be imagined, is to be ascribed to small, but continual and regular impulses of pleasurable surprise from the metrical arrangement. – On the other hand (what it must be allowed will much more frequently happen) if the Poet's words should be incommensurate with the passion, and inadequate to raise the Reader to a height of desirable excitement, then (unless the

Poet's choice of his metre has been grossly injudicious) in the feelings of pleasure which the Reader has been accustomed to connect with metre in general, and in the feeling, whether cheerful or melancholy, which he has been accustomed to connect with that particular movement of metre, there will be found something which will greatly contribute to impart passion to the words, and to effect the complex end which the Poet proposes to himself.

If I had undertaken a systematic defence of the theory upon which these poems are written, it would have been my duty to develope the various causes upon which the pleasure received from metrical language depends. Among the chief of these causes is to be reckoned a principle which must be well known to those who have made any of the Arts the object of accurate reflection; I mean the pleasure which the mind derives from the perception of similitude in dissimilitude. This principle is the great spring of the activity of our minds, and their chief feeder. From this principle the direction of the sexual appetite, and all the passions connected with it, take their origin: it is the life of our ordinary conversation; and upon the accuracy with which similitude in dissimilitude, and dissimilitude in similitude are perceived, depend our taste and our moral feelings. It would not have been a useless employment to have applied this principle to the consideration of metre, and to have shown that metre is hence enabled to afford much pleasure, and to have pointed out in what manner that pleasure is produced. But my limits will not permit me to enter upon this subject, and I must content myself with a general summary.

I have said that Poetry is the spontaneous overflow of powerful feelings: it takes its origin from emotion recollected in tranquillity: the emotion is contemplated till by a species of reaction the tranquillity gradually disappears, and an emotion, kindred to that which was before the subject of contemplation, is gradually produced, and does itself actually exist in the mind. In this mood successful composition generally begins, and in a mood similar to this it is carried on; but the emotion, of whatever kind and in whatever degree, from various causes is qualified by various pleasures, so that in describing any passions whatsoever, which are voluntarily described, the mind will upon the whole be in a state of enjoyment. Now, if Nature be thus cautious in preserving in a state of enjoyment a being thus employed, the Poet ought to profit by the lesson thus held forth to him, and ought especially to take care, that whatever passions he communicates to his Reader, those passions, if his Reader's mind be sound and vigorous, should always be accompanied with an overbalance of pleasure. Now the music of harmonious metrical language, the sense of difficulty overcome, and the blind association of pleasure which has been previously received from works of rhyme or metre of the same or similar construction, an indistinct perception perpetually renewed of language closely resembling that of real life, and yet, in the circumstance of metre, differing from it so widely – all these imperceptibly make up a complex feeling of delight, which is of the most important use in tempering the painful feeling which will always be found intermingled with powerful descriptions of the deeper passions. This effect is always produced in pathetic and impassioned poetry; while, in lighter compositions, the ease and gracefulness with which the Poet manages his numbers are themselves confessedly a principal source of the gratification of the Reader. I might perhaps include all which it is *necessary* to say upon this subject by affirming, what few persons will deny, that, of two descriptions, either of passions, manners, or characters, each of them equally well executed, the one in prose and the other in verse, the verse will be read a hundred times where the prose is read once. We see that Pope, by the power of verse alone, has contrived to render the plainest common sense interesting, and even frequently to invest it with the appearance of passion. In consequence of these convictions I related in metre the Tale of GOODY BLAKE AND HARRY GILL, which is one of the rudest of this collection. I wished to draw attention to the truth, that the power of the human imagination is sufficient to produce such changes even in our physical nature as might almost appear miraculous. The truth is an important one; the fact (for it is a *fact*) is a valuable illustration of it. And I have the satisfaction of knowing that it has been communicated to many hundreds of people who would never have heard of it, had it not been narrated as a Ballad, and in a more impressive metre than is usual in Ballads.

Having thus explained a few of the reasons why I have written in verse, and why I have chosen subjects from common life, and endeavoured to bring my language near to the real language of men, if I have been too minute in pleading my own cause, I have at the same time been treating a subject of general interest; and it is for this reason that I request the Reader's permission to add a few words with reference solely to these particular poems, and to some defects which will probably be found in them. I am sensible that my associations must have sometimes been particular instead of general, and that, consequently, giving to things a false importance, sometimes from diseased impulses I may have written upon unworthy subjects; but I am less apprehensive on this account, than that my language may frequently have suffered from those arbitrary connexions of feelings and ideas with particular words and phrases, from which no man can altogether protect himself. Hence I have no doubt, that, in some instances, feelings even of the ludicrous may be given to my Readers by expressions which appeared to me tender and pathetic. Such faulty expressions, were I convinced they were faulty at present, and that they must necessarily continue to be so, I would willingly take all reasonable pains to correct. But it is dangerous to make these alterations on the simple authority of a few individuals, or even of certain classes of men; for where the understanding of an Author is not convinced, or his feelings altered, this cannot be done without great injury to himself: for his own feelings are his stay and support, and, if he sets them aside in one instance, he may be induced to repeat this act till his mind loses all confidence in itself, and becomes utterly debilitated. To this it may be added, that the Reader ought never to forget that he is himself exposed to the same errors as the Poet, and perhaps in a much greater degree: for there can be no presumption in saying, that it is not probable he will be so well acquainted with the various stages of meaning through which words have passed, or with the fickleness or stability of the relations of particular ideas to each other; and above all, since he is so much less interested in the subject, he may decide lightly and carelessly.

Long as I have detained my Reader, I hope he will permit me

to caution him against a mode of false criticism which has been applied to Poetry in which the language closely resembles that of life and nature. Such verses have been triumphed over in parodies of which Dr Johnson's Stanza is a fair specimen.

> 'I put my hat upon my head,
> And walked into the Strand,
> And there I met another man
> Whose hat was in his hand.'

Immediately under these lines I will place one of the most justly admired stanzas of the '*Babes in the Wood*.'

> 'These pretty Babes with hand in hand
> Went wandering up and down;
> But never more they saw the Man
> Approaching from the Town.'

In both these stanzas the words, and the order of the words, in no respect differ from the most unimpassioned conversation. There are words in both, for example, 'the Strand,' and 'the Town,' connected with none but the most familiar ideas; yet the one stanza we admit as admirable, and the other as a fair example of the superlatively contemptible. Whence arises this difference? Not from the metre, not from the language, not from the order of the words; but the *matter* expressed in Dr Johnson's stanza is contemptible. The proper method of treating trivial and simple verses, to which Dr Johnson's stanza would be a fair parallelism, is not to say, this is a bad kind of poetry, or this is not poetry; but this wants sense; it is neither interesting in itself, nor can *lead* to anything interesting; the images neither originate in that sane state of feeling which arises out of thought, nor can excite thought or feeling in the Reader. This is the only sensible manner of dealing with such verses: Why trouble yourself about the species till you have previously decided upon the genus? Why take pains to prove that an ape is not a Newton, when it is self-evident that he is not a man?

I have one request to make of my Reader, which is, that in judging these Poems he would decide by his own feelings genuinely, and not by reflection upon what will probably be the

890 PREFACE TO LYRICAL BALLADS

judgement of others. How common is it to hear a person say, 'I myself do not object to this style of composition, or this or that expression, but to such and such classes of people it will appear mean or ludicrous.' This mode of criticism, so destructive of all sound unadulterated judgement, is almost universal: I have therefore to request, that the Reader would abide independently by his own feelings, and that if he finds himself affected he would not suffer such conjectures to interfere with his pleasure.

If an Author by any single composition has impressed us with respect for his talents, it is useful to consider this as affording a presumption, that, on other occasions where we have been displeased, he nevertheless may not have written ill or absurdly; and, further, to give him so much credit for this one composition as may induce us to review what has displeased us with more care than we should otherwise have bestowed upon it. This is not only an act of justice, but, in our decisions upon poetry especially, may conduce in a high degree to the improvement of our own taste: for an *accurate* taste in poetry, and in all the other arts, as Sir Joshua Reynolds has observed, is an *acquired* talent, which can only be produced by thought and a long continued intercourse with the best models of composition. This is mentioned, not with so ridiculous a purpose as to prevent the most inexperienced Reader from judging for himself (I have already said that I wish him to judge for himself); but merely to temper the rashness of decision, and to suggest, that, if Poetry be a subject on which much time has not been bestowed, the judgement may be erroneous; and that in many cases it necessarily will be so.

I know that nothing would have so effectually contributed to further the end which I have in view, as to have shown of what kind the pleasure is, and how that pleasure is produced, which is confessedly produced by metrical composition essentially different from that which I have here endeavoured to recommend: for the Reader will say that he has been pleased by such composition; and what can I do more for him? The power of any art is limited; and he will suspect, that, if I propose to furnish him with new friends, it is only upon condition of his abandoning his old friends. Besides, as I have said, the Reader is himself conscious of the pleasure which he has received from such composition, composition to which he has peculiarly attached the endearing name of Poetry; and all men feel an habitual gratitude, and something of an honourable bigotry for the objects which have long continued to please them: we not only wish to be pleased, but to be pleased in that particular way in which we have been accustomed to be pleased. There is a host of arguments in these feelings; and I should be the less able to combat them successfully, as I am willing to allow, that, in order entirely to enjoy the Poetry which I am recommending, it would be necessary to give up much of what is ordinarily enjoyed. But, would my limits have permitted me to point out how this pleasure is produced, I might have removed many obstacles, and assisted my Reader in perceiving that the powers of language are not so limited as he may suppose; and that it is possible that poetry may give other enjoyments, of a purer, more lasting, and more exquisite nature. This part of my subject I have not altogether neglected; but it has been less my present aim to prove, that the interest excited by some other kinds of poetry is less vivid, and less worthy of the nobler powers of the mind, than to offer reasons for presuming, that, if the object which I have proposed to myself were adequately attained, a species of poetry would be produced, which is genuine poetry; in its nature well adapted to interest mankind permanently, and likewise important in the multiplicity and quality of its moral relations.

From what has been said, and from a perusal of the Poems, the Reader will be able clearly to perceive the object which I have proposed to myself: he will determine how far I have attained this object; and, what is a much more important question, whether it be worth attaining; and upon the decision of these two questions will rest my claim to the approbation of the public.

APPENDIX TO THE PREFACE (1802)

As perhaps I have no right to expect from a Reader of an introduction to a volume of Poems that attentive perusal without which it is impossible, imperfectly as I have been compelled to express my meaning, that what I have said in the Preface should throughout be fully understood, I am the more anxious to give an exact notion of the sense in which I use the phrase *poetic diction*; and for this purpose I will here add a few words concerning the origin of the phraseology which I have condemned under that name. – The earliest Poets of all nations generally wrote from passion excited by real events; they wrote naturally, and as men: feeling powerfully as they did, their language was daring, and figurative. In succeeding times, Poets, and men ambitious of the fame of Poets, perceiving the influence of such language, and desirous of producing the same effect, without having the same animating passion, set themselves to a mechanical adoption of those figures of speech, and made use of them, sometimes with propriety, but much more frequently applied them to feelings and ideas with which they had no natural connexion whatsoever. A language was thus insensibly produced, differing materially from the real language of men in *any situation*. The Reader or Hearer of this distorted language found himself in a perturbed and unusual state of mind: when affected by the genuine language of passion he had been in a perturbed and unusual state of mind also: in both cases he was willing that his common judgement and understanding should be laid asleep, and he had no instinctive and infallible perception of the true to make him reject the false; the one served as a passport for the other. The agitation and confusion of mind were in both cases delightful, and no wonder if he confounded the one with the other, and believed them both to be produced by the same, or similar causes. Besides, the Poet spake to him in the character of a man to be looked up to, a man of genius and authority. Thus, and from a variety of other causes, this distorted language was received with admiration; and Poets, it is probable, who had before contented themselves for the most part with misapplying only expressions which at first had been dictated by real passion, carried the abuse still further, and introduced phrases composed apparently in the spirit of the original figurative language of passion, yet altogether of their own invention, and distinguished by various degrees of wanton deviation from good sense and nature.

It is indeed true that the language of the earl'est Poets was felt to differ materially from ordinary language, because it was the language of extraordinary occasions; but it was really spoken by men, language which the Poet himself had uttered when he had been affected by the events which he described, or which he had heard uttered by those around him. To this language it is probable that metre of some sort or other was early superadded. This separated the genuine language of Poetry still further from common life, so that whoever read or heard the poems of these earliest Poets felt himself moved in a way in which he had not been accustomed to be moved in real life, and by causes manifestly different from those which acted upon him in real life. This was the great temptation to all the corruptions which have followed: under the protection of this feeling succeeding Poets constructed a phraseology which had one thing, it is true, in common with the genuine language of poetry, namely, that it was not heard in ordinary conversation; that it was unusual. But the first Poets, as I have said, spake a language which, though unusual, was still the language of men. This circumstance, however, was disregarded by their successors; they found that they could please by easier means: they became proud of a language which they themselves had invented, and which was uttered only by themselves; and, with the spirit of a fraternity, they arrogated it to themselves as their own. In process of time metre became a symbol or promise of this unusual language, and whoever took upon him to write in metre, according as he possessed more or less of true poetic genius, introduced less or more of this adulterated phraseology into his compositions, and the true and the false became so inseparably interwoven that the taste of men was gradually perverted; and this language was received as a natural language; and at length, by the influence of books upon men, did to a certain degree really become so. Abuses of this kind were imported from one nation to another, and with the progress of refinement this diction became daily more and more corrupt, thrusting out of sight the plain humanities of nature by a motley masquerade of tricks, quaintnesses, hieroglyphics, and enigmas.

It would be highly interesting to point out the causes of the pleasure given by this extravagant and absurd language; but this is not the place; it depends upon a great variety of causes, but upon none perhaps more than its influence in impressing a notion of the peculiarity and exaltation of the Poet's character, and in flattering the Reader's self-love by bringing him nearer to a sympathy with that character; an effect which is accomplished by unsettling ordinary habits of thinking, and thus assisting the Reader to approach to that perturbed and dizzy state of mind in which if he does not find himself, he imagines that he is *balked* of a peculiar enjoyment which poetry can, and ought to bestow.

The sonnet which I have quoted from Gray, in the Preface, except the lines printed in Italics, consists of little else but this diction, though not of the worst kind; and indeed, if I may be permitted to say so, it is far too common in the best writers, both ancient and modern. Perhaps I can in no way, by positive example, more easily give my Reader a notion of what I mean by the phrase *poetic diction* than by referring him to a comparison between the metrical paraphrases which we have of passages in the Old and New Testament, and those passages as they exist in our common Translation. See Pope's 'Messiah' throughout, Prior's 'Did sweeter sounds adorn my flowing tongue,' &c. &c. 'Though I speak with the tongues of men and of angels,' &c. &c. See 1st Corinthians, chapter xiiith. By way of immediate example, take the following of Dr Johnson:

> 'Turn on the prudent Ant thy heedless eyes,
> Observe her labours, Sluggard, and be wise;
> No stern command, no monitory voice,
> Prescribes her duties, or directs her choice;
> Yet timely provident she hastes away
> To snatch the blessings of a plenteous day;
> When fruitful Summer loads the teeming plain,
> She crops the harvest and she stores the grain.
> How long shall sloth usurp thy useless hours,
> Unnerve thy vigour, and enchain thy powers?
> While artful shades thy downy couch enclose,
> And soft solicitation courts repose,
> Amidst the drowsy charms of dull delight,
> Year chases year with unremitted flight,
> Till want now following, fraudulent and slow,
> Shall spring to seize thee, like an ambushed foe.'

From this hubbub of words pass to the original. 'Go to the Ant, thou Sluggard, consider her ways, and be wise: which having no guide, overseer, or ruler, provideth her meat in the summer, and gathereth her food in the harvest. How long wilt thou sleep, O Sluggard? when wilt thou arise out of thy sleep? Yet a little sleep, a little slumber, a little folding of the hands to sleep. So shall thy poverty come as one that travaileth, and thy want as an armed man.' *Proverbs*, chap. 6th.

One more quotation and I have done. It is from Cowper's verses supposed to be written by Alexander Selkirk:

> 'Religion! what treasure untold
> Resides in that heavenly word!
> More precious than silver and gold,
> Or all that this earth can afford.
> But the sound of the church-going bell
> These valleys and rocks never heard,
> Ne'er sighed at the sound of a knell,
> Or smiled when a sabbath appeared.
>
> Ye winds, that have made me your sport,
> Convey to this desolate shore
> Some cordial endearing report
> Of a land I must visit no more.
> My Friends, do they now and then send
> A wish or a thought after me?
> O tell me I yet have a friend,
> Though a friend I am never to see.'

I have quoted this passage as an instance of three different styles of composition. The first four lines are poorly expressed; some Critics would call the language prosaic; the fact is, it would be bad prose, so bad, that it is scarcely worse in metre. The epithet 'church-going' applied to a bell, and that by so chaste a writer as Cowper, is an instance of the strange abuses which Poets have introduced into their language till they and their Readers take them as matters of course, if they do not single them out expressly as objects of admiration. The two lines 'Ne'er sighed at the sound,' &c. are, in my opinion, an instance of the language of passion wrested from its proper use, and, from the mere circumstance of the composition being in metre, applied upon an occasion that does not justify such violent expressions; and I should condemn the passage, though perhaps few Readers will agree with me, as vicious poetic diction. The last stanza is throughout admirably expressed: it would be equally good whether in prose or verse, except that the Reader has an exquisite pleasure in seeing such natural language so naturally connected with metre. The beauty of this stanza tempts me here to add a sentiment which ought to be the pervading spirit of a system, detached parts of which have been imperfectly explained in the Preface, – namely, that in proportion as ideas and feelings are valuable, whether the composition be in prose or in verse, they require and exact one and the same language.

Descriptive Sketches 1793

Were there, below, a spot of holy ground,
By Pain and her sad family unfound,
Sure, Nature's GOD that spot to man had given,
Where murmuring rivers join the song of even;
Where falls the purple morning far and wide
In flakes of light upon the mountain-side;
Where summer Suns in ocean sink to rest,
Or moonlight Upland lifts her hoary breast;
Where Silence, on her wing of night, o'erbroods
10 Unfathomed dells and undiscovered woods;
Where rocks and groves the power of waters shakes
In cataracts, or sleeps in quiet lakes.
    But doubly pitying Nature loves to shower
Soft on his wounded heart her healing power,
Who plods o'er hills and vales his road forlorn,
Wooing her varying charms from eve to morn.
No sad vacuities his heart annoy,
Blows not a Zephyr but it whispers joy;
For him lost flowers their idle sweets exhale;
20 He tastes the meanest note that swells the gale;
For him sod-seats the cottage-door adorn,
And peeps the far-off spire, his evening bourn!
Dear is the forest frowning o'er his head,
And dear the green-sward to his velvet tread;
Moves there a cloud o'er mid-day's flaming eye?
Upward he looks – and calls it luxury;
Kind Nature's charities his steps attend,
In every babbling brook he finds a friend,

While chastening thoughts of sweetest use, bestowed
30 By Wisdom, moralize his pensive road.
Host of his welcome inn, the noon-tide bower,
To his spare meal he calls the passing poor;
He views the Sun uprear his golden fire,
Or sink, with heart alive like Memnon's lyre;
Blesses the Moon that comes with kindest ray
To light him shaken by his viewless way.
With bashful fear no cottage children steal
From him, a brother at the cottage meal,
His humble looks no shy restraint impart,
40 Around him plays at will the virgin heart.
While unsuspended wheels the village dance,
The maidens eye him with inquiring glance,
Much wondering what sad stroke of crazing Care
Or desperate Love could lead a wanderer there.

Me, lured by hope her sorrows to remove,
A heart, that could not much itself approve,
O'er Gallia's wastes of corn dejected led,
Her road elms rustling thin above my head,
Or through her truant pathway's native charms,
50 By secret villages and lonely farms,
To where the Alps, ascending white in air,
Toy with the Sun, and glitter from afar.

Even now I sigh at hoary Chartreuse' doom
Weeping beneath his chill of mountain gloom.
Where now is fled that Power whose frown severe
Tamed 'sober Reason' till she crouched in fear?
That breathed a death-like peace these woods around, ⎫
Broke only by the unvaried torrent's sound, ⎬
Or prayer-bell by the dull cicada drowned. ⎭
60 The cloister startles at the gleam of arms,
And Blasphemy the shuddering fane alarms;
Nod the cloud-piercing pines their troubled heads,
Spires, rocks, and lawns, a browner night o'erspreads.
Strong terror checks the female peasant's sighs,
And start the astonished shades at female eyes.
The thundering tube the agéd angler hears,

And swells the groaning torrent with his tears.
From Bruno's forest screams the frighted jay,
And slow the insulted eagle wheels away.
70 The cross with hideous laughter Demons mock,
By angels planted on the aërial rock.
The 'parting Genius' sighs with hollow breath
Along the mystic streams of Life and Death.
Swelling the outcry dull, that long resounds
Portentous, through her old woods' trackless bounds,
Deepening her echoing torrents' awful peal
And bidding paler shades her form conceal,
Vallombre, 'mid her falling fanes, deplores,
For ever broke, the sabbath of her bowers.
80   More pleased, my foot the hidden margin roves
Of Como bosomed deep in chestnut groves.
No meadows thrown between, the giddy steeps
Tower, bare or sylvan, from the narrow deeps.
To towns, whose shades of no rude sound complain,
To ringing team unknown and grating wain,
To flat-roofed towns, that touch the water's bound,
Or lurk in woody sunless glens profound,
Or from the bending rocks obtrusive cling,
And o'er the whitened wave their shadows fling;
90 Wild round the steeps the little pathway twines,
And Silence loves its purple roof of vines.
The viewless lingerer hence, at evening, sees
From rock-hewn steps the sail between the trees;
Or marks, 'mid opening cliffs, fair dark-eyed maids
Tend the small harvest of their garden glades,
Or, led by distant warbling notes, surveys,
With hollow ringing ears and darkening gaze,
Binding the charmèd soul in powerless trance,
Lip-dewing Song and ringlet-tossing Dance,
100 Where sparkling eyes and breaking smiles illume
The bosomed cabin's lyre-enlivened gloom;
Or stops the solemn mountain-shades to view
Stretch, o'er their pictured mirror, broad and blue,
Tracking the yellow sun from steep to steep,

As up the opposing hills, with tortoise foot, they creep.
Here half a village shines, in gold arrayed
Bright as the moon, half hides itself in shade.
From the dark sylvan roofs the restless spire
Inconstant glancing, mounts like springing fire,
110 There, all unshaded, blazing forests throw
Rich golden verdure on the waves below.
Slow glides the sail along the illumined shore,
And steals into the shade the lazy oar.
Soft bosoms breathe around contagious sighs,
And amourous music on the water dies.
Heedless how Pliny, musing here, surveyed
Old Roman boats and figures through the shade,
Pale Passion, overpowered, retires and woos
The thicket, where the unlistened stockdove coos.
120   How blessed, delicious Scene! the eye that greets
Thy open beauties, or thy lone retreats;
The unwearied sweep of wood thy cliffs that scales,
The never-ending waters of thy vales;
The cots, those dim religious groves embower,
Or, under rocks that from the water tower
Insinuated, sprinkling all the shore,
Each with his household boat beside the door,
Whose flaccid sails in forms fantastic droop,
Brightening the gloom where thick the forests stoop;
130 – Thy torrents shooting from the clear-blue sky,
Thy towns, like swallows' nests that cleave on high;
That glimmer hoar in eve's last light, descried
Dim from the twilight water's shaggy side,
Whence lutes and voices down the enchanted woods
Steal, and compose the oar-forgotten floods,
While Evening's solemn bird melodious weeps,
Heard, by star-spotted bays, beneath the steeps;
– Thy lake, 'mid smoking woods, that blue and grey
Gleams, streaked or dappled, hid from morning's ray
140 Slow-travelling down the western hills, to fold
Its green-tinged margin in a blaze of gold;
From thickly-glittering spires the matin-bell

Calling the woodman from his desert cell,
A summons to the sound of oars, that pass,
Spotting the steaming deeps, to early mass;
Slow swells the service o'er the water born,
While fill each pause the ringing woods of morn.
    Farewell! those forms that, in thy noon-tide shade,
Rest, near their little plots of wheaten glade;
150 Those stedfast eyes, that beating breasts inspire
To throw the 'sultry ray' of young Desire;
Those lips, whose tides of fragrance come, and go,
Accordant to the cheek's unquiet glow;
Those shadowy breasts in love's soft light arrayed,
And rising, by the moon of passion swayed.
    – Thy fragrant gales and lute-resounding streams,
Breathe o'er the failing soul voluptuous dreams;
While Slavery, forcing the sunk mind to dwell
On joys that might disgrace the captive's cell,
160 Her shameless timbrel shakes along thy marge,
And winds between thine isles the vocal barge.
    Yet, arts are thine that rock the unsleeping heart,
And smiles to Solitude and Want impart.
I loved, 'mid thy most desert woods astray,
With pensive step to measure my slow way,
By lonely, silent cottage-doors to roam,
The far-off peasant's day-deserted home;
Once did I pierce to where a cabin stood,
The redbreast peace had buried it in wood,
170 There, by the door a hoary-headed sire
Touched with his withered hand an agéd lyre;
Beneath an old-grey oak as violets lie,
Stretched at his feet with stedfast, upward eye,
His children's children joined the holy sound,
A hermit – with his family around.
    Hence shall we seek where fair Locarno smiles
Embowered in walnut slopes and citron isles,
Or charms that smile on Tusa's evening stream,
While 'mid dim towers and woods her waters gleam;
180 From the bright wave, in solemn gloom, retire

The dull-red steeps, and darkening still, aspire,
To where afar rich orange lustres glow
Round undistinguished clouds, and rocks, and snow;
Or, led where Viamala's chasms confine
The indigant waters of the infant Rhine,
Bend o'er the abyss? – the else impervious gloom
His burning eyes with fearful light illume.
The Grison gypsy here her tent has placed,
Sole human tenant of the piny waste;
190 Her tawny skin, dark eyes, and glossy locks,
Bend o'er the smoke that curls beneath the rocks.

  – The mind condemned, without reprieve, to go
O'er life's long deserts with its charge of woe,
With sad congratulation joins the train,   ⎫
Where beasts and men together o'er the plain   ⎬
Move on, – a mighty caravan of pain;   ⎭
Hope, strength, and courage, social suffering brings,
Freshening the waste of sand with shades and springs.
  – She solitary through the desert drear
200 Spontaneous wanders, hand in hand with Fear.
  A giant moan along the forest swells
Protracted, and the twilight storm foretells,
And, ruining from the cliffs their deafening load
Tumbles, the wildering Thunder slips abroad;
On the high summits Darkness comes and goes,
Hiding their fiery clouds, their rocks, and snows;
The torrent, traversed by the lustre broad,
Starts like a horse beside the flashing road;
In the roofed bridge, at that despairing hour,
210 She seeks a shelter from the battering shower.
  – Fierce comes the river down; the crashing wood
Gives way, and half its pines torment the flood;
Fearful, beneath, the Water-spirits call,
And the bridge vibrates, tottering to its fall.
  – Heavy, and dull, and cloudy is the night,
No star supplies the comfort of its light,
Glimmer the dim-lit Alps, dilated, round,

And one sole light shifts in the vale profound;
While, opposite, the waning moon hangs still,
220 And red, above her melancholy hill.
By the deep quiet gloom appalled, she sighs,
Stoops her sick head, and shuts her weary eyes.
– Breaking the ascending roar of desert floods,
And insect buzz, that stuns the sultry woods,
She hears, upon the mountain forest's brow,
The death-dog, howling loud and long, below;
On viewless fingers counts the valley-clock,
Followed by drowsy crow of midnight cock.
– Bursts from the troubled Larch's giant boughs
230 The pie, and chattering breaks the night's repose.
Low barks the fox; by Havoc roused the bear,
Quits, growling, the white bones that strew his lair;
The dry leaves stir as with the serpent's walk,
And, far beneath, Banditti voices talk;
Behind her hill the Moon, all crimson, rides,
And his red eyes the slinking Water hides;
Then all is hushed; the bushes rustle near,
And with strange tinglings sings her fainting ear.
– Vexed by the darkness, from the piny gulf
240 Ascending, nearer howls the famished wolf,
While through the stillness scatters wild dismay,
Her babe's small cry, that leads him to his prey.

    Now, passing Urseren's open vale serene,
Her quiet streams, and hills of downy green,
Plunge with the Russ embrowned by Terror's breath,
Where danger roofs the narrow walks of death;
By floods, that, thundering from their dizzy height,
Swell more gigantic on the stedfast sight;
Black drizzling crags, that beaten by the din,
250 Vibrate, as if a voice complained within;
Bare steeps, where Desolation stalks, afraid,
Unstedfast, by a blasted yew upstayed;
By cells whose image, trembling as he prays,
Awe struck, the kneeling peasant scarce surveys;
Loose-hanging rocks the Day's blessed eye that hide,

And crosses reared to Death on every side,
Which with cold kiss Devotion planted near,
And, bending, watered with the human tear,
Soon fading 'silent' from her upward eye,
260 Unmoved with each rude form of Danger nigh,
Fixed on the anchor left by him who saves
Alike in whelming snows and roaring waves.
    On as we move, a softer prospect opes.
Calm huts, and lawns between, and sylvan slopes.
While mists, suspended on the expiring gale,
Moveless o'er-hang the deep secluded vale,
The beams of evening, slipping soft between,
Light up of tranquil joy a sober scene;
Winding its dark-green wood and emerald glade,
270 The still vale lengthens underneath the shade;
While in soft gloom the scattering bowers recede,
Green dewy lights adorn the freshened mead,
Where solitary forms illumined stray
Turning with quiet touch the valley's hay,
On the low brown wood-huts delighted sleep
Along the brightened gloom reposing deep.
While pastoral pipes and streams the landscape lull,
And bells of passing mules that tinkle dull,
In solemn shapes before the admiring eye
280 Dilated hang the misty pines on high,
Huge convent domes with pinnacles and towers,
And antique castles seen through drizzling showers.
    From such romantic dreams my soul awake,
Lo! Fear looks silent down on Uri's lake,
By whose unpathwayed margin still and dread
Was never heard the plodding peasant's tread.
Tower like a wall the naked rocks, or reach
Far o'er the secret water dark with beech,
More high, to where creation seems to end,
290 Shade above shade the desert pines ascend,
And still, below, where 'mid the savage scene
Peeps out a little speck of smiling green,
There with his infants man undaunted creeps

And hangs his small wood-hut upon the steeps.
A garden-plot the desert air perfumes,
'Mid the dark pines a little orchard blooms,
A zig-zag path from the domestic skiff
Threading the painful crag surmounts the cliff.
– Before those hermit doors, that never know
300 The face of traveller passing to and fro,
No peasant leans upon his pole, to tell
For whom at morning tolled the funeral bell,
Their watch-dog ne'er his angry bark forgoes,
Touched by the beggar's moan of human woes,
The grassy seat beneath their casement shade
The pilgrim's wistful eye hath never stayed.
– There, did the iron Genius not disdain
The gentle Power that haunts the myrtle plain,
There might the love-sick maiden sit, and chide
310 The insuperable rocks and severing tide,
There watch at eve her lover's sun-gilt sail
Approaching, and upbraid the tardy gale,
There list at midnight till is heard no more,
Below, the echo of his parting oar,
There hang in fear, when growls the frozen stream,
To guide his dangerous tread the taper's gleam.
   'Mid stormy vapours ever driving by,
Where ospreys, cormorants, and herons cry,
Where hardly given the hopeless waste to cheer
320 Denied the bread of life the foodful ear,
Dwindles the pear on autumn's latest spray,
And apple sickens pale in summer's ray,
Even here Content has fixed her smiling reign
With Independence child of high Disdain.
Exulting 'mid the winter of the skies,   ⎫
Shy as the jealous chamois, Freedom flies, ⎬
And often grasps her sword, and often eyes, ⎭
Her crest a bough of Winter's bleakest pine,
Strange 'weeds' and alpine plants her helm entwine,
330 And wildly-pausing oft she hangs aghast,
While thrills the 'Spartan fife' between the blast.

'Tis storm; and hid in mist from hour to hour
All day the floods a deeper murmur pour,
And mournful sounds, as of a Spirit lost,
Pipe wild along the hollow-blustering coast,
'Till the Sun walking on his western field
Shakes from behind the clouds his flashing shield.
Triumphant on the bosom of the storm,
Glances the fire-clad eagle's wheeling form;
340 Eastward, in long perspective glittering, shine
The wood-crowned cliffs that o'er the lake recline;
Wide o'er the Alps a hundred streams unfold,
At once to pillars turned that flame with gold;
Behind his sail the peasant strives to shun
The west that burns like one dilated sun,
Where in a mighty crucible expire
The mountains, glowing hot, like coals of fire.
    But lo! the boatman, over-awed, before
The pictured fane of Tell suspends his oar;
350 Confused the Marathonian tale appears,
While burn in his full eyes the glorious tears.
And who but feels a power of strong controul,
Felt only there, oppress his labouring soul,
Who walks, where honoured men of ancient days
Have wrought with god-like arm the deeds of praise?
Say, who, by thinking on Canadian hills,
Or wild Aosta lulled by Alpine rills,
On Zutphen's plain; or where with softened gaze
The old grey stones the plaided chief surveys,
360 Can guess the high resolve, the cherished pain
Of him whom passion rivets to the plain,
Where breathed the gale that caught Wolfe's happiest
    sigh,
And the last sun-beam fell on Bayard's eye,
Where bleeding Sydney from the cup retired,
And glad Dundee in 'faint huzza's' expired.

    But now with other soul I stand alone
Sublime upon this far-surveying cone,

And watch from pike to pike amid the sky
Small as a bird the chamois-chaser fly.
370 'Tis his with fearless step at large to roam
Through wastes, of Spirits winged the solemn home,
Through vacant worlds where Nature never gave
A brook to murmur or a bough to wave,
Which unsubstantial Phantoms sacred keep;
Through worlds where Life and Sound, and Motion
    sleep,
Where Silence still her death-like reign extends,
Save when the startling cliff unfrequent rends:
In the deep snow the mighty ruin drowned,
Mocks the dull ear of Time with deaf abortive sound;
380 – To mark a planet's pomp and steady light
In the least star of scarce-appearing night,
And neighbouring moon, that coasts the vast profound,
Wheel pale and silent her diminished round,
While far and wide the icy summits blaze
Rejoicing in the glory of her rays;
The star of noon that glitters small and bright,
Shorn of his beams, insufferably white,
And flying fleet behind his orb to view
The interminable sea of sable blue.
390 – Of cloudless suns no more ye frost-built spires
Refract in rainbow hues the restless fires!
Ye dewy mists the arid rocks o'er-spread
Whose slippery face derives his deathful tread!
– To wet the peak's impracticable sides
He opens of his feet the sanguine tides,
Weak and more weak the issuing current eyes
Lapped by the panting tongue of thirsty skies.
– At once bewildering mists around him close,
And cold and hunger are his least of woes;
400 The Demon of the snow with angry roar
Descending, shuts for aye his prison door.
Crazed by the strength of hope at morn he eyes
As sent from heaven the raven of the skies,
Then with despair's whole weight his spirits sink,

No bread to feed him, and the snow his drink,
While ere his eyes can close upon the day,
The eagle of the Alps o'ershades his prey.
– Meanwhile his wife and child with cruel hope
All night the door at every moment ope;
410 Haply that child in fearful doubt may gaze,
Passing his father's bones in future days,
Start at the reliques of that very thigh,
On which so oft he prattled when a boy.
    Hence shall we turn where, heard with fear afar,
Thunders through echoing pines the headlong Aar?
Or rather stay to taste the mild delights
Of pensive Underwalden's pastoral heights?
    – Is there who 'mid these awful wilds has seen
The native Genii walk the mountain green?
420 Or heard, while other worlds their charms reveal,
Soft music from the aërïal summit steal?
While o'er the desert, answering every close,
Rich steam of sweetest perfume comes and goes.
– And sure there is a secret Power that reigns
Here, where no trace of man the spot profanes,
Naught but the herds that pasturing upward creep,
Hung dim-discovered from the dangerous steep,
Or summer hamlet, flat and bare, on high
Suspended, 'mid the quiet of the sky.
430 How still! no irreligious sound or sight
Rouzes the soul from her severe delight.
An idle voice the sabbath region fills
Of Deep that calls to Deep across the hills,
Broke only by the melancholy sound
Of drowsy bells for ever tinkling round;
Faint wail of eagle melting into blue
Beneath the cliffs, and pine-woods steady sugh;
The solitary heifer's deepened low;
Or rumbling heard remote of falling snow.
440 Save that, the stranger seen below, the boy
Shouts from the echoing hills with savage joy.
When warm from myrtle bays and tranquil seas,

Comes on, to whisper hope, the vernal breeze,
When hums the mountain bee in May's glad ear,
And emerald isles to spot the heights appear,
When shouts and lowing herds the valley fill,
And louder torrents stun the noon-tide hill,
When fragrant scents beneath the enchanted tread
Spring up, his little all around him spread,
450 The pastoral Swiss begins the cliffs to scale,
To silence leaving the deserted vale,
Up the green mountain tracking Summer's feet,
Each twilight earlier called the Sun to meet,
With earlier smile the ray of morn to view
Fall on his shifting hut that gleams 'mid smoking dew;
Blessed with his herds, as in the patriarch's age,
The summer long to feed from stage to stage;
O'er azure pikes serene and still, they go,
And hear the rattling thunder far below;
460 Or lost at eve in sudden mist the day
Attend, or dare with minute-steps their way;
Hang from the rocks that tremble o'er the steep,
And tempt the icy valley yawning deep,
O'er-walk the chasmy torrent's foam-lit bed,
Rocked on the dizzy larch's narrow tread,
Whence Danger leans, and pointing ghastly, joys
To mock the mind with 'desperation's toys';
Or steal beneath loose mountains, half-deterred,
That sigh and shudder to the lowing herd.
470 – I see him, up the midway cliff he creeps
To where a scanty knot of verdure peeps,
Thence down the steep a pile of grass he throws
The fodder of his herds in winter snows.
Far different life to what tradition hoar
Transmits of days more blessed in times of yore.
Then Summer lengthened out his season bland,
And with rock-honey flowed the happy land.
Continual fountains welling cheered the waste,
And plants were wholesome, now of deadly taste.
480 Nor Winter yet his frozen stores had piled

Usurping where the fairest herbage smiled;
Nor Hunger forced the herds from pastures bare
For scanty food the treacherous cliffs to dare.
Then the milk-thistle bad those herds demand
Three times a day the pail and welcome hand.
But human vices have provoked the rod
Of angry Nature to avenge her God.
Thus does the father to his sons relate,
On the lone mountain top, their changed estate.
490   Still, Nature, ever just, to him imparts
Joys only given to uncorrupted hearts.
– 'Tis morn: with gold the verdant mountain glows,
More high, the snowy peaks with hues of rose.
Far stretched beneath the many-tinted hills
A mighty waste of mist the valley fills,
A solemn sea! whose vales and mountains round
Stand motionless, to awful silence bound.
A gulf of gloomy blue, that opens wide
And bottomless, divides the midway tide.
500   Like leaning masts of stranded ships appear
The pines that near the coast their summits rear;
Of cabins, woods, and lawns a pleasant shore
Bounds calm and clear the chaos still and hoar;
Loud through that midway gulf ascending, sound
Unnumbered streams with hollow roar profound.
Mounts through the nearer mist the chaunt of
      birds,
And talking voices, and the low of herds,
The bark of dogs, the drowsy tinkling bell,
And wild-wood mountain lutes of saddest swell.
510   Think not, suspended from the cliff on high
He looks below with undelighted eye.
– No vulgar joy is his, at even tide
Stretched on the scented mountain's purple side.
For as the pleasures of his simple day
Beyond his native valley hardly stray,
Naught round its darling precincts can he find
But brings some past enjoyment to his mind,

While Hope that ceaseless leans on Pleasure's urn
Binds her wild wreathes, and whispers his return.
520   Once Man entirely free, alone and wild,
Was blessed as free – for he was Nature's child.
He, all superior but his God disdained,
Walked none restraining, and by none restrained,
Confessed no law but what his reason taught,
Did all he wished, and wished but what he ought.
As Man in his primaeval dower arrayed
The image of his glorious sire displayed,
Even so, by vestal Nature guarded, here
The traces of primaeval Man appear.
530   The native dignity no forms debase,
The eye sublime, and surly lion-grace.
The slave of none, of beasts alone the lord,
He marches with his flute, his book, and sword,
Well taught by that to feel his rights, prepared
With this 'the blessings he enjoys to guard.'
   And as on glorious ground he draws his breath,
Where Freedom oft, with Victory and Death,
Hath seen in grim array amid their Storms
Mixed with auxiliar Rocks, three hundred Forms;
540   While twice ten thousand corselets at the view
Dropped loud at once, Oppression shrieked, and flew.
Oft as those sainted Rocks before him spread,
An unknown power connects him with the dead.
For images of other worlds are there,
Awful the light, and holy is the air.
Uncertain through his fierce uncultured soul
Like lighted tempests troubled transports roll;
To viewless realms his Spirit towers amain,
Beyond the senses and their little reign.
550   And oft, when passed that solemn vision by,
He holds with God himself communion high,
When the dread peal of swelling torrents fills
The sky-roofed temple of the eternal hills,
And savage Nature humbly joins the rite,
While flash her upward eyes severe delight.

Or gazing from the mountain's silent brow
Bright stars of ice and azure worlds of snow,
Where needle peaks of granite shooting bare
Tremble in ever-varying tints of air,
560 Great joy by horror tamed dilates his heart,
And the near heavens their own delights impart.
– When the Sun bids the gorgeous scene farewell,
Alps overlooking Alps their state upswell;
Huge Pikes of Darkness named, of Fear and Storms,
Lift, all serene, their still, illumined forms,
In sea-like reach of prospect round him spread,
Tinged like an angel's smile all rosy red.
  When downward to his winter hut he goes,
Dear and more dear the lessening circle grows,
570 That hut which from the hills his eyes employs
So oft, the central point of all his joys.
And as a swift by tender cares oppressed
Peeps often ere she dart into her nest,
So to the untrodden floor, where round him looks
His father helpless as the babe he rocks,
Oft he descends to nurse the brother pair,
Till storm and driving ice blockade him there;
There hears, protected by the woods behind,
Secure, the chiding of the baffled wind,
580 Hears Winter, calling all his Terrors round,
Rush down the living rocks with whirlwind sound.
Through Nature's vale his homely pleasures glide
Unstained by envy, discontent, and pride,
The bound of all his vanity to deck
With one bright bell a favourite heifer's neck;
Content upon some simple annual feast,
Remembered half the year, and hoped the rest,
If dairy produce, from his inner hoard,
Of thrice ten summers consecrate the board.
590 – Alas ! in every clime a flying ray
Is all we have to cheer our wintry way,
Condemned, in mists and tempests ever rife,
To pant slow up the endless Alp of life.

'Here,' cried a swain, whose venerable head
Bloomed with the snow-drops of Man's narrow
    bed,
Last night, while by his dying fire, as closed
The day, in luxury my limbs reposed,
'Here Penury oft from misery's mount will guide
Even to the summer door his icy tide,
600 And here the avalanche of Death destroy
The little cottage of domestic Joy.
But, ah! the unwilling mind may more than trace
The general sorrows of the human race:
The churlish gales, that unremitting blow
Cold from necessity's continual snow,
To us the gentle groups of bliss deny
That on the noon-day bank of leisure lie.
Yet more; the tyrant Genius, still at strife
With all the tender Charities of life,
610 When close and closer they begin to strain,
No fond hand left to staunch the unclosing vein,
Tearing their bleeding ties leaves Age to groan
On his wet bed, abandoned and alone.
For ever, fast as they of strength become
To pay the filial debt, for food to roam,
The father, forced by Powers that only deign
That solitary Man disturb their reign,
From his bare nest amid the storms of heaven
Drives, eagle-like, his sons as he was driven,
620 His last dread pleasure! watches to the plain –
And never, eagle-like, beholds again.'
    When the poor heart has all its joys resigned,
Why does their sad remembrance cleave behind?
Lo! by the lazy Seine the exile roves,
Or where thick sails illume Batavia's groves;
Soft o'er the waters mournful measures swell,
Unlocking bleeding Thought's 'memorial cell;'
At once upon his heart Despair has set
Her seal, the mortal tear his cheek has wet;
630 Strong poison not a form of steel can brave

Bows his young hairs with sorrow to the grave.
   Gay lark of hope thy silent song resume!
Fair smiling lights the purpled hills illume!
Soft gales and dews of life's delicious morn,
And thou, lost fragrance of the heart return!
Soon flies the little joy to man allowed,
And tears before him travel like a cloud.
For come Diseases on, and Penury's rage,
Labour, and Pain, and Grief, and joyless Age,
640 And Conscience dogging close his bleeding way
Cries out, and leads her Spectres to their prey,
Till Hope-deserted, long in vain his breath
Implores the dreadful untried sleep of Death.
– Mid savage rocks and seas of snow that shine
Between interminable tracts of pine,
Round a lone fane the human Genii mourn,
Where fierce the rays of woe collected burn.
– From viewless lamps a ghastly dimness falls,
And ebbs uncertain on the troubled walls,
650 Dim dreadful faces through the gloom appear,
Abortive Joy, and Hope that works in fear,
While strives a secret Power to hush the crowd,
Pain's wild rebellious burst proclaims her rights aloud.
   Oh give not me that eye of hard disdain
That views undimmed Einsiedlen's wretched fane.
'Mid muttering prayers all sounds of torment meet,
Dire clap of hands, distracted chase of feet,
While loud and dull ascends the weeping cry,
Surely in other thoughts contempt may die.
660 If the sad grave of human ignorance bear
One flower of hope – Oh pass and leave it there.
– The tall Sun, tiptoe on an Alpine spire,
Flings o'er the desert blood-red streams of fire.
At such an hour there are who love to stray,
And meet the gladdening pilgrims on their way.
   – Now with joy's tearful kiss each other greet,
Nor longer naked be your way-worn feet,
For ye have reached at last the happy shore,

Where the charmed worm of pain shall gnaw no
    more.
670 How gayly murmur and how sweetly taste
The fountains reared for you amid the waste!
Yes I will see you when ye first behold
Those turrets tipped by hope with morning gold,
And watch, while on your brows the cross ye make,
Round your pale eyes a wintry lustre wake.
– Without one hope her written griefs to blot,
Save in the land where all things are forgot,
My heart, alive to transports long unknown,
Half wishes your delusion were its own.
680   Last let us turn to where Chamouny shields,
Bosomed in gloomy woods, her golden fields,
Five streams of ice amid her cots descend,
And with wild flowers and blooming orchards blend,
A scene more fair than what the Grecian feigns
Of purple lights and ever vernal plains.
Here lawns and shades by breezy rivulets fanned,
Here all the Seasons revel hand in hand.
– Red stream the cottage lights; the landscape fades,
Erroneous wavering 'mid the twilight shades.
690 Alone ascends that mountain named of white,
That dallies with the Sun the summer night.
Six thousand years amid his lonely bounds
The voice of Ruin, day and night, resounds.
Where Horror-led his sea of ice assails,
Havoc and Chaos blast a thousand vales,
In waves, like two enormous serpents, wind
And drag their length of deluge train behind.
Between the pine's enormous boughs descried
Serene he towers, in deepest purple dyed;
700 Glad Day-light laughs upon his top of snow,
Glitter the stars above, and all is black below.
    At such an hour I heaved the human sigh,
When roared the sullen Arve in anger by,
That not for thee, delicious vale! unfold
Thy reddening orchards, and thy fields of gold;

That thou, the slave of slaves, art doomed to pine,
While no Italian arts their charms combine
To teach the skirt of thy dark cloud to shine;
For thy poor babes that, hurrying from the door,
710 With pale-blue hands, and eyes that fixed implore,
Dead muttering lips, and hair of hungry white,
Besiege the traveller whom they half affright.
– Yes, were it mine, the cottage meal to share
Forced from my native mountains bleak and bare;
O'er Anet's hopeless seas of marsh to stray,
Her shrill winds roaring round my lonely way;
To scent the sweets of Piedmont's breathing rose,
And orange gale that o'er Lugano blows;
In the wide range of many a weary round,
720 Still have my pilgrim feet unfailing found,
As despot courts their blaze of gems display,
Even by the secret cottage far away
The lily of domestic joy decay;
While Freedom's farthest hamlets blessings share,
Found still beneath her smile, and only there.
The casement shade more luscious woodbine binds,
And to the door a neater pathway winds,
At early morn the careful housewife, led
To cull her dinner from its garden bed,
730 Of weedless herbs a healthier prospect sees,
While hum with busier joy her happy bees;
In brighter rows her table wealth aspires,
And laugh with merrier blaze her evening fires;
Her infant's cheeks with fresher roses glow,
And wilder graces sport around their brow;
By clearer taper lit a cleanlier board
Receives at supper hour her tempting hoard;
The chamber hearth with fresher boughs is spread,
And whiter is the hospitable bed.
740 – And thou! fair favoured region! which my soul
Shall love, till Life has broke her golden bowl,
Till Death's cold touch her cistern-wheel assail,
And vain regret and vain desire shall fail;

Though now, where erst the grey-clad peasant strayed,
To break the quiet of the village shade
Gleam war's discordant habits through the trees,
And the red banners mock the sullen breeze;
'Though now no more thy maids their voices suit
To the low-warbled breath of twilight lute,
750 And heard, the pausing village hum between,
No solemn songstress lull the fading green,
Scared by the fife, and rumbling drum's alarms,
And the short thunder, and the flash of arms;
While, as Night bids the startling uproar die,
Sole sound, the sourd renews his mournful cry:
— Yet, hast thou found that Freedom spreads her power
Beyond the cottage hearth, the cottage door:
All nature smiles; and owns beneath her eyes
Her fields peculiar, and peculiar skies.
760 Yes, as I roamed where Loiret's waters glide
Through rustling aspins heard from side to side,
When from October clouds a milder light
Fell, where the blue flood rippled into white,
Methought from every cot the watchful bird
Crowed with ear-piercing power till then unheard;
Each clacking mill, that broke the murmuring streams,
Rocked the charmed thought in more delightful dreams;
Chasing those long long dreams the falling leaf
Awoke a fainter pang of moral grief;
770 The measured echo of the distant flail
Winded in sweeter cadence down the vale;
A more majestic tide the water rolled,
And glowed the sun-gilt groves in richer gold:
— Though Liberty shall soon, indignant, raise
Red on his hills his beacon's comet blaze;
Bid from on high his lonely cannon sound,
And on ten thousand hearths his shout rebound;
His larum-bell from village-tower to tower
Swing on the astounded ear its dull undying roar:
780 Yet, yet rejoice, though Pride's perverted ire
Rouse Hell's own aid, and wrap thy hills in fire.

Lo! from the innocuous flames, a lovely birth!
With its own Virtues springs another earth:
Nature, as in her prime, her virgin reign
Begins, and Love and Truth compose her train;
With pulseless hand, and fixed unwearied gaze,
Unbreathing Justice her still beam surveys:
No more, along thy vales and viny groves,
Whole hamlets disappearing as he moves,
790 With cheeks o'erspread by smiles of baleful glow,
On his pale horse shall fell Consumption go.
    Oh give, great God, to Freedom's waves to ride
Sublime o'er Conquest, Avarice, and Pride,
To break, the vales where Death with Famine scowers,
And dark Oppression builds her thick-ribbed towers;
Where Machination her fell soul resigns,
Fled panting to the centre of her mines;
Where Persecution decks with ghastly smiles
Her bed, his mountains mad Ambition piles;
800 Where Discord stalks dilating, every hour,
And crouching fearful at the feet of Power,
Like Lightnings eager for the almighty word,
Look up for sign of havoc, Fire, and Sword;
– Give them, beneath their breast while Gladness
        springs,
To brood the nations o'er with Nile-like wings;
And grant that every sceptred child of clay,
Who cries, presumptuous, 'here their tides shall stay,'
Swept in their anger from the affrighted shore,
With all his creatures sink – to rise no more.
810   Tonight, my friend, within this humble cot
Be the dead load of mortal ills forgot,
Renewing, when the rosy summits glow
At morn, our various journey, sad and slow.

Notes

References to letters and journals are by dates rather than by page numbers of particular editions. The 1850 version of *The Prelude* (J. C. Maxwell's edition, Penguin Books, 1971) is being cited unless otherwise noted. Brackets around a title indicate that the title was not given to the poem by Wordsworth.

A number of abbreviations are used. '*I. F. note*' indicates a note dictated by Wordsworth in 1843 to Isabella Fenwick. 'W.' at the end of a note designates that it is Wordsworth's. If no date is given in parentheses, the note was contained in his last edition (1849–50); otherwise the note was contained in the editions indicated by the dates. '*P.W.*' refers to Ernest de Selincourt's standard edition of Wordsworth's *Poetical Works*.

In the case of other complete editions of Wordsworth's poetry the editor's name alone is cited; unless otherwise indicated, the citation can be found in the notes to the poem in question in the last edition by that editor. The dates and exact title of the complete editions can be found in the bibliography. The term 'data' refers to information about composition, publication, and categorization that is contained in the first paragraph of each head-note.

Information concerning the classical citations is taken from the Loeb Classics edition unless otherwise indicated.

Notes

LINES WRITTEN AS A SCHOOL EXERCISE

Composed probably about (almost certainly not after) June 1785; first published in 1851. The version printed here follows D.C.MS.I.

Wordsworth's Autobiographical Memoranda: '. . . I was called upon, among other scholars, to write verses upon the completion of the second centenary from the foundation of the school [at Hawkshead] in 1585, by Archbishop Sandys. These verses were much admired, far more than they deserved, for they were but a tame imitation of Pope's versification, and a little in his style.' – Christopher Wordsworth's *Memoirs* (1851), I, 10.

3 *Science* learning.

7, 11 *she* her: MS.

13 *Academus' grove* scene of Plato's school.

16 '*Softened the terrors of her awful mien*' unidentified quotation; perhaps invented by Wordsworth.

20 *Hebe* handmaiden of the gods; associated with youthfulness.

56 *Edward's* Edward III, whose reign fell during the Hundred Years War.

65 *Sandys* See head-note above. A note to the MS points out that the name is pronounced as a monosyllable.

ANACREON

Composed probably about (almost certainly not after) 7 August 1786; first published in 1940.

An imitation, not a close translation, of Anacreon's *Ode* LXIX, *To a Painter*, which consists of eight lines.

1 *Reynolds* probably Sir Joshua Reynolds (1723–92), English portrait-painter.

8 *Apelles* a celebrated Hellenistic painter, whose most admired painting was a portrait of Aphrodite.

34 *Graces* three sister goddesses, bestowers of beauty.

THE DOG – AN IDYLLIUM

Composed perhaps late 1786; first published in 1940.

The Latin motto is made up of (1) a reworking of Catullus, *Verse* III, 1–2 ('Mourn for whoever is loved by the Graces') and (2) Horace, *Ode*, III, xiii, 13 ('you too one day will gain noble eminence').

1–6 See *Lycidas* 50–56.

6 *Winander's stream* Lake Windermere.

20–23 Compare *The Prelude* (1805), IV, 104–107.

SEPTIMIUS AND ACME

Translated probably between the beginning of 1786 and the end of 1791 (very likely during the earlier of these years); first published in 1940.

A fairly close translation of Catullus, *Verse* XLV.

TRANSLATION OF A CELEBRATED GREEK SONG

Translated probably 1786-91 (inclusive), probably around 1786; first published 13 February 1798 in the *Morning Post.*

A fairly close translation of the *Harmodiou Melos*, a famous Greek scolion or drinking song written by Callistratus and translated here from the version in four quatrains given by Athenaeus. The Greek and a prose translation are given in C. M. Bowra, *Greek Lyric Poetry* (1936), pp. 416-17. The historical background of the Greek poem is also given by Bowra, pp. 415-21.

TO MELPOMENE

Composed probably 1786 or 1787; first published in the present edition.

Melpomene was the Muse of Tragedy.

THE DEATH OF A STARLING

Composed perhaps 1786; the last eight lines were first published by Coleridge as *Morienti Superstes* in the *Morning Post*, 10 May 1798; the first eight lines were first published in Coleridge's *Literary Remains* (1836). For information regarding Coleridge's borrowing from Wordsworth, see J. W. Smyser, 'Coleridge's Use of Wordsworth's Juvenilia', *PMLA*, LXV (1950), pp. 419-26.

The motto verse consists of two quotations linked by the dash. The first is from Virgil's *Aeneid* I, 462, which in his own later translation (I, 633-34), Wordsworth renders as 'Tears for the frail estate of human kind are shed.' The second is the opening line to Catullus's *Verse* III, on the death of a sparrow – 'Mourn you Loves, and Venus' (see line 3). Wordsworth's poem is not a translation of Catullus's poem.

15 *thought* in North-country dialect rhymed with 'remote'.

LESBIA

Translated perhaps 1786; first published by Coleridge in the *Morning Post*, 11 April 1798.

A reasonably close translation of Catullus's *Verse* V.

5 *posting to the main* hastening to set in the sea.

BEAUTY AND MOONLIGHT

Composed perhaps 1786; first published in highly altered form by Coleridge (as *Lewti*) in the *Morning Post* 13 April 1798; first published in its present form in 1940.

SONNET ON SEEING MISS HELEN MARIA WILLIAMS WEEP AT A TALE OF DISTRESS

Composed probably early 1787 (before about March); first published anonymously in the *European Magazine*, XL (March 1787), p. 202.

This is the first poem published by Wordsworth, but it was never collected by him.

Helen Maria Williams (1762–1827) was a minor poetess of the period who lived in Paris for many years, where Wordsworth apparently first met her in 1820 (Moorman, *Life* II, p. 387). The signature ' Axiologus) is a Greek compound for 'Words-Worth'. F. W. Bateson nevertheless has questioned the auth nticity of the attribution of this sonnet to Wordsworth (*Wordsworth: A Reinterpretation*, p. 82n). See also Mark Reed, *Wordsworth, The Chronology of the Early Years*, p. 71n.

SONNET WRITTEN BY MR — IMMEDIATELY AFTER THE DEATH OF HIS WIFE

Composed probably about 2 March 1787 (almost certainly not after); first published in 1940.

The widower remains unidentified, if indeed Wordsworth was referring in the title to a real person.

[A BALLAD]

Composed probably about (almost certainly not after) 23 and 24 March 1787; first published in 1940.

6 *The fairest maid* recently identified as Mary Rigge of Colthouse; see T. W. Thompson, *Wordsworth's Hawkshead* (1970), pp. 65–8, and the note to line 909 of *Peter Bell* (p. 952, be.ow).

21 *Reflected* modifies 'mind' (line 22).

34 *waft* a wraith; a supernatural appearance of one whose death is imminent.

THE VALE OF ESTHWAITE

Composed probably in the spring and summer 1787, perhaps some parts as early as 1786 and some as late as early 1788; first published in 1940.

Some phrases and short passages were used later in *An Evening Walk*. The poem may originally have been longer: ' 1000' was written in the margin by line 241 in one MS.

There are three manuscripts extant of the poem, one long version (D.C. MS. 3) with a number of pages missing, and two sets of passages. In *PW*, I, 368, de Selincourt implies that where the long version is missing he places passages from the other two manuscripts, but this occurs only once (lines 137–212), although lines 388–406 were added by him to the text from the back of the long manuscript. The rest of de Selincourt's version is fitted together from overlapping passages in the three manuscripts. I have decided to give the text as in *P W* rather than dabble in further speculation regarding the two sections mentioned above. I have also added one six-line passage (lines 163–8) overlooked in one manuscript and a couplet (lines 443–4) omitted from transcription of another.

73 *gingling* obsolete form of 'jingling'.

80 *Philomela's* a nightingale.

97–8 Repeated (with changes) in *An Evening Walk*, 214–15. See the note to that passage.

183 unidentified quotation.

225 *joined* rhymes with 'mind'.

341 *eugh* obsolete form of 'yew'.

380 *Edmund* probably King Edmund the Elder, who conquered Cumbria in 946 and blinded the two sons of Dunmail.

425–36 Compare *The Prelude* (1805), XI, 345–89.

477 *Friend* The Rev. John Fleming (baptized 14 May 1768 – died 11 January 1835) of Rayrigg, Windermere; see line 553.

506 *'hang a tale'* Compare *Othello* III, i, 9, and elsewhere in Shakespeare's plays.

519 *Phoebus* the sun.

519–24 An early version of lines 9–14 of *Extract from the Conclusion of a Poem.*

EXTRACT FROM THE CONCLUSION OF A POEM

Composed probably spring or summer 1787, and early 1788, with some composition as early as 1786; first published in 1815 (the earliest poem to be included by Wordsworth in his collected poems); from 1815 included among 'Poems Written in Youth'.

I. F. note: 'Hawkshead. The beautiful image with which this poem concludes, suggested itself to me while I was resting in a boat along with my companions under the shade of a magnificent row of Sycamores, which then extended their branches from the shore of the promontory upon which stands the ancient, and at that time the more picturesque, Hall of Coniston, the seat of the Le Flemings from very early times.' See *The Prelude*, VIII, 458–75.

'WHAT IS IT THAT TELLS MY SOUL THE SUN IS SETTING'

Composed perhaps about 23 October 1787; first published in 1974.

ON THE DEATH OF AN UNFORTUNATE LADY

Composed probably 1787; first published in the present edition.

A WINTER'S EVENING

Composed probably 1787; first published in the present edition.

DIRGE SUNG BY A MINSTREL

Composed in late 1787 and January 1788 (and possibly shortly after); first published in 1940. A number of additional stanzas referring to the death of a boy can be found in *PW*, I, 268–9.

9–11 Compare Chatterton's *Aella* (1777), 965–7.

[FRAGMENTS ON A HEROIC THEME]

Composed probably 1787 or 1788, but possibly as early as 1784 (probably after 20 September) and 1785; first published in Z. S. Fink, *The Early Wordsworthian Milieu* (1958). For variants, see Fink.

6–9 Compare *Paradise Lost* IV, 985–9: 'On the other side *Satan* alarmed / Collecting all his might dilated stood, / Like *Teneriff* or *Atlas* unremoved: / His stature reached the Sky, and on his Crest / Sat horror plumed'.

10–14 See *The Prelude IV*, 85–92 and Fink, pp. 6–7.

39 *Elfrida* name of the heroine of a poem with a similar heroic theme, *Elfrida* (1752), by William Mason.

61 *Turrita nubes* deep-embattled cloud. See *An Evening Walk* 39 and note.

[FRAGMENT OF AN INTENDED POEM ON MILTON]

Composed perhaps about early 1788; first published in 1949.

[ORPHEUS AND EURYDICE]

Translated probably early 1788 (perhaps by late spring); first published in 1940.

A relatively close translation of Virgil's *Georgics* IV, 464–77, 485–527.

7 *griesly* obsolete form of 'grisly'.

12 *Erebus* the dark region under the earth through which the Shades pass into Hades.

43 *Strymon's* a Macedonian river.

62 *Tanais* a river often considered in classical times the boundary between Europe and Asia and by some thought to have its source in the Rhipaean mountains, which are situated somewhere to the north.

65 *plain* mourn.

68 *Ciconian* Thracian.

74 *Oeagrian Hebrus* a Thessalian river.

[IN PART FROM MOSCHUS'S LAMENT FOR BION]

Composed probably about summer and autumn 1788, or perhaps in 1789–90; first published in 1940.

The first eight lines are a comparatively close translation (with flowers replacing herbs) of Moschus's *Lament for Bion* 99–104.

[THE HORSE]

Translated probably late summer or autumn 1788 (possibly slightly later); first published in 1940.

A fairly close translation of Virgil's *Georgics* III, 75–81 83–94.

17 *Cyllarus* the horse of Castor, whose brother was Pollux (line 18).

23 *Pelion* mountain range in Thessaly.

ODE TO APOLLO

Translated probably late summer or autumn 1788, or perhaps in 1789–90; first published in 1940.

A fairly faithful translation of Horace's *Ode* I, xxxi.

5 *Calabria's* the peninsula that forms south-west Italy.

7 *Liris'* a river in central Italy.

11 *Calenian* a region in south-west Italy noted for its wines.

19 *Latona's honied boy* Apollo.

AN EVENING WALK

Composed 1788–9, probably mostly later 1788 and 1789, especially the summer of 1789; first published in 1793 (29 January); from 1815 included among 'Poems Written in Youth'. The version printed here is the heavily revised final form published in 1849–50.

I. F. note: 'The young Lady to whom this was addressed was my Sister. It was composed at school, and during my two first College vacations. There is not an image in it which I have not observed; and now, in my seventy-third year, I recollect the time and place where most of them were noticed. . . . I will conclude my notice of this poem by observing that the plan of it has not been confined to a particular walk or an individual place; – a proof (of which I was unconscious at the time) of my unwillingness to submit the poetic spirit to the chains of fact and real circumstance. The country is idealized rather than described in any one of its local aspects.'

This poem contains many borrowings and echoes of previous poets as noted below, but the first published version of 1793 had many more, which were subsequently deleted.

4 *Lodore* a waterfall.

9 *Winander* Windermere Lake. 'These lines are applicable only to the middle part of that lake.' – W.

11 *endear* enhance the value of.

20 'In the beginning of winter these mountains are frequented by woodcocks, which in dark nights retire into the woods.' – W.

39 *deep-embattled clouds* Charlotte Smith, *Written September, 1791* 3; see also James Beattie, *The Minstrel* (1771–4), II, xii.

48 *still-twinkling* twinkling continually. See *The Prelude* (1805), I, 481.

49 *intake* 'The word *intake* is local, and signifies a mountain-inclosure.' – W.

53 *huddling rill* Milton's *Comus* 495: 'huddling brook'.

54 *ghyll* 'Ghyll is also, I believe, a term confined to this country: ghyll and dingle have the same meaning.' – W. 'A short and, for the most part, a steep, narrow valley, with a stream running through it.' – W. (note to *The Idle Shepherd Boys*).

57–69 'The reader, who has made the tour of this country, will recognize, in this description, the features which characterize the lower waterfall in the grounds of Rydal.' – W.

66–67 Compare *As You Like It* II, i, 31–32: 'Under an oak tree whose antique root peeps out / Upon the brook that brawls along this wood.'

72–73 An allusion to Horace's 'O fons Bandusiae' (*Odes* III, 13).

Wordsworth's *Blandusia* is a variant form of the name. The next four lines contain detailed allusions to Horace's Ode.

112 *involved* enveloped.

133 *'green rings'* '"Vivid rings of green." Greenwood's *Poem on Shooting*.' – W. William Greenwood, *A Poem Written During a Shooting Excursion on the Moors* (1787), p. 18.

135 '"Down the rough slope the pond'rous waggon rings." BEATTIE.' – W. (1793). *The Minstrel* (1771–4), I, xxxix.

141 This line echoes *Paradise Lost* II, 477. N. C. Smith's note to this line suggests that *blasted* is italicized presumably because it was an unfamiliar usage at the time.

146 *Sweetly ferocious* '"Dolcemente feroce." – Tasso. In this description of the cock, I remembered a spirited one of the same animal in l'Agriculture, ou Les Georgiques Françoises of M. Roussuet.' – W. Tasso's *Gerusalemme Liberata* I, lviii.

148 *nervous* sinewy, strong.

163 *gulf profound Paradise Lost* II, 592.

174 *aspire* rise.

175 *'prospect all on fire'* Moses Browne, *Sunday Thoughts* (1752), III, 143.

182–5 'I was an eye-witness of this for the first time while crossing the Pass of Dunmail Raise.' – *I. F. note*.

190–91 'From Thomson.' – W. *The Seasons* (1730), *Summer* 1627–9: '. . . He dips his orb; / Now half-immers'd; and now, a golden curve, / Gives one bright glance, then total disappears.'

196–207 'See a description of an appearance of this kind in Clark's "Survey of the Lakes", accompanied by vouchers of its veracity, that may amuse the reader.' – W. James Clarke, *Survey of the Lakes* (1787), p. 55.

214–15 'This is feebly and imperfectly expressed, but I recollect distinctly the very spot where this first struck me. It was in the way between Hawkshead and Ambleside, and gave me extreme pleasure. The moment was important in my poetical history; for I date from it my consciousness of the infinite variety of natural appearances which had been unnoticed by the poets of any age or country, so far as I was acquainted with them; and I made a resolution to supply, in some degree, the deficiency. I could not have been at that time above fourteen years of age.' – *I. F. note*.

218-31 'The description of the swans . . . was taken from the daily opportunities I had of observing their habits, not as confined to the gentleman's park, but in a state of nature. There were two pairs of them that divided the lake of Esthwaite and its in-and-out flowing streams between them, never trespassing a single yard upon each other's separate domain. They were of the old magnificent species, bearing in beauty and majesty about the same relation to the Thames swan which that does to the goose.' – *I. F. note.*

231 'This is a fact of which I have been an eyewitness.' – W. (1793).

233 *holms* level stretches of ground by a river.

237 *'by distance made more sweet'* Collins's *Ode to Passions* (1747) 60.

250-78 'These verses relate the catastrophe of a poor woman who was found dead on Stanemoor two years ago with two children whom she had in vain attempted to protect from the storm in the manner described.' – W. (1794).

270 *like a torrent roars* compare Pope's *Essay on Criticism* 369.

279 *Sweet are the sounds* compare Goldsmith's *Deserted Village* (1770) 113.

280 *folding star* Collins's *Ode to Evening* (1747) 21.

281 *dabbles* moves in shallow water.

291 'Alluding to this passage of Spenser – "Her angel's face / As the great eye of heaven shined bright, / And made a sunshine in that [the] shady place."' – W. (1793). *The Faerie Queene* I, iii, 4.

306 Compare *The Tempest* IV, i, 155-56: 'Like this insubstantial pageant faded, / Leave not a rack behind'.

307 *overcome* to spread over, cover.

321 *tender* delicate in texture.

374 Compare Beattie's *The Minstrel* (1771-4), I, xxxix: 'Thro' rustling corn the hare astonish'd springs'.

WRITTEN IN VERY EARLY YOUTH

Composed perhaps between about late 1788 and the end of 1791, but possibly up to early 1802; first published in the *Morning Post*, 13 February 1802. From 1807 to 1843 included among 'Miscellaneous Sonnets', after that among 'Poems Written in Youth'.

8 *Home-felt* Milton's *Comus* 262.

'WHEN SLOW FROM PENSIVE TWILIGHT'S LATEST GLEAMS'

Composed perhaps between approximately late 1788 and the end of 1791 (but possibly later); first published in the present edition.

2 quotation unidentified.

14 See *The Vale of Esthwaite* 129-30.

SONNET ('If grief dismiss me not')

Probably translated between about late 1788 and the end of 1791; first published in the *Morning Post*, 13 February 1798.

Translated from Petrarch's 'Se la mia vita d'all aspro tormento'.

3–6 Compare *Descriptive Sketches, 1793*, 150–55:
> Those stedfast eyes, that beating breasts inspire
> To throw the 'sultry ray' of young Desire;
> Those lips, whose tides of fragrance come, and go,
> Accordant to the cheek's unquiet glow;
> Those shadowy breasts in love's soft light array'd,
> And rising, by the moon of passion sway'd.

5, 8   See *Twelfth Night* II, iv, 110–11: 'But let concealment, like a worm i' the bud, / Feed on her damask cheek'.

LINES WRITTEN WHILE SAILING IN A BOAT AT EVENING

Composed in earliest version possibly between about late 1788 and the end of 1791, in final version probably between 29 March 1797 and 30 May 1798; first published in 1798. From 1815 to 1843 included among 'Poems Proceeding from Sentiment and Reflection', after that among 'Poems Written in Youth'.

I. F. note: 'The title is scarcely correct. It was during a solitary walk on the banks of the Cam that I was first struck with this appearance, and applied it to my own feelings in the manner here expressed, changing the scene to the Thames, near Windsor. This, and the three stanzas of ... *Remembrance of Collins*, formed one piece: but upon the recommendation of Coleridge, the three last stanzas were separated from the other.'

7   *faithless*   delusive.

REMEMBRANCE OF COLLINS

Originally part of the previous poem, which was divided in 1800; for history of composition and publication, see the head-note to the previous poem.

Richmond was the home of James Thomson and the scene of the funeral in William Collins's *Ode on the Death of Thomson* (1749), to which Wordsworth referred in a note in the 1798 version of the poem.

1   Compare Wordsworth's *After-thought* ('*I thought of Thee*') 5: 'Still glides the Stream, and shall for ever glide'.

13   *Poet*   William Collins.

14   *later ditty*   *Ode on the Death of Thomson*.

18   Compare *Ode on the Death of Thomson* (stanza IV):
> Remembrance oft shall haunt the shore
> When Thames in summer wreaths is drest,
> And oft suspend the dashing oar,
> To bid his gentle spirit rest.

By italicizing *him* in line 18, Wordsworth indicates that he is referring to Collins, using Collins's own words.

SEPTIMI GADES

Composed perhaps late 1790 or shortly after and probably finished by late the following year; first published in 1940.

The title is the opening to Horace, *Ode* II, vi, an ode on a similar theme of the retirement of a man with his friend.

11 See *Book of Ruth*, 1:16.

25 *heartless* dejected.

49 *Phoebus* the sun.

57-71 Compare *Imitation of Anacreon* 35-47 (above).

DESCRIPTIVE SKETCHES

Some composition possibly in late 1790 and 1791, but composed for the most part probably between 6 December 1791 and perhaps late November or early December 1792 (especially after the middle of May 1792); first published 29 January 1793. In the 1815 edition of his *Poems*, Wordsworth included excerpts from the poem; it was reprinted in 1820 with a number of revisions; the poem appeared in more or less final form in 1836. The revisions mainly took the form of excising conventional diction and melancholy. From 1815 to 1832 included among 'Juvenile Pieces', in 1836 among 'Descriptive Sketches', and returned in 1845 (and thereafter) to the original category. The version printed here is from the 1849-50 edition. For the 1793 version, see Appendix B.

I. F. note : 'Much the greatest part of this poem was composed during my walks upon the banks of the Loire in the years 1791, 1792.' The poem was dedicated 'to the Rev. Robert Jones', with whom Wordsworth visited the region described in the poem.

21 *frowning* presenting a gloomy aspect.

22 Compare *Comus* 898-9: 'The Cowslip's Velvet head, / That bends not as I tread'.

24 *'and calls it luxury'* Addison's *Cato* (1713) I, iv, 71: 'Blesses his stars, and think'st it luxury'.

32 *Memnon's lyre* 'The lyre of Memnon is reported to have emitted melancholy or cheerful tones, as it was touched by the sun's evening or morning rays.' – W.

53 Compare *The Prelude* VI, 414-88.

55 *sober Reason* Samuel Rogers's *Pleasures of Memory* (1792) II, 433.

61 *thundering tube* Compare Pope's *Windsor Forest* 129-30: 'He lifts the Tube, and levels with his Eye; / Straight a short Thunder breaks the frozen Sky'.

69 *viewless* invisible (a word often later expunged by Wordsworth).

70 *The Cross, by angels planted* 'Alluding to crosses seen on the tops of the spiry rocks of Chartreuse, which have every appearance of being inaccessible.' – W.

71 *'parting Genius'* Milton's *On the Morning of Christ's Nativity* 186.

72 *Life and Death* 'Names of rivers of the Chartreuse.' – W.

75 *Vallombre* 'Name of one of the valleys of the Chartreuse.' – W.

99-100 Compare Dyer's *Grongar Hill* (1727) 51-2: 'Rushing from the woods the spires / Seem from hence ascending fires'.

157 *her waters* 'The river along whose banks you descend in crossing the Alps by the Simplon Pass.' – W.

161 *undistinguished* indistinct.

184 *bridge* 'Most of the bridges among the Alps are of wood, and covered: these bridges have a heavy appearance, and rather injure the effect of the scenery in some places.' – W.

200 *cells* 'The Catholic religion prevails here: these cells are, as is well known, very common in the Catholic countries, planted, like the Roman tombs, along the roadside.' – W.

202 *death-cross* 'Crosses, commemorative of the deaths of travellers, by the fall of snow and other accidents, are very common along this dreadful road.' – W.

214 *wood-cottages* 'The houses in the more retired Swiss valleys are all built of wood.' – W.

222 '... The description of the valley filled with mist, beginning – "In solemn shapes", was taken from that beautiful region of which the principal features are Lungarn and Sarnen. Nothing that I ever saw in nature left a more delightful impression on my mind than that which I have attempted, alas, how feebly! to convey to others in these lines. These two lakes have always interested me especially, from bearing, in their size and other features, a resemblance to those of the North of England.' – *I. F. note.*

269 *Spartan fife* Collins's *Ode to Liberty* (1747) 1.

286 *Tell* William Tell (died ca. 1350), the Swiss patriot.

293 *Canadian hills* John Langhorne's *Country Justice* (1774), I, 163.

299 *Wolfe's* General James Wolfe (1727-1759), who died taking Quebec ('the Canadian hills').

300 *Bayard's* Seigneur de Bayard (1473?-1524), a French hero killed in Italy.

301 *Sidney* Sir Philip Sidney, who was killed in battle on Zutphen's plain.

302 *'faint huzzas'* Burns's *The Author's Earnest Cry and Prayer* (1786) XXIX. The phrase was connected to Dundee in Gilpin's *Observations* (1789), I, 137. Dundee is John Graham, Viscount Dundee (1649?-1689), Jacobite leader who died in battle at Killiecrankie.

306 *abrupt* steep.

307 'For most of the images in the next sixteen verses, I am indebted to M. Raymond's interesting observations, annexed to his translation of Coxe's Tour in Switzerland.' – W.

339 *pensive Underwalden's* 'The people of this Canton are supposed to be of a more melancholy disposition than the other inhabitants of the Alps; this, if true, may proceed from their living more secluded.' – W.

343 Compare *Paradise Lost* V, 547-8: 'Cherubic Songs by night from neighbouring Hills / Aereal Music send'.

344 *answering every close* Compare Milton's *On the Morning of Christ's Nativity*, 99-100: 'The Air such pleasure loth to lose, / With thousand echoes still prolongs each heavenly close'.

345 *Rich steam of sweetest perfume* Compare *Comus* 556: 'Rose like a stream of rich distilled Perfumes'.

348 *chalets* 'This picture is from the middle region of the Alps. *Chalets* are summer huts for the Swiss herdsmen.' – W.

355 Compare *Psalms*, 42:7: 'Deep calleth unto deep . . .'

357 Compare Gray's *Elegy* 8: 'And drowsy tinklings lull the distant folds'.

359 *sugh* 'A Scotch word expressive of the sound of the wind through the trees.' – W.

367 *the southern breeze* 'This wind, which announces the spring to the Swiss, is called in their language FOEN; and is according to M. Raymond the Syroco of the Italians.' – W. (1793).

387 *times of yore* 'This tradition of the golden age of the Alps, as M. Raymond observes, is highly interesting, interesting not less to the philosopher than to the poet . . .' – W. (1793).

408–22 Partly influenced by Raymond and partly by Beattie's *Minstrel* (1771–4), I, xxi (see *PW*, I, 328). See also *The Prelude* XIV, 40–62.

448 *'the blessings he enjoys to guard'* Compare Smollett's *To Leven Water* (1771), 28.

452 *few in arms* 'Alluding to several battles which the Swiss in very small numbers have gained over their oppressors, the House of Austria; and, in particular, to one fought at Naeffels near Glarus, where three hundred and thirty men are said to have defeated an army of between fifteen and twenty thousand Austrians . . .'. – W.

463 *peal* loud outburst of sound.

472 'As Schreck-Horn, the pike of terror; Wetter-Horn, the pike of storms, etc., etc.' – W.

475 *an angel's smile all rosy red* *Paradise Lost* VIII, 618–19: 'To whom the angel with a smile that glow'd / Celestial rosy red, Love's proper hue'.

497 *hoped* looked forward to.

520 *Batavia's* Holland.

527 'The well-known effect of the famous air, called in French Ranz des Vaches, upon the Swiss troops.' – W.

Also, compare *Genesis* 42:38: 'Then shall ye bring down my gray hairs with sorrow to the grave'.

532 *'Optima quaeque dies, etc.'* – W. (1793). Virgil's *Georgics* III, 66–8: 'Life's fairest days are always the first to flee from unhappy mortals. Diseases and sad old age come on, and work; and stern death takes them off unseasonably.'

534 *installed* filled with.

538 *confide* to put trust in.

546 *Ensiedlen's wretched fane* 'This shrine is resorted to, from a hope of relief, by multitudes, from every corner of the Catholic world, labouring under mental or bodily afflictions.' – W.

550 Compare Wordsworth's *Composed in One of the Catholic Cantons* (Vol. II, p. 416) for sentiment, especially the first stanza.

560 *The fountains* 'Rude fountains built and covered with sheds for the accommodation of the Pilgrims, in their ascent of the mountain.' – W.

613 *fluctuate* wave.

619 *Sourd* 'An insect so called, which emits a short, melancholy cry, heard at the close of the summer evenings, on the banks of the Loire.' – W.

623 *peculiar* having a property exclusively its own.

631 Compare Milton's *Areopagitica*: 'There be delights, there be recreations and jolly pastimes that will fetch the day about from sun to sun, and rock the tedious year as in a delightful dream.'

636 *course* 'The duties upon many parts of the French rivers were so exorbitant, that the poorer people, deprived of the benefit of water carriage, were obliged to transport their goods by land.' – W.

658 Compare Gray's *The Alliance of Education and Government* (1748), 101, 103: 'Where Nile . . . broods o'er Egypt with his wat'ry wings.'

664 Compare John Langhorne's *Owen of Carron* (1778), XXIX: 'She saw – and sunk to rise no more.'

'SWEET WAS THE WALK'

Composed probably between June 1789 and April 1792, probably shortly before the latter date; first published in 1889.

9 *idle*] *idol*: MS. letter.

THE BIRTH OF LOVE

Translated probably between 1792 and 23 May 1794; first published in the *Morning Chronicle*, 21 August 1795.

A fairly close translation of Vicomte de Ségur's *L'Education de l'Amour* (1792).

2 *Cythera's* Venus, mother of Eros, or Love (line 1).

15 *joined* rhymes with 'behind'.

26–7 Compare Thomas Gray's *Progress of Poetry* (1757) 87–8: 'The dauntless Child / Stretched forth his little arms, and smiled.'

[AT THE ISLE OF WIGHT]

Composed probably summer 1793 (between perhaps late June, more likely early July, and late July or early August); first published in 1940.

'IN VAIN DID TIME AND NATURE TOIL TO THROW'

Composed probably between late July and September 1793; first published in the present edition.

The last ten lines of this sonnet have been substantially lost: part of the manuscript page was torn out.

'THE WESTERN CLOUDS A DEEPENING GLOOM DISPLAY'

Composed probably between late July and September 1793; first published in the present edition.

GUILT AND SORROW

In part composed in 1791, but probably written mainly between late July and September 1793, and first version almost certainly completed by 23 May 1794 (some further work on the poem probably 1795, 1799–1800); first published in this form in 1842, but 30 stanzas (XXII–XXXIV and XXXVII–L) were published in 1798 as *The Female Vagrant*. From 1845 included among 'Poems Written in Youth'. For a study of the poem, see Enid Welsford, *Salisbury Plain* (Blackwell, 1966). For the most recent standard edition of the various versions, see Stephen Gill, ed., *The Salisbury Plain Poems of William Wordsworth*, Cornell University Press, 1975.

In a letter to Francis Wrangham (20 November 1795) Wordsworth remarked about the purpose of the poem: 'Its object is partly to expose the vices of the penal law and the calamities of war as they affect individuals.' The poem underwent many subsequent revisions aimed both at improving the poem artistically and at softening the social criticism.

As usual with Wordsworth's verse much of the poem was drawn from life. In the *I. F. note*, he remarks about the female vagrant: 'All that relates to her sufferings as a sailor's wife in America, and her condition of mind during her voyage home, were faithfully taken from the report made to me of her own case by a friend who had been subjected to the same trials and affected in the same way.' At the end of the 'Advertisement', Wordsworth warns: '. . . to obviate some distraction in the minds of those who are well acquainted with Salisbury Plain, it may be proper to say that, of the features described as belonging to it, one or two are taken from other desolate parts of England.'

Some of Wordsworth's artistic considerations are present in the continuation of the *I. F. note*: 'Mr Coleridge, when I first became acquainted with him, was so much impressed with this poem, that it would have encouraged me to publish the whole as it then stood; but the mariner's fate appeared to me so tragical as to require a treatment more subdued and yet more strictly applicable in expression than I had at first given to it. This fault was corrected nearly fifty years afterwards, when I determined to publish the whole. It may be worthwhile to remark, that, though the incidents of this attempt do only in a small degree produce each other, and it deviates accordingly from the general rule by which narrative pieces ought to be governed, it is not therefore wanting in continuous hold upon the mind, or in unity, which is effected by the identity of moral interest that places the two personages upon the same footing in the reader's sympathies. My rambles over many parts of Salisbury Plain put me . . . upon writing this poem, and left on my mind imaginative impressions the force of which I have felt to this day.'

81 'From a short MS. poem read to me when an undergraduate by my

school-fellow and friend, Charles Farish, long since deceased. The verses were by a brother of his, a man of promising genius, who died young.' – W. John Bernard Farish (1754–1778 ?), *The Heath*, printed in T. W. Thompson's *Wordsworth's Hawkshead* (1970), pp. 319–20.

107-8 Compare *An Evening Walk* 248–9.

150 *Spital* a shelter for travellers.

275 *strain* to clasp tightly.

297 *devoted* doomed.

371 *hopeless* despairing.

401 *amazed* bewildered.

493 *griding* piercing (a word with a long literary history; see, for example, *Paradise Lost* VI, 329).

INSCRIPTION FOR A SEAT BY THE PATHWAY SIDE

Composed probably between early April and almost certainly 23 May 1794; first published in 1940.

[TRANSLATION OF HORACE'S *ODE* III, xiii]

Translated probably between early April and late 1794; first published in 1940 (*PW*, I, 10n); originally a note to *An Evening Walk* (1794) 72–85.

A fairly close translation of Horace.

[IMITATION OF JUVENAL – SATIRE VIII]

Pieced together from three fragments pobably written between 15 August 1795 and April 1796; first published in 1940.

Parts of an imitation of Juvenal's *Satire* VIII, which was to have been a collaborative effort of Wordsworth and Francis Wrangham (1769–1842). The first twenty-eight lines have no parallel in Juvenal; the next 134 lines (29–162) parallel passages in Juvenal's *Satire* VIII, 163–275; and the last eleven lines correspond loosely to lines 85–90 and the conclusion of Juvenal's poem.

6 *hides the diminished head* cf. *Paradise Lost* IV, 35.

9-10 *majesty ... grace* puns on 'His Majesty' and 'His Grace'. These two lines were contributed by Robert Southey and were considered by Wordsworth 'the two best' of the first 28 lines.

12 *Eden's* William Eden (1744–1814), 1st Lord Auckland, the ambassador to the Hague 1791–93.

13 *Lonsdale's* Sir James Lowther, Earl of Lonsdale (1736–1802), a notable tyrant of the period, who was responsible for withholding from the Wordsworth children their inheritance. The reference to 'honour' is a pun on 'The Honourable', a title held by M.P.s – some of whom were controlled by Lord Lonsdale.

16 *Pharaoh-plague* pun on Faro, a widely prevalent form of gambling.

17-18 *reverent, Worship* puns on 'His Reverence' and 'His Worship'.

21 *Thurlow* Edward Thurlow (1731–1806), 1st Baron Thurlow. Apis was the sacred bull of Egypt.

23 *Charlotte's* The Queen, wife of George III.

26 *Anubis* Egyptian dog-god.

28 *Grenville* William Wyndham, Baron Grenville (1759–1834).

37 *York* Frederick, Duke of York (1763–1827), led a disastrous campaign in Holland in 1794, during which the English were beaten at Dunkirk. Part of the reason for the defeat was the separation of the English (Guards) and Austrians (Uhlans, or lancers); another reason is thought to have been the dissipation of Frederick, alluded to in lines 39–40. Partridge and Moore were astrologers and almanac makers earlier in the century.

45 *Percy* Hugh Percy (1742–1817).

51 *Woolwich docks* imprisonment in a dismantled ship.

56 *gartered grace* Percy was made Knight of the Garter in 1788.

58 *worse remains behind* *Hamlet* III, iv, 179.

59-60 Probably an allusion to George Hobart, Third Earl of Buckingham-shire (1732–1804), and his wife, notorious for gaming and interested in amateur theatricals.

70 *Scrub* a character in Farquhar's *The Beaux' Stratagem*.

72 *Buffo's* a character in Pope's *Epistle to Dr Arbuthnot*, where the name is spelt 'Bufo'.

74 *Smithfield* location of Bartholomew Fair, where farces were performed.

85 *westren bridge* Westminster Bridge.

91 *St. Stephen's* a chapel in the Palace of Westminster.

95 *Norfolk* the Dukes of Norfolk have the hereditary right to grant armorial bearings.

102 *More or Henry* Sir Thomas More was beheaded by Henry VIII.

104 *a Raleigh and a James* Sir Walter Raleigh was executed by James I.

105 *Buchanan* tutor of James I.

114 *Legions of devils* a reference to the *Demonology* (1597) of James I.

116 *Pym's, Hampden's* M.P.s who resisted royal abuses.

117 *scoundrels* this word is blank in both D.C. MS. 11 and Wordsworth's letter to Wrangham (25 February 1797).

119 *The nation's hope* the Prince of Wales.

129 *Henry's tomb* the tomb of Henry V, with saddle, shield, and helmet depicted.

134 *Edward* Edward the Black Prince (1330–1376), whose tomb is decorated with his armour.

138 *Plantagenet* Edward III.

144 *self-devoted* self-doomed.

154 *Franklin* Benjamin Franklin (1706–90) was apprenticed to a printer as a youth.

156 *The bastard* William the Conqueror.

166 [*Wilston*?], *Wright* probably two provisioners of the period.

168 *Graham's* James Graham (1745–94), a well-known quack who built a 'Temple of Health' at the Adelphi.

'THE HOUR-BELL SOUNDS, AND I MUST GO'

Translated probably early 1796 (after 2 January); first published 10 May 1798 in the *Morning Post*.

This poem is a fairly close translation of a French poem in three stanzas, supposedly written by two French prisoners and printed (and translated) by Helen Maria Williams in *Letters Containing a Sketch of the Politics of France* (1795), pp. 24–6.

In the *Morning Post*, the poem was signed 'Mortimer' (originally the name of the hero of *The Borderers*) and was prefixed by the following note: 'The two following Verses from the French, never before published, were written by a French Prisoner, as he was preparing to go to the Guillotine.' This poem was originally thought to be Coleridge's (see his *Literary Remains*, 1836).

'THE ROAD EXTENDED O'ER A HEATH'

Composed perhaps early 1796, but more probably between 21 March and early October (very likely begun before late May); first published in 1940. A blank-verse version of a fragment of a tale possibly intended for *The Female Vagrant*; see the next poem for a version in Spenserian stanzas.

29 *viewless* invisible.

'NO SPADE FOR LEAGUES HAD WON A ROOD OF EARTH'

For details of composition and publication, see the previous note. A version of the same fragment in irregular Spenserian stanzas.

37 *blame* chide.

37–45 stanza deleted in MS.

THE CONVICT

Composed 1796, perhaps early, but more probably between 21 March and early October; first published in the *Morning Post*, 14 December 1797 – signed 'Mortimer', the original name of the hero of *The Borderers*; also published in *Lyrical Ballads* (1798 only).

41–2 Compare Wordsworth's *Lament of Mary Queen of Scots* 66–7.

51–2 Note the Godwinian preference for transportation of criminals.

[FRAGMENT OF A 'GOTHIC' TALE]

The bulk composed perhaps early 1796, but more probably between 21 March and early October 1796 (with one description as early as summer 1788); first published in 1940.

This fragment was pieced together (especially near the beginning) by Ernest de Selincourt from scattered bits and pieces of drafts, cancellations, and corrections.

Many parallels and echoes exist between this *Fragment* and Wordsworth's *The Borderers*; see *PW*, I, 351.

22 *dim-discovered*   See Collins's *Ode to Evening* (1747) 37 and *The Manners* (1747) 2.
38 *cutlass*   mistake for *kerchief*? (see line 169).
67 *the unimaginable touch of time*   See Wordsworth's *Mutability* 14.
69-70 *towers that stately stood ... though shattered*   an echo of *Paradise Lost* I, 613-14.
205 *devoted* doomed.
209 *uncouth* strange, unknown.

ADDRESS TO THE OCEAN

Composed probably between mid-April and (certainly) 21 November 1796; first published in the *Weekly Entertainer*, 21 November 1796. This poem is an imitation of Ossian parallel to one written by Coleridge. See S. M. Parrish, *The Art of the Lyrical Ballads*, 1973, pp. 63-4.
1 Compare Coleridge's *The Complaint of Ninathoma* 1: 'How long will ye round me be swelling'. Wordsworth's borrowing was acknowledged in a note to the first published version.

ARGUMENT FOR SUICIDE

Composed probably between the second half of 1796 and early 1797 (possibly as late as summer); first published in 1940.

THE BORDERERS

Composed probably between the second half (probably late) 1796 and late February 1797 with some composition possible as late as summer 1797; first published in 1842; included from 1845 among 'Poems Written in Youth'.
  Wordsworth had a good deal to say about this, his only drama. *I. F. note*:

> Had it been the work of a later period of life, it would have been different in some respects from what it is now. The plot would have been something more complex, and a greater variety of characters introduced to relieve the mind from the pressure of incidents so mournful. The manners also would have been more attended to. My care was almost exclusively given to the passions and the characters, and the position in which the persons in the Drama stood relatively to each other, that the reader (for I had then no thought of the Stage) might be moved, and to a degree instructed, by lights penetrating somewhat into the depths of our nature. In this endeavour, I cannot think, upon a very late review, that I have failed. As to the scene and period of action, little more was required for my purpose than the absence of established Law and Government; so that the agents might be at liberty to act on their impulses ...'

Psychology and politics are also discussed in Wordsworth's *note* of 1842:

> The study of human nature suggests this awful truth, that, as in the trials to which life subjects us, sin and crime are apt to start from their very

opposite qualities, so are there no limits to the hardening of the heart, and the perversion of the understanding to which they may carry their slaves. During my long residence in France, while the revolution was rapidly advancing to its extreme of wickedness, I had frequent opportunities of being an eye-witness of this process, and it was while that knowledge was fresh upon my memory, that the Tragedy of 'The Borderers' was composed.

One character, Oswald, was selected for special comment in the *I. F. note*:

... While I was composing this Play I wrote a short essay illustrative of that constitution and those tendencies of human nature which make the apparently *motiveless* actions of bad men intelligible to careful observers. This was partly done with reference to the character of Oswald, and his persevering endeavour to lead the man he disliked into so heinous a crime, but still more to preserve in my distinct remembrance what I had observed of transition in character, and the reflections I had been led to make during the time I was a witness of the changes through which the French Revolution passed.

The essay on Oswald is reprinted in *PW*, I, 345–9.

The Borderers won the enthusiastic acclaim of Coleridge; in a letter to Joseph Cottle (8 June 1797), he observed:

His Drama is absolutely wonderful. You know, I do not commonly speak in such abrupt and unmingled phrases – and therefore will the more readily believe me. – There are in the piece those *profound* touches of the human heart, which I find three or four times in 'The Robbers' of Schiller, and often in Shakespeare – but in Wordsworth there are no *inequalities*.

The influence of Shakespeare is noticeable throughout, especially in parallel situations and characterization. Some distinct verbal echoes are indicated in the following notes.

92–5 See Othello's description of the beginnings of Desdemona's love for him, I, iii, 128–70.

762 *natural tears   Paradise Lost* XII, 645.

779 Compare *Macbeth* III, iv, 102–3: 'Take any shape but that, and my firm nerves / Shall never tremble'.

967–72 Compare *Macbeth* II, ii, 13–14 for a similar sentiment.

1002 *mortal instruments   Julius Caesar* II, i, 66.

1022–3 The action of the play is thus set in August of 1265, after the Battle of Evesham.

1060 *draw tears from iron*   Compare Milton's *Il Penseroso* 107.

1304 *squeak and gibber   Hamlet* I, i, 116.

1493–6 a Godwinian belief.

1539–44 used as the first six lines of the motto poem for *The White Doe of Rylstone*.

2309–11 See *Macbeth* V, vii, 1–2, for a similar image.

ANIMAL TRANQUILLITY AND DECAY

Composed probably between the second half of 1796 and early June 1797; first published in *Lyrical Ballads* (1798) as *Old Man Travelling; Animal Tranquillity and Decay, A Sketch*; from 1815 included among 'Poems Referring to the Period of Old Age'. Six lines were deleted from the end in 1815:

> I asked him whither he was bound, and what
> The object of his journey: he replied
> That he was going many miles to take
> A last leave of his son, a mariner,
> Who from a sea-fight had been brought to Falmouth,
> And there was dying in an hospital.

I. F. note: 'If I recollect right these verses were an overflowing from *The Old Cumberland Beggar*.'

[FRAGMENT: 'YET ONCE AGAIN']

Composed probably between July 1796 and early June 1797; first published in 1949.

Although taken 'from the verso of a loose foolscap sheet on which an early draft of "The Old Cumberland Beggar" is written' (the title in *PW*), this fragment sounds more like an early version of Wordsworth's *Tintern Abbey*, specially of lines 4-5, 10, 106-7 of that poem.

[FRAGMENT: THE BAKER'S CART]

Composed probably between the latter half of 1796 (most likely late) and about March 1797; first published in 1940.

This fragment was possibly intended for *The Ruined Cottage*.

INSCRIPTION FOR A SEAT BY A ROADSIDE

Composed probably between about 28 November 1796 and 4 June 1797; first published in the *Morning Post*, 21 October 1800 (signed 'Ventifrons' – French for 'Windy Brow', a farm where the poem was written) with many variants (possibly by Coleridge) from the MS version printed here.

THE THREE GRAVES. Parts I* and II

Part I is of questionable authorship. Both parts composed probably between about 28 November 1796 and 4 June 1797; first published in *The Poetical Works of Samuel Taylor Coleridge*, ed. J. D. Campbell (1893). Shortly after it was written, Wordsworth handed over the unfinished poem to Coleridge, who wrote Parts III and IV, which were published in *The Friend* in 1809.

6 *jeer* companion

13 This line reads so in MS. Apparently the stanza was never completed.

35 *gear* property

37 *fere* spouse

42-45 This stanza may have been deleted in MS.

52 '*course of wooing*' *Othello* III, iii, 112.

57 This line reads so in MS.

58-77 These first five stanzas of Part II are also of questionable authorship.

98-105 These lines were cancelled in MS.

205 *sultry* excessively hot (poetical).

ADDRESS TO SILENCE

Of questionable authorship. If written by Wordsworth, composed probably in 1796; first published in the *Weekly Entertainer*, 6 March 1797, with the bracketed note: 'Read at a Literary Club'. For information on the possible authorship, see Helen Darbishire, 'An Approach to Wordsworth's Genius', in *English Studies Today*, ed. C. L. Wrenn and G. Bullough, 1951, pp. 150-52, and S. M. Parrish, *The Art of the Lyrical Ballads*, 1973, p. 64n.

20 *Hecla's* a volcano in south-west Iceland.

50 Compare Wordsworth's *On the Power of Sound* 217-18: 'O Silence! are Man's noisy years / No more than moments of thy life?' and *Ode : Intimations* 155-6: 'Our noisy years seem moments in the being / Of the eternal Silence'.

LINES LEFT UPON A SEAT IN A YEW-TREE

Probably composed for the most part early 1797 (perhaps after 8 February and by July), some lines possibly earlier (mid-1787); first published in *Lyrical Ballads* (1798); classed among 'Poems of Sentiment and Reflection' from 1815 to 1843 and thereafter among 'Poems Written in Youth'.

I. F. note: 'The tree has disappeared, and the slip of Common on which it stood, that ran parallel to the lake, and lay open to it, has long been enclosed; so that the road has lost much of its attraction. This spot was my favourite walk in the evenings during the latter part of my school-time.' The yew-tree was located on the eastern side of the lake, less than a mile from Hawkshead; according to one source, the decaying tree was chopped down in 1820 because it was thought to be poisoning the cattle.

8 *Who he was* 'The individual whose habits and character are here given, was a gentleman of the neighbourhood, a man of talent and learning who had been educated at one of our Universities, and returned to pass his time in seclusion on his own estate.' – *I. F. note*. He was the Rev. Mr W. Braithwaite of Satterhow.

27 This line, revised in 1815, was returned to its original published version in 1820, probably at the request of Charles Lamb.

38 According to Knight, this line was Coleridge's contribution, but no authority was given.

48-64 This passage constitutes a rejection of Godwinism. These lines, however, may have been written by Coleridge; see S. M. Parrish, *The Art of the Lyrical Ballads*, 1973, pp. 66-70.

INCIPIENT MADNESS

Composed probably between about March and 4-7 June 1797; first published in 1940.

Lines 4-6, 16-18 were later used in *The Ruined Cottage*, the early version of Book I of *The Excursion* (see *PW*, V, 377).

THE FARMER OF TILSBURY VALE

Composed between probably 30 March 1797 and 18 July 1800; first published in the *Morning Post*, 21 July 1800; first included in Wordsworth's poems in 1815 among 'Poems Referring to the Period of Old Age', in which category it remained.

Wordsworth's *note*: 'With this picture, which was taken from real life, compare the imaginative one of "The Reverie of Poor Susan", and see (to make up the deficiencies of this class) "The Excursion", passim.' In the *I. F. note*, Wordsworth added:

> The character of this man was described to me, and the incident upon which the verses turn was told me, by Mr Poole of Nether Stowey . . . If I seem in these verses to have treated the weaknesses of the farmer, and his transgression, too tenderly, it may in part be ascribed to my having received the story from one so averse to all harsh judgement . . . The latter part of the poem, perhaps, requires some apology as being too much of an echo to the 'Reverie of Poor Susan'.

THE REVERIE OF POOR SUSAN

Composed between probably 30 March 1797 and 13 August 1800; first published in *Lyrical Ballads* (1800) – as *Poor Susan*. The expanded title is a translation of the title of a poem by Gottfried August Bürger, *Das Arme Süsschen's Traum* (1781). From 1815 included among 'Poems of the Imagination'.

All three of the streets mentioned in the poem (Wood, Lothbury, and Cheapside) are situated in the City of London, the mercantile district.

I. F. note: 'This arose out of my observation of the affecting music of these birds hanging in this way in the London streets during the freshness and stillness of the Spring morning.' See also Wordsworth's note to the previous poem.

A final stanza was deleted in 1802:

> Poor Outcast! return – to receive thee once more
> The house of thy Father will open its door,
> And thou once again, in thy plain russet gown,
> May'st hear the thrush sing from a tree of its own.

A CHARACTER

Probably composed between 30 March 1797 and 15 October 1800, with the present version probably dating from between 15 September and 15 October 1800. First published in *Lyrical Ballads* (1800) – with the title, *A Character in the Antithetical Manner* – and dropped from editions 1802-32. It was included from 1836 among 'Poems of Sentiment and Reflection'.
I. F. note: 'The principal features are taken from my friend Robert Jones.' Jones was the friend who accompanied Wordsworth on the continental tour described in *Descriptive Sketches*.

A NIGHT-PIECE

Probably composed mainly 25 January 1798; first published in 1815 and included from then on among 'Poems of the Imagination'.
I. F. note: 'Composed on the road between Nether Stowey and Alfoxden, extempore. I distinctly recollect the very moment when I was struck, as described "He looks up at the clouds, etc."' A description of the same phenomena occurs in Dorothy Wordsworth's *Journal* (25 January 1798):

> Went to Poole's after tea. The sky spread over with one continuous cloud, whitened by the light of the moon, which, though her dim shape were seen, did not throw forth so strong a light as to chequer the earth with shadows. At once the clouds seemed to cleave asunder, and left her in the centre of a black-blue vault. She sailed along, followed by multitudes of stars, small, and bright, and sharp. Their brightness seemed concentrated (half-moon).

24 See *Tintern Abbey* 94: 'A presence that disturbs me with the joy'.

THE OLD CUMBERLAND BEGGAR

Composed probably between 25 January and 5 March 1798, with much revision before 10 October 1800; first published in *Lyrical Ballads* (1800); from 1815 included among 'Poems Referring to the Period of Old Age'.
I. F. note: 'Observed, and with great benefit to my own heart, when I was a child: written at Racedown and Alfoxden ... The political economists were about that time beginning their war upon mendicity in all its forms, and by implication, if not directly, on Almsgiving also.'

49 *hill and dale* Paradise Lost VI, 641.
61 *the cottage curs* Beattie's *The Minstrel* (1771-4), I, 39.
116 *easy* comfortable.
123 *monitor* reminder.
175 *chartered* privileged, unrestrained.
179 *HOUSE, misnamed of INDUSTRY* a workhouse set up in a parish where work was supposed to be provided (but sometimes wasn't) for paupers.

944 NOTES FOR PP. 267-74

For a description of the new changes in the Poor Laws, see T. W. Thompson, *Wordsworth's Hawkshead* (1970), pp. 276-81.

183 *free of* allowed the use or enjoyment of.

[FRAGMENTS FROM THE ALFOXDEN NOTE-BOOK (i)]

Composed probably between 25 January and 19 March 1798; first published in 1949.

Possibly intended for *The Ruined Cottage*, the first version of Book I of *The Excursion*.

TO MY SISTER

Composed probably between 1 and 9 (most probably 6, 8, or 9) March 1798; first published in *Lyrical Ballads* (1798); from 1815 included among 'Poems of Sentiment and Reflection'. The original title of the poem was 'Lines Written at a Small Distance from My House, and Sent, by My Little Boy to the Person to Whom They Are Addressed'.

I. F. note: 'Composed in front of Alfoxden House. My little boy-messenger on this occasion was the son of Basil Montagu. The larch mentioned in the first stanza was standing when I revisited the place in May, 1841, more than forty years after.'

5-9 Compare *The Prelude* (1805) I, 1-4: 'O there is blessing in this gentle breeze / That blows from the green fields and from the clouds / And from the sky: it beats against my cheek, / And seems half-conscious of the joy it gives'.

33-4 Compare *Lines Written . . . above Tintern Abbey* 100-102: 'A motion and a spirit, that . . . rolls through all things'.

GOODY BLAKE AND HARRY GILL

Composed probably between 7 March and about 16 May 1798; first published in *Lyrical Ballads* (1798); in 1815 included among 'Poems of the Imagination' because, although it and *The Horn of Egremont Castle* (as Wordsworth pointed out in a footnote to the latter poem in the edition of 1815) 'rather refer to the imagination than are produced by it', he wished 'to avoid a needless multiplication of the Classes'. In 1845, the poem was finally moved to 'Miscellaneous Poems'.

In the *Advertisement* to the 1798 edition, Wordsworth claimed the poem was 'founded on a well-authenticated fact which happened in Warwickshire', and in the *I. F. note* we learn the source: 'Written at Alfoxden. The incident from Dr Darwin's "Zoönomia" [1794-6].' Wordsworth's version of the story differs very little from his source. In the Preface to the 1802 edition, Wordsworth made further comments on the poem (see Appendix A, p. 887).

9 *July* rhymes in North-country dialect with *truly* (line 11).

39 *canty* cheerful (North-country dialect).

THE COMPLAINT OF A FORSAKEN INDIAN WOMAN

Composed probably between early March and about 16 May 1798; first published in *Lyrical Ballads* (1798); from 1815 included among 'Poems Founded on the Affections'.

I. F. note: 'Written at Alfoxden in 1798, where I read Hearne's Journey with deep interest. It was composed for the volume of Lyrical Ballads.' From Samuel Hearne's *A Journey from Prince of Wales's Fort in Hudson Bay to the Northern Ocean* (London 1795), Wordsworth got the information and even some of the wording for the note he prefixed to the poem.

Wordsworth refers to the poem in the Preface of 1802 (see Appendix A, p. 871).

HER EYES ARE WILD

Composed probably between early March and about 16 May 1798; first published in *Lyrical Ballads* (1798); from 1815 to 1820 included among 'Poems Founded on the Affections', then transferred to 'Poems of the Imagination' from 1827 to 1832, and finally returned to 'Poems Founded on the Affections' in subsequent editions. Originally entitled *The Mad Mother* (1798-1805).

I. F. note: 'Alfoxden, 1798. The subject was reported to me by a Lady of Bristol who had seen the poor creature.' There are, nevertheless, some sources for the poem in Bishop Percy's *Reliques* [1765], as indicated in the notes below. Much the most considerable of the sources was *Lady Anne Bothwell's Lament*, also a monologue, which has a similar theme and stanza form, as well as verbal echoes.

Wordsworth refers to the poem in the Preface of 1802 (see Appendix A, p. 871).

10 *English tongue* Wordsworth explained this detail in a letter to John Kenyon (late autumn, 1836):

... Though she came from far, English was her native tongue – which shows her either to be of these Islands, or a North American. On the latter supposition, while the distance removes her from us, the fact of her speaking our language brings us at once into close sympathy with her.

21 Compare the opening line of *The Frantic Lady*: 'I burn, my brain consumes to ashes'. See also *The Thorn* 120-21.

39-40 Coleridge in his *Notebooks*, ed. K. Coburn (1962) II, 2112, selected these lines as demonstrating imagination, and in his *Biographia Literaria* (Chapter XXII) he praised them as

so expressive of that deranged state, in which from the increased sensibility the sufferer's attention is abruptly drawn off by every trifle, and in the same instant plucked back again by the one despotic thought, and bringing home with it, by the blending, *fusing* power of Imagination and Passion, the alien object to which it had been so abruptly diverted, no longer an alien but an ally and an inmate.

41-2 Compare *Lady Anne Bothwell's Lament* 5: 'Balow, my boy, thy mother's joy.'

54 *hollow* empty, vacant.

61 Compare *Lament* 13-14: 'But now I see, most cruel he / Cares neither for my babe nor me'.

100 Compare *Lament* 35: 'My babe and I'll together live'.

THE IDIOT BOY

Composed probably between early March and about 16 May 1798; first published in *Lyrical Ballads* (1798); from 1815 included among 'Poems Founded on the Affections'.

I. F. note:

> Alfoxden 1798. The last stanza – 'The Cocks did crow to-whoo, to-whoo, And the sun did shine so cold' – was the foundation of the whole. The words were reported to me by my dear friend, Thomas Poole; but I have since heard the same repeated of other Idiots. Let me add that this long poem was composed in the groves of Alfoxden, almost extempore; not a word, I believe, being corrected, though one stanza was omitted. I mention this in gratitude to those happy moments, for, in truth, I never wrote anything with so much glee.

This poem was the subject of a long defence by Wordsworth in a letter to John Wilson (7 June 1802). Wordsworth always had a very high opinion of this poem. He refers to the poem in the Preface of 1802 (see Appendix A, p. 821).

104 *curr* make a low murmuring sound.

115-16 Compare Cowper's *John Gilpin* (1782), xxiv: 'His horse . . . / What thing upon his back had got / Did wonder more and more'.

240 *cattle* any livestock.

278 *road* rhymes in North-country dialect with 'abroad' (line 281).

338 *fourteen years* Jack Stillinger, in his selected edition of Wordsworth's poetry (1965), suggested that this number is possibly intended to show that the narrator is a bit slow-witted, since seven years was the ordinary period of apprenticeship.

THE LAST OF THE FLOCK

Composed probably between early March and about 16 May 1798; first published in *Lyrical Ballads* (1798); in 1815 and thereafter included among 'Poems Founded on the Affections'.

I. F. note : 'Produced at the same time and for the same purpose [as *The Complaint of a Forsaken Indian Woman*]. The incident occurred in the village of Holford, close by Alfoxden.' In justifying the use of the word *alone* in line 4, Wordsworth expanded on the background of the poem:

> Funerals, alas! we have all attended, and most of us must have seen then weeping in the public roads . . . I was a witness to a sight of this kind the

other day in the Streets of Kendal ... But for my own part, notwithstanding what has here been said in verse, I never in my whole life saw a man weep *alone* in the roads; but a friend of mine did see this poor man weeping *alone*, with the Lamb, the last of his flock, in his arms (Wordsworth to John Kenyon, late autumn, 1836).

41 *six*] *1800*; ten: *1798*.

WE ARE SEVEN

Composed probably between early March and about 16 May 1798; first published in *Lyrical Ballads* (1798); from 1815 included among 'Poems Referring to the Period of Childhood'.

I. F. note:

Written at Alfoxden in the spring of 1798, under circumstances somewhat remarkable. The little girl who is the heroine I met within the area of Goodrich Castle in the year 1793 ... I composed it while walking in the grove at Alfoxden. My friends will not deem it too trifling to relate that while walking to and fro I composed the last stanza first having begun with the last line. When it was all but finished, I came in and recited to Mr Coleridge and my Sister, and said, 'A prefatory stanza must be added, and I should sit down to our little tea-meal with greater pleasure if my task were finished.' I mentioned in substance what I wished to be expressed, and Coleridge immediately threw off the stanza thus:
'A little child, dear brother Jem,' –
I objected to the rhyme, 'dear brother Jem,' as being ludicrous, but we all enjoyed the joke of hitching-in our friend, James Tobin's name, who was familiarly called Jem.

On revisiting Goodrich Castle in 1841, Wordsworth could not find traces of the girl, as he 'did not even know her name'. In 1815 the opening line was shortened to its present form.

In the Preface to *Lyrical Ballads* (1802) Wordsworth described the poem as dealing with 'the perplexity and obscurity which in childhood attend our notion of death, or rather our utter inability to admit that notion'. As a child, Wordsworth himself had such perplexity, as we are informed in the *I. F. note* to the *Ode: Intimations*:

Nothing was more difficult for me in childhood than to admit the notion of death as a state applicable to my own being. I have said elsewhere – [first stanza of *We Are Seven* is quoted]. But it was not so much from [feelings] of animal vivacity that *my* difficulty came as from a sense of the indomitableness of the spirit within me.

19 *Conway* a seaport in North Wales.

SIMON LEE, THE OLD HUNTSMAN

Composed probably between early March and about 16 May 1798; first published in *Lyrical Ballads* (1798); from 1815 included among 'Poems of Sentiment and Reflection'. This poem was heavily revised over the years, especially the first seven stanzas.

I. F. note: 'This old man had been huntsman to the Squires of Alfoxden, which, at the time we occupied it, belonged to a minor. The old man's cottage stood upon the common, a little way from the entrance to Alfoxden Park. . . . The fact was as mentioned in the poem; and I have, after an interval of 45 years, the image of the old man as fresh before my eyes as if I had seen him yesterday.'

Wordsworth refers to the poem in the Preface of 1802 (see Appendix A, pp. 871–2).

1 *Cardigan* a county in Central Wales. Wordsworth has fictionalized the background (see *I. F. note* above).
6 *huntsman* often the man in charge of the hounds.
24 'The expression when the hounds are out, "I dearly love their voices," was word for word from [the old man's] own lips.' – *I. F. note*.
25 *But, oh the heavy change! Lycidas* 37.

'A WHIRL-BLAST FROM BEHIND THE HILL'

Composed probably 19 March 1798; first published in *Lyrical Ballads* (1800); from 1815 included among 'Poems of the Fancy'. Four lines were dropped from the end of the poem in 1815:

Oh! grant me, Heaven, a heart at ease,
That I may never cease to find,
Even in appearances like these,
Enough to nourish and to stir my mind!

I. F. note: 'Observed in the holly grove at Alfoxden, where these verses were written. . . .' The entry in Dorothy Wordsworth's *Journal* for 18 March 1798 reads: 'On our return [from Nether Stowey to Alfoxden], sheltered under the hollies during a hailshower. The withered leaves danced with the hailstones. William wrote a description of the storm.'

20 *Robin Good-fellow* Puck.

THE THORN

Composed probably between 19 March and about 16 May 1798; first published in *Lyrical Ballads* (1798); from 1815 included among the 'Poems of the Imagination'. Numerous revisions were made, especially after 1815.
I. F. note:

Alfoxden. 1798. Arose out of my observing, on the ridge of Quantock Hill, on a stormy day, a thorn which I had often passed in calm and bright weather without noticing it. I said to myself, 'Cannot I by some invention do as much to make this Thorn permanently an impressive object as the storm has made it to my eyes at this moment?' I began the poem accordingly, and composed it with great rapidity.

The entry in Dorothy Wordsworth's *Journal* for 19 March 1798 reads: 'William and Basil and I walked to the hill-tops, a very cold, bleak day. We were met on our return by a severe hailstorm. William wrote some lines describing a stunted thorn;' and for 20 April 1798: 'Came home the Crookham way, by the thorn, and the "little muddy pond".'

In the *Advertisement* to *Lyrical Ballads* of 1798, Wordsworth wrote: 'The poem of The Thorn, as the reader will soon discover, is not supposed to be spoken in the author's own person: the character of the loquacious narrator will sufficiently show itself in the course of the story.' On the persona of this narrator, Wordsworth expanded in a note to later editions of *Lyrical Ballads*:

This Poem ought to have been preceded by an introductory Poem, which I have been prevented from writing by never having felt myself in a mood when it was probable that I should write it well. The character which I have here introduced speaking is sufficiently common. The Reader will perhaps have a general notion of it, if he has ever known a man, a Captain of a small trading vessel, for example, who being past the middle age of life, had retired upon an annuity or small independent income to some village or country town of which he was not a native, or in which he had not been accustomed to live. Such men, having little to do, become credulous and talkative from indolence; and from the same cause, and other predisposing causes by which it is probable that such men may have been affected, they are prone to superstition. On which account it appeared to me proper to select a character like this to exhibit some of the general laws by which superstition acts upon the mind. Superstitious men are almost always men of slow faculties and deep feelings; their minds are not loose, but adhesive; they have a reasonable share of imagination, by which word I mean the faculty which produces impressive effects out of simple elements; but they are utterly destitute of fancy, the power by which pleasure and surprise are excited by sudden varieties of situation and an accumulated imagery.

It was my wish in this poem to show the manner in which such men cleave to the same ideas; and to follow the turns of passion, always different, yet not palpably different, by which their conversation is swayed. I had two objects to attain; first, to represent a picture which should not be unimpressive, yet consistent with the character that should describe it; secondly, while I adhered to the style in which such persons describe, to take care that words, which in their minds are impregnated with passion, should likewise convey passion to Readers who are not accustomed to sympathize with men feeling in that manner or using such language. It seemed to me that this might be done by calling in the assistance of Lyrical and rapid Metre. It was necessary that the Poem, to be natural, should in reality move slowly; yet I hoped that, by the aid of the metre, to those who should at all enter into the spirit of the Poem, it would appear to move quickly. The Reader will have the kindness to excuse this note, as I am sensible that an introductory Poem is necessary to give this Poem its full effect.

Several literary sources for *The Thorn* have been pointed out. One is William Taylor of Norwich's translation of Bürger's ballad, called by Taylor *The Lass of Fair Wone*, published in the *Monthly Magazine* in 1796, which ballad has similar incidents and even the detail of the pond (see also the note to lines 32-3 below). The other sources are variants of an anonymous ballad which likewise contains similar incidents, as well as the detail of the thorn bush – Wordsworth had copied one of these ballads in a commonplace book.

32-3] *1820*; 'I've measured it from side to side: / 'Tis three feet long, and two feet wide' *1798-1815*. Compare Bürger's ballad (see head-note), lines 179-80: '[Her skull] seems to eye the barren grave / Three spans in length, below.'
105 *Martha Ray* name of the mother of Basil Montagu, Wordsworth's companion on the walk (see head-note) on 19 March. She was the well-known mistress of the Earl of Sandwich and had been shot in public by a rejected suitor in 1779. Wordsworth must have known she was Montagu's mother.

[FRAGMENTS FROM THE ALFOXDEN NOTE-BOOK (ii)]

Composed probably between 19 March and about 16 May 1798; first published in 1949.

LINES WRITTEN IN EARLY SPRING

Composed between probably early April (possibly early March) and about 16 May 1798; first published in *Lyrical Ballads* (1798); from 1815 included among 'Poems Proceeding from Sentiment and Reflection'.
  I. F. note: 'Actually composed while I was sitting by the side of the brook that runs down from the Comb, in which stands the village of Alford, through the grounds of Alfoxden. It was a chosen resort of mine. [The scene is then described in considerable detail].'
1 *notes* rhymes with 'thoughts' in North-country pronunciation.
11-20 The idea of the sensibility of plants is probably attributable to Erasmus Darwin's *Zoönomia* (1794-6).

ANECDOTE FOR FATHERS

Composed between probably early April (possibly early March) and about 16 May 1798; first published in *Lyrical Ballads* (1798); from 1815 included among 'Poems Referring to the Period of Childhood'. This poem underwent considerable revision.
  I. F. note: 'This was suggested in front of Alfoxden. The boy was a son of my friend, Basil Montagu, who had been two or three years under our care.'
  From 1798 to 1843, the poem carried a subtitle: 'showing how the Practice

of Lying may be taught.' In 1845, this was replaced by the present motto, which is a Latin translation by Eusebius (*Preparatio Evangelica* VI, v) of a Greek line from Porphyro that purports to be the warning of Apollo to any who would try to coerce the oracle – 'Restrain your violence, for I shall lie if you force me.'

3 *cast in beauty's mould* Bishop Percy's version of *The Children in the Wood* **20**: 'framed in beauty's mold'.

10 *Kilve's* 'a village on the Bristol Channel, about a mile from Alfoxden' – *I. F. note*: Equivalent to Racedown in Wordsworth's life.

24 *Liswyn farm* 'taken from a beautiful spot on the Wye' – *I. F. note*. Equivalent to Alfoxden in Wordsworth's life.

PETER BELL

First version composed probably between 20 April and about 16 May 1798 with revisions and additions, especially in late 1801 and early 1802, also in 1806–7 and 1812; first published in 1819; from 1820 included among 'Poems of the Imagination'.

I. F. note:

> Alfoxden. 1798. Founded upon an anecdote, which I read in a newspaper, of an ass being found hanging his head over a canal in a wretched posture. Upon examination a dead body was found in the water and proved to be the body of its master. The countenance, gait, and figure of Peter, were taken from a wild rover with whom I walked from Builth, on the river Wye, downwards nearly as far as the town of Hay ... The number of Peter's wives was taken from the trespasses in this way of a lawless creature who lived in the county of Durham ... In the woods of Alfoxden I used to take great delight in noticing the habits, tricks, and physiognomy of asses; and I have no doubt that I was thus put upon writing the poem out of liking for the creature that is so often dreadfully abused ... The worship of the Methodists or Ranters is often heard during the stillness of the summer evening in the country with affecting accompaniments of rural beauty. In both the psalmody and the voice of the preacher there is, not unfrequently, much solemnity likely to impress the feelings of the rudest characters under favourable circumstances.

The first epigraph is from *Romeo and Juliet* (II, ii, 43) and the second from *Julius Caesar* (I, ii, 146).

128 *some ambitious Youth* from the context, often taken to be Samuel Taylor Coleridge.

192–5 Changed in 1820 from: 'It gave three miserable groans; / "'Tis come then to a pretty pass," / Said Peter to the groaning Ass, / "But I will *bang* your bones!"' The last three of these lines were also deleted at lines 448–50.

201 *Potter* 'In the dialect of the North, a hawker of earthenware is thus designated.' – W. (1819, 2nd ed.)

212 *Sarum* Salisbury.

227 *scars* deep, narrow valleys.

236 *the Fleet* a prison for debtors.

273 *Carl* a churl; a base man.

311 *furred* furrowed.

325 *Swale* a river in Yorkshire.

515 After 1819 a stanza was deleted following this line: 'Is it a party in a parlour? / Cramm'd just as they on earth were cramm'd – / Some sipping punch, some sipping tea, / But, as you by their faces see, / All silent and all damn'd!' Used by Shelley as an epigraph for *Peter Bell the Third* (1819). According to Wordsworth it was deleted in order 'not to offend the pious' (letter to Barron Field, 24 October 1828).

572 *resigned* absorbed.

578–80 Compare *The Prelude* V, 448–50.

681–2 scenery probably taken from the Valley of the Rocks in Devon.

790 *argument* theme.

909 *Benoni* Genesis 35:18. 'Benoni, or the child of sorrow, I knew when I was a school-boy.' – *I. F. note*. David Benoni, natural son of Mary Rigge of Colthouse – see the notes to *A Ballad* (p. 923 above), and T. W. Thompson's *Wordsworth's Hawkshead* (1970), p. 65.

973–4 'The notion is very general, that the Cross on the back and shoulders of this Animal has the origin here alluded to.' – W. (1819).

976 'I cannot suffer this line to pass, without noticing that it was suggested by Mr Haydon's noble picture of Christ's Entry into Jerusalem.' – W. (1820).

ANDREW JONES

Composed probably between 20 April 1798 and certainly 13 August 1800; first published in *Lyrical Ballads* (1800); in 1815 included among 'Poems of Sentiment and Reflection', but not subsequently reprinted. Most of the poem was apparently written as part of *Peter Bell*.

'I LOVE UPON A STORMY NIGHT'

Composed probably between 20 April 1798 and about 5 June 1800; first published in 1944. This poem was probably a draft or an overflow of the Prologue of *Peter Bell*.

2 *slender* slight, weak.

'AWAY, AWAY, IT IS THE AIR'

Composed perhaps between 20 April and about 16 May 1798 or shortly thereafter; first published in 1947.

[FRAGMENTS FROM THE ALFOXDEN NOTE-BOOK (iii)]

Perhaps composed between 20 April and about 16 May 1798, or shortly thereafter; first published in 1949.

The first fragment could fit into *Lines Composed a Few Miles above Tintern Abbey* after 'To blow against thee' (line 137); see W. J. B. Owen, 'Notes on Wordsworth', *Notes and Queries* CXCVI (1951), 209.

EXPOSTULATION AND REPLY

Composed probably 23 May 1798 or very shortly after (by 12 June 1798 almost certainly); first published in *Lyrical Ballads* (1798); from 1815 included among 'Poems of Sentiment and Reflection'.

I. F. note: 'This poem is a favourite among the Quakers, as I have learnt on many occasions. It was composed in front of the house at Alfoxden in the spring of 1798.'

In the *Advertisement* to *Lyrical Ballads* of 1798, Wordsworth claims the setting of the poem 'arose out of conversation with a friend who was somewhat unreasonably attached to modern books of Moral Philosophy'. This friend is usually thought to have been William Hazlitt, who argued with Wordsworth about metaphysics at Nether Stowey, where Hazlitt visited Coleridge in 1798 (see Hazlitt's essay, 'My First Acquaintance with Poets'). See also note to line 15 below.

15 *Matthew* most often identified with William Taylor, the master at Hawkshead Grammar School. Matthew, however, was a composite portrait; see head-note to *Matthew* below.

17-20 But see *The Prelude* XII, 127-51 for Wordsworth's attack on the despotism of the senses.

THE TABLES TURNED

For all data, see the head-note to the previous poem.

26-8 *Our meddling intellect ... to dissect.* Compare Wordsworth's later *I. F. note* (to '*This Lawn, a carpet all alive*'):

> Some are of opinion that the habit of analysing, decomposing, and anatomizing is inevitably unfavourable to the perception of beauty. People are led into this mistake by over-looking the fact that such processes being to a certain extent within the reach of a limited intellect, we are apt to ascribe to them that insensibility of which they are in truth the effect and not the cause. Admiration and love, to which all knowledge truly vital must tend, are felt by men of real genius in proportion as their discoveries in natural Philosophy are enlarged; and the beauty in form of a plant or an animal is not made less but more apparent as a whole by more accurate insight into its constituent properties and powers. A *Savant* who is not also a Poet in soul and a religionist in heart is a feeble and unhappy Creature.

LINES COMPOSED A FEW MILES ABOVE TINTERN ABBEY

Composed probably between 11 and 13 July 1798 (possibly begun 10 July); first published in *Lyrical Ballads* (1798); from 1815 included among 'Poems of the Imagination'.

There is a striking general verbal and tonal resemblance between Words-worth's poem and Charlotte Smith's *The Emigrants* (1793); see B. C. Hunt, 'Wordsworth and Charlotte Smith', *The Wordsworth Circle* I (1970), 93–6.

I. F. note:

> July 1798. No poem of mine was composed under circumstances more pleasant for me to remember than this. I began it upon leaving Tintern, after crossing the Wye, and concluded it just as I was entering Bristol in the evening, after a ramble of 4 or 5 days, with my sister. Not a line of it was altered, and not any part of it written down till I reached Bristol. It was published immediately after. . . .

In a note appended to the poem from 1800 to 1805, Wordsworth commented further: 'I have not ventured to call this Poem an Ode; but it was written with a hope that in the transitions, and the impassioned music of the versification would be found the principal requisites of that species of composition.'

4 *With a soft inland murmur* 'The river is not affected by the tides a few miles above Tintern.' – W.

7–8 *connect | The landscape with the quiet of the sky* Compare the end of the following passage from Gilpin's *Observations on the River Wye* (1782): 'Many of the furnaces, on the banks of the river, consume charcoal, which is manu-factured on the spot; and the smoke, which is frequently seen issuing from the sides of the hills; and spreading its thin veil over a part of them, beauti-fully breaks their lines, and unites them with the sky' (p. 12).

17 *wreaths of smoke* See the preceding note.

33 *that best portion of a good man's life* Compare Milton's Preface to *The Judgment of Martin Bucer Concerning Divorce*: '. . . Whereby good men in the best portion of their lives.'

106 'This line has a close resemblance to an admirable line of Young's, the exact expression of which I do not recollect.' – W. Young's *Night Thoughts* VI (1742–4), 417, 424: 'Senses . . . half create the wondrous world they see.'

110 *The guide, the guardian of my heart* Compare Akenside's *Pleasures of Imagination* (1744) 22: 'The guide, the guardian of their lovely sports.'

113 *genial* cheerful *and* creative (a play on words, pointing up their com-mon root, often made by Coleridge).

128 *evil tongues Paradise Lost* VII, 26.

THERE WAS A BOY

Composed probably between 6 October and late November/early December 1798; first published in *Lyrical Ballads* (1800); included from 1815 among 'Poems of the Imagination'; also incorporated into *The Prelude* V, 364–97.

I. F. note:

> Written in Germany. This is an extract from the poem on my own poetical education. This practice of making an instrument of their own fingers is known to most boys, though some are more skilful at it than others.

William Raincock of Rayrigg, a fine spirited lad, took the lead of all my schoolfellows in this art.

The earliest drafts of this poem are written in the first person.

2 *Winander* Windermere.

18–25 Wordsworth once told Thomas De Quincey:

I have remarked from my earliest days, that, if under any circumstances the attention is energetically braced up to an act of steady observation, or of steady expectation, then, if this intense condition of vigilance should suddenly relax, at that moment any beautiful, any impressive visual object, or collection of objects, falling upon the eye, is carried to the heart with a power not known under other circumstances.

(Edward Sackville-West, ed., *Recollections of the Lake Poets* [1948], p. 144 [matter omitted in the Masson edition]). The process is also discussed in the Preface to the *Poems* of 1815.

28 *vale* the vale of Esthwaite. The village-school (line 30) is the Hawkshead Grammar School.

ALCAEUS TO SAPPHO

Composed probably between 6 October and December 1798 (possibly January 1799); first published in the *Morning Post*, 24 November 1800, having been sent there by Coleridge, who gave it its present title and perhaps also was involved in some revision. In a letter to Coleridge (27 February 1799) Wordsworth commented that he did 'not care a farthing' for the poem.

Alcaeus was a Greek poet of Lesbos and a contemporary of Sappho.

'A SLUMBER DID MY SPIRIT SEAL'

Composed probably between 6 October and December 1798 (possibly January 1799); first published in *Lyrical Ballads* (1800). From 1815 on included among 'Poems of the Imagination'. A 'Lucy poem'.

In a letter to Thomas Poole (6 April 1799), Coleridge quotes the poem and remarks: 'Some months ago Wordsworth transmitted to me a most sublime epitaph – whether it had any reality, I cannot say. – Most probably, in some gloomier moment he had fancied the moment in which his sister might die.'

5 *motion, force* terms used in Newtonian physics.

INFLUENCE OF NATURAL OBJECTS

Composed probably between 6 October and probably 21 or 28 December (possibly as early as 14 December) 1798; first published in *The Friend*, 28 December 1809, as *Growth of Genius from the Influence of Natural Objects, on the Imagination in Boyhood, and Early Youth*. Incorporated into *The Prelude* I, 401–63 (the 'Unpublished Poem' of the present subtitle). From 1815, included among 'Poems Referring to the Period of Childhood'.

55 *spinning still* N. C. Smith suggests *spinning* has reference to a spinning wheel and *still* means 'continuously'.

'SHE DWELT AMONG THE UNTRODDEN WAYS'

Composed probably between 6 October and probably 21 or 28 December (possibly by 14 December) 1798; first published in *Lyrical Ballads* (1800); included from 1815 among 'Poems Founded on the Affections'. One of the 'Lucy poems' – Lucy is often identified with Dorothy, the poet's sister. An additional stanza of a draft was dropped from the beginning of the poem before publication:

My hope was one, from cities far,
Nursed on a lonesome heath;
Her lips were red as roses are,
Her hair a woodbine wreath.

An additional stanza appeared in the same draft between the second and third stanzas of the present version:

And she was graceful as the broom
That flowers by Carron's side;
But slow distemper checked her bloom,
And on the Heath she died.

2 *Dove* Three rivers in England have this name, any one of which Wordsworth may have had in mind.

'STRANGE FITS OF PASSION HAVE I KNOWN'

All data identical with the preceding poem. A final stanza was dropped from a draft of this poem:

I told her this: her laughter light
Is ringing in my ears:
And when I think upon that night
My eyes are dim with tears.

6 Compare *Dulcina* 17 (in Percy's *Reliques*): 'And cheeks, as fresh as rose in June'.

NUTTING

Dates of composition and publication identical with the preceding poem; from 1815 included among 'Poems of the Imagination'.

I. F. note:

Written in Germany; intended as part of a poem on my own life, but struck out as not being wanted there. Like most of my schoolfellows I was an impassioned nutter. For this pleasure, the vale of Esthwaite, abounding in coppice-wood, furnished a very wide range. These verses arose out of the remembrance of feelings I had often had when a boy, and particularly, in the extensive woods that still stretch from the side of Esthwaite Lake towards Graythwaite, the seat of the ancient family of Sandys.

A fifty-two-line opening addressed to 'Lucy', which was discarded, survives (*PW*, II, 504-6).
11 *Dame* Ann Tyson, with whom Wordsworth stayed while attending Hawkshead School.

THE DANISH BOY

Composed probably between 6 October 1798 and 23 February 1799 (almost certainly by late April 1799); first published in *Lyrical Ballads* (1800); from 1815 included among 'Poems of the Fancy'. Until 1836, the title was merely *A Fragment*. A stanza was dropped between stanzas IV and V after 1800:

When near this blasted tree you pass,
Two sods are plainly to be seen
Close at its root, and each with grass
Is covered fresh and green.
Like turf upon a new-made grave
These two green sods together lie,
Nor heat, nor cold, nor rain, nor wind
Can these two sods together bind,
Nor sun, nor earth, nor sky,
But side by s.de the two are laid,
As if just severed by the spade.

I. F. note: 'Written in Germany 1799. It was entirely a fancy, but intended as a prelude to a ballad poem never written.' In a note to the 1827 edition of his *Poems*, Wordsworth further explained:

These stanzas were designed to introduce a Ballad upon the Story of a Danish Prince who had fled from Battle, and, for the sake of the valuables about him, was murdered by the Inhabitant of a Cottage in which he had taken refuge. The House fell under a curse, and the Spirit of the Youth, it was believed, haunted the Valley where the crime had been committed.

N. C. Smith has pointed out the similarity of *The Danish Boy* to *The Thorn* in rhythm, metre, and style.

RUTH

Dates of composition and publication identical with the preceding poem; from 1815 to 1820 included among 'Poems Founded on the Affections', and thereafter among 'Poems of the Imagination'. This poem underwent considerable revision.
I. F. note: 'Written in Germany 1799. Suggested by an account I had of a wanderer in Somersetshire.'

20-24 The frontispiece of Bartram's *Travels* (see note to line 64 below) contains a portrait of an Indian chief wearing such feathers.

28-9 in 1783, after the War of Independence.

32 *tones* accents.

61 *magnolia* 'Magnolia grandiflora.' – W. (1800).

64 *flowers that with one scarlet gleam* 'The splendid appearance of these scarlet flowers, which are scattered with such profusion over the hills in the southern parts of North America, is frequently mentioned by Bartram in his Travels.' – W. (1800). William Bartram, *Travels Through North and South Carolina, Georgia* (1791).

203 *knell* a ringing sound, as of bells.

214 *Banks of Tone* 'The Tone is a river of Somersetshire at no great distance from the Quantock Hills. These hills, which are alluded to a few stanzas below, are extremely beautiful, and in most places richly covered with Coppice woods.' – W. (1800).

TO A SEXTON

Dates of composition and publication identical with the preceding poem; from 1815 included among 'Poems of the Fancy'.

I. F. note: 'Written in Germany, 1799.'

MATTHEW

Dates of composition and publication identical with the preceding poem; from 1815 included among 'Poems of Sentiment and Reflection'. Entitled in the table of contents (1800–20) 'Lines Written on a Tablet in a School' and (1827–32) 'If Nature, for a Favourite Child,' with no title in text. The present title was added in 1837.

I. F. note:

Such a Tablet as is here spoken of continued to be preserved in Hawkshead School, though the inscriptions were not brought down to our time. This and other poems connected with Matthew would not gain by a literal detail of facts. Like the Wanderer in 'The Excursion', this Schoolmaster was made up of several both of his class and men of other occupations. I do not ask pardon for what there is of untruth in such verses, considered strictly as matters of fact. It is enough if, being true and consistent in spirit, they move and teach in a manner not unworthy of a Poet's calling.

T. W. Thompson, in any event, has recently suggested three contemporaries as forming part of Matthew's portrait; see *Wordsworth's Hawkshead* (1970), pp. 171–90.

THE TWO APRIL MORNINGS

All data identical with the preceding poem. One of the 'Matthew poems'; see head-note for the preceding poem.

THE FOUNTAIN

All data identical with the preceding poem. One of the 'Matthew poems'; see head-note to *Matthew* (above).

54 *approved* proven good.

'COULD I THE PRIEST'S CONSENT HAVE GAINED'

Date of composition identical with the preceding poem; first published in 1947. One of the 'Matthew poems'; see head-note to *Matthew* (above).

25-8 Identical stanza with lines 17-20 of *Elegy Written in the Same Place*.

ELEGY WRITTEN IN THE SAME PLACE

All data identical with the preceding poem. This poem so titled in D.C. MS. 16.

7 *silly* simple.

17-20 Identical stanza with lines 25-8 of *'Could I the priest's consent have gained'*.

25-32 All but identical with lines 37-40 and 33-6 of *Address to the Scholars of the Village School of* ———.

44 *Glencarn* Glencairn, a parish in Dumfries, Scotland.

ADDRESS TO THE SCHOLARS OF THE VILLAGE SCHOOL OF —

Composed probably between 6 October 1798 and 23 February 1799 (almost certainly by late April 1799); first published in 1842; from 1845 included among 'Epitaphs and Elegiac Pieces'.

I. F. note: 'Composed at Goslar, in Germany.'

In a note to the last line of the poem, Wordsworth commented: 'See upon the subject of the three foregoing pieces *The Fountain, &c.*' The three poems referred to, *The Fountain, Matthew,* and *The Two April Mornings,* belong to the 'Matthew poems'. 'Matthew' is usually identified with the Rev. William Taylor (1754-86), master of the *Hawkshead School* – the name omitted in the title. But, even though here Wordsworth probably has Taylor especially in mind, 'Matthew' is most likely a composite (see note to line 15 of *Expostulation and Reply* above, and T. W. Thompson's *Wordsworth's Hawkshead* [1970], pp. 151n, 162).

3-4 'Taylor died while Wordsworth was still at school: and just before his death, he sent for the upper boys into his chamber . . . and there took leave of them on his death-bed.' Christopher Wordsworth, *Memoirs* I, 38. See also *The Prelude* X, 534-52.

48 *deplore* mourn for.

LUCY GRAY

Composed probably between 6 October 1798 and 23 February 1799; first published in *Lyrical Ballads* (1800). From 1815 included among 'Poems Referring to the Period of Childhood'.

I. F. note:

> Written at Goslar in Germany in 1799. It was founded on a circumstance told me by my Sister, of a little girl who, not far from Halifax in Yorkshire, was bewildered in a snow-storm. Her footsteps were traced by her parents to the middle of the lock of a canal, and no other vestige of her, backward or forward, could be traced. The body however was found in the canal. The way in which the incident was treated and the spiritualizing of the character might furnish hints for contrasting the imaginative influences which I have endeavoured to throw over common life with Crabbe's matter of fact style of treating subjects of the same kind.

According to Henry Crabb Robinson (*Diary* for 11 September 1816), Wordsworth told him his 'object was to exhibit poetically entire *solitude* . . .' – see the subtitle of the poem.

20 *yonder is the moon* H. C. Robinson recorded Wordsworth as saying that 'he represents the child as observing the day-*moon*, which no town or village girl would ever notice' (see head-note above).

30–32 Compare the stanza Wordsworth quoted from *The Babes in the Wood* in the 1800 *Preface* as 'one of the most justly admired stanzas' of the ballad: 'Those pretty babes with hand in hand / Went wandering up and down; / But never more they saw the Man / Approaching from the town.'

WRITTEN IN GERMANY

Composed probably between 6 October 1798 and 23 February 1799, possibly on 25 December 1798; first published in *Lyrical Ballads* (1800); from 1815 included among 'Poems of Sentiment and Reflection'.

I. F. note: '1798 and 1799. A bitter winter it was when these verses were composed by the side of my Sister, in our lodgings at a draper's house in the romantic imperial town of Goslar, on the edge of the Hartz Forest.'

3 *that horse* See the note prefixed to the poem.

A POET'S EPITAPH

Composed probably between 6 October 1798 and 23 February 1799; first published in *Lyrical Ballads* (1800); from 1815 included among 'Poems of Sentiment and Reflection'.

I. F. note (for *Written in Germany*): In Goslar 'I walked daily on the ramparts, or in a sort of public ground or garden ... During these walks I composed the poem that follows, *The* [sic] *Poet's Epitaph*.'

Compare Theocritus, *Epigram* XIX: 'Here lies the poet Hipponax! If thou art a sinner draw not near this tomb, but if thou art a true man, and the son of righteous sires, sit boldly down here, yea, and sleep if thou wilt.' – trans. Lang. See also Burns, *A Bard's Epitaph* (1786), with its similar repeated questions.

1 *Statist* statesman, politician.
9 *a Man of purple cheer* a clergyman or Doctor (line 11) of Divinity.
18 *Philosopher* natural scientist.
38 *russet brown* Compare Thomson's *Castle of Indolence* II (1748), xxxiii: 'the bard . . . In russet brown bedight'.

ELLEN IRWIN

Composed probably between 6 October 1798 and 23 February 1799 (possibly as late as 29 July 1800); first published in *Lyrical Ballads* (1800); in 1815 and 1820 included among 'Poems Founded on the Affections', then among 'Memorials of a Tour in Scotland, 1803'.

I. F. note:

. . . As there are Scotch Poems on the subject in the simple ballad strain, I thought it would be both presumptuous and superfluous to attempt treating it in the same way; and, accordingly, I chose a construction of stanza quite new in our language; in fact the same as that of Bürger's *Leonora*, except that the first and third line do not, in my stanzas, rhyme. At the outset I threw out a classical image to prepare the reader for the style in which I meant to treat the story, and so to preclude all comparison.

2 *the braes of Kirtle* 'The Kirtle is a river in the southern part of Scotland, on the banks of which the events here related took place.' – W. A *brae* is a steep bank bounding a river valley.

[FRAGMENT: 'FOR LET THE IMPEDIMENT']

Composed probably between 6 October 1798 and late October 1800; first published in 1949.
Compare *The Prelude* XIII, 195–202.

[FRAGMENT: REDUNDANCE]

Composed probably between early 1799 and late October 1800; first published in 1949 (in *PW*, V, 346 as V, ii).

'THREE YEARS SHE GREW IN SUN AND SHOWER'

Composed probably between 23 and 27 February 1799; first published in *Lyrical Ballads* (1800); from 1815 included in 'Poems of the Imagination'. One of the 'Lucy poems'.
I. F. note: '1799. Composed in the Hartz Forest.'

8 *impulse* incitement, impetus.

THE BROTHERS

Composition begun certainly by 24 December 1799 (probably shortly before) and finished probably in early 1800; first published in *Lyrical Ballads* (1800); from 1815 included among 'Poems Founded on the Affections'.

I. F. note:

> 1800. This poem was composed in a grove at the north-eastern end of Grasmere Lake ... The poem arose out of the fact, mentioned to me at Ennerdale, that a shepherd had fallen asleep upon the top of the rock called The Pillar, and perished as here described, his staff being left midway on the rock.

Coleridge, during a tour with Wordsworth in the Lake Country, recorded the same incident in his diary (12 November 1799), with the additional detail of the mouldering of the staff.

Wordsworth's note to the poem (1800-32): 'This poem was intended to be the concluding poem of a series of pastorals, the scene of which was laid among the mountains of Cumberland and Westmoreland. I mention this to apologise for the abruptness with which the poem begins.'

Coleridge referred to the poem in the *Biographia Literaria* (Chapter XVIII) as 'that model of English pastoral, which I have never yet read with unclouded eye'. Wordsworth also mentioned the poem in the Preface of 1802 (see Appendix A, p. 871).

13 *neither epitaph nor monument* See note to line 183 below.
16 *homely* kindly, simple.
65 'This description of the Calenture [a tropical fever] is sketched from an imperfect recollection of an admirable one in prose, by Mr Gilbert, author of the *Hurricane* [1796].' – W.
141-5 'This actually took place upon Kidstow Pike at the head of Hawes-water.' – W. (1815-36).
183 'There is not anything more worthy of remark in the manners of the inhabitants of these mountains, than the tranquillity, I might say indifference, with which they think and talk upon the subject of death. Some of the country churchyards, as here described, do not contain a single tombstone, and most of them have a very small number.' – W. *Essays on Epitaphs* (1800).
267 *piety* faithfulness to family responsibilities.
310-11 In a note, Wordsworth identified Great Gable, a mountain, the Liza and Ehen Rivers, and Egremont, a town – all in Cumberland.

TO M. H.

Composed between 20 and 28 December 1799 (probably on or shortly before 28 December); first published in *Lyrical Ballads* (1800); from 1815 included among 'Poems on the Naming of Places'.

I. F. note: 'To Mary Hutchinson, two years before our marriage. The pool alluded to is in Rydal Upper Park.'

HART-LEAP WELL

Composed probably early 1800 (certainly by about early June); first published in *Lyrical Ballads* (1800); from 1815 included among 'Poems of the Imagination'.

I. F. note:

> Town-End. 1800. *Grasmere*. The first eight stanzas were composed extempore one winter evening in the cottage; when, after having tired myself with labouring at an awkward passage in 'The Brothers', I started with a sudden impulse to this to get rid of the other, and finished it in a day or two. My sister and I had past the place a few weeks before in our wild winter journey from Sockburn on the banks of the Tees to Grasmere. A peasant whom we met near the spot told us the story so far as concerned the name of the well, and the hart, and pointed out the stones. Both the stones and the well are objects that may easily be missed; the tradition by this time may be extinct in the neighbourhood: the man who related it to us was very old.

The central incident of the curse on the cruel hunter, as well as the moral, are similar to Bürger's *Der Wilde Jäger* (1778).

1 *Wensley Moor* situated in Yorkshire between the Rivers Swale (line 75) and Ure (line 76).

75–6 *Swale, Ure* See note to line 1 above.

97 *moving accident* Compare *Othello* I, iii, 135.

THE VOICE FROM THE SIDE OF ETNA

Of questionable authorship. If by Wordsworth, possibly composed early 1800 (at least by 13 October); first published 13 October 1800 in the *Morning Post* (signed 'Cassiani, jun.').

Possibly a parody by Coleridge, to whom it was ascribed in 1804: see S. M. Parrish and D. V. Erdman, 'Who Wrote *The Mad Monk*? A Debate', *Bulletin of the New York Public Library* LXIV (1960), 209–37, and R. S. Woof, 'Wordsworth's Poetry and Stuart's Newspapers: 1797–1803', *Studies in Bibliography* XV (1962), 174–6.

Mrs Radcliffe of the subtitle was the author of numerous 'gothic' novels.

9–16 Compare *Ode: Intimations* 1–6.

'THERE IS AN EMINENCE'

Composed probably 1800 (certainly by 18 December), possibly for the most part about January 1800; first published in *Lyrical Ballads* (1800); from 1815 included among 'Poems on the Naming of Places'.

I. F. note: '1800. It is not accurate that the Eminence here alluded to could be seen from our orchard-seat. It rises above the road by the side of Grasmere lake, towards Keswick, and its name is Stone-Arthur.'

14 *She* usually identified as Dorothy Wordsworth.

'IT WAS AN APRIL MORNING: FRESH AND CLEAR'

Composed probably 1800 (perhaps between April and 13 October 1800, certainly by 15 October); first published in *Lyrical Ballads* (1800); from 1815 included among 'Poems on the Naming of Places'.

I. F. note: 'Grasmere, 1800. This poem was suggested on the banks of the brook that runs through Easedale, which is, in some parts of its course, as wild and beautiful as brook can be. I have composed thousands of verses by the side of it.'

10 *various* undergoing change.

39 *MY EMMA* always identified as Dorothy Wordsworth.

WRITTEN WITH A PENCIL UPON A STONE

Composed probably by early June 1800 (at least by 13 August); first published in *Lyrical Ballads* (1800); from 1815 included among 'Inscriptions'.

6 *Vitruvius* Marcus Vitruvius Pollio, a famous Roman architect of the age of Augustus.

THE IDLE SHEPHERD-BOYS

Composed probably 1800 (certainly by 29 July); first published in *Lyrical Ballads* (1800); from 1815 included among 'Poems Referring to the Period of Childhood'.

I. F. note:

Grasmere Town-End, 1800 ... When Coleridge and Southey were walking together upon the Fells, Southey observed that, if I wished to be considered a faithful painter of rural manners, I ought not to have said that my Shepherd-boys trimmed their rustic hats as described in the poem. Just as the words had passed his lips two boys appeared with the very plant entwined round their hats.

20 *rusty* worn, shabby.

27-30 Compare *Ode: Intimations* 36-40.

THE TWO THIEVES

Composed probably 1800 (probably by 29 July); first published in *Lyrical Ballads* (1800); from 1815 included among 'Poems Referring to the Period of Old Age'.

I. F. note: 'This is described from the life as I was in the habit of observing when a boy at Hawkshead School. Daniel was more than 80 years older than myself when he was daily thus occupied, under my notice.' The old man has recently been identified as Daniel Mackreth (1693-1788); see T. W. Thompson, *Wordsworth's Hawkshead* (1970), pp. 191-2.

1 *Bewick* Thomas Bewick (1753-1828), English painter and wood-engraver, especially known for his illustrations for the *History of British Birds*.

'A NARROW GIRDLE OF ROUGH STONES AND CRAGS'

Composed probably between 23 July and 6 November 1800; first published in *Lyrical Ballads* (1800); from 1815 included among 'Poems on the Naming of Places'.

I. F. note: '1800. The character of the eastern shore of Grasmere Lake is quite changed, since these verses were written, by the public road being carried along its side. The friends spoken of were Coleridge and my Sister, and the fact occurred strictly as recorded.'

16 *wreck* heap of drifted matter.
33-4 *that tall fern ... named* Osmunda regalis, or royal fern.

ON SEEING SOME TOURISTS

Composed probably between 1800 and early April 1807 (possibly about late July 1800); first published in 1897.

WRITTEN WITH A SLATE PENCIL UPON A STONE, THE LARGEST OF A HEAP

Composed probably 1800 (certainly by 4 August) – final version of lines 1–9 probably about (at least by) 13 August; first published in *Lyrical Ballads* (1800); from 1815 included among 'Inscriptions'.

8 *Sir William* Sir William Fleming (d. 1736) of Rydal Hall.
31 *In snow-white splendour* Wordsworth objected to white as a colour for houses in the Lake District; see 'Colouring of buildings' in his *Guide to the Lakes.*

THE OAK AND THE BROOM

Composed probably 1800 (certainly by 4 August); first published in *Lyrical Ballads* (1800); from 1815 included among 'Poems of the Fancy'. This and the following poem were probably suggested by John Langhorne's *Fables of Flora* (1771).

I. F. note: '1800. Suggested upon the mountain pathway that leads from Upper Rydal to Grasmere. The ponderous block of stone, which is mentioned in the poem, remains, I believe, to this day, a good way up Nab-Scar. Broom grows under it and in many places on the side of the precipice.' According to Henry Crabb Robinson's *Diary* (11 September 1816), Wordsworth claimed in conversation that the broom was a substitute for a rose he had seen.

THE WATERFALL AND THE EGLANTINE

All data identical with the preceding poem.

I. F. note: 'Suggested nearer [than was *The Oak and the Broom*] to Grasmere on the same mountain track. The eglantine remained many years afterwards, but is now gone.'

1 *fond* foolish.

14 *fibres* small roots.

15 *tyrannous and strong* Compare *The Ancient Mariner* 40–41 (first appearing in the 1817 version): 'And now the storm blast came and he / Was tyrannous and strong'.

SONG FOR THE WANDERING JEW

Composed probably 1800 (certainly by 13 August); first published in *Lyrical Ballads* (1800); from 1815 included among 'Poems of the Fancy'.

The story of the Wandering Jew dates at least as far back as the thirteenth century: a man, during Christ's Passion, had struck him and was required to remain alive until the Second Coming. The tale is told in a ballad included in Percy's *Reliques* (1765). This poem underwent considerable revision.

''TIS SAID, THAT SOME HAVE DIED FOR LOVE'

Composed probably 1800 (certainly by 13 August); first published in *Lyrical Ballads* (1800); from 1815 included among 'Poems Founded on the Affections'.

FOR THE SPOT WHERE THE HERMITAGE STOOD

Composed probably 1800 (certainly by 13 August); first published in *Lyrical Ballads* (1800); in 1815 included among 'Poems Referring to the Period of Old Age', afterwards among 'Inscriptions'. This poem underwent considerable revision.

THE SEVEN SISTERS

Composed probably about (but at least by) 17 August 1800; first published in the *Morning Post* 14 October 1800; from 1815 included among 'Poems of the Fancy'.

'The story of this poem is from the German of Frederica Brun [1765–1835].' – W. (1807). The German ballad was entitled *Die Sieben Hügel* (1793). The name Binnorie is from the refrain of the well-known Scottish ballad, *The Two Sisters*.

A note to the poem when first printed in the *Morning Post* acknowledges that the metre (except in the burden) is taken from *The Haunted Beach* (1800) by Mary Robinson.

TO JOANNA

Composed probably about (but at least by) 23 August 1800; first published in *Lyrical Ballads* (1800); from 1815 included among 'Poems on the Naming of Places'.

I. F. note:

Grasmere, 1800. The effect of her laugh is an extravagance; though the effect of the reverberation of voices in some parts of the mountains is very striking. There is, in the Excursion, an allusion to the bleat of a lamb thus re-echoed, and described without any exaggeration, as I heard it, on the side of Stickle Tarn, from the precipice that stretches on to Langdale Pikes.

In a notebook, Wordsworth made the following analysis of the poem:

The poem supposes that at the Rock something had taken place in my mind either then, or afterwards in thinking upon what then took place which, if related, will cause the Vicar to smile. For something like this you are prepared by the phrase 'Now, by those dear immunities', *etc.* [lines 32-5]. I begin to relate the story, meaning in a certain degree to divert or partly play upon the Vicar. I begin – my mind partly forgets its purpose, being softened by the images of beauty in the description of the rock, and the delicious morning, and when I come to the 2 lines 'The Rock, like something' *etc.* [lines 54-5], I am caught in the trap of my own imagination. I entirely lose sight of my first purpose. I take fire in the lines 'that ancient Woman' [lines 56-65]. I go on in that strain of fancy 'old Skiddaw' and terminate the description in tumult 'And Kirkstone' *etc.* [line 65], describing what for a moment I believed either actually took place at the time, or when I have been reflecting on what did take place I have had a temporary belief, in some fit of imagination, did really or might have taken place. When the description is closed, or perhaps partly before I waken from the dream and see that the Vicar thinks I have been extravagating, as I intended he should, I then tell the story as it happened really; and as the recollection of it exists permanently and regularly in my mind, mingling allusions suffused with humour, partly to the trance in which I have been, and partly to the trick I have been playing on the Vicar. The poem then concludes in a strain of deep tenderness.

20 *the old steeple-tower* St Oswald's, Grasmere.

28 *I, like a Runic Priest* 'In Cumberland and Westmoreland are several Inscriptions, upon the native rock, which, from the wasting of time, and the rudeness of the workmanship, have been mistaken for Runic. They are without doubt Roman.' – W.

31 *the Rotha* '. . . The river which, flowing through the lakes of Grasmere and Rydal, falls into Wynandermere.' – W.

42 *that tall rock* According to Knight, part of Helm-crag (line 56).

54-65 Coleridge in *Biographia Literaria* (Chapter XX) notes the influence of Drayton's *Polyolbion* (Song XXX, lines 155-64) on this image of echoes.

56-7 'On Helm-crag, that impressive single mountain at the head of the Vale of Grasmere, is a rock which from most points of view bears a striking resemblance to an old Woman cowering. Close by this rock is one of those fissures or caverns, which in the language of the country are called dungeons. Most of the mountains here mentioned immediately surround the Vale of Grasmere; of the others, some are at a considerable distance, but they belong to the same cluster.' – W.

'WHEN, TO THE ATTRACTIONS OF THE BUSY WORLD'

First version composed 29–30 August 1800, with additions and revisions possibly until about late 1805, and the final 1815 version probably between 9 September and late October 1814; first published in 1815; from 1815 included among 'Poems on the Naming of Places'.

I. F. note: '. . . The grove still exists, but the plantation has been walled in, and is not so accessible as when my brother John wore the path in the manner here described. The grove was a favourite haunt with us all while we lived at Town-End.'

67 *Esthwaite's pleasant shore* Hawkshead.

THE CHILDLESS FATHER

Composed probably 1800 (certainly by 15 September); first published in *Lyrical Ballads* (1800); from 1815 included among 'Poems Founded on the Affections'.

I. F. note:

Town-End, 1800. When I was a child at Cockermouth, no funeral took place without a basin filled with sprigs of boxwood being placed upon a table covered with a white cloth in front of the house [taken by each mourner to be thrown into the grave]. The huntings on foot, in which the Old Man is supposed to join as here described, were of common, almost habitual, occurrence in our vales when I was a boy; and the people took much delight in them. They are now less frequent.

THE PET-LAMB

Composed probably 1800 (certainly by 15 September); first published in *Lyrical Ballads* (1800); from 1815 included among 'Poems Referring to the Period of Childhood'.

I. F. note: 'Town-End, 1800. Barbara Lewthwaite, now [1843] living at Ambleside, though much changed as to beauty, was one of two most lovely sisters . . . [She] was not in fact the child whom I had seen and overheard as engaged in the poem. I chose the name for reasons implied in the above . . .'

RURAL ARCHITECTURE

Composed probably 1800 (certainly by 10 October); first published in *Lyrical Ballads* (1800); from 1815 included among 'Poems Referring to the Period of Childhood'.

I. F. note: 'These structures . . . are common among our hills, being built by shepherds as conspicuous marks, occasionally by boys in sport. It was written at Town-End, in 1801.'

3 *the height of a counsellor's bag* barristers at one time carried their brief-bags over their shoulders.

4 *GREAT HOW* 'a single and conspicuous hill which rises towards the foot of Thirlmere, on the western side of the beautiful dale of Legberthwaite, along the high road between Keswick and Ambleside.' – W.

12 *Magog* a legendary English giant.

MICHAEL

Composed probably between about early October (certainly by 11 October) and perhaps 9 December (certainly by 19 December) 1800; first published in *Lyrical Ballads* (1800); from 1815 included among 'Poems Founded on the Affections'.

I. F. note:

> Town-End, 1801. Written about the same time as *The Brothers*. The sheepfold, on which so much of the poem turns, remains, or rather the ruins of it. The character and circumstances of Luke were taken from a family to whom had belonged, many years before, the house we lived in at Town-End, along with some fields and woodlands on the eastern shore of Grasmere. The name of the Evening Star was not in fact given to this house but to another on the same side of the valley more to the north.

In Christopher Wordsworth's *Memoirs* (II, 305), Wordsworth is recorded to have told Mr Justice Coleridge that '"Michael" was founded on the son of an old couple having become dissolute and run away from his parents; and on an old shepherd having been seven years in building up a sheepfold in a solitary valley . . .' In a letter to Thomas Poole (9 April 1801), Wordsworth wrote of *Michael*:

> I have attempted to give a picture of a man, of strong mind and lively sensibility, agitated by two of the most powerful affections of the human heart; the parental affection, and the love of property, *landed* property, including the feelings of inheritance, home, and personal and family independence . . . I had a still further wish that this poem should please you, because in writing it I had your character often before my eyes, and sometimes thought I was delineating such a man as you yourself would have been under the same circumstances.

Wordsworth wrote to Charles James Fox (14 January 1801) that in *Michael* (and in *The Brothers*) he was describing the 'domestic affections' of the North-country small landowner, whose 'little tract of land serves as a kind of permanent rallying-point for their domestic feelings . . .'

In *PW* (II, 479–84) are given a number of MS passages probably intended for *Michael*.

2 *Green-head Ghyll* a ghyll is 'a steep, narrow valley, with a stream running through it' – W. (note to *The Idle Shepherd-Boys*). Green-head Ghyll is located in the north-east of Grasmere Vale.

11 *kites* birds of prey.

40 *forest-side* at the eastern side of Grasmere Lake.

50 *the South* the south wind.

169 *the CLIPPING TREE* 'Clipping is the word used in the north of England for shearing.' – W.

258 *Richard Bateman* 'The story alluded to here is well known in the country. The chapel is called Ings Chapel and is on the road leading from Kendal to Ambleside.' – W. (1802–5).

259 *parish-boy* a poor boy supported by the parish.

324 *a Sheep-fold* '... A sheepfold in these mountains is an unroofed building of stone walls, with different divisions. It is generally placed by the side of a brook . . .' – W. (1802–5).

414 *a covenant* probably an Old Testament allusion here.

[FRAGMENTS FROM THE 'CHRISTABEL' NOTE-BOOK]

Composed probably between about early October (certainly by 11 October) and perhaps 9 December (certainly by 19 December) 1800; first published in 1949 (in *PW*, V, 342–44 as Fragments IV, i–viii).

I

5–8 Compare *The Excursion* III, 70–73.

II

Compare *The Prelude* (1805), III, 539–41.

III

See *PW*, V, 480–81.

IV

9–12 Compare Coleridge's *The Nightingale* (1798) 24–9: 'Poet who hath been building up the rhyme / When he had better far have stretched his limbs / Beside a brook in mossy forest-dell, / By sun or moon-light, to the influxes / Of shapes and sounds and shifting elements / Surrendering his whole spirit . . .'.

12–23 See Wordsworth's description of the process of 'emotion recollected in tranquillity' in the 1802 *Preface*, p. 886 above.

[FRAGMENT: A SOMERSETSHIRE TRAGEDY]

Composed perhaps 1800 (by late October); first published in the present edition.

According to Robert Woof's introduction to T. W. Thompson's *Wordsworth's Hawkshead* (1970), p. xvi, the story concerned Jack Walford, a murderer, and was told to Wordsworth by Thomas Poole.

[FRAGMENT: 'Witness thou']

Composed probably between 1800 and 4 October 1802 (fairly certainly by 18 March 1804); first published in 1889.

Possibly intended for *The Recluse*.

[FRAGMENT FROM DOVE COTTAGE MANUSCRIPT 44 (i)]

Composed probably between 1800 and 6 March 1804 (perhaps about but not before 22 April 1802); first published in 1947.

MOTTO INTENDED FOR POEMS ON THE NAMING OF PLACES

Composed probably between 1800 and 6 March 1804; first published in 1944.

THE AFFLICTION OF MARGARET —

Composed probably between about 1800 and about early January 1807 (perhaps especially about 1800, spring 1802, or between late March 1804 and about early January 1807); first published in 1807; included from 1815 among 'Poems Founded on the Affections'.
  I. F. note:

  Town-End, Grasmere. 1804. This was taken from the case of a poor widow who lived in the town of Penrith. Her sorrow was well known to Mary, to my Sister, and, I believe, to the whole town. She kept a shop, and when she saw a stranger passing by, she was in the habit of going out into the street to inquire of him after her son.

  Cited by Coleridge (*Biographia Literaria*, Chapter XXII) as an example of 'meditative pathos, . . . a sympathy with man as man'. Coleridge referred to the poem as 'that most affecting composition, . . . which no mother, and, if I may judge by my own experience, no parent can read without a tear'.

THE FORSAKEN

Composed probably between about 1800 and about early January 1807 (perhaps especially about 1800, spring 1802, or between late March 1804 and about early January 1807); first published in 1842; included from 1845 among 'Poems Founded on the Affections'.
  I. F. note:

  This was an overflow from the 'Affliction of Margaret —', and was excluded as superfluous there, but preserved in the faint hope that it may turn to account by restoring a shy lover to some forsaken damsel. My poetry has been complained of as deficient in interests of this sort, – a charge which the piece beginning, 'Lyre! though such power do in thy magic live', will scarcely tend to obviate. The natural imagery of these verses was supplied by frequent, I might say intense, observation of the Rydal torrent.

THE ORCHARD PATHWAY

Composed probably between 1800 and late February 1807; first published in 1897.

'I TRAVELLED AMONG UNKNOWN MEN'

Composed probably shortly before 29 April 1801; first published in 1807; from 1815 included among 'Poems Founded on the Affections'. One of the 'Lucy poems'.

REPENTANCE

Composed probably basically between 24 November 1801 and mid-1802 (perhaps about April 1802), fairly certainly completed between about March 1815 and about early 1820; first published in 1820; included in 1820 among 'Poems of Sentiment and Reflection' and from 1827 among 'Poems Founded on the Affections'.

I. F. note: 'Town-End, Grasmere. 1804. Suggested by the conversation of our next neighbour, Margaret Ashburner.'

I. F. note (to *Mark the Concentred Hazels*): '. . . No inconsiderable part [of *Repentance*] . . . was taken verbatim from the language of the speaker herself.'

Dorothy Wordsworth's *Journal* (24 November 1801):

> [Peggy Ashburner] talked about Thomas's having sold his land. 'Ay,' says she, 'I said many a time he's not come fra London to buy our land, however.' Then she told me with what pains and industry they had made up their taxes, interest, etc. etc., how they all got up at 5 o'clock in the morning to spin and Thomas carded, and that they had paid off a hundred pounds of the interest. She said he used to take such pleasure in the cattle and sheep. 'O how pleased I used to be when they fetched them down, and when I had been a bit poorly I would gang out upon a hill and look over t' fields and see them, and it used to do me so much good you cannot think.'

THE MANCIPLE'S TALE

Modernized from Chaucer probably 2 and about 3 December 1801 (some corrections perhaps 28 April 1802); first published in 1947.

Wordsworth intended to publish this translation in 1841 with his other translations from Chaucer, but then decided to withdraw it on the advice of friends who thought it indelicate, although he himself disagreed with their judgement. In a letter to Dora Wordsworth (spring 1840) Wordsworth objected to the '*narrow*' view of the spirit of the Manciple's Tale, especially as concerns its *morality*'. 'The formal prosing at the end,' he continued,

> and the selfishness that pervades it flows from the genius of Chaucer, mainly as characteristic of the narrator whom he describes in the Prologue as eminent for shrewdness and clever worldly Prudence. The main lesson, and the most important one, is inculcated as a Poet ought chiefly to inculcate his lessons, not formally, but by implication; as when Phoebus in a transport of passion slays a wife whom he loved so dearly. How could

the mischief of telling truth, merely because it *is* truth, be more feelingly exemplified? The Manciple himself is not, in his understanding, conscious of this; but his heart dictates what was natural to be felt and the moral, without being intended, forces itself more or less upon every Reader. Then how vividly is impressed the mischief of jealous vigilance, and how truly and touchingly in contrast with the world's judgements are the transgressions of a woman in a low rank of life and one in high estate placed on the same level, treated.

THE PRIORESS' TALE

Modernized from Chaucer probably 4 and 5 December 1801 (some correction perhaps 28 April 1802); first published in 1820; included from 1820 to 1827 in an untitled category (with *The White Doe*), in 1832 by itself in an untitled category, in 1837 among 'Poems Founded on the Affections', and from 1845 among 'Selections from Chaucer Modernized'.

The motto is from Milton's *Il Penseroso* 109–10.

51 *scholar* better rendering: chorister.
61 not in Chaucer; an extra line to the stanza.
66 *with an earnest cheer* not in Chaucer.
113 *our* so reads the edition of Chaucer used by Wordsworth; modern editions read *your*.
231 *uncorrupted* Chaucer reads 'litel'.
233–9 last stanza contains irregular metre and rhyme.

THE CUCKOO AND THE NIGHTINGALE

Modernized from the original 7 to 9 December 1801; first published in 1841; from 1845 included among 'Selections from Chaucer Modernized'.

The original was thought by Wordsworth and his contemporaries to have been written by Chaucer, but it is now attributed to Sir Thomas Clanvowe (fl. 1390–1404). Wordsworth's source contained a number of corruptions, which show up in his translation (see *PW*, IV, 444–5).

201 'From a manuscript in the Bodleian, as are also stanzas 44 and 45, which are necessary to complete the sense.' – W.

TROILUS AND CRESIDA

Modernized from Chaucer perhaps about December 1801; first published in 1841; from 1845 included among 'Selections from Chaucer Modernized'.

A translation of Chaucer's *Troilus and Criseyde* V, 519–686.

8 *to cover his intent* in the original: 'his meine for to blend', to hoodwink the domestics.
21 *continuance* a mistake for the original's 'countenance'.
105 *his weakness* not in the original, but compare the whole line with *Hamlet* II, ii, 630: 'Out of my weakness and my melancholy'.

118 *With a soft voice* 1842–50: 'with a soft night voice', now considered an error in transcription or printing.

123 *with wind I steer and sail* in the original: 'with wind in stere I sayle' (with wind in the stern I sail).

138 *about* 1841–50: 'above', now considered an error for the original's 'aboute'.

WRITTEN IN A GROTTO

Usually considered by editors to have been written by Wordsworth. If so, composed possibly early 1802; first published 9 March 1802 in the *Morning Post*. For discussion of the attribution, made entirely on stylistic grounds, see *PW* III, 576.

10 *Smyrna's shepherds* 'The Shepherds of Smyrna show a cave, where, as they say, LUNA descended to ENDYMION, and a bed under a large oak, which was the scene of their loves. – See Chandler's Travels into Asia Minor.' – note in the *Morning Post*.

TO A YOUNG LADY

Composed perhaps between 23 and 27 January 1802 (certainly by 9 February); first published 12 February 1802 in the *Morning Post*; from 1815 to 1832 included among 'Poems of Sentiment and Reflection', and thereafter among 'Poems of the Imagination'.

I. F. note: 'Composed at the same time and on the same view as "I met Louisa in the shade". Indeed, they were designed to make one piece.'

The 'young lady' of the title has been variously identified as Joanna Hutchinson and Dorothy Wordsworth, who said she had been rebuked in 1794 by her aunt for 'rambling about the country on foot' (letter to Mrs C. Crackenthorpe, 21 April 1794).

LOUISA

Composed perhaps between 23 and 27 January 1802 (certainly by 9 February); first published in 1807; from 1815 included among 'Poems Founded on the Affections'.

Louisa has been variously identified as Dorothy Wordsworth, Joanna Hutchinson, and Mary Hutchinson.

7–12 I follow several editors in including this stanza, inexplicably deleted in editions from 1845 on.

19 *'beneath the moon'* *King Lear* IV, vi, 26.

THE SAILOR'S MOTHER

Composed 11, 12 March 1802; first published in 1807; from 1815 included among 'Poems Founded on the Affections'.

I. F. note: 'Town-End, 1800. I met this woman near the Wishing-Gate, on the high-road that then led from Grasmere to Ambleside. Her appearance was exactly as here described, and such was her account, nearly to the letter.' Coleridge observed (*Biographia Literaria*, Chapter xviii) that the last three stanzas 'furnish the only fair instance that I have been able to discover in all Mr. W.'s writings, of an *actual* adoption, or true imitation, of the *real* and *very* language of *low and rustic life*, freed from provincialisms'.

ALICE FELL

Composed 12, 13 March 1802; first published in 1807; from 1815 included among 'Poems Referring to the Period of Childhood' (but the poem was deleted from editions 1820-32 inclusive).

I. F. note:

Written to gratify Mr Graham of Glasgow, brother of the Author of the Sabbath. He was a zealous coadjutor of Mr Clarkson, and a man of ardent humanity. The incident had happened to himself, and he urged me to put it into verse for humanity's sake. The humbleness, meanness if you like, of the subject, together with the homely mode of treating it, brought upon me a world of ridicule by the small critics, so that in policy I excluded it from many editions of my poems, till it was restored at the request of my son-in-law, Edward Quillinan.

Dorothy Wordsworth's *Journal* (16 February 1802):

Mr Graham said he wished Wm had been with him the other day – he was riding in a post-chaise and he heard a strange cry that he could not understand, the sound continued, and he called to the chaise driver to stop. It was a little girl that was crying as if her heart would burst. She had got up behind the chaise, and her cloak had been caught by the wheel, and was jammed in, and it hung there. She was crying after it. Poor thing. Mr Graham took her into the chaise, and her cloak was released from the wheel, but the child's misery did not cease, for her cloak was torn to rags; it had been a miserable cloak before, but she had no other, and it was the greatest sorrow that could befall her. Her name was Alice Fell. She had no parents, and belonged to the next town. At the next town Mr G. left money with some respectable people in the town, to buy her a new cloak.

BEGGARS

Composed 13, 14 March 1802; first published in 1807; from 1815 contained among 'Poems of the Imagination'.

I. F. note: 'Town-End, 1802. Met, and described to me by my Sister, near the quarry at the head of Rydal Lake, a place still a chosen resort of vagrants travelling with their families.'

Dorothy Wordsworth's *Journal* (10 June 1800):

On Tuesday May 27th [1800] a very tall woman, tall much beyond the measure of tall women, called at the door. She had on a very long brown cloak, and a very white cap without Bonnet – her face was excessively brown, but it had plainly once been fair. She led a little bare-footed child about two years old by the hand, and said her husband, who was a tinker, was gone before with the other children. I gave her a piece of Bread. Afterwards on my road to Ambleside, beside the Bridge at Rydal, I saw her husband sitting by the roadside, his two asses feeding beside him, and the young children at play upon the grass. The man did not beg. I passed on and about a quarter of a mile further I saw two boys before me, one about 10, the other about 8 years old, at play chasing a butterfly. They were wild figures, not very ragged, but without shoes and stockings. The hat of the elder was wreathed round with yellow flowers; the younger, whose hat was only a rimless crown, had stuck it round with laurel leaves. They continued at play till I drew very near, and then they addressed me with the Beggars' cant and the whining voice of sorrow. I said 'I served your mother this morning' (the Boys were so like the woman who had called at the door that I could not be mistaken). 'O!' says the elder, 'you could not serve my mother, for she's dead, and my father's on at the next town – he's a potter.' I persisted in my assertion, and that I would give them nothing. Says the elder, 'Come, let's away,' and away they flew like lightning.

Wordsworth had difficulty avoiding Dorothy's exact wording (see her *Journal* 13 March 1802); see especially lines 21–6. This poem underwent considerable revision. Wordsworth wrote a sequel; see Volume II, p. 365.

Wordsworth told Henry Crabb Robinson (Edith J. Morley, *Henry Crabb Robinson on Books and Their Writers* [1938], I, 10–11) that he wrote the poem 'to exhibit the power of physical beauty and health and vigour in childhood even in a state of moral depravity'.

18 *weed of glorious feature* Compare Spenser's *Muiopotmos* 213.

TO A BUTTERFLY ('Stay near me')

Composed 14 March 1802; first published in 1807; in 1807 included in the group 'Moods of My Own Mind'; from 1815 included among 'Poems Referring to the Period of Childhood'.

I. F. note: 'Grasmere Town-End. Written in the Orchard ... My sister and I were parted immediately after the death of our Mother who died in 1778, both being very young.'

Dorothy Wordsworth's *Journal* (14 March 1802): 'The thought first came upon him as we were talking about the pleasure we both always feel at the sight of a Butterfly. I told him that I used to chase them a little, but that I was afraid of brushing the dust off their wings, and did not catch them – He told me how they used to kill all the white ones when he went to school because they were Frenchmen.'

12 *Emmeline* often identified as Dorothy Wordsworth.

THE EMIGRANT MOTHER

Composed 16, 17 March 1802; first published in 1807; from 1815 included among 'Poems Founded on the Affections'. Until 1820 the poem had no title.

I. F. note: '1802. Suggested by what I have noticed in more than one French fugitive during the time of the French Revolution.' Lines 55-64 were quoted by Coleridge (*Biographia Literaria*, Chapter XXII) as demonstrating 'inconstancy' or 'disharmony' of style.

11 *Endeavouring, in our English tongue* Compare Milton's *At a Vacation Exercise* 2: 'my first endeavouring tongue'.

TO THE CUCKOO ('O blithe New-comer!')

Composed perhaps largely 23-26 March 1802 (with further composition possible about 14 May and about 3 June); first published in 1807; in 1807 included in the group 'Moods of My Own Mind'; from 1815 included among 'Poems of the Imagination'.

Preface of 1815:

> This concise interrogation ['Shall I call thee Bird' etc.] characterizes the seeming ubiquity of the voice of the cuckoo, and dispossesses the creature almost of a corporeal existence; the Imagination being tempted to this exertion of her power by a consciousness in the memory that the cuckoo is almost perpetually heard throughout the season of spring, but seldom becomes an object of sight.

In his *Guide to the Lakes*, 3rd ed. (1822), p. 106, Wordsworth further observes: 'There is also an imaginative influence in the voice of the cuckoo, when that voice has taken possession of a deep mountain valley ...' Similarities have been noted between this poem and Michael Bruce's *Ode: To the Cuckoo* (1770).

'MY HEART LEAPS UP'

Composed probably 26 March 1802; first published in 1807; in 1807 included in the group 'Moods of My Own Mind'; from 1815 included among 'Poems Referring to the Period of Childhood'.

7-9 In 1815 placed as an epigraph to *Ode: Intimations*, which was begun the following day in 1802. In the same edition the entire poem '*My Heart Leaps Up*' was placed first.

TO H. C., SIX YEARS OLD

Composed possibly between 27 March and about 17 June 1802, or more probably early (by 6 March) 1804; first published in 1807; included from 1815 among 'Poems Referring to the Period of Childhood'. 'H.C.' was Hartley Coleridge, eldest son of Samuel Taylor Coleridge.

6-9 'See Carver's Description of his Situation upon one of the Lakes of

America.' – W. (1807). Jonathan Carver, *Travels Through the Interior Parts of North America* (1778), p. 133: 'The water at this time was as pure and transparent as air; and my canoe seemed as if it hung suspended in that element.'

ODE: INTIMATIONS OF IMMORTALITY

Composed probably between 27 March 1802 and probably early 1804 (by 6 March); first published in 1807; placed last and not included among any classification from 1815 on. In 1807 the poem was entitled simply *Ode* and the motto was 'Paulo majora canamus' ('Let us sing a little higher'); from 1815 the poem carried the present title and motto poem.

I. F. note:

> This was composed during my residence at Town-End, Grasmere; two years at least passed between the writing of the four first stanzas and the remaining part. To the attentive and competent reader the whole sufficiently explains itself; but there may be no harm in adverting here to particular feelings or *experiences* of my own mind on which the structure of the poem partly rests. Nothing was more difficult for me in childhood than to admit the notion of death as a state applicable to my own being. I have said elsewhere –

> > 'A simple child,
> > That lightly draws its breath,
> > And feels its life in every limb,
> > What should it know of death!' –

> But it was not so much from [feelings] of animal vivacity that *my* difficulty came as from a sense of the indomitableness of the spirit within me. I used to brood over the stories of Enoch and Elijah, and almost to persuade myself that, whatever might become of others, I should be translated, in something of the same way, to heaven. With a feeling congenial to this, I was often unable to think of external things as having external existence, and I communed with all that I saw as something not apart from, but inherent in, my own immaterial nature. Many times while going to school have I grasped at a wall or tree to recall myself from this abyss of idealism to the reality. At that time I was afraid of such processes. In later periods of life I have deplored, as we have all reason to do, a subjugation of an opposite character, and have rejoiced over the remembrances, as is expressed in the lines –

> > 'Obstinate questionings
> > Of sense and outward things,
> > Fallings from us, vanishings;' etc.

To that dream-like vividness and splendour which invest objects of sight in childhood, every one, I believe, if he would look back, could bear testimony, and I need not dwell upon it here: but having in the Poem regarded it as presumptive evidence of a prior state of existence, I think it right to protest against a conclusion, which has given pain to some good and pious persons, that I meant to inculcate such a belief. It is far too shadowy a notion to be recommended to faith, as more than an element in our instincts of immortality. But let us bear in mind that, though the idea is not advanced in revelation, there is nothing there to contradict it, and the fall of Man presents an analogy in its favor. Accordingly, a pre-existent state has entered into the popular creeds of many nations; and, among all persons acquainted with classic literature, is known as an ingredient in Platonic philosophy. Archimedes said that he could move the world if he had a point whereon to rest his machine. Who has not felt the same aspirations as regards the world of his own mind? Having to wield some of its elements when I was impelled to write this Poem on the 'Immortality of the Soul', I took hold of the notion of pre-existence as having sufficient foundation in humanity for authorizing me to make for my purpose the best use of it I could as a Poet.

In Christopher Wordsworth, *Memoirs* II, 476, Wordsworth observed further:

In my Ode on the *Intimations of Immortality in Childhood*, I do not profess to give a literal representation of the state of the affections and of the moral being in childhood. I record my own feelings at that time – my absolute spirituality, my 'all-soulness,' if I may so speak. At that time I could not believe that I should lie down quietly in the grave, and that my body would moulder into dust.

In the same *Memoirs* (II, 480), R. P. Graves is quoted as reporting:

I remember Mr Wordsworth saying that, at a particular stage of his mental progress, he used to be frequently so rapt into an unreal transcendental world of ideas that the external world seemed no longer to exist in relation to him, and he had to reconvince himself of its existence by *clasping a tree*, or something that happened to be near him.

In a letter to Mrs Clarkson (January 1815), Wordsworth further observed of the ode:

This poem rests entirely upon two recollections of childhood, one that of a splendour in the objects of sense which is passed away, and the other an indisposition to bend to the law of death, as applying to our particular case. A Reader who has not a vivid recollection of these feelings having existed in his mind cannot understand that poem.

1-9 Compare *The Voice from the Side of Etna* (possibly by Wordsworth) 9-16: 'There was a time when earth, and sea, and skies, / The bright green vale and forest's dark recess, / When all things lay before my eyes / In steady loveliness. / But now I feel on earth's uneasy scene / Such motions as will never cease! / I only ask for peace – / Then wherefore must I know that such a time has been?'

23 *A timely utterance* usually considered to be a reference to *'My Heart Leaps Up'*, composed the day before Wordsworth began the Ode – see the motto poem.

28 *the fields of sleep* Thomas Hutchinson suggests: 'the west, those on which the sun has not yet risen'.

36-40 Compare Wordsworth's *The Idle Shepherd-Boys* 27-30.

74-5 Compare Wordsworth's *The Barberry-Tree* 63-4.

86 *the Child* usually considered a reference to Hartley Coleridge, eldest son of Samuel Taylor Coleridge.

103 *cons* commits to memory.

104 *'humorous stage'* Daniel's dedicatory sonnet (line 1) to Fulke Greville in *Musophilus*. *Humorous* means 'fanciful'.

105 *Persons* dramatis personae.

109-21 Coleridge (*Biographia Literaria*, Chapter XXII) objected to this passage as '*mental* bombast'.

119-20 *thy Immortality Broods like the Day* Compare Wordsworth's *Essay upon Epitaphs* (fifth paragraph): 'If we look back upon the days of childhood, we shall find that the time is not in remembrance when, with respect to our own individual Being, the mind was without this assurance [of immortality].'

121 Following this line, Wordsworth after 1815 deleted the following passage to which Coleridge objected in the *Biographia Literaria* (Chapter XXII): 'To whom the grave / Is but a lonely bed without the sense or sight / Of day or the warm light, / A place of thought where we in waiting lie.' Coleridge disliked the 'frightful notion of lying *awake* in the grave', but a passage in Dorothy Wordsworth's *Journal* (29 April 1802) evinces a quite different attitude: 'We then went to John's Grove, sate a while at first. Afterwards William lay, and I lay, in the trench under the fence . . . He thought that it would be as sweet thus to lie so in the grave, to hear the *peaceful* sounds of the earth, and just to know that our dear friends were near.'

127-8 Compare *The Prelude* XIV, 157-9: 'The tendency, too potent in itself, / Of use and custom to bow down the soul / Under a growing weight of vulgar sense . . .'

155-6 *Our noisy years . . . Silence* Compare *Address to Silence* (probably by Wordsworth) 50: 'Our little years are moments of thy [Silence's] life', and Wordsworth's *On the Power of Sound* 217-18: 'O Silence! are Man's noisy years / No more than moments of thy life?'

161 *abolish or destroy* Compare *Paradise Lost* II, 92-3: 'More destroyed than thus / We should be quite abolisht and expire'.

182 *primal sympathy* Compare *The Prelude* I, 555-8: 'To those first-born affinities that fit / Our new existence to existing things, / And, in our dawn of being, constitute / The bond of union between life and joy'.

190 *in my heart of hearts* Hamlet III, ii, 78.

203 *the meanest flower* Compare Gray's *Ode on the Pleasure Arising from Vicissitude* (1754), 49: 'The meanest floweret of the vale'.

THE SPARROW'S NEST

Composed probably about March–April 1802 (certainly by 7 May); first published in 1807; in 1807 included in a group of poems entitled 'Moods of My Own Mind'; from 1815 to 1843 it was included among 'Poems Founded on the Affections', and thereafter among 'Poems Referring to the Period of Childhood'.

I. F. note:

> The Orchard, Grasmere Town-End, 1801. At the end of the garden at my Father's house at Cockermouth was a high terrace . . . The terrace-wall, a low one, was covered with closely clipt privet and roses, which gave an almost impervious shelter to birds that built their nests there. The latter of these stanzas alludes to one of these nests.

9 *Emmeline* 'Dorothy' in the MS sent to the printer.
15-17 Compare Charles Churchill's *Independence* (1764) 42-3: 'The blessing she [Nature] bestow'd – she gave them eyes, / And they could see; she gave them ears – they heard . . .'
18 Compare *The Prelude* XIV, 230: 'Of humble cares and delicate desires'.

TO A SKY-LARK ('Up with me')

Composed probably between about March and 29 July 1802; first published in 1807; included from 1815 among 'Poems of the Fancy'.

In a letter to Barron Field (October 1828), Wordsworth explained his considerable revisions:

> After having succeeded in the second *Skylark* ['Ethereal Minstrel . . .'] and in the conclusion of the poem entitled *A Morning Exercise*, in my notice of this bird, I became indifferent to this poem, which Coleridge used severely to condemn and to treat contemptuously. I like, however, the beginning of it [lines 1–7] so well that, for the sake of that, I tacked to it the respectably-tame conclusion [lines 26–31].

The intervening lines (8–25), dropped in 1827, were restored in 1832.

'AMONG ALL LOVELY THINGS' [THE GLOW-WORM]

Composed 12 April 1802; first published in 1807 and never reprinted by Wordsworth.

In a letter to Coleridge (16 April 1802), Wordsworth commented on the poem: 'The incident . . . took place about seven years ago between Dorothy and me.' The poem had no title when first published, but in Dorothy Wordsworth's *Journal* it is referred to as *The Glow-Worm*.

WRITTEN IN MARCH

Composed 16 April 1802; first published in 1807; in 1807 included in the group 'Moods of My Own Mind'; from 1815 included among 'Poems of the Imagination'.

I. F. note: 'Extempore ... This little poem was a favourite with Joanna Baillie [1762–1851; a minor Scottish poet and dramatist].'

Dorothy Wordsworth's *Journal* (16 April 1802):

When we came to the foot of Brother's Water I left William sitting on the bridge ... When I returned I found William writing a poem descriptive of the sights and sounds we saw and heard. There was the gentle flowing of the stream, the glittering, lively lake, green fields without a living creature to be seen on them; behind us, a flat pasture with forty-two cattle feeding ... The people were at work ploughing, harrowing, and sowing; lasses spreading dung, a dog's barking now and then; cocks crowing, birds twittering; the snow in patches at the top of the highest hills .. . William finished his poem before we got to the foot of Kirkstone.

Brother's Water is a small lake near the foot of Kirkstone Pass.

THE GREEN LINNET

Composed perhaps between 16 April and 8 July 1802; first published in 1807; from 1815 included among 'Poems of the Fancy'.

I. F. note: 'Composed in the Orchard, Town-End, where the bird was often seen as here described.'

TO THE DAISY ('In youth')

Composed perhaps between 16 April and 8 July 1802; first published 1807; from 1815 included among 'Poems of the Fancy'.

I. F. note: 'Composed in Town-End Orchard ...'

Wordsworth's note (1807):

This Poem, and the two others to the same Flower, ... were written in the year 1802; which is mentioned, because in some of the ideas, though not in the manner in which those ideas are connected, and likewise even in some of the expressions, there is a resemblance to passages in a Poem (lately published) of Mr Montgomery entitled A Field Flower ...

The motto poem is from George Wither's *The Shepherd's Hunting* (1615), *Eclogue* IV, 366–78 (slightly misquoted).

22 *remote* rhymes with 'naught' and 'thought' in North-country dialect.

25 *secret mews* Compare *The Faerie Queene* II, vii, 19: 'But safe I have them kept in secret mew'.

34-6 In a letter to Lady Beaumont (postmarked 3 February 1807) Words-worth comments: '... In the month of April I have passed many an hour under the shade of a green Holly, glad to find it in my walk, and unwilling to quit it because I had not the courage to face the sun.'

39 *scare* drive off.

64 *careful* troubled.

80 'See in Chaucer and elder Poets, the honours formerly paid to this flower.' – W.

TO THE DAISY ('Bright Flower!')

Composed perhaps at least partly between 16 April and 8 July 1802, and possibly not completed until between 6 March 1804 and about March 1805; first published in 1807; included from 1815 to 1832 among 'Poems of the Fancy', and afterwards among 'Poems of Sentiment and Reflection'.

See Wordsworth's remarks in the head-note to the preceding poem.

I. F. note: 'This and the other poems addressed to the same flower were composed at Town-End, Grasmere, during the earlier part of my residence there.'

23 I have been censured for the last line but one – 'thy function apostolical' – as being little less than profane. How could it be thought so? The word is adopted with reference to its derivation, implying something sent on a mission; and assuredly this little flower, especially when the subject of verse, may be regarded, in its humble degree, as administering both to moral and to spiritual purposes.

– *I. F. note.*

TO THE SAME FLOWER [The Daisy] ('With little')

Composed perhaps at least partly between 16 April and 8 July 1802, and possibly not completed until between 6 March 1804 and about March 1805; first published in 1807; included from 1815 among 'Poems of the Fancy'.

See Wordsworth's remarks in the head-notes to the two preceding poems.

Wordsworth's *note* (1807): This and *To the Daisy* ('Bright flower') 'were overflowings of the mind in composing' *To the Daisy* ('In youth').

6 *homely* simple, unadorned.

THE REDBREAST CHASING THE BUTTERFLY

Composed 18 April 1802; first published in 1807; from 1815 included among 'Poems of the Fancy'.

I. F. note: 'Observed as described in the then beautiful Orchard at Town-End.' Dorothy Wordsworth's *Journal* (17 April 1802): 'I saw a robin chasing a scarlet butterfly this morning.'

2 *The pious bird* Compare: 'And Robin redbreasts whom men praise / For pious birds,' attributed by Knight to Cowley. See also the note to lines 22–3 below.

12 'See "Paradise Lost," Book XI., where Adam points out to Eve the ominous sign of the Eagle chasing "two Birds of gayest plume," and the gentle Hart and Hind pursued by their enemy.' – W.

22-3 See Bishop Percy's *Reliques*, 'The Children in the Wood' 125-8: 'No burial this pretty fair / Of any man receives, / Till Robin-red-breast piously/ Did cover them with leaves.'

TO A BUTTERFLY ('I've watched you now')

Composed 20 April 1802; first published in 1807; in 1807 included in the group 'Moods of My Own Mind'; from 1815 included among 'Poems Founded on the Affections'.

[FRAGMENTS FROM DOVE COTTAGE MS. 44 (ii)]

Composed probably about ('*I have thoughts*' certainly by) 22 April 1802; first published in 1947.

Dorothy Wordsworth's *Journal* (22 April 1802):

> We walked into Easedale ... The waters were high, for there had been a great quantity of rain in the night. I ... sate upon the grass till [William and Coleridge] came from the Waterfall ... When they returned William was repeating the poem 'I have thoughts that are fed by the sun' [line 13]. It had been called to his mind by the dying away of the stunning of the waterfall when he came behind a stone.

THE TINKER

Composed 27-29 April 1802; first published in 1897.

A tinker is an itinerant craftsman who mends pots and pans.

FORESIGHT

Composed 28 April 1802; first published in 1807; from 1815 included among 'Poems Referring to the Period of Childhood'.

Dorothy Wordsworth's *Journal* (28 April 1802): 'William was in the Orchard. I went to him ... I happened to say that when I was young I would not have pulled a strawberry blossom.' From 1807 to 1832 the poem had the subtitle 'or the Charge of a Child to his Younger Companion'.

TO THE SMALL CELANDINE ('Pansies, lilies')

Composed probably 30 April – 1 May 1802; first published in 1807; from 1815 included among 'Poems of the Fancy'.

I. F. note: 'It is remarkable that this flower, coming out so early in the Spring as it does, and so bright and beautiful, and in such profusion, should not have been noticed earlier in English verse.' In a note to the title Wordsworth identified the celandine as a 'Common Pilewort'.

THE BARBERRY-TREE

Composed probably between late April and June 1802 (possibly 28 May 1802); first published 31 July 1964 in the *New Statesman*. This poem was recently found in a letter from Charles Abraham Elton to his sister Julia, wife of Henry Hallam, the historian, dated 22 September 1807. The case for its authenticity has been convincingly made by Jonathan Wordsworth in *College English* XXVII (1966), 455–65.

5 *nodded in the breeze* Compare *Ruth* 23: 'The feathers nodded in the breeze'.
6 *rustled in mine ear* Compare *The Pet Lamb* 28: 'And that green corn all day is rustling in thy ears'.
9–24 Compare *'I Wandered Lonely as a Cloud'* 1–10, 17–18 for general resemblance.
42 *I cannot tell, I do not know* Compare *Anecdote for Fathers* 39: '"I cannot tell, I do not know"'.
55 *Peter Grimes* the main character in the poem by George Crabbe published in 1810.
63–4 Compare *Ode: Intimations* 73–4: 'And by the vision splendid / Is on his way attended'. Also compare *Guilt and Sorrow* 90: 'But, when the trance was gone, feebly pursued his way'.
67–72 Compare *The Solitary Reaper* 29–32 for general resemblance.
85 *Jacob Jones* unidentified.
87–90 Words are missing where the seal of the letter was torn off.

TO THE SAME FLOWER [The Small Celandine] ('Pleasures newly found')

Composed probably 1 May 1802; first published in 1807; from 1815 included among 'Poems of the Fancy'.

33–40 'What adds much to the interest that attaches to [the celandine] is its habit of shutting itself up and opening out according to the degree of light and temperature of the air.' – *I. F. note* (to *To the Small Celandine* ['Pansies, lilies']).
50 *'beneath our shoon'* Compare *Comus* 634–5: 'And the dull swain / Treads on it daily with his clouted shoon'.

RESOLUTION AND INDEPENDENCE

First version composed 3–7 May 1802, with revisions 9 May and heavy revisions perhaps between 14 June and 4 July 1802; first published in 1807; from 1815 included among 'Poems of the Imagination'.
I. F. note:

This old man I met a few hundred yards from my cottage at Town-End, Grasmere; and the account of him is taken from his own mouth. I was in the state of feeling described in the beginning of the poem, while crossing over Barton Fell from Mr Clarkson's, at the foot of Ullswater, towards Askam. The image of the hare I then observed on the ridge of the Fell.

Dorothy Wordsworth's *Journal* (3 October 1800):

When William and I returned from accompanying Jones, we met an old man almost double. He had on a coat, thrown over his shoulders above his waistcoat and coat. Under this he carried a bundle, and had an apron on and a nightcap. His face was interesting. He had dark eyes and a long nose. John, who afterwards met him at Wytheburn, took him for a Jew. He was of Scotch parents, but had been born in the army. He had had a wife, and 'a good woman, and it pleased God to bless us with ten children'. All these were dead but one, of whom he had not heard for many years, a sailor. His trade was to gather leeches, but now leeches are scarce, and he had not strength for it. He lived by begging, and was making his way to Carlisle, where he should buy a few godly books to sell. He said leeches were very scarce, partly owing to the dry season, but many years they have been scarce. He supposed it owing to their being much sought after, that they did not breed fast, and were of slow growth. Leeches were formerly 2s. 6d. [per] 100; now they are 30s.

Wordsworth offers an interpretation of the poem in a letter to Sara Hutchinson (14 June 1802) [some of the quotations given are from an early draft – see *PW*, II, 536]:

I describe myself as having been exalted to the highest pitch of delight by the joyousness and beauty of Nature and then as depressed, even in the midst of those beautiful objects, to the lowest dejection and despair. A young Poet in the midst of the happiness of Nature is described as over-whelmed by the thought of the miserable reverses which have befallen the happiest of all men, viz Poets – I think of this till I am so deeply impressed by it, that I consider the manner in which I was rescued from my dejection and despair almost as an interposition of Providence. 'Now whether it was by peculiar grace, A leading from above'. A person reading this Poem with feelings like mine will have been awed and controuled, expecting almost something spiritual or supernatural – What is brought forward? 'A lonely place, a Pond' 'by which an old man *was*, far from all house or home' – not stood, not sat, but *'was'* – the figure presented in the most naked simplicity possible. This feeling of spirituality or supernaturalness is again referred to as being strong in my mind in this passage – *'How came he here* thought I or what can he be doing?' I then describe him, whether ill or well is not for me to judge with perfect confidence, but this I can *confidently* affirm, that, though I believe God has given me a strong imagination, I cannot conceive a figure more impressive than that of an old Man like this, the survivor of a Wife and ten children, travelling alone among the mountains and all lonely places, carrying with him his own fortitude, and the necessities which an unjust state of society has entailed upon him. You say and Mary (that is you can say no more than that) the

Poem is *very well* after the introduction of the old man; this is not true, if it is not more than very well it is very bad, there is no intermediate state. You speak of his speech as tedious: everything is tedious when one does not read with the feelings of the Author – *'The Thorn'* is tedious to hundreds; and so is the *Idiot Boy* to hundreds. It is in the character of the old man to tell his story in a manner which an *impatient* reader must necessarily feel as tedious. But Good God! Such a figure, in such a place, a pious self-respecting, miserably infirm, and [   ] Old Man telling such a tale!

My dear Sara, it is not a matter of indifference whether you are pleased with this figure and his employment; it may be comparatively so, whether you are pleased or not with *this Poem*; but it is of the utmost importance that you should have had pleasure from contemplating the fortitude, independence, persevering spirit, and the general moral dignity of this old man's character.

5 *the Stock-dove broods*

The Stock-dove is said to *coo*, a sound well imitating the note of the bird; but, by intervention of the metaphor *broods*, the affections are called in by the imagination to assist in marking the manner in which the bird reiterates and prolongs her soft note, as if herself delighting to listen to it, and participating of a still and quiet satisfaction, like that which may be supposed inseparable from the continuous process of incubation.

– W. (Preface of 1815).

39 *genial* cheerful *and* creative (a common play-on-words, pointing up their common root, often made by Coleridge).

43 *Chatterton* Thomas Chatterton (1752–70). Chatterton's *Excellent Ballade of Charitie* has the same stanza form as *Resolution and Independence* and a similar focus on an old man.

45-6 'Him' is Robert Burns.

56 The following stanza, which originally came after line 56, was deleted in 1820, probably because it was criticized by Coleridge for demonstrating 'inconstancy of style' (*Biographia Literaria*, Chapter XXII): 'My course I stopped as soon as I espied / The Old Man in that naked wilderness: / Close by a Pond, upon the further side, / He stood alone: a minute's space I guess / I watched him, he continuing motionless: / To the Pool's further margin then I drew; / He being all the while before me full in view.'

57-65 Quoted (along with lines 75–7) in the 1815 Preface with the observation: 'In these images, the conferring, the abstracting, and the modifying powers of the Imagination, immediately and mediately acting, are all brought into conjunction.' Wordsworth continues by describing how each image prepares for the next.

TRAVELLING

Composed perhaps about (but by) 4 May 1802 (revised slightly before 6 March 1804); first published in 1947.

Dorothy Wordsworth's *Journal* (4 May 1802): 'I repeated verses to William while he was in bed; he was soothed and I left him. "This is the spot" over and over again.'

STANZAS WRITTEN IN MY POCKET-COPY

Composed probably 9, 10, 11 May 1802; first published in 1815; from 1815 included among 'Poems Founded on the Affections'.

I. F. note: 'Composed in the Orchard, Grasmere, Town-End. Coleridge was living with us much at the time; his son Hartley has said, that his father's character and habits are here preserved in a livelier way than anything that has been written about him.' The last four stanzas refer to Coleridge, the first four to Wordsworth himself. Wordsworth's portrait of himself owes a good deal to Beattie's characterization of Edwin, the hero of *The Minstrel* (1771-4).

The poem should be read with Thomson's *Castle of Indolence* (1748) fresh in mind, for Wordsworth's poem imitates Thomson's style and mood.

27 *like a naked Indian* Compare *The Prelude* I, 300.

58 *deftly* softly (North-country dialect).

1801 ('I grieved for Buonaparté!')

Composed probably 21 May 1802; first published 16 September 1802 in the *Morning Post*; from 1815 included among 'Poems Dedicated to National Independence and Liberty'.

'METHOUGHT I SAW THE FOOTSTEPS OF A THRONE'

Composed probably between 21 May and about late 1802 (possibly late July or 25 December 1802); first published in 1807; from 1815 included among 'Miscellaneous Sonnets'.

I. F. note: 'The latter part ... was a great favourite with my Sister Sara Hutchinson.'

1 *Methought I saw* Possibly an echo of Milton's sonnet *'Methought I Saw My Late Espousèd Saint'*.

'GREAT MEN HAVE BEEN AMONG US'

Composed probably between 21 May and about late 1802 (possibly by 25 December); first published in 1807; from 1815 included among 'Poems Dedicated to National Independence and Liberty'.

3-4 Algernon Sidney (1622-83), Andrew Marvell (1621-78), James Harrington (1611-77), Sir Henry Vane the Younger (1613-62). All of these men were active in the Commonwealth.

'ENGLAND! THE TIME IS COME'

All data identical with the preceding poem.

'IT IS NOT TO BE THOUGHT OF'

Composed probably between 21 May and about late 1802 (possibly by 25 December); first published 16 April 1803 in the *Morning Post*; from 1815 included among 'Poems Dedicated to National Independence and Liberty'.

4 *'with pomp of waters, unwithstood'* Samuel Daniel's *Civil Wars* II, 7.
5–6 *1827–50*; 'Road by which all might come and go that would, / And bear out freights of worth to foreign Lands' *1803–20*. Note the growing conservatism reflected in this revision.

'THERE IS A BONDAGE WORSE'

Composed probably between 21 May and about late 1802 (possibly by 25 December); first published in 1807; from 1815 included among 'Poems Dedicated to National Independence and Liberty'.

'WHEN I HAVE BORNE IN MEMORY'

Composed probably between 21 May and about late 1802 (possibly by 25 December); first published 17 September 1803 in the *Morning Post* (with the title *England*); from 1815 included among 'Poems Dedicated to National Independence and Liberty'.

TO SLEEP ('O gentle Sleep!')

Composed probably between 21 May and about late 1802 (possibly by 25 December); first published in 1807; from 1815 included among 'Miscellaneous Sonnets'.

TO SLEEP ('A flock of sheep')

All data identical with the preceding poem.

2–4 Compare *The Faerie Queene* I, i, 41: 'And more, to lull him in his slumber soft, / A trickling stream from high rock tumbling down / And ever-drizzling raine upon the loft, / Mixt with a murmuring wind, much like the sowne, / Of swarming Bees, did cast him in a swowne'.

TO SLEEP ('Fond words')

All data identical with the preceding poem.

'"BELOVED VALE!" I SAID, "WHEN I SHALL CON"'

Composed probably between 21 May and about late 1802 (possibly by 25 December); first published in 1807; from 1815 included among 'Miscellaneous Sonnets'.

1 *Vale* undoubtedly the Vale of Esthwaite.

'BROOK! WHOSE SOCIETY THE POET SEEKS'

Composed probably between 21 May and about late 1802 (possibly by 25 December); first published in 1815; from 1815 included among 'Miscellaneous Sonnets'.

'WHAT IF OUR NUMBERS BARELY COULD DEFY'

Composed probably between 21 May and about late 1802 (possibly by 25 December); first published in 1837; from 1837 included among 'Poems Dedicated to National Independence and Liberty'. The earliest version, which differs considerably from the poem printed in the text, can be found in *PW*, III, 456.

'THERE IS A LITTLE UNPRETENDING RILL'

Composed in early version probably between 21 May and about late 1802 (possibly by 25 December), in first published version perhaps by late October 1814; first published in 1820; from 1820 included among 'Miscellaneous Sonnets'.

  I. F. note:

  The rill trickles down the hill-side into Windermere, near Lowwood. My sister and I, on our first visit together to this part of the country, walked from Kendal, and we rested to refresh ourselves by the side of the lake where the streamlet falls into it. The sonnet was written some years after in recollection of that happy ramble, that most happy day and hour.

'I FIND IT WRITTEN OF SIMONIDES'

Composed probably between 21 May 1802 and 7 October 1803; first published 10 October 1803 in the *Morning Post*. Never reprinted by Wordsworth.

  The story is told in prose in Wordsworth's *Essay on Epitaphs* I (1810) (fourth paragraph); Wordsworth probably found the original in Valerius Maximus I, viii ('De Miraculis') or Cicero's *De Divinatione* I.

'HOW SWEET IT IS'

Composed probably between 21 May 1802 and 6 March 1804; first published in 1807; from 1815 included among 'Miscellaneous Sonnets'.

  Henry Crabb Robinson in his *Diary* (3 June 1812) claimed Wordsworth said this was nearly his only sonnet 'of pure fancy'.

PERSONAL TALK

Composed probably between 21 May 1802 and 6 March 1804; first published in 1807; included in 1815 among 'Poems of Sentiment and Reflection'. from

1820 to 1843 among 'Miscellaneous Sonnets', and replaced in the original category in 1845.

I. F. note: 'Written at Town-End. The last line but two [of Sonnet I] stood, at first, better and more characteristically thus: "By my half-kitchen and half-parlour fire." My Sister and I were in the habit of having the tea-kettle in our little sitting-room . . .'

6 *maidens withering on the stalk* 'Miss Fenwick . . . has always stigmatized one line . . . as vulgar, and worthy only of having been composed by a country Squire' – *I. F. note*. Compare *Comus* 743–4: 'If you let slip time, like a neglected rose / It withers on the stalk . . .' See also *A Midsummer-Night's Dream* I, i, 76–8.

7–8 *Forms . . . floors* lines to guide the dancers.

26 *by distance made more sweet* Collins's *Ode, The Passions* (1747) 60. Previously quoted in *An Evening Walk* 237.

32 *with the lofty sanctifies the low* See *The Prelude* XIV, 271, and *Epitaph from Chiabrera* ('There never breathed') 24.

41–2 See *Othello* and *The Faerie Queene* I.

44 *remote* in North-country dialect rhymed with 'sought' (line 45).

51–6 Inscribed on the pedestal of Wordsworth's statue in Westminster Abbey.

'PELION AND OSSA'

Composed probably between 21 May 1802 and 6 March 1804; first published in 1815; from 1815 included among 'Miscellaneous Sonnets'.

1 *Pelion and Ossa* adjoining mountains in Greece.

4–5 *'did divide . . . forehead wide'* See Spenser's *Virgil's Gnat* 21–4: 'Or whereas mount *Parnasse*, the Muses brood, / Doth his broad forehead like two horns divide, / And the sweet waves of sounding *Castaly* / With liquid foot doth slide down easily'.

14 *more sweet than Castaly* See note to lines 4–5 above.

'THE WORLD IS TOO MUCH WITH US'

Composed probably between 21 May 1802 and 6 March 1804; first published in 1807; from 1815 included among 'Miscellaneous Sonnets'.

11 *pleasant lea* Spenser's *Colin Clouts Come Home Againe* 283.

13 *Proteus rising from the sea* Compare *Paradise Lost* III, 603–4: 'and call up unbound / In various shapes old *Proteus* from the Sea'.

14 *Triton blow his wreathèd horn* Compare *Colin Clouts* 245: '*Triton* blowing loud his wreathèd horne'.

TO THE MEMORY OF RAISLEY CALVERT

All data identical with the preceding poem.

I. F. note: 'This young man, Raisley Calvert, to whom I was so much indebted [for a legacy], died at Penrith, 1795.'

11–12 *the lays Of higher mood* Compare *Lycidas* 87: 'That strain I heard was of a higher mood'.

'WHERE LIES THE LAND'

All data identical with the preceding poem.

In Henry Crabb Robinson's *Diary* (3 June 1812) Wordsworth is quoted as saying the poem 'expressed the delight he had felt on thinking of the first feelings of men before navigation had so completely made the world known, and while a ship exploring unknown regions was an object of high interest and sympathy'.

"'WITH HOW SAD STEPS, O MOON'"

Composed probably between 21 May 1802 and 6 March 1804; first published in 1807. This sonnet began as a quinzain placed among 'Poems Composed During a Tour, Chiefly on Foot' in 1807, was included among 'Poems of the Fancy' in 1815, and was reduced to fourteen lines in 1820 and placed among 'Miscellaneous Sonnets'. It was heavily revised.

1–2 'From a Sonnet of Sir Philip Sydney.' – W. (1807–15). *Astrophel and Stella* XXXI.

'WITH SHIPS THE SEA WAS SPRINKLED'

Composed probably between 21 May 1802 and 6 March 1804; first published in 1807; from 1815 included among 'Miscellaneous Sonnets'.

In a letter to Lady Beaumont (21 May 1807), Wordsworth attempts an explication of the poem, the main point of which is as follows:

> There is scarcely one of my Poems which does not aim to direct the attention to some moral sentiment, or to some general principle, or law of thought, or of our intellectual constitution. For instance, in the present case, who is there that has not felt that the mind can have no rest among a multitude of objects, of which it either cannot make one whole or from which it cannot single out one individual, whereupon may be concentrated the attention divided among or distracted by a multitude? After a certain time we must either select one image or object, which must put out of view the rest wholly, or must subordinate them to itself while it stands forth as a Head . . .

5–8 'From a passage in Skelton which I cannot here insert, not having the Book at hand.' – W. (1807). Skelton's *Bowge of Court* 36–8: 'Methought I saw a ship, goodly of sail, / Come sailing forth into that haven broad, / Her tackling rich and of high apparel.'

'IT IS NO SPIRIT WHO FROM HEAVEN HATH FLOWN'

Composed probably between 21 May 1802 and 6 March 1804 (perhaps between 8 November 1802 and 7 January 1803 or between 1 and 28 April

1803); first published in 1807; in 1807 included in the group 'Moods of My Own Mind'; from 1815 included among 'Poems of the Imagination'.

I. F. note: '1803. Town-End. I remember the instant my sister S.[ara] H.[utchinson], called me to the window of our Cottage, saying, "Look how beautiful is yon star? It has the sky all to itself." I composed the verses immediately.'

ON THE EXTINCTION OF THE VENETIAN REPUBLIC

Composed probably between 21 May 1802 and early February 1807; first published in 1807; from 1815 included among 'Poems Dedicated to National Independence and Liberty'.

1–2 At her highest peak in the fifteenth century, Venice was a considerable commercial power as a centre of trade with the East. She was also a bulwark against Turkish invasion of Europe.

8 *espouse the everlasting Sea* In an annual ceremony, the Doge of Venice wedded his city and the Adriatic.

12 *its final day* In 1797 Napoleon brought an end to the Republic of Venice.

A FAREWELL

Composed probably for the most part about late May (by 29 May) 1802, with revision between 30 May and 14 June 1802; first published in 1815; from 1815 included among 'Poems Founded on the Affections'.

I. F. note: '1802. Composed just before my Sister and I went to fetch Mary from Gallow-hill, near Scarborough.' In a letter to Mary Hutchinson (14 June 1802), Wordsworth refers to the poem as 'Spenserian', thus allowing it to accommodate slightly more extravagant imagery.

1 *little Nook of mountain-ground* Dove cottage.

22 *Bright gowan* the globe-flower.

56 *one song The Sparrow's Nest.*

'THE SUN HAS LONG BEEN SET'

Composed 8 June 1802; first published in 1807, placed among 'Moods of My Own Mind'. Not published 1815–32; from 1835 included among 'Evening Voluntaries'.

10–11 *'parading', 'masquerading'* Burns, *The Twa Dogs* (1786), 153–4: 'at operas and plays parading, / Mortgaging, gambling, masquerading'.

COMPOSED UPON WESTMINSTER BRIDGE

Composition begun perhaps 31 July 1802 (probably completed 3 September 1802); first published in 1807; from 1815 included among 'Miscellaneous Sonnets'.

I. F. note: 'Composed on the roof of a coach on my way to France Sept. 1802.' Dorothy Wordsworth's *Journal* (for 31 July 1802):

> ... We left London on Saturday morning at half past five or six, the 31st of July (I have forgot which). We mounted the Dover Coach at Charing Cross. It was a beautiful morning. The City, St Paul's, with the River and a multitude of little Boats, made a most beautiful sight as we crossed Westminster Bridge. The houses were not overhung by their cloud of smoke, and they were spread out endlessly, yet the sun shone so brightly, with such a pure light, that there was even something like the purity of one of nature's own grand spectacles.

4-5 *like a garment, wear ... bare* '... The contradiction is in the *words* only – bare, as not being covered with smoke or vapour; – clothed, as being attired in the beams of morning.' – W. (letter to John Kenyon, late autumn 1836).

COMPOSED NEAR CALAIS

Composed probably 1 or 7 August 1802; first published in 1807; from 1815 included among 'Poems Dedicated to National Independence and Liberty'.

Autobiographical Memoir (Christopher Wordsworth, *Memoir* I, 14): 'In August, 1790, I set off for the continent in companionship with Robert Jones, a Welshman, a fellow-collegean. We crossed from Dover and landed at Calais on the eve of the day when the king was to swear fidelity to the new constitution ...'

3 *day* '14th July, 1790.' – W.

CALAIS, AUGUST, 1802

Composed probably between 1 and 29 August 1802; first published 13 January 1803 in the *Morning Post*; from 1815 included among 'Poems Dedicated to National Independence and Liberty'.

1-2 *Matthew* 11:7.

3-7 Napoleon was made First Consul for life on 2 August 1802. Sir Francis Romilly's *Diary* (October 1802): 'I had been disgusted at the eagerness with which the English crowded to do homage at the new court of a usurper and a tyrant ...'

COMPOSED BY THE SEA-SIDE

Composed probably between 1 and 29 August 1802; first published in 1807; from 1815 included among 'Poems Dedicated to National Independence and Liberty'.

Dorothy Wordsworth's *Journal* (August 1802): '... We had delightful walks after the heat of the day was passed away – seeing far off in the west the Coast of England like a cloud crested with Dover Castle, which was but like the summit of the cloud. The Evening star and the glory of the sky.'

'IT IS A BEAUTEOUS EVENING'

Composed probably between 1 and 29 August 1802; first published in 1807; from 1815 included among 'Miscellaneous Sonnets'.

I. F. note: 'This was composed on the beach near Calais in the autumn of 1802.' Dorothy Wordsworth's *Journal* (August 1802): 'The weather was very hot. We walked by the seashore almost every evening with Annette and Caroline, or William and I alone . . . It was also beautiful, on the calm hot night . . . Caroline was delighted.'

9 *Dear Child* Caroline, Wordsworth's daughter by Annette Vallon, was ten years old at the time.

12 *Abraham's bosom Luke* 16:22.

TO TOUSSAINT L'OUVERTURE

Composed possibly between 1 and 29 August 1802; first published in the *Morning Post*, 2 February 1803; from 1815 included among 'Poems Dedicated to National Independence and Liberty'.

François Dominique Toussaint, surnamed L'Ouverture, was the son of a Negro slave; as governor of Haiti, he resisted Napoleon's re-establishment of slavery and was imprisoned in 1802.

14 *unconquerable mind* Gray's *The Progress of Poesy* (1757) 65.

CALAIS, AUGUST 15, 1802

Composed probably 15 August 1802; first published 26 February 1803 in the *Morning Post*; from 1815 included among 'Poems Dedicated to National Independence and Liberty'.

SEPTEMBER 1, 1802

Composed perhaps between 29 August and 1 September 1802; first published 11 February 1803 in the *Morning Post* (with the title *The Banished Negroes*); from 1815 included among 'Poems Dedicated to National Independence and Liberty'. This sonnet was heavily revised over the years.

COMPOSED IN THE VALLEY NEAR DOVER

Composed probably 30 August 1802; first published in 1807; from 1815 included among 'Poems Dedicated to National Independence and Liberty'.

Dorothy Wordsworth's *Journal of a Tour on the Continent* (10 July 1820):

When within a mile of Dover, saw crowds of people at a Cricket-Match, the numerous combatants dressed in 'white-sleeved shirts', and it was in the very same field where, when we 'trod the grass of England' once again, twenty years ago, we had seen an Assemblage of Youths engaged in the same sport, so very like the present that all might have been the same!

SEPTEMBER, 1802. NEAR DOVER

Composed probably 30 August 1802 (or shortly after); first published in 1807; from 1815 included among 'Poems Dedicated to National Independence and Liberty'.

Dorothy Wordsworth's *Journal* (30 August 1802): 'We . . . sate upon the Dover Cliffs, and looked upon France with many a melancholy and tender thought. We could see the shores almost as plain as if it were but an English Lake.'

LONDON, 1802

Composed probably September (by 22 September) 1802; first published in 1807; from 1815 included among 'Poems Dedicated to National Independence and Liberty'.

WRITTEN IN LONDON, SEPTEMBER, 1802

All data identical with the preceding poem.
   I. F. note:

   This was written immediately after my return from France to London, when I could not but be struck, as here described, with the vanity and parade of our own country, especially in great towns and cities, as contrasted with the quiet, and I may say the desolation, that the revolution had produced in France. This must be borne in mind, or else the reader may think that in this and the succeeding sonnets I have exaggerated the mischief engendered and fostered among us by undisturbed wealth.

1   *O Friend*]   Coleridge: MS.
9   *Rapine, avarice*   Compare Milton's *Sonnet to Fairfax* 13–14: 'In vain doth Valour bleed / While Avarice and Rapine share the land'.

COMPOSED AFTER A JOURNEY ACROSS THE HAMBLETON HILLS

Composed probably 4 October 1802; first published in 1807; from 1815 included among 'Miscellaneous Sonnets'. This sonnet was heavily revised.

   I. F. note: 'Composed . . . on a day memorable to me – the day of my marriage. The horizon commanded by those hills is most magnificent . . .'

   Dorothy Wordsworth's *Journal* (4 October 1802 – but written at a later date):

   . . . Before we had crossed the Hambleton Hills, and reached the point overlooking Yorkshire, it was quite dark. We had not wanted, however, fair prospects before us, as we drove along the flat plain of the high hill. Far, far off us, in the western sky, we saw the shapes of castles, ruins among groves, a great spreading wood, rocks, and single trees, a minster with its tower unusually distinct, minarets in another quarter, and a round Grecian Temple also; the colours of the sky of a bright grey, and the forms of a sober grey, with a dome.

It is now thought that the poem and journal entry probably derived from the conversation during the time in question.

'THOSE WORDS WERE UTTERED'

Composed probably between 4 October 1802 and 6 March 1804; first published in 1807; from 1815 included among 'Miscellaneous Sonnets'.

The prefatory lines are from the end of Wordsworth's *Composed After a Journey Across the Hambleton Hills*.

[TRANSLATION OF ARIOSTO]

Translated probably between 7 and perhaps about 19 November 1802; first published in 1947.

The extant passage is taken from the *Orlando Furioso* I, v–xiv; Wordsworth apparently translated the whole of the first two books – see his letter to Sir George Beaumont of 17 October 1805.

SONNET TRANSLATED FROM THE ITALIAN OF MILTON

Translated perhaps between about November 1802 and early January 1803; first published 5 October 1803 in the *Morning Post*.

A translation of Milton's Italian sonnet, 'Giovane piano e semplicetto amante'.

CANTATA, FROM METASTASIO

Possibly translated by Wordsworth. If so, translated perhaps between about November 1802 and early January 1803; first published 17 October 1803 in the *Morning Post*.

For a discussion of Wordsworth's possible authorship, see R. S. Woof, 'Wordsworth's Poetry and Stuart's Newspapers: 1797–1803', *Studies in Bibliography* XV (1962), 185–6.

[TRANSLATIONS FROM METASTASIO]

Translated perhaps between about November 1802 and early January 1803; first published as indicated below.

I

First published 22 October 1803 in the *Morning Post*. A translation of 'Alla selva, al prato, al fonte'.

II

First published 2 November 1803 in the *Morning Post*. A translation of 'Rodinella, a cui rapità'.

III

First published 12 December 1803 in the *Morning Post*. A translation of 'Quanto mai felici fiete'.

IV

First published in 1947. A translation of 'Sarò qual madre amante'.

V

First published 15 November 1803 in the *Morning Post*. A translation of *Amor Timido* ('Placido zeffiretto').

'NUNS FRET NOT'

Composed perhaps about late 1802; first published in 1807; from 1815 included among 'Miscellaneous Sonnets', where it served as the prefatory sonnet until 1827.

1 *narrow room* '[The music of Milton's sonnets] has an energetic and varied flow of sound crowding into narrow room more of the combined effect of rhyme and blank verse than can be done by any other kind of verse I know of.' – W. (letter to ?, November 1802).

6 *Furness-fells* the hills west of Lake Windermere.

[TRANSLATION OF THE SESTET OF A SONNET BY TASSO]

Translated possibly 1802-5; first published in 1896.

A translation of the sestet of Tasso's sonnet 'Vasco, le cui felici ardite antenne'. A translation (by an unknown hand) of the octave is printed in *PW*, IV, 475.

1 *Camoëns* Portuguese poet (1524-80).

AT THE GRAVE OF BURNS

Composed in part possibly 18 August 1803 (or shortly after) with the earliest complete version probably between late March 1804 and early April 1807; first published in 1842; included from 1845 among 'Memorials of a Tour in Scotland, 1803'.

I. F. note: 'For illustration see my Sister's Journal.'

Dorothy Wordsworth's *Recollections of a Tour Made in Scotland* (18 August 1803): '... Went on to visit his grave; he lies at a corner of the churchyard, and his second son, Francis Wallace, beside him; there is no stone to mark the spot ... We looked at the grave with melancholy and painful reflections repeating to each other his own [poet's epitaph].'

20 *'glinted' forth* Compare Burns's *To a Mountain Daisy* (1786), 15: 'Yet cheerfully thou glinted forth'.

34-6 *And showed my youth ... truth* 'With the Poems of Burns I became acquainted almost immediately upon their first appearance in the volume printed at Kilmarnock in 1786.' – W. (1842 MS note to *Thoughts Suggested the Day Following*).

39–40 *Huge Criffel's hoary top . . . By Skiddaw seen*

Drayton has prettily described the connection, which this neighbourhood has with ours, when he makes Skiddaw say, – 'Scurffel [Criffel], from the sky / That Annandale doth crown, with a most amorous eye / Salutes me every day, or at my pride looks grim, / Oft threatening me with clouds, as I oft threatening him.'

– Dorothy Wordsworth's *Recollections* (18 August 1803).

41–2 *Neighbours . . . might have been* '. . . We talked of Burns, and of the prospect he must have had, perhaps from his own door, of Skiddaw and his companions, indulging ourselves in the fancy that we *might* have been personally known to each other, and he have looked upon those objects with more pleasure for our sakes.' – Dorothy Wordsworth's *Journal* (18 August 1803).

47 *joined* rhymes with 'entwined'.

50 '*poor Inhabitant below*' Burns's *A Bard's Epitaph* (1786), 19.

THOUGHTS SUGGESTED THE DAY FOLLOWING

Some conception perhaps formed 19 August 1803, with part of the composition within a few years but the last stanza early or mid-December (before 23 December) 1839; first published in 1842; included from 1845 among 'Memorials of a Tour in Scotland, 1803'.

I. F. note: This poem 'though felt at the time [1803], was not composed till many years after'.

65–6 *The best . . . forgive!* 'The more I reflect upon this last exclamation, the more I feel . . . justified in attaching comparatively small importance to any literary monument that I may be enabled to leave behind.' – W. (letter to Henry Reed, 23 December 1839).

ADDRESS TO KILCHURN CASTLE

Composed 31 August 1803 (lines 1–3) and the remainder probably between 1820 and 1827; first published in 1827; included from 1827 among 'Memorials of a Tour in Scotland, 1803'.

I. F. note: 'The first three lines were thrown off at the moment I first caught sight of the Ruin from a small eminence by the wayside; the rest was added many years after.'

Dorothy Wordsworth, *Recollections of a Tour in Scotland* (31 August 1803): 'We . . . sate a long time . . . looking on the castle and the huge mountain cove opposite, and William, addressing himself to the ruin, poured out these verses [lines 1-3].'

43 'The tradition is, that the Castle was built by a Lady during the absence of her Lord in Palestine.' – W.

SONNET COMPOSED AT ————————— CASTLE

Composed probably for the most part 18 September 1803; first published in 1807; included among 'Miscellaneous Sonnets' from 1815 to 1820, then among 'Memorials of a Tour in Scotland, 1803'.

I. F. note: '1803. The Castle here mentioned was Nidpath near Peebles. The person alluded to was the then Duke of Queensbury. The fact was told me by Walter Scott.'

According to John Veitch's *Border History and Poetry* (1893) II, 319, 'To spite his heir chiefly, the last Douglas of Queensbury of his line ordered the cutting down of the old forest-trees that had grown up through the centuries ... This was carried out, and the steep sides of the picturesque gorge of the Tweed ... were left defaced and bare ...'.

'FLY, SOME KIND HARBINGER'

Composed probably in whole or in part 25 September 1803 (fairly certainly by 21 November 1803); first published in 1815; included among 'Miscellaneous Sonnets' (with the title 'On Approaching home') from 1815 to 1820; then among 'Memorials of a Tour in Scotland'.

I. F. note: 'This was actually composed the last day of our tour between Dalston and Grasmere.'

TO THE MEN OF KENT. OCTOBER, 1803

Composed probably between 25 September and 14 October 1803; first published in 1807; from 1815 included among 'Poems Dedicated to National Independence and Liberty'.

9-11   Wordsworth is here drawing on the legend that the men of Kent (east of the Medway) had their charters confirmed by the Normans.

ANTICIPATION. OCTOBER, 1803

Composed perhaps between 1 and 14 October 1803; first published 28 October 1803 in the *Courier*; from 1815 included among 'Poems Dedicated to National Independence and Liberty'.

SONNET, IN THE PASS OF KILLICRANKY

Composed perhaps between 14 and 31 October 1803; first published in 1807; from 1815 to 1820 included among 'Sonnets Dedicated to Liberty', from 1827 among 'Memorials of a Tour in Scotland, 1803'.

Dorothy Wordsworth's *Recollections of a Tour Made in Scotland* (8 September 1803):

Before breakfast we walked to the Pass of Killiecrankie ... When we were travelling in Scotland an invasion was hourly looked for, and one could not but think with some regret of the times when from the now depopulated Highlands forty or fifty thousand men might have been poured down for the defence of the country, under such leaders as the Marquis of Montrose or [Viscount Dundee].

11 'See an anecdote related in Mr Scott's *Border Minstrelsy*.' – W. (1807). Scott's anecdote is as follows:

[Viscount Dundee] is still remembered in the Highlands as the most successful leader of their clans. An old soldier told the editor that on the field of battle at Sheriffmuir an old veteran urged the Earl of Mar to order the Highlanders to charge before the regular army of Argyle had formed their line. Mar repeatedly answered that it was not yet time, till the old chieftain turned from him in disdain and despair, and stamping with rage exclaimed aloud 'O for one hour of Dundee!'

LINES ON THE EXPECTED INVASION

Composed probably basically between 14 October 1803 and early January 1804 (possibly by 31 October 1803); first published in 1842; from 1845 contained among 'Poems Dedicated to National Independence and Liberty'.

3, 4 *Falkland ... Montrose* Lucius Cary, Second Viscount Falkland (1610?-43) and James Graham, First Marquis of Montrose (1612-50) remained loyal to Charles I.
7 *Pyms* John Pym (1584-1643), who was, like John Milton, a Republican.

OCTOBER, 1803 ('One might')

Composed probably between 14 October 1803 and early January 1804 (possibly by 31 October 1803); first published in 1807; from 1815 included among 'Poems Dedicated to National Independence and Liberty'.

OCTOBER, 1803 ('These times')

All data identical with the previous poem.

OCTOBER, 1803 ('When, looking')

All data identical with the preceding poem.

TO A HIGHLAND GIRL

Composed probably between 14 October 1803 and 6 March 1804, possibly by 21 November (probably early or mid-November 1803); first published in 1807; from 1815 to 1820 included among 'Poems of the Imagination' and thereafter among 'Memorials of a Tour in Scotland, 1803'.
I. F. note:

This delightful creature and her demeanour are particularly described in my Sister's Journal. The sort of prophecy with which the verses conclude has, through God's goodness, been realized; and now, approaching on the close of my 73rd year, I have a most vivid remembrance of her and the beautiful objects with which she was surrounded. She is alluded to in the poem of the 'Three Cottage Girls' among my Continental Memorials.

Dorothy Wordsworth's *Recollections* (28 August 1803):

When beginning to descend the hill towards Loch Lomond, we overtook two girls, who told us we could not cross the ferry till evening . . . One of the girls was exceedingly beautiful; . . . they answered us so sweetly that we were quite delighted, at the same time that they stared at us with an innocent look of wonder . . .

YARROW UNVISITED

Composed probably between 14 October 1803 and 6 March 1804 (possibly by 21 November, especially early or mid-November 1803); first published in 1807; from 1815 to 1820 included among 'Poems of the Imagination' and thereafter among 'Memorials of a Tour in Scotland, 1803'.

Dorothy Wordsworth's *Recollections of a Tour in Scotland* (18 September 1803): 'At Clovenford, being so near to the Yarrow, we could not but think of the possibility of going thither, but came to the conclusion of reserving the pleasure for some future time, in consequence of which, after our return, William wrote the poem . . .'

In a letter to Sir Walter Scott (16 January 1805) Wordsworth sent the poem and commented: 'A few stanzas, which I hope, for the subject at least, will give you some pleasure. I wrote them, not without a view of pleasing you, soon after our return from Scotland . . . They are in the same sort of metre as the *Leader Haughs* . . .'. The *Leader Haughs* was a ballad written by the Border poet Nicol Burne (flourished 1581). It was but one of the many ballads involving Yarrow (see the Prefatory note and the notes below); Helen Darbishire, in her edition of the *Poems in Two Volumes*, suggests that the use of the river in traditional song was at least partly responsible for Wordsworth's reluctance to visit it. In any event, in the *I. F. note* to *Yarrow Revisited* Wordsworth claimed that in 1803 they 'declined going in search of this celebrated stream, not altogether . . . for the reasons assigned in the poem on the occasion'.

The poem referred to in the Prefatory note is *The Braes of Yarrow* (1724) by William Hamilton of Bangour.

6 *Marrow* companion (see Prefatory note).
20 *lintwhites* linnets (a form found in *Leader Haughs*).
35 'See Hamilton's Ballad as above.' – W. Line 51.
37 *Strath* a wide valley.
38, 40 *thorough . . . Yarrow* This rhyme occurs in the *Dowie Dens of Yarrow*, a traditional ballad.
42 *Burn-mill* In *Leader Haughs* occurs the name 'Burnmill bog'. In the letter to Scott (see head-note above), Wordsworth asked Scott to suggest

another name actually located in the Yarrow Valley, but Scott's recommended change ('Broad Meadow') was never made.

64 *Leader Haughs* 88.

AT APPLETHWAITE

Composed probably between 14 October 1803 and 6 March 1804 (perhaps early 1804); first published in 1842; from 1845 included among 'Miscellaneous Sonnets'.

I. F. note: 'This place was presented to me by Sir George Beaumont with a view to the erection of a house upon it, for the sake of being near to Coleridge, then living, and likely to remain, at Greta Hall near Keswick. The *severe* necessities [line 8] that prevented this arose from his domestic situation.'

When published in 1842, Wordsworth added the following note: 'This biographical Sonnet, if so it may be called, . . . [has] long been suppressed from feelings of personal delicacy.'

'SHE WAS A PHANTOM OF DELIGHT'

Composed probably between 14 October 1803 and 6 March 1804 (perhaps early 1804); first published in 1807; included from 1815 among 'Poems of the Imagination'.

In Christopher Wordsworth's *Memoirs* II, 306, Wordsworth is quoted as having said the poem was written 'on "his dear wife"'.

I. F. note: '1804 Town-End. The germ of this poem was four lines composed as part of the verses on the Highland Girl [*To a Highland Girl*]. Though beginning in this way, it was written from my heart, as is sufficiently obvious.'

22 *machine* term 'applied to the human and animal frame as a combination of several parts' – NED. Compare William Bartram's *Travels Through North and South Carolina* (1791), which Wordsworth knew well: 'At the return of the morning, by the powerful influence of light, the pulse of nature becomes more active, and the universal vibration of life insensibly and irresistibly moves the wondrous machine' (p. 179).

THE SMALL CELANDINE

Composed possibly 1803 or early 1804 (by 6 March); first published in 1807; in 1807 included in the group 'Moods of My Own Mind'; from 1815 included among 'Poems Referring to the Period of Old Age'.

2–4 'What adds much to the interest that attaches [to the flower] is its habit of shutting itself up and opening out according to the degree of light and temperature of the air.' – *I. F. note* (for *To the Small Celandine*).

[FRAGMENT: 'Along the mazes of this song I go']

Composed possibly between about 14 January 1804 and about January 1805; first published in 1889.

Very likely written for *The Prelude*.

ODE TO DUTY

Composed probably basically early 1804 (by 6 March) with the first stanza probably added between late March 1804 and early December 1806; first published in 1807; from 1815 included among 'Poems of Sentiment and Reflection'.

I. F. note:

> This Ode, written 1805, is on the model of Gray's Ode to Adversity which is copied from Horace's Ode to Fortune. . . . Many and many a time have I been twitted by my wife and sister for having forgotten this dedication of myself to the stern lawgiver. Transgressor indeed I have been, from hour to hour, from day to day; I would fain hope, however, not more flagrantly nor in a worse way than most of my tuneful brethren. But these last words are in a wrong strain. We should be rigorous to ourselves, and forbearing if not indulgent to others, and if we make comparisons at all it ought to be with those who have morally excelled us.

The Latin motto, added in 1837, is taken from Seneca's description of a man of perfect virtue in his *Moral Epistles* CXX, 10 (with a change to the first person) and reads in English: 'Not only consciously good but so habituated by training that I not only can act rightly but cannot act otherwise.' This poem underwent considerable revision.

1 *Daughter of the Voice of God* Compare *Paradise Lost* IX, 652-3: 'God so commanded, and left that Command / Sole Daughter of his voice.'

41-8 In line with the policy followed by later editors, the sixth stanza, deleted by Wordsworth after 1807, is here replaced. This stanza makes the transition in thought clearer, but was excised by Wordsworth perhaps because it tends to qualify his submission in a manner that could be mistaken for latent wilfulness.

46 *'precepts over dignified'* Adapted from Milton's Dedication to *The Doctrine and Discipline of Divorce*: 'empty and over-dignified precepts'.

55-6 In a letter to *The Friend* (4 January 1810), Wordsworth remarked:

> . . . When, in his character of philosophical Poet, having thought of Morality as implying in its essence voluntary obedience, and producing the effect of order, [the poet] transfers in the transport of imagination, the law of moral to physical natures, and, having contemplated, through the medium of that order, all modes of existence as subservient to one spirit, concludes his address to the power of Duty in the following words: [last stanza quoted].

61   *lowly wise   Paradise Lost* VIII, 173.
63   *confidence of reason*   Dr Johnson's *Life of Addison.*

THE MATRON OF JEDBOROUGH

Composed probably between late March 1804 and 1 November 1805; first published in 1807; included from 1815 to 1820 among 'Poems Referring to the Period of Old Age' and thereafter among 'Memorials of a Tour in Scotland, 1803'.

Dorothy Wordsworth's *Recollections* (20 September 1803):

> We were received with hearty welcome by a good woman, who, though above seventy years old, moved about as briskly as if she were only seventeen . . . She was a most remarkable person; . . . she had a quick eye, and keen strong features, and a joyousness in her motions . . . I found afterwards that she had been subject to fits of dejection and ill-health: we then conjectured that her overflowing gaiety and strength might in part be attributed to the same cause as her former dejection. Her husband was deaf and infirm, and sate in a chair with scarcely the power to move a limb – an affecting contrast!

THE BLIND HIGHLAND BOY

Composed probably between late March 1804 and about March 1806; first published in 1807; included among 'Poems Referring to Childhood' 1815–20, and from 1827 among 'Memorials of a Tour in Scotland, 1803'.

I. F. note: 'The story was told me by George Mackereth, for many years parish-clerk of Grasmere. He had been an eye-witness of the occurrence. The vessel in reality was a washing-tub, which the little fellow had met with on the shore of the Loch.'

119   *Amphitrite*   goddess of the sea.
122   *Vaga's*   Latin name for the Wye.

ADMONITION

Composed probably between late March 1804 and early April 1807; first published in 1807; from 1815 included among 'Miscellaneous Sonnets'.

'WHO FANCIED WHAT A PRETTY SIGHT'

Composed probably between late March 1804 and early April 1807; first published in 1807, placed among 'Moods of My Own Mind'; from 1815 included among 'Poems of the Fancy'.

3   *snow-drops*   an early blooming white flower.

'I WANDERED LONELY AS A CLOUD'

Composed probably between late March 1804 and early April 1807 (possibly by the end of 1804); first published in 1807, placed among 'Moods of My

Own Mind'; included from 1815 among 'Poems of the Imagination' (in 1815 with the following note: 'The subject of these Stanzas is rather an elementary feeling and simple impression [approaching to the nature of an ocular spectrum] upon the imaginative faculty, than an *exertion* of it . . .').

I. F. note: 'Town-End, 1804 . . . The daffodils grew and still grow on the margin of Ullswater and probably may be seen to this day as beautiful in the month of March, nodding their golden heads beside the dancing and foaming waves.'

Dorothy Wordsworth's *Journal* (15 April 1802):

> . . . We saw a few daffodils close to the water-side. We fancied that the lake had floated the seeds ashore, and that the little colony had so sprung up. But as we went along there were more and yet more; and at last, under the boughs of the trees, we saw that there was a long belt of them along the shore, about the breadth of a country turnpike road. I never saw daffodils so beautiful. They grew among the mossy stones about and about them; some rested their heads upon these stones as on a pillow for weariness; and the rest tossed and reeled and danced, and seemed as if they verily laughed with the wind that blew upon them over the lake; they looked so gay, ever glancing, ever changing. This wind blew directly over the lake to them. There was here and there a little knot, and a few stragglers a few yards higher up; but they were so few as not to disturb the simplicity, and unity, and life of that one busy highway.

7–12 The second stanza was added in 1815.
21–2 These two lines, written by Wordsworth's wife, he considered the 'two best lines in it' (*I. F. note*). Coleridge, however, thought them an example of '*mental* bombast' (*Biographia Literaria*, Chapter XXII).

ADDRESS TO MY INFANT DAUGHTER, DORA

Composed probably basically 16 September 1804; first published in 1815; included among 'Poems of the Fancy' from 1815.

Preface of 1815 (passage deleted 1845): '. . . "An address to an Infant" . . . exhibits something of this communion and interchange of instruments and functions between the two powers [fancy and imagination], and is, accordingly, placed last in the class [Fancy], as a preparation for that of Imagination which follows.'

15 *'heaven's eternal year'* Dryden's *To the Pious Memory of . . . Mrs Anne Killigrew* 15.

YEW–TREES

Partly (lines 1–13) composed possibly 24 September 1804 (or shortly after) and completed by late October 1814; first published in 1815; from 1815 included among 'Poems of the Imagination'.

I. F. note:

Grasmere, 1803. These yew-trees are still standing, but the spread of that at Lorton is much diminished by mutilation. I will here mention that a little way up the hill, on the road leading from Rosthwaite to Stonethwaite, lay the trunk of a yew-tree ... Calculating upon what I have observed of the slow growth of this tree in rocky situations, and of its durability, I have often thought that the one I am describing must have been as old as the Christian era ... In no part of England, or of Europe, have I ever seen a yew-tree at all approaching this in magnitude, as it must have stood ...

Both Wordsworth (Henry Crabb Robinson's *Diary*, 9 May 1815) and Coleridge (*Biographia Literaria*, Chapter XXII) considered *Yew-Trees* among Wordsworth's most imaginative poems.

5 *Umfraville . . . Percy* probably Robert de Umfraville (1277–1325) and Sir Henry Percy (1364–1403), both of whom fought against the Scots.
7–8 *Azincour, Crecy, Poictiers* three battles of the Hundred Years War.
25 *ghostly Shapes* See the *Aeneid* VI, 273–84 for a similar congregation of allegorical figures, 'And in the midst an ancient elm spreads its shadowing arms' (282–3).

VAUDRACOUR AND JULIA

Composed probably between early October and late autumn 1804; first published in 1820; from 1820 included among 'Poems Founded on the Affections'.

I. F. note:

Town-End, 1805. Faithfully narrated, though with the omission of many pathetic circumstances, from the mouth of a French Lady, who had been an eye-and-ear-witness of all that was done and said. Many long years after, I was told that Dupligne was then a monk in the Convent of La Trappe.

The poem was taken from *The Prelude*, Book IX, where the passage stands in the 1805 version (lines 555–934). The story can also be found in Helen Maria Williams's *Letters Written in France* (1790).

8 *Vaudracour* possibly adapted from the name of Lieutenant de Vaudrecourt, an officer in Beaupuy's battalion.
15 *ingenuous* of honourable birth.
93–4 *Romeo and Juliet* III, v, 7–8: 'what envious streaks / Do lace the severing clouds in yonder east'.

[FRAGMENT: 'There was a spot']

Composed probably between early October and late Autumn 1804; first published in 1949.

THE KITTEN AND FALLING LEAVES

Composed possibly between early October 1804 and early 1805 (perhaps between late 1805 and early 1806); first published in 1807; from 1815 included among 'Poems of the Fancy'.

I. F. note: 'Seen at Town-End Grasmere. The Elder-bush has long since disappeared: it hung over the wall near the cottage, and the kitten continued to leap up catching the leaves as here described. The infant was Dora.' Until after Dora's death in 1847, 'Dora's' in line 104 read 'Laura's'.

Henry Crabb Robinson's *Diary* (11 September 1816): Wordsworth 'quoted some of . . . "The Kitten and Falling Leaves" to show how he had connected *even the kitten with the great, awful and mysterious powers of nature*'.

FRENCH REVOLUTION

Composed probably about late November or December 1804; first published 26 October 1809 in *The Friend*; from 1815 included among 'Poems of the Imagination'.

I. F. note: 'An extract from the long poem on my own poetical education [*The Prelude* XI, 105-44]. It was first published by Coleridge in his "Friend", which is the reason of its having had a place in every edition of my poems since.'

36 *subterranean fields* probably the Utopia found in Ludvig Holberg's *Nicolai Klimii Iter Subterraneum* (1741).

[INSCRIPTION FOR THE MOSS-HUT]

Composed probably shortly before 25 December 1804; first published in 1887.

In a letter to Sir George Beaumont (25 December 1804), Wordsworth enclosed the poem and commented:

> We have lately built in our little rocky orchard a little circular Hut, lined with moss, like a wren's nest, and coated on the outside with heath, that stands most charmingly, with several views from the different sides of it, of the Lake, the Valley and the Church . . . The little retreat is most delightful . . . I will copy a dwarf inscription which I wrote for it the other day, before the building was entirely finished, which indeed it is not yet.

THE SIMPLON PASS

Composed probably 1804 (perhaps 1799); first published in 1845; from 1845 included among 'Poems of the Imagination'. This poem occurs also as a passage in *The Prelude* VI, 621-40.

THE KING OF SWEDEN

Composed probably between late 1804 and early February 1807; first published in 1807; from 1815 included among 'Poems Dedicated to National Independence and Liberty'.

> In this and a succeeding sonnet on the same subject ['Call not the royal Swede unfortunate'], let me be understood as a Poet availing himself of the situation which the King of Sweden occupied, and of the principles AVOWED IN HIS MANIFESTOES; as laying hold of these advantages for the purpose of embodying moral truths . . .

– W.

In a letter to John Scott (25 February 1816), Wordsworth commented on the poem and its hero:

> . . . He stood forth at that time as the only Royal Advocate of the only truths by which, if judiciously applied, Europe could be delivered from Bondage. I seized on him as an outstanding object in which to embody certain principles of action which human nature has thousands of times proved herself capable of being governed by.

2 *crownèd Youth* Gustavus IV was crowned in 1792 at the age of fourteen.

GLEN-ALMAIN

Composed probably between about 20 May and 11 June 1805; first published in 1807; from 1815 to 1820 included among 'Poems of the Imagination' and thereafter among 'Memorials of a Tour in Scotland, 1803'.

Dorothy Wordsworth's *Recollections* (9 September 1803):

> The prospect was very extensive . . . in harmony with the secluded dell, and fixing its own peculiar character of removedness from the world, and the secure possession of the quiet of nature more deeply in our minds. The . . . poem was written by William on hearing of a tradition relating to it, which we did not know when we were there.

ELEGIAC STANZAS

Composed probably between about 20 May and 27 June 1806; first published in 1807; included from 1815 among 'Epitaphs and Elegiac Pieces'.

I. F. note: 'Sir George Beaumont painted two pictures on this subject, one of which he gave to Mrs Wordsworth . . .'

1-2 Peele (or Piel) Castle is situated near Barrow-in-Furness in North Lancashire; Wordsworth stayed in near-by Rampside in the summer of 1794. **14-16** *add the gleam . . . the Poet's dream 1807-15, 1832-50;* 'add a gleam, / Of lustre, known to neither sea nor land / But borrowed from the youthful Poet's dream' – *1820-27.* On the insistence of a friend, Wordsworth restored the original reading in 1832.

35 *A power . . . nothing can restore* Compare Wordsworth's comment on the death of his brother in a letter to James Losh (16 March 1805): 'I feel that there is something cut out of my life which cannot be restored.'

36   *A deep distress*   the death of John Wordsworth, lost at sea 6 February 1805.

42   *deplore*   mourn.

54   *the Kind*   humankind.

'DISTRESSFUL GIFT!'

Composed perhaps between about 20 May and 5 July (possibly shortly before 5 July) 1805; first published in 1947.

5   *my Friend*   John Wordsworth, who died at sea 6 February 1805. The book (line 1) was one in which Wordsworth's poems were copied for John to take with him.

TO THE DAISY ('Sweet Flower!')

Composed perhaps between about 20 May and 5 July (possibly shortly before 5 July) 1805; first published in 1815; included from 1815 among 'Epitaphs and Elegiac Pieces'.

In a letter to Lady Beaumont (7 August 1805), Wordsworth wrote:

> The following was written in remembrance of a beautiful letter of my Brother John, sent to us from Portsmouth, when he had left us at Grasmere, and first taken the command of his unfortunate ship, more than four years ago. Some of the expressions in the Poem are the very words he used in his letter [see note to lines 19–28 below]. N. B. I have written two Poems to the same flower before – this is partly alluded to in the first stanza.

19–28   In a letter to Dorothy Wordsworth (2 April 1801), John Wordsworth observed (see head-note above):

> We are painting the Ship, and make all as smart – Never Ship was like ours – indeed we are not a *little* proud. . . . I have been on shore this afternoon to stretch my legs upon the Isle of White [sic]. The Primroses are beautiful and the daisy's [sic] after sunset are like little *white* stars upon the dark green fields.

70   *senseless*   said of death, the grave (obsolete).

STEPPING WESTWARD

Composed probably 3 June 1805; first published in 1807; included among 'Poems of the Imagination' from 1815 to 1820, and thereafter among 'Memorials of a Tour in Scotland, 1803'.

Dorothy Wordsworth's *Recollections* (for 11 September 1803):

> The sun had been set for some time, when, being within a quarter of a mile of the ferryman's hut, our path having led us close to the shore of the calm lake, we met two neatly dressed women, without hats, who had

probably been taking their Sunday evening's walk. One of them said to us
in a friendly, soft tone of voice, 'What! you are stepping westward?' I
cannot describe how affecting this simple expression was in that remote
place, with the western sky in front, *yet* glowing with the departed sun.
William wrote this poem long after in remembrance of his feelings and
mine.

ELEGIAC VERSES

Composed probably 8 June 1805; first published in 1842; included in 1845
among 'Epitaphs and Elegiac Pieces'.
16 *this unknown Flower* 'Moss Campion (Silene acaulis): This most
beautiful plant is scarce in England, though it is found in great abundance
upon the mountains of Scotland.' – W.
21 *Here did we stop* 'The point is 2 or 3 yards below the outlet of Grisdale
Tarn on a foot-road by which a horse may pass to Patterdale, a ridge of
Helvellyn on the left, and the summit of Fairfield on the right.' – *I. F. note*.
63-4 *Here let . . . Stand* Lines 21-4 and 61-4 were inscribed on a rock
placed near the spot in 1882 by the Wordsworth Society.

FIDELITY

Composed probably between 14 August and 10 November 1805, certainly
by 2 March 1806; first published in 1807; included from 1815 among 'Poems
of Sentiment and Reflection'.
I. F. note:

The young man whose death gave occasion to this poem was named
Charles Gough, and had come early in the spring [April 1805] to Patter-
dale for the sake of angling. While attempting to cross over Helvellyn to
Grasmere he slipped from a steep part of the rock where the ice was not
thawed, and perished. His body was discovered as is told in this poem.
Walter Scott heard of the accident, and both he [in *Helvellyn*] and I,
without either of us knowing that the other had taken up the subject, each
wrote a poem in admiration of the dog's fidelity . . .

According to Henry Crabb Robinson in his *Diary* (for 11 September 1816),
Wordsworth

says he purposely made the narrative as prosaic as possible in order that
no discredit might be thrown on the truth of the incident. In the descrip-
tion at the beginning and in the moral at the end he has alone indulged in
a poetic vein – and these parts he thinks he has peculiarly succeeded in.

20 *tarn* 'a *small* Mere or Lake, mostly high up in the mountains'. – W.
62-5 '. . . The sentiment in the last four lines . . . was uttered by a shepherd
with such exactness, that a traveller, who afterwards reported his account in
print, was induced to question the man whether he had read them, which he
had not.' – *I. F. note*.

INCIDENT CHARACTERISTIC OF A FAVOURITE DOG

Composed probably between 14 August 1805 and 23 December 1806 (certainly after the preceding poem); first published in 1807; included from 1815 among 'Poems of Sentiment and Reflection'.

I. F. note: 'This dog I knew well. It belonged to Mrs Wordsworth's brother, Mr Thomas Hutchinson ...'

24 *over-head* submerged.

TRIBUTE TO THE MEMORY OF THE SAME DOG

All data identical with the preceding poem.

I. F. note: 'The Dog "Music" died, aged and blind, by falling into a draw-well at Gallow Hill.'

FROM THE ITALIAN OF MICHELANGELO ('Yes! hope may')

Translated probably 1805, by 24 August; first published in 1806 in Richard Duppa's *Life and Works of Michael Angelo Buonarroti*; from 1815 included among 'Miscellaneous Sonnets'.

This poem is a translation of Sonnet LX of Michelangelo ('Ben può talor col mio ardente desio').

I. F. note: 'Translations from Michael Angelo, done at the request of Mr Duppa, whose acquaintance I made through Mr Southey. Mr Duppa was engaged in writing the life of Michael Angelo, and applied to Mr Southey and myself to furnish him some specimens of his poetic genius.'

In a letter to Sir George Beaumont (17 October 1805), Wordsworth called this sonnet 'the only one I was able to finish' – 'it is far from being the best, or most characteristic, but the others were too much for me.' The original poetry, he explained, was at fault: '... It is the most difficult to construe I ever met with, but just what you would expect from such a man, showing abundantly how conversant his soul was with great things ...; so much meaning has been put by Michael Angelo into so little room, and that meaning sometimes so excellent in itself, that I found the difficulty of translating him insurmountable.'

ROB ROY'S GRAVE

Composed probably between early September 1805 and 21 February 1806; first published in 1807; included among 'Poems of Sentiment and Reflection' 1815 and 1820, and thereafter among 'Memorials of a Tour in Scotland, 1803'.

I. F. note: 'I have since been told that I was misinformed as to the burial-place of Rob Roy.'

Dorothy Wordsworth's *Recollections* (for 12 September 1803): 'We ... went up to the burying-ground that stood so sweetly near the water-side....

There were several tombstones, but the inscriptions were either worn-out or unintelligible to us, and the place was choked up with nettles and brambles.'

5 *ROB ROY* Robert MacGregor, Highland outlaw (1671–1734).

10 *And wondrous length . . . of arm* 'The people of the neighbourhood of Loch Ketterine, in order to prove the extraordinary length of their Hero's arm, tell you that "he could garter his Tartan Stockings below the knee when standing upright".' – W. (1807).

95 *her present Boast* Napoleon.

TO THE SONS OF BURNS

Composed probably partly (stanzas II–IV, VIII) between early September 1805 and 21 February 1806 with the remaining stanzas added 1820–27; first published in 1807; included among 'Poems of Sentiment and Reflection' from 1815 to 1820, and thereafter among 'Memorials of a Tour in Scotland, 1803'.

I. F. note: 'See, in connexion with these verses, two other Poems upon Burns, one composed actually at the time [*At the Grave of Burns*], and the other [*Thoughts Suggested the Day Following*], though then felt, not put into words till several years afterwards.'

Dorothy Wordsworth's *Recollections* (for 18 August 1803): '. . . The grave of Burns's son, which we had just seen by the side of his father, and some stories heard at Dumfries respecting the dangers his surviving children were exposed to, filled us with melancholy concern, which had a kind of connexion with ourselves.'

31 *'lonely heights and hows'* Burns's *To James Smith* (1786), 53.

41–2 *'light . . . Heaven'* adapted from Burns's *The Vision* (1786), Duan II, 239–40.

THE SOLITARY REAPER

Composed probably 5 November 1805; first published in 1807; included among 'Poems of the Imagination' 1815 and 1820, and thereafter among 'Memorials of a Tour in Scotland, 1803'.

Wordsworth's note (1807): 'This poem was suggested by a beautiful sentence in a MS. Tour in Scotland written by a friend, the last line being taken from it *verbatim*.' The passage, from Thomas Wilkinson's *Tours to the British Mountains* (finally published 1824), is as follows (p. 12): 'Passed a female who was reaping alone: she sung in Erse as she bended over her sickle; the sweetest human voice I ever heard: her strains were tenderly melancholy, and felt delicious, long after they were heard no more.'

Dorothy Wordsworth's *Recollections* (for 13 September 1803): 'It was harvest time, and the fields were quietly – might I be allowed to say pensively? – enlivened by small companies of reapers. It is not uncommon in the more lonely parts of the Highlands to see a single person so employed.'

FROM THE ITALIAN OF MICHELANGELO. TO THE SUPREME BEING

Translated perhaps 1805–6, probably between 7 November 1805 and early 1806 (certainly before 1 August); first published in 1807; from 1815 included among 'Miscellaneous Sonnets'.

This poem is a translation of Sonnet LXXXIX of Michelangelo ('Ben sarien dolce le preghiere mie').

For more comment by Wordsworth, see the head-note to *From the Italian of Michelangelo* (p. 1012 above).

FROM THE ITALIAN OF MICHELANGELO ('No mortal object')

Translated probably between 7 November 1805 and 8 September 1806; first published in 1807; from 1815 included among 'Miscellaneous Sonnets'.

This poem is a translation of Sonnet LII of Michelangelo ('Non vider gli occhi miei cosa mortale').

For more comment by Wordsworth, see the head-note to *From the Italian of Michelangelo* (p. 1012 above).

FROM THE ITALIAN OF MICHELANGELO ('Well-nigh')

Of doubtful authorship. If by Wordsworth, translated probably 1805; first published in 1806 in Richard Duppa's *Life and Works of Michel Angelo Buonarroti*. For authorship, see Mark Reed, *Chronology of the Middle Years*, p. 278 n.

This poem is a translation of Sonnet LXV of Michelangelo ('Giunto è già 'l corso della vita mia').

FROM THE ITALIAN OF MICHELANGELO ('Rid of a vexing')

Translated in completed form probably between 7 November 1805 and early April 1807; first published in 1896. Wordsworth published a later version of the poem in 1842; see 'Eternal Lord' (Vol. II, p. 862).

CHARACTER OF THE HAPPY WARRIOR

Composed probably between about 6 December 1805 and early January 1806; first published in 1807; included from 1815 among 'Poems of Sentiment and Reflection'.

Wordsworth's *note* (1807): 'The above verses were written soon after tidings had been received of the Death of Lord Nelson [d. 21 October 1805], which event directed the Author's thoughts to the subject . . .'

I. F. note:

The course of the great war with the French naturally fixed one's attention upon the military character, and, to the honour of our country, there were many illustrious instances of the qualities that constitute its highest excellence. Lord Nelson carried most of the virtues that the trials he was exposed to in his department of the service necessarily call forth and sustain ... Many elements of the character here portrayed were found in my brother John, who perished by shipwreck as mentioned elsewhere. His messmates used to call him the Philosopher, from which it must be inferred that the qualities and dispositions I allude to had not escaped their notice.

Wordsworth was also apparently influenced by Samuel Daniel's *Funeral Poem Upon the Earl of Devonshire* in both style and content – see notes to *PW*.

Having been told by Harriet Martineau that the poem was admired by Dr Channing, Wordsworth replied (Harriet Martineau, *Autobiography* [1877] II, 237): 'Ay, that was not on account of the *poetic conditions* being best fulfilled in that poem: but because it is [solemnly] a chain of extremely *valooable* thoughts.'

49 *joined* rhymes with 'kind'.

63 *approve* demonstrate.

75-6 *persevering ... From well to better* '"For Knightes ever should be persevering / To seek honour without feintise or slouth / Fro well to better in all manner thing." CHAUCER. – *The Floure and the Leafe*.' – W. (1807). The poem in question is no longer attributed to Chaucer.

THE COTTAGER TO HER INFANT

The first three stanzas were written by Dorothy Wordsworth, the last two by William Wordsworth (from a MS, composed probably between 1805 and 1815). The first three stanzas composed probably between 28 November and about 6 December 1805; the first three stanzas were first published in 1815, Wordsworth's MS. stanzas were first published in 1896; included from 1815 among 'Poems Founded on the Affections'.

I. F. note: 'Suggested to [my sister] while beside my sleeping children.'

[TRANSLATIONS FROM MICHELANGELO: A FRAGMENT]

Translated probably between 1805 and early May 1807; first published in 1807 in Richard Duppa's *Life and Works of Michel Angelo Buonarroti* (second edition).

MICHELANGELO IN REPLY

Translated possibly between 1805 and 1807, not certainly before some time between about 1836 and about 1840; first published in 1883. The originals are given in *PW*, IV, 474.

[TRANSLATION: 'COME, GENTLE SLEEP']

Translated possibly between 1805 and 1807, not certainly before between about 1836 and about 1840; first published in 1883.

This quatrain is a fairly close translation of a Latin poem (1787) by Thomas Warton, the Younger.

THE WAGGONER

Composed basically between 1 and 14 January 1806; first published in 1819; placed first among 'Poems of the Fancy' in 1820, then between 'Poems Founded on the Affections' and 'Poems of the Fancy' from 1827 to 1836, and finally placed last among 'Poems of the Fancy' from 1845.

I. F. note: 'Written at Town-End, Grasmere. The characters and story from fact.'

Wordsworth's *note* (1836):

> Several years after the event that forms the subject of the poem, in company with my friend, the late Mr Coleridge, I happened to fall in with the person to whom the name of Benjamin is given. Upon our expressing regret that we had not, for a long time, seen upon the road either him or his wagon, he said: – 'They could not do without me; and as to the man who was put in my place, no good could come out of him; he was a man of no *ideas*.'
>
> The fact of my discarded hero's getting the horses out of a great difficulty with a word, as related in the poem, was told me by an eye-witness.

Justice Coleridge recorded in his *Memoranda* (for 10 October 1836) that Wordsworth

> read much of *The Waggoner* to me. It seems a very favourite poem of his, and he read me splendid descriptions from it. He said his object in it had not been understood. It was a play of the fancy on a domestic incident and lowly character: he wished by the opening descriptive lines to put his reader into the state of mind in which he wished it to be read. If he failed in doing that, he wished him to lay it down. He pointed out, with the same view, the glowing lines on the state of exaltation in which Ben and his companion are under the influence of liquor. Then he read the sickening languor of the morning walk, contrasted with the glorious uprising of Nature, and the songs of the birds. Here he has added about six most exquisite lines [IV, 71-82].

– Christopher Wordsworth, *Memoirs* II, 310. The motto verse, added in 1845, is from Thomson's *Seasons: Summer* 977-9.

I, 3 *The buzzing dor-hawk* 'When the poem was first written the note of the bird was thus described: "The Night-hawk is singing his frog-like tune, / Twirling his watchman's rattle about –" but from unwillingness to startle the reader at the outset by so bold a mode of expression, the passage was altered as it now stands.' – W. (1836-7).
I, 26 *The far-off tinkling's drowsy cheer* Compare Gray's *Elegy* 8: 'And drowsy tinklings lull the distant folds'.
I, 53 *the DOVE and OLIVE-BOUGH* Dove Cottage, in which Wordsworth lived at Town-End, Grasmere, was once an inn.
I, 90 *painted by the Host* 'This rude piece of self-taught art (such is the

progress of refinement) has been supplanted by a professional production.' – W.

I, 168 *Helm-crag* 'A mountain of Grasmere, the broken summit of which presents two figures, full as distinctly shaped as that of the famous Cobbler near Arroquhar in Scotland.' – W. Sidrophel (line 171) is the name of the astrologer in Butler's *Hudibras* II, iii.

I, 197–9 *1836*;

> By peals of thunder, clap on clap!
> And many a terror-striking flash; –
> And somewhere, as it seems, a crash   *1819–32*

I, 210 *King Dunmail's bones* Dunmail, the last king of Cumberland, according to tradition is buried under a cairn at the top of Dunmail Raise, the boundary between Cumberland and Westmoreland.

II, 6 *crazy* damaged.

II, 30 *MERRY-NIGHT* 'A term well known in the North of England, and applied to rural Festivals where young persons meet in the evening for the purpose of dancing.' – W.

II, 42 *vibrate* vacillate.

II, 81 *A Caesar past the Rubicon!* Caesar's crossing of the Rubicon river on his return to Rome to fight Pompey signified an irreversible step.

II, 97 *The fiddle's squeak* 'At the close of each strathspey, or jig, a particular note from the fiddle summons the Rustic to the agreeable duty of saluting his partner.' – W.

II, 115 *at the Nile* Nelson fought the French in the Battle of the Nile in 1798.

II, 128–34 Compare Sterne's *Tristram Shandy* (IX, xxviii): 'And this, said he, is the town of *Namur* – and this the citadel – and there lay the French – and here lay his honour and myself.'

III, 28

After [this line] followed in the MS. an incident which has been kept back. Part of the suppressed verses shall here be given as a gratification of private feeling, which the well-disposed reader will find no difficulty in excusing. They are now printed for the first time:

> Can any mortal clog come to her?
> It can: ...
>
> .   .   .   .
>
> But Benjamin, in his vexation,
> Possesses inward consolation;
> He knows his ground, and hopes to find
> A spot with all things to his mind,
> An upright mural block of stone,
> Moist with pure water trickling down.
> A slender spring; but kind to man
> 10 It is, a true Samaritan;

Close to the highway, pouring out
Its offering from a chink or spout;
Whence all, howe'er athirst, or dropping
With toil, may drink, and without stooping.

Cries Benjamin "Where is it, where?
Voice hath it none, but must be near."
– A star, declining towards the west,
Upon the watery surface threw
Its image tremulously imprest,
20 That just marked out the object and withdrew,
Right welcome service! . . .

.   .   .   .

ROCK OF NAMES!

Light is the strain, but not unjust
To Thee and Thy memorial-trust
That once seemed only to express
Love that was love in idleness;
Tokens, as year hath followed year
How changed, alas, in character!
For they were graven on thy smooth breast
By hands of those my soul loved best;
30 Meek women, men as true and brave
As ever went to a hopeful grave:
Their hands and mine, when side by side
With kindred zeal and mutual pride,
We worked until the Initials took
Shapes that defied a scornful look. –
Love as for us a genial feeling
Survives, or one in need of healing,
The power, dear Rock, around thee cast,
Thy monumental power, shall last
40 For me and mine! O thought of pain,
That would impair it or profane!
Take all in kindness then, as said
With a staid heart but playful head;
And fail not Thou, loved Rock! to keep
Thy charge when we are laid asleep.

– W. (1836)

III, 92 *foundrous* likely to cause to stick fast or break down.
IV, 21 *Ghimmer-crag* 'The crag of the ewe lamb'. – W. Identified by
Knight as the rock now known as Fisher Crag.
IV, 47–8 *Sir Lancelot . . . Clifford* See *Song at the Feast of Brougham
Castle* 95–101.
IV, 123 *pricked* rode (archaic, with a Spenserian flavour – see *The Faerie
Queene* I, i, 1).

IV, 198 *adventurous song* Compare *Paradise Lost* I, 13: 'Invoke thy aid to my adventurous Song'.
IV, 259 *heartless* dejected.

POWER OF MUSIC

Composed probably between 4 April and 10 November 1806; first published in 1807; included from 1815 among 'Poems of the Imagination'.
I. F. note: 'Taken from life, 1806.'

STRAY PLEASURES

Composed probably between 4 April and 10 November 1806; first published in 1807; included from 1815 among 'Poems of the Fancy'.
I. F. note:

> Suggested on the Thames by the sight of one of those floating mills that used to be seen there. This I noticed on the Surrey side between Somerset House and Blackfriars Bridge. Charles Lamb was with me at the time; and I thought it remarkable that I should have to point out to *him*, an idolatrous Londoner, a sight so interesting as the happy group dancing on the platform.

13–19 Thomas De Quincey, 'On Wordsworth's Poetry' (*Works*, ed. Masson XI, 302):

> Undeniably there is (and without ground for complaint there is) even here, where the spirit of gaiety is professedly invoked, an oblique though evanescent image flashed upon us of a sadness that lies deep behind the laughing figures, and of a solitude that is the real possessor in fee of all things, but is waiting an hour or so for the dispossession of the dancing men and maidens who for that transitory hour are the true, but alas! the fugitive tenants.

33–4 Compare Drayton's *The Muses' Elysium* (Nymphal VI, 4, 6): 'The wind had no more strength than this . . . To make one leaf the next to kiss . . .'

STAR-GAZERS

Composed probably between 4 April and 14 November 1806; first published in 1807; included from 1815 among 'Poems of the Imagination'.
I. F. note: 'Observed by me in Leicester Square as here described, 1806.'

21 *rude* unpolished, unlearned.

'YES, IT WAS THE MOUNTAIN ECHO'

Composed 15 June 1806 or shortly thereafter; first published in 1807; from 1815 included among 'Poems of the Imagination'.
I. F. note: 'Town-End . . . The echo came from Nab-Scar, when I was walking on the opposite side of Rydal Mere . . . On my return from my walk I recited these verses to Mary . . .'

Wordsworth in his *Guide to the Lakes* (3rd ed., 1822), p. 106, comments on the 'imaginative influence in the voice of the cuckoo, when that voice has taken possession of a deep mountain valley, very different from anything which can be excited by the same sound in a flat country'.

THE RECLUSE. HOME AT GRASMERE

Partly composed perhaps early 1800; composed for the most part probably between about late June and early September 1806; first published in 1888.

As the full title indicates, *Home at Grasmere* was intended as the first book of the first part of *The Recluse*, the only entire part of which to reach completion was *The Excursion* – see the head-notes to that poem (Vol. II, p. 951).

6 *devious* rambling.

152–78 A prose version of this journey is contained in a letter from Wordsworth to Coleridge (24 December 1799).

334 *bield* shelter.

339 *Norman Curfew's* a curfew was established by William the Conqueror.

559 *wanton boys King Lear* IV, i, 38.

654 *a Stranger of our Father's House* John Wordsworth.

658–9 *Sisters ... Brother* Mary Hutchinson and her sisters; Samuel Taylor Coleridge.

755 The remainder of the first book (106 lines here omitted) serves as the 'Prospectus' of *The Excursion*.

WATER FOWL

Composed probably between about late June and early September 1806; first published in 1823; from 1827 included among 'Poems of the Imagination'. Except for the opening line, which may have been written in 1812, this poem occurs as a passage in *Home at Grasmere*, lines 203–29.

14 *indefatigable flight* Compare *Paradise Lost* II, 407–8: '... Spread his aerie flight / Upborn with indefatigable wings'.

TO THE EVENING STAR

Composed probably July 1806; lines 1–10 first published in 1889, lines 11–12 in 1896.

Possibly intended to be part of the description of Grasmere in *Home at Grasmere* (lines 117–28) – see note to line 8 below.

8 Identical to line 120 of *Home at Grasmere*.

TO THE SPADE OF A FRIEND

Composed probably between 18 August and 26 October 1806; first published in 1807; included from 1815 among 'Poems of Sentiment and Reflection'.

I. F. note:

This person was Thomas Wilkinson, a Quaker by religious profession; by natural constitution of mind, or shall I venture to say, by God's grace, he was something better. He had inherited a small estate, and built a house upon it near Yanwath, upon the banks of the Emont . . . As represented in this poem, he employed his leisure hours in shaping pleasant walks by the side of his beloved river . . .

In a letter to Wilkinson (November 1806), Wordsworth sent the poem with the comment that it was 'supposed to have been composed that afternoon when you and I were labouring together in your pleasure-ground, an afternoon I often think of with pleasure'. Wilkinson wrote the account of the solitary reaper that inspired Wordsworth's poem of that name.

13 *the Poet* Wilkinson was also a poet.

[FRAGMENT: 'THE RAINS AT LENGTH HAVE CEASED']

Composed probably about early September 1806 (before the following poem); first published in 1889.

Extracted from Dorothy Wordsworth's Grasmere journal.

LINES, COMPOSED AT GRASMERE

Composed probably about early September 1806; first published in 1807; included from 1815 among 'Epitaphs and Elegiac Pieces'.

For Wordsworth's estimation of Charles James Fox (died 13 September 1806), see his letter to Fox of 14 January 1801, which accompanied a presentation copy of the *Lyrical Ballads*.

10 'Importuna e grave salma. – Michael Angelo.' – W. From the first line of Sonnet CIII of Michelangelo, translated later by Wordsworth in its entirety – see *Memorials of a Tour in Italy*, XXII.

THE HORN OF EGREMONT CASTLE

Composed possibly between 30 October and early December 1806; first published in 1807; included from 1815 to 1843 among 'Poems of the Imagination' (in 1815 with a note that 'as [it] rather [refers] to the imagination than [is] produced by it, would not have been placed here but to avoid a needless multiplication of the Classes'), and afterwards among 'Miscellaneous Poems'.

Wordsworth's *note*: 'This story is a Cumberland tradition . . .'

I. F. note: 'A tradition transferred from the ancient mansion of Hutton John, the seat of the Hudlestons, to Egremont Castle.'

THOUGHT OF A BRITON

Composed probably between 30 October 1806 and late February 1807; first published in 1807; from 1815 included among 'Poems Dedicated to National Independence and Liberty'.

I. F. note: 'This was composed while pacing to and fro between the Hall of Coleorton, then rebuilding, and the principal Farm-house of the Estate, in which we lived for nine or ten months.'

Coleridge (*The Friend*, 21 December 1809) thought this 'one of the noblest Sonnets in our language' and Wordsworth (in a letter to Richard Sharp, 27 September 1808) considered it 'as being the best I had written'.

The French subjugated Switzerland in 1802.

NOVEMBER, 1806

Composed probably between 30 October 1806 and late February 1807 (perhaps by early December, especially 7 December); first published in 1807; from 1815 included among 'Poems Dedicated to National Independence and Liberty'.

2 Prussia, the last Continental power thought strong enough to resist Napoleon, was defeated at the Battle of Jena, 14 October 1806.

13-14 'These two lines are from Lord Brooke's *Life of Sir Philip Sidney*.' – W. (1807). Chapter VIII (near the beginning): '. . . The stirring spirits sent abroad as fuel, to keep the flame far off: and the effeminate made judges of danger which they fear and honour which they understand not.'

SONG AT THE FEAST OF BROUGHAM CASTLE

Composed probably between 30 October 1806 and early April 1807; first published in 1807; included from 1815 among 'Poems of the Imagination'.

I. F. note: 'This poem was composed at Coleorton . . .'

Wordsworth in a *note* (1807), described a portion of the history of the Wars of the Roses pertinent to the poem:

> Henry Lord Clifford, . . . the subject of this poem, was the son of John, Lord Clifford, who was slain at Towton Field [and who] after the battle of Wakefield slew, in the pursuit, the young Earl of Rutland, son of the Duke of York . . . 'in part of revenge, for the Earl's Father had slain his' . . . But independent of this act, at best a cruel and savage one, the family of Clifford had done enough to draw upon them the vehement hatred of the House of York: so that after the Battle of Towton, there was no hope for them but in flight and concealment. Henry, the subject of the poem, was deprived of his estate and honours during the space of twenty-four years; all which time he lived as a shepherd in Yorkshire, or in Cumberland, where the estate of his father-in-law [step-father] (Sir Lancelot Threlkeld) lay. He was restored to his estate and honours in the first year of Henry the Seventh.

6 *red rose* emblem of the House of Lancaster, as the white rose was the emblem of York.

7 *thirty years* 1455-85, the Wars of the Roses.

9-10 Compare Butler's *Hudibras* II, i, 567-8: 'That shall infuse Eternal Spring, / And everlasting flourishing'.

13 *the two . . . are blended* the Houses of Lancaster and York were joined through marriage in 1486.

27 'This line is from *The Battle of Bosworth Field* [1629] by Sir John Beaumont . . .' – W. (1807). Line 100: 'The earth assists thee with the cry of blood.'

36–49 All the castles mentioned were part of the Clifford estate.

122 *the undying fish* 'It is imagined by the people of the Country that there are two immortal Fish, Inhabitants of this Tarn, which lies in the mountains not far from Threlkeld. – Blencathara, mentioned before, is the old and proper name of the mountain vulgarly called Saddle-back.' – W. (1807).

142–3 'The martial character of the Cliffords is well known to the readers of English History; but it may not be improper here to say . . . that, besides several others, who perished in the same manner, the four immediate progenitors of the person in whose hearing this is supposed to be spoken, all died in the Field.' – W.

'THOUGH NARROW BE THAT OLD MAN'S CARES'

Composed probably between 30 October 1806 and early April 1807; first published in 1807; in 1815 included among 'Poems Referring to the Period of Old Age' and thereafter among 'Miscellaneous Sonnets'.

I. F. note:

1807. Coleorton. This old man's name was Mitchell. He was, in all his ways and conversation, a great curiosity, both individually and as a representative of past times. His chief employment was keeping watch at night by pacing round the house, at that time building, to keep off depradators. He has often told me gravely of having seen the Seven Whistlers and the Hounds as here described.

The motto verse is from *A Midsummer Night's Dream* V, i, 16–17.

10, 12 *SEVEN WHISTLERS, GABRIEL'S HOUNDS* 'Both these superstitions are prevalent in the midland Counties of England; that of "Gabriel's Hounds" appears to be very general over Europe, being the same as the one upon which the German Poet, Bürger, has founded his ballad of the "Wild Huntsman".' – W. (1807–15).

A COMPLAINT

Composed probably between 30 October 1806 and early April 1807 (possibly by 7 December 1806); first published in 1807; included from 1815 among 'Poems Founded on the Affections'.

I. F. note: 'Town-End 1806. Suggested by a change in the manner of a friend [Coleridge].'

SONG FOR THE SPINNING WHEEL

Composed possibly 1806 (or more probably 1812); first published in 1820; from 1820 included among 'Poems of the Fancy'.

I. F. note: '1806. The belief on which this is founded I have often heard expressed by an old neighbour of Grasmere.'

'THROUGH CUMBRIAN WILDS'

Composed perhaps between 1806 and late October 1814; first published in 1896.

A PROPHECY

Composed probably February 1807; first published in 1807; from 1815 included among 'Poems Dedicated to National Independence and Liberty'.
4 *ARMINIUS* the German who defeated the Roman Army under Varus in 9 A.D.
10 *Those new-born Kings* the twelve lesser German sovereigns who in 1806 put themselves under the Protectorate of Napoleon.
12 *that Bavarian* Frederick Augustus, Elector of Saxony, admitted into the Protectorate later in 1806.

'O NIGHTINGALE!'

Composed probably between early February and early April 1807; first published in 1807 (among 'Moods of My Own Mind'); included from 1815 among 'Poems of the Imagination'.

2 *'fiery heart'* *III Henry VI*, I, iv, 87.
6 *Valentine* i.e., lover. On St Valentine's Day birds were supposed to select their mates – see Chaucer's *Parlement of Foules*.
13 *His voice was buried among trees*

> ... A metaphor expressing the love of *seclusion* by which this Bird is marked; and characterising its note as not partaking of the shrill and the piercing, and therefore more easily deadened by the intervening shade; yet a note so peculiar and withal so pleasing, that the breeze, gifted with that love of the sound which the Poet feels, penetrates the shades in which it is entombed, and conveys it to the ear of the listener.

– W. (Preface of 1815).

TO LADY BEAUMONT

Composed probably about early February 1807 (by 15 February); first published in 1807; from 1815 included among 'Miscellaneous Sonnets'.

I. F. note: '1807. The winter garden of Coleorton, fashioned out of an old quarry under the superintendence and direction of Mrs Wordsworth and my sister Dorothy, during the winter and spring of the year we resided there.'

GYPSIES

Composed probably about (but not before) 26 February 1807; first published in 1807; in 1807 included in the group 'Moods of My Own Mind'; included from 1815 among 'Poems of the Imagination'.

I. F. note: 'Composed at Coleorton, 1807. I had observed them, as here described, near Castle Donnington, on my way to and from Derby.'

Coleridge (*Biographia Literaria*, Chapter XXII) attacked the poem for '*mental* bombast', or 'thoughts and images too great for the subject'.

25-28 added 1820. Wordsworth in a letter to Barron Field (24 October 1828) promised to drop 'the concluding apology' but failed to do so.

TO THOMAS CLARKSON

Composed probably 26 March 1807 (or shortly after); first published in 1807; from 1815 included among 'Poems Dedicated to National Independence and Liberty'.

Thomas Clarkson (1760-1846), a prominent agitator in the English anti-slavery movement, was a friend of Wordsworth.

5 *Didst first lead forth that enterprise*
This honour has, I am told, been denied to Mr Clarkson by the sons of Mr Wilberforce, in the account of his life lately published by them, and priority of exertion in this cause ... claimed for their father ... I shall avail myself of some future occasion to make public the grounds of evidence ...

– W. (1838).

TO THE POET, JOHN DYER

Composed perhaps between April 1807 and early 1811; first published in 1815; from 1815 included among 'Miscellaneous Sonnets'. John Dyer (1700?-1758).

1 *Bard of the Fleece* Dyer's *The Fleece* (1757).

5-6 Dyer's *The Fleece* III, 437-8 (with slight changes).

13 Compare *The Fleece* I, 192-5: 'Darwent's naked peaks, / Snowden and blue of Plynlymmon, and the wide / Aërial sides of Cader-Yddris huge'.

14 *Grongar Hill* Dyer's *Grongar Hill* (1726).

'GRIEF, THOU HAST LOST AN EVER READY FRIEND'

Composed perhaps between April 1807 and late October 1814; first published in 1819; from 1820 included among 'Miscellaneous Sonnets'.

I. F. note: 'I could write a treatise of lamentation upon the changes brought about among the cottages of Westmoreland by the silence of the Spinning-Wheel. During long winter nights and wet days, the wheel upon which wool was spun gave employment to a great part of the family.'

14 *mantling* Frothing, sparkling to a 'head' (as with fermented liquids).

'MARK THE CONCENTRED HAZELS'

Composed perhaps between April 1807 and late October 1814; first published in 1815; from 1815 included among 'Miscellaneous Sonnets'.
I. F. note: 'Suggested in the wild hazel-wood at the foot of Helm-crag, where the stone still lies, with others of like form and character, though much of the wood that veiled it from the glare of day has been felled.'

'THE SHEPHERD, LOOKING EASTWARD'

Composed perhaps between April 1807 and late October 1814; first published in 1815; from 1815 included among 'Miscellaneous Sonnets'.

'WEAK IS THE WILL OF MAN'

Composed perhaps between April 1807 and late October 1814; first published in 1815; in 1820 included among 'Miscellaneous Sonnets', in 1820 used as a motto prefixed to *The White Doe*, then returned from 1827 to 'Miscellaneous Sonnets'; also used as a motto in the 1815 edition of *The White Doe*.

COMPOSED BY THE SIDE OF GRASMERE LAKE

Composed possibly 1807, after 10 July (fairly certainly by late October 1814); first published in 1819 with *The Waggoner*; in 1820 included among 'Miscellaneous Sonnets' and thereafter among 'Poems Dedicated to National Independence and Liberty'.

THE FORCE OF PRAYER

Composed perhaps about 18 September 1807; first published in 1815 with *The White Doe of Rylstone*; included from the collected edition of 1815 among 'Poems of Sentiment and Reflection'.
I. F. note: 'An Appendage to *The White Doe*. My friend, Mr Rogers, has also written on the subject [*The Boy of Egremond*]. The story is preserved in Dr. Whitaker's "History of Craven" [1805] . . .' Samuel Rogers (1763–1855).

1 *bene* prayer.
19 *Wharf*, the river which runs beside Bolton Abbey.
21 *striding-place* crossing-place.
1
THE WHITE DOE OF RYLSTONE

Composed probably between 16 October 1807 and 16 January 1808 (under revision until at least 19 April 1809); first published 2 June 1815, first collected in 1820, and revised extensively again for the 1836–7 edition.
Wordsworth's Prefatory *note* (1820):

The Poem of the White Doe of Rylstone is founded on a local tradition and on the Ballad in Percy's Collection, entitled 'The Rising of the North'. The tradition is as follows: – 'About [at] this time', not long after

the Dissolution, 'a White Doe', say the aged people in the neighbour-
hood, 'long continued to make a weekly pilgrimage from Rylstone over
the fells of [to] Bolton, and was constantly found in the Abbey Church-
yard during divine service; after the close of which she returned home
as regularly as the rest of the congregation.' – DR WHITAKER'S
History of the Deanery of Craven. – Rylstone was the property and resid-
ence of the Nortons, distinguished in that ill-advised and unfortunate
Insurrection; which led me to connect with this tradition the principal
circumstance of their fate, as recorded in the Ballad.

Dr Thomas Dunham Whitaker's *The History and Antiquities of the
Deanery of Craven* (1805), p. 383. The ballad *The Rising of the North* was
reprinted at the end of Wordsworth's long note (cut short above) and can be
found in *PW*, III, 538–42.

In the *I. F. note*, besides describing the locale of the composition of the
poem (which is not quite accurate), Wordsworth offered an analysis of the
poem:

Let me here say a few words of this Poem in the way of criticism. The
subject being taken from feudal times has led to its being compared to
some of Walter Scott's poems that belong to the same age and state of
society. The comparison is inconsiderate. Sir Walter pursued the
customary and very natural course of conducting an action, presenting
various turns of fortune, to some outstanding point on which the mind
might rest as a termination or catastrophe. The course I attempted to
pursue is entirely different. Everything that is attempted by the principal
personages in 'The White Doe' fails, so far as its object is external and
substantial. So far as it is moral and spiritual it succeeds. The heroine of
the Poem knows that her duty is not to interfere with the current of
events, either to forward or delay them, but
                                    To abide
                    The shock, and finally secure
                    O'er pain and grief a triumph pure.

This she does in obedience to her brother's injunction, as most suitable to
a mind and character that, under previous trials, had been proved to
accord with his. She achieves this not without aid from the communica-
tion with the inferior Creature, which often leads her thoughts to revolve
upon the past with a tender and humanizing influence that exalts rather
than depresses her. The anticipated beatification, if I may so say, of her
mind, and the apotheosis of the companion of her solitude, are the points
at which the Poem aims, and constitute its legitimate catastrophe, far too
spiritual a one for instant or widely spread sympathy, but not therefore
the less fitted to make a deep and permanent impression upon that class of
minds who think and feel more independently, than the many do, of the
surfaces of things and interests transitory because belonging more to the
outward and social forms of life than to its internal spirit. How insignifi-
cant a thing, for example, does personal prowess appear compared with

the fortitude of patience and heroic martyrdom; in other words, with struggles for the sake of principle, in preference to victory gloried in for its own sake.

In a letter to Francis Wrangham (18 January 1816), Wordsworth expanded upon this analysis:

> ... As the Poem thus begins and ends with pure and lofty Imagination, every motive and impulse that actuates the persons introduced is from the same source; a kindred spirit pervades, and is intended to harmonise, the whole. Throughout, objects (the Banner, for instance) derive their influence, not from properties inherent in them, not from what they are actually in themselves, but from such as are bestowed upon them by the minds of those who are conversant with or affected by those objects. Thus the Poetry, if there be any in the work, proceeds, whence it ought to do, from the soul of Man, communicating its creative energies to the images of the external world.

In Christopher Wordsworth's *Memoirs* (II, 311), Wordsworth is quoted as considering '*The White Doe* as, in conception, the highest work he had ever produced'.

Dedication

2 *MARY* Mary Wordsworth, the poet's wife.

5 *Spenser's Lay* The Faerie Queene.

11 *sorrow's thrilling dart* Compare *The Faerie Queene* I, vii, 25: 'And thrilling sorrow thrown his utmost dart'.

14 *The milk-white Lamb which in a line she led* Compare *The Faerie Queene* I, i, 4: 'And by her, in a line a milk white lamb she led'. The phrase 'in a line' means 'on a lead'.

19 *specious* apparently real.

22 *lamentable change* Wordsworth lost two children in 1812.

23 *The Faerie Queene* II, viii, 44: 'That bliss may not abide in state of mortal men'.

38-9 *High over hill ... we wandered* Compare *The Faerie Queene* I, vii, 28: 'High over hills, and low adown the dale, She wandered'.

39 *wandered, willing to partake* Compare *The Faerie Queene* I, iii, 44: 'To be partaker of her wandering woe'.

The Verse Motto ('*Action is transitory*')

Wordsworth's *note*: 'This and the five lines that follow were either read or recited by me, more than thirty years since, to the late Mr Hazlitt, who quoted some expressions in them (imperfectly remembered) in a work of his [*Spirit of the Age* (1825)] published several years ago.' In 1815 and 1820, the sonnet *Weak Is the Will of Man* was the motto verse, and in 1827 and 1832 there was none; these lines became the verse motto in 1837.

The first six lines are part of *The Borderers* (lines 1539-44), while the remainder were added to make up the motto.

The Prose Motto

Taken from Bacon's *Of Atheism*, the prose motto appeared in all editions of *The White Doe*.

Cantos I–VII

1 *tower* 'It is to be regretted that at the present day Bolton Abbey wants this ornament; but the Poem, according to the imagination of the Poet, is composed in Queen Elizabeth's time.' – W.

6 *Wharf* the river which runs beside Bolton Abbey.

11 *grooms* boys.

17 *fifty years* The Abbey was taken over by the Crown early in 1540. Thus the scene takes place approximately twenty years after the Rebellion of 1569.

94 *cunning* skill.

161 *several* separate.

186 *From Rylstone* Rylstone is seven miles from Bolton Abbey.

212 *characters* features.

226 *When Lady Aäliza mourned* 'The detail of this tradition may be found in Dr Whitaker's book, and in a Poem of this collection, "The Force of Prayer".' – W.

242-53

'At the East end of the North aisle of Bolton Priory Church is a chantry belonging to Bethmesly Hall, and a vault, where, according to tradition, the Claphams' (who inherited this estate, by the female line, from the Mauleverers) 'were interred upright.' John de Clapham, of whom this ferocious act is recorded, was a man of great note in his time: 'he was a vehement partisan of the house of Lancaster, in whom the spirit of his chieftains, the Cliffords, seemed to survive.'

– W.

244 *griesly* obsolete form of grisly.

266 *conceit* opinion.

268 '[See] "Song at the Feast of Brougham Castle, upon the Restoration of Lord Clifford, the Shepherd, to the Estates and Honours of his Ancestors." To that Poem is annexed an account of this personage, chiefly extracted from Burns and Nicholson's History of Cumberland and Westmoreland.' – W. Wordsworth here added 'further particulars concerning him, from Dr Whitaker'.

294 *Barden's lowly quietness* Barden Tower is two miles from Bolton Priory.

357 Compare *The Rising in the North* 108: 'And the five wounds our Lord did bear'.

400 *dying fall* *Twelfth Night* I, i, 4; Pope's *Ode on St Cecilia's Day* 21; Thomson's *Spring* 725.

479 *fearless* a transferred epithet: Marmaduke is fearless.

511 Compare *The Rising in the North* 90: 'Unarmed and naked will I be'.

515 'See the Old Ballad, "The Rising of the North".' – W.

527 *I could prophesy* *I Henry IV*, V, iv, 83.

588 Compare *Paradise Lost* VIII, 452: 'He ended, or I heard no more'.

595 *Brancepeth* 'Brancepeth Castle stands near the river Were, a few miles from the city of Durham. It formerly belonged to the Nevilles, Earls of Westmoreland. See Dr Percy's account.' – W.

596 *telling* counting.

667 *the blessed Dove* the Holy Spirit.

687 *Saint Cuthbert* Durham Cathedral.

696 *Raby Hall* Raby Castle, six miles from Barnard Castle.

716–17 Compare *The Rising in the North* 99–100: 'At Wetherby they mustered their host, / Thirteen thousand fair to see'. Wetherby is on the Wharf River in Yorkshire.

787 *Dudley* Ambrose Dudley, Earl of Warwick (1528?–1590).

796 Compare *The Rising in the North* 144: 'Against so many could not stay'.

800 *Lord Dacre* Leonard Dacre (d. 1573), one of the chief rebels.

801 *Howard's* Thomas Howard, Fourth Duke of Norfolk (1536–72).

814–15 *Thurston...conquered!* 'See the Historians for the account of this memorable battle, usually denominated the Battle of the Standard.' – W.

828 *that other day* Henry Percy defeated the Scotch at the Battle of Neville's Cross in 1346.

918 *joined* rhymes with 'find'.

933 *prove* test.

937 A manuscript continuation of thirty-seven lines to Canto Three is printed in *PW*, III, 552–3.

940 *Town* the town of Barnard Castle.

972–1002 Compare the description of the doe with Dorothy Wordsworth's description of a dog in her *Journal* (8 November 1805): 'Mrs Luff's large white dog lay in the moonshine upon the round knoll under the old yew-tree, a beautiful and romantic image – the dark tree with its dark shadow, and the elegant creature as fair as a spirit.'

974 *herb* herbage, grass.

1069 *Her duty is to stand and wait* Compare Milton's *On His Blindness* 14: 'They also serve who only stand and wait'. The italics (and capitalization in lines 1071–2) were added in 1820, possibly, Nowell C. Smith suggests, to point up the theme of the poem.

1087 *enjoined* rhymes with 'mind'.

1168 *Norton Tower* 'It is so called to this day.' – W.

1175 Compare *The Battle of Flodden Field* V, 9: 'From Penigent to Pendle Hill'.

1328 *Sussex* Sir Thomas Radcliffe, Third Earl of Sussex (1526?–83).

1387 *blank awe* *Comus* 452.

1446 *Sir George Bowes* (1527–80), Provost Marshal.
Motto to Canto VII added in 1837; taken from Wordsworth's *Address to Kilchurn Castle* 6–9.
1587 *brave* fine.
1589 *birds'* *bird's: 1815–50.* I follow de Selincourt in making this change.
1721 *From looks conceiving her desire* Compare *The Faerie Queene* I, iii, 9: 'And ever by her looks conceived her intent'.
1762 '𝕲𝖔𝖉 𝖚𝖘 𝖆𝖞𝖉𝖊' 'On one of the bells of Rylstone Church, which seems coeval with the building of the tower, is this cypher, "𝕵. 𝕹." for John Norton, and the motto, "𝕲𝖔𝖉 𝖚𝖘 𝖆𝖞𝖉𝖊."' – W. From Whitaker's *History*, p. 384.
1803 *Pound* compound, a trap for game.
1862 *joined* rhymes with 'mind'.

SONNET ON MILTON

Composed probably about early 1808; first published in 1946.
   On the bottom of a MS, Wordsworth wrote: 'This Sonnet is suggested by Symond's [sic] Life.' Charles Symmons's *Life of Milton* (1806).

9–10 *Norway's bleak domain . . . stately Pine* an allusion to *Paradise Lost* I, 292–3: 'the tallest Pine, / Hewn on *Norwegian* hills'.

[ST PAUL'S]

Composed probably between 6 April and early autumn 1808; first published in 1947.
   In a letter to Sir George Beaumont (8 April 1808), Wordsworth described the scene of the poem:

   I left Coleridge at seven o'clock on Sunday morning, and walked towards the City in a very thoughtful and melancholy state of mind. I had passed through Temple Bar and by St Dunstan's, noticing nothing, and entirely occupied with my own thoughts, when, looking up, I saw before me the avenue of Fleet Street, silent, empty, and pure white, with a sprinkling of new-fallen snow, not a cart or carriage to obstruct the view, no noise, only a few soundless and dusky foot-passengers here and there. You remember the elegant curve of Ludgate Hill in which this avenue would terminate, and beyond, towering above it, was the huge and majestic form of St Paul's, solemnised by a thin veil of falling snow. I cannot say how much I was affected at this unthought-of sight in such a place, and what a blessing I felt there is in habits of exalted Imagination. My sorrow was controlled, and my uneasiness of mind – not quieted and relieved altogether – seemed at once to receive the gift of an anchor of security.

THE TUFT OF PRIMROSES

Composed probably between 6 April and early autumn 1808; first published in 1949.

1–19 Wordsworth apparently intended to change the poem from the second to the third person, for such revisions had been made in MS for these lines.

24 *conceit* conception.

37 *a Friend* Sara Hutchinson.

74 John Wordsworth, brother of the poet, had died in 1805, and estrangement with Coleridge was felt as early as 1806.

103 *blanc* Miltonic spelling; see *Paradise Lost* III, 48.

143–85 used to compose *The Excursion* VII, 242–91, the story of the Sympsons.

156–7 *A consummation . . . to be wished for* Compare *Hamlet* III, i, 63–4: 'A Consummation/Devoutly to be wished'.

164 *Emma* Dorothy Wordsworth. 'Mary' (line 167) is Mary Wordsworth, wife of the poet.

264–95 used to compose *The Excursion* III, 367–405.

296 *St Basil* (329 ?–?379 A.D.) scholar and theologian, usually considered the founder of monasticism.

318–420 The description of the retreat and Basil's invitation to St Gregory of Nazianzus are taken from Basil's Letter XIV.

356–8 used in *The Excursion* VII, 980–82 and originally taken, according to Wordsworth's note to *The Excursion*, from 'the introduction to the Foundation-charter . . . of the Abbey of St Mary's Furness'.

372–3 Compare *Paradise Lost* I, 743: 'from Noon to dewy Eve' and *Lycidas* 178–9: 'There entertain him all the Saints above, / In solemn troops, and sweet Societies'.

402 *Pard* leopard.

434 *Amphilochius* (d. 394) Bishop of Iconium.

494–508 lines crossed out in the MS.

510–69 used to compose *The Prelude* VI, 424–71. See also *Descriptive Sketches* 52–76 for the earliest version of Wordsworth's visit to Chartreuse.

TO THE CLOUDS

Composed probably between 6 April and early autumn 1808; first published in 1842; included from 1845 among 'Poems of the Imagination'.

I. F. note: 'These verses were suggested while I was walking on the foot-road between Rydal Mount and Grasmere. The clouds were driving over the top of Nab Scar across the vale; they set my thoughts agoing, and the rest followed almost immediately.'

77 *a Cyclades* cluster of islands in the Aegean.

82 *the god of verse* Apollo.

ELEGIAC STANZAS COMPOSED IN THE CHURCHYARD OF GRASMERE

Composed perhaps 7 or 8 April 1808 (or shortly after); first published September 1839 by Thomas De Quincey in *Tait's Edinburgh Magazine* (never published by Wordsworth).

In a letter to Coleridge (19 April 1808), Wordsworth sent the poem with the title: 'Elegiac Stanzas composed in the Churchyard of Grasmere, Westmoreland, a few days after the Interment there of a Man and his Wife, Inhabitants of the Vale, who were lost upon the neighbouring Mountains, on the night of the nineteenth of March last.' Wordsworth commented further: '. . . In passing through the churchyard I stopped at the grave of the poor Sufferers and immediately afterwards composed the following stanzas; *composed* I have said, I ought rather to have said effused, for it is the mere pouring out of my own feeling . . .'

[PELAYO]

Composed possibly about late June, perhaps about early July 1808; first published in 1946.

Pelayo (d. 737) was a Spanish leader who, after fighting a guerrilla war in the Asturian mountains, finally overthrew the Moors in 718. After the Spanish revolt against Napoleon in 1810, Pelayo became a type of the Spanish hero.

5 *Deva's* a river in northern Spain.
8 *Auseva's* a mountain in Asturias, site of the Battle of Covadonga.
49-50 Napoleon placed his brother, Joseph, on the Spanish throne.

COMPOSED WHILE THE AUTHOR WAS ENGAGED

Composed probably between about mid-November 1808 and 26 March 1809 (or even possibly by 31 December 1808); first published in 1815; from 1815 included among 'Poems Dedicated to National Independence and Liberty'.

The Convention of Cintra conceded to the beaten French what many thought dishonourably favourable terms; in a letter to Daniel Stuart (5 February 1809) Wordsworth commented: '. . . My heart is deeply interested in this affair. Never did any public event cause in my mind so much sorrow as the Convention of Cintra . . .'

COMPOSED AT THE SAME TIME

All data identical with the previous poem.

1810 ('Ah! where is Palafox?')

Composed fairly certainly between 14 March 1809 and sometime in 1810 (perhaps about late March [after 14 March] 1809); first published in 1815;

from 1815 included among 'Poems Dedicated to National Independence and Liberty'.

1 *Palafox* Don Joseph Palafox-y-Melzi (1780–1847), the defender of Saragossa. See note to line 2 of *'Is There a Power'* (below).

7 *that imperial Slave* Napoleon.

'HAIL, ZARAGOZA!'

All data identical with the preceding poem.

Wordsworth's *note* (1815): 'The beginning is imitated from an Italian Sonnet.'

1 *Zaragoza* Saragossa, a city in Spain beseiged by the French, fell 20 February 1809.

'IS THERE A POWER'

All data identical with the preceding poem.

2 *the captive chieftain* Most probably Don Joseph Palafox-y-Melzi (1780–1847), the defender of Saragossa. He was kept in prison for nearly five years.

'AVAUNT ALL SPECIOUS PLIANCY OF MIND'

Composed perhaps between about March 1809 and 1810; first published in 1815; from 1815 included among 'Poems Dedicated to National Independence and Liberty'.

THE FRENCH AND THE SPANISH GUERILLAS

All data identical with the preceding poem.

'SAY, WHAT IS HONOUR?'

All data identical with the preceding poem.

'CALL NOT THE ROYAL SWEDE UNFORTUNATE'

Composed perhaps about early April (probably not before 30 March) 1809; first published in 1815; from 1815 included among 'Poems Dedicated to National Independence and Liberty'.

1 *the royal Swede* Gustavus IV, who abdicated in 1809. See *The King of Sweden.*
5 *'perished by his choice, and not his fate'* unidentified quotation.

'LOOK NOW ON THAT ADVENTURER'

All data identical with the preceding poem.

Napoleon ('that adventurer') is probably here being contrasted with Gustavus IV – see the previous poem.

'BRAVE SCHILL! BY DEATH DELIVERED'

Composed perhaps about, but not before, 19 June 1809; first published in 1815; from 1815 included among 'Poems Dedicated to National Independence and Liberty'.

Ferdinand von Schill (1773–1809) was a Prussian who attempted to rally the Germans against Napoleon.

2 *Prussia's timid region* Prussia had maintained neutrality during a good many years of the Napoleonic wars.

'ALAS! WHAT BOOTS'

Composed probably between 22 June and 16 November 1809; first published 16 November 1809 in *The Friend*, where it was entitled *Sonnet suggested by the efforts of the Tyrolese, contrasted with the present state of Germany*; from 1815 included among 'Poems Dedicated to National Independence and Liberty'.

1 *Alas! what boots* *Lycidas* 64.

'AND IS IT AMONG RUDE'

Composed probably between 22 June and 21 December (possibly between 22 and 29 June) 1809; first published 21 December 1809 in *The Friend*; from 1815 included among 'Poems Dedicated to National Independence and Liberty'.

10 *Palafox* Don Joseph Palafox-y-Melzi (1780–1847), Spanish general famous for his defence of Saragossa in 1808–9, using the local citizens.

FEELINGS OF THE TYROLESE

All data identical with the preceding poem.

12 *self-devoted* self-doomed.

'O'ER THE WIDE EARTH'

All data identical with the previous poem.

3 *universal P A N* *Paradise Lost* IV, 266 (source acknowledged in a note in *The Friend*).

[PASSAGE FROM JOHN WILSON'S THE ANGLER'S TENT]

Wordsworth helped John Wilson to compose these lines possibly about 29 June 1809, or possibly between 8 and 13 September 1809; first published in 1812.

For the background of the collaboration, see Martha Gordon's *Christopher North*, 2nd ed. (1879), pp. 92–3.

'ADVANCE – COME FORTH'

Composed probably 10 October 1809; first published in *The Friend*, 26 October 1809; from 1815 included among 'Poems Dedicated to National Independence and Liberty'.

3 *Sweet Nymph, O rightly of the mountains named* Compare *L'Allegro* 36: 'The Mountain Nymph, sweet Liberty'.

HOFER

All data identical with the preceding poem.
Andreas Hofer (1767–1810) was an inn-keeper who led the Tyrolese mountaineers against the French in 1796 and 1809.

3 *Tell's* William Tell (died c. 1350), the Swiss patriot.
5 *Phoebus* the sun.

ON THE FINAL SUBMISSION OF THE TYROLESE

Composed probably between 24 October and 21 December 1809; first published 21 December 1809 in *The Friend* with the title *On the Report of the Submission of the Tyrolese*; from 1815 included among 'Poems Dedicated to National Independence and Liberty'.

EPITAPH (FROM CHIABRERA): 'Not without heavy grief'

Translated probably late 1809 (by 11 December); first published 4 January 1810 in *The Friend*; from 1815 included among 'Epitaphs and Elegiac Pieces'. Gabriello Chiabrera (1552–1617) was an Italian poet who worked with classical forms.
A translation of Epitaph IX on Monsignor Abbate Francesco Pozzobonello ('Non senza gran cordoglio il Zio ripose').

15 'In justice to the Author, I subjoin the original: " ————— e degli amici / Non lasciava languire i bei pensieri".' – W.

EPITAPH (FROM CHIABRERA): 'Destined to war'

Translated probably late 1809 (by 22 December); first published in *The Friend*, 28 December 1809; from 1815 included among 'Epitaphs and Elegiac Pieces'.
A translation of Epitaph XIX on Roberto Dati ('Ancora entro i confin di fanciullezza').

13 *Arno* river that runs through Florence.

EPITAPH (FROM CHIABRERA): 'Pause, courteous Spirit!'

All data identical with the preceding poem.
A translation of Epitaph XXVII ('Alma cortese, che quinci oltrepassi') on Bernardino Baldi of Urbino (1553–1617).

In his *Essays on Epitaphs* III, Wordsworth analyses this epitaph at some length – passage reprinted in *PW*, IV, 450.

9 *the Stagyrite* Aristotle.
14 *Permessus* a river in Boeotia that descends from Mount Helicon.
16 *the songs* the Psalms.

EPITAPH (FROM CHIABRERA): 'There never breathed'

Translated probably late 1809 (by 22 December); first published in *The Friend*, 28 December 1809; from 1815 included among 'Epitaphs and Elegiac Pieces'.

A translation of Epitaph XXV on Giambattista Feo ('Uomo non è, che pervenuto a morte').

13 *Auster and Boötes* the South and North winds.
15 *Pelorus* Cape Faro, in north-east Sicily. The 'Atlantic pillars' are the straits of Gibraltar.
24 *the lofty and the low* See *The Prelude* XIV, 271, and *Personal Talk* 32.

EPITAPH (FROM CHIABRERA): 'O Thou who movest'

Translated probably late 1809 or early 1810 (certainly by 22 February 1810); first published 22 February 1810 in *The Friend*; included from 1815 among 'Epitaphs and Elegiac Pieces'.

A translation of Epitaph VIII ('O tu, che muovi alla tua strada intento') on Giuseppe Ferreri, Archbishop of Urbino.

EPITAPH (FROM CHIABRERA): 'Perhaps some needful service'

For all data, see the head-note to the previous poem.

A translation of Epitaph XIV ('Forse ragion di buon governo trasse') on Roberto Titi.

11 *Nestorian* full of wisdom.
13 'Ivi vivea giocondo e i suoi pensieri / Erano tutti rose. The Translator had not skill to come nearer to his original.' – W.

[EPITAPH (FROM CHIABRERA) ON TASSO]

Translated probably late 1809 or early 1810 (by about late February); first published in 1876.

EPITAPH (FROM CHIABRERA): 'Weep not'

Translated possibly in part late 1809 or early 1810 (by about late February); first published in 1837; included from 1837 among 'Epitaphs and Elegiac Pieces'.

A translation of Epitaph I ('Non spargete sospir, diletti amici') on Francesco Ceni.

EPITAPH (FROM CHIABRERA): 'True is it'

All data identical with the preceding poem.

A translation of Epitaph VII ('Fu ver che Ambrosio Salinero a torto') on Ambrosio Salinero.

10 *Parnassian* Parnassus, a mountain in Greece sacred to Apollo.
12 *Hippocrene* a fountain on Mount Helicon sacred to the Muses.
22 *Permessus* a river that descends from Mount Helicon.

EPITAPH (FROM CHIABRERA): 'O flower'

All data identical with the preceding poem.

A translation of Epitaph XXIV ('O Lelio, o fior gentil di gentilezza') on Lelio Pavese. Another version (*'O Lelius, beauteous flower of gentleness'*) was written by Wordsworth in 1809-10. See head-note to the following poem.

4 *Aglaia* one of the Graces.
10 *Sebeto* a river near Naples.

[EPITAPH (FROM CHIABRERA): 'O Lelius']

Translated probably late 1809 or early 1810 (certainly by 28 February 1810); first published in 1876.

A translation of Epitaph XXIV ('O Lelio, o fior gentil di gentilezza') on Lelio Pavese. Another version (*'O flower of all that springs from gentle blood'*) was also written by Wordsworth (see previous poem).

Wordsworth's *Prefatory Comment*: In Chiabrera's

> mixed manner, exemplifying some of the points in which he has erred . . . This Epitaph is not without some tender thoughts, but . . . Chiabrera has here neglected to ascertain whether the passions expressed were in kind and degree a dispensation of reason, or at least commodities issued under her licence and authority.

– *Prose Works*, ed. Owen and Smyser II, 90.

2 *Aglaia's* one of the Graces.
9 *Sebeto* a river near Naples.

'THE MARTIAL COURAGE OF A DAY'

Composed perhaps about (but not before) 15 March 1810; first published in 1815; from 1815 included among 'Poems Dedicated to National Independence and Liberty'.

5-6 *a strain | Of triumph* In May 1809, Archduke Charles prevented Napoleon from crossing the Danube at the Battle of Marchfield.
10 *a Daughter of her Throne* Arch-Duchess Marie Louise was married to Napoleon by proxy 11 March 1810.

11 *her Tyrolean Champion* Andreas Hofer, who was shot in February 1810. (See *Hofer* above.)

INDIGNATION OF A HIGH-MINDED SPANIARD

Composed perhaps 1810; first published in 1815; from 1815 included among 'Poems Dedicated to National Independence and Liberty'.

1-3 Compare the comment of the Castilians on the proclamation of their 'apostate countrymen at Bayonne': Napoleon 'carries his audacity the length of holding out to us offers of happiness and peace, while he is laying waste our country, pulling down our churches, and slaughtering our brethren. . . .' Quoted in Wordsworth's *Convention of Cintra* tract.

'IN DUE OBSERVANCE'

All data identical with the preceding poem.

FEELINGS OF A NOBLE BISCAYAN

All data identical with the preceding poem.

THE OAK OF GUERNICA

All data identical with the preceding poem.

2 *Dodona* site of the oldest oracle in Greece. The oracle responded from a grove of oak trees.

1810 ('O'erweening Statesmen')

All data identical with the preceding poem.

13-14 'See Laborde's Character of the Spanish people; from him the sentiment of these last two lines is taken.' – W. Alexandre de Labor de, *A View of Spain* (1809).

ON A CELEBRATED EVENT

Composed probably between about 20 and 30 March 1811; first published in 1815; from 1815 included among 'Poems Dedicated to National Independence and Liberty'.

1 *A Roman Master* Titus Quinctius Flaminius (230?–?174 B.C.), who, after defeating Philip V of Macedon in 197, proclaimed the independence of the Greek states the following year.

UPON THE SAME EVENT

All data identical with the previous poem.

4-9 The Aetolians demanded from Flaminius that the Macedonians be expelled.

14 *Pelion's* a mountain in Thessaly.

UPON THE SIGHT OF A BEAUTIFUL PICTURE

Composed perhaps about early June (and not later than 28 August) 1811; first published in 1815; from 1815 included among 'Miscellaneous Sonnets'.

I. F. note:

> This was written when we dwelt in the Parsonage at Grasmere. The principal features of the picture are Bredon Hill and Cloud Hill near Coleorton. I shall never forget the happy feeling with which my heart was filled when I was impelled to compose this Sonnet. We resided only two years in this house; and during the last half of the time, which was after this poem had been written, we lost our two children, Thomas and Catharine. Our sorrow upon these events often brought it to my mind, and cast me upon the support to which the last line of it gives expression –
>
> 'The appropriate calm of blest eternity.'

It is scarcely necessary to add that we still possess the picture.

In a letter to Sir George Beaumont (28 August 1811), Wordsworth sent the sonnet with the following comment:

> A few days after I had enjoyed the pleasure of seeing in different moods of mind your Coleorton landscape from my fireside, it *suggested* to me the following Sonnet, which, having walked out to the side of Grasmere Brook, where it murmurs through the meadows near the Church, I composed immediately . . . The images of the smoke and the Travellers are taken from your Picture; the rest were added, in order to place the thought in a clear point of view, and for the sake of variety.

EPISTLE TO SIR GEORGE HOWLAND BEAUMONT

Composed probably for the most part about 26–28 August 1811 (finished 1842); first published in 1842; included from 1845 among 'Miscellaneous Poems'.

I. F. note:

> The journey, of which the first part is here described, was from Grasmere to Bootle on the south-west coast of Cumberland, the whole among mountain roads through a beautiful country, and we had fine weather. The verses end with our breakfast at the head of Yewdale in a yeoman's house. . . . Our hostess married a Mr Oldfield, a Lieut. in the Navy: they lived together for some time at Hackett, where she still resides as his widow. It was in front of that house, on the mountain side, near which stood the Peasant who, while we were passing at a distance, saluted us, waving a kerchief in her hand as described in the Poem . . . The dog which we met with soon after our starting belonged to Mr Rowlandson, who for forty years was curate of Grasmere in place of the rector . . . The "Epistle" to which these notes refer . . . was carefully revised so late as 1842, previous to its publication. I am loth to add, that it was never seen by the person to whom it is addressed.

See *Upon Perusing the Epistle* [to Sir George Howland Beaumont] *Thirty Years After its Composition* below (Vol. II, p. 871).

40–41 (*like Phoebus . . . attendant on Thessalian flocks*) Apollo tended the sheep of Admetus in Thessaly as a punishment inflicted by Zeus.

66 *the HOUSE OF KEYS* the Manx House of Commons.

84 *telegraph* a device for visual signalling, such as semaphore.

113 *those Infants* Catharine and Thomas Wordsworth, both of whom died the following year.

153 *Archimago's* the arch-villain of *The Faerie Queene*.

166 *Loughrigg-tarn* 'This beautiful pool and the surrounding scene are minutely described in my little Book upon the Lakes.' – *I. F. note.*

175 *craggy bield* rough cottage.

246–7 *butter fit to lie | Upon a lordly dish* Compare *Judges* 5:25: 'she brought forth butter in a lordly dish'.

DEPARTURE FROM THE VALE OF GRASMERE

Composed probably for the most part about 26–8 August 1811; first published in 1827; from 1827 included among 'Memorials of a Tour in Scotland 1803'.

I. F. note: '. . . transplanted from my epistle to Sir G. Beaumont.'

6 *crystal battlements* *Paradise Lost* I, 742.

10 *tracts of darkness* Compare *Paradise Lost* I, 28: 'the deep Tract of Hell'.

11 *aëry flight* *Paradise Lost* II, 407.

30–32 *brief absence . . . sweet return* Compare *Paradise Lost* IX, 248–50: '. . . to short absence I could yield. For . . . short retirement urges sweet return.'

VIEW FROM THE TOP OF BLACK COMB

Composed probably between late August 1811 and about 1813; first published in 1815; from 1815 included among 'Poems of the Imagination'.

I. F. note: '1813. Mary and I, as mentioned in the "Epistle to Sir G. Beaumont", lived for some time under its shadow.'

Wordsworth's Prefatory *note*: 'Black Comb stands at the southern extremity of Cumberland: its base covers a much greater extent of ground than any other mountain in those parts; and, from its situation, the summit commands a more extensive view than any other point in Britain.'

20 *cultured* cultivated.

28 *Look homeward now!* Compare *Lycidas* 163: 'Look homeward Angel now'.

WRITTEN WITH A SLATE PENCIL ON A STONE, ON THE SIDE OF THE MOUNTAIN

Dates of composition and publication identical with the preceding poem; from 1815 included among 'Inscriptions'.

I. F. note: 'The circumstance alluded to at the conclusion of these verses was told me by Dr Satterthwaite, who was Incumbent of Bootle, a small town at the foot of Black Comb. He had the particulars from one of the engineers who was employed in making trigonometrical surveys of that region.'

INSCRIPTION IN THE GROUNDS OF COLEORTON

Composed perhaps basically about mid-October (probably by 26 October) 1811, with alterations probably about, but by, 30 October; first published in 1815; from 1815 included among 'Inscriptions'.

I. F. note: 'In the Grounds of Coleorton these verses are engraved on a stone placed near the Tree, which was thriving and spreading when I saw it in the summer of 1841.'

17 *the haunt of him* Sir John Beaumont (1583-1627), author of *Bosworth Field*.

19 *that famous Youth* Francis Beaumont (1584-1616), the dramatist and brother of Sir John.

WRITTEN AT THE REQUEST OF SIR GEORGE BEAUMONT

All data identical with the preceding poem.

6 *that awful Pile* St Paul's, burial place of Sir Joshua Reynolds (1723-92), the portrait painter.

INSCRIPTION IN A GARDEN OF THE SAME [COLEORTON]

Composed probably about, but by, 29 October 1811; first published in 1815; from 1815 included among 'Inscriptions'.

I. F. note:

> This Niche is in the sandstone-rock in the winter-garden at Coleorton, which garden, as has been elsewhere said, was made under our direction out of an old unsightly quarry. While the labourers were at work, Mrs Wordsworth, my Sister, and I used to amuse ourselves occasionally in scooping this seat out of the soft stone. It is of the size, with something of the appearance, of a Stall in a Cathedral. This inscription is not engraven, as the former and the two following are, in the grounds.

FOR A SEAT IN THE GROVES OF COLEORTON

Composed 19 November 1811; first published in 1815; from 1815 included among 'Inscriptions'.

The poem was sent by Wordsworth in a letter to Lady Beaumont (20 November 1811) with the following comment:

> The following I composed yesterday morning, in a walk from Brathay, whither I had been to accompany my sister ... Grace Dieu is itself so

interesting a spot, and has naturally and historically such a connexion with Coleorton, that I could not deny myself the pleasure of paying it this mark of attention.

18 *And things of holy use unhallowed lie* In the letter cited above, Wordsworth acknowledged the debt to Daniel's *Musophilus* 289: 'Straight all that holy was unhallowed lies.'

1811 ('Here pause')

Composed perhaps 1811; first published in 1815; from 1815 included among 'Poems Dedicated to National Independence and Liberty'.

1811 ('The power of Armies')

All data identical with the previous poem.

7 *a fatal place* apparently 'a place appointed for its doom or annihilation' – N. C. Smith. Contrast to armies, 'circumscribed in time and space' (line 2).

SPANISH GUERILLAS

All data identical with the previous poem.

3-4 *to open and to close | The ridges of grim war* Compare *Paradise Lost* VI, 235-6: 'open when, and when to close / The ridges of grim War'.
10 *Viriathus* Lusitanian Guerilla leader who fought the Romans (*c.* 150–140 B.C.).
11 *Mina* Don Esprez y Mina, Guerilla leader of Navarre, who was educated for the Church.
12 *that great Leader* Sertorius (c. 112–72 B.C.), a Roman general who held Spain against the dictator Sulla. In Plutarch's *Lives*, Sertorius is said to have heard from sailors stories of islands in the Atlantic and to have desired to leave warfare and dwell there.

'THE FAIREST, BRIGHTEST, HUES'

Composed probably 28 July 1812 (or shortly after), but possibly early September (by 8 September) 1812; first published in 1815; from 1815 included among 'Miscellaneous Sonnets'.

I. F. note: 'Suggested at Hacket, which is on the craggy ridge that rises between the two Langdales and looks toward Windermere . . . The musician mentioned in the Sonnet was the Rev S. Tillbrook of Peter-house . . .'

In a letter to Mrs Clarkson (31 July 1812), Dorothy Wordsworth described the outing: 'We spent Tuesday afternoon in a walk to Hacket, where we drank tea with our old Servant's Mother . . . Tillbrook stationed himself upon a rock and sounded his flute to the great delight of our party, the cows in the field, and a group of rustic children.'

5 'See the "Vision of Mirza" in the "Spectator".' – W. Essay No. 159 (1 September 1711) by Joseph Addison.

'EVEN AS A DRAGON'S EYE'

Composed perhaps about early September (by 8 September) 1812; first published in 1815; from 1815 included among 'Miscellaneous Sonnets'.

3 *Sullenly glaring* in some editions, including the 1849-50, 'sullenly' reads 'suddenly'.

'HAIL, TWILIGHT'

All data identical with the preceding poem.

COMPOSED ON THE EVE OF THE MARRIAGE OF A FRIEND

Composed perhaps 1 November 1812; first published in 1815; from 1815 included among 'Miscellaneous Sonnets'.

2 *These humble nuptials* Thomas Hutchinson, Wordsworth's brother-in-law, was married to Mary Monkhouse, Wordsworth's cousin and sister of his friend Thomas Monkhouse.

EPITAPH

Composed perhaps between 1 December 1812 and 19 September 1822 (probably during the later of these years); first published in 1837; included from 1837 among 'Epitaphs and Elegiac Pieces'.

1 Thomas Wordsworth died 1 December 1812.

CHARACTERISTICS OF A CHILD THREE YEARS OLD

Composed possibly 1811, probably between 3 January 1813 and about late May 1814; first published in 1815; from 1815 included among 'Poems Referring to the Period of Childhood'.

I. F. note: 'Written at Allan Bank, Grasmere 1811. Picture of my Daughter Catharine, who died the year after.'

12-13 *solitude to her Is blithe society* Compare *Paradise Lost* IX, 249: 'for solitude sometimes is best society'.

[FRAGMENT FROM DOVE COTTAGE MANUSCRIPT 69]

Composed perhaps between 3 January 1813 and about late May 1814; first published in 1949 (in *PW*, V, 346, as number VI).

'COME YE THAT ARE DISTURBED'

Composed perhaps between 3 January 1813 and about late May 1814; first published in 1949.

According to de Selincourt (*PW*, V, 429), these lines are an early version of *The Excursion* IV, 1158-87.

MATERNAL GRIEF

Composed probably for the most part between 3 January 1813 and about late May 1814; first published in 1842; included from 1845 among 'Poems Founded on the Affections'.

I. F. note:

This was in part an overflow from the Solitary's description of his own and his wife's feelings upon the decease of their children [*The Excursion* III, 650-79], and, I will venture to add *for private notice only*, is faithfully set forth from my Wife's feelings and habits after the loss of our two children within half a year of each other.

NOVEMBER, 1813

Composed perhaps about mid-November 1813 (after 5 November); first published in the *Courier* 1 January 1814; from 1815 included among 'Poems Dedicated to National Independence and Liberty'.

5 *in twofold night* George III was both blind and insane.
14 *The triumphs of this hour* the defeat of Napoleon at Leipzig 16-19 October 1813.

'IF THOU INDEED DERIVE THY LIGHT'

Composed possibly 1813 (after May); first published in 1827; from 1827 to 1832 included among 'Poems of Sentiment and Reflection'; in 1837 (with three lines added) it was made the motto poem of the fifth volume, and from 1845 it was placed at the beginning of Wordsworth's collected poems, where it was intended 'to serve as a sort of preface' (letter to Edward Moxon, 5 November 1845).

I. F. note:

These verses were written some time after we had become residents at Rydal Mount; and I will take occasion from them to observe upon the beauty of that situation, as being backed and flanked by lofty fells, which bring the heavenly bodies to touch, as it were, the earth upon the mountain-tops, while the prospect in front lies open to a length of level valley, the extended lake, and a terminating ridge of low hills; so that it gives an opportunity to the inhabitants of the place of noticing the stars in both the positions here alluded to, namely, on the tops of the mountains, and as winter-lamps at a distance among the leafless trees.

'SURPRISED BY JOY'

Composed probably between sometime in 1813 and about the middle of October 1814; first published in 1815; from 1815 included among 'Miscellaneous Sonnets'.

I. F. note : 'This was in fact suggested by my daughter Catharine, long after her death.' She died on 4 June 1812 at the age of three.

Index of Titles

Address to Kilchurn Castle, upon Loch Awe 592
Address to My Infant Daughter, Dora 620
Address to Silence 252
Address to the Ocean 160
Address to the Scholars of the Village School 389
Admonition 618
Advance – Come Forth from Thy Tyrolean Ground 828
Affliction of Margaret –, The 472
'Alas! What Boots the Long Laborious Quest' 826
Alcaeus to Sappho 363
Alice Fell 514
Among All Lovely Things 531
Anacreon 40
A Narrow Girdle of Rough Stones and Crags 430
'And Is It Among Rude Untutored Dales' 827
Andrew Jones 351
Anecdote for Fathers 313
Animal Tranquillity and Decay 242
Anticipation. October, 1803 595
Argument for Suicide 161
'A Slumber Did My Spirit Seal' 364
At Applethwaite, near Keswick 602
At the Grave of Burns 587
At the Isle of Wight 116
'Avaunt All Specious Pliancy of Mind' 823
'Away, Away, It Is the Air' 354
'A Whirl-blast from behind the Hill' 303

Baker's Cart, a Fragment, The 242
Ballad, A 48
Banished Negroes, The 578
Barberry-Tree, The 546
Beauty and Moonlight 46
Beggars 516
' "Beloved Vale!" I Said, "When I Shall Con" ' 563
Birth of Love, The 114
Blind Highland Boy, The 610
Borderers, The 163
'Brave Schill! by Death Delivered, Take Thy Flight' 826

'Brook! Whose Society the Poet Seeks' 564
Brothers, The 402

Calais, August, 1802 575
Calais, August 15, 1802 577
'Call Not the Royal Swede Unfortunate' 825
Cantata, from Metastasio 584
Character, A 261
Characteristics of a Child Three Years Old 858
Character of the Happy Warrior 662
Childless Father, The 451
'Come Ye That Are Disturbed, This Steady Voice' 859
Complaint A 731
Complaint of a Forsaken Indian Woman, The 275
Composed after a Journey across the Hambleton Hills 580
Composed at the Same Time 821
Composed by the Sea-Side 576
Composed by the Side of Grasmere Lake 739
Composed in the Valley near Dover 578
Composed near Calais 575
Composed on the Eve of the Marriage of a Friend 857
Composed upon Westminster Bridge 574
Composed While the Author Was Engaged in Writing a Tract 821
Convict, The 152
Cottager to Her Infant, The 664
'Could I the Priest's Consent Have Gained' 385
Cuckoo and the Nightingale – [A Modernization], The 494

Danish Boy, The 369
Death of a Starling, The 44
Departure from the Vale of Grasmere 849
Descriptive Sketches [1850] 94
Descriptive Sketches 1793 897
Dirge Sung by a Minstrel 68
'Distressful Gift! This Book Receives' 642
Dog – An Idyllium, The 41
1801 ('I grieved for Buonaparté') 558
1810 ('Ah! where is Palafox?') 822
1810 ('O'erweening Statesmen') 839
1811 ('Here pause') 854
1811 ('The power of Armies') 855

Elegiac Stanzas Composed in the Churchyard of Grasmere 817
Elegiac Stanzas Suggested by a Picture of Peele Castle 639
Elegiac Verses in Memory of My Brother 646
Elegy Written in the Same Place Upon the Same Occasion 387

Ellen Irwin 397
Emigrant Mother, The 518
England 561
'England! the Time Is Come When Thou Shouldst Wean' 560
Epistle to Sir George Howland Beaumont 841
Epitaph 858
Epitaph Translated from Chiabrera: 'Destined to war' 831
Epitaph Translated from Chiabrera: 'Not without heavy grief' 830
Epitaph Translated from Chiabrera: 'O flower' 835
Epitaph Translated from Chiabrera: 'O Lelius' 836
Epitaph Translated from Chiabrera: 'O Thou who movest' 833
Epitaph Translated from Chiabrera: 'Pause, courteous Spirit!' 831
Epitaph Translated from Chiabrera: 'Perhaps some needful service' 833
Epitaph Translated from Chiabrera: 'There never breathed' 832
Epitaph Translated from Chiabrera: 'True is it' 835
Epitaph Translated from Chiabrera: 'Weep not' 834
[Epitaph on Tasso Translated from Chiabrera] 834
'Even as a Dragon's Eye That Feels the Stress' 856
Evening Walk, An 77
Expostulation and Reply 355
Extract from the Conclusion of a Poem 66

'Fairest, Brightest, Hues of Ether Fade, The' 856
Farewell, A 572
Farmer of Tilsbury Vale, The 257
Feelings of a Noble Biscayan 838
Feelings of the Tyrolese 827
Female Vagrant, The 118
Fidelity 649
'Fly, Some Kind Harbinger, to Grasmere-dale' 594
For a Seat in the Groves of Coleorton 854
Force of Prayer, The 739
Foresight 543
Forsaken, The 475
For the Spot Where the Hermitage Stood 442
Fountain, The 383
Fragment, A 369
Fragment: 'Along the Mazes of This Song I Go' 605
Fragment: A Somersetshire Tragedy 471
Fragment: 'For Let the Impediment Be What It May' 399
Fragment: Redundance 400
Fragment: The Baker's Cart 242
Fragment: 'The Rains at Length Have Ceased' 720
Fragment: 'There Was a Spot' 632
Fragment: 'Witness Thou' 471
Fragment: 'Yet Once Again' 242

Fragment from Dove Cottage Manuscript 44 (i) 472
Fragment from Dove Cottage Manuscript 69 859
Fragment of a 'Gothic' Tale 153
Fragment of an Intended Poem on Milton 72
Fragments from Dove Cottage Manuscript 44 (ii) 541
Fragments from the Alfoxden Note-Book (i) 268
Fragments from the Alfoxden Note-Book (ii) 311
Fragments from the Alfoxden Note-Book (iii) 355
Fragments from the 'Christabel' Notebook 468
Fragments on a Heroic Theme 70
French and the Spanish Guerillas, The 824
French Revolution 636
From the Greek 43
From the Italian of Michelangelo ('No mortal object') 661
From the Italian of Michelangelo ('Rid of a vexing') 662
From the Italian of Michelangelo ('Well-nigh') 661
From the Italian of Michelangelo ('Yes! hope may') 653
From the Italian of Michelangelo. To the Supreme Being 660
From the Verso of a Loose Foolscap Sheet 242

George and Sarah Green 817
Glen-Almain; Or, The Narrow Glen 638
Glow-Worm, The 531
Goody Blake and Harry Gill 271
'Great Men Have Been among Us; Hands That Penned' 559
Green Linnet, The 533
'Grief, Thou Hast Lost an Ever Ready Friend' 737
Growth of Genius 364
Guilt and Sorrow 118
Gypsies 735

'Hail, Twilight, Sovereign of One Peaceful Hour!' 857
'Hail, Zaragoza! If with Unwet Eye' 822
Hart-Leap Well 415
Her Eyes Are Wild 277
Hofer 829
Home at Grasmere 697
Horn of Egremont Castle, The 721
Horse, The 75
'Hour-Bell Sounds, and I Must Go, The' 147
'How Sweet It Is, When Mother Fancy Rocks' 566

Idiot Boy, The 281
Idle Shepherd-Boys, The 425
'I Find It Written of SIMONIDES' 565
'If Nature, for a Favourite Child' 380

'If Thou Indeed Derive Thy Light from Heaven' 863
'I Love upon a Stormy Night' 352
Imitation of Juvenal – Satire VIII 142
Incident Characteristic of a Favourite Dog 651
Incipient Madness 256
Indignation of a High-Minded Spaniard 837
In Due Observance of an Ancient Rite 837
Influence of Natural Objects 364
In Part from Moschus's Lament for Bion 74
Inscription for a Seat by a Roadside 243
Inscription for a Seat by the Pathway Side 141
Inscription for the Moss-Hut at Dove Cottage 637
Inscription in a Garden of the Same 853
Inscription in the Grounds of Coleorton 852
Intimations Ode 523
'In Vain Did Time and Nature Toil to Throw' 116
'Is There a Power That Can Sustain and Cheer' 823
'It Is a Beauteous Evening, Calm and Free' 576
'It Is No Spirit Who from Heaven Hath Flown' 571
'It Is Not To Be Thought of That the Flood' 560
'I Travelled among Unknown Men' 476
'It Was an April Morning: Fresh and Clear' 423
'I Wandered Lonely as a Cloud' 619

King of Sweden, The 638
Kitten and Falling Leaves, The 632

Last of the Flock, The 295
Leechgatherer 551
[Lesbia] 45
Lines Composed a Few Miles above Tintern Abbey 357
Lines, Composed at Grasmere 720
Lines (Left upon a Seat in a Yew-tree) 254
Lines on the Expected Invasion 1803 596
Lines Written as a School Exercise at Hawkshead 37
Lines Written at a Small Distance 269
Lines Written in Early Spring 312
Lines Written on a Tablet 380
Lines Written While Sailing in a Boat at Evening 89
London, 1802 579
'Look Now on That Adventurer Who Hath Paid' 825
Louisa 511
Lucy Gray 392
Lucy Poems
      'A Slumber Did My Spirit Seal' 364
      'She Dwelt among the Untrodden Ways' 366

'Strange Fits of Passion Have I Known' 366
'I Travelled among Unknown Men' 476
'Three Years She Grew in Sun and Shower' 400

Mad Monk, The 421
Mad Mother, The 277
Manciple's Tale – [A Modernization], The 478
'Mark the Concentred Hazels That Enclose' 737
'Martial Courage of a Day Is Vain, The' 836
Maternal Grief 860
Matron of Jedborough and Her Husband, The 607
Matthew 380
Matthew Poems
    Address to the Scholars of the Village School 389
    Matthew 380
    The Two April Mornings 381
    The Fountain 383
    'Could I the Priest's Consent Have Gained' 385
    Elegy Written in the Same Place 387
'Methought I Saw the Footsteps of a Throne' 559
Michael 455
Michelangelo in Reply to the Passage upon His Statue 666
Motto Intended for Poems on the Naming of Places 472
'My Heart Leaps Up When I Behold' 522

'Narrow Girdle of Rough Stones and Crags, A' 430
Night-Piece, A 262
'No Spade for Leagues Had Won a Rood of Earth' 149
November, 1806 725
November, 1813 862
'Nuns Fret Not at Their Convent's Narrow Room' 586
Nutting 367

Oak and the Broom, The 434
Oak of Guernica, The 838
October, 1803 ('One might') 596
October, 1803 ('These times') 597
October, 1803 ('When, looking') 597
Ode: Intimations of Immortality 523
Ode to Apollo 76
Ode to Duty 605
'O'er the Wide Earth, on Mountain and on Plain' 828
Old Cumberland Beggar, The 262
Old Man Travelling 242
On a Celebrated Event in Ancient History 840
On Approaching Home 594

'O Nightingale! Thou Surely Art' 734
On Seeing Some Tourists 432
On the Death of an Unfortunate Lady 67
On the Extinction of the Venetian Republic 571
On the Final Submission on the Tyrolese 829
On the Report of the Submission of the Tyrolese 829
Orchard Pathway, The 475
Orpheus and Eurydice 72

Passage from John Wilson's *The Angler's Tent* 828
[Pelayo] 819
Pelion and Ossa Flourish Side by Side 568
Personal Talk 566
Peter Bell 315
Pet-Lamb, The 452
Poet's Epitaph, A 395
Poor Susan 260
Power of Music 691
Prioress' Tale – [A Modernization], The 485
Prophecy, A 733

Recluse, The 697
Redbreast Chasing the Butterfly, The 539
Redundance, a Fragment 400
'Remembering How Thou Didst Beguile' 387
Remembrance of Collins 90
Repentance 476
Resolution and Independence 551
Reverie of Poor Susan, The 260
Road Extended O'er a Heath, The 147
Rob Roy's Grave 653
Rural Architecture 454
Ruth 371

Sailor's Mother, The 512
St Paul's 798
Salisbury Plain 118
'Say, What Is Honour? – 'Tis the Finest Sense' 824
September 1, 1802 578
September, 1802. Near Dover 579
Septimi Gades 91
Septimius and Acme 42
Seven Sisters, The 443
'She Dwelt among the Untrodden Ways' 366
'Shepherd, Looking Eastward, Softly Said, The' 738
'She Was a Phantom of Delight' 603

Simon Lee 300
Simplon Pass, The 637
'Six Months to Six Years Added He Remained' 858
'Slumber Did My Spirit Seal, A' 364
Small Celandine, The 604
Solitary Reaper, The 659
Solitude 392
Somersetshire Tragedy, a Fragment, A 471
Song at the Feast of Brougham Castle 726
Song for the Spinning Wheel 732
Song for the Wandering Jew 439
Sonnet Composed at — Castle 593
Sonnet ('If grief dismiss me not') 89
Sonnet, in the Pass of Killicranky 595
Sonnet on Milton 797
Sonnet on Seeing Miss Helen Maria Williams Weep 47
Sonnet Suggested by the Efforts of the Tyrolese 826
Sonnet Translated from the Italian of Milton 584
Sonnet Written by Mr — Immediately after the Death of His Wife 47
Spanish Guerillas 1811 855
Sparrow's Nest, The 529
Stanzas Written in My Pocket-Copy 556
Star-Gazers 694
Stepping Westward 645
'Strange Fits of Passion Have I Known' 366
Stray Pleasures 693
'Sun Has Long Been Set, The' 574
'Surprised by Joy – Impatient as the Wind' 863
'Sweet Was the Walk along the Narrow Lane' 114

Tables Turned, The 356
'The Fairest, Brightest, Hues of Ether Fade' 856
'The Hour-Bell Sounds, and I Must Go' 147
'The Martial Courage of a Day Is Vain' 836
'There Is a Bondage Worse, Far Worse, To Bear' 561
'There Is a Little Unpretending Rill' 565
'There Is an Eminence, – of These Our Hills' 422
There Was a Boy 362
Thorn, The 304
'Those Words Were Uttered as in Pensive Mood' 581
'Though Narrow Be That Old Man's Cares, and Near' 731
Thought of a Briton on the Subjugation of Switzerland 725
Thoughts Suggested the Day Following 590
Three Graves, The. Parts I and II 245
'Three Years She Grew in Sun and Shower' 400
'Through Cumbrian Wilds, in Many a Mountain Cove' 733

Tinker, The 542
Tintern Abbey 357
''Tis Said, That Some Have Died for Love' 440
To a Butterfly ('I've watched you now') 540
To a Butterfly ('Stay near me') 517
To a Highland Girl 598
To a Sexton 379
To a Sky-Lark ('Up with me!') 530
To a Young Lady 511
To H. C., Six Years Old 522
To Joanna 445
To Lady Beaumont 734
To Melpomene 44
To M. H. 414
To My Sister 269
To Sleep ('A flock of sheep') 562
To Sleep ('Fond words') 563
To Sleep ('O gentle Sleep!') 562
To the Clouds 815
To the Cuckoo ('O blithe New-comer!') 521
To the Daisy ('Bright Flower!') 537
To the Daisy ('In youth') 534
To the Daisy ('Sweet Flower!') 643
To the Daisy ('With little') 537
To the Evening Star over Grasmere Water 718
To the Memory of Raisley Calvert 569
To the Men of Kent. October, 1803 594
To the Poet, John Dyer 736
To the Same Flower [The Daisy] ('With little') 537
To the Same Flower [The Small Celandine] ('Pleasures newly found') 549
To the Small Celandine ('Pansies, lilies') 544
To the Small Celandine ('Pleasures newly found') 549
To the Sons of Burns 657
To the Spade of a Friend 719
To Thomas Clarkson 736
To Toussaint L'Ouverture 577
Translation: 'Come, Gentle Sleep' 667
Translation of a Celebrated Greek Song 43
Translation of Ariosto 581
Translation of Horace's Ode III, xiii 141
Translation of the Sestet of a Sonnet by Tasso 587
Translations from Metastasio 585
Translations from Michelangelo. A Fragment 665
Travelling 556
Tribute to the Memory of the Same Dog 652
Troilus and Cressida – [A Modernization] 505

Tuft of Primroses, The 799
Two April Mornings, The 381
Two Thieves, The 428

Upon the Same Event 840
Upon the Sight of a Beautiful Picture 841

Vale of Esthwaite, The 50
Vaudracour and Julia 623
View from the Top of Black Comb 850
Voice from the Side of Etna, The 421

Waggoner, The 667
Waterfall and the Eglantine, The 437
Water Fowl 717
Weak Is the Will of Man, His Judgement Blind 738
We Are Seven 298
'Western Clouds a Deepening Gloom Display, The' 117
'What If Our Numbers Barely Could Defy' 564
'What Is It That Tells My Soul the Sun Is Setting' 67
'When I Have Borne in Memory What Has Tamed' 561
'When Slow from Pensive Twilight's Latest Gleams' 88
'When, to the Attractions of the Busy World' 448
'Where Lies the Land to Which Yon Ship Must Go?' 569
Whirl-blast from behind the Hill, A 303
White Doe of Rylstone, The 741
'Who Fancied What a Pretty Sight' 618
Winter's Evening, A 68
'With How Sad Steps, O Moon, Thou Climb'st the Sky' 570
'With Ships the Sea Was Sprinkled Far and Nigh' 570
'World Is Too Much With Us; Late and Soon, The' 568
Written at the Request of Sir George Beaumont, Bart. 853
Written in a Grotto 510
Written in Germany 394
Written in London, September, 1802 580
Written in March 532
Written in Very Early Youth 88
Written with a Pencil upon a Stone 424
Written with a Slate Pencil on a Stone, on the Side of the Mountain 851
Written with a Slate Pencil upon a Stone, the Largest of a Heap 433

Yarrow Unvisited 600
'Yes, It Was the Mountain Echo' 696
Yew-Trees 622

Index of First Lines

A barking sound the Shepherd hears 649
Advance – come forth from thy Tyrolean ground 828
A famous man is Robin Hood 653
A few bold Patriots, Reliques of the Fight 819
A flock of sheep that leisurely pass by 562
Age! twine thy brows with fresh spring flowers 607
Ah! have you seen a bird of sweetest tone 67
Ah me! the lowliest children of the spring 74
Ah! where is Palafox? Nor tongue nor pen 822
Alas! what boots the long laborious quest 826
Along a precipice they wound their way 153
Along the mazes of this song I go 605
A Manciple there was, one of a Temple 478
Amid the dark control of lawless sway 797
Amid the smoke of cities did you pass 445
Among all lovely things my Love had been 531
A narrow girdle of rough stones and crags 430
and beneath the star 355
And has the Sun his flaming chariot driven 37
And is it among rude untutored Dales 827
– And I will bear my vengeful blade 43
And sweet it is to see in summer time 665
'And will you leave me thus alone 48
An Orpheus! an Orpheus! yes, Faith may grow bold 691
Another year – another deadly blow! 725
A plague on your languages, German and Norse! 394
A plain youth, Lady, and a simple lover 584
Army of Clouds! ye wingèd Host in troops 815
A Roman Master stands on Grecian ground 840
Art thou a Statist in the van 395
Art thou the bird whom Man loves best 539
– A simple Child 298
A slumber did my spirit seal 364
As the fresh wine the poet pours 76
As when, upon the smooth pacific deep 859
A Traveller on the skirt of Sarum's Plain 119
At the corner of Wood Street, when daylight appears 260
Avaunt all specious pliancy of mind 823
[?] avaunt! with tenfold pleasure 50

Away, away, it is the air 354
A whirl-blast from behind the hill 303

Bandusian Spring than glass more brightly clear 141
Bard of the Fleece, whose skilful genius made 736
Beaumont! it was thy wish that I should rear 602
Before I see another day 275
'Begone, thou fond presumptuous Elf 437
Behold her, single in the field 659
Behold, within the leafy shade 529
'Beloved Vale!' I said, 'when I shall con 563
Beneath these fruit-tree boughs that shed 533
Beneath this thorn when I was young 245
Beneath yon eastern ridge, the craggy bound 854
Between two sister moorland rills 369
Brave Schill! by death delivered, take thy flight 826
Bright Flower! whose home is everywhere 537
– Brook and road 637
Brook! whose society the Poet seeks 564
– But hark! the Curfew tolls! and lo! the night 68
By their floating mill 693

Call not the royal Swede unfortunate 825
Calm is all nature as a resting wheel 88
Calvert! it must not be unheard by them 569
Camoëns, he the accomplished and the good 587
Child of loud-throated War! the mountain Stream 592
Clarkson! it was an obstinate hill to climb 736
Clouds, lingering yet, extend in solid bars 739
Come, gentle Sleep, Death's image though thou art 667
Come then in robe of darkest blue 44
Come ye that are disturbed, this steady voice 859
Come ye – who, if (which Heaven avert!) the Land 596
Could I the priest's consent have gained 385

Dark and more dark the shades of evening fell 580
Dear Child of Nature, let them rail! 511
Dear native regions, I foretell 66
Degenerate Douglas! oh, the unworthy Lord! 593
Departed Child! I could forget thee once 860
Destined to war from very infancy 831
Distressful gift! this Book receives 642

Earth has not anything to show more fair 574
England! the time is come when thou shouldst wean 560

Ere the Brothers through the gateway 721
Even as a dragon's eye that feels the stress 856

Fair Ellen Irwin, when she sate 397
Fair Star of evening, Splendour of the west 576
Farewell, thou little Nook of mountain-ground 572
Far from my dearest Friend, 'tis mine to rove 77
Far from our home by Grasmere's quiet Lake 841
Festivals have I seen that were not names 577
Five years have past; five summers, with the length 357
Fly, some kind Harbinger, to Grasmere-dale! 594
Fond words have oft been spoken to thee, Sleep! 563
For let the impediment be what it may 399
From Bolton's old monastic tower 744
From Stirling castle we had seen 600

Gentle Zephyr 586
Glide gently, thus for ever glide 90
Grateful is Sleep, more grateful still to be 667
Grateful is Sleep, my life in stone bound fast 666
Great men have been among us; hands that penned 559
Grief, thou hast lost an ever ready friend 737

Hail, Twilight, sovereign of one peaceful hour! 857
Hail, Zaragoza! If with unwet eye 822
– Hast thou then survived 620
Here, on our native soil, we breathe once more 578
Here pause: the poet claims at least this praise 854
Her eyes are wild, her head is bare 277
He wandering far along the lonely main 72
High deeds, O Germans, are to come from you 733
High in the breathless Hall the Minstrel sate 726
High o'er the silver rocks I roved 46
His armour glittered in the [   ] 70
His simple truths did Andrew glean 434
How long will ye round me be roaring 160
How richly glows the water's breast 89
How sweet it is, when mother Fancy rocks 566
How sweet the walk along the woody steep 116
How sweet, when crimson colours dart 363
Hunger, and sultry heat, and nipping blast 824

I am not One who much or oft delight 566
I come, ye little noisy Crew 389
I crossed the dreary moor 256
I dropped my pen; and listened to the Wind 821

If from the public way you turn your steps 455
If grief dismiss me not to them that rest 89
I find it written of SIMONIDES 565
If Nature, for a favourite child 380
If thou indeed derive thy light from Heaven 863
If thou in the dear love of some one Friend 442
I grieved for Buonaparté, with a vain 558
I hate that Andrew Jones: he'll breed 351
I have a boy of five years old 313
I have been here in the Moon-light 472
I have seen the Baker's horse 242
I heard a thousand blended notes 312
I heard a voice from Etna's side 421
Ill fared it now with his poor wife I ween 471
I love upon a stormy night 352
I marvel how Nature could ever find space 261
I met Louisa in the shade 511
In distant countries have I been 295
In due observance of an ancient rite 837
Inland, within a hollow vale, I stood 579
In the sweet shire of Cardigan 300
In this still place, remote from men 638
In trellised shed with clustering roses gay 742
In vain did Time and Nature toil to throw 116
In youth from rock to rock I went 534
I saw an aged Beggar in my walk 263
I shiver, Spirit fierce and bold 587
Is it a reed that's shaken by the wind 575
Is there a power that can sustain and cheer 823
It is a beauteous evening, calm and free 576
It is no Spirit who from heaven hath flown 571
It is not to be thought of that the Flood 560
It is the first mild day of March 269
I travelled among unknown men 476
— It seems a day 367
It was a *moral* end for which they fought 829
It was an April morning: fresh and clear 423
I've watched you now a full half-hour 540
I wandered lonely as a cloud 619
I was thy neighbour once, thou rugged Pile! 639
I will be that fond Mother 586

Jones! as from Calais southward you and I 575

Lady! the songs of Spring were in the grove 734
Late on a breezy vernal eve 546

LAURA, farewell my LAURA! 584
Let thy wheel-barrow alone 379
Lie here, without a record of thy worth 652
List! the bell-Sprite stuns my ears 68
Long had I stood and looked into the west 470
Look now on that Adventurer who hath paid 825
Loud is the Vale! the Voice is up 720
lovely as the fairy day 312
Loving she is, and tractable, though wild 858

Mark how the feathered tenants of the flood 717
Mark the concentred hazels that enclose 737
Methought I saw the footsteps of a throne 559
'Mid crowded obelisks and urns 658
Milton! thou shouldst be living at this hour 579
My heart leaps up when I behold 522
My Lesbia let us love and live 45

Nay, Traveller! rest. This lonely Yew-tree stands 254
Next morning Troilus began to clear 505
No mortal object did these eyes behold 661
No spade for leagues had won a rood of earth 149
Not 'mid the World's vain objects that enslave 821
Not the more 400
Not without heavy grief of heart did He 830
No whimsy of the purse is here 637
Now that all hearts are glad, all faces bright 862
Now we are tired of boisterous joy 610
Nuns fret not at their convent's narrow room 586

Oak of Guernica! Tree of holier power 839
O blithe New-comer! I have heard 521
O'er the wide earth, on mountain and on plain 828
O'erweening Statesmen have full long relied 839
O flower of all that springs from gentle blood 835
Of mortal parents is the Hero born 829
O Friend! I know not which way I must look 580
Oft I had heard of Lucy Gray 392
Oft is the medal faithful to its trust 853
Of unknown modes of being which on earth 269
O gentle Sleep! do they belong to thee 562
O happy time of youthful lovers (thus 623
Oh! blessed all bliss above 585
Oh! pleasant exercise of hope and joy! 636
Oh thou, whose fixed bewildered eye 91
Oh 'tis a joy divine on summer days 469

Oh! what's the matter? what's the matter? 271
O Lelius, beauteous flower of gentleness 836
'O Lord, our Lord! how wondrously,' (quoth she) 486
O Moon! if e'er I joyed when thy soft light 510
Once did She hold the gorgeous east in fee 571
Once in a lonely hamlet I sojourned 518
Once more I welcome Thee, and Thou, fair Plant 799
Once to the verge of yon steep barrier came 697
One might believe that natural miseries 596
One morning (raw it was and wet – 512
On his morning rounds the Master 651
O Nightingale! thou surely art 734
O now that the genius of Bewick were mine 428
On Religion's holy hill 72
Orchard Pathway, to and fro 475
Orlando who great length of time had been 581
O Thou who movest onward with a mind 833
O thou! whose fancies from afar are brought 522
Our walk was far among the ancient trees 414

Pansies, lilies, kingcups, daisies 544
Pause, courteous Spirit! – Baldi supplicates 831
Pelion and Ossa flourish side by side 568
Perhaps some needful service of the State 833
Pity mourns in plaintive tone 44
Pleasures newly found are sweet 549
Praised by the Art whose subtle power could stay 841
Pressed with conflicting thoughts of love and fear 798

Remembering how thou didst beguile 387
Reynolds, come, thy pencil prove 40
Rid of a vexing and a heavy load 662
Rude is this Edifice, and Thou hast seen 424

Say, what is Honour? – 'Tis the finest sense 824
Send this man to the mine, this to the battle 161
Septimius thus his [   ] love addressed 42
Seven Daughters had Lord Archibald 443
She dwelt among the untrodden ways 366
She had a tall man's height or more 516
She was a Phantom of delight 603
She wept. – Life's purple tide began to flow 47
Shout, for a mighty Victory is won! 595
SILENCE! calm, venerable majesty 252
Six months to six years added he remained 858
Six thousand veterans practised in war's game 595

Solemn dreams 311
Some minds have room alone for pageant stories 472
Spade! with which Wilkinson hath tilled his lands 719
Stay, bold Adventurer; rest awhile thy limbs 851
Stay near me – do not take thy flight! 517
Stern Daughter of the Voice of God! 605
Strange fits of passion have I known 366
Stranger! this hillock of mis-shapen stones 433
Surprised by joy – impatient as the Wind 863
Sweet Flower! belike one day to have 643
Sweet Highland Girl, a very shower 598
Sweet was the walk along the narrow lane 114
Swiftly turn the murmuring wheel! 732

That is work of waste and ruin – 543
That way look, my Infant, lo! 632
The clouds are standing still in the mid heavens 469
The Cock is crowing 532
The days are cold, the nights are long 664
The dew was falling fast, the stars began to blink 452
The embowering rose, the acacia, and the pine 852
The fairest, brightest, hues of ether fade 856
The fields which with covetous spirit we sold 476
The foal of generous breed along the plains 75
The gentlest Shade that walked Elysian plains 849
The glory of evening was spread through the west 152
The God of Love – *ah, benedicite!* 494
The hour-bell sounds, and I must go 147
The Knight had ridden down from Wensley Moor 415
The Lake is thine 718
The Land we from our fathers had in trust 827
The leaves stir not 469
The little hedgerow birds 242
The martial courage of a day is vain 836
The moon is in the East, I see her not 471
The peace which others seek they find 475
The placid lake that rested far below 828
The post-boy drove with fierce career 514
The power of Armies is a visible thing 855
The prayers I make will then be sweet indeed 660
The rains at length have ceased, the winds are stilled 720
There is a bondage worse, far worse, to bear 561
There is a change – and I am poor 731
There is a Flower, the lesser Celandine 604
There is a little unpretending Rill 565
There is an Eminence, – of these our hills 422

'There is a Thorn – it looks so old 304
There is Yew-tree, pride of Lorton Vale 622
There is creation in the eye 470
There never breathed a man who, when his life 832
There's George Fisher, Charles Fleming, and Reginald Shore 454
There's something in a flying horse 316
There was a Boy; ye knew him well ye cliffs 362
There was a roaring in the wind all night 551
There was a spot 632
There was a time when meadow, grove, and stream 523
there would he stand 268
The road extended o'er a heath 147
These Chairs they have no words to utter 541
these populous slopes 355
These times strike monied worldlings with dismay 597
'These Tourists, heaven preserve us! needs must live 402
The Sheep-boy whistled loud, and lo! 649
The Shepherd, looking eastward, softly said 738
– The sky is overcast 262
The sl[ender] dandelion bows his head 469
The sun has long been set 574
The Sun is dead – ye heard the curfew toll 47
The Swallow, that hath lost 585
The Troop will be impatient; let us hie 164
The valley rings with mirth and joy 425
The Voice of song from distant lands shall call 638
The western clouds a deepening gloom display 117
The world is too much with us; late and soon 568
They seek, are sought; to daily battle led 855
This Height a ministering Angel might select 850
This is the spot: – how mildly does the sun 556
Those words were uttered as in pensive mood 581
Though narrow be that old Man's cares, and near 731
Though the torrents from their fountains 439
Thou issuest from a fissure in the rock 468
Thou, who in youthful vigour rich, and light 243
Three years she grew in sun and shower 400
Through Cumbrian wilds, in many a mountain cove 733
'Tis eight o'clock, – a clear March night 281
'Tis not for the unfeeling, the falsely refined 257
'Tis said, that some have died for love 440
'Tis spent – this burning day of June! 668
Too frail to keep the lofty vow 590
Torquato Tasso rests within this tomb 834
To the grove, the meadow, the well 585
Toussaint, the most unhappy man of men! 577

True is it that Ambrosia Salinero 835
Two Voices are there; one is of the sea 725

Up, Timothy, up with your staff and away! 451
Up! up! my Friend, and quit your books 356
Up with me! up with me into the clouds! 530

Vanguard of Liberty, ye men of Kent 594

Weak is the will of Man, his judgement blind 738
We can endure that He should waste our lands 837
Weep not, beloved Friends! nor let the air 834
We had a female Passenger who came 578
Well mayst thou halt – and gaze with brightening eye! 618
Well-nigh the voyage now is overpast 661
Were there, below, a spot of holy ground (1850) 95
Were there, below, a spot of holy ground (1793) 897
We talked with open heart, and tongue 383
We walked along, while bright and red 381
What crowd is this? what have we here! we must not pass it by 694
What if our numbers barely could defy 564
'What is good for a bootless bene?' 739
What is it that tells my soul the Sun is setting 67
What need of clamorous bells, or ribands gay 857
What waste in the labour of Chariot and Steed! 432
'What, you are stepping westward?' – 'Yea.' 645
When, far and wide, swift as the beams of morn 840
When I have borne in memory what has tamed 561
When, looking on the present face of things 597
When LOVE was born of heavenly line 114
When Ruth was left half desolate 371
When slow from pensive twilight's latest gleams 88
When, to the attractions of the busy world 448
Where art thou, my beloved Son 472
Where lies the Land to which yon Ship must go? 569
Where truth 355
Where were ye, nymphs, when the remorseless deep 41
Who fancied what a pretty sight 618
Who is the happy Warrior? Who is he 662
Who leads a happy life 542
Who weeps for strangers? Many wept 817
Why is it we feel 268
'Why, William, on that old grey stone 355
Wisdom and Spirit of the universe! 364
'With how sad steps, O Moon, thou climb'st the sky 570
Within our happy Castle there dwelt One 556

With little here to do or see 537
With Ships the sea was sprinkled far and nigh 570
Witness thou 471
'Would ye come here, ye maiden vile 247

Ye kings, in wisdom, sense and power, supreme 142
Ye Lime-trees, ranged before this hallowed Urn 853
Yes! hope may with my strong desire keep pace 653
Yes, it was the mountain Echo 696
Yet are they here the same unbroken knot 735
Yet once again do I behold the forms 242
Yet, yet, Biscayans! we must meet our Foes 838
Ye, who with buoyant spirits blessed 141